THE LOST BOOKS
OF THE BIBLE

AND

THE FORGOTTEN
BOOKS OF EDEN

The Lost Books
of the Bible

AND

The Forgotten
Books of Eden

A MERIDIAN BOOK

NEW AMERICAN LIBRARY

TIMES MIRROR

NEW YORK AND SCARBOROUGH, ONTARIO

MERIDIAN TRADEMARK REG. PAT. OFF. AND FOREIGN COUNTRIES
REGISTERED TRADEMARK—MARCA REGISTRADA
HECHO EN WESTFORD, MASS., U.S.A.

SIGNET, SIGNET CLASSICS, MENTOR, PLUME, MERIDIAN AND
NAL BOOKS are published *in the United States* by
The New American Library, Inc.,
1633 Broadway, New York, New York 10019,
in Canada by The New American Library of Canada Limited,
81 Mack Avenue, Scarborough, Ontario M1L 1M8
First Printing/World Publishing Company, 1963
First Printing/New American Library, November, 1974

8   9   10   11   12   13   14

PRINTED IN THE UNITED STATES OF AMERICA

MEMBERS OF THE COUNCIL OF NICE PRESENTING THEIR DECISION TO THE EMPEROR CONSTANTINE: FOURTH CENTURY.

FROM AN EARLY GREEK MANUSCRIPT.

THE
Lost Books
OF THE
BIBLE

BEING ALL THE GOSPELS, EPISTLES, AND OTHER PIECES NOW
EXTANT ATTRIBUTED IN THE FIRST FOUR CENTURIES

TO

JESUS CHRIST

HIS APOSTLES AND THEIR COMPANIONS

NOT INCLUDED, BY ITS COMPILERS, IN THE AUTHORIZED NEW
TESTAMENT; AND, THE RECENTLY DISCOVERED SYRIAC
MSS. OF PILATE'S LETTERS TO TIBERIUS, ETC.

TRANSLATED FROM THE ORIGINAL TONGUES

ILLUSTRATED FROM ANCIENT PAINTINGS AND MISSALS

---

*"Christ was the joyous boy of the fields. We are not
permitted to think that the shadows of Calvary darkened
His pathway as a youth, and the Apocryphal Books of
the New Testament show a great deal of the early life of
Christ not to be found in the four Evangelists."*
— DR. TALMAGE

LIST OF ILLUSTRATIONS

INTRODUCTION TO
THE LOST BOOKS OF THE BIBLE

By Dr. Frank Crane

THE great things in this world are growths.
This applies to books as well as to institutions.
The Bible is a growth. Many people do not understand that it is not a book written by a single person, but it is a library of several books which were composed by various people in various countries. It is interesting to know how this library grew and upon what principle some books were accepted and some rejected.

Of course we may take people's word for the reasons why certain books were chosen, but it is always satisfactory to come to our own conclusions by examining our own evidence.

This is what this *Lost Books of the Bible* enables us to do. We can examine the books of the Scriptures which we have in the authorized version, and then in this book we can read those scriptures which have been eliminated by various councils in order to make up our standard Bible.

It is safe to say that a comparison of the accepted books with those rejected may be relied upon, for those books which were accepted are far superior in value to the others.

These others which are included in the *Lost Books of the Bible* comprise all kinds of stories, tales and myths.

No great figure appears in history without myths growing up about him. Every great personage becomes a nucleus or center about which folk tales cluster.

There are apocryphal tales about Napoleon, about

INTRODUCTION

Charlemagne, about Julius Cæsar and other outstanding characters.

It is impossible that a man representing so great a force as Jesus of Nazareth should appear in the world without finding many echoes of His personality in contemporary literature—many stories which grew up about Him as time elapsed.

What these tales and stories are, just how He appears to the fictional minds of His day and afterwards, it is interesting to note.

Very often the fiction writer depicts life and the great truth of life better than the historian. He does not pretend to write down what is exactly true, but he tinges all things with his imagination. His feelings, however, may be just and reliable.

The reading of this *Lost Books of the Bible* is interesting as a matter of course. All who in any way are attracted by the personage of Jesus are interested to know any stories that may have grown up about Him.

They are also valuable because they enable us to get many a point of view which otherwise would have been lost.

History may be true, but in a sense tradition is even truer. It has been said that history records what has been, but tradition tells what ought to have been.

It must be remembered also that such a thing as historical accuracy is a comparatively novel product. The older writers never dreamed of it. They wrote in order to be interesting, not to tell the truth. And it is a remarkable fact that the events recorded in the Holy Scriptures, as far as we can find out, were most of them veritable, and the chroniclers were truthful.

In this volume all these apocryphal volumes are presented without argument or commentation. The reader's own judgment and common sense are appealed to. It makes no difference whether he is Catholic or Protestant or Hebrew. The facts are plainly laid before him. These facts for a long time have been the peculiar esoteric property of the learned. They were available only in the original Greek and Latin and so forth. Now they have been translated and brought in plain English before the eye of every reader.

The ordinary man has therefore the privilege of seeing upon what grounds the commonly accepted Scriptures rest. He can examine the pile of evidence and do his own sifting.

Thousands of people to-day look to the New Testament narrative as their leader and guide. It is important to know upon what authority this rests, and many a man will be delighted to find the evidence thus clearly presented before him.

The Lost Books of the Bible present all sorts of matter before the curious eye. There are stories about Mary and instances of her personal life. There are other stories about the boyhood of Jesus and instances about His crucifixion. All of these become important because of the central figure about whom they revolve.

No man has ever appealed to the imagination of the world and so played upon its feelings as has Jesus of Nazareth.

It is interesting to know what forms of stories and speculations about Him took place in the early period of the Christian era.

In other words, the ordinary man is invited to take his place in that council chamber which accepts and rejects the various writings of Scripture. It is safe to say that the conclusions desired can safely be left to his common sense. It can no longer be said that our Scriptures were accepted by learned men; you do not know that, but you must accept their conclusions. Now it is shown you upon what grounds these conclusions rest.

As a believer in the authenticity of our accepted Scriptures I have no hesitancy in saying that I am perfectly satisfied to let the common sense of the world decide upon the superiority of the accepted text.

The publication of this book will do good because it takes away the veil of secrecy that has hidden for many years the act of the church in accepting certain Scriptures and rejecting others. All of the grounds are rendered perfectly intelligible to the common man.

THE

ORDER OF ALL THE BOOKS

OF THE

LOST BOOKS of the BIBLE

WITH

Their proper Names and Number of Chapters.

THE EMPEROR CONSTANTINE PRESENTING THE LABORS OF THE COUNCIL OF NICE TO
CHRIST FOR HIS BLESSING.

FROM AN EARLY GREEK MANUSCRIPT.

PREFACE

YOU will find between these covers all the ecclesiastical writings of early Christian authorities that are known to exist, and yet were omitted from the authorized New Testament.

They are published here as a matter of record. Whether they are canonical or not, at least these writings are of very great antiquity.

Origins are noted in paragraphs at the front of each book. This will enable the reader to form his own conclusions as to the genuineness of the writings. These writings are a vivid picture of the minds of men in the post-Apostolic period of the Church. Discount the statements from the historical viewpoint as you will—there remains in these gospels and epistles an earnestness of purpose, and zeal to express a message, similar to that of our authorized Bible.

An interesting question naturally arises as to why these writings were cast out in the selection of the material that has come down to us in the authorized version.

The compilation of the Bible was not an act of any definite occurrence. It was a matter complicated and abstruse. It was an evolution at the hands of Churchmen of various beliefs and purposes. In the formulation of early church doctrines there was dissension, personal jealousy, intolerance, persecution, bigotry. That out of this welter should have arisen the Bible, with its fine inspiration, would seem to present a plausible basis for belief in its Divine origin.

But who can deny that under such vicious and human circumstances much writing of as pure purpose and as profound sincerity as other that is included in the authorized Bible, must have been omitted? The story of the first council of Nice, when Arius was commanded by the Bishop of Alexandria to quit his beliefs or be declared a heretic, and his writings were ordered destroyed, is eloquent of many things that happened. Good men were engaged on both sides of the ecclesiastical controversies.

About two thirds of this volume is occupied with epistles. Beginning on page 91 you will discover otherwise generally unknown letters of Paul; and the illuminating letters of Clement and others, concluding with correspondence and reports of Herod, Pontius Pilate, and Tiberius Cæsar.

Concerning these epistles Archbishop of Canterbury Wake, who translated them from the originals, says that here is a full and perfect collection of "all the genuine writings that remain to us of the Apostolic Fathers, and carry on the antiquity of the Church from the time of the Holy Scriptures of the New Testament to about a hundred and fifty years after Christ; that except the Holy Scriptures, there is nothing remaining of the truly genuine Christian antiquity more early; that they contain all that can with any certainty be depended upon of the most Primitive Fathers, who had not only the advantage of living in the apostolical times, of hearing the Holy Apostles, and conversing with them, but were most of them persons of a very eminent character in the church, too: that we cannot with any reason doubt of what they deliver to us as the Gospel of Christ, but ought to receive it, if not with equal veneration, yet but a little less respect than we do the Sacred Writings of those who were their masters and instructors;" and, "if," says the Archbishop, "it shall be asked how I came to choose the drudgery of a translator, rather than the more ingenious part of publishing somewhat of my own composing, it was, in short, this; because I hoped that such writings as these would find a more general and unprejudiced acceptance with all sorts of men than anything that could be written by anyone now living."

This collection of *The Lost Books of the Bible*, is published, without prejudice or motive, save that the reader may find whatever pleases and instructs him, and may be free to enjoy his own speculation and hold his own opinion of these ancient and beautiful writings.

R.H.P., Jr.

New York, January 1, 1926.

THE BIRTH OF THE VIRGIN.

FROM A GREEK DIPTYCHON OF THE THIRTEENTH OR FOURTEENTH CENTURY.

THE

Lost Books of the Bible

The GOSPEL of the BIRTH OF MARY.

[In the primitive ages there was a Gospel extant bearing this name, attributed to St. Matthew, and received as genuine and authentic by several of the ancient Christian sects. It is to be found in the works of Jerome, a Father of the Church, who flourished in the fourth century, from whence the present translation is made. His contemporaries, Epiphanius, Bishop of Salamis, and Austin, also mention a Gospel under this title. The ancient copies differed from Jerome's, for from one of them the learned Faustus, a native of Britain, who became Bishop of Riez, in Provence, endeavoured to prove that Christ was not the Son of God till after his baptism; and that he was not of the house of David and tribe of Judah, because, according to the Gospel he cited, the Virgin herself was not of this tribe, but of the tribe of Levi; her father being a priest of the name of Joachim. It was likewise from this Gospel that the sect of the Collyridians, established the worship and offering of manchet bread and cracknels, or fine wafers, as sacrifices to Mary, whom they imagined to have been born of a Virgin, as Christ is related in the Canonical Gospel to have been born of her. Epiphanius likewise cites a passage concerning the death of Zacharias, which is not in Jerome's copy, viz. "That it was the occasion of the death of Zacharias in the temple, that when he had seen a vision, he, through surprise, was willing to disclose it, and his mouth was stopped. That which he saw was at the time of his offering incense, and it was a man standing in the form of an ass. When he was gone out, and had a mind to speak thus to the people, *Woe unto you, whom do ye worship?* he who had appeared to him in the temple took away the use of his speech. Afterwards when he recovered it, and was able to speak, he declared this to the Jews, and they slew him. They add (viz. the Gnostics in this book), that on this very account the high-priest was appointed by their lawgiver (by God to Moses), to carry little bells, that whensoever he went into the temple to sacrifice, he, whom they worshipped, hearing the noise of the bells, might have time enough to hide himself, and not be caught in that ugly shape and figure."—The principal part of this Gospel is contained in the Protevangelion of James, which follows next in order.]

CHAP. I.

1 *The parentage of Mary. 7 Joachim her father, and Anna her mother, go to Jerusalem to the feast of the dedication. 9 Issachar the high priest reproaches Joachim for being childless.*

THE blessed and ever glorious Virgin Mary, sprung from the royal race and family of David, was born in the city of Nazareth, and educated at Jerusalem, in the temple of the Lord.

2 Her father's name was Joachim, and her mother's Anna. The family of her father was of Galilee and the city of Nazareth. The family of her mother was of Bethlehem.

3 Their lives were plain and right in the sight of the Lord, pious and faultless before men. For they divided all their substance into three parts:

4 One of which they devoted

17

to the temple and officers of the temple; another they distributed among strangers, and persons in poor circumstances; and the third they reserved for themselves and the uses of their own family.

5 In this manner they lived for about twenty years chastely, in the favour of God, and the esteem of men, without any children.

6 But they vowed, if God should favour them with any issue, they would devote it to the service of the Lord; on which account they went at every feast in the year to the temple of the Lord.[1]

7 ¶ And it came to pass, that when the feast of the dedication drew near, Joachim, with some others of his tribe, went up to Jerusalem, and at that time, Issachar was high-priest;

8 Who, when he saw Joachim along with the rest of his neighbours, bringing his offering, despised both him and his offerings, and asked him,

9 Why he, who had no children, would presume to appear among those who had? Adding, that his offerings could never be acceptable to God, who was judged by him unworthy to have children; the Scripture having said, Cursed is every one who shall not beget a male in Israel.

10. He further said, that he ought first to be free from that curse by begetting some issue, and then come with his offerings into the presence of God.

11 But Joachim being much confounded with the shame of such reproach, retired to the shepherds, who were with the cattle in their pastures;

12 For he was not inclined to return home, lest his neighbours, who were present and heard all this from the high-priest, should publicly reproach him in the same manner.

CHAP. II.

1 *An angel appears to Joachim,* 9 *and informs him that Anna shall conceive and bring forth a daughter, who shall be called Mary,* 11 *be brought up in the temple,* 12 *and while yet a virgin, in a way unparalleled, bring forth the Son of God:* 13 *gives him a sign,* 14 *and departs.*

BUT when he had been there for some time, on a certain day when he was alone, the angel of the Lord stood by him with a prodigious light.

2 To whom, being troubled at the appearance, the angel who had appeared to him, endeavouring to compose him said:

3 Be not afraid, Joachim, nor troubled at the sight of me, for I am an angel of the Lord sent by him to you, that I might inform you, that your prayers are heard, and your alms ascended in the sight of God.[2]

4 For he hath surely seen your shame, and heard you unjustly reproached for not having children: for God is the avenger of sin, and not of nature;

5 And so when he shuts the womb of any person, he does it for this reason, that he may in a more wonderful manner again open it, and that which is born appear to be not the product of lust, but the gift of God.

6 For the first mother of your nation Sarah, was she not barren even till her eightieth year: And yet even in the end of her old age brought forth Isaac, in whom the promise was made a blessing to all nations.[3]

---

[1] Sam. i. 6, 7, &c.   [2] Acts x. 4.   [3] Gen. xvi. 2, &c. and xviii. 10, &c.

18

7 Rachel also, so much in favour with God, and beloved so much by holy Jacob, continued barren for a long time, yet afterwards was the mother of Joseph, who was not only governor of Egypt, but delivered many nations from perishing with hunger.[1]

8 Who among the judges was more valiant than Samson, or more holy than Samuel? And yet both their mothers were barren.[2]

9 But if reason will not convince you of the truth of my words, that there are frequent conceptions in advanced years, and that those who were barren have brought forth to their great surprise; therefore Anna your wife shall bring you a daughter, and you shall call her name Mary;

10 She shall, according to your vow, be devoted to the Lord from her infancy, and be filled with the Holy Ghost from her mother's womb;[3]

11 She shall neither eat nor drink anything which is unclean, nor shall her conversation be without among the common people, but in the temple of the Lord ; that so she may not fall under any slander or suspicion of what is bad.

12 So in the process of her years, as she shall be in a miraculous manner born of one that was barren, so she shall, while yet a virgin, in a way unparalleled, bring forth the Son of the most High God, who shall, be called Jesus, and, according to the signification of his name, be the Saviour of all nations.[4]

13 And this shall be a sign to you of the things which I declare, namely, when you come to the golden gate of Jerusalem, you shall there meet your wife Anna, who being very much troubled that you returned no sooner, shall then rejoice to see you.

14 When the angel had said this he departed from him.

CHAP. III.

1 *The angel appears to Anna ; 2 tells her a daughter shall be born unto her, 3 devoted to the service of the Lord in the temple, 5, who, being a virgin and not knowing man, shall bring forth the Lord, 6 and gives her a sign therefore. 8 Joachim and Anna meet and rejoice, 10 and praise the Lord. 11 Anna conceives, and brings forth a daughter called Mary.*

AFTERWARDS the angel appeared to Anna his wife saying: Fear not, neither think that which you see is a spirit.[5]

2 For I am that angel who hath offered up your prayers and alms before God, and am now sent to you, that I may inform you, that a daughter will be born unto you, who shall be called Mary, and shall be blessed above all women.[6]

3 She shall be, immediately upon her birth, full of the grace of the Lord, and shall continue during the three years of her weaning in her father's house, and afterwards, being devoted to the service of the Lord, shall not depart from the temple, till she arrives to years of discretion.

4 In a word, she shall there serve the Lord night and day in fasting and prayer,[7] shall abstain from every unclean thing, and never know any man ;

5 But, being an unparalleled instance without any pollution or defilement, and a virgin not

---

[1] Gen. xxx. 1—22, and xli. 1, &c. [2] Judg. xiii. 2. and 1 Sam. 6, &c.
[3] Luke i. 15. [4] Matth. i. 21. [5] Matth. xiv. 26. [6] Luke i. 28. [7] Luke ii. 37.

19

knowing any man, shall bring forth a son, and a maid shall bring forth the Lord, who both by his grace and name and works, shall be the Saviour of the world.

6 Arise therefore, and go up to Jerusalem, and when you shall come to that which is called the golden gate (because it is gilt with gold), as a sign of what I have told you, you shall meet your husband, for whose safety you have been so much concerned.

7 When therefore you find these things thus accomplished, believe that all the rest which I have told you, shall also undoubtedly be accomplished.

8 ¶ According therefore to the command of the angel, both of them left the places where they were, and when they came to the place specified in the angel's prediction, they met each other.

9 Then, rejoicing at each other's vision, and being fully satisfied in the promise of a child, they gave due thanks to the Lord, who exalts the humble.

10 After having praised the Lord, they returned home, and lived in a cheerful and assured expectation of the promise of God.

11 ¶ So Anna conceived, and brought forth a daughter, and, according to the angel's command, the parents did call her name Mary.

CHAP. IV.

1 *Mary brought to the temple at three years old.* 6 *Ascends the stairs of the temple by miracle.* 8 *Her parents sacrificed and returned home.*

AND when three years were expired, and the time of her weaning complete, they brought the Virgin to the temple of the Lord with offerings.

2 And there were about the temple, according to the fifteen Psalms of degrees,[1] fifteen stairs to ascend.

3 For the temple being built in a mountain, the altar of burnt-offering, which was without, could not be come near but by stairs;

4 The parents of the blessed Virgin and infant Mary put her upon one of these stairs;

5 But while they were putting off their clothes, in which they had travelled, and according to custom putting on some that were more neat and clean,

6 In the mean time the Virgin of the Lord in such a manner went up all the stairs one after another, without the help of any to lead or lift her, that any one would have judged from hence that she was of perfect age.

7 Thus the Lord did, in the infancy of his Virgin, work this extraordinary work, and evidence by this miracle how great she was like to be hereafter.

8 But the parents having offered up their sacrifice, according to the custom of the law, and perfected their vow, left the Virgin with other virgins in the apartments of the temple, who were to be brought up there, and they returned home.

CHAP. V.

2 *Mary ministered unto by angels.* 4 *The high-priest orders all virgins of fourteen years old to quit the temple and endeavour to be married.* 5 *Mary refuses,* 6 *having vowed her virginity to the Lord.* 7 *The high-priest commands a meeting of the chief persons of Jerusalem,* 11 *who seek the Lord for counsel in the matter.* 13 *A voice from the mercy-seat.* 15 *The*

---

[1] Those Psalms are from the 120th to the 134th, including both.

high-priest obeys it by ordering all the unmarried men of the house of David to bring their rods to the altar, 17 that his rod which should flower, and on which the Spirit of God should sit, should betroth the Virgin.

BUT the Virgin of the Lord, as she advanced in years, increased also in perfections, and according to the saying of the Psalmist, her father and mother forsook her, but the Lord took care of her.

2 For she every day had the conversation of angels, and every day received visitors from God, which preserved her from all sorts of evil, and caused her to abound with all good things;

3 So that when at length she arrived to her fourteenth year, as the wicked could not lay anything to her charge worthy of reproof, so all good persons, who were acquainted with her, admired her life and conversation.

4 At that time the high-priest made a public order. That all the virgins who had public settlements in the temple, and were come to this age, should return home, and, as they were now of a proper maturity, should, according to the custom of their country, endeavour to be married.

5 To which command, though all the other virgins readily yielded obedience, Mary the Virgin of the Lord alone answered, that she could not comply with it.

6 Assigning these reasons, that both she and her parents had devoted her to the service of the Lord; and besides, that she had vowed virginity to the Lord, which vow she was resolved never to break through by lying with a man.

7 The high priest being hereby brought into a difficulty,

8 Seeing he durst neither on the one hand dissolve the vow, and disobey the Scripture, which says, Vow and pay,[1]

9 Nor on the other hand introduce a custom, to which the people were strangers, commanded,

10 That at the approaching feast all the principal persons both of Jerusalem and the neighbouring places should meet together, that he might have their advice, how he had best proceed in so difficult a case.

11 When they were accordingly met, they unanimously agreed to seek the Lord, and ask counsel from him on this matter.[2]

12 And when they were all engaged in prayer, the high-priest, according to the usual way, went to consult God.

13 And immediately there was a voice from the ark, and the mercy seat, which all present heard, that it must be inquired or sought out by a prophecy of Isaiah to whom the Virgin should be given and be betrothed;

14 For Isaiah saith, there shall come forth a rod out of the stem of Jesse, and a flower shall spring out of its root,

15 And the Spirit of the Lord shall rest upon him, the Spirit of Wisdom and Understanding, the Spirit of Counsel and Might, the Spirit of Knowledge and Piety, and the Spirit of the fear of the Lord shall fill him.

16 Then, according to this prophecy, he appointed, that all

---

[1] Eccles. v. 4, 5, 6; and Psalm lxxvi. 11.

[2] Num. xxvii. 21, compared with Exod. xxviii. 30; Lev. viii. 8; Deut. xxxiii. 8; Ezra ii. 63; Nehem. vii. 65.

the men of the house and family of David, who were marriageable, and not married, should bring their several rods to the altar,

17 And out of whatsoever person's rod after it was brought, a flower should bud forth, and on the top of it the Spirit of the Lord should sit in the appearance of a dove, he should be the man to whom the Virgin should be given and be betrothed.

CHAP. VI.

1 *Joseph draws back his rod.* 5 *The dove pitches on it. He betroths Mary and returns to Bethlehem.* 7 *Mary returns to her parents' house at Galilee.*

AMONG the rest there was a man named Joseph, of the house and family of David, and a person very far advanced in years, who drew back his rod, when every one besides presented his.

2 So that when nothing appeared agreeable to the heavenly voice, the high-priest judged it proper to consult God again,

3 Who answered that he to whom the Virgin was to be betrothed was the only person of those who were brought together, who had not brought his rod.

4 Joseph therefore was betrayed.

5 For, when he did bring his rod, and a dove coming from Heaven pitched upon the top of it, every one plainly saw, that the Virgin was to be betrothed to him:

6 Accordingly, the usual ceremonies of betrothing being over, he returned to his own city of Bethlehem, to set his house in order, and make the needful provisions for the marriage.

7 But the Virgin of the Lord,

Mary, with seven other virgins of the same age, who had been weaned at the same time, and who had been appointed to attend her by the priest, returned to her parents' house in Galilee.

CHAP. VII.

7 *The salutation of the Virgin by Gabriel, who explains to her that she shall conceive, without lying with a man, while a Virgin,* 19 *by the Holy Ghost coming upon her without the heats of lust.* 21 *She submits.*

NOW at this time of her first coming into Galilee, the angel Gabriel was sent to her from God, to declare to her the conception of our Saviour, and the manner and way of her conceiving him.

2 Accordingly going into her, he filled the chamber where she was with a prodigious light, and in a most courteous manner saluting her, he said,

3 Hail, Mary! Virgin of the Lord most acceptable! O Virgin full of Grace! The Lord is with you, you are blessed above all women, you are blessed above all men, that have been hitherto born.[1]

4 But the Virgin, who had before been well acquainted with the countenances of angels, and to whom such light from heaven was no uncommon thing,

5 Was neither terrified with the vision of the angel, nor astonished at the greatness of the light, but only troubled about the angel's words:

6 And began to consider what so extraordinary a salutation should mean, what it did portend, or what sort of end it would have.[2]

7 To this thought the angel, divinely inspired, replies;

8 Fear not, Mary, as though

[1] Luke i. 28.

[2] Luke i. 29.

I intended anything inconsistent with your chastity in this salutation:

9 For you have found favour with the Lord, because you made virginity your choice.

10 Therefore while you are a Virgin, you shall conceive without sin, and bring forth a son.

11 He shall be great, because he shall reign from sea to sea, and from the rivers to the ends of the earth.[1]

12 And he shall be called the Son of the Highest; for he who is born in a mean state on earth reigns in an exalted one in heaven.

13 And the Lord shall give him the throne of his father David, and he shall reign over the house of Jacob for ever, and of his kingdom there shall be no end.

14 For he is the King of Kings, and Lord of Lords, and his throne is for ever and ever.

15 To this discourse of the angel the Virgin replied not, as though she were unbelieving, but willing to know the manner of it.

16 She said, How can that be? For seeing, according to my vow, I have never known any man, how can I bear a child without the addition of a man's seed?

17 To this the angel replied and said, Think not, Mary, that you shall conceive in the ordinary way.

18 For, without lying with a man, while a Virgin, you shall conceive; while a Virgin, you shall bring forth; and while a Virgin shall give suck.

19 For the Holy Ghost shall come upon you, and the power of the Most High shall overshadow you, without any of the heats of lust.

20 So that which shall be born of you shall be only holy, because it only is conceived without sin, and being born, shall be called the Son of God.

21 Then Mary stretching forth her hands, and lifting her eyes to heaven, said, Behold the handmaid of the Lord! Let it be unto me according to thy word.[2]

CHAP. VIII.

1 *Joseph returns to Galilee to marry the Virgin he had betrothed. 4 perceives she is with child, 5 is uneasy, 7 purposes to put her away privily, 8 is told by the angel of the Lord it is not the work of man but the Holy Ghost, 12 Marries her, but keeps chaste, 13 removes with her to Bethlehem, 15 where she brings forth Christ.*

JOSEPH therefore went from Judæa to Galilee, with intention to marry the Virgin who was betrothed to him:

2 For it was now near three months since she was betrothed to him.

3 At length it plainly appeared she was with child, and it could not be hid from Joseph:

4 For going to the Virgin in a free manner, as one espoused, and talking familiarly with her, he perceived her to be with child.

5 And thereupon began to be uneasy and doubtful, not knowing what course it would be best to take;

6 For being a just man, he was not willing to expose her, nor defame her by the suspicion of being a whore, since he was a pious man.

7 He purposed therefore privately to put an end to their agreement, and as privately to put her away.

8 But while he was meditating these things,[3] behold the angel of the Lord appeared to him in

[1] Luke i. 31, &c.   [2] Luke i. 38.   [3] Matt. i. 19.

23

his sleep, and said Joseph, son of David, fear not;

9 Be not willing to entertain any suspicion of the Virgin's being guilty of fornication, or to think any thing amiss of her, neither be afraid to take her to wife;

10 For that which is begotten in her and now distresses your mind, is not the work of man, but the Holy Ghost.

11 For she of all women is that only Virgin who shall bring forth the Son of God, and you shall call his name Jesus, that is, Saviour : for he will save his people from their sins.

12 Joseph thereupon, according to the command of the angel, married the Virgin, and did not know her, but kept her in chastity.

13 And now the ninth month from her conception drew near, when Joseph took his wife and what other things were necessary to Bethlehem, the city from whence he came.

14 And it came to pass, while they were there, the days were fulfilled for her bringing forth.

15 And she brought forth her first-born son, as the holy Evangelists have taught, even our Lord Jesus Christ, who with the Father, Son, and Holy Ghost, lives and reigns to everlasting ages.

The PROTEVANGELION ; or, An Historical Account of the BIRTH of CHRIST, and the Perpetual VIRGIN MARY, his Mother, by JAMES THE LESSER, Cousin and Brother of the Lord Jesus, chief Apostle and first Bishop of the Christians in Jerusalem.

[This Gospel is ascribed to James. The allusions to it in the ancient Fathers are frequent, and their expressions indicate that it had obtained a very general credit in the Christian world. The controversies founded upon it chiefly relate to the age of Joseph at the birth of Christ, and to his being a widower with children, before his marriage with the Virgin. It seems material to remark, that the legends of the latter ages affirm the virginity of Joseph, notwithstanding Epiphanius, Hilary, Chrysostom, Cyril, Euthymius, Thephylact, Occumenius, and indeed all the Latin Fathers till Ambrose, and the Greek Fathers afterwards, maintain the opinions of Joseph's age and family, founded upon their belief in the authenticity of this book. It is supposed to have been originally composed in Hebrew. Postellus brought the MS. of this Gospel from the Levant, translated it into Latin, and sent it to Oporimus, a printer at Basil, where Bibliander, a Protestant Divine, and the Professor of Divinity at Zurich, caused it to be printed in 1552. Postellus asserts that it was publicly read as canonical in the eastern churches, they making no doubt that James was the author of it. It is, nevertheless, considered apocryphal by some of the most learned divines in the Protestant and Catholic churches.]

CHAP. I.

1 *Joachim, a rich man,* 2 *offers to the Lord,* 3 *is opposed by Reuben the high-priest, because he has not begotten issue in Israel,* 6 *retires into the wilderness and fasts forty days and forty nights.*

IN the history of the twelve tribes of Israel we read there was a certain person called Joachim, who being very rich, made double[1] offerings to the Lord God, having made this resolu-

[1] That is, gave as much more as he was obliged to give.

ELIZABETH RECEIVING THE VISIT OF MARY.

FROM A GREEK DIPTYCHON OF THE THIRTEENTH OR FOURTEENTH CENTURY.

tion: my substance shall be for the benefit of the whole people, and that I may find mercy from the Lord God for the forgiveness of my sins.

2 But at a certain great feast of the Lord, when the children of Israel offered their gifts, and Joachim also offered his, Reuben the high-priest opposed him, saying it is not lawful for thee to offer thy gifts, seeing thou hast not begot any issue in Israel.

3 At this Joachim being concerned very much, went away to consult the registries of the twelve tribes, to see whether he was the only person who had begot no issue.

4 But upon inquiry he found that all the righteous had raised up seed in Israel:

5 Then he called to mind the patriarch Abraham, How that God in the end of his life had given him his son Isaac; upon which he was exceedingly distressed, and would not be seen by his wife:

6 But retired into the wilderness, and fixed his tent there, and fasted forty days and forty nights, saying to himself,

7 I will not go down either to eat or drink, till the Lord my God shall look down upon me, but prayer shall be my meat and drink.[1]

CHAP. II.

1 *Anna, the wife of Joachim, mourns her barrenness, 6 is reproached with it by Judith her maid, 9 sits under a laurel tree and prays to the Lord.*

IN the meantime his wife Anna was distressed and perplexed on a double account, and said I will mourn both for my widowhood and my barrenness.

2 Then drew near a great feast of the Lord, and Judith her maid said, How long will you thus afflict your soul? The feast of the Lord is now come, when it is unlawful for any one to mourn.

3 Take therefore this hood which was given by one who makes such things, for it is not fit that I, who am a servant, should wear it, but it well suits a person of your greater character.

4 But Anna replied, Depart from me, I am not used to such things; besides, the Lord hath greatly humbled me.

5 I fear some ill-designing person hath given thee this, and thou art come to pollute me with my sin.

6 Then Judith her maid answered, What evil shall I wish you when you will not hearken to me?

7 I cannot wish you a greater curse than you are under, in that God hath shut up your womb, that you should not be a mother in Israel.

8 At this Anna was exceedingly troubled, and having on her wedding garment, went about three o'clock in the afternoon to walk in her garden.

9 And she saw a laurel-tree, and sat under it, and prayed unto the Lord, saying,

10 O God of my fathers, bless me and regard my prayer as thou didst bless the womb of Sarah, and gavest her a son Isaac.[2]

CHAP. III.

1 *Anna perceiving a sparrow's nest in the laurels bemoans her barrenness.*

[1] In imitation of the forty days and nights fast of Moses, recorded Exod. xxiv. 11, xxxiv. 28; Deut. ix. 9; of Elijah, 1 Kings xix. 8; and Christ's, Matt. iv. 2.   [2] Gen. xxi. 2.

AND as she was looking towards heaven she perceived a sparrow's nest in the laurel,

2 And mourning within herself, she said, Wo is me, who begat me? and what womb did bear me, that I should be thus accursed before the children of Israel, and that they should reproach and deride me in the temple of my God: Wo is me, to what can I be compared?

3 I am not comparable to the very beasts of the earth, for even the beasts of the earth are fruitful before thee, O Lord! Wo is me, to what can I be compared?

4 I am not comparable to the brute animals, for even the brute animals are fruitful before thee, O Lord! Wo is me, to what am I comparable?

5 I cannot be compared to these waters, for even the waters are fruitful before thee, O Lord! Wo is me, to what can I be compared?

6 I am not comparable to the waves of the sea; for these, whether they are calm, or in motion, with the fishes which are in them, praise thee, O Lord! Wo is me, to what can I be compared?

7 I am not comparable to the very earth, for the earth produces its fruits, and praises thee, O Lord!

CHAP. IV.

1 An Angel appears to Anna and tells her she shall conceive; two angels appear to her on the same errand. 5 Joachim sacrifices. 8 Anna goes to meet him, 9 rejoicing that she shall conceive.

THEN an angel of the Lord stood by her and said, Anna, Anna, the Lord hath heard thy prayer; thou shalt conceive and bring forth, and thy progeny shall be spoken of in all the world.

2 And Anna answered, As the Lord my God liveth, whatever I bring forth, whether it be male or female, I will devote it to the Lord my God, and it shall minister to him in holy things, during its whole life.

3 And behold there appeared two angels, saying unto her, Behold Joachim thy husband is coming with his shepherds.

4 For an angel of the Lord hath also come down to him, and said, The Lord God hath heard thy prayer, make haste and go hence, for behold Anna thy wife shall conceive.

5 And Joachim went down and called his shepherds, saying Bring me hither ten she-lambs without spot or blemish, and they shall be for the Lord my God.

6 And bring me twelve calves without blemish, and the twelve calves shall be for the priests and the elders.

7 Bring me also a hundred goats, and the hundred goats shall be for the whole people.

8 And Joachim went down with the shepherds, and Anna stood by the gate and saw Joachim coming with the shepherds.

9 And she ran, and hanging about his neck, said, Now I know that the Lord hath greatly blessed me:

10 For behold, I who was a widow am no longer a widow, and I who was barren shall conceive.

CHAP. V.

1 Joachim abides the first day in his house, but sacrifices on the morrow. 2 consults the plate on the priest's forehead. 3 And is without sin. 6 Anna brings forth a daughter, 9 whom she calls Mary.

AND Joachim abode the first day in his house, but on the morrow he brought his offerings and said,

2 If the Lord be propitious to me let the plate which is on the priest's forehead[1] make it manifest.

3 And he consulted the plate which the priest wore, and saw it, and behold sin was not found in him.

4 And Joachim said, Now I know that the Lord is propitious to me, and hath taken away all my sins.

5 And he went down from the temple of the Lord justified, and he went to his own house.

6 And when nine months were fulfilled to Anna, she brought forth, and said to the midwife, What have I brought forth?

7 And she told her, a girl.

8 Then Anna said, the Lord hath this day magnified my soul; and she laid her in bed.

9 And when the days of her purification were accomplished, she gave suck to the child, and called her name Mary.

CHAP. VI.

1 *Mary at nine months old, walks nine steps, 3 Anna keeps her holy, 4 When she is a year old, Joachim makes a great feast. 7 Anna gives her the breast, and sings a song to the Lord.*

AND the child increased in strength every day, so that when she was nine months old, her mother put her upon the ground to try if she could stand; and when she had walked nine steps, she came again to her mother's lap.

2 Then her mother caught her up, and said, As the Lord my God liveth, thou shalt not walk again on this earth till I bring thee into the temple of the Lord.

3 Accordingly she made her chamber a holy place, and suffered nothing uncommon or unclean to come near her, but invited certain undefiled daughters of Israel, and they drew her aside.

4 But when the child was a year old, Joachim made a great feast, and invited the priests, scribes, elders, and all the people of Israel;

5 And Joachim then made an offering of the girl to the chief priests, and they blessed her, saying, The God of our fathers bless this girl, and give her a name famous and lasting through all generations. And all the people replied, So be it, Amen.

6 Then Joachim a second time offered her to the priests, and they blessed her, saying, O most high God, regard this girl, and bless her with an everlasting blessing.

7 Upon this her mother took her up, and gave her the breast, and sung the following song to the Lord.[2]

8 I will sing a new song unto the Lord my God, for he hath visited me, and taken away from me the reproach of mine enemies, and hath given me the fruit of his righteousness, that it may now be told the sons of Reuben, that Anna gives suck.

9 Then she put the child to rest in the room which she had consecrated, and she went out and ministered unto them.

10 And when the feast was ended, they went away rejoicing and praising the God of Israel.

[1] Such an instrument God had appointed the high-priest to wear for such discoveries. See Exod. xxviii. 36, &c., and Spencer de Urim et Thummim.
[2] Compare 1 Sam. ii., &c., with Luke i. 46.

CHAP. VII.

3 *Mary being three years old, Joachim causes certain virgins to light each a lamp, and goes with her to the temple.* 5 *The high-priest places her on the third step of the altar, and she dances with her feet.*

BUT the girl grew, and when she was two years old, Joachim said to Anna, Let us lead her to the temple of the Lord, that we may perform our vow, which we have vowed unto the Lord God, lest he should be angry with us, and our offering be unacceptable.

2 But Anna said, Let us wait the third year, lest she should be at a loss to know her father. And Joachim said, Let us then wait.

3 And when the child was three years old, Joachim said, Let us invite the daughters of the Hebrews, who are undefiled, and let them take each a lamp, and let them be lighted, that the child may not turn back again, and her mind be set against the temple of the Lord.

4 And they did thus till they ascended into the temple of the Lord. And the high-priest received her, and blessed her, and said, Mary, the Lord God hath magnified thy name to all generations, and to the very end of time by thee will the Lord shew his redemption to the children of Israel.

5 And he placed her upon the third step of the altar, and the Lord gave unto her grace, and she danced with her feet, and all the house of Israel loved her.

CHAP. VIII.

2 *Mary fed in the temple by angels,* 3 *when twelve years old the priests consult what to do with her.* 6 *The angel of the Lord warns Zacharias*
to call together all the widowers, each bringing a rod. 7 *The people meet by sound of trumpet.* 8 *Joseph throws away his hatchet, and goes to the meeting,* 11 *a dove comes forth from his rod, and alights on his head.* 12 *He is chosen to betroth the Virgin.* 13 *refuses because he is an old man,* 15 *is compelled,* 16 *takes her home, and goes to mind his trade of building.*

AND her parents went away filled with wonder, and praising God, because the girl did not return back to them.

2 But Mary continued in the temple as a dove educated there, and received her food from the hand of an angel.

3 And when she was twelve years of age, the priests met in a council, and said, Behold, Mary is twelve years of age; what shall we do with her, for fear lest the holy place of the Lord our God should be defiled?

4 Then replied the priests to Zacharias the high-priest, Do you stand at the altar of the Lord, and enter into the holy place, and make petitions concerning her, and whatsoever the Lord shall manifest unto you, that do.

5 Then the high-priest entered into the Holy of Holies, and taking away with him the breast-plate of judgment[1] made prayers concerning her;

6 And behold the angel of the Lord came to him, and said, Zacharias, Zacharias, Go forth and call together all the widowers among the people, and let every one of them bring his rod, and he by whom the Lord shall shew a sign shall be the husband of Mary.

7 And the criers went out through all Judæa, and the trumpet of the Lord sounded, and all the people ran and met together.

---

[1] See Exod. xxviii. 22, &c.

8 ¶ Joseph also, throwing away the hatchet, went out to meet them; and when they were met, they went to the high-priest, taking every man his rod.

9 After the high-priest had received their rods, he went into the temple to pray;

10 And when he had finished his prayer, he took the rods, and went forth and distributed them, and there was no miracle attended them.

11 The last rod was taken by Joseph, and behold a dove proceeded out of the rod, and flew upon the head of Joseph.

12 And the high-priest said, Joseph, Thou art the person chosen to take the Virgin of the Lord, to keep her for him:

13 But Joseph refused, saying, I am an old man, and have children, but she is young, and I fear lest I should appear ridiculous in Israel.

14 Then the high-priest replied, Joseph, fear the Lord thy God, and remember how God dealt with Dathan, Korah, and Abiram, how the earth opened and swallowed them up, because of their contradiction.

15 Now therefore, Joseph, fear God, lest the like things should happen in your family.

16 Joseph then being afraid, took her unto his house, and Joseph said unto Mary, Behold, I have taken thee from the temple of the Lord, and now I will leave thee in my house; I must go to mind my trade of building. The Lord be with thee.

CHAP. IX.

1 *The priests desire a new veil for the temple, 3 seven virgins cast lots for making different parts of it, 4 the lot to spin the true purple falls to* Mary. 5 *Zacharias, the high-priest becomes dumb.* 7 *Mary takes a pot to draw water, and hears a voice, 8 trembles and begins to work, 9 an angel appears, and salutes her, and tells her she shall conceive by the Holy Ghost, 17 she submits, 19 visits her cousin Elizabeth, whose child in her womb leaps.*

AND it came to pass, in a council of the priests, it was said, Let us make a new veil for the temple.

2 And the high-priest said, Call together to me seven undefiled virgins of the tribe of David.

3 And the servants went and brought them into the temple of the Lord, and the high-priest said unto them Cast lots before me now, who of you shall spin the golden thread, who the blue, who the scarlet, who the fine linen, and who the true purple.

4 Then the high-priest knew Mary, that she was of the tribe of David; and he called her, and the true purple fell to her lot to spin, and she went away to her own house.

5 But from that time Zacharias the high-priest became dumb, and Samuel was placed in his room till Zacharias spoke again.

6 But Mary took the true purple, and did spin it.

7 ¶ And she took a pot, and went out to draw water, and heard a voice saying unto her, Hail thou who art full of grace,[1] the Lord is with thee; thou art blessed among women.

8 And she looked round to the right and to the left (to see) whence that voice came, and then trembling went into her house, and laying down the water-pot she took the purple, and sat down in her seat to work it.

[1] Luke i. 28, &c.

29

9 And behold the angel of the Lord stood by her, and said, Fear not, Mary, for thou hast found favour in the sight of God;

10 Which when she heard, she reasoned with herself what that sort of salutation meant.

11 And the angel said unto her, The Lord is with thee, and thou shalt conceive:

12 To which she replied, What! shall I conceive by the living God, and bring forth as all other women do?

13 But the angel returned answer, Not so, O Mary, but the Holy Ghost shall come upon thee, and the power of the Most High shall overshadow thee;

14 Wherefore that which shall be born of thee shall be holy, and shall be called the Son of the Living God, and thou shalt call his name Jesus; for he shall save his people from their sins.

15 And behold thy cousin Elizabeth, she also hath conceived a son in her old age.

16 And this now is the sixth month with her, who was called barren; for nothing is impossible with God.

17 And Mary said, Behold the handmaid of the Lord; let it be unto me according to thy word.

18 ¶ And when she had wrought her purple, she carried it to the high-priest, and the high-priest blessed her, saying, Mary, the Lord God hath magnified thy name, and thou shalt be blessed in all the ages of the world.

19 Then Mary, filled with joy, went away to her cousin Elizabeth, and knocked at the door.

20 Which when Elizabeth heard, she ran and opened to her, and blessed her, and said,

Whence is this to me, that the mother of my Lord should come unto me?

21 For lo! as soon as the voice of thy salutation reached my ears, that which is in me leaped and blessed thee.

22 But Mary, being ignorant of all those mysterious things which the archangel Gabriel had spoken to her, lifted up her eyes to heaven, and said, Lord! What am I, that all the generations of the earth should call me blessed?

23 But perceiving herself daily to grow big, and being afraid, she went home, and hid herself from the children of Israel; and was fourteen years old when all these things happened.

CHAP. X.

1 *Joseph returns from building houses, finds the Virgin grown big, being six months' gone with child, 2 is jealous and troubled, 8 reproaches her, 10 she affirms her innocence, 13 he leaves her, 16 determines to dismiss her privately, 17 is warned in a dream that Mary is with child by the Holy Ghost, 20 and glorifies God who hath shewn him such favour.*

AND when her sixth month was come, Joseph returned from his building houses abroad, which was his trade, and entering into the house, found the Virgin grown big:

2 Then smiting upon his face, he said, With what face can I look up to the Lord my God? or, what shall I say concerning this young woman?

3 For I received her a Virgin out of the temple of the Lord my God, and have not preserved her such!

4 Who has thus deceived me? Who has committed this evil in my house, and seducing the Virgin from me, hath defiled her?

¹ Luke ii. 39, &c.

30

5 Is not the history of Adam exactly accomplished in me?

6 For in the very instant of his glory, the serpent came and found Eve alone, and seduced her.

7 Just after the same manner it has happened to me.

8 Then Joseph arising from the ground, called her, and said, O thou who hast been so much favoured by God, why hast thou done this?

9 Why hast thou thus debased thy soul, who wast educated in the Holy of Holies, and received thy food from the hand of angels?

10 But she, with a flood of tears, replied, I am innocent, and have known no man.

11 Then said Joseph, How comes it to pass you are with child?

12 Mary answered, As the Lord my God liveth, I know not by what means.

13 ¶ Then Joseph was exceedingly afraid, and went away from her, considering what he should do with her; and he thus reasoned with himself:[1]

14 If I conceal her crime, I shall be found guilty by the law of the Lord ;

15 And if I discover her to the children of Israel, I fear, lest she being with child by an angel, I shall be found to betray the life of an innocent person:

16 What therefore shall I do? I will privately dismiss her.

17 Then the night was come upon him, when behold an angel of the Lord appeared to him in a dream, and said,

18 Be not afraid to take that young woman, for that which is within her is of the Holy Ghost;

19 And she shall bring forth a son, and thou shalt call his name Jesus, for he shall save his people from their sins.

20 Then Joseph arose from his sleep, and glorified the God of Israel, who had shown him such favour, and preserved the Virgin.

CHAP. XI.

3 Annas visits Joseph, perceives the Virgin big with child, 4 informs the high priest that Joseph had privately married her. 8 Joseph and Mary brought to trial on the charge. 17 Joseph drinks the water of the Lord as an ordeal, and receiving no harm, returns home.

THEN came Annas the scribe, and said to Joseph, Wherefore have we not seen you since your return?

2 And Joseph replied, Because I was weary after my journey, and rested the first day.

3 But Annas turning about perceived the Virgin big with child.

4 And went away to the priest, and told him, Joseph in whom you placed so much confidence, is guilty of a notorious crime, in that he hath defiled the Virgin whom he received out of the temple of the Lord, and hath privately married her, not discovering it to the children of Israel.

5 Then said the priest, Hath Joseph done this?

6 Annas replied, If you send any of your servants, you will find that she is with child.

7 And the servants went, and found it as he said.

8 Upon this both she and Joseph were brought to their trial, and the priest said unto her, Mary, what hast thou done?

9 Why hast thou debased thy

---

[1] See Matt. i. 18.

31

soul, and forgot thy God, seeing thou wast brought up in the Holy of Holies, and didst receive thy food from the hands of angels, and heardest their songs?

10 Why hast thou done this?

11 To which with a flood of tears she answered, As the Lord my God liveth, I am innocent in his sight, seeing I know no man.

12 Then the priest said to Joseph, Why hast thou done this?

13 And Joseph answered, As the Lord my God liveth, I have not been concerned with her.

14 But the priest said, Lie not, but declare the truth; thou hast privately married her, and not discovered it to the children of Israel, and humbled thyself under the mighty hand (of God), that thy seed might be blessed.

15 And Joseph was silent.

16 Then said the priest (to Joseph), You must restore to the temple of the Lord the Virgin which you took thence.

17 But he wept bitterly, and the priest added, I will cause you both to drink the water of the Lord,[1] which is for trial, and so your iniquity shall be laid open before you.

18 Then the priest took the water, and made Joseph drink, and sent him to a mountainous place.

19 And he returned perfectly well, and all the people wondered that his guilt was not discovered.

20 So the priest said, Since the Lord hath not made your sins evident, neither do I condemn you.

21 So he sent them away.

22 Then Joseph took Mary, and went to his house, rejoicing and praising the God of Israel.

CHAP. XII.

1 *A decree from Augustus for taxing the Jews. 5 Joseph puts Mary on an ass, to return to Bethlehem, 6 she looks sorrowful, 7 she laughs, 8 Joseph inquires the cause of each, 9 she tells him she sees two persons, one mourning and the other rejoicing, 10 the delivery being near, he takes her from the ass, and places her in a cave.*

AND it came to pass, that there went forth a decree[2] from the Emperor Augustus, that all the Jews should be taxed, who were of Bethlehem in Judæa:

2 And Joseph said, I will take care that my children be taxed: but what shall I do with this young woman?

3 To have her taxed as my wife I am ashamed; and if I tax her as my daughter, all Israel knows she is not my daughter.

4 When the time of the Lord's appointment shall come, let him do as seems good to him.

5 And he saddled the ass, and put her upon it, and Joseph and Simon followed after her, and arrived at Bethlehem within three miles.

6 Then Joseph turning about saw Mary sorrowful, and said within himself, Perhaps she is in pain through that which is within her.

7 But when he turned about again he saw her laughing, and said to her,

8 Mary, how happens it, that I sometimes see sorrow, and sometimes laughter and joy in thy countenance?

9 And Mary replied to him, I see two people with mine eyes,

---

[1] Num. v. 18.　　　　[2] Luke ii. 1.

THE BIRTH OF CHRIST.

FROM A "BOOK OF THE EVANGELISTS." GREEK MANUSCRIPT OF THE TWELFTH CENTURY.

the one weeping and mourning, the other laughing and rejoicing.

10 And he went again across the way, and Mary said to Joseph, Take me down from the ass, for that which is in me presses to come forth.

11 But Joseph replied, Whither shall I take thee? for the place is desert.

12 Then said Mary again to Joseph, take me down, for that which is within me mightily presses me.

13 And Joseph took her down.

14 And he found there a cave, and let her into it.

CHAP. XIII.

1 *Joseph seeks a Hebrew midwife,* 2 *perceives the fowls stopping in their flight,* 3 *the working people at their food not moving,* 8 *the sheep standing still,* 9 *the shepherd fixed and immoveable,* 10 *and kids with their mouths touching the water but not drinking.*

AND leaving her and his sons in the cave, Joseph went forth to seek a Hebrew midwife in the village of Bethlehem.

2 But as I was going (said Joseph) I looked up into the air, and I saw the clouds astonished, and the fowls of the air stopping in the midst of their flight.

3 And I looked down towards the earth, and saw a table spread, and working people sitting around it, but their hands were upon the table, and they did not move to eat.

4 They who had meat in their mouths did not eat.

5 They who lifted their hands up to their heads did not draw them back:

6 And they who lifted them up to their mouths did not put anything in;

7 But all their faces were fixed upwards.

8 And I beheld the sheep dispersed, and yet the sheep stood still.

9 And the shepherd lifted up his hand to smite them, and his hand continued up.

10. And I looked unto a river, and saw the kids with their mouths close to the water, and touching it, but they did not drink.

CHAP. XIV.

1 *Joseph finds a midwife.* 10 *A bright cloud overshadows the cave.* 11 *A great light in the cave, gradually increases until the infant is born.* 13 *The midwife goes out, and tells Salome that she has seen a virgin bring forth.* 17 *Salome doubts it.* 20 *her hand withers,* 22 *she supplicates the Lord,* 28 *is cured,* 30 *but warned not to declare what she had seen.*

THEN I beheld a woman coming down from the mountains, and she said to me, Where art thou going, O man?

2 And I said to her, I go to inquire for a Hebrew midwife.

3 She replied to me, Where is the woman that is to be delivered?

4 And I answered, In the cave, and she is betrothed to me.

5 Then said the midwife, Is she not thy wife?

6 Joseph answered, It is Mary, who was educated in the Holy of Holies, in the house of the Lord, and she fell to my lot, and is not my wife, but has conceived by the Holy Ghost.

7 The midwife said, Is this true?

8 He answered, Come and see.

9 And the midwife went along with him, and stood in the cave.

10 Then a bright cloud overshadowed the cave, and the mid-

33

wife said, This day my soul is magnified, for mine eyes have seen surprising things, and salvation is brought forth to Israel.

11 But on a sudden the cloud became a great light in the cave, so that their eyes could not bear it.

12 But the light gradually decreased, until the infant appeared, and sucked the breast of his mother Mary.

13 Then the midwife cried out, and said, How glorious a day is this, wherein mine eyes have seen this extraordinary sight!

14 And the midwife went out from the cave, and Salome met her.

15 And the midwife said to her, Salome, Salome, I will tell you a most surprising thing which I saw,

16 A virgin hath brought forth, which is a thing contrary to nature.

17 To which Salome replied, As the Lord my God liveth, unless I receive particular proof of this matter, I will not believe that a virgin hath brought forth.

18 ¶ Then Salome went in, and the midwife said, Mary, shew thyself, for a great controversy is risen concerning thee.

19 And Salome received satisfaction.

20 But her hand was withered, and she groaned bitterly.

21 And said, Woe to me, because of mine iniquity; for I have tempted the living God, and my hand is ready to drop off.

22 Then Salome made her supplication to the Lord, and said, O God of my fathers, remember me, for I am of the seed of Abraham, and Isaac, and Jacob.

23 Make me not a reproach among the children of Israel, but restore me sound to my parents.

24 For thou well knowest, O Lord, that I have performed many offices of charity in thy name, and have received my reward from thee.

25 Upon this an angel of the Lord stood by Salome, and said, The Lord God hath heard thy prayer, reach forth thy hand to the child, and carry him, and by that means thou shalt be restored.

26 Salome, filled with exceeding joy, went to the child, and said, I will touch him:

27 And she purposed to worship him, for she said, This is a great king which is born in Israel.

28 And straightway Salome was cured.

29 Then the midwife went out of the cave, being approved by God.

30 And lo! a voice came to Salome, Declare not the strange things which thou hast seen, till the child shall come to Jerusalem.

31 So Salome also departed, approved by God.

CHAP. XV.

1 *Wise men come from the east.* 3. *Herod alarmed; 8 desires them if they find the child, to bring him word.* 10 *They visit the cave, and offer the child their treasure,* 11 *and being warned in a dream, do not return to Herod, but go home another way.*

THEN Joseph was preparing to go away, because there arose a great disorder in Bethlehem by the coming of[1] some wise men from the east,

---

[1] Matt. ii. 1, &c.

2 Who said, Where is the king of the Jews born? For we have seen his star in the east, and are come to worship him.

3 When Herod heard this, he was exceedingly troubled, and sent messengers to the wise men, and to the priests, and inquired of them in the town-hall,

4 And said unto them, Where have you it written concerning Christ the king, or where should he be born?

5 Then they say unto him, In Bethlehem of Judæa; for thus it is written: And thou Bethlehem in the land of Judah, art not the least among the princes of Judah, for out of thee shall come a ruler, who shall rule my people Israel.

6 And having sent away the chief priests, he inquired of the wise men in the town-hall, and said unto them, What sign was it ye saw concerning the king that is born?

7 They answered him, We saw an extraordinary large star shining among the stars of heaven, and so out-shined all the other stars, as that they became not visible, and we knew thereby that a great king was born in Israel, and therefore we are come to worship him.

8 Then said Herod to them, Go and make diligent inquiry; and if ye find the child, bring me word again, that I may come and worship him also.

9 So the wise men went forth, and behold, the star which they saw in the east went before them, till it came and stood over the cave where the young child was with Mary his mother.

10 Then they brought forth out of their treasures, and offered unto him gold and frankincense, and myrrh.

11 And being warned in a dream by an angel, that they should not return to Herod through Judæa, they departed into their own country by another way.

CHAP. XVI.

1 Herod enraged, orders the infants in Bethlehem to be slain. 2 Mary puts her infant in an ox manger. 3 Elizabeth flees with her son John to the mountains. 6 A mountain miraculously divides and receives them. 9 Herod incensed at the escape of John, causes Zacharias to be murdered at the altar, 23 the roofs of the temple rent, the body miraculously conveyed, and the blood petrified. 25 Israel mourns for him. 27 Simeon chosen his successor by lot.

THEN Herod[1] perceiving that he was mocked by the wise men, and being very angry, commanded certain men to go and to kill all the children that were in Bethlehem, from two years old and under.

2 But Mary hearing that the children were to be killed, being under much fear, took the child, and wrapped him up in swaddling clothes, and laid him in an ox-manger,[2] because there was no room for them in the inn.

3 Elizabeth also, hearing that her son John was about to be searched for, took him and went up unto the mountains, and looked around for a place to hide him;

4 And there was no secret place to be found.

5 Then she groaned within herself, and said, O mountain of the Lord, receive the mother with the child.

6 For Elizabeth could not climb up.

[1] Matt. ii. 16. [2] Luke ii. 7 is alluded to, though misapplied as to time.

35

7 And instantly the mountain was divided and received them.

8 And there appeared to them an angel of the Lord, to preserve them.

9 ¶ But Herod made search after John, and sent servants to Zacharias, when he was (ministering) at the altar, and said unto him, Where hast thou hid thy son?

10 He replied to them, I am a minister of God, and a servant at the altar; how should I know where my son is?

11 So the servants went back, and told Herod the whole; at which he was incensed, and said, Is not this son of his like to be king in Israel?

12 He sent therefore again his servants to Zacharias, saying, Tell us the truth, where is thy son, for you know that your life is in my hand.

13 So the servants went and told him all this:

14 But Zacharias replied to them, I am a martyr for God, and if he shed my blood, the Lord will receive my soul.

15 Besides know that ye shed innocent blood.

16 However Zacharias was murdered in the entrance of the temple and altar, and about the partition;

17 But the children of Israel knew not when he was killed.

18 ¶ Then at the hour of salutation the priests went into the temple, but Zacharias did not according to custom meet them and bless them;

19 Yet they still continued waiting for him to salute them;

20 And when they found he did not in a long time come, one of them ventured into the holy place where the altar was, and he saw blood lying upon the ground congealed;

21 When, behold, a voice from heaven said, Zacharias is murdered, and his blood shall not be wiped away, until the revenger of his blood come.

22 But when he heard this, he was afraid, and went forth and told the priests what he had seen and heard; and they all went in, and saw the fact.

23 Then the roofs of the temple howled, and were rent from the top to the bottom:

24 And they could not find the body, but only blood made hard like stone.

25 And they went away, and told the people, that Zacharias was murdered, and all the tribes of Israel heard thereof, and mourned for him, and lamented three days.[1]

---

[1] There is a story both in the Jerusalem and Babylonish Talmud very similar to this. It is cited by Dr. Lightfoot, *Talmud, Hierosol, in Taannith,* fol. 69; and *Talmud, Babyl. in Sanhedr.,* fol. 96. "Rabbi Jochanan said, Eighty thousand priests were slain for the blood of Zacharias. Rabbi Judas asked Rabbi Achan, Where did they kill Zacharias? Was it in the woman's court, or in the court of Israel? He answered: Neither in the court of Israel, nor in the court of women, but in the court of the priests; and they did not treat his blood in the same manner as they were wont to treat the blood of a ram or a young goat. For of these it is written, He shall pour out his blood, and cover it with dust. But it is written here, The blood is in the midst of her: she set it upon the top of the rock; she poured it not upon the ground. (Ezek. xxiv. 7.) But why was this? That it might cause fury to come up to take vengeance: I have set his blood upon the top of a rock, that it should not be covered. They committed seven evils that day: they murdered a priest, a prophet, and a

26 Then the priests took counsel together concerning a person to succeed him.

27 And Simeon and the other priests cast lots, and the lot fell upon Simeon.

28 For he had been assured by the Holy Spirit, that he should not die, till he had seen Christ come in the flesh.[1]

¶ *I James wrote this History in Jerusalem: and when the disturbance was I retired into a desert place, until the death of Herod. And the disturbance ceased at Jerusalem. That which remains is, that I glorify God that he hath given me such wisdom to write unto you who are spiritual, and who love God: to whom (be ascribed) glory and dominion for ever and ever, Amen.*

king; they shed the blood of the innocent: they polluted the court: that day was the Sabbath: and the day of expiation. When therefore Nebuzaradan came there (viz. Jerusalem), he saw his blood bubbling, and said to them, What meaneth this? They answered, It is the blood of calves, lambs, and rams, which we have offered upon the altar. He commanded then, that they should bring calves, and lambs, and rams, and said I will try whether this be their blood: accordingly they brought and slew them, but the blood of (Zacharias) still bubbled, but the blood of these did not bubble. Then he said, Declare to me the truth of the matter, or else I will comb your flesh with iron combs. Then said they to him, He was a priest, prophet, and judge, who prophesied to Israel all these calamities which we have suffered from you; but we arose against him, and slew him. Then, said he, I will appease him: then he took the rabbins and slew them upon his (viz. Zacharias's) blood, and he was not yet appeased. Next he took the young boys from the schools, and slew them upon his blood, and yet it bubbled. Then he brought the young priests and slew them in the same place, and yet it still bubbled. So he slew at length ninety-four thousand persons upon his blood, and it did not as yet cease bubbling. Then he drew near to it, and said, O Zacharias, Zacharias, thou hast occasioned the death of the chief of thy countrymen; shall I slay them all? then the blood ceased, and did bubble no more."

[1] Luke ii. 26.

The first Gospel of the INFANCY of JESUS CHRIST.

[Mr. Henry Sike, Professor of Oriental Languages at Cambridge, first translated and published this Gospel in 1697. It was received by the Gnostics, a sect of Christians in the second century, and several of its relations were credited in the following ages by other Christians, viz., Eusebius, Athanasius, Epiphanius, Chrysostom, &c. Sozomen says, he was told by many, and he credits the relations, of the idols in Egypt falling down on Joseph, and Mary's flight thither with Christ; and of Christ making a well to wash his clothes in a sycamore tree, from whence balsam afterwards proceeded. These stories are from this Gospel. Chemnitius, out of Stipulensis, who had it from Peter Martyr, Bishop of Alexandria, in the third century, says, that the place in Egypt where Christ was banished is now called Matarea, about ten miles beyond Cairo; that the inhabitants constantly burn a lamp in remembrance of it; and that there is a garden of trees yielding a balsam, which were planted by Christ when a boy. M. La Crosse cites a synod at Angamala, in the mountains of Malabar, A.D. 1599, which condemns this Gospel as commonly read by the Nestorians in that country. Ahmed Ibu Idris, a Mahometan divine, says, it was used by some Christians in common with the other four Gospels; and Ocobius de Castro mentions a Gospel of Thomas, which he says, he saw and had translated to him by an Armenian Archbishop at Amsterdam, that was read in very many churches of Asia and Africa, as the only rule of their faith. Fabricius takes it to be this Gospel. It has been supposed, that Mahomet and his coadjutors used it in compiling the Koran. There are several stories believed of Christ proceeding from this Gospel; as that which Mr. Sike relates out of La Brosse's Persic Lexicon, that Christ practised the trade of a dyer, and his working a miracle with the colours; from whence the Persian dyers honour him as their patron, and call a dye-house the shop of Christ. Sir John Chardin mentions Persian legends concerning Christ's dispute with his schoolmaster about his A B C; and his lengthening the cedar-board which Joseph sawed too short.]

CHAP. I.

1 *Caiaphas relates, that Jesus when in his cradle, informed his mother, that he was the Son of God.* 5 *Joseph and Mary going to Bethlehem to be taxed, Mary's time of bringing forth arrives, and she goes into a cave.* 8 *Joseph fetches in a Hebrew woman, the cave filled with great lights.* 11 *The infant born,* 17 *cures the woman,* 19 *arrival of the shepherds.*

THE following accounts we found in the book of Joseph the high-priest, called by some Caiaphas:

2 He relates, that Jesus spake even when he was in the cradle, and said to his mother:

3 Mary, I am Jesus the Son of God, that word which thou didst bring forth according to the declaration of the angel Gabriel to thee, and my father hath sent me for the salvation of the world.

4 ¶ In the three hundred and ninth year of the æra of Alexander, Augustus published a decree that all persons should go to be taxed in their own country.

5 Joseph therefore arose, and with Mary his spouse he went to Jerusalem, and then came to Bethlehem, that he and his family might be taxed in the city of his fathers.

6 And when they came by the cave, Mary confessed to Joseph that her time of bringing forth was come, and she could not go on to the city, and said, Let us go into this cave.

7 At that time the sun was very near going down.

8 But Joseph hastened away, that he might fetch her a midwife; and when he saw an old Hebrew woman who was of Jeru-

38

salem, he said to her, Pray come hither, good woman, and go into that cave, and you will there see a woman just ready to bring forth.

9 It was after sunset, when the old woman and Joseph with her reached the cave, and they both went into it.

10 And behold, it was all filled with lights, greater than the light of lamps and candles, and greater than the light of the sun itself.

11 The infant was then wrapped up in swaddling clothes, and sucking the breasts of his mother St. Mary.

12 When they both saw this light, they were surprised; the old woman asked St. Mary, Art thou the mother of this child?

13 St. Mary replied, She was.

14 On which the old woman said, Thou art very different from all other women.

15 St. Mary answered, As there is not any child like to my son, so neither is there any woman like to his mother.

16 The old woman answered, and said, O my Lady, I am come hither that I may obtain an everlasting reward.

17 Then our Lady, St. Mary, said to her, Lay thine hands upon the infant; which, when she had done, she became whole.

18 And as she was going forth, she said, From henceforth, all the days of my life, I will attend upon and be a servant of this infant.

19 After this, when the shepherds came, and had made a fire, and they were exceedingly rejoicing, the heavenly host appeared to them, praising and adoring the supreme God.

20 And as the shepherds were engaged in the same employ-ment, the cave at that time seemed like a glorious temple, because both the tongues of angels and men united to adore and magnify God, on account of the birth of the Lord Christ.

21 But when the old Hebrew woman saw all these evident miracles, she gave praises to God, and said, I thank thee, O God, thou God of Israel, for that mine eyes have seen the birth of the Saviour of the world.

CHAP II.

1 *The child circumcised in the cave,* 2 *and the old woman preserving his fore-skin or navel-string in a box of spike-nard, Mary afterwards anoints Christ with it.* 5 *Christ brought to the temple,* 6 *shines,* 7 *angels stand around him adoring.* 8 *Simeon praises Christ.*

AND when the time of his circumcision was come, namely, the eighth day, on which the law commanded the child to be circumcised, they circumcised him in the cave.

2 And the old Hebrew woman took the foreskin (others say she took the navel-string), and preserved it in an alabaster-box of old oil of spikenard.

3 And she had a son who was a druggist, to whom she said, Take heed thou sell not this alabaster box of spikenard-ointment, although thou shouldst be offered three hundred pence for it.

4 Now this is that alabaster-box which Mary the sinner procured, and poured forth the ointment out of it upon the head and the feet of our Lord Jesus Christ, and wiped it off with the hairs of her head.

5 Then after ten days they brought him to Jerusalem, and on the fortieth day from his birth they presented him in the

39

temple before the Lord, making the proper offerings for him, according to the requirement of the law of Moses: namely, that every male which opens the womb shall be called holy unto God.

6 At that time old Simeon saw him shining as a pillar of light, when St. Mary the Virgin, his mother, carried him in her arms, and was filled with the greatest pleasure at the sight.

7 And the angels stood around him, adoring him, as a king's guards stand around him.

8 Then Simeon going near to St. Mary, and stretching forth his hands towards her, said to the Lord Christ, Now, O my Lord, thy servant shall depart in peace, according to thy word;

9 For mine eyes have seen thy mercy, which thou hast prepared for the salvation of all nations; a light to all people, and the glory of thy people Israel.

10 Hannah the prophetess was also present, and drawing near, she gave praises to God, and celebrated the happiness of Mary.

CHAP. III.

1 The wise men visit Christ. Mary gives them one of his swaddling clothes. 3 An angel appears to them in the form of a star. They return and make a fire, and worship the swaddling cloth, and put it in the fire, where it remains unconsumed

AND it came to pass, when the Lord Jesus was born at Bethlehem, a city of Judæa, in the time of Herod the King; the wise men came from the East to Jerusalem, according to the prophecy of Zoradascht,[1] and brought with them offerings: namely, gold, frankincense, and myrrh, and worship-

ped him, and offered to him their gifts.

2 Then the Lady Mary took one of his swaddling clothes in which the infant was wrapped, and gave it to them instead of a blessing, which they received from her as a most noble present.

3 And at the same time there appeared to them an angel in the form of that star which had before been their guide in their journey; the light of which they followed till they returned into their own country.

4 ¶ On their return their kings and princes came to them inquiring, What they had seen and done? What sort of journey and return they had? What company they had on the road?

5 But they produced the swaddling cloth which St. Mary had given to them, on account whereof they kept a feast.

6 And having, according to the custom of their country, made a fire, they worshipped it.

7 And casting the swaddling cloth into it, the fire took it, and kept it.

8 And when the fire was put out, they took forth the swaddling cloth unhurt, as much as if the fire had not touched it.

9 Then they began to kiss it, and put it upon their heads and their eyes, saying, This is certainly an undoubted truth, and it is really surprising that the fire could not burn it, and consume it.

10 Then they took it, and with the greatest respect laid it up among their treasures.

CHAP. IV.

1 Herod intends to put Christ to death. 3 An angel warns Joseph to take the child and its mother into Egypt. 6 Consternation on their arrival. 13

[1] Zoroaster.

THE ADORATION OF THE MAGI.

FROM A BAS-RELIEF OF THE TWELFTH CENTURY OVER THE DOOR OF THE CHURCH OF ST. ANDREW, PISTOJA.

The idols fall down. 15 *Mary washes Christ's swaddling clothes, and hangs them to dry on a post.* 16 *A son of the chief priest puts one on his head, and being possessed of devils, they leave him.*

NOW Herod, perceiving that the wise men did delay, and not return to him, called together the priests and wise men and said, Tell me in what place the Christ should be born?

2 And when they replied, in Bethlehem, a city of Judæa, he began to contrive in his own mind the death of the Lord Jesus Christ.

3 But an angel of the Lord appeared to Joseph in his sleep, and said, Arise, take the child and his mother, and go into Egypt as soon as the cock crows. So he arose, and went.

4 ¶ And as he was considering with himself about his journey, the morning came upon him.

5 In the length of the journey the girts of the saddle broke.

6 And now he drew near to a great city, in which there was an idol, to which the other idols and gods of Egypt brought their offerings and vows.

7 And there was by this idol a priest ministering to it, who, as often as Satan spoke out of that idol, related the things he said to the inhabitants of Egypt, and those countries.

8 This priest had a son three years old, who was possessed with a great multitude of devils, who uttered many strange things, and when the devils seized him, walked about naked with his clothes torn, throwing stones at those whom he saw.

9 Near to that idol was the inn of the city, into which when Joseph and St. Mary were come, and had turned into that inn, all the inhabitants of the city were astonished.

10 And all the magistrates and priests of the idols assembled before that idol, and made inquiry there, saying, What means all this consternation, and dread, which has fallen upon all our country?

11 The idol answered them, The unknown God is come hither, who is truly God; nor is there any one besides him, who is worthy of divine worship; for he is truly the Son of God.

12 At the fame of him this country trembled, and at his coming it is under the present commotion and consternation; and we ourselves are affrighted by the greatness of his power.

13 And at the same instant this idol fell down, and at his fall all the inhabitants of Egypt, besides others, ran together.

14 ¶ But the son of the priest, when his usual disorder came upon him, going into the inn, found there Joseph and St. Mary, whom all the rest had left behind and forsook.

15 And when the Lady St. Mary had washed the swaddling clothes of the Lord Christ, and hanged them out to dry upon a post, the boy possessed with the devil took down one of them, and put it upon his head.

16 And presently the devils began to come out of his mouth, and fly away in the shape of crows and serpents.

17 From that time the boy was healed by the power of the Lord Christ, and he began to sing praises, and give thanks to the Lord who had healed him.

18 When his father saw him restored to his former state of

41

health, he said, My son, what has happened to thee, and by what means wert thou cured?

19 The son answered, When the devils seized me, I went into the inn, and there found a very handsome woman with a boy, whose swaddling clothes she had just before washed, and hanged out upon a post.

20 One of these I took, and put it upon my head, and immediately the devils left me, and fled away.

21 At this the father exceedingly rejoiced, and said, My son, perhaps this boy is the son of the living God, who made the heavens and the earth.

22 For as soon as he came amongst us, the idol was broken, and all the gods fell down, and were destroyed by a greater power.

23 Then was fulfilled the prophecy which saith, Out of Egypt I have called my son.

CHAP. V.

1 *Joseph and Mary leave Egypt.* 3 *Go to the haunts of robbers,* 4 *Who, hearing a mighty noise as of a great army, flee away.*

NOW Joseph and Mary, when they heard that the idol was fallen down and destroyed, were seized with fear and trembling, and said, When we were in the land of Israel, Herod, intending to kill Jesus, slew for that purpose all the infants at Bethlehem, and that neighbourhood.

2 And there is no doubt but the Egyptians if they come to hear that this idol is broken and fallen down, will burn us with fire.

3 They went therefore hence to the secret places of robbers, who robbed travellers as they pass by, of their carriages and

their clothes, and carried them away bound.

4 These thieves upon their coming heard a great noise, such as the noise of a king with a great army and many horses, and the trumpets sounding at his departure from his own city; at which they were so affrighted as to leave all their booty behind them, and fly away in haste.

5 Upon this the prisoners arose, and loosed each other's bonds, and taking each man his bags, they went away, and saw Joseph and Mary coming towards them, and inquired, Where is that king, the noise of whose approach the robbers heard, and left us, so that we are now come off safe?

6 Joseph answered, He will come after us.

CHAP. VI.

1 *Mary looks on a woman in whom Satan had taken up his abode, and she becomes dispossessed.* 5 *Christ kissed by a bride made dumb by sorcerers, cures her,* 11 *miraculously cures a gentlewoman in whom Satan had taken up his abode.* 16 *A leprous girl cured by the water in which he was washed, and becomes the servant of Mary and Joseph.* 20 *The leprous son of a prince's wife cured in like manner.* 37 *His mother offers large gifts to Mary, and dismisses her.*

THEN they went into another city where there was a woman possessed with a devil, and in whom Satan, that cursed rebel, had taken up his abode.

2 One night, when she went to fetch water, she could neither endure her clothes on, nor to be in any house; but as often as they tied her with chains or cords, she brake them, and went out into desert places, and sometimes standing where roads crossed, and in churchyards, would throw stones at men.

3 When St. Mary saw this woman, she pitied her; whereupon Satan presently left her, and fled away in the form of a young man, saying, Wo to me, because of thee, Mary, and thy son.

4 So the woman was delivered from her torment; but considering herself naked, she blushed, and avoided seeing any man, and having put on her clothes, went home, and gave an account of her case to her father and relations, who, as they were the best of the city, entertained St. Mary and Joseph with the greatest respect.

5 The next morning having received a sufficient supply of provisions for the road, they went from them, and about the evening of the day arrived at another town, where a marriage was then about to be solemnized; but by the arts of Satan and the practices of some sorcerers, the bride was become so dumb, that she could not so much as open her mouth.

6 But when this dumb bride saw the Lady St. Mary entering into the town, and carrying the Lord Christ in her arms, she stretched out her hands to the Lord Christ, and took him in her arms, and closely hugging him, very often kissed him, continually moving him and pressing him to her body.

7 Straightway the string of her tongue was loosed, and her ears were opened, and she began to sing praises unto God, who had restored her.

8 So there was great joy among the inhabitants of the town that night, who thought that God and his angels were come down among them.

9 ¶ In this place they abode three days, meeting with the greatest respect and most splendid entertainment.

10 And being then furnished by the people with provisions for the road, they departed and went to another city, in which they were inclined to lodge, because it was a famous place.

11 There was in this city a gentlewoman, who, as she went down one day to the river to bathe, behold cursed Satan leaped upon her in the form of a serpent,

12 And folded himself about her belly, and every night lay upon her.

13 This woman seeing the Lady St. Mary, and the Lord Christ the infant in her bosom, asked the Lady St. Mary, that she would give her the child to kiss, and carry in her arms.

14 When she had consented, and as soon as the woman had moved the child, Satan left her, and fled away, nor did the woman ever afterwards see him.

15 Hereupon all the neighbours praised the Supreme God, and the woman rewarded them with ample beneficence.

16 On the morrow the same woman brought perfumed water to wash the Lord Jesus; and when she had washed him, she preserved the water.

17 And there was a girl there, whose body was white with a leprosy, who being sprinkled with this water, and washed, was instantly cleansed from her leprosy.

18 The people therefore said Without doubt Joseph and Mary, and that boy are Gods, for they do not look like mortals.

19 And when they were making ready to go away, the girl, who had been troubled with the leprosy, came and desired they would permit her to go along

43

with them; so they consented, and the girl went with them till they came to a city, in which was the palace of a great king, and whose house was not far from the inn.

20 Here they staid, and when the girl went one day to the prince's wife, and found her in a sorrowful and mournful condition, she asked her the reason of her tears.

21 She replied, Wonder not at my groans, for I am under a great misfortune, of which I dare not tell any one.

22 But, says the girl, if you will entrust me with your private grievance, perhaps I may find you a remedy for it.

23 Thou, therefore, says the prince's wife, shalt keep the secret, and not discover it to any one alive!

24 I have been married to this prince, who rules as king over large dominions, and lived long with him, before he had any child by me.

25 At length I conceived by him, but alas! I brought forth a leprous son; which, when he saw, he would not own to be his, but said to me,

26 Either do thou kill him, or send him to some nurse in such a place, that he may be never heard of; and now take care of yourself; I will never see you more.

27 So here I pine, lamenting my wretched and miserable circumstances. Alas, my son! alas, my husband! Have I disclosed it to you?

28 The girl replied, I have found a remedy for your disease, which I promise you, for I also was leprous, but God hath cleansed me, even he who is called Jesus, the son of the Lady Mary.

29 The woman inquiring where that God was, whom she spake of, the girl answered He lodges with you here in the same house.

30 But how can this be? says she; where is he? Behold, replied the girl, Joseph and Mary; and the infant who is with them is called Jesus: and it is he who delivered me from my disease and torment.

31 But by what means, says she, were you cleansed from your leprosy? Will you not tell me that?

32 Why not? says the girl; I took the water with which his body had been washed, and poured it upon me, and my leprosy vanished.

33 The prince's wife then arose and entertained them, providing a great feast for Joseph among a large company of men.

34 And the next day took perfumed water to wash the Lord Jesus, and afterwards poured the same water upon her son, whom she had brought with her, and her son was instantly cleansed from his leprosy.

35 Then she sang thanks and praises unto God, and said, Blessed is the mother that bare thee, O Jesus!

36 Dost thou thus cure men of the same nature with thyself, with the water with which thy body is washed?

37 She then offered very large gifts to the Lady Mary, and sent her away with all imaginable respect.

CHAP. VII.

1 *A man who could not enjoy his wife, freed from his disorder.* 5 *A young man who had been bewitched, and turned into a mule, miraculously cured by Christ being put on his back.* 28 *and is married to the girl who had been cured of leprosy.*

THEY came afterwards to another city, and had a mind to lodge there.

2 Accordingly they went to a man's house, who was newly married, but by the influence of sorcerers could not enjoy his wife:

3 But they lodging at his house that night, the man was freed of his disorder:

4 And when they were preparing early in the morning to go forward on their journey, the new married person hindered them, and provided a noble entertainment for them?

5 But going forward on the morrow, they came to another city, and saw three women going from a certain grave with great weeping.

6 When St. Mary saw them, she spake to the girl who was their companion, saying, Go and inquire of them, what is the matter with them, and what misfortune has befallen them?

7 When the girl asked them, they made her no answer, but asked her again, Who are ye, and where are ye going? For the day is far spent, and the night is at hand.

8 We are travellers, saith the girl, and are seeking for an inn to lodge at.

9 They replied, Go along with us, and lodge with us.

10 They then followed them, and were introduced into a new house, well furnished with all sorts of furniture.

11 It was now winter-time, and the girl went into the parlour where these women were, and found them weeping and lamenting, as before.

12 By them stood a mule, covered over with silk, and an ebony collar hanging down from his neck, whom they kissed, and were feeding.

13 But when the girl said, How handsome, ladies, that mule is! they replied with tears, and said, This mule, which you see, was our brother, born of this same mother as we:

14 For when our father died, and left us a very large estate, and we had only this brother, and we endeavoured to procure him a suitable match, and thought he should be married as other men, some giddy and jealous woman bewitched him without our knowledge.

15 And we, one night, a little before day, while the doors of the house were all fast shut, saw this our brother was changed into a mule, such as you now see him to be:

16 And we, in the melancholy condition in which you see us, having no father to comfort us, have applied to all the wise men, magicians, and diviners in the world, but they have been of no service to us.

17 As often therefore as we find ourselves oppressed with grief, we rise and go with this our mother to our father's tomb, where, when we have cried sufficiently we return home.

18 When the girl had heard this, she said, Take courage, and cease your fears, for you have a remedy for your afflictions near at hand, even among you and in the midst of your house,

19 For I was also leprous; but when I saw this woman, and this little infant with her, whose name is Jesus, I sprinkled my body with the water with which his mother had washed him, and I was presently made well.

20 And I am certain that he is also capable of relieving you

under your distress. Wherefore, arise, go to my mistress, Mary, and when you have brought her into your own parlour, disclose to her the secret, at the same time, earnestly beseeching her to compassionate your case.

21 As soon as the women had heard the girl's discourse, they hastened away to the Lady St. Mary, introduced themselves to her, and sitting down before her, they wept.

22 And said, O our Lady St. Mary, pity your handmaids, for we have no head of our family, no one older than us; no father, or brother to go in and out before us.

23 But this mule, which you see, was our brother, which some woman by witchcraft have brought into this condition which you see: we therefore entreat you to compassionate us.

24 Hereupon St. Mary was grieved at their case, and taking the Lord Jesus, put him upon the back of the mule.

25 And said to her son, O Jesus Christ, restore (or heal) according to thy extraordinary power this mule, and grant him to have again the shape of a man and a rational creature, as he had formerly.

26 This was scarce said by the Lady St. Mary, but the mule immediately passed into a human form, and became a young man without any deformity.

27 Then he and his mother and the sisters worshipped the Lady St. Mary, and lifting the child upon their heads, they kissed him, and said, Blessed is thy mother, O Jesus, O Saviour of the world! Blessed are the eyes which are so happy as to see thee.

28 Then both the sisters told

46

their mother, saying, Of a truth our brother is restored to his former shape by the help of the Lord Jesus Christ, and the kindness of that girl, who told us of Mary and her son.

29 And inasmuch as our brother is unmarried, it is fit that we marry him to this girl their servant.

30 When they had consulted Mary in this matter, and she had given her consent, they made a splendid wedding for this girl.

31 And so their sorrow being turned into gladness, and their mourning into mirth, they began to rejoice, and to make merry, and sing, being dressed in their richest attire, with bracelets.

32 Afterwards they glorified and praised God, saying, O Jesus son of David who changest sorrow into gladness, and mourning into mirth!

33 After this Joseph and Mary tarried there ten days, then went away, having received great respect from those people;

34 Who, when they took their leave of them, and returned home, cried,

35 But especially the girl.

CHAP. VIII.

1 *Joseph and Mary pass through a country infested by robbers,* 3 *Titus, a humane thief, offers Dumachus, his comrade, forty groats to let Joseph and Mary pass unmolested.* 6 *Jesus prophesies that the thieves, Dumachus and Titus, shall be crucified with him, and that Titus shall go before him into Paradise.* 10 *Christ causes a well to spring from a sycamore tree, and Mary washes his coat in it.* 11 *A balsam grows there from his sweat: They go to Memphis, where Christ works more miracles. Return to Judæa.* 15 *being warned, depart for Nazareth.*

IN their journey from hence they came into a desert country, and were told it was infested with robbers; so Joseph and St. Mary prepared to pass through it in the night.

2 And as they were going along, behold they saw two robbers asleep in the road, and with them a great number of robbers, who were their confederates, also asleep.

3 The names of these two were Titus and Dumachus; and Titus said to Dumachus, I beseech thee let those persons go along quietly, that our company may not perceive anything of them:

4 But Dumachus refusing, Titus again said, I will give thee forty groats, and as a pledge take my girdle, which he gave him before he had done speaking, that he might not open his mouth, or make a noise.

5 When the Lady St. Mary saw the kindness which this robber did shew them, she said to him, The Lord God will receive thee to his right hand, and grant thee pardon of thy sins.

6 Then the Lord Jesus answered, and said to his mother, When thirty years are expired, O mother, the Jews will crucify me at Jerusalem;

7 And these two thieves shall be with me at the same time upon the cross, Titus on my right hand, and Dumachus on my left, and from that time Titus shall go before me into paradise:

8 And when she had said, God forbid this should be thy lot, O my son, they went on to a city in which were several idols; which, as soon as they came near to it, was turned into hills of sand.

9 ¶ Hence they went to that sycamore tree, which is now called Matarea;

10 And in Matarea the Lord Jesus caused a well to spring forth, in which St. Mary washed his coat;

11 And a balsam is produced, or grows, in that country from the sweat which ran down there from the Lord Jesus.

12 Thence they proceeded to Memphis, and saw Pharaoh, and abode three years in Egypt.

13 And the Lord Jesus did very many miracles in Egypt, which are neither to be found in the Gospel of the Infancy nor in the Gospel of Perfection.

14 ¶ At the end of three years he returned out of Egypt, and when he came near to Judæa, Joseph was afraid to enter;

15 For hearing that Herod was dead, and that Archelaus his son reigned in his stead, he was afraid;

16 And when he went to Judæa, an angel of God appeared to him, and said, O Joseph, go into the city Nazareth, and abide there.

17 It is strange indeed that he, who is the Lord of all countries, should be thus carried backward and forward through so many countries.

CHAP. IX.

2 *Two sick children cured by water wherein Christ was washed.*

WHEN they came afterwards into the city Bethlehem, they found there several very desperate distempers, which became so troublesome to children by seeing them, that most of them died.

2 There was there a woman who had a sick son, whom she brought, when he was at the point of death, to the Lady St. Mary, who saw her when she was washing Jesus Christ.

3 Then said the woman, O my

47

Lady Mary, look down upon this my son, who is afflicted with most dreadful pains.

4. St. Mary hearing her, said, Take a little of that water with which I have washed my son, and sprinkle it upon him.

5 Then she took a little of that water, as St. Mary had commanded, and sprinkled it upon her son, who being wearied with his violent pains, had fallen asleep; and after he had slept a little, awaked perfectly well and recovered.

6 The mother being abundantly glad of this success, went again to St. Mary, and St. Mary said to her, Give praise to God, who hath cured this thy son.

7 There was in the same place another woman, a neighbour of her, whose son was now cured.

8 This woman's son was afflicted with the same disease, and his eyes were now almost quite shut, and she was lamenting for him day and night.

9 The mother of the child which was cured, said to her, Why do you not bring your son to St. Mary, as I brought my son to her, when he was in the agonies of death; and he was cured by that water, with which the body of her son Jesus was washed?

10 When the woman heard her say this, she also went, and having procured the same water, washed her son with it, whereupon his body and his eyes were instantly restored to their former state.

11 And when she brought her son to St. Mary, and opened his case to her, she commanded her to give thanks to God for the recovery of her son's health, and tell no one what had happened.

48

CHAP. X.

1 *Two wives of one man, each have a son sick.* 2 *One of them, named Mary, and whose son's name was Caleb, presents the Virgin with a handsome carpet, and Caleb is cured; but the son of the other wife dies,* 4 *which occasions a difference between the women.* 5 *The other wife puts Caleb into a hot oven, and he is miraculously preserved;* 9 *she afterwards throws him into a well, and he is again preserved;* 11 *his mother appeals to the Virgin against the other wife,* 12, *whose downfall the Virgin prophesies,* 13 *and who accordingly falls into the well,* 14 *therein fulfilling a saying of old.*

THERE were in the same city two wives of one man, who had each a son sick. One of them was called Mary and her son's name was Caleb.

2 She arose, and taking her son, went to the Lady St. Mary, the mother of Jesus, and offered her a very handsome carpet, saying, O my Lady Mary accept this carpet of me, and instead of it give me a small swaddling cloth.

3 To this Mary agreed, and when the mother of Caleb was gone, she made a coat for her son of the swaddling cloth, put it on him, and his disease was cured; but the son of the other wife died.

4 ¶ Hereupon there arose between them, a difference in doing the business of the family by turns, each her week.

5 And when the turn of Mary the mother of Caleb came, and she was heating the oven to bake bread, and went away to fetch the meal, she left her son Caleb by the oven;

6 Whom, the other wife, her rival, seeing to be by himself, took and cast him into the oven, which was very hot, and then went away.

7 Mary on her return saw her son Caleb lying in the middle of

THE BIRTH OF JOHN THE BAPTIST.

FROM A "BOOK OF THE EVANGELISTS." GREEK MANUSCRIPT OF THE TWELFTH CENTURY.

the oven laughing, and the oven quite as cold as though it had not been before heated, and knew that her rival the other wife had thrown him into the fire.

8 When she took him out, she brought him to the Lady St. Mary, and told her the story, to whom she replied, Be quiet, I am concerned lest thou shouldest make this matter known.

9 After this her rival, the other wife, as she was drawing water at the well, and saw Caleb playing by the well, and that no one was near, took him, and threw him into the well.

10 And when some men came to fetch water from the well, they saw the boy sitting on the superficies of the water, and drew him out with ropes, and were exceedingly surprised at the child, and praised God.

11 Then came the mother and took him and carried him to the Lady St. Mary, lamenting and saying, O my Lady, see what my rival hath done to my son, and how she hath cast him into the well, and I do not question but one time or other she will be the occasion of his death.

12 St. Mary replied to her, God will vindicate your injured cause.

13 Accordingly a few days after, when the other wife came to the well to draw water, her foot was entangled in the rope, so that she fell headlong into the well, and they who ran to her assistance, found her skull broken, and bones bruised.

14 So she came to a bad end, and in her was fulfilled that saying of the author, They digged a well, and made it deep, but fell themselves into the pit which they prepared.

CHAP. XI.

1 *Bartholomew, when a child and sick, miraculously restored by being laid on Christ's bed.*

ANOTHER woman in that city had likewise two sons sick.

2 And when one was dead, the other, who lay at the point of death, she took in her arms to the Lady St. Mary, and in a flood of tears addressed herself to her, saying,

3 O my Lady, help and relieve me; for I had two sons, the one I have just now buried, the other I see is just at the point of death, behold how I (earnestly) seek favour from God, and pray to him.

4 Then she said, O Lord, thou art gracious, and merciful, and kind; thou hast given me two sons; one of them thou hast taken to thyself, O spare me this other.

5 St. Mary then perceiving the greatness of her sorrow, pitied her and said, Do thou place thy son in my son's bed, and cover him with his clothes.

6 And when she had placed him in the bed wherein Christ lay, at the moment when his eyes were just closed by death; as soon as ever the smell of the garments of the Lord Jesus Christ reached the boy, his eyes were opened, and calling with a loud voice to his mother, he asked for bread, and when he had received it, he sucked it.

7 Then his mother said, O Lady Mary, now I am assured that the powers of God do dwell in you, so that thy son can cure children who are of the same sort as himself, as soon as they touch his garments.

8 This boy who was thus

49

cured, is the same who in the Gospel is called Bartholomew.

CHAP. XII.

1 A leprous woman healed by Christ's washing water. 7 A princess healed by it and restored to her husband.

AGAIN there was a leprous woman who went to the Lady St. Mary, the mother of Jesus, and said, O my Lady, help me.

2 St. Mary replied, what help dost thou desire? Is it gold or silver, or that thy body be cured of its leprosy?

3 Who, says the woman, can grant me this?

4 St. Mary replied to her, Wait a little till I have washed my son Jesus, and put him to bed.

5 The woman waited; as she was commanded; and Mary when she had put Jesus in bed, giving her the water with which she had washed his body, said, Take some of the water, and pour it upon thy body;

6 Which when she had done, she instantly became clean, and praised God, and gave thanks to him.

7 ¶ Then she went away, after she had abode with her three days:

8 And going into the city, she saw a certain prince, who had married another prince's daughter;

9 But when he came to see her, he perceived between her eyes the signs of leprosy like a star, and thereupon declared the marriage dissolved and void.

10 When the woman saw these persons in this condition, exceedingly sorrowful, and shedding abundance of tears, she inquired of them the reason of their crying.

11 They replied, Inquire not into our circumstances; for we are not able to declare our misfortunes to any person whatsoever.

12 But still she pressed and desired them to communicate their case to her, intimating, that perhaps she might be able to direct them to a remedy.

13 So when they shewed the young woman to her, and the signs of the leprosy, which appeared between her eyes,

14 She said, I also, whom ye see in this place, was afflicted with the same distemper, and going on some business to Bethlehem, I went into a certain cave, and saw a woman named Mary, who had a son called Jesus.

15 She seeing me to be leprous, was concerned for me, and gave me some water with which she had washed her son's body; with that I sprinkled my body, and became clean.

16 Then said these women, Will you, Mistress, go along with us, and shew the Lady St. Mary to us?

17 To which she consenting, they arose and went to the Lady St. Mary, taking with them very noble presents.

18 And when they came in and offered their presents to her, they showed the leprous young woman what they brought with them to her.

19 Then said St. Mary, The mercy of the Lord Jesus Christ rest upon you;

20 And giving them a little of that water with which she had washed the body of Jesus Christ, she bade them wash the diseased person with it; which when they had done, she was presently cured;

21 So they, and all who were

present, praised God; and being filled with joy, they went back to their own city, and gave praise to God on that account.

22 Then the prince hearing that his wife was cured, took her home and made a second marriage, giving thanks unto God for the recovery of his wife's health.

CHAP. XIII.

1 *A girl, whose blood Satan sucked, receives one of Christ's swaddling clothes from the Virgin.* 14 *Satan comes like a dragon, and she shews it to him; flames and burning coals proceed from it and fall upon him;* 19 *he is miraculously discomfited, and leaves the girl.*

THERE was also a girl, who was afflicted by Satan;

2 For that cursed spirit did frequently appear to her in the shape of a dragon, and was inclined to swallow her up, and had so sucked out all her blood, that she looked like a dead carcase.

3 As often as she came to herself, with her hands wringed about her head she would cry out, and say, Wo, Wo is me, that there is no one to be found who can deliver me from that impious dragon!

4 Her father and mother, and all who were about her and saw her, mourned and wept over her;

5 And all who were present would especially be under sorrow and in tears, when they heard her bewailing, and saying, My brethren and friends, is there no one who can deliver me from this murderer?

6 Then the prince's daughter, who had been cured of her leprosy, hearing the complaint of that girl, went upon the top of her castle, and saw her with her hands twisted about her head, pouring out a flood of tears, and all the people that were about her in sorrow.

7 Then she asked the husband of the possessed person, Whether his wife's mother was alive? He told her, That her father and mother were both alive.

8 Then she ordered her mother to be sent to her: to whom, when she saw her coming, she said, Is this possessed girl thy daughter? She moaning and bewailing said, Yes, madam, I bore her.

9 The prince's daughter answered, Disclose the secret of her case to me, for I confess to you that I was leprous, but the Lady Mary, the mother of Jesus Christ, healed me.

10 And if you desire your daughter to be restored to her former state, take her to Bethlehem, and inquire for Mary the mother of Jesus, and doubt not but your daughter will be cured; for I do not question but you will come home with great joy at your daughter's recovery.

11 As soon as ever she had done speaking, she arose and went with her daughter to the place appointed, and to Mary, and told her the case of her daughter.

12 When St. Mary had heard her story, she gave her a little of the water with which she had washed the body of her son Jesus, and bade her pour it upon the body of her daughter.

13 Likewise she gave her one of the swaddling cloths of the Lord Jesus, and said, Take this swaddling cloth and shew it to thine enemy as often as thou seest him; and she sent them away in peace.

14 ¶ After they had left that city and returned home, and the time was come in which Satan was wont to seize her, in the same moment this cursed spirit appear-

51

ed to her in the shape of a huge dragon, and the girl seeing him was afraid.

15 The mother said to her, Be not afraid daughter; let him alone till he come nearer to thee! then shew him the swaddling cloth, which the Lady Mary gave us, and we shall see the event.

16 Satan then coming like a dreadful dragon, the body of the girl trembled for fear.

17 But as soon as she had put the swaddling cloth upon her head, and about her eyes, and shewed it to him, presently there issued forth from the swaddling cloth flames and burning coals, and fell upon the dragon.

18 Oh! how great a miracle was this, which was done : as soon as the dragon saw the swaddling cloth of the Lord Jesus, fire went forth and was scattered upon his head and eyes ; so that he cried out with a loud voice, What have I to do with thee, Jesus, thou son of Mary, Whither shall I flee from thee?

19 So he drew back much affrighted, and left the girl.

20 And she was delivered from this trouble, and sang praises and thanks to God, and with her all who were present at the working of the miracle.

CHAP. XIV.

1 Judas when a boy possessed by Satan, and brought by his parents to Jesus to be cured, whom he tries to bite, 7 but failing, strikes Jesus and makes him cry out. Whereupon Satan goes from Jesus in the shape of a dog.

ANOTHER woman likewise lived there, whose son was possessed by Satan.

2 This boy, named Judas, as often as Satan seized him, was inclined to bite all that were present; and if he found no one else

near him, he would bite his own hands and other parts.

3 But the mother of this miserable boy, hearing of St. Mary and her son Jesus, arose presently, and taking her son in her arms, brought him to the Lady Mary.

4 In the meantime, James and Joses had taken away the infant, the Lord Jesus, to play at a proper season with other children ; and when they went forth, they sat down and the Lord Jesus with them.

5 Then Judas, who was possessed, came and sat down at the right hand of Jesus.

6 When Satan was acting upon him as usual, he went about to bite the Lord Jesus.

7 And because he could not do it, he struck Jesus on the right side, so that he cried out.

8 And in the same moment Satan went out of the boy, and ran away like a mad dog.

9 This same boy who struck Jesus, and out of whom Satan went in the form of a dog, was Judas Iscariot, who betrayed him to the Jews.

10 And that same side, on which Judas struck him, the Jews pierced with a spear.

CHAP. XV.

1 Jesus and other boys play together, and make clay figures of animals. 4 Jesus causes them to walk, 6 also makes clay birds, which he causes to fly, and eat and drink. 7 The children's parents alarmed, and take Jesus for a sorcerer. 8 He goes to a dyer's shop, and throws all the cloths into the furnace, and works a miracle therewith. 15 Whereupon the Jews praise God.

AND when the Lord Jesus was seven years of age, he was on a certain day with other boys his companions about the same age.

2 Who when they were at play,

made clay into several shapes, namely, asses, oxen, birds, and other figures,

3 Each boasting of his work, and endeavouring to exceed the rest.

4 Then the Lord Jesus said to the boys, I will command these figures which I have made to walk.

5 And immediately they moved, and when he commanded them to return, they returned.

6 He had also made the figures of birds and sparrows, which, when he commanded to fly, did fly, and when he commanded to stand still, did stand still; and if he gave them meat and drink, they did eat and drink.

7 When at length the boys went away, and related these things to their parents, their fathers said to them, Take heed, children, for the future, of his company, for he is a sorcerer; shun and avoid him, and from henceforth never play with him.

8 ¶ On a certain day also, when the Lord Jesus was playing with the boys, and running about, he passed by a dyer's shop, whose name was Salem.

9 And there were in his shop many pieces of cloth belonging to the people of that city, which they designed to dye of several colours.

10 Then the Lord Jesus going into the dyer's shop, took all the cloths, and threw them into the furnace.

11 When Salem came home, and saw the cloths spoiled, he began to make a great noise, and to chide the Lord Jesus, saying,

12 What hast thou done to me, O thou Son of Mary? Thou hast injured both me and my neighbours; they all desired their cloths of a proper colour; but

thou hast come, and spoiled them all.

13 The Lord Jesus replied, I will change the colour of every cloth to what colour thou desirest;

14 And then he presently began to take the cloths out of the furnace, and they were all dyed of those same colours which the dyer desired.

15 And when the Jews saw this surprising miracle, they praised God.

CHAP. XVI.

1 *Christ miraculously widens or contracts the gates, milk-pails, sieves, or boxes, not properly made by Joseph,* 4 *he not being skilful at his carpenter's trade.* 5 *The King of Jerusalem gives Joseph an order for a throne.* 6 *Joseph works on it for two years in the king's palace, and makes it two spans too short. The king being angry with him,* 10 *Jesus comforts him,* 13 *commands him to pull one side of the throne, while he pulls the other, and brings it to its proper dimensions.* 14 *Whereupon the bystanders praise God.*

AND Joseph, wheresoever he went in the city, took the Lord Jesus with him, where he was sent for to work to make gates, or milk-pails, or sieves, or boxes; the Lord Jesus was with him wheresoever he went.

2 And as often as Joseph had anything in his work, to make longer or shorter, or wider, or narrower, the Lord Jesus would stretch his hand towards it.

3 And presently it became as Joseph would have it.

4 So that he had no need to finish anything with his own hands, for he was not very skilful at his carpenter's trade.

5 ¶ On a certain time the King of Jerusalem sent for him, and said, I would have thee make me a throne of the same dimen-

53

sions with that place in which I commonly sit.

6 Joseph obeyed, and forthwith began the work, and continued two years in the king's palace before he finished it.

7 And when he came to fix it in its place, he found it wanted two spans on each side of the appointed measure.

8 Which, when the king saw, he was very angry with Joseph;

9 And Joseph afraid of the king's anger, went to bed without his supper, taking not any thing to eat.

10 Then the Lord Jesus asked him, What he was afraid of?

11 Joseph replied, Because I have lost my labour in the work which I have been about these two years.

12 Jesus said to him, Fear not, neither be cast down;

13 Do thou lay hold on one side of the throne, and I will the other, and we will bring it to its just dimensions.

14 And when Joseph had done as the Lord Jesus said, and each of them had with strength drawn his side, the throne obeyed, and was brought to the proper dimensions of the place:

15 Which miracle when they who stood by saw, they were astonished, and praised God.

16 The throne was made of the same wood, which was in being in Solomon's time, namely, wood adorned with various shapes and figures.

CHAP. XVII.

1 *Jesus plays with boys at hide and seek.* 3 *Some women put his playfellows in a furnace, 7 where they are transformed by Jesus into kids. 10 Jesus calls them to go and play, and they are restored to their former shape.*

ON another day the Lord Jesus going out into the
54

street, and seeing some boys who were met to play, joined himself to their company:

2 But when they saw him, they hid themselves, and left him to seek for them:

3 The Lord Jesus came to the gate of a certain house, and asked some women who were standing there, Where the boys were gone?

4 And when they answered, That there was no one there; the Lord Jesus said, Who are those whom ye see in the furnace?

5 They answered, They were kids of three years old.

6 Then Jesus cried out aloud, and said, Come out hither, O ye kids, to your shepherd;

7 And presently the boys came forth like kids, and leaped about him; which when the women saw, they were exceedingly amazed, and trembled.

8 Then they immediately worshipped the Lord Jesus, and beseeched him, saying, O our Lord Jesus, son of Mary, thou art truly that good shepherd of Israel! have mercy on thy handmaids, who stand before thee, who do not doubt, but that thou, O Lord, art come to save, and not to destroy.

9 After that, when the Lord Jesus said, the children of Israel are like Ethiopians among the people; the women said, Thou, Lord, knowest all things, nor is any thing concealed from thee; but now we entreat thee, and beseech of thy mercy that thou wouldst restore those boys to their former state.

10 Then Jesus said, Come hither O boys, that we may go and play; and immediately, in the presence of these women, the kids were changed and returned into the shape of boys.

CHAP. XVIII.

1 Jesus becomes the king of his playfellows, and they crown him with flowers, 4 miraculously causes a serpent who had bitten Simon the Cananite, then a boy, to suck out all the poison again ; 16 the serpent bursts, and Christ restores the boy to health.

IN the month Adar Jesus gathered together the boys, and ranked them as though he had been a king.

2 For they spread their garments on the ground for him to sit on ; and having made a crown of flowers, put it upon his head, and stood on his right and left as the guards of a king.

3 And if any one happened to pass by, they took him by force, and said, Come hither, and worship the king, that you may have a prosperous journey.

4 ¶ In the mean time, while these things were doing, there came certain men, carrying a boy upon a couch ;

5 For this boy having gone with his companions to the mountain to gather wood, and having found there a partridge's nest, and put his hand in to take out the eggs, was stung by a poisonous serpent, which leaped out of the nest ; so that he was forced to cry out for the help of his companions : who, when they came, found him lying upon the earth like a dead person.

6 After which his neighbours came and carried him back into the city.

7 But when they came to the place where the Lord Jesus was sitting like a king, and the other boys stood around him like his ministers, the boys made haste to meet him, who was bitten by the serpent, and said to his neighbours, Come and pay your respects to the king ;

8 But when, by reason of their sorrow, they refused to come, the boys drew them, and forced them against their wills to come.

9 And when they came to the Lord Jesus, he inquired, On what account they carried that boy ?

10 And when they answered, that a serpent had bitten him, the Lord Jesus said to the boys, Let us go and kill that serpent.

11 But when the parents of the boy desired to be excused, because their son lay at the point of death ; the boys made answer, and said, Did not ye hear what the king said ? Let us go and kill the serpent ; and will not ye obey him ?

12 So they brought the couch back again, whether they would or not.

13 And when they were come to the nest, the Lord Jesus said to the boys, Is this the serpent's lurking place? They said, It was.

14 Then the Lord Jesus calling the serpent, it presently came forth and submitted to him ; to whom he said, Go and suck out all the poison which thou hast infused into that boy ;

15 So the serpent crept to the boy, and took away all its poison again.

16 Then the Lord Jesus cursed the serpent so that it immediately burst asunder, and died.

17 And he touched the boy with his hand to restore him to his former health ;

18 And when he began to cry, the Lord Jesus said, Cease crying, for hereafter thou shalt be my disciple ;

19 And this is that Simon the Canaanite, who is mentioned in the Gospel.

CHAP. XIX.

1 *James being bitten by a viper, Jesus blows on the wound and cures him.* 4. *Jesus charged with throwing a boy from the roof of a house,* 10 *miraculously causes the dead boy to acquit him,* 12 *fetches water for his mother, breaks the pitcher and miraculously gathers the water in his mantle and brings it home,* 16 *makes fish-pools on the sabbath,* 20 *causes a boy to die who broke them down,* 22 *another boy run against him, whom he also causes to die.*

ON another day Joseph sent his son James to gather wood and the Lord Jesus went with him ;

2 And when they came to the place where the wood was, and James began to gather it, behold, a venomous viper bit him, so that he began to cry, and make a noise.

3 The Lord Jesus seeing him in this condition, came to him, and blowed upon the place where the viper had bit him, and it was instantly well.

4 ¶ On a certain day the Lord Jesus was with some boys, who were playing on the house-top, and one of the boys fell down, and presently died.

5 Upon which the other boys all running away, the Lord Jesus was left alone on the house-top.

6 And the boy's relations came to him and said to the Lord Jesus, Thou didst throw our son down from the house-top.

7 But he denying it, they cried out, Our son is dead, and this is he who killed him.

8 The Lord Jesus replied to them, Do not charge me with a crime, of which you are not able to convict me, but let us go ask the boy himself, who will bring the truth to light.

9 Then the Lord Jesus going down stood over the head of the dead boy, and said with a loud voice, Zeinunus, Zeinunus, who threw thee down from the house-top ?

10 Then the dead boy answered, thou didst not throw me down, but such a one did.

11 And when the Lord Jesus bade those who stood by to take notice of his words, all who were present praised God on account of that miracle.

12 ¶ On a certain time the Lady St. Mary had commanded the Lord Jesus to fetch her some water out of the well ;

13 And when he had gone to fetch the water, the pitcher, when it was brought up full, brake.

14 But Jesus spreading his mantle gathered up the water again, and brought it in that to his mother.

15 Who, being astonished at this wonderful thing, laid up this, and all the other things which she had seen, in her memory.

16 ¶ Again on another day the Lord Jesus was with some boys by a river and they drew water out of the river by little channels, and made little fish-pools.

17 But the Lord Jesus had made twelve sparrows, and placed them about his pool on each side, three on a side.

18 But it was the Sabbath day, and the son of Hanani a Jew came by, and saw them making these things, and said, Do ye thus make figures of clay on the Sabbath? And he ran to them, and broke down their fish-pools.

19 But when the Lord Jesus clapped his hands over the sparrows which he had made, they fled away chirping.

20 At length the son of Hanani

THE PRESENTATION IN THE TEMPLE.

FROM A GREEK PAINTING IN DISTEMPER ON WOOD.

coming to the fish-pool of Jesus to destroy it, the water vanished away, and the Lord Jesus said to him,

21 In like manner as this water has vanished, so shall thy life vanish; and presently the boy died.

22 ¶ Another time, when the Lord Jesus was coming home in the evening with Joseph, he met a boy, who ran so hard against him, that he threw him down;

23 To whom the Lord Jesus said, As thou hast thrown me down, so shalt thou fall, nor ever rise.

24 And that moment the boy fell down and died.

CHAP. XX.

1 Sent to school to Zaccheus to learn his letters, and teaches Zaccheus. 13 Sent to another schoolmaster. 14 refuses to tell his letters, and the schoolmaster going to whip him his hand withers and he dies.

THERE was also at Jerusalem one named Zaccheus, who was a schoolmaster.

2 And he said to Joseph, Joseph, why dost thou not send Jesus to me, that he may learn his letters?

3 Joseph agreed, and told St. Mary;

4 So they brought him to that master; who, as soon as he saw him, wrote out an alphabet for him.

5 And he bade him say Aleph; and when he had said Aleph, the master bade him pronounce Beth.

6 Then the Lord Jesus said to him, Tell me first the meaning of the letter Aleph, and then I will pronounce Beth.

7 And when the master threatened to whip him, the Lord Jesus explained to him the meaning of the letters Aleph and Beth;

8 Also which were the straight figures of the letters, which the oblique, and what letters had double figures; which had points, and which had none; why one letter went before another; and many other things he began to tell him, and explain, of which the master himself had never heard, nor read in any book.

9 The Lord Jesus farther said to the master, Take notice how I say to thee; then he began clearly and distinctly to say Aleph, Beth, Gimel, Daleth, and so on to the end of the alphabet.

10 At this the master was so surprised, that he said, I believe this boy was born before Noah;

11 And turning to Joseph, he said, Thou hast brought a boy to me to be taught, who is more learned than any master.

12 He said also unto St. Mary, This your son has no need of any learning.

13 ¶ They brought him then to a more learned master, who, when he saw him, said, say Aleph.

14 And when he had said Aleph, the master bade him pronounce Beth; to which the Lord Jesus replied, Tell me first the meaning of the letter Aleph, and then I will pronounce Beth.

15 But this master, when he lift up his hand to whip him, had his hand presently withered, and he died.

16 Then said Joseph to St. Mary, henceforth we will not allow him to go out of the house; for every one who displeases him is killed.

CHAP. XXI.

1 Disputes miraculously with the doctors in the temple; 7 on law, 9 on astronomy, 12 on physics and metaphysics, 21 is worshipped by a philosopher, 28 and fetched home by his mother.

AND when he was twelve years old, they brought him to Jerusalem to the feast; and when the feast was over, they returned.

2 But the Lord Jesus continued behind in the temple among the doctors and elders, and learned men of Israel; to whom he proposed several questions of learning, and also gave them answers:

3 For he said to them, Whose son is the Messiah? They answered, the son of David:

4 Why then, said he, does he in the spirit call him Lord? when he saith, The Lord said to my Lord, sit thou at my right hand, till I have made thine enemies thy footstool.

5 Then a certain principal Rabbi asked him, Hast thou read books?

6 Jesus answered, he had read both books, and the things which were contained in books.

7 And he explained to them the books of the law, and precepts, and statutes: and the mysteries which are contained in the books of the prophets; things which the mind of no creature could reach.

8 Then said that Rabbi, I never yet have seen or heard of such knowledge! What do you think that boy will be!

9 ¶ When a certain astronomer, who was present, asked the Lord Jesus, Whether he had studied astronomy?

10 The Lord Jesus replied, and told him the number of the spheres and heavenly bodies, as also their triangular, square, and sextile aspect; their progressive and retrograde motion; their size and several prognostications; and other things which the reason of man had never discovered.

11 ¶ There was also among them a philosopher well skilled in physic and natural philosophy, who asked the Lord Jesus, Whether he had studied physic?

12 He replied, and explained to him physics and metaphysics.

13 Also those things which were above and below the power of nature;

14 The powers also of the body, its humours, and their effects.

15 Also the number of its members, and bones, veins, arteries, and nerves;

16 The several constitutions of body, hot and dry, cold and moist, and the tendencies of them;

17 How the soul operated upon the body;

18 What its various sensations and faculties were;

19 The faculty of speaking, anger, desire;

20 And lastly the manner of its composition and dissolution; and other things, which the understanding of no creature had ever reached.

21 Then that philosopher arose, and worshipped the Lord Jesus, and said, O Lord Jesus, from henceforth I will be thy disciple and servant.

22 ¶ While they were discoursing on these and such like things, the Lady St. Mary came in, having been three days walking about with Joseph, seeking for him.

23 And when she saw him sitting among the doctors, and in his turn proposing questions to them, and giving answers, she said to him, My son, why hast thou done thus by us? Behold I and thy father have been at much pains in seeking thee.

24 He replied, Why did ye seek me? Did ye not know that

I ought to be employed in my father's house?

25 But they understood not the words which he said to them.

26 Then the doctors asked Mary, Whether this was her son? And when she said, He was, they said, O happy Mary, who hast borne such a son.

27 Then he returned with them to Nazareth, and obeyed them in all things.

28 And his mother kept all these things in her mind;

29 And the Lord Jesus grew in stature and wisdom, and favour with God and man.

CHAP. XXII.

1 *Conceals his miracles,* 2 *studies the law and is baptized.*

NOW from this time Jesus began to conceal his miracles and secret works,

2 And he gave himself to the study of the law, till he arrived to the end of his thirtieth year;

3 At which time the Father publicly owned him at Jordan, sending down this voice from heaven, This is my beloved son, in whom I am well pleased;

4 The Holy Ghost being also present in the form of a dove.

5 This is he whom we worship with all reverence, because he gave us our life and being, and brought us from our mother's womb.

6 Who, for our sakes, took a human body, and hath redeemed us, so that he might so embrace us with everlasting mercy, and shew his free, large, bountiful grace and goodness to us.

7 To him be glory and praise, and power, and dominion, from henceforth and for evermore, Amen.

¶ *The end of the whole Gospel of the Infancy, by the assistance of the Supreme God, according to what we found in the original.*

THOMAS'S GOSPEL of the INFANCY of JESUS CHRIST.

[The original in Greek, from which this translation is made, will be found printed by Cotelerius, in his notes on the constitutions of the Apostles, from a MS. in the French King's Library, No. 2279—It is attributed to Thomas, and conjectured to have been originally connected with the Gospel of Mary.]

¶ *An Account of the* ACTIONS *and* MIRACLES *of our Lord and* *Saviour* JESUS CHRIST *in his* INFANCY.

CHAP. I.

2 *Jesus miraculously clears the water after rain.* 4 *plays with clay sparrows, which he animates on the sabbath day.*

I THOMAS, an Israelite, judged it necessary to make known to our brethren among the Gentiles, the actions and miracles of Christ in his childhood, which our Lord and God Jesus Christ wrought after his birth in Bethlehem in our country, at which I myself was astonished; the beginning of which was as followeth.

2 ¶ When the child Jesus was five years of age and there had been a shower of rain, which was now over, Jesus was playing with other Hebrew boys by a running stream; and the water running over the banks, stood in little lakes;

3 But the water instantly became clear and useful again; he having smote them only by his word, they readily obeyed him.

4 Then he took from the bank of the stream some soft clay, and formed out of it twelve sparrows; and there were other boys playing with him.

5 But a certain Jew seeing the things which he was doing, namely, his forming clay into the figures of sparrows on the sabbath day, went presently away, and told his father Joseph, and said,

6 Behold, thy boy is playing by the river side, and has taken clay, and formed it into twelve sparrows, and profaneth the sabbath.

7 Then Joseph came to the place where he was, and when he saw him, called to him, and said, Why doest thou that which it is not lawful to do on the sabbath day?

8 Then Jesus clapping together the palms of his hands, called to the sparrows, and said to them: Go, fly away; and while ye live remember me.

9 So the sparrows fled away, making a noise.

10 The Jews seeing this, were astonished, and went away, and told their chief persons what a

60

strange miracle they had seen wrought by Jesus.

CHAP. II.

2 *Causes a boy to wither who broke down his fish pools, 6 partly restores him, 7 kills another boy, 16 causes blindness to fall on his accusers, 18 for which Joseph pulls him by the ear.*

BESIDES this, the son of Anna the scribe was standing there with Joseph, and took a bough of a willow tree, and scattered the waters which Jesus had gathered into lakes.

2 But the boy Jesus seeing what he had done, became angry, and said to him, Thou fool, what harm did the lake do thee, that thou shouldest scatter the water?

3 Behold, now thou shalt wither as a tree, and shalt not bring forth either leaves, or branches, or fruit.

4 And immediately he became withered all over.

5 Then Jesus went away home. But the parents of the boy who was withered, lamenting the misfortune of his youth, took and carried him to Joseph, accusing him, and said, Why dost thou keep a son who is guilty of such actions?

6 Then Jesus at the request of all who were present did heal him, leaving only some small member to continue withered, that they might take warning.

7 ¶ Another time Jesus went forth into the street, and a boy running by, rushed upon his shoulder;

8 At which Jesus being angry, said to him, thou shalt go no farther.

9 And he instantly fell down dead:

10 Which when some persons saw, they said, Where was this boy born, that everything which he says presently cometh to pass?

11 Then the parents of the dead boy going to Joseph complained, saying, You are not fit to live with us, in our city, having such a boy as that:

12 Either teach him that he bless and not curse, or else depart hence with him, for he kills our children.

13 ¶ Then Joseph calling the boy Jesus by himself, instructed him saying, Why doest thou such things to injure the people so, that they hate us and prosecute us?

14 But Jesus replied, I know that what thou sayest is not of thyself, but for thy sake I will say nothing;

15 But they who have said these things to thee, shall suffer everlasting punishment.

16 And immediately they who had accused him became blind.

17 And all they who saw it were exceedingly afraid and confounded, and said concerning him, Whatsoever he saith, whether good or bad, immediately cometh to pass: and they were amazed.

18 And when they saw this action of Christ, Joseph arose, and plucked him by the ear, at which the boy was angry, and said to him, Be easy;

19 For if they seek for us, they shall not find us: thou hast done very imprudently.

20 Dost thou not know that I am thine? Trouble me no more.

CHAP. III.

1 *Astonishes his schoolmaster by his learning.*

A CERTAIN schoolmaster named Zacchæus, standing in a certain place, heard Jesus

61

speaking these things to his father.

2 And he was much surprised, that being a child, he should speak such things; and after a few days he came to Joseph, and said,

3 Thou hast a wise and sensible child, send him to me, that he may learn to read.

4 When he sat down to teach the letters to Jesus, he began with the first letter Aleph;

5 But Jesus pronounced the second letter Mpeth (Beth) Cghimel (Gimel), and said over all the letters to him to the end.

6 Then opening a book, he taught his master the prophets: but he was ashamed, and was at a loss to conceive how he came to know the letters.

7 And he arose and went home, wonderfully surprised at so strange a thing.

CHAP. IV.

1 *Fragment of an adventure at a dyer's.*

AS Jesus was passing by a certain shop, he saw a young man dipping (or dyeing) some cloths and stockings in a furnace, of a sad colour, doing them according to every person's particular order;

2 The boy Jesus going to the young man who was doing this, took also some of the cloths.

*   *   *   *   *   *

¶ *Here endeth the Fragment of Thomas's Gospel of the Infancy of Jesus Christ*

THE EPISTLES of JESUS CHRIST and ABGARUS KING of EDESSA.

[The first writer who makes any mention of the Epistles that passed between Jesus Christ and Abgarus, is Eusebius, Bishop of Cæsarea, in Palestine, who flourished in the early part of the fourth century. For their genuineness, he appeals to the public registers and records of the City of Edessa in Mesopotamia, where Abgarus reigned, and where he affirms that he found them written, in the Syriac language. He published a Greek translation of them, in his Ecclesiastical History.[1] The learned world have been much divided on this subject; but, notwithstanding that the erudite Grabe, with Archbishop Cave, Dr. Parker, and other divines, has strenuously contended for their admission into the canon of Scripture, they are deemed apocryphal. The Rev. Jeremiah Jones observes, that the common people in England have this Epistle in their houses, in many places, fixed in a frame, with the picture of Christ before it; and that they generally, with much honesty and devotion, regard it as the word of God, and the genuine Epistle of Christ.]

CHAP. I.

A copy of a letter written by King Abgarus to Jesus, and sent to him by Ananias, his footman, to Jerusalem, 5 *inviting him to Edessa.*

ABGARUS, king of Edessa, to Jesus the good Saviour, who appears at Jerusalem, greeting.

2 I have been informed concerning you and your cures, which are performed without the use of medicines and herbs.

3 For it is reported, that you cause the blind to see, the lame to walk, do both cleanse lepers, and cast out unclean spirits and devils, and restore them to health

[1] L. i. c. 13.

who have been long diseased, and raisest up the dead;

4 All which when I heard, I was persuaded of one of these two, viz: either that you are God himself descended from heaven, who do these things, or the son of God.

5 On this account therefore I have wrote to you, earnestly to desire you would take the trouble of a journey hither, and cure a disease which I am under.

6 For I hear the Jews ridicule you, and intend you mischief.

7 My city is indeed small, but neat, and large enough for us both.

CHAP. II.

The answer of Jesus by Ananias the footman to Abgarus the king, 3 declining to visit Edessa.

ABGARUS, you are happy, forasmuch as you have believed on me, whom ye have not seen.

2 For it is written concerning me, that those who have seen me should not believe on me, that they who have not seen might believe and live.

3 As to that part of your letter, which relates to my giving you a visit, I must inform you, that I must fulfil all the ends of my mission in this country, and after that be received up again to him who sent me.

4 But after my ascension I will send one of my disciples, who will cure your disease, and give life to you, and all that are with you.

The GOSPEL of NICODEMUS, formerly called the ACTS of PONTIUS PILATE.

[Although this Gospel is, by some among the learned, supposed to have been really written by Nicodemus, who became a disciple of Jesus Christ, and conversed with him; others conjecture that it was a forgery towards the close of the third century by some zealous believer, who observing that there had been appeals made by the Christians of the former age, to the Acts of Pilate, but that such Acts could not be produced, imagined it would be of service to Christianity to fabricate and publish this Gospel; as it would both confirm the Christians under persecution, and convince the Heathens of the truth of the Christian religion. The Rev. Jeremiah Jones says, that such pious frauds were very common among Christians even in the first three centuries; and that a forgery of this nature, with the view above mentioned, seems natural and probable. The same author, in noticing that Eusebius, in his Ecclesiastical history, charges the Pagans with having forged and published a book, called "The Acts of Pilate," takes occasion to observe, that the internal evidence of this Gospel shows it was not the work of any Heathen; but that if in the latter end of the third century we find it in use among Christians (as it was then certainly in some churches) and about the same time find a forgery of the Heathens under the same title, it seems exceedingly probable that some Christians, at that time, should publish such a piece as this, in order partly to confront the spurious one of the Pagans, and partly to support those appeals which had been made by former Christians to the Acts of Pilate; and Mr. Jones says, he thinks so more particularly as we have innumerable instances of forgeries by the faithful in the primitive ages, grounded on less plausible reasons. Whether it be canonical or not, it is of very great antiquity, and is appealed to by several of the ancient Christians. The present translation is made from the Gospel published by Grynæus in the Orthodoxographa, vol. i. tom. ii. p. 643.]

The Gospel of NICODEMUS *the disciple, concerning the Sufferings and Resurrection of our Master and Saviour* JESUS CHRIST.

CHAP. I.

1 *Christ accused to Pilate by the Jews of healing on the sabbath,* 9 *summoned before Pilate by a messenger who does him honour,* 20 *worshipped by the standards bowing down to him.*

ANNAS and Caiaphas, and Summas, and Datam, Gamaliel, Judas, Levi, Nepthalim, Alexander, Cyrus, and other Jews, went to Pilate about Jesus, accusing him with many bad crimes.

2 And said, We are assured that Jesus is the son of Joseph the carpenter,[1] and born of Mary, and that he declares himself the Son of God, and a king;[2] and not only so, but attempts the dissolution of the sabbath,[3] and the laws of our fathers.

3 Pilate replied; What is it which he declares? and what is it which he attempts dissolving?

4 The Jews told him, We have a law which forbids doing cures on the sabbath day;[4] but he cures both the lame and the deaf, those afflicted with the palsy, the blind, and lepers, and demoniacs, on that day by wicked methods.

5 Pilate replied, How can he do this by wicked methods? They answered, He is a conjurer, and casts out devils by the prince of the devils;[5] and so all things become subject to him.

6 Then said Pilate, Casting out devils seems not to be the work of an unclean spirit, but to proceed from the power of God.

7 The Jews replied to Pilate, We entreat your highness to summon him to appear before your tribunal, and hear him yourself.

8 Then Pilate called a messenger and said to him, By what means will Christ be brought hither?

9 Then went the messenger forth, and knowing Christ, worshipped him; and having spread the cloak which he had in his hand upon the ground, he said, Lord, walk upon this, and go in, for the governor calls thee.

10 When the Jews perceived what the messenger had done they exclaimed (against him) to Pilate, and said, Why did you not give him his summons by a beadle, and not by a messenger?— For the messenger, when he saw him, worshipped him, and spread the cloak which he had in his hand upon the ground before him, and said to him, Lord, the governor calls thee.

11 Then Pilate called the messenger, and said, Why hast thou done thus?

12 The messenger replied, When thou sentest me from Jerusalem to Alexander, I saw Jesus sitting in a mean figure upon a she-ass, and the children of the Hebrews cried out, Hosannah, holding boughs of trees in their hands.

13 Others spread their garments in the way, and said, Save us, thou who art in heaven; blessed is he who cometh in the name of the Lord.[7]

14 Then the Jews cried out, against the messenger, and said, The children of the Hebrews made their acclamations in the Hebrew language; and how couldst thou, who art a Greek, understand the Hebrew?

---

[1] Matt. xiii. 55, and John vi. 42.   [2] John v. 17, 18.   Mark xv. 2.
[3] Matt. xii. 2, &c.; Luke xiii. 14. John, v. 18.   [4] Exod. xx. 8, &c.   [5] Matt. vi. 24, and xi. 5.   [6] Matt. iv. 34, and xii. 24, &c.   [7] Matt. xxi. 8, 9, &c.

MARY OFFERING IN THE TEMPLE.

FROM A GREEK DIPTYCHON OF THE THIRTEENTH OR FOURTEENTH CENTURY.

15 The messenger answered them and said, I asked one of the Jews and said, What is this which the children do cry out in the Hebrew language?

16 And he explained it to me, saying, they cry out Hosannah, which being interpreted, is, O, Lord, save me; or, O Lord, save.

17 Pilate then said to them, Why do you yourselves testify to the words spoken by the children, namely, by your silence? In what has the messenger done amiss? And they were silent.

18 Then the governor said unto the messenger, Go forth and endeavour by any means to bring him in.

19 But the messenger went forth, and did as before; and said, Lord, come in, for the governor calleth thee.

20 And as Jesus was going in by the ensigns, who carried the standards, the tops of them bowed down and worshipped Jesus.

21 Whereupon the Jews exclaimed more vehemently against the ensigns.

22 But Pilate said to the Jews, I know it is not pleasing to you that the tops of the standards did of themselves bow and worship Jesus; but why do ye exclaim against the ensigns, as if they had bowed and worshipped?

23 They replied to Pilate, We saw the ensigns themselves bowing and worshipping Jesus.

24 Then the governor called the ensigns and said unto them, Why did you do thus?

25 The ensigns said to Pilate, We are all Pagans and worship the gods in temples; and how should we think anything about worshipping him? We only held the standards in our hands and they bowed themselves and worshipped him.

26 Then said Pilate to the rulers of the synagogue, Do ye yourselves choose some strong men, and let them hold the standards, and we shall see whether they will then bend of themselves.

27 So the elders of the Jews sought out twelve of the most strong and able old men, and made them hold the standards and they stood in the presence of the governor.

28 Then Pilate said to the messenger, Take Jesus out, and by some means bring him in again. And Jesus and the messenger went out of the hall.

29 And Pilate called the ensigns who before had borne the standards, and swore to them, that if they had not borne the standards in that manner when Jesus before entered in, he would cut off their heads.

30 Then the governor commanded Jesus to come in again.

31 And the messenger did as he had done before, and very much entreated Jesus that he would go upon his cloak, and walk on it, and he did walk upon it, and went in.

32 And when Jesus went in, the standards bowed themselves as before, and worshipped him.

CHAP. II.

2 Is compassionated by Pilate's wife, 7 charged with being born in fornication. 12 Testimony to the betrothing of his parents. Hatred of the Jews to him.

NOW when Pilate saw this, he was afraid, and was about to rise from his seat.

2 But while he thought to rise, his own wife who stood at a distance, sent to him, saying

65

Have thou nothing to do with that just man; for I have suffered much concerning him in a vision this night.[1]

3 When the Jews heard this they said to Pilate, Did we not say unto thee, He is a conjuror? Behold, he hath caused thy wife to dream.

4 Pilate then calling Jesus, said, thou hast heard what they testify against thee, and makest no answer?

5 Jesus replied, If they had not a power of speaking, they could not have spoke; but because every one has the command of his own tongue, to speak both good and bad, let him look to it.

6 But the elders of the Jews answered, and said to Jesus, What shall we look to?

7 In the first place, we know this concerning thee, that thou wast born through fornication; secondly, that upon the account of thy birth the infants were slain in Bethlehem; thirdly, that thy father and mother Mary fled into Egypt, because they could not trust their own people.

8 Some of the Jews who stood by spake more favourably, We cannot say that he was born through fornication; but we know that his mother Mary was betrothed to Joseph, and so he was not born through fornication.

9 Then said Pilate to the Jews who affirmed him to be born through fornication, This your account is not true, seeing there was a betrothment, as they testify who are of your own nation.

10 Annas and Caiaphas spake to Pilate, All this multitude of people is to be regarded, who cry out, that he was born through fornication, and is a conjuror; but they who deny him to be born through fornication, are his proselytes and disciples.

11 Pilate answered Annas and Caiaphas, Who are the proselytes? They answered, They are those who are the children of Pagans, and are not become Jews, but followers of him.

12 Then replied Eleazer, and Asterius, and Antonius, and James, Caras and Samuel, Isaac and Phinees, Crispus and Agrippa, Annas and Judas, We are not proselytes, but children of Jews, and speak the truth, and were present when Mary was betrothed.

13 Then Pilate addressing himself to the twelve men who spake this, said to them, I conjure you by the life of Cæsar, that ye faithfully declare whether he was born through fornication, and those things be true which ye have related.

14 They answered Pilate, We have a law, whereby we are forbid to swear, it being a sin: Let them swear by the life of Cæsar that it is not as we have said, and we will be contented to be put to death.

15 Then said Annas and Caiaphas to Pilate, Those twelve men will not believe that we know him to be basely born, and to be a conjuror, although he pretends that he is the son of God, and a king:[2] which we are so far from believing, that we tremble to hear.

16 Then Pilate commanded every one to go out except the twelve men who said he was not born through fornication, and Jesus to withdraw to a distance, and said to them, Why have the Jews a mind to kill Jesus?

---

[1] Matt. xxvii. 19.   [2] John v. 17, 18; Mark xv. 2.

17 They answered him, They are angry because he wrought cures on the sabbath day. Pilate said, Will they kill him for a good work?[1] They say unto him, Yes, Sir.

CHAP. III.

1 *Is exonerated by Pilate.* 11 *Disputes with Pilate concerning Truth.*

THEN Pilate, filled with anger, went out of the hall, and said to the Jews, I call the whole world to witness that I find no fault in that man.[2]

2 The Jews replied to Pilate, If he had not been a wicked person, we had not brought him before thee.

3 Pilate said to them, Do ye take him and try him by your law.

4 Then the Jews said, It is not lawful for us to put any one to death.

5 Pilate said to the Jews, The command, therefore thou shalt not kill,[3] belongs to you, but not to me.

6 And he went again into the hall, and called Jesus by himself, and said to him, Art thou the king of the Jews?

7 And Jesus answering, said to Pilate, Dost thou speak this of thyself, or did the Jews tell it thee concerning me?

8 Pilate answering, said to Jesus, Am I a Jew? The whole nation and rulers of the Jews have delivered thee up to me. What hast thou done?

9 Jesus answering, said, My kingdom is not of this world: if my kingdom were of this world, then would my servants fight, and I should not have been delivered to the Jews; but now my kingdom is not from hence.

10 Pilate said, Art thou a king then? Jesus answered, Thou sayest that I am a king : to this end was I born, and for this end came I into the world; and for this purpose I came, that I should bear witness to the truth; and every one who is of the truth, heareth my voice.

11 Pilate saith to him, What is truth?

12 Jesus said, Truth is from heaven.

13 Pilate said, Therefore truth is not on earth.

14 Jesus said to Pilate, Believe that truth is on earth among those, who when they have the power of judgment, are governed by truth, and form right judgment.

CHAP. IV.

1 *Pilate finds no fault in Jesus.* 16 *The Jews demand his crucifixion.*

THEN Pilate left Jesus in the hall, and went out to the Jews, and said, I find not any one fault in Jesus.

2 The Jews say unto him, But he said, I can destroy the temple of God, and in three days build it up again.

3 Pilate saith unto them, What sort of temple is that of which he speaketh?

4 The Jews say unto him, That which Solomon was forty-six years in building,[4] he said he would destroy, and in three days build up.

5 Pilate said to them again, I am innocent from the blood of that man; do ye look to it.[5]

---

[1] John x. 32.   [2] John xviii. 31, &c.   [3] Exod. xx. 13.   [4] John ii. 19.
[5] Matt. xxvii. 24.

6 The Jews say to him, His blood be upon us and our children. Then Pilate calling together the elders and scribes, priests and Levites, saith to them privately, Do not act thus; I have found nothing in your charge (against him) concerning his curing sick persons, and breaking the sabbath, worthy of death.

7 The Priests and Levites replied to Pilate, By the life of Cæsar, if any one be a blasphemer, he is worthy of death ;[1] but this man hath blasphemed against the Lord.

8 Then the governor again commanded the Jews to depart out of the hall; and calling Jesus, said to him, What shall I do with thee?

9 Jesus answered him, Do according as it is written.

10 Pilate said to him, How is it written?

11 Jesus saith to him, Moses and the prophets have prophesied concerning my suffering and resurrection.

12 The Jews hearing this, were provoked, and said to Pilate, Why wilt thou any longer hear the blasphemy of that man?

13 Pilate saith to them, If these words seem to you blasphemy, do ye take him, bring him to your court, and try him according to your law.

14 The Jews reply to Pilate, Our law saith, he shall be obliged to receive nine and thirty stripes, but if after this manner he shall blaspheme against the Lord, he shall be stoned.

15 Pilate saith unto them, If that speech of his was blasphemy, do ye try him according to your law.

16 The Jews say to Pilate, Our law commands us not to put any one to death :[2] we desire that he may be crucified, because he deserves the death of the cross.

17 Pilate saith to them, It is not fit he should be crucified: let him be only whipped and sent away.[3]

18 But when the governor looked upon the people that were present and the Jews, he saw many of the Jews in tears, and said to the chief priests of the Jews, All the people do not desire his death.

19 The elders of the Jews answered to Pilate, We and all the people came hither for this very purpose, that he should die.

20 Pilate saith to them, Why should he die?

21 They said to him, Because he declares himself to be the Son of God, and a King.

CHAP. V.

1 *Nicodemus speaks in defence of Christ, and relates his miracles.* 12 *Another Jew,* 26 *with Veronica,* 34 *Centurio, and others, testify of other miracles.*

BUT Nicodemus, a certain Jew, stood before the governor, and said, I entreat thee, O righteous judge, that thou wouldst favour me with the liberty of speaking a few words.

2 Pilate said to him, Speak on.

3 Nicodemus said, I spake to the elders of the Jews, and the scribes, and priests and Levites, and all the multitude of the Jews, in their assembly; What is it ye would do with this man?

4 He is a man who hath wrought many useful and glorious miracles, such as no man on earth ever wrought before,

---

[1] Leviticus xxiv. 16.   [2] Exodus xx. 13.   [3] Luke xxiii. 16.

nor will ever work.[1] Let him go, and do him no harm; if he cometh from God, his miracles, (his miraculous cures) will continue; but if from men, they will come to nought.[2]

5 Thus Moses, when he was sent by God into Egypt, wrought the miracles which God commanded him, before Pharaoh king of Egypt; and though the magicians of that country, Jannes and Jambres,[3] wrought by their magic the same miracles which Moses did, yet they could not work all which he did;

6 And the miracles which the magicians wrought, were not of God, as ye know, O Scribes and Pharisees; but they who wrought them perished, and all who believed them.[5]

7 And now let this man go; because the very miracles for which ye accuse him, are from God; and he is not worthy of death.

8 The Jews then said to Nicodemus, Art thou become his disciple, and making speeches in his favour?

9 Nicodemus said to them, Is the governor become his disciple also, and does he make speeches for him? Did not Cæsar place him in that high post?

10 When the Jews heard this they trembled, and gnashed their teeth at Nicodemus, and said to him, Mayest thou receive his doctrine for truth, and have thy lot with Christ!

11 Nicodemus replied, Amen; I will receive his doctrine, and my lot with him, as ye have said.

12 ¶ Then another certain Jew rose up, and desired leave of the governor to hear him a few words.

13 And the governor said, Speak what thou hast a mind.

14 And he said, I lay for thirty-eight years by the sheep-pool at Jerusalem, labouring under a great infirmity, and waiting for a cure which should be wrought by the coming of an angel, who at a certain time troubled the water; and whosoever first after the troubling of the water stepped in, was made whole of whatsoever disease he had.

15 And when Jesus saw me languishing there, he said to me, Wilt thou be made whole? And I answered, Sir, I have no man, when the water is troubled, to put me into the pool.

16 And he said unto me, Rise, take up thy bed and walk. And I was immediately made whole, and took up my bed and walked.[6]

17 The Jews then said to Pilate, Our Lord Governor, pray ask him what day it was on which he was cured of his infirmity.

18 The infirm person replied, It was on the sabbath.

19 The Jews said to Pilate, Did we not say that he wrought his cures on the sabbath, and cast out devils by the prince of devils?

20 Then another certain[7] Jew came forth, and said, I was blind, could hear sounds, but could not see any one; and as Jesus was going along, I heard the multitude passing by, and I asked what was there?

21 They told me that Jesus was passing by: then I cried out, saying, Jesus, Son of David, have mercy on me. And he

[1] John iii. 2.   [2] Acts v. 38.
[3] These are mentioned also as the names of the magicians, 2 Tim. iii. 8.
[4] Exod. viii. 18, &c.   [5] Acts v. 35. An allusion to Gamaliel's speech.
[6] John v. 1, 2, &c.   [7] Mark x. 46.

stood still, and commanded that I should be brought to him, and said to me, What wilt thou?

22 I said, Lord, that I may receive my sight.

23 He said to me, Receive thy sight: and presently I saw, and followed him, rejoicing and giving thanks.

24 Another Jew also came forth, and said, [1] I was a leper, and he cured me by his word only, saying, I will, be thou clean; and presently I was cleansed from my leprosy.

25 And another Jew came forth, and said, I was crooked, and he made me straight by his word.[2]

26 ¶ And a certain woman named Veronica, said, [3] I was afflicted with an issue of blood twelve years, and I touched the hem of his garments, and presently the issue of my blood stopped.

27 The Jews then said, We have a law, that a woman shall not be allowed as an evidence.

28 And, after other things, another Jew said, [4] I saw Jesus invited to a wedding with his disciples, and there was a want of wine in Cana of Galilee;

29 And when the wine was all drank, he commanded the servants that they should fill six pots which were there with water, and they filled them up to the brim, and he blessed them, and turned the water into wine, and all the people drank, being surprised at this miracle.

30 And another Jew stood forth, and said, [5] I saw Jesus teaching in the synagogue at Capernaum; and there was in the synagogue a certain man who had a devil; and he cried out, saying, let me alone; what have we to do with thee, Jesus of Nazareth? Art thou come to destroy us? I know that thou art the Holy One of God.

31 And Jesus rebuked him, saying, Hold thy peace, unclean spirit, and come out of the man; and presently he came out of him, and did not at all hurt him.

32 The following things were also said by a Pharisee; I saw that a great company came to Jesus from Galilee and Judæa, and the sea-coast, and many countries about Jordan, and many infirm persons came to him, and he healed them all.[6]

33 And I heard the unclean spirits crying out, and saying,[7] Thou art the Son of God. And Jesus strictly charged them, that they should not make him known.

34 ¶ After this another person, whose name was Centurio, said,[8] I saw Jesus in Capernaum, and I entreated him, saying, Lord, my servant lieth at home sick of the palsy.

35 And Jesus said to me, I will come and cure him.

36 But I said, Lord, I am not worthy that thou shouldst come under my roof; but only speak the word, and my servant shall be healed.

37 And Jesus said unto me, Go thy way; and as thou hast believed, so be it done unto thee. And my servant was healed from that same hour.

---

[1] Matt. viii. 11, &c.   [2] Luke xiii. 11.

[3] Matt. ix. 20, &c. See concerning this woman called Veronica, on whom this miracle was performed, and the statue which she erected to the honour of Christ, in Euseb. Hist. Eccl. 1. 7, c. 18.

[4] John ii. 1, &c.   [5] Luke iv. 33, &c.   [6] Matt. v. 23.
[7] Mark iii. 11.   [8] Matt. viii. 5, &c.

38 Then a certain nobleman said, I had a son in Capernaum, who lay at the point of death; and when I heard that Jesus was come into Galilee, I went and besought him that he would come down to my house, and heal my son, for he was at the point of death.

39 He said to me, Go thy way, thy son liveth.

40 And my son was cured from that hour.

41 Besides these, also many others of the Jews, both men and women, cried out and said, He is truly the Son of God, who cures all diseases only by his word, and to whom the devils are altogether subject.

42 Some of them farther said, This power can proceed from none but God.

43 Pilate said to the Jews, Why are not the devils subject to your doctors?

44 Some of them said, The power of subjecting devils cannot proceed but from God.

45 But others said to Pilate, That he had [1] raised Lazarus from the dead, after he had been four days in his grave.

46 The governor hearing this, trembling said to the multitude of the Jews, What will it profit you to shed innocent blood?

CHAP. VI.

1 *Pilate dismayed by the turbulence of the Jews, 5 who demand Barabbas to be released, and Christ to be crucified, 9 Pilate warmly expostulates with them, 20 washes his hands of Christ's blood, 23 and sentences him to be whipped and crucified.*

THEN Pilate having called together Nicodemus, and the fifteen men who said that Jesus was not born through fornication, said to them, What shall I do, seeing there is like to be a tumult among the people.[2]

2 They said unto him, We know not; let them look to it who raise the tumult.

3 Pilate then called the multitude again, and said to them, Ye know that ye have a custom, that I should release to you one prisoner at the feast of the passover;

4 I have a noted prisoner, a murderer, who is called Barabbas, and Jesus who is called Christ, in whom I find nothing that deserves death; which of them therefore have you a mind that I should release to you?[3]

5 They all cry out, and say, Release to us Barabbas.

6 Pilate saith to them, What then shall I do with Jesus who is called Christ?

7 They all answer, Let him be crucified.

8 Again they cry out and say to Pilate, You are not the friend of Cæsar, if you release this man?[4] for he hath declared that he is the Son of God, and a king. But are you inclined that he should be king, and not Cæsar?

9 Then Pilate filled with anger said to them, Your nation hath always been seditious, and you are always against those who have been serviceable to you?

10 The Jews replied, Who are those who have been serviceable to us?

11 Pilate answered them, Your God who delivered you from the hard bondage of the Egyptians, and brought you over the Red Sea as though it had been dry land, and fed you in the wilderness with manna and the flesh of

[1] John xi. 17, &c.　　[2] Matt. xxvii. 24.　　[3] Matt. xxvii. 21.
[4] John xix.12.

quails, and brought water out of the rock, and gave you a law from heaven :

12 Ye provoked him all ways, and desired for yourselves a molten calf, and worshipped it, and sacrificed to it, and said, These are Thy Gods, O Israel, which brought thee out of the land of Egypt !

13 On account of which your God was inclined to destroy you ; but Moses interceded for you, and your God heard him, and forgave your iniquity.

14 Afterwards ye were enraged against, and would have killed your prophets, Moses and Aaron, when they fled to the tabernacle, and ye were always murmuring against God and his prophets.

15 And arising from his judgment seat, he would have gone out ; but the Jews all cried out, We acknowledge Cæsar to be king, and not Jesus.

16 Whereas this person, as soon as he was born, the wise men came and offered gifts unto him ; which when Herod heard, he was exceedingly troubled, and would have killed him.

17 When his father knew this, he fled with him and his mother Mary into Egypt. Herod, when he heard he was born, would have slain him ; and accordingly sent and slew all the children which were in Bethlehem, and in all the coasts thereof, from two years old and under.[1]

18 When Pilate heard this account, he was afraid ; and commanding silence among the people, who made a noise, he said to Jesus, Art thou therefore a king ?

19 All the Jews replied to Pilate, he is the very person whom Herod sought to have slain.

20 Then Pilate taking water, washed his hands before the people and said, I am innocent of the blood of this just person ; look ye to it.[2]

21 The Jews answered and said, His blood be upon us and our children.

22 Then Pilate commanded Jesus to be brought before him, and spake to him in the following words :

23 Thy own nation hath charged thee as making thyself a king ; wherefore I, Pilate, sentence thee to be whipped according to the laws of former governors ; and that thou be first bound, then hanged upon a cross in that place where thou art now a prisoner ; and also two criminals with thee, whose names are Dimas and Gestas.

CHAP. VII.

1 Manner of Christ's crucifixion with the two thieves.

THEN Jesus went out of the hall, and the two thieves with him.

2 And when they came to the place which is called Golgotha,[3] they stript him of his raiment, and girt him about with a linen cloth, and put a crown of thorns upon his head, and put a reed in his hand.

3 And in like manner did they to the two thieves who were crucified with him, Dimas on his right hand and Gestas on his left.

4 But Jesus said, My Father, forgive them ; For they know not what they do.

5 And they divided his garments, and upon his vesture they cast lots.

6 The people in the mean time stood by, and the chief priests

---

[1] Matt. ii.   [2] Matt. xxvii. 24, &c.   [3] Matt. xxvii. 33.

THE BIRTH OF CHRIST.

FROM A PAINTING ON WOOD BY FRA FILIPPO LIPPI.

THE MURDER OF THE INNOCENTS.

FROM A PAINTING ON WOOD BY MATTEO DI GIOVANNI.

and elders of the Jews mocked him, saying, he saved others, let him now save himself if he can; if he be the son of God, let him now come down from the cross.

7 The soldiers also mocked him, and taking vinegar and gall offered it to him to drink, and said to him, If thou art king of the Jews deliver thyself.

8 Then Longinus, a certain soldier, taking a spear,[1] pierced his side, and presently there came forth blood and water.

9 And Pilate wrote the title upon the cross in Hebrew, Latin, and Greek letters, viz. This is the king of the Jews.[2]

10 But one of the two thieves who were crucified with Jesus, whose name was Gestas, said to Jesus, If thou art the Christ, deliver thyself and us.

11 But the thief who was crucified on his right hand, whose name was Dimas, answering, rebuked him, and said, Dost not thou fear God, who art condemned to this punishment? We indeed receive rightly and justly the demerit of our actions; but this Jesus, what evil hath he done?

12 After this groaning, he said to Jesus, Lord, remember me when thou comest into thy kingdom.

13 Jesus answering, said to him, Verily I say unto thee, that this day thou shalt be with me in Paradise.

CHAP. VIII.

1 *Miraculous appearance at his death.*
10 *The Jews say the eclipse was natural.*
12 *Joseph of Arimathœa embalms Christ's body and buries it.*

AND it was about the sixth hour,[3] and darkness was upon the face of the whole earth until the ninth hour.

2 And while the sun was eclipsed, behold the vail of the temple was rent from the top to the bottom; and the rocks also were rent, and the graves opened, and many bodies of saints, which slept, arose.

3 And about the ninth hour Jesus cried out with a loud voice, saying, Hely, Hely, lama zabacthani? which being interpreted, is, My God, My God, why hast thou forsaken me?

4 And after these things, Jesus said, Father, into thy hands I commend my spirit; and having said this, he gave up the ghost.

5 But when the centurion saw that Jesus thus crying out gave up the ghost, he glorified God, and said, Of a truth this was a just man.

6 And all the people who stood by, were exceedingly troubled at the sight; and reflecting upon what had passed, smote upon their breasts, and then returned to the city of Jerusalem.

7 The centurion went to the governor, and related to him all that had passed;

8 And when he had heard all these things, he was exceeding sorrowful;

9 And calling the Jews together, said to them, Have ye seen the miracle of the sun's eclipse, and the other things which came to pass, while Jesus was dying?

10 Which when the Jews heard, they answered to the governor, The eclipse of the sun happened according to its usual custom.

11 But all those who were the acquaintance of Christ, stood at a distance, as did the women who had followed Jesus from Galilee, observing all these things.

[1] John xix. 34.   [2] John xix. 19.   [3] Matt. xxvii. 45, &c.

73

12 And [1] behold a certain man of Arimathæa, named Joseph, who also was a disciple of Jesus, but not openly so, for fear of the Jews, came to the governor, and entreated the governor that he would give him leave to take away the body of Jesus from the cross.

13 And the governor gave him leave.

14 And Nicodemus came, bringing with him a mixture of myrrh and aloes about a hundred pound weight; and they took down Jesus from the cross with tears, and bound him with linen cloths with spices, according to the custom of burying among the Jews,

15 And placed him in a new tomb, which Joseph had built, aud caused to be cut out of a rock, im which never any man had been put; and they rolled a great stone to the door of the sepulchre.

CHAP. IX.

1 *The Jews angry with Nicodemus; 5 and with Joseph of Arimathœa, 7 whom they imprison.*

WHEN the unjust Jews heard that Joseph had begged and buried the body of Jesus, they sought after Nicodemus; and those fifteen men who had testified before the Governor, that Jesus was not born through fornication, and other good persons who had shewn any good actions towards him.

2 But when they all concealed themselves through fear of the Jews Nicodemus alone shewed himself to them, and said, How can such persons as these enter into the synagogue?

3 The Jews answered him, But how durst thou enter into the synagogue who wast a confederate with Christ? Let thy lot be along with him in the other world.

4 Nicodemus answered, Amen; so may it be, that I may have my lot with him in his kingdom.

5 In like manner Joseph, when he came to the Jews, said to them Why are ye angry with me for desiring the body of Jesus of Pilate? Behold, I have put him in my tomb, and wrapped him up in clean linen, and put a stone at the door of the sepulchre:

6 I have acted rightly towards him; but ye have acted unjustly aginst that just person, in crucifying him, giving him vinegar to drink, crowning him with thorns, tearing his body with whips, and prayed down the guilt of his blood upon you.

7 The Jews at the hearing of this were disquieted, and troubled; and they seized Joseph, and commanded him to be put in custody before the sabbath, and kept there till the sabbath was over.

8 And they said to him, Make confession; for at this time it is not lawful to do thee any harm, till the first day of the week come. But we know that thou wilt not be thought worthy of a burial; but we will give thy flesh to the birds of the air, and the beasts of the earth.

9 Joseph answered, That speech is like the speech of proud Goliath, who reproached the living God in speaking against David. But ye scribes and doctors know that God saith by the prophet, Vengeance is mine, and I

[1] John xix. 38.

74

will repay to you[1] evil equal to that which ye have threatened to me.

10 The God whom you have hanged upon the cross, is able to deliver me out of your hands. All your wickedness will return upon you.

11 For the governor, when he washed his hands, said, I am clear from the blood of this just person. But ye answered and cried out, His blood be upon us and our children. According as ye have said, may ye perish for ever.

12 The elders of the Jews hearing these words, were exceedingly enraged; and seizing Joseph, they put him into a chamber where there was no window; they fastened the door, and put a seal upon the lock;

13 And Annas and Caiaphas placed a guard upon it, and took counsel with the priests and Levites, that they should all meet after the sabbath, and they contrived to what death they should put Joseph.

14 When they had done this, the rulers, Annas and Caiaphas, ordered Joseph to be brought forth.

¶ *In this place there is a portion of the Gospel lost or omitted, which cannot be supplied.*

CHAP. X.

1 *Joseph's escape.* 2 *The soldiers relate Christ's resurrection.* 18 *Christ is seen preaching in Galilee.* 21 *The Jews repent of their cruelty to him.*

WHEN all the assembly heard this, they admired and were astonished, because they found the same seal upon the lock of the chamber, and could not find Joseph.

2 Then Annas and Caiaphas

went forth, and while they were all admiring at Joseph's being gone, behold one of the soldiers, who kept the sepulchre of Jesus, spake in the assembly.

3 That [2] while they were guarding the sepulchre of Jesus, there was an earthquake; and we saw an angel of God roll away the stone of the sepulchre and [3]sit upon it;

4 And his countenance was like lightning and his garment like snow; and we became through fear like persons dead.

5 And we heard an angel saying to the women at the sepulchre of Jesus, Do not fear; I know that you seek Jesus who was crucified; he is risen as he foretold.

6 Come and see the place where he was laid; and go presently, and tell his disciples that he is risen from the dead, and he will go before you into Galilee; there ye shall see him as he told you.

7 Then the Jews called together all the soldiers who kept the sepulchre of Jesus, and said to them, Who are those women, to whom the angel spoke? Why did ye not seize them?

8 The soldiers answered and said, We know not whom the women were; besides we became as dead persons through fear, and how could we seize those women?

9 The Jews said to them, As the Lord liveth we do not believe you.

10 The soldiers answering said to the Jews, when ye saw and heard Jesus working so many miracles, and did not believe him, how should ye believe us? Ye well said, As the Lord liveth, for the Lord truly does live.

---

[1] Deut. xxxii. 35; Heb. x. 40.   [2] Matt. xxviii. 11, 12, &c.
[3] Matt. xxviii. 1, 2, &c.

11 We have heard that ye shut up Joseph, who buried the body of Jesus, in a chamber, under a lock which was sealed; and when ye opened it, found him not there.

12 Do ye then produce Joseph whom ye put under guard in the chamber, and we will produce Jesus whom we guarded in the sepulchre.

13 The Jews answered and said, We will produce Joseph, do ye produce Jesus. But Joseph is in his own city of Arimathæa.

14 The soldiers replied, If Joseph be in Arimathæa, and Jesus in Galilee, we heard the angel inform the women.

15 The Jews hearing this, were afraid, and said among themselves, If by any means these things should become public, then every body will believe in Jesus.

16 Then they gathered a large sum of money, and gave it to the soldiers, saying, Do ye tell the people that the disciples of Jesus came in the night when ye were asleep and stole away the body of Jesus; and if Pilate the governor should hear of this, we will satisfy him and secure you.

17 The soldiers accordingly took the money, and said as they were instructed by the Jews; and their report was spread abroad among all the people.

18 ¶ But a certain priest Phinees, Ada a schoolmaster, and a Levite, named Ageus, they three came from Galilee to Jerusalem, and told the chief priests and all who were in the synagogues, saying,

19 We have seen Jesus, whom ye crucified, talking with his eleven disciples, and sitting in the midst of them in Mount Olivet, and saying to them,[1]

20 Go forth into the whole world, preach the Gospel to all nations, baptizing them in the name of the Father, and the Son, and the Holy Ghost; and whosoever shall believe and be baptized, shall be saved.

21 And when he had said these things to his disciples, we saw him ascending up to heaven.

22 When the chief priests, and elders, and Levites heard these things, they said to these three men, Give glory to the God of Israel, and make confession to him, whether those things are true, which ye say ye have seen and heard.

23 They answering said, As the Lord of our fathers liveth, the God of Abraham, and the God of Isaac, and the God of Jacob, according as we heard Jesus talking with his disciples, and according as we saw him ascending up to heaven, so we have related the truth to you.

24 And the three men farther answered, and said, adding these words, If we should not own the words which we heard Jesus speak, and that we saw him ascending into heaven, we should be guilty of sin.

25 Then the chief priests immediately rose up, and holding the book of the law in their hands, conjured these men, saying, Ye shall no more hereafter declare those things which ye have spoke concerning Jesus.

26 And they gave them a large sum of money, and sent other persons along with them, who should conduct them to their own country, that they might not by any means make any stay at Jerusalem.

[1] Matt. xxviii. 16. and Mark xvi. 16.

27 Then the Jews did assemble all together, and having expressed the most lamentable concern, said, What is this extraordinary thing which is come to pass in Jerusalem?

28 But Annas and Caiaphas comforted them, saying, Why should we believe the soldiers who guarded the sepulchre of Jesus, in telling us, that an angel rolled away the stone from the door of the sepulchre?

29 Perhaps his own disciples told them this, and gave them money that they should say so, and they themselves took away the body of Jesus.

30 Besides, consider this, that there is no credit to be given to foreigners,[1] because they also took a large sum of us, and they have declared to us according to the instructions which we gave them. They must either be faithful to us, or to the disciples of Jesus.

CHAP. XI.

1 *Nicodemus counsels the Jews.* 6 *Joseph found.* 11 *Invited by the Jews to return.* 19 *Relates the manner of his miraculous escape.*

THEN Nicodemus arose, and said, Ye say right, O sons of Israel, ye have heard what those three men have sworn by the Law of God, who said, We have seen Jesus speaking with his disciples upon Mount Olivet, and we saw him ascending up to heaven.

2 And the scripture teacheth us that the blessed prophet Elijah was taken up to heaven; and Elisha being asked by the sons of the prophets, Where is our father Elijah? He said to them, that he is taken up to heaven.

3 And the sons of the prophets said to him, Perhaps the spirit hath carried him into one of the mountains of Israel, there perhaps we shall find him. And they besought Elisha, and he walked about with them three days, and they could not find him.

4 And now hear me, O sons of Israel, and let us send men into the mountains of Israel, lest perhaps the spirit hath carried away Jesus, and there perhaps we shall find him, and be satisfied.

5 And the counsel of Nicodemus pleased all the people; and they sent forth men who sought for Jesus, but could not find him: and they returning, said, We went all about, but could not find Jesus, but we have found Joseph in his city of Arimathea.

6 The rulers hearing this, and all the people, were glad, and praised the God of Israel, because Joseph was found, whom they had shut up in a chamber, and could not find.

7 And when they had formed a large assembly, the chief priests said, By what means shall we bring Joseph to us to speak with him?

8 And taking a piece of paper, they wrote to him, and said, Peace be with thee, and all thy family. We know that we have offended against God and thee. Be pleased to give a visit to us your fathers, for we were perfectly surprised at your escape from prison.

9 We know that it was malicious counsel which we took against thee, and that the Lord took care of thee, and the Lord himself delivered thee from our designs. Peace be unto thee, Joseph, who art honourable among all the people.

10 And they chose seven of

---

[1] Heathens.

Joseph's friends, and said to them, When ye come to Joseph, salute him in peace, and give him this letter.

11 Accordingly, when the men came to Joseph, they did salute him in peace, and gave him the letter.

12 And when Joseph had read it, he said, Blessed be the Lord God, who didst deliver me from the Israelites, that they could not shed my blood. Blessed be God, who has protected me under thy wings.

13 And Joseph kissed them, and took them into his house. And on the morrow, Joseph mounted his ass, and went along with them to Jerusalem.

14 And when all the Jews heard these things, they went out to meet him, and cried out, saying, Peace attend thy coming hither, father Joseph.

15 To which he answered, Prosperity from the Lord attend all the people.

16 And they all kissed him; and Nicodemus took him to his house, having prepared a large entertainment.

17 But on the morrow, being a preparation-day, Annas, and Caiaphas, and Nicodemus, said to Joseph, Make confession to the God of Israel, and answer to us all those questions which we shall ask thee;

18 For we have been very much troubled, that thou didst bury the body of Jesus; and that when we had locked thee in a chamber, we could not find thee; and we have been afraid ever since, till this time of thy appearing among us. Tell us therefore before God, all that came to pass.

19 Then Joseph answering, said, Ye did indeed put me under confinement, on the day of preparation, till the morning.

20 But while I was standing at prayer in the middle of the night, the house was surrounded with four angels; and I saw Jesus as the brightness of the sun, and fell down upon the earth for fear.

21 But Jesus laying hold on my hand, lifted me from the ground, and the dew was then sprinkled upon me; but he, wiping my face, kissed me, and said unto me, Fear not, Joseph; look upon me, for it is I.

22 Then I looked upon him, and said, Rabboni Elias! He answered me, I am not Elias, but Jesus of Nazareth, whose body thou didst bury.

23 I said to him, Shew me the tomb in which I laid thee.

24 Then Jesus, taking me by the hand, led me unto the place where I laid him, and shewed me the linen clothes, and napkin which I put round his head. Then I knew that it was Jesus, and worshipped him, and said, Blessed be he who cometh in the name of the Lord.

25 Jesus again taking me by the hand, led me to Arimathæa to my own house, and said to me, Peace be to thee; but go not out of thy house till the fortieth day; but I must go to my disciples.

CHAP. XII.

1 *The Jews astonished and confounded.* 17 *Simeon's two sons, Charinus and Lenthius, rise from the dead at Christ's crucifixion.* 19 *Joseph proposes to get them to relate the mysteries of their resurrection.* 21 *They are sought and found,* 22 *brought to the synagogue,* 23 *privately sworn to secrecy,* 25 *and undertake to write what they had seen.*

WHEN the chief priests and Levites heard all these

things, they were astonished, and fell down with their faces on the ground as dead men, and crying out to one another said, What is this extraordinary sign which is come to pass in Jerusalem? We know the father and mother of Jesus.

2 And a certain Levite said, I know many of his relations, religious persons, who are wont to offer sacrifices and burnt-offerings to the God of Israel, in the temple, with prayers.

3 And when the high priest Simeon took him up in his arms. he said to him, [1]Lord, now lettest thou thy servant depart in peace, according to thy word; for mine eyes have seen thy salvation, which thou hast prepared before the face of all people: a light to enlighten the Gentiles, and the glory of thy people Israel.

4 Simeon in like manner blessed Mary the mother of Jesus, and said to her, I declare to thee concerning that child; He is appointed for the fall and rising again of many, and for a sign which shall be spoken against.

5 Yea, a sword shall pierce through thine own soul also, and the thoughts of many hearts shall be revealed.

6 Then said all the Jews, Let us send to those three men, who said they saw him talking with his disciples in Mount Olivet.

7 After this, they asked them what they had seen; who answered with one accord, In the presence of the God of Israel we affirm, that we plainly saw Jesus talking with his disciples in Mount Olivet, and ascending up to heaven.

8 Then Annas and Caiaphas took them into separate places, and examined them separately; who unanimously confessed the truth, and said, they had seen Jesus.

9 Then Annas and Caiaphas said "Our law saith, By the mouth of two or three witnesses every word shall be established."[2]

10 But what have we said? The blessed Enoch pleased God, and was translated by the word of God; and the burying-place of the blessed Moses is known.

11 But Jesus was delivered to Pilate, whipped, crowned with thorns, spit upon, pierced with a spear, crucified, died upon the cross, and was buried, and his body the honorable Joseph buried in a new sepulchre, and he testifies that he saw him alive.

12 And besides these men have declared, that they saw him talking with his disciples in Mount Olivet, and ascending up to heaven.

13 ¶ Then Joseph rising up. said to Annas and Caiaphas, Ye may be justly under a great surprise, that you have been told, that Jesus is alive, and gone up to heaven.

14 It is indeed a thing really surprising, that he should not only himself arise from the dead, but also raise others from their graves, who have been seen by many in Jerusalem.[3]

15 And now hear me a little: We all knew the blessed Simeon, the high-priest, who took Jesus when an infant into his arms in the temple.

16 This same Simeon had two sons of his own, and we were all present at their death and funeral.

17 Go therefore and see their tombs, for these are open, and

---

[1] Luke, ii. 29.   [2] Deut. xvii. 6.   [3] Matt. xxvii. 53.

they are risen: and behold, they are in the city of Arimathæa, spending their time together in offices of devotion.

18 Some, indeed, have heard the sound of their voices in prayer, but they will not discourse with any one, but they continue as mute as dead men.

19 But come, let us go to them, and behave ourselves towards them with all due respect and caution. And if we can bring them to swear, perhaps they will tell us some of the mysteries of their resurrection.

20 When the Jews heard this, they were exceedingly rejoiced.

21 Then Annas and Caiaphas, Nicodemus, Joseph, and Gamaliel, went to Arimathæa, but did not find them in their graves; but walking about the city, they found them on their bended knees at their devotions:

22 Then saluting them with all respect and deference to God, they brought them to the synagogue at Jerusalem: and having shut the gates, they took the book of the law of the Lord,

23 And putting it in their hands, swore them by God Adonai, and the God of Israel, who spake to our fathers by the law and the prophets, saying, If ye believe him who raised you from the dead, to be Jesus, tell us what ye have seen, and how ye were raised from the dead.

24 Charinus and Lenthius, the two sons of Simeon, trembled when they heard these things, and were disturbed, and groaned; and at the same time looking up to heaven, they made the sign of the cross with their fingers on their tongues,

25 And immediately they spake, and said, Give each of us some paper, and we will write down for you all those things which we have seen. And they each sat down and wrote, saying,

CHAP. XIII.

1 *The narrative of Charinus and Lenthius commences.* 3 *A great light in hell.* 7 *Simeon arrives, and announces the coming of Christ.*

O LORD Jesus and Father, who art God, also the resurrection and life of the dead, give us leave to declare thy mysteries, which we saw after death, belonging to thy cross; for we are sworn by thy name.

2 For thou hast forbid thy servants to declare the secret things, which were wrought by thy divine power in hell.

3 ¶ When we were placed with our fathers in the depth of hell, in the blackness of darkness, on a sudden there appeared the colour of the sun like gold, and a substantial purple-coloured light enlightening the place.

4 Presently upon this, Adam, the father of all mankind, with all the patriarchs and prophets, rejoiced and said, That light is the author of everlasting light, who hath promised to translate us to everlasting light.

5 Then Isaiah the prophet cried out, and said,[1] This is the light of the Father, and the Son of God, according to my prophecy, when I was alive upon earth.

6 The land of Zabulon, and the land of Nephthalim beyond Jordan, a people who walked in darkness, saw a great light; and to them who dwelled in the region of the shadow of death, light is arisen. And now he is

---

[1] Isai. xi. 1   Matt. iv. 16.

80

ST. JOHN THE BAPTIST.

FROM A TRIPTYCHON BY AN ITALIAN PAINTER OF THE THIR-
TEENTH OR FOURTEENTH CENTURY.

come, and hath enlightened us who sat in death.

7 And while we were all rejoicing in the light which shone upon us, our father Simeon came among us, and congratulating all the company, said, Glorify the Lord Jesus Christ the Son of God.

8 Whom I took up in my arms when an infant in the temple, and being moved by the Holy Ghost, said to him, and acknowledged,[1] That now mine eyes have seen thy salvation, which thou hast prepared before the face of all people, a light to enlighten the Gentiles and the glory of thy people Israel.

9 All the saints who were in the depth of hell, hearing this, rejoiced the more.

10 Afterwards there came forth one like a little hermit, and was asked by every one, Who art thou?

11 To which he replied, I am the voice of one crying in the wilderness, John the Baptist, and the prophet of the Most High, who went before his coming to prepare his way, to give the knowledge of salvation to his people for the forgiveness of sins.

12 And I John, when I saw Jesus coming to me, being moved by the Holy Ghost, I said, Behold the Lamb of God, behold him who takes away the sins of the world.

13 And I baptized him in the river Jordan, and saw the Holy Ghost descending upon him in the form of a dove, and heard a voice from heaven, saying, This is my beloved Son, in whom I am well pleased.

14 And now while I was going before him, I came down hither to acquaint you, that the Son of God will next visit us, and, as the day-spring from on high, will come to us, who are in darkness and the shadow of death.

CHAP. XIV.

1 *Adam causes Seth to relate what he heard from Michael the archangel, when he sent him to Paradise to entreat God to anoint his head in his sickness.*

BUT when the first man our father Adam heard these things, that Jesus was baptized in Jordan,[2] he called out to his son, Seth, and said,

2 Declare to your sons, the patriarchs and prophets, all those things, which thou didst hear from Michael, the archangel, when I sent thee to the gates of Paradise, to entreat God that he would anoint my head when I was sick.

3 Then Seth, coming near to the patriarchs and prophets, said, I Seth, when I was praying to God at the gates of Paradise, beheld the angel of the Lord, Michael appear unto me saying, I am sent unto thee from the Lord; I am appointed to preside over human bodies.

4 I tell thee Seth, do not pray to God in tears, and entreat him for the oil of the tree of mercy wherewith to anoint thy father Adam for his head-ache;

5 Because thou canst not by any means obtain it till the last day and times, namely, till five thousand and five hundred years be past.

6 Then will Christ, the most merciful Son of God, come on earth to raise again the human body of Adam, and at the same time to raise the bodies of the

[1] Luke ii. 29.   [2] Matt. iii. 13.

dead, and when he cometh he will be baptized in Jordan:

7 Then with the oil of his mercy he will anoint all those who believe on him; and the oil of his mercy will continue to future generations, for those who shall be born of the water and the Holy Ghost unto eternal life.

8 And when at that time the most merciful Son of God, Christ Jesus, shall come down on earth, he will introduce our father Adam into Paradise, to the tree of mercy.

9 When all the patriarchs and prophets heard all these things from Seth, they rejoiced more.

CHAP. XV.

1 Quarrel between Satan and the prince of hell concerning the expected arrival of Christ in hell.

WHILE all the saints were rejoicing, behold Satan, the prince and captain of death, said to the prince of hell,[1]

2 Prepare to receive Jesus of Nazareth himself, who boasted that he was the Son of God, and yet was a man afraid of death, and said, [2] My soul is sorrowful even to death.

3 Besides he did many injuries to me and to many others; for those whom I made blind and lame and those also whom I tormented with several devils, he cured by his word; yea, and those whom I brought dead to thee, he by force takes away from thee.

4 To this the prince of hell replied to Satan, Who is that so-powerful prince, and yet a man who is afraid of death?

5 For all the potentates of the earth are subject to my power, whom thou broughtest to subjection by thy power.

6 But if he be so powerful in his human nature, I affirm to thee for truth, that he is almighty in his divine nature, and no man can resist his power.

7 When therefore he said he was afraid of death, he designed to ensnare thee, and unhappy it will be to thee for everlasting ages.

8 Then Satan replying, said to the prince of hell, Why didst thou express a doubt, and wast afraid to receive that Jesus of Nazareth, both thy adversary and mine?

9 As for me, I tempted him and stirred up my old people the Jews with zeal and anger against him?

10 I sharpened the spear for his suffering; I mixed the gall and vinegar, and commanded that he should drink it; I prepared the cross to crucify him, and the nails to pierce through his hands and feet; and now his death is near at hand, I will bring him hither, subject both to thee and me.

11 Then the prince of hell answering, said, Thou saidst to me just now, that he took away the dead from me by force.

12 They who have been kept here till they should live again upon earth, were taken away hence, not by their own power, but by prayers made to God, and their almighty God took them from me.

13 Who then is that Jesus of Nazareth that by his word hath taken away the dead from me without prayer to God?

14 Perhaps it is the same who

---

[1] St. Jerome affirms that the soul of Christ went to hell.
[2] Matt. xxvi. 38.

took away from me Lazarus, after he had been four days dead, and did both stink and was rotten, and of whom I had possession as a dead person, yet he brought him to life again by his power.

15 Satan answering, replied to the prince of hell, It is the very same person, Jesus of Nazareth.

16 Which when the prince of hell heard, he said to him, I adjure thee by the powers which belong to thee and me, that thou bring him not to me.

17 For when I heard of the power of his word, I trembled for fear, and all my impious company were at the same time disturbed;

18 And we were not able to detain Lazarus,[1] but he gave himself a shake, and with all the signs of malice, he immediately went away from us; and the very earth, in which the dead body of Lazarus was lodged, presently turned him out alive.

19 And I know now that he is Almighty God who could perform such things, who is mighty in his dominion, and mighty in his human nature, who is the Saviour of mankind.

20 Bring not therefore this person hither, for he will set at liberty all those whom I hold in prison under unbelief, and bound with the fetters of their sins, and will conduct them to everlasting life.

CHAP. XVI.

1 *Christ's arrival at hell-gates; the confusion thereupon.* 10 *He descends into hell.*

AND while Satan and the prince of hell were discoursing thus to each other, on a sudden there was a voice as of thunder and the rushing of winds, saying, [2] Lift up your gates, O ye princes; and be ye lift up, O everlasting gates, and the King of Glory shall come in.

2 When the prince of hell heard this, he said to Satan, Depart from me, and begone out of my habitations; if thou art a powerful warrior, fight with the King of Glory. But what hast thou to do with him?

3 And he cast him forth from his habitations.

4 And the prince said to his impious officers, Shut the brass gates of cruelty, and make them fast with iron bars, and fight courageously, lest we be taken captives.

5 But when all the company of the saints heard this they spake with a loud voice of anger to the prince of hell:

6 Open thy gates that the King of Glory may come in.

7 And the divine prophet David, cried out saying, [3] Did not I when on earth truly prophesy and say, O that men would praise the Lord for his goodness, and for his wonderful works to the children of men.

8 For he hath broken the gates of brass, and cut the bars of iron in sunder. He hath taken them because of their iniquity, and because of their unrighteousness they are afflicted.

9 After this another prophet,[4] namely, holy Isaiah, spake in like manner to all the saints, did not I rightly prophesy to you when I was alive on earth?

10 The dead men shall live, and they shall rise again who are in their graves, and they shall rejoice who are in earth; for the dew which is from the Lord shall bring deliverance to them.

---

[1] John xi.   [2] Psalm xxiv. 7, &c.   [3] Psalm cvii. 15, &c.   [4] Isaiah xxvi. 19.

11 And I said in another place, O death, where is thy victory? O death, where is thy sting?

12 When all the saints heard these things spoken by Isaiah, they said to the prince of hell,[1] Open now thy gates, and take away thine iron bars; for thou wilt now be bound, and have no power.

13 Then there was a great voice, as of the sound of thunder saying, Lift up your gates, O princes; and be ye lifted up, ye gates of hell, and the King of Glory will enter in.

14 The prince of hell perceiving the same voice repeated, cried out as though he had been ignorant, Who is that King of Glory?

15 David replied to the prince of hell, and said, I understand the words of that voice, because I spake them by his spirit. And now, as I have above said, I say unto thee, the Lord strong and powerful, the Lord mighty in battle: he is the King of Glory, and he is the Lord in heaven and in earth;

16 He hath looked down to hear the groans of the prisoners, and to set loose those that are appointed to death.[2]

17 And now, thou filthy and stinking prince of hell, open thy gates, that the King of Glory may enter in; for he is the Lord of heaven and earth.

18 While David was saying this, the mighty Lord appeared in the form of a man, and enlightened those places which had ever before been in darkness,

19 And broke asunder the fetters which before could not be broken; and with his invincible power visited those who sate in the deep darkness by iniquity, and the shadow of death by sin.[3]

CHAP. XVII.

1 *Death and the devils in great horror at Christ's coming.* 13 *He tramples on death, seizes the prince of hell, and takes Adam with him to heaven.*

IMPIOUS Death and her cruel officers hearing these things, were seized with fear in their several kingdoms, when they saw the clearness of the light,

2 And Christ himself on a sudden appearing in their habitations; they cried out therefore, and said, We are bound by thee; thou seemest to intend our confusion before the Lord.

3 Who art thou, who hast no sign of corruption, but that bright appearance which is a full proof of thy greatness, of which yet thou seemest to take no notice?

4 Who art thou, so powerful and so weak, so great and so little, a mean and yet a soldier of the first rank, who can command in the form of a servant as a common soldier?

5 The King of Glory, dead and alive, though once slain upon the cross?

6 Who layest dead in the grave, and art come down alive to us, and in thy death all the creatures trembled, and all the stars were moved, and now hast thou thy liberty among the dead, and givest disturbance to our legions?

7 Who art thou, who dost release the captives that were held in chains by original sin, and bringest them into their former liberty?

8 Who art thou, who dost

---

[1] Psalm xxiv. 7, &c.   [2] Psalm cii. 19, 20.   [3] Luke i. 79.

spread so glorious and divine a light over those who were made blind by the darkness of sin?

9 In like manner all the legions of devils were seized with the like horror, and with the most submissive fear cried out, and said,

10 Whence comes it, O thou Jesus Christ, that thou art a man so powerful and glorious in majesty, so bright as to have no spot, and so pure as to have no crime? For that lower world of earth, which was ever till now subject to us, and from whence we received tribute, never sent us such a dead man before, never sent such presents as those to the princes of hell.

11 Who therefore art thou, who with such courage enterest among our abodes, and art not only not afraid to threaten us with the greatest punishments, but also endeavourest to rescue all others from the chains in which we hold them?

12 Perhaps thou art that Jesus, of whom Satan just now spoke to our prince, that by the death of the cross thou wert about to receive the power of death.

13 Then the King of Glory trampling upon death, seized the prince of hell, deprived him of all his power, and took our earthly father Adam with him to his glory.

CHAP. XVIII.

1 *Beelzebub, prince of hell, vehemently upbraids Satan for persecuting Christ and bringing him to hell.* 4. *Christ gives Beelzebub dominion over Satan for ever, as a recompense for taking away Adam and his sons.*

THEN the prince of hell took Satan, and with great indignation said to him, O thou prince of destruction, author of Beelzebub's defeat and banishment, the scorn of God's angels and loathed by all righteous persons! What inclined thee to act thus?

2 Thou wouldst crucify the King of Glory, and by his destruction, hast made us promises of very large advantages, but as a fool wert ignorant of what thou wast about.

3 For behold now that Jesus of Nazareth, with the brightness of his glorious divinity, puts to flight all the horrid powers of darkness and death;

4 He has broke down our prisons from top to bottom, dismissed all the captives, released all who were bound, and all who were wont formerly to groan under the weight of their torments have now insulted us, and we are like to be defeated by their prayers.

5 Our impious dominions are subdued, and no part of mankind is now left in our subjection, but on the other hand, they all boldly defy us;

6 Though, before, the dead never durst behave themselves insolently towards us, nor, being prisoners, could ever on any occasion be merry.

7 ¶ O Satan, thou prince of all the wicked, father of the impious and abandoned, why wouldest thou attempt this exploit, seeing our prisoners were hitherto always without the least hopes of salvation and life?

8 But now there is not one of them does ever groan, nor is there the least appearance of a tear in any of their faces.

9 O prince Satan, thou great keeper of the infernal regions, all thy advantages which thou didst acquire by the forbidden tree, and the loss of Paradise,

85

thou hast now lost by the wood of the cross;

10 And thy happiness all then expired, when thou didst crucify Jesus Christ the King of Glory.

11 Thou hast acted against thine own interest and mine, as thou wilt presently perceive by those large torments and infinite punishments which thou art about to suffer.

12 O Satan, prince of all evil, author of death, and source of all pride, thou shouldest first have inquired into the evil crimes of Jesus of Nazareth, and then thou wouldest have found that he was guilty of no fault worthy of death.

13 Why didst thou venture, without either reason or justice, to crucify him, and hast brought down to our regions a person innocent and righteous, and thereby hast lost all the sinners, impious and unrighteous persons in the whole world?

14 While the prince of hell was thus speaking to Satan, the King of Glory said to Beelzebub, the prince of hell, Satan, the prince shall be subject to thy dominion for ever, in the room of Adam and his righteous sons, who are mine.

CHAP. XIX.

1 *Christ takes Adam by the hand, the rest of the saints join hands, and they all ascend with him to Paradise.*

THEN Jesus stretched forth his hand, and said, Come to me, all ye my saints, who were created in my image, who were condemned by the tree of forbidden fruit, and by the devil and death;

2 Live now by the wood of my cross; the devil, the prince of this world, is overcome, and death is conquered.

3 Then presently all the saints were joined together under the hand of the most high God; and the Lord Jesus laid hold on Adam's hand and said to him, Peace be to thee, and all thy righteous posterity, which is mine.

4 Then Adam, casting himself at the feet of Jesus, addressed himself to him, with tears, in humble language, and a loud voice, saying,[1]

5 I will extol thee, O Lord, for thou hast lifted me up, and hast not made my foes to rejoice over me. O Lord my God, I cried unto thee, and thou hast healed me.

6 O Lord thou hast brought up my soul from the grave; thou hast kept me alive, that I should not go down to the pit.

7 Sing unto the Lord, all ye saints of his, and give thanks at the remembrance of his holiness. For his anger endureth but for a moment; in his favour is life.

8 In like manner all the saints, prostrate at the feet of Jesus, said with one voice, Thou art come, O Redeemer of the world, and hast actually accomplished all things, which thou didst foretell by the law and thy holy prophets.

9 Thou hast redeemed the living by thy cross, and art come down to us, that by the death of the cross thou mightest deliver us from hell, and by thy power from death.

10 O, Lord, as thou hast put the ensigns of thy glory in heaven, and hast set up the sign of

---

[1] Psalm xxx. 1, &c.

thy redemption, even thy cross on earth ! so, Lord, set the sign of the victory of thy cross in hell, that death may have dominion no longer.

11 Then the Lord stretching forth his hand, made the sign of the cross upon Adam, and upon all his saints.

12 And taking hold of Adam by his right hand, he ascended from hell, and all the saints of God followed him.

13 Then the royal prophet David boldly cried, and said,[1] O sing unto the Lord a new song, for he hath done marvellous things; his right hand and his holy arm have gotten him the victory.

14 The Lord hath made known his salvation, his righteousness hath he openly shewn in the sight of the heathen.

15 And the whole multitude of saints answered, saying,[2] This honour have all his saints, Amen, Praise ye the Lord.

16 Afterwards, the prophet Habakkuk[3] cried out, and said, Thou wentest forth for the salvation of thy people, even for the salvation of thy people.

17 And all the saints said,[4] Blessed is he who cometh in the name of the Lord ; for the Lord hath enlightened us. This is our God for ever and ever ; he shall reign over us to everlasting ages, Amen.

18 In like manner all the prophets spake the sacred things of his praise, and followed the Lord.

CHAP. XX.

1 *Christ delivers Adam to Michael the archangel.* 3. *They meet Enoch and Elijah in heaven,* 5 *and also the*

blessed thief, who relates how he came to Paradise.

THEN the Lord holding Adam by the hand, delivered him to Michael the archangel; and he led them into Paradise, filled with mercy and glory;

2 And two very ancient men met them, and were asked by the saints, Who are ye, who have not yet been with us in hell, and have had your bodies placed in Paradise ?

3 One of them answering, said, I am Enoch, who was translated by the word of God :[5] and this man who is with me, is Elijah the Tishbite, who was translated in a fiery chariot.[6]

4 Here we have hitherto been, and have not tasted death, but are now about to return at the coming of Antichrist, being armed with divine signs and miracles, to engage with him in battle, and to be slain by him at Jerusalem, and to be taken up alive again into the clouds, after three days and a half.[7]

5 ¶ And while the holy Enoch and Elias were relating this, behold there came another man in a miserable figure carrying the sign of the cross upon his shoulders.

6 And when all the saints saw him, they said to him, Who art thou? For thy countenance is like a thief's ; and why dost thou carry a cross upon thy shoulders?

7 To which he answering, said, Ye say right, for I was a thief, who committed all sorts of wickedness upon earth.

8 And the Jews crucified me with Jesus ; and I observed the surprising things which hap-

---

[1] Psalm xcviii. 1, &c.   [2] Psalm cxlix. 2.   [3] Hab. iii. 13.   [4] Matt. xxiii. 39.
[5] Gen. v. 24.   [6] Kings ii. 11.   [7] Rev. xi. 11.

pened in the creation at the crucifixion of the Lord Jesus.

9 And I believed him to be the Creator of all things, and the Almighty King; and I prayed to him, saying, Lord, remember me, when thou comest into thy kingdom.

10 He presently regarded my supplication, and said to me, Verily I say unto thee, this day thou shalt be with me in Paradise.[1]

11 And he gave me this sign of the cross saying, Carry this, and ᵹᴏ to Paradise; and if the angel who is the guard of Paradise will not admit thee, shew him the sign of the cross, and say unto him: Jesus Christ who is now crucified, hath sent me hither to thee.

12 When I did this, and told the angel who is the guard of Paradise all these things, and he heard them, he presently opened the gates, introduced me, and placed me on the right-hand in Paradise,

13 Saying, Stay here a little time, till Adam, the father of all mankind, shall enter in, with all his sons, who are the holy and righteous servants of Jesus Christ, who was crucified.

14 When they heard all this account from the thief, all the patriarchs said with one voice, Blessed be thou, O Almighty God, the Father of everlasting goodness, and the Father of mercies, who hast shewn such favour to those who were sinners against him, and hast brought them to the mercy of Paradise, and hast placed them amidst thy large and spiritual provisions, in a spiritual and holy life. Amen.

CHAP. XXI.

1 *Charinus and Lenthius being only allowed three days to remain on earth,* 7 *deliver in their narratives, which miraculously correspond; they vanish,* 13 *and Pilate records these transactions.*

THESE are the divine and sacred mysteries which we saw and heard. I, Charinus and Lenthius are not allowed to declare the other mysteries of God, as the archangel Michael ordered us,

2 Saying, ye shall go with my brethren to Jerusalem, and shall continue in prayers, declaring and glorifying the resurrection of Jesus Christ, seeing he hath raised you from the dead at the same time with himself.

3 And ye shall not talk with any man, but sit as dumb persons till the time come when the Lord will allow you to relate the mysteries of his divinity.

4 The archangel Michael farther commanded us to go beyond Jordan, to an excellent and fat country, where there are many who rose from the dead along with us for the proof of the resurrection of Christ.

5 For we have only three days allowed us from the dead, who arose to celebrate the passover of our Lord with our parents, and to bear our testimony for Christ the Lord, and we have been baptized in the holy river of Jordan. And now they are not seen by any one.

6 This is as much as God allowed us to relate to you; give ye therefore praise and honour to him, and repent, and he will have mercy upon you. Peace be to you from the Lord God Jesus

[1] Luke xxiii. 43.

THE BAPTISM OF CHRIST IN THE JORDAN.

FROM A "BOOK OF THE EVANGELISTS," GREEK MANUSCRIPT OF THE TWELFTH CENTURY.

Christ, and the Saviour of us all. Amen, Amen, Amen.

7 And after they had made an end of writing and had wrote in two distinct pieces of paper, Charinus gave what he wrote into the hands of Annas, and Caiaphas, and Gamaliel.

8 Lenthius likewise gave what he wrote into the hands of Nicodemus and Joseph; and immediately they were changed into exceeding white forms and were seen no more.

9 But what they had wrote was found perfectly to agree, the one not containing one letter more or less than the other.

10 When all the assembly of the Jews heard all these surprising relations of Charinus and Lenthius, they said to each other, Truly all these things were wrought by God, and blessed be the Lord Jesus for ever and ever, Amen.

11 And they went about with great concern, and fear, and trembling, and smote upon their breasts and went away every one to his home.

12 But immediately all these things which were related by the Jews in their synagogues concerning Jesus, were presently told by Joseph and Nicodemus to the governor.

13 And Pilate wrote down all these transactions, and placed all these accounts in the public records of his hall.

CHAP. XXII.

1 Pilate goes to the temple; calls together the rulers, and scribes, and doctors. 2 Commands the gates to be shut; orders the book of the Scripture; and causes the Jews to relate what they really knew concerning Christ. 14 They declare that they crucified Christ in ignorance, and that they now know him to be the Son of God, according to the testimony of the Scriptures; which, after they put him to death, they are examined.

AFTER these things Pilate went to the temple of the Jews, and called together all the rulers and scribes, and doctors of the law, and went with them into a chapel of the temple.

2 And commanding that all the gates should be shut, said to them, I have heard that ye have a certain large book in this temple; I desire you therefore, that it may be brought before me.

3 And when the great book, carried by four ministers of the temple, and adorned with gold and precious stones, was brought, Pilate said to them all, I adjure you by the God of your Fathers, who made and commanded this temple to be built, that ye conceal not the truth from me.

4 Ye know all the things which are written in that book; tell me therefore now, if ye in the Scriptures have found any thing of that Jesus whom ye crucified, and at what time of the world he ought to have come: shew it me.

5 Then having sworn Annas and Caiaphas, they commanded all the rest who were with them to go out of the chapel.

6 And they shut the gates of the temple and of the chapel, and said to Pilate, Thou hast made us to swear, O judge, by the building of this temple, to declare to thee that which is true and right.

7 After we had crucified Jesus, not knowing that he was the Son of God, but supposing he wrought his miracles by some magical arts, we summoned a large assembly in this temple.

8 And when we were deliberating among one another about

the miracles which Jesus had wrought, we found many witnesses of our own country, who declared that they had seen him alive after his death, and that they heard him discoursing with his disciples, and saw him ascending unto the height of the heavens, and entering into them ;

9 And we saw two witnesses, whose bodies Jesus raised from the dead, who told us of many strange things which Jesus did among the dead, of which we have a written account in our hands.

10 And it is our custom annually to open this holy book before an assembly, and to search there for the counsel of God.

11 And we found in the first of the seventy books, where Michael the archangel is speaking to the third son of Adam the first man, an account that after five thousand five hundred years, Christ the most beloved Son of God was come on earth,

12 And we further considered, that perhaps he was the very God of Israel who spoke to Moses, Thou shalt make the ark of the testimony ; two cubits and a half shall be the length thereof, and a cubit and a half the breadth thereof, and a cubit and a half the height thereof.[1]

13 By these five cubits and a half for the building of the ark of the Old Testament, we perceived and knew that in five thousand years and a half (one thousand) years, Jesus Christ was to come in the ark or tabernacle of a body ;

14 And so our scriptures testify that he is the son of God, and the Lord and King of Israel.

15 And because after his suffering, our chief priests were surprised at the signs which were wrought by his means, we opened that book to search all the generations down to the generation of Joseph and Mary the mother of Jesus, supposing him to be of the seed of David ;

16 And we found the account of the creation, and at what time he made the heaven and the earth and the first man Adam, and that from thence to the flood, were two thousand, two hundred and twelve years.

17 And from the flood to Abraham, nine hundred and twelve. And from Abraham to Moses, four hundred and thirty. And from Moses to David the king, five hundred and ten.

18 And from David to the Babylonish captivity, five hundred years. And from the Babylonish captivity to the incarnation of Christ, four hundred years.

19 The sum of all which amounts to five thousand and half (a thousand).

20 And so it appears, that Jesus whom we crucified, is Jesus Christ the Son of God, and true and Almighty God. Amen.

In the name of the Holy Trinity, thus end the Acts of our Saviour Jesus Christ, which the Emperor Theodosius the Great found at Jerusalem, in the hall of Pontius Pilate among the public records ; the things were acted in the nineteenth year of Tiberius Cæsar, Emperor of the Romans, and in the seventeenth year of the government of Herod the son of Herod king of Galilee, on the eighth of the calends of April, which is the twenty-

---

[1] Exod. xxv. 10.

third day of the month of March, in the CCIId *Olympiad, when Joseph and Caiaphas were Rulers of the Jews; being a History written in Hebrew by Nicodemus, of what happened after our Saviour's crucifixion.*

———

The APOSTLES' CREED.

[It is affirmed by Ambrose, "that the twelve Apostles, as skilful artificers assembled together, and made a key by their common advice, that is, the Creed; by which the darkness of the devil is disclosed, that the light of Christ may appear."[1] Others fable that every Apostle inserted an article, by which the creed is divided into twelve articles; and a sermon, fathered upon St. Austin, and quoted by the Lord Chancellor King, fabricates that each particular article was thus inserted by each particular Apostle:—

" *Peter.*—1. I believe in God the Father Almighty;

" *John.*—2. Maker of heaven and earth;

" *James.*—3. And in Jesus Christ his only Son, our Lord;

" *Andrew.*—4. Who was conceived by the Holy Ghost, born of the Virgin Mary;

" *Philip.*—5. Suffered under Pontius Pilate, was crucified, dead and buried;

" *Thomas.*—6. He descended into hell, the third day he rose again from the dead;

" *Bartholomew.*—7. He ascended into heaven, sitteth at the right hand of God the Father Almighty;

" *Matthew.*—8. From thence he shall come to judge the quick and the dead;

" *James, the son of Alpheus.*—9. I believe in the Holy Ghost, the holy Catholic Church;

" *Simon Zelotes.*—10. The communion of saints, the forgiveness of sins;

" *Jude the brother of James.*—11. The resurrection of the body;

" *Matthias.*—12. Life everlasting. Amen."[2]

Archbishop WAKE says: "With respect to the Apostles being the authors of this Creed, it is not my intention to enter on any particular examination of this matter, which has been so fully handled, not only by the late critics of the Church of Rome, Natalis Alexander,[3] Du Pin,[4]

[1] Amb. Opera, tom. iii. Serm. 38, p. 265. [2] King's Hist. Apost. Creed, 8vo, p. 26. [3] Nat. Alex., §1, vol. i., p. 490, &c. [4] Du Pin, Biblioth. Eccles., vol. i., p. 25.

&c., but yet more especially by Archbishop Usher,[1] Gerard Vossius,[2] Suicer,[3] Spanhemius,[4] Tentzelius,[5] and Sam. Basnage,[6] among the Protestants. It shall suffice to say, that as it is not likely, that had any such thing as this been done by the Apostles, St. Luke would have passed it by, without taking the least notice of it: so the diversity of Creeds in the ancient Church, and that not only in expression, but in some whole Articles too, sufficiently shows, that the Creed which we call by that name, was not composed by the twelve Apostles, much less in the same form in which it now is."[7]

Mr. Justice BAILEY says: " It is not to be understood that this Creed was framed by the Apostles, or indeed that it existed as a Creed in their time;"[8] and after giving the Creed as it existed in the year 600, and which is here copied from his Common Prayer Book, he says, "how long this form had existed before the year 600 is not exactly known. The additions were probably made in opposition to particular heresies and errors."

The most important "addition," since the year of Christ 600, is that which affirms, that Christ *descended into hell.* This has been proved not only to have been an invention after the Apostles' time, but even after the time of Eusebius. Bishop Pearson says,[9] that the descent into hell was not in the ancient creeds or rules of faith. "It is not to be found in the rules of faith delivered by Irenæus,[10] by Origen,[11] or by Tertullian.[12] It is not expressed in those creeds which were made by the councils as larger explications of the Apostles' Creed; not in the Nicene, or Constantinopolitan; not in those of Ephesus, or Chalcedon; not in those confessions made at Sardica, Antioch, Selucia, Sirmium, &c. It is not mentioned in several confessions of faith delivered by particular persons; not in that of Eusebius Cæsariensis, presented to the council of Nice;[13] not in that of Marcellus, bishop of Ancyra, delivered to Pope Julius;[14] not in that of Arius and Euzoius, presented to Constantine;[15] not in that of Acacius, bishop of Cæsarea, delivered into the synod of Selucia;[16] not in that of Eustathius, Theophilus, and Sylvanus, sent to Liberius;[17] there is no mention of it in the creed of St. Basil;[18] in the creed of Epiphanus,[19] Gelasius, Damascus, Macarius, &c. It is not in the creed expounded by St. Cyril, though some have produced that creed to prove it. It is not in the creed expounded by St. Augustine;[20] not in that other,[21] attributed to St. Augustine in another place; not in that expounded by Maximus Taurinensis; nor in that so often interpreted by Petrus Chrysologus; nor in that of the church of Antioch, delivered by Cassianus;[22] neither is it to be seen in the MS. creeds set forth by the learned Archbishop of Armagh. It is affirmed by Ruffinus, that in his time it was neither in the Roman nor the Oriental Creeds."[23]

---

[1] Diatrib. de Symb. [2] Voss. Dissert. de tribus Symbolis. [3] Suicer. Thesaur. Eccles. tom. ii. Voce συμβολον, p. 1086, &c. [4] Spanhem, Introd. ad Hist. Eccles., § ii., c. 3. [5] Ernest. Tentzel. Exercit. select. Exercit. I. [6] Sam. Basnage Exercit. Hist. Crit. ad Ann. XLIV. num. 17, 18. [7] Wake's Apost. Fathers, 8vo, p. 103. [8] Mr. Justice Bailey's Common Prayer, 1813, p. 9. [9] Pearson on the Creed, fol. 1676, p. 225. [10] Lib. 1, c. 2. [11] Lib. de Princip. in Prœm. [12] Advers. Praxeam., c. ii., Virgin. veland., c. 1.—De Præscript. advers. Hæres., c. 13. [13] Theodoret, l. 1, c. 2. [14] Epiphan. Hæ. es. 72. [15] Socrat. l. 1, c. 19. [16] Ibid. l. 2, c. 40. [17] Ibid. l. 4, c. 12. [18] Tract. de Fide in Ascet. [19] In Anchorat., c. 120. [20] De Fide et Symbolo. [21] De Symbolo ad Catechumenos. [22] De Incarnat., lib. 6. [23] Exposit. in Symbol., Apost., § 20.

THE APOSTLES' CREED.

As it stood An. Dom. 600. Copied from Mr. Justice Bailey's Edition of the book of Common Prayer. 'Before the year 600, it was no more than this.'—Mr. Justice Bailey. p. 9 n.

1 I Believe in God the Father Almighty:

2 And in Jesus Christ his only begotten Son, our Lord;

3 Who was born of the Holy Ghost and Virgin Mary,

4 And was crucified under Pontius Pilate, and was buried;

5 And the third day rose again from the dead.

6 Ascended into heaven, sitteth on the right hand of the Father;

7 Whence he shall come to judge the quick and the dead;

8 And in the Holy Ghost;

9 The Holy Church;

10 The remission of sins;

11 And the resurrection of the flesh, Amen.

As it stands in the book of Common Prayer of the United Church of England and Ireland as by law established.

1 I Believe in God the Father Almighty, maker of heaven and earth:

2 And in Jesus Christ his only Son, our Lord:

3 Who was conceived by the Holy Ghost, born of the Virgin Mary,

4 Suffered under Pontius Pilate, was crucified, dead and buried;

5 He descended into hell;

6 The third day he rose again from the dead;

7 He ascended into heaven, and sitteth on the right hand of God the Father Almighty;

8 From thence he shall come to judge the quick and the dead.

9 ¶ I believe in the Holy Ghost;

10 The holy Catholic Church; the communion of saints;

11 The forgiveness of sins;

12 The resurrection of the body; and the life everlasting. Amen.

THE EPISTLE of PAUL the APOSTLE to the LAODICEANS.

[This Epistle has been highly esteemed by several learned men of the church of Rome and others. The Quakers have printed a translation and plead for it, as the reader may see, by consulting Poole's Annotations on Col. vi. 16. Sixtus Senensis mentions two MSS., the one in the Sorbonne Library at Paris, which is a very ancient copy, and the other in the Library of Joannes a Viridario, at Padua, which he transcribed and published, and which is the authority for the following translation. There is a very old translation of this Epistle in the British Museum, among the Harleian MSS., Cod. 1212.]

1 *He salutes the brethren.* 3 *exhorts them to persevere in good works,* 4 *and not to be moved by vain speaking.* 6 *Rejoices in his bonds,* 10 *desires them to live in the fear of the Lord.*

PAUL an Apostle, not of men, neither by man, but by Jesus Christ, to the brethren which are at Laodicea.

2 Grace be to you, and Peace, from God the Father and our Lord Jesus Christ.

3 I thank Christ in every prayer of mine, that ye may continue and persevere in good works looking for that which is promised in the day of judgment.

4 Let not the vain speeches of any trouble you who pervert the truth, that they may draw you aside from the truth of the Gospel which I have preached.

5 And now may God grant, that my converts may attain to a perfect knowledge of the truth of the Gospel, be beneficent, and doing good works which accompany salvation.

6 And now my bonds, which I suffer in Christ, are manifest, in which I rejoice and am glad.

7 For I know that this shall turn to my salvation for ever, which shall be through your prayer, and the supply of the Holy Spirit.

8 Whether I live or die; (for) to me to live shall be a life to Christ, to die will be joy.

9 And our Lord will grant us his mercy, that ye may have the same love, and be likeminded.

10 Wherefore, my beloved, as ye have heard of the coming of the Lord, so think and act in fear, and it shall be to you life eternal;

11 For it is God who worketh in you;

12 And do all things without sin.

13 And what is best, my beloved, rejoice in the Lord Jesus Christ, and avoid all filthy lucre.

14 Let all your requests be made known to God, and be steady in the doctrine of Christ.

15 And whatsoever things are sound and true, and of good report, and chaste, and just, and lovely, these things do.

16 Those things which ye have heard, and received, think on these things, and peace shall be with you.

17 All the saints salute you.

18 The grace of our Lord Jesus Christ be with your spirit. *Amen.*

19 Cause this Epistle to be read to the Colossians, and the Epistle of the Colossians to be read among you.

The EPISTLES of PAUL the APOSTLE to SENECA, with SENECA'S to PAUL.

[Several very learned writers have entertained a favourable opinion of these Epistles. They are undoubtedly of high antiquity. Salmeron cites them to prove that Seneca was one of Cæsar's household, referred to by Paul, *Philip.* iv. 22, as saluting the brethren at Philippi. In Jerome's enumeration of illustrious men, he places Seneca, on account of these Epistles, amongst the ecclesiastical and holy writers of the Christian Church. Sixtus Senensis has published them in his Bibliotheque, pp. 89, 90; and it is from thence that the present translation is made. Baronius, Bellarmine, Dr. Cave, Spanheim, and others, contend that they are not genuine.]

CHAP. I.

ANNÆUS SENECA to PAUL *Greeting.*

I SUPPOSE, Paul, you have been informed of that conversation, which passed yesterday between me and my Lucilius, concerning hypocrisy and other subjects; for there were some of your disciples in company with us;

2 For when we were retired into the Sallustian gardens, through which they were also passing, and would have gone another way, by our persuasion they joined company with us.

3 I desire you to believe, that we much wish for your conversation:

4 We were much delighted with your book of many Epistles, which you have wrote to some cities and chief towns of provinces, and contain wonderful instructions for moral conduct:

5 Such sentiments, as I suppose you were not the author of, but only the instrument of conveying, though sometimes both the author and the instrument.

6 For such is the sublimity of those doctrines, and their grandeur, that I suppose the age of a man is scarce sufficient to be instructed and perfected in the knowledge of them. I wish your welfare, my brother. Farewell.

CHAP. II.

PAUL *to* SENECA *Greeting.*

I RECEIVED your letter yesterday with pleasure : to which I could immediately have wrote an answer, had the young man been at home, whom I intended to have sent to you:

2 For you know when, and by whom, at what seasons, and to whom I must deliver every thing which I send.

3 I desire therefore you would not charge me with negligence, if I wait for a proper person.

4 I reckon myself very happy in having the judgment of so valuable a person, that you are delighted with my Epistles:

5 For you would not be esteemed a censor, a philosopher, or be the tutor of so great a prince, and a master of every thing, if you were not sincere. I wish you a lasting prosperity.

CHAP. III.

ANNÆUS SENECA *to* PAUL *Greeting.*

I HAVE completed some volumes, and divided them into their proper parts.

2 I am determined to read them to Cæsar, and if any favourable opportunity happens, you also shall be present, when they are read;

3 But if that cannot be, I will appoint and give you notice of a day, when we will together read over the performance.

4 I had determined, if I could with safety, first to have your opinion of it, before I published it to Cæsar, that you might be convinced of my affection to you. Farewell, dearest Paul.

CHAP. IV.

PAUL to SENECA Greeting.

AS often as I read your letters, I imagine you present with me; nor indeed do I think any other, than that you are always with us.

2 As soon therefore as you begin to come, we shall presently see each other. I wish you all prosperity.

CHAP. V.

ANNÆUS SENECA to PAUL Greeting.

WE are very much concerned at your too long absence from us.

2 What is it, or what affairs are they, which obstruct your coming?

3 If you fear the anger of Cæsar, because you have abondoned your former religion, and made proselytes also of others, you have this to plead, that your acting thus proceeded not from inconstancy, but judgment. Farewell.

CHAP. VI.

PAUL to SENECA and LUCILIUS Greeting.

CONCERNING those things about which ye wrote to me it is not proper for me to mention anything in writing with pen and ink: the one of which leaves marks, and the other evidently declares things.

2 Especially since I know that there are near you, as well as me, those who will understand my meaning.

3 Deference is to be paid to all men, and so much the more, as they are more likely to take occasions of quarrelling.

4 And if we show a submissive temper, we shall overcome effectually in all points, if so be they are, who are capable of seeing

96

and acknowledging themselves to have been in the wrong. Farewell.

CHAP. VII.

ANNÆUS SENECA to PAUL Greeting.

I PROFESS myself extremely pleased with the reading your letters to the Galatians, Corinthians, and people of Achaia.

2 For the Holy Ghost has in them by you delivered those sentiments which are very lofty, sublime, deserving of all respect, and beyond your own invention.

3 I could wish therefore, that when you are writing things so extraordinary, there might not be wanting an elegancy of speech agreeable to their majesty.

4 And I must own my brother, that I may not at once dishonestly conceal anything from you, and be unfaithful to my own conscience, that the emperor is extremely pleased with the sentiments of your Epistles;

5 For when he heard the beginning of them read, he declared, That he was surprised to find such notions in a person, who had not had a regular education.

6 To which I replied, That the Gods sometimes made use of mean (innocent) persons to speak by, and gave him an instance of this in a mean countryman, named Vatienus, who, when he was in the country of Reate, had two men appeared to him, called Castor and Pollux, and received a revelation from the gods. Farewell.

CHAP. VIII.

PAUL to SENECA Greeting.

ALTHOUGH I know the emperor is both an admirer and favourer of our (religion), yet give me leave to advise you against your suffering any injury, (by shewing favour to us.)

THE LAST JUDGMENT.

FROM A PERSIAN MINIATURE OF THE EIGHTH CENTURY.

2 I think indeed you ventured upon a very dangerous attempt, when you would declare (to the emperor) that which is so very contrary to his religion, and way of worship; seeing he is a worshipper of the heathen gods.

3 I know not what you particularly had in view, when you told him of this; but I suppose you did it out of too great respect for me.

4 But I desire that for the future you would not do so; for you had need be careful, lest by shewing your affection for me, you should offend your master:

5 His anger indeed will do us no harm, if he continue a heathen; nor will his not being angry be of any service to us:

6 And if the empress act worthy of her character, she will not be angry; but if she acts as a woman, she will be affronted. Farewell.

CHAP. IX.

ANNÆUS SENECA *to* PAUL *Greeting.*

I KNOW that my letter, wherein I acquainted you, that I had read to the Emperor your Epistles, does not so much affect you as the nature of the things (contained in them),

2 Which do so powerfully divert men's minds from their former manners and practices, that I have always been surprised, and have been fully convinced of it by many arguments heretofore.

3 Let us therefore begin afresh; and if any thing heretofore has been imprudently acted, do you forgive.

4 I have sent you a book *de copia verborum.* Farewell, dearest Paul.

CHAP. X.

PAUL *to* SENECA *Greeting.*

A S often as I write to you, and place my name before yours, I do a thing both disagreeable to myself, and contrary to our religion:

2 For I ought, as I have often declared, to become all things to all men, and to have that regard to your quality, which the Roman law has honoured all senators with; namely, to put my name last in the (inscription of the) Epistle, that I may not at length with uneasiness and shame be obliged to do that which it was always my inclination to do. Farewell, most respected master. Dated the fifth of the calends of July, in the fourth consulship of Nero, and Messala.

CHAP. XI.

ANNÆUS SENECA *to* PAUL *Greeting.*

A LL happiness to you, my dearest Paul.

2 If a person so great, and every way agreeable as you are, become not only a common, but a most intimate friend to me, how happy will be the case of Seneca!

3 You therefore, who are so eminent, and so far exalted above all, even the greatest, do not think yourself unfit to be first named in the inscription of an Epistle;

4 Lest I should suspect you intend not so much to try me, as to banter me; for you know yourself to be a Roman citizen.

5 And I could wish to be in that circumstance or station which you are, and that you were in the same that I am. Farewell, dearest Paul. Dated the xth of the calends of April, in the consulship of Aprianus and Capito.

97

CHAP. XII.

ANNÆUS SENECA *to* PAUL *Greeting.*

ALL happiness to you, my dearest Paul. Do you not suppose I am extremely concerned and grieved that your innocence should bring you into sufferings?

2 And that all the people should suppose you (Christians) so criminal, and imagine all the misfortunes that happen to the city, to be caused by you?

3 But let us bear the charge with a patient temper, appealing (for our innocence) to the court (above), which is the only one our hard fortune will allow us to address to, till at length our misfortunes shall end in unalterable happiness.

4 Former ages have produced (tyrants) Alexander the son of Philip, and Dionysius; ours also has produced Caius Cæsar; whose inclinations were their only laws.

5 As to the frequent burnings of the city of Rome, the cause is manifest; and if a person in my mean circumstances might be allowed to speak, and one might declare these dark things without danger, every one should see the whole of the matter.

6 The Christians and Jews are indeed commonly punished for the crime of burning the city; but that impious miscreant, who delights in murders and butcheries, and disguises his villanies with lies, is appointed to, or reserved till, his proper time.

7 And as the life of every excellent person is now sacrificed instead of that one person (who is the author of the mischief), so this one shall be sacrificed for many, and he shall be devoted to be burnt with fire instead of all.

8 One hundred and thirty-two houses, and four whole squares (or islands) were burnt down in six days: the seventh put an end to the burning. I wish you all happiness.

9 Dated the fifth of the calends of April, in the consulship of Frigius and Bassus.

CHAP. XIII.

ANNÆUS SENECA *to* PAUL *Greeting.*

ALL happiness to you, my dearest Paul.

2 You have wrote many volumes in an allegorical and mystical style, and therefore such mighty matters and business being committed to you, require not to be set off with any rhetorical flourishes of speech, but only with some proper elegance.

3 I remember you often say, that many by affecting such a style do injury to their subjects, and lose the force of the matters they treat of.

4 But in this I desire you to regard me, namely, to have respect to true Latin, and to choose just words, that so you may the better manage the noble trust which is reposed in you.

5 Farewell. Dated vth of the names of July, Leo and Savinus consuls.

CHAP. XIV.

PAUL *to* SENECA *Greeting.*

YOUR serious consideration requited with these discoveries, which the Divine Being has granted but to few.

2 I am thereby assured that I sow the most strong seed in a fertile soil, not anything material, which is subject to corruption, but the durable word of God, which shall increase and bring forth fruit to eternity.

3 That which by your wisdom you have attained to, shall abide without decay for ever.

4 Believe that you ought to avoid the superstitions of Jews and Gentiles.

5 The things which you have in some measure arrived to, prudently make known to the emperor, his family, and to faithful friends;

6 And though your sentiments will seem disagreeable, and not be comprehended by them, seeing most of them will not regard your discourses, yet the Word of God once infused into them, will at length make them become new men, aspiring towards God.

7 Farewell Seneca, who art most dear to us. Dated on the Calends of August, in the consulship of Leo and Savinus.

The ACTS of PAUL and THECLA.

[Tertullian says that this piece was forged by a Presbyter of Asia, who being convicted, "confessed that he did it out of respect of Paul," and Pope Gelasius, in his Decree against apocryphal books, inserted it among them. Notwithstanding this, a large part of the history was credited, and looked upon as genuine among the primitive Christians. Cyprian, Eusebius, Epiphanius, Austin, Gregory Nazianzen, Chrysostom, and Severus Sulpitius, who all lived within the fourth century, mention Thecla, or refer to her history. Basil of Seleucia wrote her acts, sufferings, and victories, in verse; and Euagrius Scholasticus, an ecclesiastical historian, about 590, relates that "after the Emperor Zeno had abdicated his empire, and Basilik had taken possession of it, he had a vision of the holy and excellent martyr Thecla, who promised him the restoration of his empire; for which, when it was brought about, he erected and dedicated a most noble and sumptuous temple to this famous martyr Thecla, at Seleucia, a city of Isauria, and bestowed upon it very noble endowments, which (says the author) are preserved even till this day." Hist. Eccl., lib. 3, cap. 8.—Cardinal Baronius, Locrinus, Archbishop Wake, and others; and also the learned Grabe, who edited the Septuagint, and revived the Acts of Paul and Thecla, consider them as having been written in the Apostolic age; as containing nothing superstitious, or disagreeing from the opinions and belief of those times; and, in short, as a genuine and authentic history. Again, it is said, that this is not the original book of the early Christians; but however that may be, it is published from the Greek MS. in the Bodleian Library at Oxford, which Dr. Mills copied and transmitted to Dr. Grabe.]

The Martyrdom of the holy and glorious first Martyr and Apostle Thecla.

CHAP. I.

1 *Demas and Hermogenes become Paul's companions.* 4 *Paul visits Onesiphorus.* 8 *Invited by Demas and Hermogenes.* 11 *Preaches to the household of Onesiphorus.* 12 *His sermon.*

WHEN Paul went up to Iconium, after his flight from Antioch, Demas and Hermogenes became his companions, who were then full of hypocrisy.

2 But Paul looking only at the goodness of God, did them no harm, but loved them greatly.

3 Accordingly he endeavoured to make agreeable to them, all

99

the oracles and doctrines of Christ, and the design of the Gospel of God's well-beloved Son, instructing them in the knowledge of Christ, as it was revealed to him.

4 ¶ And a certain man named Onesiphorus, hearing that Paul was come to Iconium, went out speedily to meet him, together with his wife Lectra, and his sons Simmia and Zeno, to invite him to their house.

5 For Titus had given them a description of Paul's personage, they as yet not knowing him in person, but only being acquainted with his character.

6 They went in the king's highway to Lystra, and stood there waiting for him, comparing all who passed by, with that description which Titus had given them.

7 At length they saw a man coming (namely Paul), of a low stature, bald (or shaved) on the head, crooked thighs, handsome legs, hollow-eyed; had a crooked nose; full of grace; for sometimes he appeared as a man, sometimes he had the countenance of an angel. And Paul saw Onesiphorus, and was glad.

8 ¶ And Onesiphorus said: Hail, thou servant of the blessed God. Paul replied, The grace of God be with thee and thy family.

9 But Demas and Hermogenes were moved with envy, and, under a show of great religion, Demas said, And are not we also servants of the blessed God? Why didst thou not salute us?

10 Onesiphorus replied, Because I have not perceived in you the fruits of righteousness; nevertheless, if ye are of that sort, ye shall be welcome to my house also.

100

11 Then Paul went into the house of Onesiphorus, and there was great joy among the family on that account: and they employed themselves in prayer, breaking of bread, and hearing Paul preach the word of God concerning temperance and the resurrection, in the following manner:

12 ¶ Blessed are the pure in heart; for they shall see God.

13 Blessed are they who keep their flesh undefiled (or pure); for they shall be the temple of God.

14 Blessed are the temperate (or chaste); for God will reveal himself to them.

15 ¶ Blessed are they who abandon their secular enjoyments; for they shall be accepted of God.

16 Blessed are they who have wives, as though they had them not; for they shall be made angels of God.

17 Blessed are they who tremble at the word of God; for they shall be comforted.

18 Blessed are they who keep their baptism pure; for they shall find peace with the Father, Son, and Holy Ghost.

19 ¶ Blessed are they who pursue the wisdom (or doctrine) of Jesus Christ; for they shall be called the sons of the Most High.

20 Blessed are they who observe the instructions of Jesus Christ; for they shall dwell in eternal light.

21 Blessed are they, who for the love of Christ abandon the glories of the world; for they shall judge angels, and be placed at the right hand of Christ, and shall not suffer the bitterness of the last judgment.

22 ¶ Blessed are the bodies and

souls of virgins; for they are acceptable to God, and shall not lose the reward of their virginity; for the word of their (heavenly) Father shall prove effectual to their salvation in the day of his Son, and they shall enjoy rest for evermore.

CHAP. II.

1 *Thecla listens anxiously to Paul's preaching.* 5 *Thamyris, her admirer, concerts with Theoclia her mother to dissuade her,* 12 *in vain.* 14 *Demas and Hermogenes vilify Paul to Thamyris.*

WHILE Paul was preaching this sermon in the church which was in the house of Onesiphorus, a certain virgin, named Thecla (whose mother's name was Theoclia, and who was betrothed to a man named Thamyris) sat at a certain window in her house.

2 From whence, by the advantage of a window in the house where Paul was, she both night and day heard Paul's sermons concerning God, concerning charity, concerning faith in Christ, and concerning prayer;

3 Nor would she depart from the window, till with exceeding joy she was subdued to the doctrines of faith.

4 At length, when she saw many women and virgins going in to Paul, she earnestly desired that she might be thought worthy to appear in his presence, and hear the word of Christ; for she had not yet seen Paul's person, but only heard his sermons, and that alone.

5 ¶ But when she would not be prevailed upon to depart from the window, her mother sent to Thamyris, who came with the greatest pleasure, as hoping now to marry her. Accordingly he said to Theoclia, Where is my Thecla?

6 Theoclia replied, Thamyris, I have something very strange to tell you; for Thecla, for the space of three days, will not move from the window not so much as to eat or drink, but is so intent in hearing the artful and delusive discourses of a certain foreigner, that I perfectly admire, Thamyris, that a young woman of her known modesty, will suffer herself to be so prevailed upon.

7 For that man has disturbed the whole city of Iconium, and even your Thecla, among others, All the women and young men flock to him to receive his doctrine; who, besides all the rest, tells them that there is but one God, who alone is to be worshipped, and that we ought to live in chastity.

8 ¶ Notwithstanding this, my daughter Thecla, like a spider's web fastened to the window, is captivated by the discourses of Paul, and attends upon them with prodigious eagerness, and vast delight; and thus, by attending on what he says, the young woman is seduced. Now then do you go, and speak to her, for she is betrothed to you.

9 Accordingly Thamyris went, and having saluted her, and taking care not to surprise her, he said, Thecla, my spouse, why sittest thou in this melancholy posture? What strange impressions are made upon thee? Turn to Thamyris, and blush.

10 Her mother also spake to her after the same manner, and said, Child, why dost thou sit so melancholy, and, like one astonished, makest no reply?

11 Then they wept exceedingly, Thamyris, that he had lost

101

his spouse; Theoclia, that she had lost her daughter; and the maids, that they had lost their mistress; and there was an universal mourning in the family.

12 But all these things made no impression upon Thecla, so as to incline her so much as to turn to them, and take notice of them; for she still regarded the discourses of Paul.

13 Then Thamyris ran forth into the street to observe who they were who went into Paul, and came out from him; and he saw two men engaged in a very warm dispute, and said to them;

14 ¶ Sirs, what business have you here? and who is that man within, belonging to you, who deludes the minds of men, both young men and virgins, persuading them, that they ought not to marry, but continue as they are?

15 I promise to give you a considerable sum, if you will give me a just account of him; for I am the chief person of this city.

16 Demas and Hermogenes replied, We cannot so exactly tell who he is; but this we know, that he deprives young men of their (intended) wives, and virgins of their (intended) husbands, by teaching, There can be no future resurrection, unless ye continue in chastity, and do not defile your flesh.

CHAP. III.

1 They betray Paul. 7 Thamyris arrests him with officers.

THEN said Thamyris, Come along with me to my house, and refresh yourselves. So they went to a very splendid entertainment, where there was wine in abundance, and very rich provision.

2 They were brought to a table richly spread, and made to drink plentifully by Thamyris, on account of the love he had for Thecla and his desire to marry her.

3 Then Thamyris said, I desire ye would inform me what the doctrines of this Paul are, that I may understand them; for I am under no small concern about Thecla, seeing she so delights in that stranger's discourses, that I am in danger of losing my intended wife.

4 ¶ Then Demas and Hermogenes answered both together, and said, Let him be brought before the governor Castellius, as one who endeavours to persuade the people into the new religion of the Christians, and he, according to the order of Cæsar, will put him to death, by which means you will obtain your wife;

5 While we at the same time will teach her, that the resurrection which he speaks of is already come, and consists in our having children; and that we then arose again, when we came to the knowledge of God.

6 Thamyris having this account from them, was filled with hot resentment:

7 And rising early in the morning he went to the house of Onesiphorus, attended by the magistrates, the jailor, and a great multitude of people with staves, and said to Paul;

8 Thou hast perverted the city of Iconium, and among the rest, Thecla, who is betrothed to me, so that now she will not marry me. Thou shalt therefore go with us to the governor Castellius.

9 And all the multitude cried out, Away with this impostor

(magician), for he has perverted the minds of our wives, and all the people hearken to him.

CHAP. IV.

1 *Paul accused before the governor by Thamyris.* 5 *Defends himself.* 9 *Is committed to prison,* 10 *and visited by Thecla.*

THEN Thamyris standing before the governor's judgment-seat, spake with a loud voice in the following manner.

2 O governor, I know not whence this man cometh; but he is one who teaches that matrimony is unlawful. Command him therefore to declare before you for what reason he publishes such doctrines.

3 While he was saying thus, Demas and Hermogenes (whispered to Thamyris, and) said; Say that he is a Christian, and he will presently be put to death.

4 But the governor was more deliberate, and calling to Paul, he said, Who art thou? What dost thou teach? They seem to lay gross crimes to thy charge.

5 Paul then spake with a loud voice, saying, As I am now called to give an account, O governor, of my doctrines, I desire your audience.

6 That God, who is a God of vengeance, and who stands in need of nothing but the salvation of his creatures, has sent me to reclaim them from their wickedness and corruptions, from all (sinful) pleasures, and from death; and to persuade them to sin no more.

7 On this account, God sent his Son Jesus Christ, whom I preach, and in whom I instruct men to place their hopes as that person who only had such compassion on the deluded world, that it might not, O governor,

be condemned, but have faith, the fear of God, the knowledge of religion, and the love of truth.

8 So that if I only teach those things which I have received by revelation from God, where is my crime?

9 When the governor heard this, he ordered Paul to be bound, and to be put in prison, till he should be more at leisure to hear him more fully.

10 But in the night, Thecla taking off her ear-rings, gave them to the turnkey of the prison, who then opened the doors to her, and let her in;

11 And when she made a present of a silver looking-glass to the jailor, was allowed to go into the room where Paul was; then she sat down at his feet, and heard from him the great things of God.

12 And as she perceived Paul not to be afraid of suffering, but that by divine assistance he behaved himself with courage, her faith so far increased that she kissed his chains.

CHAP. V.

1 *Thecla sought and found by her relations.* 4 *Brought with Paul before the governor.* 9 *Ordered to be burnt, and Paul to be whipt.* 15 *Thecla miraculously saved.*

AT length Thecla was missed, and sought for by the family and by Thamyris in every street, as though she had been lost, but one of the porter's fellow-servants told them, that she had gone out in the night-time.

2 Then they examined the porter, and he told them, that she was gone to the prison to the strange man.

3 They went therefore according to his direction, and there

found her; and when they came out, they got a mob together, and went and told the governor all that happened.

4 Upon which he ordered Paul to be brought before his judgment seat.

5 Thecla in the mean time lay wallowing on the ground in the prison, in that same place where Paul had sat to teach her; upon which the governor also ordered her to be brought before his judgment-seat; which summons she received with joy, and went.

6 When Paul was brought thither, the mob with more vehemence cried out, He is a magician, let him die.

7 Nevertheless the governor attended with pleasure upon Paul's discourses of the holy works of Christ; and, after a council called, he summoned Thecla, and said to her, Why do you not, according to the law of the Iconians, marry Thamyris?

8 She stood still, with her eyes fixed upon Paul; and finding she made no reply, Theoclia, her mother, cried out, saying, Let the unjust creature be burnt; let her be burnt in the midst of the theatre, for refusing Thamyris, that all women may learn from her to avoid such practices.

9 Then the governor was exceedingly concerned, and ordered Paul to be whipt out of the city, and Thecla to be burnt.

10 So the governor arose, and went immediately into the theatre; and all the people went forth to see the dismal sight.

11 But Thecla, just as a lamb in the wilderness looks every way to see his shepherd, looked around for Paul;

12 And as she was looking upon the multitude, she saw the

Lord Jesus in the likeness of Paul, and said to herself, Paul is come to see me in my distressed circumstances. And she fixed her eyes upon him; but he instantly ascended up to heaven, while she looked on him.

13 Then the young men and women brought wood and straw for the burning of Thecla; who, being brought naked to the stake, extorted tears from the governor, with surprise beholding the greatness of her beauty.

14 And when they had placed the wood in order, the people commanded her to go upon it; which she did, first making the sign of the cross.

15 Then the people set fire to the pile; though the flame was exceeding large, it did not touch her, for God took compassion on her, and caused a great eruption from the earth beneath, and a cloud from above to pour down great quantities of rain and hail;

16 Insomuch that by the rupture of the earth, very many were in great danger, and some were killed, the fire was extinguished, and Thecla preserved.

CHAP. VI.

1 *Paul with Onesiphorus in a cave.* 7 *Thecla discovers Paul;* 12 *proffers to follow him:* 13 *he exhorts her not for fear of fornication.*

IN the mean time Paul, together with Onesiphorus, his wife and children, was keeping a fast in a certain cave, which was in the road from Iconium to Daphne.

2 And when they had fasted for several days, the children said to Paul, Father, we are hungry, and have not wherewithal to buy bread; for Onesiphorus had left all his substance to follow Paul with his family.

HELL.

PAINTED IN FRESCO BY ANDREA ORCAGNA IN THE CHURCH OF ST MARIA NOVELLO AT FLORENCE.

KEY TO THE PLATE "HELL."

1. Entrance to the confines of Hell.
2. Charon in his bark.
3. The Minotaur roaring at the approach of condemned souls.
4. Souls agitated by the impure breath of evil spirits.
5. Cerberus devouring the souls of gourmands.
6. The avaricious and prodigal condemned to carry burdens.
7. The envious and angry cast into the Styx.
8. Tower and wall of the evil city.
9. In this ditch are those who have sinned against their neighbors; Centaurs shoot arrows at them.
10. Those who have sinned against themselves are here tormented by Harpies.
11. Rain of fire for those who have sinned against God.
12. Soul of the tyrant Gerion cast into the flames.
13. Debauchees and corruptors of youth flogged by devils.
14. Poisonous gulf into which flatterers are plunged.
15. Lake of fire in the caldrons into which Simonaics are cast.
16. Sorcerers and diviners, their faces turned backward.
17. Bog of boiling pitch for cheats, thieves, and deceivers.
18. Hypocrite crucified.
19. Perfidious advisers plunged into a flaming ditch.
20. For scandalous persons: one holds his head in his hand.
21. Robbers and other criminals tormented by a centaur armed with serpents.
22. Alchemists and quacks a prey to leprosy.
23. Well of ice, for traitors and the ungrateful.
24. Pluto in the midst of a glacier devouring the damned.
25. The holy city of Jerusalem.

3 Then Paul, taking off his coat, said to the boy, Go, child, and buy bread, and bring it hither.

4 But while the boy was buying the bread, he saw his neighbour Thecla and was surprised, and said to her. Thecla, where are you going?

5 She replied, I am in pursuit of Paul, having been delivered from the flames.

6 The boy then said, I will bring you to him, for he is under great concern on your account, and has been in prayer and fasting these six days.

7 ¶ When Thecla came to the cave, she found Paul upon his knees praying and saying, O holy Father, O Lord Jesus Christ, grant that the fire may not touch Thecla; but be her helper, for she is thy servant.

8 Thecla then standing behind him, cried out in the following words: O sovereign Lord, Creator of heaven and earth, the Father of thy beloved and holy Son, I praise thee that thou hast preserved me from the fire, to see Paul again.

9 Paul then arose, and when he saw her, said, O God, who searchest the heart, Father of my Lord Jesus Christ, I praise thee that thou hast answered my prayer.

10 ¶ And there prevailed among them in the cave an entire affection to each other; Paul, Onesiphorus, and all that were with them being filled with joy.

11 They had five loaves, some herbs and water, and they solaced each other in reflections upon the holy works of Christ.

12 Then said Thecla to Paul, If you be pleased with it, I will follow you whithersoever you go.

13 He replied to her, Persons are now much given to fornication, and you being handsome, I am afraid lest you should meet with greater temptation than the former, and should not withstand, but be overcome by it.

14 Thecla replied, Grant me only the seal of Christ, and no temptation shall affect me.

15 Paul answered, Thecla, wait with patience, and you shall receive the gift of Christ.

CHAP. VII.

1 *Paul and Thecla go to Antioch.* 2 *Alexander, a magistrate, falls in love with Thecla:* 4 *kisses her by force:* 5 *she resists him:* 6 *is carried before the governor, and condemned to be thrown to wild beasts.*

THEN Paul sent back Onesiphorus and his family to their own home, and taking Thecla along with him, went for Antioch;

2 And as soon as they came into the city, a certain Syrian, named Alexander, a magistrate, in the city, who had done many considerable services for the city during his magistracy, saw Thecla and fell in love with her, and endeavoured by many rich presents to engage Paul in his interest.

3 But Paul told him, I know not the woman of whom you speak, nor does she belong to me.

4 But he being a person of great power in Antioch, seized her in the street and kissed her; which Thecla would not bear, but looking about for Paul, cried out in a distressed loud tone, Force me not, who am a stranger; force me not, who am a servant of God; I am one of the principal persons of Iconium, and was obliged to leave that city because I would not be married to Thamyris.

5 Then she laid hold on Alexander, tore his coat, and took his crown off his head, and made him appear ridiculous before all the people.

6 But Alexander, partly as he loved her, and partly being ashamed of what had been done, led her to the governor, and upon her confession of what she had done,[1] he condemned her to be thrown among the beasts.

CHAP. VIII.

2 Thecla entertained by Trifina; 3 brought out to the wild beasts; a she-lion licks her feet. 5 Trifina upon a vision of her deceased daughter, adopts Thecla, 11 who is taken to the amphitheatre again.

WHICH when the people saw, they said: The judgments passed in this city are unjust. But Thecla desired the favour of the governor, that her chastity might not be attacked, but preserved till she should be cast to the beasts.

2 The governor then inquired, Who would entertain her; upon which a certain very rich widow, named Trifina, whose daughter was lately dead, desired that she might have the keeping of her; and she began to treat her in her house as her own daughter.

3 At length a day came, when the beasts were to be brought forth to be seen; and Thecla was brought to the amphitheatre, and put into a den in which was an exceeding fierce she-lion, in the presence of a multitude of spectators.

4 Trifina, without any surprise, accompanied Thecla, and the she-lion licked the feet of Thecla. The title written which denotes her crime, was, Sacrilege. Then the woman cried out, O God, the judgments of this city are unrighteous.

5 After the beasts had been shewn, Trifina took Thecla home with her, and they went to bed; and behold, the daughter of Trifina, who was dead, appeared to her mother, and said; Mother, let the young woman, Thecla, be reputed by you as your daughter in my stead; and desire her that she should pray for me, that I may be translated to a state of happiness.

6 Upon which Trifina, with a mournful air, said, My daughter Falconilla has appeared to me, and ordered me to receive you in her room; wherefore I desire, Thecla, that you would pray for my daughter, that she may be translated into a state of happiness, and to life eternal.

7 When Thecla heard this, she immediately prayed to the Lord, and said: O Lord God of heaven and earth, Jesus Christ, thou Son of the Most High, grant that her daughter Falconilla may live forever. Trifina hearing this groaned again, and said: O unrighteous judgments! O unreasonable wickedness! that such a creature should (again) be cast to the beasts!

8 ¶ On the morrow, at break of day, Alexander came to Trifina's house, and said: The governor and the people are waiting; bring the criminal forth.

9 But Trifina ran in so violent-

---

[1] There being something wanting here in the old Greek MS., it is supplied out of the old Latin version, which is in the Bodleian Library, Cod. Digb. 39, rather than out of Simeon Metaphrastes, a writer of the eleventh century.

106

ly upon him, that he was affrighted, and ran away. Trifina was one of the royal family; and she thus expressed her sorrow, and said; Alas! I have trouble in my house on two accounts, and there is no one who will relieve me, either under the loss of my daughter, or my being unable to save Thecla. But now, O Lord God, be thou the helper of Thecla thy servant.

10 While she was thus engaged, the governor sent one of his own officers to bring Thecla. Trifina took her by the hand, and, going with her, said: I went with Falconilla to her grave, and now must go with Thecla to the beasts.

11 When Thecla heard this, she weeping prayed, and said: O Lord God, whom I have made my confidence and refuge, reward Trifina for her compassion to me, and preserving my chastity.

12 Upon this there was a great noise in the amphitheatre; the beasts roared, and the people cried out, Bring in the criminal.

13 But the woman cried out, and said: Let the whole city suffer for such crimes; and order all of us, O governor, to the same punishment. O unjust judgment! O cruel sight!

14 Others said, Let the whole city be destroyed for this vile action. Kill us all, O governor. O cruel sight! O unrighteous judgment.

CHAP. IX.

1 *Thecla thrown naked to the wild beasts;* 2 *they all refuse to attack her;* 8 *throws herself into a pit of water.* 10 *other wild beasts refuse her.* 11 *Tied to wild bulls.* 13 *Miraculously saved.* 1 *Released.* 24 *Entertained by Trifina.*

THEN Thecla was taken out of the hand of Trifina, stripped naked, had a girdle put on, and thrown into the place appointed for fighting with the beasts: and the lions and the bears were let loose upon her.

2 But a she-lion, which was of all the most fierce, ran to Thecla, and fell down at her feet. Upon which the multitude of women shouted aloud.

3 Then a she-bear ran fiercely towards her; but the she-lion met the bear, and tore it to pieces.

4 Again, a he-lion, who had been wont to devour men, and which belonged to Alexander, ran towards her; but the she-lion encountered the he-lion, and they killed each other.

5 Then the women were under a greater concern, because the she-lion, which had helped Thecla, was dead.

6 Afterwards they brought out many other wild beasts; but Thecla stood with her hands stretched towards heaven, and prayed; and when she had done praying, she turned about, and saw a pit of water, and said, Now it is a proper time for me to be baptized.

7 Accordingly she threw herself into the water, and said, In thy name, O my Lord Jesus Christ, I am this last day baptized. The women and the people seeing this, cried out, and said, Do not throw yourself into the water. And the governor himself cried out, to think that the fish (sea-calves) were like to devour so much beauty.

8 ¶ Notwithstanding all this, Thecla threw herself into the water, in the name of our Lord Jesus Christ.

9 But the fish (sea-calves,) when they saw the lighting and fire, were killed, and swam dead upon the surface of the water, and a cloud of fire surrounded

Thecla, so that as the beasts could not come near her, so the people could not see her nakedness.

10 Yet they turned other wild beasts upon her; upon which they made a very mournful outcry; and some of them scattered spikenard, others cassia, others amomus (a sort of spikenard, or the herb of Jerusalem, or ladies-rose) others ointment; so that the quantity of ointment was large, in proportion to the number of people; and upon this all the beasts lay as though they had been fast asleep, and did not touch Thecla.

11 Whereupon Alexander said to the Governor, I have some very terrible bulls; let us bind her to them. To which the governor, with concern, replied, You may do what you think fit.

12 Then they put a cord round Thecla's waist, which bound also her feet, and with it tied her to the bulls, to whose privy-parts they applied red-hot irons, that so they being the more tormented, might more violently drag Thecla about, till they had killed her.

13 The bulls accordingly tore about, making a most hideous noise; but the flame which was about Thecla, burnt off the cords which were fastened to the members of the bulls, and she stood in the middle of the stage, as unconcerned as if she had not been bound.

14 But in the mean time Trifina, who sat upon one of the benches, fainted away and died; upon which the whole city was under a very great concern.

15 And Alexander himself was afraid, and desired the governor, saying: I entreat you, take compassion on me and the city, and release this woman, who has

108

fought with the beasts; lest, both you and I, and the whole city be destroyed:

16 For if Cæsar should have any account of what has passed now, he will certainly immediately destroy the city, because Trifina, a person of royal extract, and a relation of his, is dead upon her seat.

17 Upon this the governor called Thecla from among the beasts to him, and said to her, Who art thou? and what are thy circumstances, that not one of the beasts will touch thee?

18 Thecla replied to him; I am a servant of the living God; and as to my state, I am a believer on Jesus Christ his Son, in whom God is well pleased; and for that reason none of the beasts could touch me.

19 He alone is the way to eternal salvation, and the foundation of eternal life. He is a refuge to those who are in distress; a support to the afflicted, hope and defence to those who are hopeless; and, in a word, all those who do not believe on him, shall not live, but suffer eternal death.

20 ¶ When the governor heard these things, he ordered her clothes to be brought, and said to her put on your clothes.

21 Thecla replied: May that God who clothed me when I was naked among the beasts, in the day of judgment clothe your soul with the robe of salvation. Then she took her clothes, and put them on; and the governor immediately published an order in these words; I release to you Thecla the servant of God.

22 Upon which the women cried out together with a loud voice, and with one accord gave praise unto God, and said; There is but one God, who is the God

of Thecla; the one God who hath delivered Thecla.

23 So loud were their voices that the whole city seemed to be shaken; and Trifina herself heard the glad tidings, and arose again, and ran with the multitude to meet Thecla; and embracing her, said: Now I believe there shall be a resurrection of the dead; now I am persuaded that my daughter is alive. Come therefore home with me, my daughter Thecla, and I will make over all that I have to you.

24 So Thecla went with Trifina, and was entertained there a few days, teaching her the word of the Lord, whereby many young women were converted; and there was great joy in the family of Trifina.

25 But Thecla longed to see Paul, and inquired and sent everywhere to find him; and when at length she was informed that he was at Myra, in Lycia, she took with her many young men and women; and putting on a girdle, and dressing herself in the habit of a man, she went to him to Myra in Lycia, and there found Paul preaching the word of God; and she stood by him among the throng.

CHAP. X.

1 *Thecla visits Paul.* 6 *Visits Onesiphorus.* 8 *Visits her mother.* 9 *Who repulses her.* 12 *Is tempted by the devil. Works miracles.*

BUT it was no small surprise to Paul when he saw her and the people with her; for he imagined some fresh trial was coming upon them;

2 Which when Thecla perceived, she said to him: I have been baptized, O Paul; for he who assists you in preaching, has assisted me to baptize.

3 Then Paul took her, and led her to the house of Hermes; and Thecla related to Paul all that had befallen her in Antioch, insomuch that Paul exceedingly wondered, and all who heard were confirmed in the faith, and prayed for Trifina's happiness.

4 Then Thecla arose, and said to Paul, I am going to Iconium. Paul replied to her: Go, and teach the word of the Lord.

5 But Trifina had sent large sums of money to Paul, and also clothing by the hands of Thecla, for the relief of the poor.

6 ¶ So Thecla went to Iconium. And when she came to the house of Onesiphorus, she fell down upon the floor where Paul had sat and preached, and, mixing tears with her prayers, she praised and glorified God in the following words:

7 O Lord the God of this house, in which I was first enlightened by thee; O Jesus, son of the living God, who wast my helper before the governor, my helper in the fire, and my helper among the beasts; thou alone art God forever and ever. Amen.

8 ¶ Thecla now (on her return) found Thamyris dead, but her mother living. So calling her mother, she said to her: Theoclia, my mother, is it possible for you to be brought to a belief, that there is but one Lord God, who dwells in the heavens? If you desire great riches, God will give them to you by me; if you want your daughter again, here I am.

9 These and many other things she represented to her mother, (endeavouring) to persuade her (to her own opinion). But her mother Theoclia gave no credit to the things which were said by the martyr Thecla.

109

10 So that Thecla perceiving she discoursed to no purpose, signing her whole body with the sign (of the cross), left the house and went to Daphine; and when she came there, she went to the cave, where she had found Paul with Onesiphorus, and fell down on the ground; and wept before God.

11 When she departed thence, she went to Seleucia, and enlightened many in the knowledge of Christ.

12 ¶ And a bright cloud conducted her in her journey.

13 And after she had arrived at Seleucia she went to a place out of the city, about the distance of a furlong, being afraid of the inhabitants, because they were worshippers of idols.

14 And she was led (by the cloud) into a mountain called Calamon, or Rodeon. There she abode many years, and underwent a great many grievous temptations of the devil, which she bore in a becoming manner, by the assistance which she had from Christ.

15 At length certain gentlewomen hearing of the virgin Thecla, went to her, and were instructed by her in the oracles of God, and many of them abandoned this world, and led a monastic life with her.

16 Hereby a good report was spread everywhere of Thecla, and she wrought several (miraculous) cures, so that all the city and adjacent countries brought their sick to that mountain, and before they came as far as the door of the cave, they were instantly cured of whatsoever distemper they had.

17 The unclean spirits were cast out, making a noise; all received their sick made whole, and glorified God, who had bestowed such power on the virgin Thecla;

18 Insomuch that the physicians of Seleucia were now of no more account, and lost all the profit of their trade, because no one regarded them; upon which they were filled with envy, and began to contrive what methods to take with this servant of Christ.

CHAP. XI.

1 *Is attempted to be ravished,* 12 *escapes by a rock opening,* 17 *and closing miraculously.*

THE devil then suggested bad advice to their minds; and being on a certain day met together to consult, they reasoned among each other thus: The virgin is a priestess of the great goddess Diana, and whatsoever she requests from her, is granted, because she is a virgin, and so is beloved by all the gods.

2 Now then let us procure some rakish fellows, and after we have made them sufficiently drunk, and given them a good sum of money, let us order them to go and debauch this virgin, promising them, if they do it, a larger reward.

3 (For they thus concluded among themselves, that if they be able to debauch her, the gods will no more regard her, nor Diana cure the sick for her.)

4 They proceeded according to this resolution, and the fellows went to the mountain, and as fierce as lions to the cave, knocking at the door.

5 The holy martyr Thecla, relying upon the God in whom she believed, opened the door, although she was before apprized of their design, and said to them,

Young men, what is your business?

6 They replied, Is there any one within, whose name is Thecla? She answered, What would you have with her? They said, We have a mind to lie with her.

7 The blessed Thecla answered: Though I am a mean old woman, I am the servant of my Lord Jesus Christ; and though you have a vile design against me, ye shall not be able to accomplish it. They replied: It is impossible but we must be able to do with you what we have a mind.

8 And while they were saying this, they laid hold on her by main force, and would have ravished her. Then she with the (greatest) mildness said to them: Young men have patience, and see the glory of the Lord.

9 And while they held her, she looked up to heaven and said; O God most reverend, to whom none can be likened; who makest thyself glorious over thine enemies; who didst deliver me from the fire, and didst not give me up to Thamyris, didst not give me up to Alexander; who deliveredst me from the wild beasts; who didst preserve me in the deep waters; who hast everywhere been my helper, and hast glorified thy name in me;

10 Now also deliver me from the hands of these wicked and unreasonable men, nor suffer them to debauch my chastity which I have hitherto preserved for thy honour; for I love thee and long for thee, and worship thee, O Father, Son, and Holy Ghost, for evermore. Amen.

11 Then came a voice from heaven, saying, Fear not, Thecla, my faithful servant, for I am with thee. Look and see the place which is opened for thee: there thy eternal abode shall be; there thou shalt receive the beatific vision.

12 The blessed Thecla observing, saw the rock opened to as large a degree as that a man might enter in; she did as she was commanded, bravely fled from the vile crew, and went into the rock, which instantly so closed, that there was not any crack visible where it had opened.

13 The men stood perfectly astonished at so prodigious a miracle, and had no power to detain the servant of God; but only, catching hold of her veil, or hood, they tore off a piece of it;

14 And even that was by the permission of God, for the confirmation of their faith who should come to see this venerable place, and to convey blessings to those in succeeding ages, who should believe on our Lord Jesus Christ from a pure heart.

15 Thus suffered that first martyr and apostle of God, and virgin, Thecla; who came from Iconium at eighteen years of age; afterwards, partly in journeys and travels, and partly in a monastic life in the cave, she lived seventy-two years; so that she was ninety years old when the Lord translated her.

16 Thus ends her life.

17 The day which is kept sacred to her memory, is the twenty-fourth of September, to the glory of the Father, and the Son, and the Holy Ghost, now and for evermore. Amen.

111

The FIRST EPISTLE of CLEMENT to the CORINTHIANS.

Clement was a disciple of Peter, and afterwards Bishop of Rome. Clemens Alexandrinus calls him an apostle. Jerome says he was an apostolical man, and Rufinus that he was almost an apostle. Eusebius calls this the wonderful Epistle of St. Clement, and says that it was publicly read in the assemblies of the primitive church. It is included in one of the ancient collections of the Canon Scripture. Its genuineness has been much questioned, particularly by Photius, patriarch of Constantinople, in the ninth century, who objects that Clement speaks of worlds beyond the ocean; that he has not written worthily of the divinity of Christ; and that to prove the possibility of a future resurrection, he introduces the fabulous story of the phœnix's revival from its own ashes. To the latter objection, Archbishop Wake replies that the generality of the ancient Fathers have made use of the same instance in proof of the same point; and asks if St. Clement really believed that there was such a bird, and that it did revive out of the cinders of the body after burning, where was the great harm either in giving credit to such a wonder, or, believing it, to make such a use as he here does of it?—The present is the Archbishop's translation from the ancient Greek copy of the Epistle, which is at the end of the celebrated Alexandrine MS. of the Septuagint and New Testament, presented by Cyril, patriarch of Alexandria, to King Charles the First, now in the British Museum. The Archbishop, in prefacing his translation, esteems it a great blessing that this " Epistle" was at last so happily found out for the increase and confirmation both of our faith and our charity.

CHAP. I.

He commends them for their excellent order and piety in Christ, before their schism broke out.

THE Church of God which [1]is at Rome, to the Church of God which is at Corinth, [2]elect, sanctified [3]by the will of God, through Jesus Christ our Lord: grace and peace from the Almighty God, by Jesus Christ be multiplied unto you.[4]

2 ¶ Brethren, the [5]sudden and unexpected dangers and calamities that have fallen upon us, have, we fear, made us the more slow in our consideration of those things which you inquired of us:

3 [6]As also of that wicked and detestable sedition, so [7]unbecoming the elect of God, which a few heady and self-willed men have fomented to such a degree of madness, that your venerable and renowned name, so worthy of all men to be beloved, is greatly blasphemed thereby.

4 For who that has [8]ever been among you has not experimented the firmness of your faith, [9]and its fruitfulness in all good works; and admired the temper and moderation of your religion in Christ; and published abroad the magnificence of your hospitality, and thought you happy in your perfect and certain knowledge of the Gospel ?

[1] Sojourneth. [2] Called. See Hammond on Matt. xx. [3] Gr. in. - See Bp. Pearson's note on this place. Ed. Colomesii. p. 2. [5] Ibid. [6] And. [7] Gr. Strange to. [8] Gr. Lodged as a stranger. [9] Adorned with all manner of virtues.

112

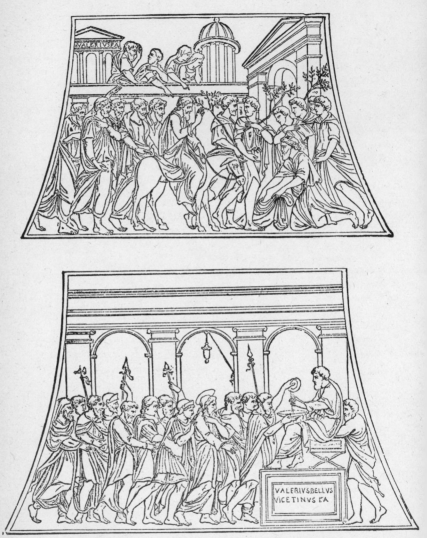

CHRIST'S ENTRY INTO JERUSALEM, AND CHRIST BEFORE PILATE.

FROM INTAGLIOS IN A BOX OF ROCK CRYSTAL, BY A EARLY VENETIAN ARTIST.

5 For ye did all things without respect of persons and walked [1]according to the laws of God; being subject to those who had the rule over you, and giving the honour that was fitting to the [2]aged among you.

6 Ye commanded the young men to think those things that were modest and grave.

7 The women ye exhorted to do all things with an unblameable and seemly, and pure conscience; loving their own husbands, as was fitting: and that keeping themselves within the [3]bounds of a due obedience, they should [4] order their houses gravely, with all [5]discretion.

8 [6]Ye were all of you humble minded, not [7]boasting of any thing: desiring rather to be subject than to govern; to [8]give than to receive; being [9]content with the portion God hath dispensed to you;

9 And hearkening diligently to his word, ye [10]were enlarged in your bowels, having his [11] suffering always before your eyes.

10 Thus a firm, and [12]blessed and profitable peace was given unto you; and an unsatiable desire of doing good; and a plentiful effusion of the Holy Ghost was upon all of you.

11 And being full of [13] good designs, ye did with [14] great readiness of mind, and with a religious confidence stretch forth your hands to God Almighty; beseeching him to be merciful unto you, if in any thing ye had unwillingly sinned against him.

12 Ye contended day and night for the whole brotherhood; that [15] with compassion and a good conscience, the number of his elect might be saved.

13 Ye were sincere, and without offence towards each other; not mindful of injuries; all sedition and schism was an abomination unto you.

14 Ye bewailed every one his neighbour's sins, esteeming their defects your own.

15 Ye [16] were kind one to another without grudging; being ready to every good work. And being adorned with a conversation altogether virtuous and religious, ye did all things in the fear of God; whose [17]commandments were written upon the tables of your heart.

CHAP. II.

How their divisions began.

ALL honour and enlargement was given unto you; and so was fulfilled that which is written, [18]my beloved did eat and drink, he was enlarged and waxed fat, and he kicked.

2 From hence came emulation, and envy, and strife, and sedition; persecution and [19]disorder, war and captivity.

3 So they who were of no renown, lifted up themselves against the honourable; those of no reputation, against those who were in respect; the foolish against the wise; the young men against the aged.

---

[1] In.   [2] Presbyters.   [3] Canon, rule.   [4] Themselves do their own business. Vid. Not. Junii in loc.   [5] Temperance, sobriety.   [6] 1 Pet. v. 5.   [7] Proud. [8] Acts, xx. 35.   [9] 1 Tim. vi. 8.   [10] Embraced it in your very bowels. [11] παθηματα. See Dr. Grabe's Addit. to Bp. Bull's Def. fid. Nic. p. 60, 61. [12] Gr. λιπαρα.   [13] Holy counsel, or purpose, or will.   [14] Gr. good.   [15] With mercy and conscience.   [16] Ye were without repentance in all well-doing. Titus iii. 1.   [17] Prov. vii. 3.   [18] Deut. xxxii. 15.   [19] Confusion, tumults, &c.

4 Therefore righteousness and peace are departed from you, because every one hath forsaken the fear of God ; and is grown blind in his faith ; nor walketh by the rule of God's commandments nor liveth as is fitting in Christ :

5 But every one [1] follows his own wicked lusts : having taken up an unjust and wicked envy, by which death first entered into the world.

CHAP. III.

Envy and emulation the original of all strife and disorder. Examples of the mischiefs they have occasioned.

FOR thus it is written, [2] And in process of time it came to pass that Cain brought of the fruit of the ground an offering unto the Lord. And Abel, he also brought of the firstlings of his flock, and of the fat thereof :

2 And the Lord had respect unto Abel, and to his offering. But unto Cain and unto his offering he had not respect. And Cain was very sorrowful, and his countenance fell.

3 And the Lord said unto Cain, Why art thou sorrowful ? And why is thy countenance fallen ? [3] If thou shalt offer aright, but not divide aright, hast thou not sinned ? Hold thy peace : unto thee shall be his [4] desire, and thou shalt rule over him.

4 And Cain said unto Abel his brother, Let us go down into the field. And it came to pass, as they were in the field, that Cain rose up against Abel his brother, and slew him.

5 Ye see, brethren, how envy and emulation wrought [5] the death of a brother. For [6] this our father [7] Jacob fled from the face of his brother Esau.

6 It was this that caused [8] Joseph to be persecuted even unto death, and to come into bondage. Envy forced [9] Moses to flee from the face of Pharaoh king of Egypt, when he heard his own countrymen ask him, [10] Who made thee a Judge, and a ruler over us ? Wilt thou kill me as thou didst the Egyptian yesterday ?

7 Through envy Aaron and Miriam were [11] shut out of the camp, from the rest of the congregation seven days.

8 [12] Emulation [13] sent Dathan and Abiram quick into the [14] grave because they raised up a sedition against Moses the servant of God.

9 For this David [15] was not only hated of strangers, but was persecuted even by Saul the king of Israel.

10 But [16] not to insist upon antient examples, let us come to those [17] worthies that have been nearest to us ; and take the brave examples of our own age.

11 Through zeal and envy, [18] the most faithful and righteous [19] pillars of the church have been persecuted even to the most grievous deaths.

12 Let us set before our eyes the holy Apostles ; Peter by unjust envy underwent not one or

---

[1] Walketh after.   [2] Gen. iv. 3, &c.   [3] This is according to the LXX.
[4] 'Αποστροφη, conversion.   [5] Fratricide.   [6] Envy.   [7] Gen. xxviii.   [8] Gen. xxxvii.
[9] Exodus ii. 15.   [10] Exod. ii. 14.   [11] Made to lodge out.   [12] Num. xii. 14, 15.
[13] Brought.   [14] Hades.   [15] Had, or underwent the hatred, not only, &c.
[16] To cease from.   [17] Combatants, wrestlers.   [18] The faithful and most righteous.
[19] Good.

two, but many [1] sufferings; [2] till at last being martyred, he went to the place of glory that was due unto him.

13 [3] For the same cause did Paul in like manner receive the reward of his patience. Seven times [4] he was in bonds; he was whipped, was stoned; he preached both in the East and in the West; [5] leaving behind him the glorious report of his faith:

14 And so having taught the whole world righteousness, and for that end travelled even to the utmost bounds of the West; he at last suffered martyrdom [6] by the command of the governors,

15 And departed out of the world, and went unto his holy place; being become a most eminent pattern of patience unto all ages.

16 To these [7] Holy Apostles were joined a very great number of others, who having through envy undergone in like manner many pains and torments, have [8] left a glorious example to us.

17 For [9] this not only men but women have been persecuted: [10] and having suffered very grievous and [11] cruel punishments, have finished the course of their faith with firmness; and though weak in body, yet received a glorious reward.

18 [12] This has alienated the minds even of women from their husbands; and changed what was once said by our father Adam; [13] This is now bone of my bone, and flesh of my flesh.

19 In a word, envy and strife, have overturned [14] whole cities, and rooted out great nations from off the earth.

CHAP. IV.

1 *He exhorts them to live by the rules, and repent of their divisions, and they shall be forgiven.*

THESE things, beloved, we [15] write unto you, not only [16] for your instruction, but also for our own remembrance.

2 For we are all in the same [17] lists, and the same combat is [18] prepared for us all.

3 Wherefore let us lay aside all vain and empty cares; and let us come up to the glorious and venerable rule of our holy calling.

4 [19] Let us consider what is good, and acceptable and well-pleasing in the sight of him that made us.

5 Let us look steadfastly to the blood of Christ, and see how precious his blood is in the sight of God: which being shed for our salvation, [20] has obtained the grace of repentance for all the world.

6 Let us [21] search into all the ages that have gone before us; and let us learn that our Lord has [22] in every one of them still given place for repentance to all such as would [23] turn to him.

7 [24] Noah preached repentance; and as many as hearkened to him were saved. [25] Jonah denounced

---

[1] Labours. [2] And so. [3] By envy. [4] Having borne seven times bonds, &c. [5] He received the, &c. [6] Vid. Pearson de Success, c. viii. § 9. [7] Men who have lived godly, is gathered together. [8] Become an excellent example among us. [9] Envy. [10] The names of Danae and Dirce I omit.—See Junius Annot. in loc. [11] Cursed afflictions or torments. [12] Envy or emulation. [13] Gen. ii. 23. [14] Great. [15] End. [16] Instructing you, but also remembering, &c. [17] Place of encounter. [18] Imposed upon us all. [19] 1 Tim. v. 4. [20] Afforded or given to. [21] Look diligently to. [22] From age to age. [23] Be turned. [24] 2 Peter ii. 5· Genesis vii. [25] John iii.

destruction against the Ninevites :

8 Howbeit they repenting of their sins, appeased God by their prayers : and [1] were saved, though they were strangers to the covenant of God.

9 ¶ Hence we find how all the ministers of the grace of God have spoken by the Holy Spirit of repentance. And even the Lord of all has himself [2]declared with an oath concerning it ;

10 [3] As I live, saith the Lord, I desire not the death of a sinner, [4] but that he should repent. Adding farther this good sentence, saying : [5] Turn from your iniquity, O house of Israel.

11 [6] Say unto the children of my people, Though your sins should reach from earth to heaven ; and though they shall be redder than scarlet, and blacker than sackcloth ; yet if ye shall turn to me with all your heart, and shall call me father, I will hearken to you, as to a holy people.

12 And in another place he saith on this wise : [7] Wash ye, make you clean ; put away [8]the evil of your doings from before mine eyes ; cease to do evil, learn to do well ; seek judgment, relieve the oppressed, judge the fatherless, plead for the widow.

13 Come now and let us reason together, saith the Lord : though your sins be as scarlet, they shall be as white as snow ; though they be red as crimson, [9] they shall be as wool.

14 If ye be willing and obedient, ye shall eat the good of the land ; but if ye refuse and rebel, ye shall be devoured with the sword ; for the mouth of the Lord hath spoken it.

15 These things has God established by his Almighty will, desiring that all his beloved should come to repentance.

CHAP. V.

1 *He sets before them the examples of holy men, whose piety is recorded in the Scriptures.*

WHEREFORE let us obey his excellent and glorious will ; and [10] imploring his mercy and goodness, let us fall down upon our faces before him, and [11] cast ourselves upon his mercy ; laying aside all [12] vanity, and contention, and envy which leads unto death.

2 Let us look up to those who have the most perfectly ministered to his excellent glory. Let us take Enoch for our example ; who being found righteous in obedience, was [13] translated, and his death was not [14] known.

3 Noah [15] being proved to be faithful, did by his ministry preach [16] regeneration to the world ; and the Lord saved by him all the living creatures, that went [17] with one accord into the ark.

4 [18] Abraham, who was called God's friend, was in like manner found faithful ; inasmuch as he obeyed the [19] commands of God.

5 By obedience [20] he went out of his own country, and from

---

[1] Received salvation. [2] Spoken. [3] Ezekiel xxxiii. 11. [4] So much as his repentance. [5] Repent from. [6] Ezekiel xviii. 30, 23 ; Isaiah i.; Jeremiah iii. 4, 19. [7] Isaiah v. 16. [8] Evil from your souls. [9] I will make them as wool. [10] Becoming suppliants of, &c. [11] Turn ourselves to his mercy. [12] Vain labour. [13] Gen. v. 24. [14] Found. [15] Being found. [16] Gen. vi., vii., viii. [17] In unity. [18] James ii. 23; Isaiah xli. 8. [19] Words. [20] This man

his own kindred, and from his father's house: that so forsaking a small country, and a weak affinity, and a little house, he might inherit the promises of God.

6 For thus God said unto him; [1] get thee out of thy country, and from thy kindred, and from thy father's house, unto a land that I will show thee.

7 And I will make thee a great nation, and will bless thee, and make thy name great, and thou shalt be blessed. And I will bless them that bless thee, and curse them that curse thee; and in thee shall all families of the earth be blessed.

8 And again when he separated himself from Lot, God said unto him; [2] Lift up now thine eyes, and look from the place where thou art northward and southward and eastward and [3] westward for all the land which thou seest, to thee will I give it, and to thy seed for ever.

9 And I will make thy seed as the dust of the earth, so that if a man can number the dust of the earth, then shall thy seed also be numbered.

10 And again he saith: and [4] God brought forth Abraham, and said unto him; Look now toward heaven, and tell the stars, if thou be able to number them: so shall thy seed be.

11 And Abraham believed God, and it was counted to him for righteousness.

12 Through faith and hospitality, [5] he had a son given him in his old age; and through

obedience he offered him up in sacrifice to God, upon one of the mountains which God showed unto him.

CHAP. VI.

1 *And particularly such as have been eminent for their kindness and charity to their neighbours.*

BY [6] hospitality and godliness was Lot saved out of Sodom, when all the country round about was [7] destroyed by fire and brimstone:

2 The Lord thereby making it manifest, that he will not forsake those that trust in him; but [8] will bring the disobedient to punishment and correction.

3 For his wife who went out with him, being of a different mind, [9] and not continuing in the same obedience, was for that reason [10] set forth for an example, being turned into a pillar of salt unto this day.

4 That so all men may know, that those who are double minded, and distrustful of the power of God, are [11] prepared for condemnation, and to be a sign to all succeeding ages.

5 [12] By faith and hospitality was Rahab the harlot saved. For when the spies were sent by Joshua the son of Nun, to search out Jericho and the king of Jericho knew that they were come to spy out his country; [13] he sent men to take them, so that they might be put to death.

6 [14] Rahab therefore being hospitable, received them, and hid

---

[1] Gen. xii. 1. [2] Gen. xiii. 14. [3] Towards the sea. [4] Gen. xv. 5.
[5] A son was given unto him. [6] Gen. xix. 2; 2 Peter ii. 6; Jude 7.
[7] See Not. in loc. or punished with. [8] But those that turn another way, he puts, &c. [9] Not in concord. [10] Put for a sign. [11] Become. [12] Jos. ii. 1, &c.
[13] He sent men that should take them, that being taken, &c. [14] Therefore hospitable Rahab.

117

them under the stalks of flax, on the top of her house.

7 And when the [1]messengers that were sent by the king came unto her, and asked her, saying, [2]There came men unto thee to spy out the land, bring them forth, for so hath the king commanded : She answered, [3]The two men whom ye seek came unto me, but presently they departed, and are gone : [4]Not discovering them unto them.

8 Then she said to the [5]spies, [6]I know that the Lord your God [7]has given this city into your hands; for the fear of you is fallen upon all that dwell therein. When, therefore, ye shall have taken it [8]ye shall save me and my father's house.

9 And they answered her, saying, It shall be as thou hast spoken to us. [9]Therefore, when thou shalt know that we are near thou shalt gather all thy family together upon the housetop, and they shall be saved : but all that shall be found without thy house, shall be destroyed.

10 [10]And they gave her moreover a sign : that she should hang out of her house a scarlet rope ; [11]shewing thereby, that by the blood of our Lord, there should be redemption to all that believe and hope in God. Ye see, beloved, how there was not only faith, but prophecy too in this woman.

CHAP. VII.

1 *What rules are given for this purpose.*

LET us, therefore, humble ourselves, brethren, laying aside all pride, and boasting, and foolishness, and anger : And let us do as it is written.

2 For thus saith the Holy Spirit ; [12]Let not the wise man glory in his wisdom, nor the strong man in his strength, nor the rich man in his riches ; but let him that glorieth, glory in the Lord, to seek him, and to do judgment and justice.

3 Above all, remembering the words of the Lord Jesus, which he spake [13]concerning equity and long suffering, [14]saying,

4 [15]Be ye merciful and ye shall obtain mercy ; forgive, and ye shall be forgiven : as ye do, so shall it be done unto you : as ye give, so shall it be given unto you : as ye judge, so shall ye be judged ; as ye are kind to others so shall God be kind to you : with what measure ye mete, with the same shall it be measured to you again.

5 By this command, and by these rules, let us establish ourselves, that so we may always walk obediently to his holy words ; being humble minded :

6 For so says [16]the Holy Scripture ; [17]upon whom shall I look, even upon him that is poor and of a contrite spirit, and that trembles at my word.

7 ¶ It is, therefore, just and [18]righteous, men and brethren, that we should become obedient unto God, rather than follow

---

[1] Men being sent by the king, and saying.   [2] Verse 4.   [3] Verses 4, 5. [4] Vid. Conjecture. Coteler. in loc.   [5] Men.   [6] Verse 9.   [7] Given you this city.   [8] Verse 13.   [9] Verses 18, 19.   [10] Verse 18.   [11] Many of the Fathers have applied this to the same purpose.—See not. Coteler . in loc. [12] Jer. ix. 23. Comp. 2 Cor. xi. 31.   [13] Teaching us.   [14] For thus he saith. [15] Luke vi. 35.   [16] Holy Word.   [17] Isaiah lxvi. 2.   [18] Holy.

such as [1]through pride and sedition, have made themselves the ring-leaders of a detestable emulation.

8 For it is not an ordinary harm that we shall do ourselves, but rather a very great danger that we shall run, if we shall rashly give up ourselves to the wills of men who [2] promote strife and seditions, to turn us aside from that which is fitting.

9 But let us be kind to one another, according to the compassion and sweetness of him that made us.

10 For it is written, [3]The merciful shall inherit the earth; and they that are without evil shall be left upon it: [4]but the transgressors shall perish from off the face of it.

11 And again he saith, [5]I have seen the wicked in great power and spreading himself like the cedar of Libanus. I passed by, and lo! he was not; I sought his place, but it could not be found.

12 Keep innocently, and do the thing that is right, for there shall be a remnant to the peaceable man.

13 Let us, therefore, hold fast to those who [6] religiously follow peace; and not to such as [7] only pretend to desire.

14 For he saith in a certain place, [8] This people honoureth me with their lips, but their heart is far from me.

15 And again, They [9] bless with their mouths, [10] but curse in their hearts.

16 And again he saith, [11] They loved him with their mouths, and with their tongues they lied to him. For their heart was not right with him, neither were they faithful in his covenant.

17 [12] Let all deceitful lips become dumb, and the tongue that speaketh proud things. Who have said, [13] with our tongue will we prevail; our lips are our own, who is Lord over us.

18 For the oppression of the poor, for the sighing of the needy, now will I arise saith the Lord; I will set him in safety, I will deal confidently with him.

CHAP. VIII.

He advises them to be humble; and that from the examples of Jesus and of holy men in all ages.

FOR Christ is theirs who are humble, and not who exalt themselves over his flock. The sceptre of the majesty of God, our Lord Jesus Christ, came not in the [14] shew of pride and arrogance, [15] though he could have done so; but with humility as the Holy Ghost had before spoken concerning him.

2 For thus he saith, Lord, [16] who hath believed our report, and to whom is the arm of the Lord revealed? For he shall grow up before him as a tender plant, and as a root out of a dry ground.

3 He hath no form or comeliness, and when we shall see him, there is no beauty that we should desire him.

---

[1] In. [2] Prick on to.—See Junius Ann. [3] Psalm **xxxvii**. 9. [4] Prov. ii. 10.
[5] Psalm lxviii. 36. [6] With religion or godliness. [7] With hypocrisy will it.
[8] Isaiah **xxix.** 13. Psalm lxii. 4. [9] Blessed. [10] Cursed. [11] Psalm lxxviii.
36, 37. [12] Psalm xii. 3.   [13] We will magnify our tongue.   [14] Boasting.
[15] Καιπερ δυναμενος, though he were powerful. [16] Isaiah liii. according to the Hebrew.

4 He is despised and rejected of men ; a man of sorrows and acquainted with grief.

5 And we hid, as it were, our faces from him ; he was despised, and we esteemed him not.

6 Surely he hath born our griefs, and carried our sorrows : yet we did esteem him stricken, smitten of God, and afflicted.

7 But he was wounded for our transgressions ; he was bruised for our iniquities ; the chastisement of our peace was upon him ; and with his stripes we are healed.

8 All we like sheep have gone astray ; we have turned every one to his own way, and the Lord hath laid on him the iniquity of us all.

9 He was oppressed, and he was afflicted, yet he opened not his mouth : he is brought as a lamb to the slaughter ; and as a sheep before her shearers is dumb, so he openeth not his mouth.

10 He was taken from prison, and from judgment ; and who shall declare his generation? For he was cut off out of the land of the living, for the transgressions of my people was he stricken.

11 And he made his grave with the wicked, and with the rich in his death ; because he had done no violence, neither was any deceit in his mouth.

12 Yet it pleased the Lord to bruise him, he hath put him to grief ; when thou shalt make his soul an offering for sin, he shall see his seed, he shall prolong his days ; and the pleasure of the Lord shall prosper in his hand.

13 He shall see of the travail of his soul and shall be satisfied ; by his knowledge shall my righteous servant justify many : for he shall bear their iniquities.

14 Therefore will I divide him a portion with the great, and he shall divide the spoil with the strong ; because he hath poured out his soul unto death ; and he was numbered with the transgressors, and he bare the sin of many, and made intercession for the transgressors.

15 And again he himself saith, [1] I am a worm and no man, a reproach of men, and despised of the people. All they that see me laugh me to scorn ; they shoot out their lips, they shake their heads, saying : He trusted in the Lord that he would deliver him, let him deliver him seeing he delighted in him.

16 Ye see, beloved, what the pattern is that has been given to us. For if the Lord thus humbled himself, what should we do who are brought [2] by him under the yoke of his grace ?

17 Let us be followers of those who went about in goat-skins and sheep-skins ; preaching the coming of Christ.

18 [3] Such were Elias, and Elisæus, and Ezekiel the prophets. [4] And let us add to these such others as have received the like testimony.

19 Abraham has been greatly witnessed of ; having been called the friend of God. And yet he steadfastly beholding the glory of God, says with all humility, [5] I am dust and ashes.

20 Again of Job it is thus written, [6] That he was just and without blame, true ; one that served God, and abstained from all evil. Yet he accusing himself, says, [7] No man is free from pollution, no not though he should live but one day.

21 Moses was called faithful

---

[1] Psalm xxii. 6. [2] MS. *δι αυτου.* [3] We say. [4] To these, those also that have been witnessed of. [5] Gen. xviii. 27. [6] Job i. 1. [7] Job xiv. 4.

THE TWO SPIES SENT BY JOSHUA TO JERICHO, AND THEIR ESCAPE FROM
THE HOUSE FROM RAHAB.

FROM MOSAICS OF THE FIFTH CENTURY IN THE CHURCH OF ST. MARIA MAGGIORE, ROME.

in all God's House; and by his conduct [1] the Lord punished Israel by stripes and plagues.

22 And even this man, though thus greatly honoured, spake not greatly of himself; but when the oracle of God was delivered to him out of the bush he said, [2] Who am I, that thou dost send me? I am of a slender voice, and a slow tongue.

23 And again he saith, [3] I am as the smoke of the pot.

24 And what shall we say of David, so highly testified of in the Holy Scriptures? To whom God said [4] I have found a man after my own heart, David the son of Jesse, with my holy oil have I anointed him.

25 But yet he himself saith unto God, [5] Have mercy upon me, O God, according to thy loving kindness; according unto the multitude of thy tender mercies, blot out my transgressions.

26 Wash me thoroughly from mine iniquity, and cleanse me from my sin! For I acknowledge my transgressions, and my sin is ever before me.

27 Against Thee only have I sinned, and done this evil in thy sight, that thou mightest be justified when thou speakest, and be clear when thou judgest.

28 Behold I was shapen in iniquity, and in sin did my mother conceive me.

29 Behold, thou desireth truth in the inward parts; and in the hidden part thou shalt make me to know wisdom.

30 Purge me with hyssop and I shall be clean, wash me and I shall be whiter than snow.

31 Make me to hear joy and gladness, that the bones which thou hast broken may rejoice.

32 Hide thy face from my sins, and blot out all mine iniquities.

33 Create in me a clean heart O God; and renew a right spirit within me.

34 Cast me not away from thy presence, and take not thy holy spirit from me.

35 Restore unto me the joy of thy salvation, and uphold me with thy free spirit.

36 Then I will teach transgressors thy ways, and sinners shall be converted unto thee.

37 Deliver me from bloodguiltiness, O God, thou God of my salvation, and my tongue shall sing aloud of thy righteousness.

38 O Lord open thou my lips, and my mouth shall show forth thy praise.

39 For thou desirest not sacrifice, else would I give it; thou delightest not in burnt offerings.

40 The sacrifices of God are a broken spirit, a broken and a contrite heart, O God, thou wilt not despise.

CHAP. IX.

He again persuades them to compose their divisions.

THUS has the humility and [6] godly fear of these [7] great and excellent men, [8] recorded in the Scriptures, through obedience, made not only us, but also the generations before us better; even as many as have received his holy oracles [9] with fear and truth.

2 Having therefore so many,

---

[1] MS. εκρινεν ο θεος τον Ισραηλ δια των μαστιγων. [2] Exod. iii. 11. [3] Exod. iv. 10. [4] Psalm lxxxix. 20. [5] Psalm li. to v. 17, according to the Hebrew. [6] Fearfulness. [7] So great and such kind of men. [8] Witnessed of, or celebrated. [9] In.

and such great and glorious [1] examples, [2] let us return to that peace which was the mark that from the beginning was set before us ;

3 Let us look up to the Father and Creator of the whole world ; and let us hold fast to his glorious and exceeding gifts and benefits of peace.

4 Let us [3] consider and behold with the eyes of our [4] understanding his long-suffering will; and think how gentle and patient he is towards his whole creation.

5 The heavens moving by his appointment, are subject to him in peace.

6 Day and night accomplish the courses that he has allotted unto them, not disturbing one another.

7 The sun and moon, and all the several [5] companies and constellations of the stars, run the [6] courses that he has appointed to them in concord, without departing in the least from them.

8 The fruitful earth yields its food plentifully in due season both to man and beast, and to all animals that are upon it, according to his will; not [7] disputing, nor altering any thing of what was ordered by him.

9 So also the unfathomable and unsearchable floods of the deep, are kept in by his command ;

10 [8] And the [9] conflux of the vast sea, being brought together by his order into its several collections, passes not the bounds that he has set to it ;

11 But as he [10] appointed it, so it remains. For he said,[11]

Hitherto shalt thou come, and thy floods shall be broken within thee.

12 The ocean, unpassable to mankind, and the worlds that are beyond it, are governed by the same commands of their great master.

13 Spring and summer, autumn and winter, give place peaceably to each other.

14 The several [12] quarters of the winds fulfil their [13] work in their seasons, without offending one another.

15 The ever-flowing fountains, made both for pleasure and health, never fail to reach out their breasts to support the life of men.

16 Even the smallest creatures [14] live together in peace and concord with each other.

17 All these has the Great Creator and Lord of all, commanded to observe peace and concord; being good to all.

18 But especially to us who flee to his mercy through our Lord Jesus Christ ; to whom be glory and majesty for ever and ever. Amen.

CHAP. X.

He exhorts them to obedience, from the consideration of the goodness of God, and of his presence in every place.

TAKE heed, beloved, that his many blessings be not to [15] us to condemnation; except we shall walk worthy of him, doing with [16] one consent what is good and pleasing in his sight.

2 [17] The spirit of the Lord is a

---

[1] Deeds or works. [2] Let us return to the mark of peace given to us from the beginning. [3] See him with our understanding. [4] Soul. [5] Choruses.
[6] Bounds. [7] Doubting. [8] Vid. Edit. Colomes. p. 53. [9] Hollow, or depth.
[10] Commanded, so it does. [11] Job xxxiii. [12] Stations. [13] Survive. [14] Mix together. [15] All of us. [16] With concord. [17] Prov. xx. 27.

candle, searching out the inward parts of the belly.

3 Let us therefore consider how near he is to us ; and how that none of our thoughts, or reasonings which we frame within ourselves, are [1] hid from him.

4 It is therefore just that we should not forsake our rank, by doing contrary to his will.

5 Let us choose to offend a few foolish and inconsiderate men, lifted up and glorying [2] in their own pride, rather than God.

6 Let us reverence our Lord Jesus Christ whose blood was given for us.

7 Let us honour those who are set over us ; let us respect the aged that are amongst us ; and let us instruct the younger men, in the discipline and fear of the LORD.

8 Our wives let us [3] direct to do that which is good.

9 Let them show forth a lovely habit of purity in all their conversation ; with a sincere [4] affection of meekness.

10 Let the [5] government of their tongues [6] be made manifest by their silence.

11 Let their charity be without respect of persons alike towards all such as religiously fear God.

12 Let your children [7] be bred up in the instruction of Christ :

13 And especially let them learn how great a power humility has with God ; how much a pure and holy charity avails with him ; how excellent and great his fear is ; and how it will [8] save all such as turn to him with holiness in a pure mind.

14 For he is the searcher of the thoughts and counsels of the heart ; whose breath is in us, and when he pleases he can take it from us.

CHAP. XI.

Of faith, and particularly what we are to believe as to the resurrection.

BUT all these things [9] must be confirmed by the faith which is in Christ ; for so he himself bespeaks us by the Holy Ghost.

2 [10] Come ye children and hearken unto me, and I will teach you the fear of the Lord. What man is there that desireth life, and loveth to see good days ?

3 Keep thy tongue from evil, and thy lips that they speak no guile.

4 Depart from evil and do good ; seek peace and ensue it.

5 The eyes of the Lord are upon the righteous, and his ears are open unto their prayers.

6 But the face of the Lord is against them that do evil, to cut off the remembrance of them from the earth.

7 The righteous cried, and the Lord heard him, and delivered him out of all his troubles.

8 Many are the troubles of the wicked ; but they that trust in the Lord, mercy shall encompass them about.

9 Our all-merciful and beneficent Father hath bowels of compassion towards them that fear him ; and kindly and lovingly bestows his graces upon all such as come to him with a simple mind.

---

[1] That nothing is hid to him of our thoughts, or reasonings.   [2] In the pride of their own speech, or reason.   [3] Correct, or amend.   [4] Will, or counsel.   [5] Moderation.   [6] Let them manifest.   [7] Partake of.   [8] Saving.   [9] The faith confirms.   [10] Psalm xxiv. 11.

10 Wherefore let us not [1] waver, neither let us have any doubt in our hearts, of his excellent and glorious gifts.

11 [2] Let that be far from us which is written, [3] Miserable are the double-minded, and those who are doubtful in their hearts.

12 Who say these things have we heard, and our fathers have told us these things. But behold we are grown old, and none of them has happened unto us.

13 O ye fools! [4] consider the trees: take the vine for an example. First it sheds its leaves; then it buds; after that it spreads its leaves; then it flowers; then come the sour grapes; and after them follows the ripe fruit. Ye see how in a little time the fruit of the tree comes to maturity.

14 Of a truth, yet a little while and his will shall suddenly be accomplished.

15 The Holy Scripture itself bearing witness, That [5] He shall quickly come and not tarry, and that the Lord shall suddenly come to his temple, even the [6] holy ones whom ye look for.

16 Let us consider, beloved, how the Lord does continually shew us, that there shall be a future resurrection; of which he has made our Lord Jesus Christ the first fruits, raising him from the dead.

17 Let us [7] contemplate, beloved, the resurrection that is [8] continually made before our eyes.

18 Day and night manifest a resurrection to us. The night lies down, and the day arises: again the day departs, and the night comes on.

19 Let us behold the fruits of the earth. Every one sees how the seed is sown. The sower [9] goes forth, and casts it upon the earth; and the seed which when it was sown fell upon the earth dry and naked, in time dissolves.

20 And from the dissolution, the great power of the providence of the Lord raises it again; and of one seed many arise, and bring forth fruit.

CHAP. XII.
The Resurrection further proved.

LET us consider that wonderful [10] type of the resurrection which is seen in the Eastern countries; that is to say, in Arabia.

2 There is a certain bird called a Phœnix; of this there is never but one at a time: and that lives five hundred years. And when the time of its dissolution draws near, that it must die, it makes itself a nest of frankincense, and myrrh, and other spices into which when its time is fulfilled it enters and dies.

3 But its flesh putrifying, breeds a certain worm, which being nourished with the juice of the dead bird brings forth feathers; and when it is grown to a perfect state, it takes up the nest in which the bones of its parents lie, and carries it from Arabia into Egypt, to a city called Heliopolis:

4 And flying in open day in the sight of all men, lays it upon the altar of the sun, and so returns from whence it came.

5 The priests then search into the records of the time; and find that it returned precisely at the end of five hundred years.

---

[1] Be double-minded.   [2] Let the writing be far from us.   [3] James i. 8. [4] Compare yourselves unto a tree.   [5] Ex. MS. omitted by James, Hab. ii. 3; Malach. iii. 1.   [6] Coteler. Αγγελος Angel.   [7] See.   [8] Made every season. [9] Went forth, and so in the rest.   [10] Sign.

6 And [1]shall we then think it to be any very great and strange thing for the Lord of all to raise up those that religiously serve him in the assurance of a good faith, when even by a bird he shews us the greatness of his power to fulfil his promise?

7 For he says in a certain place, Thou shalt raise me up, and I shall confess unto thee.

8 And again [2]I laid me down and slept, and awaked, because thou art with me.

9 And again, Job says, [3]Thou shalt raise up this flesh of mine, that has suffered all these things.

10 Having therefore this hope, let us [4]hold fast to him who is faithful in all his promises, and righteous in all his judgments; who has commanded us not to lie: how much more will he not himself lie?

11 For nothing is impossible with God but to lie.

12 Let his faith then be stirred up again in us; and let us consider that all things are nigh unto him.

13 By the word of his [5]power he made all things; and by [6]the same word he is able (whenever he will), to destroy them.

14 Who shall say unto him, what dost thou? or who shall resist the power of his strength?[7]

15 When, and as he pleased,[8] he will do all things; and nothing shall pass away of all that has been determined by him.

16 All things are open before him; nor can anything be hid from his council.

17 [9]The heavens declare the glory of God, and the firmament sheweth his handy work. Day unto day uttereth speech, and night unto night sheweth knowledge. There is no speech nor language where their voice is not heard.

CHAP. XIII.

It is impossible to escape the vengeance of God, if we continue in sin.

SEEING then all things are seen and heard by God; let us fear him, and let us lay aside our wicked works which proceed from ill desires; that through his mercy we may be [10]delivered from the [11]condemnation to come.

2 For whither can any of us flee from his mighty hand? Or what world shall receive any of those who run away from him?

3 For thus saith the Scripture in a certain place, [12]Whither shall I flee from thy Spirit, or where shall I hide myself from thy presence?

4 If I ascend up into heaven, thou art there; if I shall go to the utmost part of the earth, there is thy right hand: If I shall make my bed in the deep, thy Spirit is there.

5 Whither then shall any one go; or whither shall he run from him that comprehends all things?

6 Let us therefore come to him with holiness of [13]heart, lifting up chaste and undefiled hands unto him; loving our gracious and merciful Father, who has made us [14]to partake of his election.

7 For so it is written, [15]When the Most High divided the nations, when he separated the sons of Adam, he set the bounds of the nations, according to the number of his angels; [16]his peo-

[1] Do. [2] Psalm iii. 5. [3] Job xix. 23. [4] Let our minds be fastened.
[5] Majesty. [6] His word. [7] Wisd. xii. 12. [8] MS. ποιησει. [9] If the, &c.,
Psalm xix. 1. [10] Covered. [11] Judgments. [12] Psalm cxxxix. 7. [13] Mind.
[14] A part. [15] Deut. xxxii. 8, 9. [16] So the LXX.

ple Jacob became the portion of the Lord, and Israel the lot of his inheritance.

8 And in another place he saith, [1] Behold the Lord taketh unto himself a nation, out of the midst of the nations, as a man taketh the first-fruits of his flower; [2] and the Most Holy shall come out of that nation.

CHAP. XIV.

How we must live that we may please God.

WHEREFORE we being a part of the Holy One, let us do all those things that pertain unto holiness:

2 Fleeing all evil-speaking against one another; all filthy and impure embraces, together with all drunkenness, youthful lusts, abominable concupiscences, detestable adultery, and execrable pride.

3 [3] For God, saith he, resisteth the proud, but giveth grace to the humble.

4 Let us therefore hold fast to those to whom [4] God has given His grace.

5 And let us put on concord, being humble, temperate; free from all whispering and detraction; and justified by our [5] actions, not our words.

6 For he saith, [6] Doth he that speaketh and heareth many things, and that is of a ready tongue, suppose that he is righteous? [7] Blessed is he that is born of a woman, that liveth but a few days: [8] use not therefore much speech.

7 Let our praise be of God, not of ourselves ; for God hateth those that [9] commend themselves.

8 Let the witness of our good actions be given to us of others, as it was given to the holy men that went before us.

9 Rashness, and arrogance, and confidence, belong to them who are accursed of God : but equity, and humility, and mildness, to such as are blessed by him.

10 Let us then lay hold of his blessing, and let us [10] consider what are the ways by which we may attain unto it.

11 Let us [11] look back upon those things that have happened from the beginning.

12 For what was our father Abraham blessed? Was it not because that through faith he wrought righteousness and truth?

13 Isaac being [12] fully persuaded of what he knew was to come, cheerfully yielded himself up for a sacrifice. Jacob with humility departed out of his own country, fleeing from his brother, and went unto Laban and served him ; and so the sceptre of the twelve tribes of Israel was given unto him.

14 Now what the greatness of [13] this Gift was, will plainly appear, if we shall take the pains distinctly to consider all the parts of it.

15 For from him came the priests and Levites, who all ministered at the altar of God.

16 From him came our Lord Jesus Christ according to the flesh.

17 From him came the kings, and princes, and rulers in Judah.

18 Nor were the rest of his

---

[1] Deut. iv. 34.   [2] Num. xxvii.   [3] Ja. iv. 9, 1 Pet. v. 5.   [4] The grace of God has been given.   [5] Works.   [6] He that speaketh many things shall also hear, &c.   [7] Job xi. 2, 3, lxx.   [8] Be not wordy.   [9] Are praised of.   [10] See what are the ways of his blessing.   [11] Unroll.   [12] Foreknowing what was to be, became a sacrifice.   [13] These gifts he shall know who will carefully consider them.

[1]tribes in any small glory: God having promised that [2] thy seed (says he) shall be as the stars of heaven.

19 They were all therefore [3] greatly glorified, not for their own sake, or for their own works, or for the righteousness that they themselves wrought, but through his will.

20 And we also being called by the same will in Christ Jesus, are not justified by ourselves, neither by our own wisdom, or knowledge, or piety, or the works which we have done [4] in the holiness of our hearts:

21 But by that faith by which God Almighty has justified all men from the beginning; to whom be glory for ever and ever. Amen.

CHAP. XV.

We are justified by faith; yet this must not lessen our care to live well, nor our pleasure in it.

WHAT shall we do therefore, brethren? Shall we be slothful in well-doing, and lay aside our charity? God forbid that any such thing should be done by us.

2 But rather let us hasten with all earnestness and readiness of mind, to perfect every good work. For even the Creator and Lord of all things himself rejoices in his own works.

3 By his [5] Almighty power he fixed the heavens, and by his incomprehensible wisdom he adorned them.

4 He also divided the earth from the water, with which it is encompassed; and fixed it as a secure tower, upon the foundation of his own will.

5 He also by his appointment,

commanded all the living creatures that are upon it, to exist.

6 So likewise the sea, and all the creatures that are in it; having first created them, he enclosed them therein by his power.

7 And above all, he with his holy and pure hands, formed man, the most excellent, and, as to his understanding, truly the greatest of all other creatures, the character of his own image.

8 For so God says, [6] Let us make man in our image, after our own likeness So God created man, male and female created he them.

9 And having thus finished all these things, he commended all that he had made, and blessed them, and said, [7] increase and multiply.

10 We see how all righteous men have been adorned with good works: Wherefore even the Lord himself, having adorned himself with his works, rejoiced.

11 Having therefore [8] such an example, let us without delay, [9]fulfil his will; and with all our strength, work the work of righteousness.

CHAP. XVI.

This enforced from the examples of the holy angels, and from the exceeding greatness of that reward which God has prepared for us.

THE good workman with confidence receives the bread of his [10] labour; but the sluggish and lazy cannot look him in the face that set him on work.

2 We must therefore be ready and forward in well doing; for from him are all things.

3 And thus he foretells us, [11] behold the Lord cometh, and

---

[1] Sceptres.　[2] Gen. xxvii. 17.　[3] Glorified.　[4] In holiness of heart.　[5] All-greatest.　[6] Gen. i. 26, 27.　[7] Gen. i. 28.　[8] This.　[9] Come to.　[10] Work-[11] Isaiah xl. 10, lxii. 11.

his reward is with him, even before his face, to render to every one according to his work.

4 He warns us therefore beforehand, with all his heart to this end, that we should not be slothful and negligent in [1] well doing.

5 Let our boasting, therefore, and our confidence be in [2] God: let us submit ourselves to his will. Let us consider the whole multitude of his angels, how ready they stand to minister unto his will.

6 As saith the scripture, [3]thousands of thousands stood before him and ten thousand times ten thousand ministered unto him. [4] And they cried, saying, Holy, holy, holy is the Lord of Sabaoth : [5] The whole earth is full of his glory.

7 Wherefore let us also, being conscientiously gathered together in concord with one another; as it were with one mouth, cry earnestly unto him, that he would make us partakers of his great and glorious promises.

8 For he saith, [6] Eye hath not seen, nor ear heard, neither have entered into the heart of man, the things which God has prepared for them that wait for him.

CHAP. XVII.

1 We must attain unto this reward by faith and obedience, which we must carry on in an orderly pursuing of the duties of our several stations, without envy or contention. 24 The necessity of different orders among men. 33 We have none of us anything but what we received of God: whom therefore we ought in every condition thankfully to obey.

HOW blessed and wonderful, beloved, are the gifts of God.

2 Life in immortality! brightness in righteousness! truth in full assurance! faith in confidence! temperance in holiness!

3 And all this has [7] God subjected to our understandings :

4 What therefore shall those things be which he has prepared for them that wait for him?

5 The Creator and Father of [8] spirits, the Most Holy ; he only knows both the [9] greatness and beauty of them.

6 Let us therefore strive with all earnestness, that we may be found in the number of those that wait for him, that so we may receive the [10] reward which he has promised.

7 But how, beloved, shall we do this? [11] We must fix our minds by faith towards God, and seek those things that are pleasing and acceptable unto him.

8 We must [12] act conformably to his holy will ; and follow the way of truth, casting off from us all unrighteousness and iniquity, together with all covetousness, strife, evil manners, deceit, whispering, detractions ; all hatred of God, pride and boasting ; vainglory and ambition ;

9 For they that do these things are odious to God ; and not only they that do them, but also [13] all such as approve of those that do them.

10 For thus saith the Scripture, [14] But unto the wicked, God said, What hast thou to do to declare my statute, or that thou shouldst take my covenant in thy mouth? Seeing that thou hatest instruction, and castest my words behind thee.

11 When thou sawest a thief, then thou consentedst with him ; and hast been partaker with adul-

---

[1] Every good work.　[2] Him.　[3] Dan. vii. 10.　[4] Isaiah vi. 3.　[5] Every creature.　[6] Isaiah lxiv. 4, 1 Cor. ii. 9.　[7] He.　[8] Ages.　[9] Quantity.　[10] Gifts. [11] If we shall.　[12] Perform those things that are agreeable.　[13] Rom. i. 32. [14] Psalm l. 15, &c., ac. to the Hebrew.

CHRIST IN THE PRÆTORIUM AND MOCKED, AND HIS DESCENT INTO HELL.

FROM INTAGLIOS IN A BOX OF ROCK CRYSTAL. BY AN EARLY VENETIAN ARTIST.

terers. Thou givest thy mouth to evil, and thy tongue frameth deceit. Thou sittest and speakest against thy brother; thou slanderest thine own mother's son.

12 These things hast thou done and I kept silence; thou thoughtest that I was altogether such a one as thyself: but I will reprove thee, and set them in order before thine eyes.

13 Now consider this ye that forget God, lest I tear you in pieces, and there be none to deliver.

14 Whoso offereth praise, glorifieth me: and to him that disposeth his way aright, will I shew the salvation of God.

15 This is the way, beloved, in which we may find [1]our Saviour, even Jesus Christ the high-priest of all our offerings, the defender and helper of our weakness.

16 By him we look up to the[2] highest heavens; and behold, as in a glass, his spotless and most excellent visage.

17 By him are the eyes of our hearts opened; by him our foolish and darkened understanding rejoiceth to behold his wonderful light.

18 By him would God have us to taste the knowledge of immortality: [3]who being the brightness of his glory, is by so much greater than the angels, as he has by inheritance obtained a more excellent name than they.

19 For so it is written, [4] who maketh his angels spirits, and his ministers a flame of fire:

20 But to his son, thus saith the Lord, [5]Thou art my Son, today have I begotten thee.

21 [6]Ask of me, and I will give thee the heathen for thy inheritance, and the utmost parts of the earth for thy possession.

22 And again he saith unto him, [7]Sit thou on my right hand until I make thine enemies my footstool.

23 But who are his enemies? even the wicked, and such who oppose their own wills to the will of God.

24 Let us therefore [8]march on, men and brethren, with all earnestness in his holy laws.

25 Let us consider those who fight under our earthly governors: How orderly, how readily, and with what exact obedience they perform those things that are commanded them.

26 All are not [9]generals, nor [10]colonels, nor [11]captains, nor [12]inferior officers:

27 But every one in his respective rank does what is commanded him by the king, and those who have the authority over him.

28 They who are great, cannot subsist without those that are little; nor the little without the great.

29 But there must be a mixture in all things, and then there will be use and profit too.

30 Let us, [13]for example, take our body: the head without the feet is nothing, neither the feet without the head.

31 And even the smallest members of our body are yet both necessary and useful to the whole body.

32 But all conspire together, and [14] are subject to one common

---

[1] That which has the power to save us. [2] Heights of heaven. [3] Heb. i. 3, 4.
[4] Psalm cix. 4. Heb. i. 7. [5] Heb. i. 5. [6] Comp. Psalm ii. 7, 8. [7] Heb. i. 13,
Psalm cv. 1. [8] War. [9] Prefects. [10] Commanders of a thousand. [11] Centurions. [12] Commanders of 50, and so on. [13] 1 Cor. xii. 13, 21. [14] Use one common subjection.

use, namely, the preservation of the whole [1] body.

33 Let therefore our whole body be saved in Christ Jesus; and let every one be subject to his neighbour, [2] according to the order in which he is placed .by the [3] gift of God.

34 Let not the strong man despise the weak; and let the weak see that he reverence the strong.

35 Let the rich man distribute to the necessity of the poor: and let the poor bless God, that he has given one unto him, by whom his want may be supplied.

36 Let the wise man shew forth his wisdom, not in words, but in good works.

37 Let him that is humble, not bear witness to himself, but let him leave it to another to bear witness of him.

38 Let him that is pure in the flesh, not grow proud of it, knowing that it was [4] from another that he received the gift of continence.

39 Let us consider therefore, brethren, [5] whereof we are made; who, and what kind of men we came into the world, as it were out of a sepulchre, and from outer darkness.

40 He that made us, and formed us, brought us into his own world; having [6] presented us with his benefits, even before we were born.

41 Wherefore, having received all these things from him, we ought in everything to give thanks unto him; to whom be glory for ever and ever. Amen.

CHAP. XVIII.

From whence he exhorts them to do everything orderly in the Church, as the only way to please God.

FOOLISH and unwise men [7] who have neither prudence nor learning may mock and deride us; being willing to set up themselves in their own conceits;

2 [8] But what can a mortal man do? Or what strength is there in him that is made out of the dust?

3 For it is written, there was no shape before mine eyes; only I heard a [9] sound and a voice.

4 [10] For what? Shall man be pure before the Lord? Shall he be blameless in his works?

5 Behold, he trusteth not in his servants; and his angels he chargeth with folly.

6 Yes, the heaven is not clean in his sight, how much less they that dwell in houses of clay; of which also we ourselves were made?

7 He smote them as a moth: and from morning even unto the evening they endure not. Because they were not able to help themselves, they perished; he breathed upon them and they died, because they had no wisdom.

8 [11] Call now if there be any that will answer thee; and to which of the angels wilt thou look?

9 For wrath killeth the foolish man, and envy slayeth him that is in error.

10 I have seen the foolish taking root, but lo, their habitation was presently consumed.

11 Their children were far from safety, they [12] perished at the gates of those who were lesser than themselves; and there was no man to [13] help them.

12 For what was prepared for them, the righteous [14] did eat: and they shall not be delivered from evil.

---

[1] MS. το σωα.   [2] As also has he placed.   [3] His gift.   [4] Another that gave him.   [5] Of what matter.   [6] Prepared for us.   [7] And impudent, and without instruction.   [8] For.   [9] An air.   [10] John iv. 16. &c., xv. 15, iv. 19.   [11] Job v. 1, &c.   [12] Were crushed upon.   [13] Deliver.   [14] Eat.

13 Seeing then these things are manifest unto us, it will behoove us, to take care that looking into the depths of the divine knowledge, we do all things in order, whatsoever our Lord has commanded us to do.

14 And particularly, that we perform our offerings and service to God, at their appointed seasons: for these he has commanded to be done, not [1]rashly and disorderly, but at certain determinate times and hours.

15 And therefore he has ordained by his supreme will and authority, both where, and by what persons, they are to be performed; that so all things being piously done unto all well-pleasing, they may be acceptable unto [2]him.

16 They therefore who make their offerings at the appointed seasons, are happy and accepted: because that obeying the commandments of the Lord, they are free from sin.

17 And the same care must be had of the persons that minister unto him.

18 [3]For the chief-priest has his proper services; and to the priests their proper place is appointed; and to the Levites appertain their proper ministries: and the layman is confined within the bounds of what is commanded to laymen.

19 Let every one of you therefore, brethren, bless God in his proper station, with [4]a good conscience, and with all gravity, not exceeding the rule of his service that is appointed to him.

20 The daily sacrifices are not offered everywhere; nor the peace-offerings, nor the sacrifices appointed for sins and transgressions; but only at Jerusalem: nor in any place there, but only at the altar before the temple; that which is offered being first diligently examined by the high-priest and the other minister we before mentioned.

21 They therefore who do anything which is not agreeable to His will are punished with death.

22 [5]Consider, brethren, that by how much the better knowledge God has vouchsafed unto us by so much the greater danger are we exposed to.

CHAP. XIX.

The orders of Ministers in Christ's Church established by the Apostles according to Christ's command, 7 after the example of Moses. 16 Therefore they who have been duly placed in the ministry according to their order cannot without great sin be put out of it.

THE Apostles have preached to us from the Lord Jesus Christ; Jesus Christ from God.

2 Christ therefore was sent by God, the Apostles by Christ; so both were orderly [6]sent, according to the will of God.

3 For having received their command, and being thoroughly assured by the resurrection of our Lord Jesus Christ; [7]and convinced by the word of God, with the [8]fulness of the Holy Spirit, they went abroad, publishing, That the kingdom of God was at hand.

4 And thus preaching through countries and cities, [9]they appointed the first fruits of their conversion to be bishops and ministers over such as should afterwards believe, having first proved them by the Spirit.

5 Nor was this any new thing:

---

[1] By chance.   [2] To his will.   [3] See Coteler. in loc.   [4] Being in a good conscience.   [5] Ye see.   [6] Done.   [7] 1 Thess. i. 5.   [8] With the full assurance.   [9] Vid. Coteler. in loc.

131

seeing that long before it was written concerning bishops and deacons.

6 For thus saith the Scripture, in a certain place: [1] I will appoint their [2] overseers in righteousness, and their ministers in faith.

7 And what wonder if they, to whom such a work was committed by God in Christ, established such officers as we before mentioned; when even that blessed and faithful servant in all his house, Moses, [3] set down in the Holy Scriptures all things that were commanded him.

8 Whom also all the rest of the prophets followed, bearing witness with one consent to those things that were appointed by him.

9 For he, perceiving an [4] emulation to arise among the tribes concerning the priesthood, and that there was a strife about it, which of them should be adorned with that glorious name; commanded their twelve captains to bring to him [5] twelve rods; every tribe being written upon its rod, according to its name.

10 And he took them and bound them together, and sealed them with the seals of the twelve princes of the tribes; and laid them up in the tabernacle of witness, upon the table of God.

11 And when he had shut the door of the tabernacle he sealed up the keys of it, in like manner [6] as he had done the rods; and said unto them, Men and brethren, whichsoever tribe shall have its rod blossom, that

tribe has God chosen to perform the office of a priest, and [7] to minister unto him in holy things.

12 And when the morning was come, he called together all Israel, six hundred thousand men; and shewed to the princes their seals; and opened the tabernacle of witness; and brought forth the rods.

13 And the rod of Aaron was found not only to have blossomed, but also to have fruit upon it.

14 What think you, beloved? Did not Moses before know [8] what should happen?

15 Yes verily: but to the end there might be no division, nor tumult in Israel, he did in this manner, that the name of the true and only God might be glorified, to him be honour for ever and ever, Amen.

16 So likewise our Apostles knew by our Lord Jesus Christ, that there should contentions arise, [9] upon account of the ministry.

17 And therefore having a perfect fore-knowledge of this, they appointed persons, as we have before said, and then [10] gave direction, how, when they should die, other chosen and approved men should succeed in their ministry.

18 Wherefore we cannot think that those may justly be thrown out of their ministry, who were either appointed by them, or afterwards chosen by other eminent men, with the consent of the whole church; and who have with all lowliness and in-

---

[1] Isaiah lx. 17.   [2] Bishops, Deacons.   [3] Signified.   [4] An emulation happening.   [5] Numb. xvii.   [6] And the Rods.   [7] To exercise the office of the priesthood, and to minister, &c.   [8] That this should be so.   [9] About the name of the bishoprick.   [10] Left a list of other chosen and approved persons, who should succeed them in their ministry. See Dr. Arden's Disc. upon this passage.   Dr. Hammond's Power of the Keys, c. iii. p. 413.

nocency ministered to the flock of Christ, in peace, and without self-interest, and were for a long time commended by all.

19 For it would be no small sin in us, should we cast off those from their [1] ministry who holily and without blame [2] fulfil the duties of it.

20 Blessed are those priests, who having finished their course before these times have obtained a fruitful and perfect dissolution: for they have no fear, lest any one should turn them out of the place which is now appointed for them.

21 But we see how you have put out some, who lived reputably among you, from the ministry, which by their innocence they had adorned.

CHAP. XX.

He exhorts them to peace from examples out of the Holy Scriptures, 20 particularly from St. Paul's exhortation to them.

YE are contentious, brethren, and zealous for things that pertain not unto salvation.

2 Look into the Holy Scriptures, which are the true words of the Holy Ghost. Ye know that there is nothing unjust or counterfeit written in them.

3 There you shall not find that righteous men were ever cast off by such as were good themselves.

4 [3] They were persecuted, but it was by the wicked and unjust.

5 They were cast into prison; but they were cast in by those that were unholy.

6 They were stoned; but it was by transgressors.

7 They were killed; but by accursed men, and such as had taken up an unjust envy against them.

8 [4] And all these things they underwent gloriously.

9 For what shall we say, brethren? Was Daniel cast into the [5] den of lions, by men fearing God? Ananias, Azarius, and Misael, were they [6] cast into the [7] fiery furnace by men, [8] professing the excellent and glorious worship of the Most High? God forbid.

10 What kind of persons then were they that did these things? They were men abominable, full of all wickedness; who were incensed to so great a degree, as to bring those into sufferings, who with a holy and unblameable purpose of mind worshipped God: not knowing that the Most High is the protector and defender of all such as with a pure conscience serve his [9] holy name: to whom be glory for ever and ever, Amen.

11 But they who with a full persuasion have endured these things, [10] are made partakers of glory and honour: and [11] are exalted and lifted up by God in their memorial throughout all ages, Amen.

12 ¶ Wherefore it will behoove us also, brethren, [12] to follow such examples as these; for it is written, Hold fast to such as are holy; for they that do so shall be sanctified.

13 And again in another place he saith, [13] With the pure thou shalt be pure, ([14] and with the elect thou shalt be elect),

---

[1] Bishoprick. [2] Offer the gifts. [3] Just men. [4] Suffering these things they underwent them gloriously. [5] Dan. vi. 16. [6] Shut into. [7] Dan. iii. 20. [8] Worshipping the worship. [9] Full of virtue. [10] Have inherited. [11] Have been exalted. [12] To cleave to. [13] Psalm xvii. 2. [14] Omitted by Junius, and now restored from the MS.

but with the perverse man thou shalt be [1] perverse.

14 Let us therefore join ourselves to the innocent and righteous; for such are the elect of God.

15 Wherefore are there strifes, and anger, and divisions, and schisms, and wars, among us?

16 [2] Have we not all one God, and one Christ? [3] Is not one spirit of grace poured out upon us all? Have we not one calling in Christ?

17 Why then do we rend and tear in pieces the members of Christ; and raise seditions against our own body? And are come to such a height of madness, as to forget that [4] we were members one of another?

18 Remember the words of our Lord Jesus, [5] how he said, Wo to that man, (by whom offences come) [6] It were better for him that he had never been born, than that he should have offended one of my elect. It were better for him, that a millstone should be tied about his neck, and he should be cast into the sea, than that he should offend one of my little ones.

19 Your schism has perverted many, has discouraged many: it has caused diffidence in many, and grief in us all. And yet your sedition continues still.

20 ¶ Take the epistle of the blessed Paul the Apostle into your hands; [7] What was it that he wrote to you at his first preaching the Gospel among you?

21 Verily he did [8] by the spirit admonish you concerning himself, and Cephas, and Apollos, because that even then ye had begun to fall into [9] parties and factions among yourselves.

22 Nevertheless your partiality then led you into a much less sin: forasmuch as ye [10] placed your affections upon Apostles, men of [11] eminent reputation in the church; and upon another, who was greatly tried and approved of by them.

23 But consider, we pray you, who are they that have now led you astray; and lessened the [12] reputation of that brotherly love that was [13] so eminent among you?

24 It is a shame, my beloved, yea, a very great shame, and unworthy of your Christian [14] profession, to hear that the most firm and [15] ancient church of the Corinthians should, by one or two persons, be led into a sedition against its priests.

25 And this report is come not only to us, but to those also that differ from us.

26 Insomuch that the name of the Lord is blasphemed through your folly; and even ye yourselves are brought into danger by it.

27 ¶ Let us therefore with all haste [16] put an end to this sedition; and let us fall down before the Lord, and beseech Him with tears that He [17] would be favourably reconciled to us, and restore us again to a [18] seemly and holy course of brotherly love.

28 For this is the gate of righteousness, opening unto life: as it is written, [19] Open unto me

---

[1] Turn aside.   [2] Eph. iv. 4.   [3] 1 Cor. xii.   [4] Rom. xii.   [5] For he said.   [6] Luke, xvii. 2.   [7] See Dodwell's add. and Pearson, Dr. Grabe, &c.   [8] Spiritually send to you.   [9] Inclinations.   [10] Inclined.   [11] Witnessed of.   [12] Gravity.   [13] So much spoken of.   [14] Institution.   [15] See Dodwell.   [16] Take away.   [17] Becoming favourable.   [18] Grave, venerable.   [19] Psalm cxviii. 19, 20.

the gates of righteousness; I will go in unto them and will praise the Lord. This is the gate of the Lord, the righteous shall enter into it.

29 Although therefore many gates are opened, yet this gate of righteousness is that gate in Christ at which blessed are they that enter in, and direct their way in holiness and righteousness, doing all things without disorder.

30 Let a man be faithful, let him be powerful in the utterance of knowledge: let him be wise in making an exact judgment of words; let him be pure in all his actions.

31 But still by how much the more he seems to be [1] above others by reason of these things, by so much the more will it behoove him to be humble-minded; and to seek what is profitable to all men, and not his own advantage.

CHAP. XXI.

1 *The value which God puts upon love and unity : the effects of a true charity, 8 which is the gift of God, and must be obtained by prayer.*

HE that has the love that is in Christ, let him keep the commandments of Christ.

2 For who is able to express the [2] obligation of the love of God? What man is sufficient to declare, and is fitting, the excellency of its beauty?

3 The height to which charity leads is inexpressible.

4 Charity [3] unites us to God; [4] charity covers the multitude of sins: [5] charity endures all things, is long-suffering in all things.

5 There is nothing base and sordid in charity; charity lifts not itself up above others; admits of no divisions; is not seditious; but does all things in peace and concord.

6 By charity were all the elect of God made perfect: Without it nothing is pleasing and acceptable in the sight of God.

7 Through charity did the Lord [6] join us unto himself; whilst for the love that he bore towards us, our Lord Jesus Christ gave his own blood for us, by the will of God; his flesh for our flesh; his soul, for our souls.

8 ¶ Ye see, beloved, how great and wonderful a thing charity is : and how that no expressions are sufficient to declare its perfection.

9 But who is fit to be found in it? Even such only as God shall vouchsafe to make so.

10 Let us therefore pray to him, and beseech him, that we may be worthy of it; that so we may live in charity; being unblamable, without human propensities, without respect of persons.

11 All the ages of the world, from Adam, even unto this day, are passed away; but they who have been made perfect in love, have by the grace of God obtained a place among the righteous; and shall be made manifest in the [7] judgment of the kingdom of Christ.

12 For it is written, [8] Enter into thy chambers for a little space, till my anger and indignation shall pass away : And I will remember the good day, and will raise you up out of your graves.

13 Happy [9] then shall we be, beloved, if we shall have fulfilled the commandments of God, in the unity of love; that so, through love, our sins may be forgiven us.

---

[1] Greater. [2] Bond. [3] Glues. [4] 1 Peter iv. 9. [5] 1 Cor. xiii. 7, &c. [6] Take us up. [7] Animadversion, or visitation. [8] Isaiah xxvi. 20. [9] Are we.

14 For so it is written, [1] Blessed are they whose iniquities are forgiven, and whose sins are covered. Blessed is the man to whom the Lord imputeth no sin, and in whose mouth there is no guile.

15 Now this blessing is fulfilled in those who are chosen by God through Jesus Christ our Lord, to whom be glory for ever and ever. Amen.

CHAP. XXII.

1 *He exhorts such as have been concerned in these divisions to repent, and return to their unity, confessing their sin to God, 7 which he enforces from the example of Moses, 10 and of many among the heathen, 23 and of Judith and Esther among the Jews.*

LET us therefore, as many as have transgressed by any of the [2] suggestions of the adversary, beg God's forgiveness.

2 And as for those who have been the [3] heads of the sedition and faction among you, [4] let them look to the common end of our hope.

3 For as many as are [5] endued with fear and charity, would rather they themselves should fall into trials than their neighbours: And choose to be themselves condemned, rather than that the good and just charity delivered to us, should suffer.

4 For it is seemly for a man to confess wherein he has transgressed.

5 [6] And not to harden his heart, as the hearts of those were hardened, who raised up sedition against Moses the servant of God; whose punishment was manifest [7] unto all men; for they went down alive into the grave, death swallowed them up.

6 [8] Pharaoh and his host, and all the rulers of Egypt, their chariots also and their horsemen, were for no other cause drowned, in the bottom of the Red Sea, and perished; but because they hardened their foolish hearts, after so many signs done in the land of Egypt, by Moses the servant of God.

7 ¶ Beloved, God is not indigent of any thing; nor does he demand any thing of us, but that we should confess our sins unto him.

8 For so says the [9] Holy David, [10] I will confess unto the Lord, and it shall please him better than a young bullock that hath horns and hoof. Let the poor see it and be glad.

9 And again he saith, [11] Offer unto God the sacrifice of praise, and pay thy vows unto the Most Highest. And call upon me in the day of trouble, and I will deliver thee, and thou shalt glorify me. [12] The sacrifice of God is a broken spirit.

10 ¶ Ye know, beloved, ye know full well the Holy Scriptures; and have thoroughly searched into the oracles of God: call them therefore to your remembrance.

11 For when Moses went up into the mount, and tarried there forty days and forty nights in fasting and humiliation; God said unto him, [13] Arise, Moses, and get thee down quickly from hence, for thy people whom thou broughtest out of the land of Egypt, have committed wicked-

---

[1] Psalm xxxii.　[2] See Junius in loc.　[3] Chief leaders.　[4] They ought.　[5] Walking according to; live in.　[6] Rather than.　[7] Num. xvi.　[8] Exod. iv.　[9] Chosen.　[10] Psalm lxix. 31.　[11] Psalm l. 14.　[12] Psalm li. 17.　[13] Exod. xxxii. Deut. ix.

THE RED SEA SWALLOWING UP THE ARMY OF PHARAOH, AFTER THE ISRAELITES HAD PASSED THROUGH.

FROM A FRAGMENT OF THE BIBLE, IN GREEK MANUSCRIPT, OF THE FOURTEENTH CENTURY.

ness: they have soon transgressed the way that I commanded them, and have made to themselves graven images.

12 And the Lord said unto him, I have spoken unto thee [1] several times, saying I have seen this people, and behold it is a stiffnecked people: let me therefore destroy them, and put out their name from under heaven. And I will make unto thee a great and a wonderful nation, that shall be much [2] larger than this.

13 But Moses said, Not so, Lord; Forgive now this people their sin; or if thou wilt not, blot me also out of the book of the living. O admirable charity! O insuperable perfection! The servant speaks freely to his Lord; He beseeches him either to forgive the people, or to [3] destroy him together with them.

14 ¶ Who is there among you that is generous? Who that is compassionate? Who that has any charity? Let him say, if this sedition, this contention, and these schisms, be upon my account, I am ready to depart; to go away whithersoever you please; and do whatsoever [4] ye shall command me: Only let the flock of Christ be in peace, with the elders that are set over it.

15 He that shall do this, shall get to himself a very great honour in the Lord; and [5] there is no place but what will be ready to receive him: [6] For the earth is the Lord's and the fulness thereof.

16 These things they who have their conversation towards God

not to be repented of, both have done and will always be ready to do.

17 ¶ [7] Nay and even the Gentiles themselves have given us examples of this kind.

18 For we read, How many kings and princes, in times of pestilence, being warned by their oracles, have given up themselves unto death: that by their own blood, they might deliver their [8] country from destruction.

19 [9] Others have forsaken their cities, so that they might put an end to the seditions of them.

20 We know how many among ourselves, have given up themselves unto bonds, that thereby they might free others from them.

21 Others have sold themselves into bondage that they might feed [10] their brethren with the price of themselves.

22 And even many women, being strengthened by the grace of God, have done many glorious and manly things on such occasions.

23 The blessed [11] Judith, when her city was besieged, desired the elders, that they would suffer her to go into the camp of [12] their enemies: and she went out exposing herself to danger for the love she bore to her country and her people that were besieged; and the Lord delivered Holofernes into the hands of a woman.

24 Nor did [13] Esther, being perfect in faith, expose herself to any less hazard, for the delivery of the twelve tribes of Israel, in danger of being destroyed. For, by fasting and humbling herself, she entreated the Great Maker

---

[1] Once and twice.   [2] More, greater.   [3] Blot out.   [4] The multitude.
[5] Every place.   [6] Psalm xxiv.   [7] But that we may bring the examples of heathens.   [8] Citizens.   [9] Many   [10] Others.   [11] Judith, viii. ix. x. xiii.
[12] The strangers.   [13] Esther, vii. viii.

of all things, the God of [1] spirits; so that beholding the humility of her soul, he delivered the people, for whose sake she was in peril.

CHAP. XXIII.

The benefit of mutual advice and correction. He entreats them to follow that which is here given to them.

WHEREFORE let us also pray for such as are fallen into [2] sin. That being endued with humility and moderation, they may submit not unto us, but to the will of God.

2 For by this means [3] they shall obtain a fruitful and perfect remembrance, with mercy, both in our prayers to God, and in our mention of them before his [4] saints.

3 Let us receive correction, at which no man ought to repine.

4 Beloved, the reproof and the correction which we exercise towards one another, is good, and exceeding profitable: for it unites us the more closely to the will of God.

5 For so says the Holy Scripture, [5] The Lord corrected me, but he did not deliver me over unto death. [6] For whom the Lord loveth he chasteneth, and scourgeth every son whom he receiveth.

6 [7] The righteous, saith he, shall instruct me in mercy and reprove me; but let not oil of sinners make fat my head.

7 And again he saith, [8] Happy is the man whom God correcteth; therefore despise not thou the chastening of the Almighty.

8 For he maketh sore and bindeth up; he woundeth and his hands make whole.

9 He shall deliver thee in six troubles; yea in seven there shall no evil touch thee. In famine he shall redeem thee from death; and in war from the power of the sword.

10 Thou shalt be hid from the scourge of the tongue; neither shalt thou be afraid of destruction when it cometh.

11 Thou shalt laugh at the wicked and sinners; neither shalt thou be afraid of the beasts of the earth. The wild beast shall be at peace with thee.

12 Then shalt thou know that thy house shall be in peace; and the habitation of thy tabernacle shall not err. Thou shalt know also that thy seed shall be great and thy offspring as the grass of the earth.

13 Thou shalt come to thy grave as the ripe corn, that is taken in due time; like as a shock of corn cometh in, in its season.

14 Ye see, beloved, how there shall be a defence to those that are corrected of the Lord. For being a good instructor, he is willing to admonish us by his holy discipline.

15 Do ye therefore who laid the first foundation of this sedition, submit yourselves unto your [9] priests; and be instructed unto repentance, bending the knees of your hearts.

16 Learn to be subject, laying aside all proud and arrogant boasting of your tongues.

17 For it is better for you to be found little, and approved, in the [10] sheepfold of Christ, than to seem to yourselves better than others, and be cast out of his [11] fold.

18 For thus speaks the excellent and all virtuous wisdom,

---

[1] Ages; who.   [2] Viz. that of schism. Fellow-Christians.   [5] Psalm xcviii.   [3] There shall be to them.   [4] i. e. our   [6] Prov. iii. 11.   [7] Psalm cxli. 5.
[8] Job v. 17, &c.   [9] Elders.   [10] See Junius in loc.   [11] See Coteler in loc.

[1] Behold I will pour out the word of my spirit upon you, I will make known my speech unto you.

19 Because I called and ye would not hear, I stretched out my words and ye regarded not.

20 But ye have set at nought all my counsel, and would none of my reproof. I will also laugh at your calamity, and mock when your fear cometh.

21 When your fear cometh as desolation, and your destruction as a whirlwind, when distress and anguish cometh upon you.

22 Then shall ye call upon me, but I will not hear you: the wicked shall seek me, but they shall not find me. For that they hated knowledge, and did not seek the fear of the Lord.

23 They would not hearken unto my counsel: they despised all my reproof. Therefore shall they eat of the fruit of their own ways; and be filled with their own wickedness.

*   *   *

CHAP. XXIV.

1 Recommends them to God. Desires speedily to hear that this Epistle has had a good effect upon them. 4 Conclusion.

NOW God, the inspector of all things, the [2] Father of Spirits, and the Lord of all flesh, who hath chosen our Lord Jesus Christ, and us by him, to be his peculiar people;

2 Grant to every soul of man that calleth upon his glorious and holy name, faith, fear, peace, long-suffering, patience, temperance, holiness and sobriety, unto all well-pleasing [3] in his sight; through our High-Priest and Protector Jesus Christ, by whom be glory, and majesty, and power, and honour, unto him now and for ever more. Amen.

3 ¶ The messengers whom we have sent unto you, Claudius, Ephebus, and Valerios Bito, with Fortunatus, send back to us again with all speed in peace, and with joy, that they may the sooner acquaint us with your peace and concord, so much prayed for and desired by us; and that we may rejoice in your good order.

4 The Grace of our Lord Jesus Christ be with you, and with all that are anywhere called by God through him: To whom be honour and glory, and might and majesty, and eternal dominion, by [4] Christ Jesus, from everlasting to everlasting. Amen.

The SECOND EPISTLE of CLEMENT to the CORINTHIANS.

[Archbishop Wake is the translator of this Second Epistle, which he says was not of so great reputation among the primitive Fathers as the first. He defends it notwithstanding; and in answer to those who objected to Clement's First Epistle, that it did not duly honour the Trinity, the Archbishop refers to this as containing proof of the writer's fulness of belief on that point.]

CHAP. I.

That we ought to value our salvation; and to shew that we do, by a sincere obedience.

BRETHREN, we ought so to think of Jesus Christ as of God: as of the judge of the living, and the dead; nor should we think any less of our salvation.

2 For if we think [5] meanly of him, we shall hope only to re-

[1] Prov. i. 23, &c.   [2] Master.   [3] To his name.   [4] Him.   [5] Little things, or meanly.

ceive some small things from him.

3 And if we [1] do so; we shall sin; not [2] considering from whence we have been called, and by whom, and to what place; and how much Jesus Christ vouchsafed to suffer for our sakes.

4 What recompense then shall we render unto him? Or what fruit that may be worthy of what he has given to us?

5 For indeed [3] how great are those advantages which we owe to him in relation to our holiness? He has illuminated us: as a father, he has called us his children; he has saved us who were lost and undone.

6 What praise shall we give to him? Or what reward that may be answerable to those things which we have received?

7 We were defective in our understandings; worshipping stones and wood; gold, and silver, and brass, the works of men's hands; and our whole life was nothing else but death.

8 Wherefore being encompassed with darkness, and having such a mist before our eyes, we have looked up, and through his will have laid aside the cloud wherewith we were surrounded.

9 For he had compassion upon us, and being moved in his bowels towards us, he saved us; having beheld in us much error, and destruction; and seen that we had no hope of salvation, but only through him.

10 For he called us who were not; and was pleased from nothing to give us being.

CHAP. II.

1 *That God had before prophesied by Isaiah, that the Gentiles should be saved.* 8 *That this ought to engage such especially to live well; without which they will still miscarry.*

REJOICE, thou barren, that bearest not, break forth and cry thou that travailest not; for she that is desolate hath many more children than she that hath an husband.[4]

2 In that he said, Rejoice thou barren that bearest not, he spake of us: for our church was barren before that children were given unto it.

3 And again; when he said, Cry thou that travailest not; he implied thus much: That after the manner of women in travail, we should not cease to put up our prayers unto God [5] abundantly.

4 And for what follows, because she that is desolate hath more children than she that hath an husband: it was therefore added, because our people which seem to have been forsaken by God, now believing in him, are become more than they who seemed to have God.

5 And another Scripture saith, [6] I came not to call the righteous but sinners (to repentance). The meaning of which is this: that those who were lost must be saved.

6 For that is, indeed, truly great and wonderful, not to confirm those things that are yet standing, but those which are falling.

7 Even so did it seem good to Christ to save what was lost; and when he came into the

---

[1] Hear as of little things. [2] Knowing. [3] How greatly holy things do we owe unto him. [4] Isaiah liv. 1. [5] Ἁπλῶς. See St. James i. 5. Compare Rom. xii. 8. 2 Cor. viii. 2, ix. 11, 13. [6] Matt. ix. 13.

world, he saved many, and called us who were already lost.

8 Seeing then he has shewed so great mercy towards us; and chiefly for that, we who are alive, do now no longer sacrifice to dead Gods, nor pay any worship to them, but have by him been brought to the knowledge of the Father of truth.

9 [1] Whereby shall we shew that we do indeed know him, but by not denying him by whom we have come to the knowledge of him?

10 For even he himself saith, [2] Whosoever shall confess me before men, him will I confess before my Father. This therefore is our reward if we shall confess him by whom we have been saved.

11 But, wherein must we confess him?—Namely, in doing those things which he saith, and not disobeying his commandments: by worshipping him not with our lips only, but with all our heart, and with all our mind. For he saith in Isaiah: [3] This people honoureth me with their lips, but their heart is far from me.

12 Let us then not only call him Lord; for that will not save us. For he saith: [4] Not every one that saith unto me Lord, Lord, shall be saved, but he that doeth righteousness.

13 Wherefore, brethren, let us confess him by our works; by loving one another; in not committing adultery, not speaking evil against each other, not envying one another; but by being temperate, merciful, good.

14 Let us also have a mutual sense of one another's sufferings; and not be covetous of money: but let us, by our good works, confess God, and not by those that are otherwise.

15 Also let us not fear men: but rather God. [5] Wherefore, if we should do such wicked things, the Lord hath said: Though ye should be joined unto me, even in my very bosom, and not keep my commandments, I would cast you off, and say unto you: [6] Depart from me; I know not whence you are, ye workers of iniquity.

CHAP. III.

1 *That whilst we secure the other world, we need not fear what can befall us in this.* 5. *That if we follow the interests of this present world, we cannot escape the punishment of the other.* 10 *Which ought to bring us to repentance and holiness,* 14 *and that presently: because in this world is the only time for repentance.*

WHEREFORE, brethren, leaving willingly for conscience sake our sojourning in this world, let us do the will of him who has called us, and not fear to depart out of this world.

2 For the Lord saith, [7] Ye shall be as sheep in the midst of wolves. Peter answered and said, What if the wolves shall tear in pieces the sheep? Jesus said unto Peter, Let not the sheep fear the wolves after death: [8] And ye also fear not those that kill you, and after that have no more that they can do unto you; but fear him who after you are dead, has power to cast both soul and body into hell-fire.

3 For consider, brethren, that the sojourning of this flesh in

---

[1] What is the knowledge which is towards him. [2] Matt. x. 32. [3] Isaiah xxix. 13. [4] Matt. vii. 21. [5] Wherefore we doing these things. [6] Matt. xii. 23; Luke xiii. 27. [7] Matt. v. 16. [8] Luke xii. 4, 5.

141

the present world, is but little, and of a short continuance, but the promise of Christ is great and wonderful, even the rest of the kingdom that is to come, and of eternal life.

4 What then must we do that we may attain unto it?—We must [1]order our conversation holily and righteously, and look upon all the things of this world as none of ours, and not desire them. For, if we desire to possess them we fall from the way of righteousness.

5 For thus saith the Lord, [2]No servant can serve two masters. If therefore we shall desire to serve God and Mammon it will be without profit to us. [3]For what will it profit, if one gain the whole world, and lose his own soul?

6 Now this world and that to come are two enemies. This speaketh of adultery and corruption, of covetousness and deceit; but renounces these things.

7 We cannot, therefore, be the friends of both; but we must resolve by forsaking the one, to enjoy the other. And we think it is better to hate the present things, as little, short-lived, and corruptible, and to love those which are to come, which are truly good and incorruptible.

8 For, if we do the will of Christ, we shall find rest: but if not, nothing shall deliver us from eternal punishment if we shall disobey his commands. For even thus saith the Scripture in the prophet Ezekiel, [4]If Noah, Job, and Daniel should rise up, they shall not deliver their children in captivity.

9 Wherefore, if such righteous men are not able by their right-

eousness to deliver their children; how can we hope to enter into the kingdom of God, except we keep our baptism holy and undefiled? Or who shall be our advocate, unless we shall be found to have done what is holy and just?

10 Let us, therefore, my brethren, contend with all earnestness, knowing that our combat is at hand; and that many go long voyages to encounter for a corruptible reward.

11 And yet all are not crowned, but they only that labour much, and strive gloriously. Let us, therefore, so contend, that we may all be crowned. Let us run in the straight road, the race that is incorruptible: and let us in great numbers pass unto it, and strive that we may receive the crown. But and if we cannot all be crowned, let us come as near to it as we are able.

12 Moreover, we must consider, that he who contends in a corruptible combat, if he be found doing anything that is not fair, is taken away and scourged, and cast out of the lists. What think ye then that he shall suffer, who does anything that is not fitting in the combat of immortality?

13 Thus speaks the prophet concerning those who keep not their seal; [5]Their worm shall not die, and their fire shall not be quenched; and they shall be for a spectacle unto all flesh.

14 Let us therefore repent, whilst we are yet upon the earth: for we are as clay in the hand of the artificer. For as the potter if he make a vessel, and it be turned amiss in his hands, or broken, again forms it anew;

[1] MS. Alexander. οσιως και δικαιως ανςρεφεσθαι. [2] Luke xvi. 13. [3] Matt. xvi. 26. [4] Ezek. xiv. 14, 20. [5] Isaiah lxvi. 24

but if he have gone so far as to throw it into the furnace of fire, he can no more bring any remedy to it.

15 So we, whilst we are in this world, [1]should repent with our whole heart for whatsoever evil we have done in the flesh; while we have yet the time of repentance, that we may be saved by the Lord.

16 For after we shall have departed out of this world, we shall no longer be able to confess our sins or repent [2]in the other.

17 Wherefore, brethren, let us doing the will of the Father, and keeping our flesh pure, and observing the commandments of the Lord, lay hold on eternal life: for the Lord saith in the gospel, [3]If ye have not kept that which was little, who will give you that which is great?—For I say unto you, he that is faithful in that which is least, is faithful also in much.

18 This, therefore, is what he saith; keep your bodies pure, and your seal without spot, that ye may receive eternal life.

CHAP. IV.

1 *We shall rise, and be judged in our bodies; therefore we must live well in them, 6 that we ought, for our own interest, to live well; though few seem to mind what really is for their advantage, 10 and not deceive ourselves: seeing God will certainly judge us, and render to all of us according to our works.*

AND let not any one among you say, that this very flesh is not judged, neither raised up. Consider, in what were you saved; in what did you look up, if not whilst you were in this flesh.

2 We must, therefore, keep our flesh as the temple of God. For in like manner as ye were called in the flesh ye shall also come to judgment in the flesh. [4]Our one Lord Jesus Christ, who has saved us, being first a spirit, was made flesh, and so called us; even so we also shall in this flesh receive the reward.

3 Let us, therefore, love one another, that we may attain unto the kingdom of God. Whilst we have time to be healed, let us deliver up ourselves to God our physician, giving our reward unto him.

4. And what reward shall we give?—Repentance out of a pure heart. For he knows all things before hand, and searches out our very hearts.

5 Let us, therefore, give praise unto him: not only with our mouths, but with all our souls; that he may receive us as children. [5]For so the Lord hath said; [6]They are my brethren, who do the will of my father.

6 ¶ Wherefore, my brethren, let us do the will of the Father, who hath called us, that we may live. Let us pursue virtue, and forsake wickedness, which leadeth us into sins; and let us flee all ungodliness, that evils overtake us not.

7 For, if we shall do our diligence to live well, peace shall follow us. [7]And yet how hard is it to find a man that does this? For almost all are led by human fears, choosing rather the present enjoyments, than the future promise.

8 For they know not how great a torment the present enjoyments bring with them; nor what delights the future promise

[1] Let us repent. [2] There. [3] Luke xvi. 10, 12. [4] MS. Alex. plane sic exhibit: εις Χριςος. [5] Vox. Θεου non est in MS. [6] Matt. xii. 50. [7] For, for this cause, we cannot find a man. Aliter Wendel. in traduct. lat. q. v.

9 And if they themselves only did this, it might the more easily be endured; but now they go on to infect innocent souls with their evil doctrines; not knowing that both themselves, and those that hear them, shall receive a double condemnation.

10 ¶ Let us, therefore, serve God with a pure heart, and we shall be righteous: but if we shall not serve him because we do not believe the promise of God, we shall be miserable.

11 For thus saith the prophet; [1] Miserable are the double minded who doubt in their heart, and say, these things we have heard, even in the time of our fathers, but we have seen none of them, though we have expected them from day to day.

12 O ye fools! compare yourselves to a tree; take the vine for an example. First it sheds its leaves, then it buds, then come the sour grapes, then the ripe fruit; even so my people have borne its disorders and afflictions, but shall hereafter receive good things.

13 Wherefore my brethren, let us not doubt in our minds, but let us expect with hope, that we may receive our reward; for he is faithful, who has promised that he will render to every one a reward according to his works.

14 If, therefore, we shall do what is just in the sight of God we shall enter into his kingdom, and shall receive the promises; [2] Which neither eye has seen, nor ear heard, nor have entered into the heart of man.

15 ¶ Wherefore let us every hour expect the kingdom of God in love and righteousness; because we know not the day of God's appearing.

CHAP. V.

A FRAGMENT.

Of the Lord's kingdom.

1 * * For the Lord himself, being asked by a certain person, When his kingdom should come? answered, When two shall be one, and that which is without as that which is within; and the male with the female, neither male nor female.

2 Now *two are one*, when we speak the truth to each other, and there is (without hypocrisy) one soul in two bodies:

3 *And that which is without as that which is within;*—He means this: he calls the soul that which is within, and the body that which is without. As therefore thy body appears, so let thy soul be seen by its good works.

4 *And the male with the female neither male nor female;*—He means this; he calls our anger the male, our concupiscence the female.

5 When therefore a man is come to such a pass that he is subject neither to the one nor the other of these (both of which, through the prevalence of custom, and an evil education, cloud and darken the reason,)

6 But rather, having dispelled the mist arising from them, and being full of shame, shall by repentance have united both his soul and spirit in the obedience of reason; then, as Paul says, there is in us neither male nor female

---

[1] See I. Clement, chap. x.   [2] 1 Cor. ii. 9.

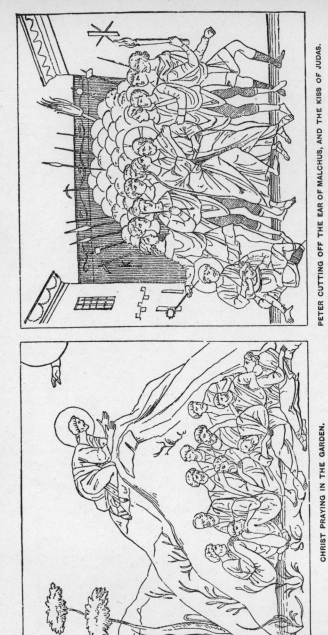

CHRIST PRAYING IN THE GARDEN.

PETER CUTTING OFF THE EAR OF MALCHUS, AND THE KISS OF JUDAS.

FROM A GREEK MANUSCRIPT, OF THE TWELFTH CENTURY, IN THE LIBRARY OF THE VATICAN.

The GENERAL EPISTLE OF BARNABAS.

Barnabas was a companion and fellow-preacher with Paul. This Epistle lays a greater claim to canonical authority than most others. It has been cited by Clemens Alexandrinus, Origen, Eusebius, and Jerome, and many ancient Fathers. Cotelerius affirms that Origen and Jerome esteemed it genuine and canonical; but Cotelerius himself did not believe it to be either one or the other; on the contrary, he supposes it was written for the benefit of the Ebionites (the christianized Jews,) who were tenacious of rites and ceremonies. Bishop Fell feared to own expressly what he seemed to be persuaded of, that it ought to be treated with the same respect as several of the books of the present canon. Dr. Bernard, Savilian professor at Oxford, not only believed it to be genuine, but that it was read throughout, in the churches at Alexandria, as the canonical scriptures were. Dodwell supposed it to have been published before the Epistle of Jude, and the writings of both the Johns. Vossius, Dupuis, Dr. Cane, Dr. Mill, Dr. S. Clark, Whiston, and Archbishop Wake also esteemed it genuine: Menardus, Archbishop Laud, Spanheim, and others, deemed it apocryphal.]

CHAP. I.
Preface to the Epistle.

ALL happiness to you my sons and daughters, in the name of our Lord Jesus Christ, who loved us, in peace.

2 Having perceived abundance of knowledge of the great and [1] excellent [2] laws of God to be in you, I exceedingly rejoice in your blessed and admirable [3] souls, because ye have so worthily received the grace which was [4] grafted in you.

3 For which cause I am full of joy, hoping the rather to be [5] saved ; inasmuch as I truly see a spirit infused into you, from the [6] pure fountain of God :

4 Having this persuasion, and being fully convinced thereof, because that since I have begun to speak unto you, I have had a more than ordinary good success in the way of [7] the law of the Lord which is in Christ.

5 For which cause [8] brethren, I also think verily that I love you above my own soul: because that therein dwelleth the greatness of faith and charity, as also the hope of that life which is to come.

6 Wherefore considering this, that if I shall take care to communicate to you a part of what I have received, it shall turn to my reward, [9] that I have served such good souls ; I gave diligence to write in a few words unto you; that together with your faith, [10] knowledge also may be perfect.

7 There are therefore three [11] things ordained by the Lord ; the hope of life; [12] the beginning and the completion of it.

8 For the Lord hath both declared unto us, by the prophets those things that [13] are past; and [14] opened to us the beginnings of those that are to come.

---

[1] Honestarum. [2] Æquitatum, Δικαιωματων, righteous judgments. [3] Spiritibus, Disposition. [4] Natural, Gr. εμφυτον. See chap. xix. εμφυτον δορεαν διδαχης ; which the Lat. Int. renders. Naturale donum Doctrinæ. Comp. Jam. i. 21. [5] Liberari : Gr. at videtur σωθηναι. [6] Honesto from the Gr. καλης. [7] Comp. Psalm 119, 33, viz. either by preaching or fulfilling the same. [8] Vid. Annot. Vos. in loc. [9] Talibus spiritibus servienti. Usser. [10] Γνωσις. [11] Δογματα κυριον, Constitutions of the Lord. [12] Viz. faith and Charity. See before. [13] Namely, which we are to believe. [14] That is, which are to be hoped for, and end in love.

9 Wherefore, it will behoove us, [1] as he has spoken, to come [2] more holily, and nearer to his altar.

10 I therefore, not as a teacher, but as one [3] of you, will endeavour to lay before you a few things by which you may, on [4] many accounts, become the more joyful.

CHAP. II.

That God has abolished the legal sacrifices to introduce the spiritual righteousness of the Gospel.

SEEING then the days are exceeding evil, and the adversary has got the power of this present [5] world we ought to give the more diligence to inquire into the [6] righteous judgments of the Lord.

2 [7] Now the assistants of our faith are fear and patience; our fellow-combatants, long-suffering and continence.

3 Whilst these remain pure in what relates unto the Lord, wisdom, and understanding, and science, and knowledge, rejoice together with them.

4 For God has manifested to us by all the prophets, that he has no occasion for our sacrifices, or burnt-offerings, or oblations: saying thus; [8] To what purpose is the multitude of your sacrifices unto me, saith the Lord.

5 I am full of the burnt-offerings of rams, and the fat of [9] fed beasts; and I delight not in the blood of bullocks, or of he-goats

6 [10] When ye come to appear before me; who hath required this at your hands? Ye shall no more tread my courts.

7 Bring no more vain obla-

tions, incense is an abomination unto me; your new moons and sabbaths; the calling of assemblies I cannot away with, it is iniquity, even the solemn meeting; your new moons and your appointed feasts my soul hateth.

8 These things therefore hath God abolished, that the new law of our Lord Jesus Christ, which is without the yoke of any such necessity, might have the spiritual offering of men themselves.

9 For so the Lord saith again to those heretofore; [11] Did I at all command your fathers when they came out of the land of Egypt concerning burnt-offerings of sacrifices?

10 But this I commanded them, saying, [12] Let none of you imagine evil in your hearts against his neighbour, and love no false oath.

11 Forasmuch then as we are not without understanding, we ought to apprehend the design [13] of our merciful Father. For he speaks to us, being willing that we who have been in the same error about the sacrifices, should seek and find how to approach unto him.

12 And therefore he thus bespeaks us, [14] The sacrifice of God (is a broken spirit,) a broken and contrite heart God will not despise.

13 Wherefore brethren, we ought the more diligently to inquire after those things that belong to our salvation, that the adversary may not have any entrance into us, and deprive us of our spiritual life.

14 Wherefore he again speaketh to them, concerning these

---

[1] Given us to know. [2] Honestius et Altius; he more honestly and highly. [3] Like yourselves. [4] In many things. [5] Age. [6] Equitus. [7] Comp. Græc. Clem. Alex. [8] Isaiah i. 11. [9] Lambs. [10] Isaiah, i. 12, 13, 14. [11] Jer. vii. 22, 23. [12] Zech. viii. 17. [13] Of the mercy of Our Father. [14] Psalm i. 19.

things; [1] Ye shall not fast as ye do this day, to make your voice to be heard on high.

15 Is it such a fast that I have chosen? a day for a man to afflict his soul? [2] Is it to bow down his head like a bulrush, and to spread sackcloth and ashes under him? Wilt thou call this a fast, and an acceptable day to the Lord?

16 But to us he saith on this wise. [3] Is not this the fast that I have chosen, to loose the bands of wickedness, to undo the heavy burdens, and to let the oppressed go free; and that ye break every yoke?

17 [4] Is it not to deal thy bread to the hungry, and that thou bring the poor that are cast out to thy house? When thou seest the naked that thou cover him, and that thou hide not thyself from thine own flesh.

18 [5] Then shall thy light break forth as the morning, and thy health shall spring forth speedily; and thy righteousness shall go before thee, the glory of the Lord shall be thy reward.

19 [6] Then shalt thou call and the Lord shall answer; thou shalt cry and he shall say, Here I am. If thou put away from the midst of thee the yoke, the putting forth of the finger, and speaking vanity; [7] and if thou draw out thy soul to the hungry; and satisfy the afflicted soul.

20 In this therefore brethren, God has manifested his [8] foreknowledge and love for us; because the people which he has purchased to his beloved Son were to believe in [9] sincerity; and therefore he has shewn these things to all of us, that we should not run as proselytes to [10] the Jewish law.

CHAP. III.

The prophecies of Daniel, concerning the ten kings, and the coming of Christ.

WHEREFORE it is necessary that searching diligently into those [11] things which are near to come to pass, we should write to you what may serve to keep you whole.

2 To which end let us flee from every evil work and hate the errors of the present time, that we may be [12] happy in that which is to come:

3 Let us not give ourselves the liberty of disputing with the wicked and sinners; lest we should chance in time to become like unto them.

4 For the consummation of [13] sin is come, as it is written, as the prophet Daniel says. And for this end the Lord hath shortened the times and the days, that his beloved might hasten his coming to his inheritance.

5 For so the prophet speaks; [14] There shall ten kings reign in the heart, and there shall rise last of all another little one, and he shall humble three kings.

6 And again Daniel speaks in like manner concerning the kingdoms; [15] and I saw the fourth beast dreadful and terrible, and strong exceedingly; and it had ten horns. [16] I considered the horns, and behold there came up among them another little horn, before which were three of the first horns plucked up by the roots.

7 We ought therefore to understand this also: And I beseech you as one of your own brethren, loving you all beyond my own life, that you look well to yourselves, and be not like to those who

[1] Isa. lviii. 4.   [2] V. 5.   [3] V. 6.   [4] V. 7.   [5] V. 8.   [6] V. 9.   [7] V. 10.   [8] Providence.   [9] Simplicity.   [10] Their.   [11] Histantibus: read Instantibus.   [12] Beloved. [13] Temptation. Dan. ix   [14] Dan. vii.   [15] V. 7.   [16] V. 8.   [17] Heap up sins.

147

[1] add sin to sin, and say: That their covenant is ours also. Nay, but it is ours only: for they have for ever lost that which Moses received.

8 For thus saith the Scripture: And Moses continued fasting forty days and forty nights in the Mount; and he received the covenant from the Lord, even the two tables of stone, written by the hand of God.

9 But having turned themselves to idols they lost it; as the Lord also said to Moses; Moses, [2] go down quickly, for thy people which thou hast brought forth out of Egypt, have corrupted themselves, and turned aside from the way which I commanded them. [3] And Moses cast the two tables out of his hands: and their covenant was broken; that the love of Jesus might be sealed in your hearts, unto the hope of his faith.

10 Wherefore let us give heed unto the last times. For all the [4] time past of our life, and our faith will profit us nothing; unless we continue to hate what is evil, and to withstand the future temptations. So the Son of God tells us; Let us resist all iniquity and hate it.

11 Wherefore consider the works of the evil way. [5] Do not withdraw yourselves from others, as if you were already justified; but coming altogether into one place, inquire what is agreeable to and profitable for the beloved of God. For the Scripture saith; [6] Wo unto them that are wise in their own eyes, and prudent in their sight.

12 Let us become spiritual, a perfect temple to God. As much as in us lies let us meditate upon the fear of God; and strive to the utmost of our power to keep his commandments; that we may rejoice in his righteous judgments.

13 For God will judge the world without respect of persons: and every one shall receive according to his works.

14 If a man shall be good, his righteousness shall go before him; if wicked, the reward of his wickedness shall follow him.

15 Take heed therefore lest sitting still, now that we are called, we fall asleep in our sins; and the wicked one getting the dominion over us, stir us up, [7] and shut us out of the kingdom of the Lord.

16 Consider this also: although you have seen so great signs and wonders done among the people of the Jews, yet this notwithstanding the Lord hath forsaken them.

17 Beware therefore, lest it happen to us; as it is written. [8] There may be many called, but few chosen.

CHAP. IV.

That Christ was to suffer: proved from the prophecies concerning him.

FOR this cause did our Lord vouchsafe to give up his body to destruction, that through the forgiveness of our sins we might be sanctified; that is, by the sprinkling of his blood.

2 Now for what concerns the things that are written about him, some belong to the people of the Jews, and some to us.

3 For thus saith the Scripture: [9] He was wounded for our transgressions, he was bruised for our iniquities, and by his blood we are

---

[1] Exod. xxxi. xxxiv.   [2] Exod. xxxvii. 7. Deut. ix. 12.   [3] V. 19.   [4] Days.
[5] Heb. x. 25.   [6] Vid. Gr. Clem. Alex. Isa. v., 21.   [7] Matt. xxv. 7—10.
[8] Matt. xxii. 14.   [9] Isa. lii. 5—7.

healed. He was led as a lamb to the slaughter, and as a sheep before his shearers is dumb, so he opened not his mouth.

4 Wherefore we ought the more to give thanks unto God, for that he hath both declared unto us what is passed, [1] and not suffered us to be without understanding of those things that are to come.

5 But to them he saith; [2] The nests are not unjustly spread for the birds.

6 This he spake, because a man will justly perish, if having the knowledge of the way of truth, he shall nevertheless not refrain himself from the way of darkness.

7 And for this cause the Lord was content to suffer for our souls, although he be the Lord of the whole earth; to whom God said before the beginning of the world, [3] Let us make man after our own image and likeness.

8 Now how he suffered for us, seeing it was by men that he underwent it, [4] I will shew you.

9 The prophets having received from him the gift of prophecy, spake before concerning him:

10 But he, that he might abolish death, and make known the resurrection from the dead, was content, as it was necessary, to appear in the flesh, that he might make good the promise before given to our fathers, and preparing himself a new people, might demonstrate to them whilst he was upon earth, that after the resurrection he would judge the world.

11 And finally teaching the people of Israel, and doing many wonders and signs among them,

he preached to them, and shewed the exceeding great love which he bare towards them.

12 And when he chose his apostles, which were afterwards to publish his Gospel, he took men who had been very great sinners; that thereby he might plainly shew, [5] That he came not to call the righteous but sinners to repentance.

13 Then he clearly manifested himself to be the Son of God. For had he not come in the flesh, how should men have been able to look upon him, that they might be saved?

14 Seeing if they beheld only the sun, which was the work of his hands, and shall hereafter cease to be, they are not able to endure steadfastly to look against the rays of it.

15 Wherefore the Son of God came in the flesh for this cause, that he might fill up the measure of their iniquity, who have persecuted his prophets unto death. And for the same reason also he suffered.

16 For God hath said of the [6] stripes of his flesh, that they were from them. And, [7] I will smite the shepherd, and the sheep of the flock shall be scattered.

17 Thus he would suffer, because it behooved him to suffer upon the cross.

18 For thus one saith, prophesying concerning him; [8] Spare my soul from the sword. And again, Pierce my flesh from thy fear.

19 And again, the congregation of wicked doers rose up against me, [9] (They have pierced my hands and my feet).

20 And again he saith, I gave

---

[1] Vid. Ed. Ox., p. 21.   [2] Prov. i. 17.   [3] Gen. i. 26.   [4] Learn.   [5] Matt. ix. 13.   [6] Namely, from the Jews.   [7] Zach. xiii. 6, 7.   [8] According to the LXX. Psalm xxii. 20. Psalm cxix. 120. Psalm xxii. 16, 17.   [9] These words

my back to the smiters, [1] and my face I set as an hard rock.

CHAP. V.

The subject continued.

AND when he had fulfilled the commandment of God, What says he? [2] Who will contend with me? Let him stand against me: or who is he that will implead me? Let him draw near to the servant of the Lord. Wo be to you! [3] Because ye shall all wax old as a garment, the moth shall eat you up.

2 And again the prophet adds, [4] He is put for a stone for stumbling. [5] Behold I lay in Zion for a foundation, a precious stone, a choice corner stone; an honourable stone. And what follows? And he that hopeth in him shall live for ever.

3 What then? Is our hope built upon a stone? God forbid. But because the Lord hath [6] hardened his flesh against sufferings, he saith, [7] I have put me as a firm rock.

4 And again the prophet adds; [8] The stone which the builders refused has become the head of the corner. And again he saith; [9] This is the great and wonderful day which the Lord hath made. [10] I write these things the more plainly to you that ye may understand: [11] For indeed I could be content even to die for your sakes.

5 But what saith the prophet again? [12] The counsel of the wicked encompassed me about. [13] They came about me, as bees about the honey-comb: and, [14] Upon my vesture they cast lots.

6 Forasmuch then as our Saviour was to appear in the flesh and suffer, his passion was hereby foretold.

7 For thus saith the prophet against Israel: [15] Wo be to their soul, because they have taken wicked counsel against themselves, saying, let us [16] lay snares for the righteous, because he is unprofitable to us.

8 Moses also in like manner speaketh to them; [17] Behold thus saith the Lord God; Enter ye into the good land of which the Lord hath sworn to Abraham, and Isaac, and Jacob, that he would give it you, and possess it; a land flowing with milk and honey.

9 Now what the spiritual meaning of this is, learn; [18] It is as if it had been said, Put your trust in Jesus, who shall be manifested to you in the flesh. For man is the earth which suffers: forasmuch as out of the [19] substance of the earth Adam was formed.

10 What therefore does he mean when he says, Into a good land flowing with milk and honey? Blessed be our Lord, who has given us wisdom, and a heart to understand his secrets. For so says the prophet, [20] Who shall understand the hard sayings of the Lord? [21] But he that

---

were doubtless cited thus by Barnabas, because that without them, those foregoing do not prove the Crucifixion of Christ. But through the repetition of the same preposition, this latter part was so early omitted, that it was not in the Latin interpreter's copy.   [1] Isaiah l. 6.   [2] Isa. l. 8, 9.   [3] Rep. In.   [4] Isa. viii. 14.   [5] Isa. xxviii. 16.   [6] Gr. put in strength, or strengthened.   [7] Isa. l. 7.   [8] Ps. cxviii. 22.   [9] V. 24. Clem. Alex. Strom. v.   [10] This is not in the Old Latin Version.   [11] Vid. Ed. Ox., p. 29, a. περιψημα της αγαπης υμων.   [12] Ps. xxii. 16.   [13] Ps. cxviii. 12.   [14] Ps. xxii. 18.   [15] Is. iii. 9.   [16] Bind.   [17] Exod. xxxiii. 1.   [18] Vid. Cot. An. Marg. ex Clem. Alex.   [19] προσωπου.   [20] Osee, xiv. ult.   [21] Prov. i. 6. Ec. i. 10.

is wise, and intelligent, and that loves his Lord.

11 Seeing therefore he has renewed us by the remission of our sins, he has [1] put us into another frame, that we should have souls [2] like those of children, forming us again himself [3] by the spirit.

12 For thus the Scripture saith concerning us, [4] where it introduceth the Father speaking to the Son; [5] Let us make man after our likeness and similitude; and let them have dominion over the beasts of the earth, and over the fowls of the air, and the fish of the sea.

13 And when the Lord saw the man which he had formed, that behold he was very good; he said, [6] Increase and multiply, and replenish the earth. And this he spake to his son.

14 I will now shew you, how he made us [7] a new creature, in the latter days.

15 The Lord saith; [8] Behold I will make the last as the first. Wherefore the prophet thus spake, [9] Enter into the land flowing with milk and honey, and have dominion over it.

16 Wherefore ye see how we are again formed anew; as also he speaks by another prophet; [10] Behold saith the Lord, I will take from them, that is, from those whom the spirit of the Lord foresaw, their hearts of stone, and I will put into them hearts of flesh.

17 Because he was about to be made manifest in the flesh and to dwell in us.

18 For, my brethren, the habitation of our heart is a [11] holy temple unto the Lord. For

the Lord saith again. [12] In what place shall I appear before the Lord my God, and be glorified?

19 He answers I will confess unto thee in the congregation in the midst of my brethren; and will sing unto thee in the church of the saints.

20 Wherefore we are they whom he has brought into that good land.

21 [13] But what signifies the milk and honey? Because as the child is nourished first with milk, and then with honey; so we being kept alive by the belief of his promises, and his word, shall live and have dominion over the land.

22 For he foretold above, saying, increase and multiply, and have dominion over the fishes, etc.

23 But who is there that is now able to have this dominion over the wild beasts, or fishes, or fowls of the air? For you know that to rule is to have power, that a man should be set over what he rules.

24 But forasmuch as this we have not now, he tells us when we shall have it; namely, when we shall become perfect, that we may be made the inheritors of the covenant of the Lord.

CHAP. VI.

The scape-goat an evident type of this.

UNDERSTAND then my beloved children, that the good God hath before manifested all things unto us, that we might know to whom we ought always to give thanks and praise.

2 If therefore the Son of God who is the Lord of all, and shall

---

[1] Gr. made us another form. [2] Vid. Ed. Ox., p. 30, b. [3] Vid. Vet. Lat. In. [4] As he saith to the Son. [5] Gen. i. 26. &c. [6] Gen. i. 28. [7] Gr. a second formation. [8] Isa. xliii. 18, 19, &c. [9] Heb. iii. [10] Ezek. xi. 19. [11] So St. Paul, 1 Cor. iii. 16, 17. [12] Ps. xlii. 2. [13] Jer. xxxii. 22.

come to judge both the quick and dead, hath suffered, that by his stripes we might live: let us believe that the Son of God could not have suffered but for us. But being crucified, they gave him vinegar and gall to drink.

3 Hear therefore how the priests of the temple did foreshew this also: [1] the Lord by his command which was written, declared that whosoever did not fast the appointed fast he [2] should die the death: because he also was himself one day to offer up his [3] body for our sins; that so the type of what was done in [4] Isaac might be fulfilled, who was offered upon the altar.

4 What therefore is it that he says by the prophet? [5] And let them eat of the goat which is offered in the day of the fast for all their sins. Hearken diligently (my brethren,) and all the priests, and they only shall eat the inwards not washed with vinegar.

5 Why so? because [6] I know that when I shall hereafter offer my flesh for the sins of a new people, ye will give me vinegar to drink mixed with gall; therefore do ye only eat, the people fasting the while, and lamenting in sackcloth and ashes.

6 And that he might foreshew that he was to suffer for them, hear then how he appointed it.

7 [7] Take, says he, two goats, fair and alike, and offer them, and let the high priest take one of them for a burnt offering. And what must be done with the other? Let it says he be accursed.

8 Consider how exactly this appears to have been a type of Jesus. [8] And let all the congregation spit upon it, and prick it; and put the scarlet wool about its head, and thus let it be carried forth into the wilderness.

9 And this being done, he that was appointed to convey the goat, led it into the wilderness, [9] and took away the scarlet wool, and put it upon a thorn bush, whose [10] young sprouts when we find them in the field we are wont to eat: so the fruit of that thorn only is sweet.

10 And to what end was this ceremony? Consider; one was offered upon the altar, the other was accursed.

11 And why was that which was accursed crowned? Because they shall see Christ in that day having a scarlet garment about his body; and shall say: Is not this he whom we crucified; having despised him, pierced him, mocked him? Certainly, this is he, who then said, that he was the Son of God.

12 [11] As therefore he shall be then like to what he was on earth, so were the Jews heretofore commanded, to take two goats fair and equal. That when they shall see (our Saviour) hereafter coming (in the clouds of heaven), they may be amazed at the likeness of the goats.

13 Wherefore [12] ye here again see a type of Jesus who was to suffer for us.

14 But what then signifies this. That the wool was to be put into the midst of the thorns?

15 This also is a figure of Jesus, sent out to the church. For as

---

[1] In same manner applied Heb. ix. spirit. [4] Gen. xxii. [5] Numb. xxix., [6] Vid. Annot. Cot. [7] Levit xi. Vid. Maimon. tract. de die Exy. Edit. du Veil, p. 350, &c. [8] Vid. Edit. Ox. p. 40 a. 41. b. [9] Vid. Maim. ib. p. 341. &c. [10] Vid. Voss. in loc. [11] The Greek is imperfect. [12] Vid. Lat. Ver. [2] Lev. xxiii. 29. [3] The vessel of his &c., Vic. Cot. in Marg. et Annot. in loc.

2

CHRIST BEARING HIS CROSS TO GOLGOTHA, FOLLOWED BY HOLY WOMEN.

The Drawings on each side of the Engraving are Enlargements of the Heads of the Principal Figures.

FROM A FRESCO OF THE TWELFTH CENTURY IN THE CHURCH OF ST. STEPHEN AT BOLOGNA.

he who would take away the scarlet wool must undergo many difficulties, because that thorn was very sharp, and with difficulty get it : [1] So they, says Christ, that will see me, and come to my kingdom, must through many afflictions and troubles attain unto me.

CHAP. VII.

The red heifer, another type of Christ.

BUT what [2] type do ye suppose it to have been, where it is commanded [3] to the people of Israel, that grown persons in whom sins are come to perfection, should offer an heifer, and after they had killed it should burn the same.

2 But then young men should take up the ashes and put them in vessels; and tie a piece of scarlet wool and hyssop upon a stick, and so the young men should sprinkle every one of the people, and they should be clear from their sins.

3 Consider how all these are delivered in a [4] figure to us.

4 This heifer is Jesus Christ; the wicked men that were to offer it are those sinners who brought him to death: who afterwards have no more to do with it; the sinners have no more the honour of handling of it:

5 But the young men that performed the sprinkling, signified those who preach to us the forgiveness of sins and the purification of the heart, to whom the Lord gave authority to preach his Gospel: being at the beginning twelve, [5] to signify the tribes, because there were twelve tribes of Israel.

6 But why were there three young men appointed to sprinkle? To denote Abraham, and Isaac, and Jacob, because they were great before God.

7 And why was the wool put upon a [6] stick? Because the kingdom of Jesus was founded upon the cross; and therefore they that put their trust in him, shall live for ever.

8 But why was the wool and hyssop put together? To signify that in the kingdom of Christ there shall be evil and filthy days, in which however we shall be saved; and [7] because he that has any disease in the flesh by some filthy humours is cured by hyssop.

9 Wherefore these things being thus done, are to us indeed evident, but to the [8] Jews they are obscure; because they hearkened not unto the voice of the Lord.

CHAP. VIII.

Of the circumcision of the ears; and how in the first institution of circumcision Abraham mystically foretold Christ by name.

AND therefore the Scripture again speaks concerning our ears, that God has circumcised them, together with our hearts. For thus saith the Lord by the holy prophets : [9] By the hearing of the ear they obeyed me.

2 And again, [10] They who are afar off, shall hear and understand what things I have done. And again, [11] Circumcise your hearts, saith the Lord.

3 And again he saith, [12] Hear O Israel! For thus saith the Lord thy God. And again the

---

[1] Acts xiv. 22.   [2] Numb. xix.   [3] That this was also a type of Christ, see Heb. ix. 13.   [4] Vid. Vet. Lat. Interpr. Simplicity, Gr. [5] Gr. to testify. [6] Wood. [7] Vid. Coteler. in loc.   [8] Them.   [9] Septuag. Psalm xvii. 45.   [10] Isaiah xxxiii. 13.   [11] Jer. iv. 4.   [12] Jer. vii. 2.

Spirit of God prophesieth, saying : [1] Who is there that would live for ever, [2] let him hear the voice of my Son.

4 And again, [3] Hear, O Heaven and give ear O Earth ! Because the Lord has spoken these things for a witness.

5 And again he saith [4] Hear the word of the Lord, ye princes of the people. And again [5] Hear O Children ! The voice of one crying in the wilderness.

6 Wherefore he has circumcised our ears that we should hear his word, and believe. But as for that circumcision, in which the Jews trust, it is abolished. For the circumcision of which God spake, was not of the flesh ;

7 But they have transgressed his commands, because the evil [6] one hath deceived them. For thus God bespeaks them ; [7] Thus saith the Lord your God (Here I find the new law) Sow not among thorns ; but circumcise yourselves to the Lord your God. And what doth he mean by this saying ? Hearken unto your Lord.

8 And again he saith, [8] Circumcise the hardness of your heart, and harden not your neck. And again, [9] Behold, saith the Lord, all the nations are uncircumcised, (they have not lost their fore-skin) : but this people is uncircumcised in heart.

9 But you will say [10]the Jews were circumcised for a sign. [11] And so are all the Syrians and Arabians, and all the idolatrous priests : but are they therefore

of the covenant of Israel ? And even the Egyptians themselves are circumcised.

10 Understand therefore, children, these things more fully, that Abraham, who was the first that brought in circumcision, looking forward in the Spirit to Jesus, circumcised, having received the mystery of three letters.

11 For the Scripture says that Abraham circumcised three hundred and eighteen men of his house. [12] But what therefore was the mystery that was made known unto him ?

12 Mark, first the eighteen, and next the three hundred. For the numeral letters of ten and eight are I H. And these denote Jesus.

13 And because the cross was that by which we were to find grace ; therefore he adds, three hundred ; the note of which is T (the figure of his cross). Wherefore by two letters he signified Jesus, and by the third his cross.

14 He who has put the engrafted gift of his doctrine within us, knows that I never taught to any one a more [13] certain truth ; but I trust that ye are worthy of it.

CHAP. IX.

That the commands of Moses concerning clean and unclean beasts, &c., were all designed for a spiritual signification.

BUT why did Moses say [14] Ye shall not eat of the swine, neither the eagle nor the hawk ; nor the crow ; nor any fish that

---

[1] Psalms xxxiii. xxxiv.   [2] Isaiah, l. 10.   [3] Isaiah, i. 2.   [4] Isaiah l. 10.   [5] Isaiah, xl. 3.   [6] Angel.   [7] Jer. iv. 3, 4.   [8] Jer. iv. 4.   [9] Deut. x. 16.   [10] That people.   [11] Vid. Cot. in loc. conter. Orig. ad Rom cap. ii. 25.   [12] That many others of the ancient Fathers have concurred with him in this, see Cot. in loc. Add. Eund. p. 34, 85, ibid. Ed., &c., &c.   [13] Genuine.   [14] That in this he goes on the received opinion of the RR. Vid. Annot. Cot. and Ed. Ox. in loc. Lev. xi. Deut. xiv. Add. Ainsworth on Lev. xi. 1, and Deut. xiv. 4.

has not a scale upon him?—answer, that in the spiritual sense, he comprehended three doctrines, that were to be [1] gathered from thence.

2 Besides which he says to them in the book of Deuteronomy, And I will give my statutes unto this people. Wherefore it is not the command of God that they should not eat these things; but Moses in the spirit spake unto them.

3 Now the sow he forbade them to eat; meaning thus much; thou shalt not join thyself to such persons as are like unto swine; who whilst they live in pleasure, forget their God; but when any want pinches them, then they know the Lord; as the sow when she is full knows not her master; but when she is hungry she makes a noise; and being again fed, is silent.

4 Neither, says he, shalt thou eat the eagle, nor the hawk, nor the kite, nor the crow; that is thou shalt not keep company with such kind of men as know not how by their labour and sweat to get themselves food: but injuriously ravish away the things of others; and watch how to lay snares for them; when at the same time they appear to live in perfect innocence.

5 ([2] So these birds alone seek not food for themselves, but) sitting idle seek how they may eat of the flesh others have provided; being destructive through their wickedness.

6 Neither, says he, shalt thou eat the lamprey, nor the polypus, nor the cuttle-fish; that is, thou shalt not be like such men, by using to converse with them; who are altogether wicked and adjudged to death. For so those fishes are alone accursed, and wallow in the mire, nor swim as other fishes, but tumble in the dirt at the bottom of the deep.

7 But he adds, neither shalt thou eat of the hare. To what end?—To signify this to us; Thou shalt not be an adulterer; nor liken thyself to such persons. For the hare every year multiplies the places of its conception; and so many years as it lives, so many it has.

8 Neither shalt thou eat of the hyena; that is, again, be not an adulterer, nor a corruptor of others; neither be like to such. And wherefore so?—Because that creature every year changes its kind, and is sometimes male and sometimes female.

9 For which cause also he justly hated the weasel; to the end that they should not be like such persons who with their mouths commit wickedness by reason of their uncleanness; nor join themselves with those impure women, who with their mouths commit wickedness. Because that animal conceives with its mouth.

10 Moses, therefore, speaking as concerning meats, delivered indeed three great precepts to them in the spiritual signification of those commands. But they according to the desires of the flesh, understood him as if he had only meant it of meats.

11 And therefore David took aright the knowledge of his threefold command, saying in like manner.

12 Blessed is the man that hath not walked in the counsel of

---

[1] In the understanding. Deut. iv.   [2] Vid. antiq. Lat. Vers.

the ungodly; as the fishes before mentioned in the bottom of the deep in darkness.

13 Nor stood in the way of sinners, as they who seem to fear the Lord, but yet sin, as the sow.

14 And hath not sat in the seat of the scorners; as those birds who sit and watch that they may devour.

15 Here you have the law concerning meat perfectly set forth, and according to the true knowledge of it.

16 But, says Moses, ye shall eat all that divideth the hoof, and cheweth the cud. Signifying thereby such an one as having taken his food, knows him that nourisheth him; and resting upon him, rejoiceth in him.

17 And in this he spake well, having respect to the commandment. What, therefore, is it that he says?—That we should hold fast to them that fear the Lord; with those who meditate on the command of the word which they have received in their heart; with those that declare the righteous judgments of the Lord, and keep his commandments;

18 In short, with those who know that to meditate is a work of pleasure, and therefore exercise themselves in the word of the Lord.

19 But why might they eat those that clave the hoof?—Because the righteous liveth in this present world; but his expectation is fixed upon the other. Sec, brethren, how admirably Moses commanded these things.

20 But how should we thus know all this, and understand it? We, therefore, understanding aright the commandments, speak as the Lord would have us. Wherefore he has circumcised our ears and our hearts, that we might know these things.

CHAP. X.

Baptism and the Cross of Christ foretold in figures under the law.

LET us now inquire whether the Lord took care to manifest anything beforehand concerning water and the cross.

2. Now for the former of these, it is written to the people of Israel how they shall not receive that baptism which brings to forgiveness of sins; but shall institute another to themselves that cannot.

3 For thus saith the prophet: [1] Be astonished, O Heaven! and let the earth tremble at it, because this people have done two great and wicked things; they have left me, the fountain of living water, and have digged for themselves broken cisterns, that can hold no water.

4 Is my holy mountain a [2] Zion, a desolate wilderness?— [3] For ye shall be as a young bird when its nest is taken away.

5 And again the prophet saith, [4] I will go before thee, and will make plain the mountains, and will break the gates of brass, and will snap in sunder the bars of iron; and will give thee dark, and hidden, and invisible treasures, that they may know that I am the Lord God.

6 And again: He shall dwell [5] in the high den of the strong rock. And then, what follows in the same prophet? His water is faithful; ye shall see the king

---

[1] Jeremiah, ii. 12.   [2] Vid. Annot. Coteler. and Ed. Oxon. in loc.   [3] Isaiah, xvi. 1, 2.   [4] Isaiah xlv. 2.   [5] Isaiah, xxxiii. 16, 17.

with glory, and your soul shall learn the fear of the Lord.

7 And again he saith in another prophet: He that does these things; [1] shall be like a tree, planted by the currents of water, which shall give its fruit in its season. Its leaf also shall not wither, and whatsoever he doth it shall prosper.

8 As for the wicked it is not so with them; but they are as the dust which the wind scattereth away from the face of the earth.

9 Therefore the ungodly shall not stand in the judgment, neither the sinners in the council of the righteous. For the Lord knoweth the way of the righteous and the way of the ungodly shall perish.

10 Consider how he has joined both the cross and the water together.

11 For thus he saith: Blessed are they who put their trust in the cross, descend into the water; for they shall have their reward in due time; then, saith he, will I give it them.

12 But as concerning the present time, he saith, their leaves shall not fall; meaning thereby that every word that shall go out of your mouth, shall through faith and charity be to the conversion and hope of many.

13 In like manner doth another prophet speak. [2] And the land of Jacob was the praise of all the earth; [3] magnifying thereby [4] the vessel of his spirit.

14 And what follows?—And there was a river running on the right hand, and beautiful trees

grew up by it; and he that shall eat of them shall live for ever. The signification of which is this: that we go down into the water full of sins and pollutions; but come up again, bringing forth fruit; having in our hearts the fear and hope which is in Jesus, by the spirit. And whosoever shall eat of them shall live for ever.

15 That is, whosoever shall hearken to those who call them, and shall believe, shall live for ever.

CHAP. XI.

The subject continued.

IN like manner he determines concerning the cross in [5] another prophet, saying: And when shall these things be fulfilled?

2 The Lord answers; When the tree that has fallen shall rise, and when blood shall drop down from the tree. Here you have again mention made, both of the cross, and of him that was to be crucified upon it.

3 [6] And yet farther he saith by Moses; (when Israel was fighting with, and beaten by, a strange people; to the end that God might put [7] them in mind how that for their sins they were delivered unto death) yea, the holy spirit put it into the heart of Moses, to represent both the sign of the cross, and of him that was to suffer; that so they might know that if they did not believe in him, they should be overcome for ever.

4 Moses therefore [8] piled up armour upon armour in the middle of a rising ground, and

---

[1] Psalm, i.   [2] Zeph. iii. 19.   [3] For τουτο λεγει and o, the Old Interpreter did not read; and Clemens Alex. lib. iii. Strom. p. 463, transcribing this passage hath them not.   [4] i. e., the body of Christ.   [5] Vid. Conject. Edit. Oxon. Comp. iv.   Esdr. v. 4, et Obs. Cotel. in loc.   [6] See St. Hier. in like manner. Annot. D. Bernard, p. 124, Edit. Oxon. Exod. xvii.   [7] That were so beaten. [8] Again set them in array, being armed. Lat. Vers.

standing up high above all of them, stretched forth his arms, and so Israel again conquered.

5 But no sooner did he let down his hands, but they were again slain. And why so?—To the end they might know, that except they trust in him they cannot be saved.

6 And in another prophet, he saith, [1] I have stretched out my hands all the day long to a people disobedient, and speaking against my righteous way.

7 And again Moses makes a [2] type of Jesus, to show that he was to die, and then that he, whom they thought to be dead, was to give life to others; in the [3] type of [4] those that fell in Israel.

8 For God caused all sorts of serpents to bite them, and they died; forasmuch as by a serpent transgression began in Eve: that so he might convince them that for their transgressions they shall be delivered into the pain of death.

9 Moses then himself, who had commanded them, saying, [5] Ye shall not make to yourselves any graven or molten image, to be your God; yet now did so himself, that he might represent to them the figure of the Lord Jesus.

10 For he made a brazen serpent, and set it up on high, and called the people together by a proclamation; where being come, they entreated Moses that he would make an atonement for them, and pray that they might be healed.

11 Then Moses spake unto them, saying: when any one among you shall be bitten, let him come unto the serpent that is set upon the pole; and let him assuredly trust in him, that though he be dead, yet he is able to give life, and presently he shall be saved; and so they did. See therefore how here also you have in this the glory of Jesus; and that [6] in him and to him are all things.

12 Again; What says Moses to Jesus the son of Nun, when he gave that name unto him, as being a prophet that all the people might hear him alone, [7] because the father did manifest all things concerning his son Jesus, in [8] Jesus the Son of Nun; and gave him that name when he sent him to spy out the land of Canaan; [9] he said: Take a book in thine hands, and write what the Lord saith: Forasmuch as Jesus the Son of God shall in the last days cut off by the roots all the house of Amalek. See here again Jesus, not the son of man, but the Son of God, made manifest in a type and in the flesh.

13 But because it might hereafter be said, that Christ was the Son of David; [10] therefore David fearing and well knowing the errors of the wicked, saith; [11] the Lord saith unto my Lord, sit thou on my right hand until I make thine enemies thy footstool.

14 And again Isaiah speaketh on this wise. The Lord said unto [12] Christ my Lord, I have laid hold on his right hand, that the

---

[1] Isaiah, lxv. 2.   [2] So Irenæus, Just. Mart. St. Chrysost., &c. Edit. Oxon. p. 77, a.   [3] Sign.   [4] Israel falling.   [5] Deut. xvii. 15.   [6] Rom. xi. 36.   [7] Deut. xviii. 15, 18.   [8] So the other Fathers. Just. Mart. &c. Vid. Edit. Oxon. page 79.   [9] Vid. Interp. Vet. Lat. Exod. xvii. 14.   [10] Comp. Vet. Lat. Interp. [11] Psalm cix. 3.   [12] Vid. Annot. Coteler, in loc. Edit. Oxon. page 78, c. Isaiah xlv. 1.

nations should obey before him, and I will break the strength of kings.

15 Behold, how doth [1] David and Isaiah call him Lord, and the Son of God.

CHAP. XII.

The promise of God not made to the Jews only, but to the Gentiles also, and fulfilled to us by Jesus Christ.

BUT let us go yet farther, and inquire whether this people be the heir, or the former; and whether the covenant be with us or with them.

2 And first, as concerning the people, hear now what the Scripture saith.

3 [2] Isaac prayed for his wife Rebekah, because she was barren; and she conceived. Afterwards Rebekah went forth to inquire of the Lord.

4 And the Lord said unto her; There are two nations in thy womb, and two people shall come from thy body; and the one shall have power over the other, and the greater shall serve the lesser. Understand here who was Isaac; who Rebekah; and of whom it was foretold, this people shall be greater than that.

5 And in another prophecy Jacob speaketh more clearly to his son Joseph saying; [3] Behold the Lord hath not deprived me of seeing thy face, bring me thy sons that I may bless them. And he brought unto his father [4] Manasseh and Ephraim, desiring that he should bless Manasseh, because he was the elder.

6 Therefore Joseph brought him to the right hand of his father Jacob. But Jacob by the spirit foresaw the figure of the people that was to come.

7 And what saith the Scripture? And Jacob crossed his hands, and put his right hand upon Ephraim, his second, and the younger son, and blessed him. And Joseph said unto Jacob; Put thy right hand upon the head of Manasseh, for he is my first-born son. And Jacob said unto Joseph; I know it, my son, I know it; but the greater shall serve the lesser; though he also shall be blessed.

8 Ye see of whom he appointed it, that they should be the first people, and heirs of the covenant.

9 If therefore God shall have yet farther taken notice of this by Abraham too; our understanding of it will then be perfectly established.

10 What then saith the Scripture to Abraham, when he [5] believed, and it was imputed unto him for righteousness? Behold I have made thee a father of the nations, which without circumcision believe in the Lord.

11 Let us therefore now inquire whether God has fulfilled the covenant, which he sware to our fathers, that he would give this people? Yes, verily, he gave it: but they were not worthy to receive it by reason of their sins.

12 For thus saith the prophet: [6] And Moses continued fasting in mount Sinai, to receive the covenant of the Lord with the people, forty days and forty nights.

13 [7] And he received of the Lord two tables written with the finger of the Lord's hand in the

---

[1] Comp. Vet. Lat. Interp.   [2] Gen. xxv. 21. Comp. St. Paul Rom. ix. Just. Mart. Tert. &c. Vid. Ed. Oxon. p. 11, a.   [3] Gen. xlviii.   [4] Vid. Lat. Interp. Vet.   [5] Gen. xv. 17. So St. Paul himself applies this: Rom. iv. 3. [3] Exod. xxiv. 18.   [7] Deut. ix. 10. Exod. xxxi. 12.

Spirit. And Moses when he had received them brought them down that he might deliver them to the people.

14 And the Lord said unto Moses; [1] Moses, Moses, get thee down quickly, for the people which thou broughtest out of the land of Egypt have done wickedly.

15 And Moses understood that they had again set up a molten image : and he cast the two tables out of his hands ; and the tables of the covenant of the Lord were broken. Moses therefore received them, but they were not worthy.

16 Now then learn how we have received them. Moses, being a servant, took them ; but the Lord himself has given them unto us, that we might be the people of his inheritance, having suffered for us.

17 He was therefore made manifest ; that they should fill up the measure of their sins, and that we [2] being made heirs by him, should receive the covenant of the Lord Jesus.

18 And again the prophet saith ; [3] Behold, I have set thee for a light unto the Gentiles, to be [4] the saviour of all the ends of the earth, saith the Lord the God who hath redeemed thee.

19 Who for that very end was prepared, that by his own appearing he might redeem our hearts, already devoured by death, and delivered over to the irregularity of error, from darkness ; and establish a covenant with us by his word.

20 For so it is written that the father commanded him by delivering us from darkness, to prepare unto himself a holy people.

21 Wherefore the prophet saith : [5] I the Lord thy God have called thee in righteousness, and I will take thee by thy hand and will strengthen thee. And give thee for a covenant of the people, for a light of the Gentiles. [6] To open the eyes of the blind, to bring out the prisoners from the prison, and them that sit in darkness out of the prison house.

22 Consider therefore from whence we have been redeemed. And again the prophet saith : [7] The spirit of the Lord is upon me, because he hath anointed me : he hath sent me to preach glad tidings to the lowly ; to heal the broken in heart ; to preach remission to the captives, and sight unto the blind ; to proclaim the acceptable year of the Lord, and the day of restitution ; to comfort all that mourn.

CHAP. XIII.

That the sabbath of the Jews was but a figure of a more glorious sabbath to come, and their temple, of the spiritual temples of God.

FURTHERMORE it is written concerning the sabbath, in the Ten [8] Commandments, which God spake in the Mount Sinai to Moses, [9] face to face ; Sanctify the sabbath of the Lord with pure hands, and with a clean heart.

2 And elsewhere he saith ; [10] If thy children shall keep my sabbaths, then will I put my mercy upon them.

3 And even in the beginning of the creation he makes men-

---

[1] Exod. xxxii. 7.   Deut. ix. 12.   [2] Vid. Lat. Interpret. Vet.   [3] Isaiah xlix. 6.   [4] For salvation unto.   [5] Isaiah xlii. 6.   [6] Verse 7.   [7] Isaiah lxi. 1, 2.   Comp. Luke, iv. 18.   [8] Words.   [9] Exod. xx. 8.   [10] Jer. xvii. 24

VERONICA AFFLICTED WITH AN ISSUE OF BLOOD.

tion of the sabbath. [1] And God made in six days the works of his hands; and he finished them on the [2] seventh day, and he rested the seventh day, and sanctified it.

4 Consider, my children, what that signifies, he finished them in six days. The meaning of it is this; that in [3] six thousand years the Lord God will bring all things to an end.

5 For with him one day is a thousand years; as himself testifieth, saying, Behold this day shall be as a thousand years. Therefore, children, in six days, that is, in six thousand years, shall [4] all things be accomplished.

6 And what is that he saith, And he rested the seventh day: he meaneth this; that when his Son shall come, and abolish the season of the [5] Wicked One, and judge the ungodly; and shall change the sun and the moon, and the stars; then he shall gloriously rest in that seventh day.

7 He adds lastly; Thou shalt sanctify it with clean hands and a pure heart. Wherefore we are greatly deceived if we imagine that any one can now sanctify that day which God has made holy, without having a heart pure in all things.

8 Behold therefore he will then truly sanctify it with blessed rest, when we (having received the righteous promise, when iniquity shall be no more, all things being renewed by the Lord) shall be able to sanctify it, being ourselves first made holy.

9 Lastly, he saith unto them: [6] Your new moons and your sabbaths I cannot bear them. Consider what he means by it; the sabbaths, says he, which ye now keep are not acceptable unto me, but those which I have made; when resting from all things I shall begin [7] the eighth day, that is, the beginning of the other world.

10 For which cause we observe the eighth day with gladness, in which Jesus rose from the dead; and having manifested himself to his disciples, ascended into heaven.

11 ¶ It remains yet that I speak to you concerning the temple how these miserable men being deceived have put their trust in the house, [8] and not in God himself who made them, as if it were the habitation of God.

12 For much after the same manner as the Gentiles, they consecrated him in the temple.

13 But learn therefore how the Lord speaketh, rendering the temple vain: [9] Who has measured the heaven with a span, and the earth with his hand? Is it not I? Thus saith the Lord,[10] Heaven is my throne, and the earth is my footstool. What is the house that ye will build me? Or what is the place of my rest? Know therefore that all their hope is vain.

14 And again he speaketh after this manner: [11] Behold they

---

[1] Gen. ii. 2. Exod. xx. 11, xxxi. 17. [2] Vid. Coteler. Annot. in loc.
[3] How general this tradition then was. See Coteler. Annot. in loc.
Edit. Oxon, page 90, a. Psalm lxxxix. 4. [4] That is, to the time of the Gospel, says Dr. Bernard, q. v. Annot. p. 127, Ed. Oxon. [5] So the Lat. Vers. [6] Isaiah, i. 13. [7] So the other Fathers, q. v. apud. Coteler. Annot. in loc. p. 36. [8] Vid. Edit. Oxon. et Vet. Lat. Interp. [9] Isaiah, xl. 12.
[10] Isaiah, lxvi. 1. [11] Isaiah, xlix. 17.

that destroy this temple, even they shall again build it up. And so it came to pass; for through their wars it is now destroyed by their enemies; and the servants of their enemies built it up.

15 Furthermore it has been made manifest, how both the city and the temple, and the people of Israel should be given up. For the Scripture saith; [1] And it shall come to pass in the last days, that the Lord will deliver up the sheep of his pasture, and their fold, and their tower into destruction. And it is come to pass, as the Lord hath spoken.

16 Let us inquire therefore, whether there be any temple of God? Yes there is; and that there, where himself declares that he would both make and perfect it. For it is written; And it shall be that as soon as the week shall be completed, the temple of the Lord shall be gloriously built in the name of the Lord.

17 I find therefore that there is a temple. But how shall it be built in the name of the Lord? I will shew you.

18 Before that we believed in God, the habitation of our heart was corruptible, and feeble, as a temple truly built with hands.

19 For it was a house full of idolatry, a house of devils; inasmuch as there was done in it whatsoever was contrary unto God. But it shall be built in the name of the Lord.

20 Consider, how that the temple of the Lord shall be very gloriously built; and by what means that shall be, learn.

21 Having received remission of our sins, and trusting in the name of the Lord, we are become renewed, being again created as it were from the beginning. Wherefore God truly dwells in our house, that is, in us.

22 But how does he dwell in us? The word of his faith, the calling of his promise, the wisdom of his righteous judgments, the commands of his doctrine; he himself prophesies within us, he himself dwelleth in us, and openeth to us who were in bondage of death the gate of our [3] temple, that is, the mouth of wisdom, having given repentance unto us; and by this means has brought us to be an incorruptible temple.

23 He therefore that desires to be saved looketh not unto the man, but unto him that dwelleth in him, and speaketh by him; being struck with wonder, forasmuch as he never either heard him speaking such words out of his mouth, nor ever desired to hear them.

24 This is that spiritual temple that is built unto the Lord.

CHAP. XIV.

Of the way of light; being a summary of what a Christian is to do, that he may be happy for ever.

AND thus, I trust, I have declared to you as much, and with as great simplicity as I could, those things which make for your salvation, so as not to have omitted anything that might be requisite thereunto.

2 For should I speak further of the things that [4] now are, and of those that are to come, you would not yet understand them, seeing they lie in parables. This therefore shall suffice as to these things.

[1] Zeph. ii. 6. just. Heb.   [2] Dan. ix. Haggai, ii.   [3] Vid. Lat. Ver. Interp.
[4] So the old Lat. Interp.

3 Let us now go on to the other kind of knowledge and doctrine. There are two ways of doctrine and power ; the one of light, the other of darkness.

4 But there is a great deal of difference between these two ways: for over one are appointed the [1] angels of God, the leaders of the way of light ; over the other, the angels of Satan. And the one is the Lord from everlasting to everlasting ; the other is the prince of the time of unrighteousness.

5 Now the way of light is this, if any one desires to attain to the place that is appointed for him, and will hasten thither by his works. And the knowledge that has been given to us for walking in it, to this effect : Thou shalt love him that made thee : thou shalt glorify him that hath redeemed thee from death.

6 Thou shalt be simple in heart, and rich in the spirit. Thou shalt not cleave to those that walk in the way of death. Thou shalt hate to do anything that is not pleasing unto God. Thou shalt abhor all dissimulation. Thou shalt not neglect any of the commands of the Lord.

7 Thou shalt not exalt thyself, but shalt be humble. Thou shalt not take honour to thyself. Thou shalt not enter into any wicked counsel against thy neighbour. Thou shalt not be over-confident in thy heart.

8 Thou shalt not commit fornication, nor adultery. Neither shalt thou corrupt thyself with mankind. Thou shalt not make use of the word of God, to any impurity.

9 Thou shalt not accept any man's person, when thou reprovest any one's faults. Thou shalt be gentle. Thou shalt be quiet. Thou shalt tremble at the words which thou hast heard. Thou shalt not keep any hatred in thy heart against thy brother. Thou shalt not entertain any doubt whether it shall be or not.

10 Thou shalt not take the name of the Lord in vain. Thou shalt love thy neighbour above thy own soul.

11 Thou shalt not destroy thy conceptions before they are brought forth ; nor kill them after they are born.

12 Thou shalt not withdraw thy hand from thy son, or from thy daughter ; but shall teach them from their youth the fear of the Lord.

13 Thou shalt not covet thy neighbour's goods; neither shalt thou be [2] an extortioner. Neither shall thy heart be joined to proud men ; but thou shalt be numbered among the righteous and the lowly. Whatever [3] events shall happen unto thee, thou shalt receive them as good.

14 Thou shalt not be doubleminded, or double-tongued ; for a double tongue is the snare of death. Thou shalt be subject unto the Lord and to inferior masters as to the representatives of God, in fear and reverence.

15 Thou shalt not be bitter in thy commands towards any of thy servants that trust in God ; lest thou chance not to fear him who is over both; because he came not to call any with respect of persons, but whomsoever the spirit had prepared.

---

[1] Vid. Coteler. in loc. et Basil. in Psalm i. [2] Greedy, $\pi\lambda\epsilon o\nu\epsilon\kappa\tau\eta\varsigma$.
[3] Effects.

16 Thou shalt communicate to thy neighbour of all thou hast; thou shalt not call anything thine own: for if ye partake in such things as are incorruptible, how much more should you do it in those that are corruptible?

17 [1] Thou shalt not be forward to speak; for the mouth is the snare of death. [2] Strive for thy soul with all thy might. [3] Reach not out thine hand to receive, and withhold it not when thou shouldest give.

18 Thou shalt love, as the apple of thine eye, every one that speaketh unto thee the Word of the Lord. [4] Call to thy remembrance, day and night, the future judgment.

19 Thou shalt seek out every day the persons of the [5] righteous: and both consider and go about to exhort others by the word, and meditate how thou mayest save a soul.

20 Thou shalt also labour with thy hands to give to the poor, [6] that thy sins may be forgiven thee. Thou shalt not deliberate whether thou shouldst give: nor, having given, murmur at it.

21 Give to every one that asks: so shalt thou know who is the good rewarder of thy gifts.

22 Keep what thou hast received; thou shalt neither add to it nor take from it.

23 Let the wicked be always thy aversion. Thou shalt judge righteous judgment. Thou shalt never cause divisions; but shalt make peace between those that are at variance, and bring them together.

24 Thou shalt confess thy sins; and not come to thy prayer with an evil conscience.

25 This is the way of light.

CHAP. XV.

Of the way of darkness; that is, what kind of persons shall be for ever cast out of the kingdom of God.

BUT the way of darkness is crooked and full of cursing. For it is the way of eternal death, with punishment; in which they that walk meet those things that destroy their own souls.

2 Such are; idolatry, confidence, pride of power, hypocrisy, double-mindedness, adultery, murder, rapine, pride, transgression, deceit, malice, arrogance, witchcraft, covetousness, and the want of the fear of God.

3 In this walk those who are the persecutors of them that are good; haters of truth; lovers of lies; who know not the reward of righteousness, nor cleave to any thing that is good.

4 Who administer not righteous judgment to the widow and orphan; who watch for wickedness, and not for the fear of the Lord:

5 From whom gentleness and patience are far off; who love vanity, and follow after rewards; having no compassion upon the poor; nor take any pains for such as are heavy laden and oppressed.

6 Ready to evil speaking, not

---

[1] See Eccles. iv. 29.   [2] Ibid., ver. 28. For so I choose to read it, υπερ της ψυχης σου αγωνευσεις, according to the conjecture of Cotelerius. [3] Ibid., ver. 36. [4] And remember him night and day. The words ημερας κριςεως, seem to have been erroneously inserted, and pervert the sense. [5] Gr. Saints. [6] Gr. For the redemption of thy sins. Comp. Dan. iv. 24. See LXX.

knowing him that made them; murderers of children; corrupters of the creatures of God; that turn away from the needy; oppress the afflicted; are the advocates of the rich, but unjust judges of the poor; being altogether sinners.

7 It is therefore fitting that learning the just commands of the Lord, which we have before mentioned, we should walk in them. For he who does such things shall be glorified in the kingdom of God.

8 But he that chooses the other part, shall be destroyed, together with his works. For this cause there shall be both a resurrection, and a retribution.

9 I beseech those that are in high estate among you, (if so be you will take the counsel which with a good intention I offer to you,) you have those with you towards whom you may do good; do not forsake them.

10 For the day is at hand in which all things shall be destroyed, together with the wicked one. The Lord is near, and his reward is with him.

11 I beseech you, therefore, again, and again, be as good lawgivers to one another; continue faithful counsellors to each other; remove from among you all hypocrisy.

12 And may God, the Lord of all the world give you wisdom, knowledge, counsel, and understanding of his judgments in patience.

13 Be ye taught of God; seeking what it is the Lord requires of you, and doing it; that ye may be saved in the day of judgment.

14 And if there be among you any remembrance of what is good, think of me; meditating upon these things, that both my desire and my watching for you may turn to a good account.

15 I beseech you; I ask it as a favour of you; whilst you are in this beautiful [1] tabernacle of the body, be wanting in none of these things; but without ceasing seek them, and fulfil every command. For these things are fitting and worthy to be done.

16 Wherefore I have given the more diligence to write unto you, according to my ability, that you might rejoice. Farewell, children, of love and peace.

17 The Lord of glory and of all grace, be with your spirit, Amen.

¶ *The end of the Epistle of Barnabas, the Apostle, and fellow-traveller of St. Paul the Apostle.*

[1] Vessel.

The EPISTLE of IGNATIUS to the EPHESIANS.

¶ OF THE EPISTLES OF IGNATIUS.

[The Epistles of Ignatius are translated by Archbishop Wake from the text of Vossius. He says that there were considerable differences in the editions; the best for a long time extant containing fabrications, and the genuine being altered and corrupted. Archbishop Usher printed old Latin translations of them at Oxford, in 1644. At Amsterdam, two years afterwards, Vossius printed six of them, in their ancient and pure Greek; and the seventh greatly amended from the ancient Latin version, was printed at Paris, by Ruinart, in 1689, in the Acts and Martyrdom of Ignatius, from a Greek uninterpolated copy. These are supposed to form the collection that Polycarp made of the Epistles of Ignatius, mentioned by Irenæus, Origen, Eusebius, Jerome, Athanasius, Theodoret, and other ancients; but many learned men have imagined all of them to be apocryphal. This supposition, the piety of Archbishop Wake, and his persuasion of their utility to the faith of the church, will not permit him to entertain; hence he has taken great pains to render the present translation acceptable, by adding numerous readings and references to the Canonical Books.]

CHAP. I.

1 *Commends them for sending Onesimus, and other members of the church to him.* 8 *Exhorts them to unity,* 13 *by a due subjection to their bishop.*

IGNATIUS, who is also called Theophorus, to the church which is at Ephesus in Asia; most deservedly happy; being blessed [1] through the greatness and fulness [2] of God the Father, and predestinated before the world began, that it should be always unto an enduring and unchangeable glory; being united and chosen [3] through his true passion, according to the will of the Father, and Jesus Christ our God; all [4] happiness, by Jesus Christ, and [5] his undefiled grace.

2 I have heard of your name much beloved in God; which ye have [6] very justly attained by a [7] habit of righteousness, according to the faith and love which is in Jesus Christ our Saviour.

3 How that being [8] followers of God, and stirring up yourselves by the blood of Christ ye have perfectly accomplished the work that was con-natural unto you.

4 For hearing that I came bound from Syria, for the common name and [9] hope, trusting through your prayers to fight with beasts at Rome; so that by [10] suffering I may become indeed the disciple of him [11] who gave himself to God, an offering and sacrifice for us; [12] (ye hastened to see me). I received, therefore, in the name of God, your whole multitude in Onesimus.

5 Who by inexpressible love is ours, but according to the flesh is your bishop; whom I beseech you, by Jesus Christ, to love; and that you would all strive to be like unto him. And blessed be God, who has granted unto you, who are so worthy of him, to [13] enjoy such an excellent bishop.

6 For what concerns my fellow servant Burrhus, and your [14] most blessed deacon in things pertaining to God; I entreat you that he may tarry longer, both for yours, and your bishop's honour.

---

[1] In. [2] See Eph. iii. 19. [3] In. [4] Health, Joy. [5] Received. Vid. Epist. Interpol. [6] Vid. Coteler. in loc. Comp. Gal. iv. 8. [7] Pearson Vind. Ignat, Par. 2, cap. 14. [8] Imitators. [9] Viz. of Christ. [10] Martyrdom. [11] Eph. v. 2. [12] See the old Lat. Ed. of Bishop Usher. [13] Possess. [14] Blessed in all things.

7 And Crocus also worthy both our God and you, whom I have received as the pattern of your love, has in all things refreshed me, as the Father of our Lord Jesus Christ shall also refresh him; together with Onesimus, and Burrhus, and Euclus, and Fronto, [1] in whom I have, as to your charity, seen all of you. And may I always, [2] have joy of you, if I shall be worthy of it.

8 It is therefore fitting that you should [3] by all means glorify Jesus Christ who hath glorified you: that [4] by a uniform obedience [5] ye may be perfectly joined together, in the same mind, and in the same judgment: and may all speak the same things concerning everything.

9 And that being subject to [6] your bishop, and the presbytery, ye may be wholly and thoroughly sanctified.

10 These things I [7] prescribe to you, not as if I were somebody extraordinary: for though I am bound [8] for his name, I am not yet perfect in Christ Jesus. [9] But now I begin to learn, and I speak to you as fellow disciples together with me.

11 For I ought to have been stirred up by you, in faith, in admonition, in patience, in longsuffering; but forasmuch as charity suffers me not to be silent [10] towards you, I have first taken upon me to exhort you, that ye would all run together according to the will of God.

12 For even Jesus Christ, our inseparable life, is sent by the [11] will of the Father; as the bishops, appointed unto the utmost bounds of the earth, are by the will of Jesus Christ.

13 [12] Wherefore it will become you to run together according to the will of your bishop, as also ye do.

14 For your [13] famous presbytery, worthy of God, is fitted as exactly to the bishop, as the strings are to the harp.

15 Therefore in your concord and agreeing charity, Jesus Christ is sung; and every single person among you makes up the chorus:

16 That so being all consonant in [14] love, and taking up the song of God, ye may in a perfect unity with one voice, sing to the Father by Jesus Christ; to the end that he may both hear you, and perceive by your works, that ye are indeed the members of his son.

17 Wherefore it is profitable for you to live in an unblameable unity, that so ye may always [15] have a fellowship with God.

CHAP. II.

1 *The benefit of subjection.* 4 *The bishop not to be respected the less because he is not forward in exacting it:* 8 *warns them against heretics; bidding them cleave to Jesus, whose divine and human nature is declared; commends them for their care to keep themselves from false teachers; and shews them the way to God.*

FOR if I in this little time have had such a familiarity with your bishop, I mean not a carnal, but spiritual acquaintance with him; how much more must I think you happy who are so joined to him, as the church is to Jesus Christ, and Jesus Christ to

---

[1] By. [2] See Philem. 20. Wisd. xxx. 2. [3] In all manner of ways. [4] In one. [5] 1 Cor. i. 10. [6] The. [7] Command you. [8] In. [9] For. [10] Concerning. [1] Mind, counsel, opinion, &c. [12] Whence. [13] Worthy to be named. [14] Concord. [15] Partake of.

the Father; that so all things may agree in the same unity?

2 Let no man deceive himself; if a man be not within the altar, he is deprived of the bread of God. For if the prayers of [1] one or two be of such force, as we are told; how much more powerful shall that of the bishop and the whole church be?

3 He therefore that does not come together in the same place with it, is [2] proud, and has already [3] condemned himself. For it is written, [4] God resisteth the proud. Let us take heed therefore, that we do not set ourselves against the bishop, that we may be subject to God.

4 [5] The more any one sees his bishop silent, the more let him revere him. For whomsoever the master of the house sends to be over his own household, we ought in like manner to receive him, as we would do him that sent him. It is therefore evident that we ought to look upon the bishop, even as we would do upon the Lord himself.

5 And indeed Onesimus himself does greatly commend your good order in God: that you all live according to the truth, and that no heresy dwells among you. For neither do ye hearken to any one more than to Jesus Christ speaking to you in truth.

6 For some there are who [6] carry about the name of Christ [7] in deceitfulness, but do things unworthy of God; whom ye must [8] flee, as ye would do so many wild beasts. For they are ravening

dogs, who bite secretly: against whom ye must guard yourselves, as men hardly to be cured.

7 There is one physician, both fleshly and spiritual; made and not made; God incarnate; true life in death; both of Mary and of God; first passible, then impassible; even Jesus Christ our Lord.

8 Wherefore let no man deceive you; as indeed neither are ye deceived, being wholly the servants of God. For inasmuch as there is no contention nor strife among you,[9] to trouble you, [10] ye must needs live according to God's will. [11] My soul be for yours; and I myself the expiatory offering for your church of Ephesus, so famous [12] throughout the world.

9 They that are of the flesh cannot do the works of the spirit; neither they that are of the spirit the works of the flesh. [13] As he that has faith cannot be an infidel; nor he that is an infidel have faith. But even those things which ye do according to the flesh are spiritual; forasmuch as ye do all things in Jesus Christ.

10 Nevertheless I have [14] heard of some who have [15] passed by you, having perverse doctrine; whom ye did not suffer to sow [16] among you; but stopped your ears, that ye might not receive those things that were sown by them; [17] as becoming the stones of the temple of the Father, prepared for [18] his building; and drawn up on high by the Cross of Christ, [19] as by an engine.

11 Using the Holy Ghost as

---

[1] Matt. xviii. 19. [2] Is already proud and has, &c. [3] Judged, or separated. [4] James, iv. 6. [5] And the. [6] Accustom themselves to carry. [7] In wicked deceit. [8] Avoid. [9] Which can. [10] Without doubt ye live. [11] Vid. Voss. Annot. in loc. Pearson, Vind. Ign. par. 2, pp. 207, 208. [12] To ages. [13] As neither is faith the things of infidelity, nor infidelity the things of faith. [14] Known. [15] Passed thither. [16] Upon. [17] Comp. Eph. ii. 20, 21, 22. 1 Pet. ii. 5. [18] The building of God the Father. [19] By the engine of the cross, etc.

the rope : your faith being your support; and your charity the way that leads unto God.

12 Ye are therefore, with all your companions in the same [1] journey, full of God; his spiritual temples, [2] full of Christ, full of holiness : adorned in all things with the commands of Christ.

13 In whom also I rejoice that I have been thought worthy by [3] this present epistle to converse, and joy together with you; that with respect to the other life, ye love nothing but God only.

CHAP. III.

1 *Exhorts them to prayer ; to be un-blameable.* 5 *To be careful of salvation ;* 11 *frequent in public devotion ;* 13 *and to live in charity.*

PRAY also without ceasing for other men: for there is hope of repentance in them, that they may attain unto God. Let them therefore at least be instructed by your works, if they will be no other way.

2 Be ye mild at their anger; humble at their boasting; to their blasphemies return your prayers: to their error, your [4] firmness in the faith : when they are cruel, be ye gentle; not endeavouring to imitate their ways.

(3 Let us be their brethren in all kindness and moderation, but let us be followers of the Lord ; [5] for who was ever more unjustly used ? More destitute ? More despised ?)

4 That so no herb of the devil may be found in you: but ye may remain in all holiness and sobriety [6] both of body and spirit, in Christ Jesus.

5 The last times [7] are come upon us : let us therefore be very reverent and fear the long-suffering of God, that it be not to us unto condemnation.

6 For let us either fear the wrath that is to come, or let us love the grace [8] that we at present enjoy: that [9] by the one, or other, of these we may be found in Christ Jesus, unto true life.

7 [10] Besides him, let nothing [11] be worthy of you ; [12] for whom also I bear about these bonds, those spiritual jewels, in which I would to God that I might arise through your prayers.

8 Of which I entreat you to make me always partaker, that I may be found in the lot of the Christians of Ephesus, who have always [13] agreed with the Apostles,[14] through the power of Jesus Christ.

9 ¶ I know both who I am, and to whom I write; I, a person condemned : ye, such as have obtained mercy : I, exposed to danger ; ye, confirmed against danger.

10 Ye are the passage of those that are killed for God ; the companions of Paul in the mysteries of the Gospel ; the Holy, the [15] martyr, the deservedly most happy Paul : at whose feet may I be found, when I shall have attained unto God; who [16] throughout all his epistle, makes mention of you in Christ Jesus.

11 Let it be your care therefore to come more fully together, to the praise and glory of God. For when ye meet fully together in the same place, the powers of

---

[1] Pearson, ib. part 2, cap. 12.   [2] Carriers.   [3] These things I write.   [4] Be ye firm.   [5] Who has been more, etc.   [6] In Jesus Christ both bodily and spiritually.   1 Cor. vii. 34.   [7] Remain: or, for it remains.   [8] Is present. [9] One of the two, only that we may be found, etc.   [10] Without him. [11] Become you.   [12] In.   [13] Assented to.   [14] In.   [15] Witnessed of.   [16] Vid. Coteler. in loc. Pears. Vind. Ign. Par 2, cap. 10.

the devil are destroyed, and his ¹mischief is dissolved by the ²unity of their faith.

12 And indeed, nothing is better than peace, by which all war both ³spiritual and earthly is abolished.

13 Of all which nothing is hid from you, if ye have perfect faith and charity in Christ Jesus, which are the beginning and end of life.

14 For the beginning is faith; the end is charity. And these two ⁴joined together, are of God: but all other things which concern a holy life are the consequences of these.

15 No man professing a true faith, sinneth; neither does he who has charity hate any.

16 ⁵The tree is made manifest by its fruit; so they who profess themselves to be Christians ⁶are known by what they do.

17 For Christianity is not the work of an outward profession; but shows itself in the power of faith, if a man be found faithful unto the end.

18 It is better for a man to hold his peace, and be; ⁷than to say he is a Christian and not to be.

19 It is good to teach; ⁸if what he says he does likewise.

20 There is therefore one master who spake, and it was done; and even those things which he did without speaking, are worthy of the Father.

21 He that possesses the word of Jesus is truly able to hear his very silence, that he may be perfect; ⁹and both do according to what he speaks, and be known

by those things of which he is silent.

22 There is nothing hid from God, but even our secrets are nigh unto him.

23 Let us therefore do all things, as becomes those who have ¹⁰God dwelling in them; that we may be his temples, and he may be our God: as also he is, and will manifest himself before our faces, by those things ¹¹for which we justly love him.

CHAP. IV.

1 *To have a care for the Gospel.* 9 *The virginity of Mary, the incarnation, and the death of Christ, were hid from the Devil.* 11 *How the birth of Christ was revealed.* 16 *Exhorts to unity.*

BE not deceived, my brethren: those that ¹²corrupt families by adultery, shall not inherit the kingdom of God.

2 If therefore they who do this according to the flesh, ¹³have suffered death; how much more shall he die, who by his wicked doctrine corrupts the faith of God, for which Christ was crucified?

3 ¹⁴He that is thus defiled, shall depart into unquenchable fire, and so also shall he that ¹⁵hearkens to him.

4 For this cause did the Lord ¹⁶suffer the ointment to be poured on his head; that he might breathe the breath of immortality unto his church.

5 Be not ye therefore anointed with the evil savour of the doctrine of the prince of this world: let him not take you captive from the life that is set before you.

6 And why are we not all

¹ Destruction. ² Concord. ³ Of things in heaven and of things on earth. ⁴ Being in unity. ⁵ Matt. xii. 38. ⁶ Shall be seen or made manifest. ⁷ Speaking, not to be. ⁸ If he who says, does. ⁹ That he may. ¹⁰ Him. ¹¹ Out of. ¹² The corrupters of houses. 1 Cor. vi. 9, 10. ¹³ 1 Cor. x. 8. ¹⁴ Such a one being become defiled. ¹⁵ Hears him. ¹⁶ Receives ointment. Psalm xliv. 8, cxxxii. 2.

wise, seeing we have received the knowledge of God, which is Jesus Christ? Why [1] do we suffer ourselves foolishly to perish; [2] not considering the gift which the Lord has truly sent to us?

7 [3] Let my life be sacrificed for the doctrine of the cross; which is indeed a scandal to the unbelievers, but to us is salvation and life eternal.

8 [4] Where is the wise man? Where is the disputer? Where is the boasting of those who are called wise?

9 For our God Jesus Christ was according to the dispensation of God [5] conceived in the womb of Mary, of the seed of David, [6] by the Holy Ghost; [7] he was born and baptized, that through his passion he might purify water, to the washing away of sin.

10 Now the Virginity of Mary, and he who was born of her, was kept in secret from the prince of this world; as was also the death of our Lord: three of the [8] mysteries the most spoken of throughout the world, yet done in [9] secret by God.

11 How then was our Saviour manifested to the world? A star shone in heaven beyond all the other stars, and its light was inexpressible, and its novelty struck terror into men's minds. All the rest of the stars, together with the sun and moon, were the chorus to this star; but that sent out its light exceedingly above them all.

12 And men [10] began to be troubled to think whence this [11] new star came so unlike to [12] all the others.

13 Hence all the power of magic became dissolved; and every bond of wickedness was [13] destroyed: men's ignorance was taken away; and the old kingdom abolished; God himself [14] appearing in the form of a man, for the renewal of eternal life.

14 From thence began what God had prepared: from thenceforth things were disturbed; forasmuch as he designed to abolish death.

15 But if Jesus Christ shall give me grace through your prayers, and it be his will, I purpose in a second epistle which I will suddenly write unto you to manifest to you more fully the dispensation of which I have now begun to speak, unto the new man, which is Jesus Christ; both in his faith, and charity; in his suffering, and in his resurrection.

16 Especially if the Lord shall [15] make known unto me, that ye all by name come together in common in one faith, and in one Jesus Christ; who was of the race of David according to the flesh; the Son of man, and Son of God; [16] obeying your bishop and the presbytery with an entire [17] affection; breaking one and the same bread, which is the medicine of immortality; our antidote that we should not die, but live forever in Christ Jesus.

17 My soul be for yours, and theirs whom ye have sent to the glory of God, even unto Smyrna, from whence also I write to you; giving thanks unto the Lord and loving Polycarp even as I do you. Remember me, as Jesus Christ does remember you.

---

[1] Are we foolishly destroyed? [2] Not knowing. [3] See Dr. Smith's note in loc. 1 Cor. i. 18, 23, 24. [4] 1 Cor. i. 20. [5] Carried. [6] But by. [7] Who was. [8] Mysteries of noise. [9] Silence or quietness. See Rom. xvi. 25. [10] There was a disorder. [11] Novelty. [12] Them. [13] Disappeared. [14] Being made manifest. [15] Reveal. [16] That ye may obey. [17] Mind.

18 Pray for the church which is in Syria, from whence I am carried bound to Rome; being the least of all the faithful which are there, as I have been thought worthy to be found to the glory of God.

19 Fare ye well in God the Father, and in Jesus Christ, our common Hope. Amen.

¶ *To the Ephesians.*

The EPISTLE of IGNATIUS to the MAGNESIANS.

CHAP. I.

4 *Mentions the arrival of Damas, their bishop, and others,* 6 *whom he exhorts them to reverence, notwithstanding he was a young man.*

IGNATIUS who is also called Theophorus; to the blessed [1] (church) [2] by the grace of God the Father in [3] Jesus Christ our Saviour: in whom I salute the church which is at Magnesia near the Mæander : and wish it all joy in God the Father and in Jesus Christ.

2 When I heard of your well ordered love and charity in God, being full of joy, I desired much to speak unto you in the faith of Jesus Christ.

3 For having [4] been thought worthy to obtain a most excellent name, [5] in the bonds which I carry about, I [6] salute the churches; wishing in them a union both of the body and spirit of Jesus Christ, our eternal life : as also of faith and charity, to which nothing is preferred : but especially of Jesus and the Father; in whom [7] if we undergo all the injuries of the prince of this present world, and escape, we shall enjoy God.

4 Seeing then I have been judged worthy to see you, by Damas your [8] most excellent bishop; and by your very worthy presbyters, Bassus and Apollonius; and by my fellow-servant Sotio, the deacon ;

5 In whom [9] I rejoice, forasmuch as he is the subject unto his bishop as to the grace of God, and to the presbytery as to the law of Jesus Christ; [10] I determined to write unto you.

6 Wherefore it will become you also not [11] to use your bishop too familiarly upon the account of his youth; but to yield all reverence to him according to the power of God the Father; as also I perceive that your holy presbyters do: not considering his [12] age, which indeed to appearance is young; but as becomes those who are prudent in God, submitting to him, or rather not to him, but to the Father of our Lord Jesus Christ, the bishop of us all.

7 It will therefore [13] behoove you [14] with all sincerity, to obey your bishop; in honour of him [15] whose pleasure it is that ye should do so.

8 Because he that does not do so, deceives not the bishop whom

---

[1] Vid. Interp. Lat. Epist. Interpol. [2] In. [3] According to. [4] Been vouchsafed a name carrying a great deal of divinity in it. [5] See Bishop Pearson. Vind. Ign. par. ii. cap. 12, p. 146. [6] Sing, commend. [7] Undergoing, escaping. [8] Worthy of God. [9] Whom may I enjoy. [10] Apud. Vet. Lat. Interp. Glorificato Deum Patrem D. nostri Jesu Christi. [11] Vid. Voss. Annot. in loc. Pearson Præf. ad Vind. Ignat. [12] Seeming youthful state. [13] It is becoming. [14] Without any hypocrisy. [15] Who willeth it.

he sees, but [1] affronts him that is invisible. [2] For whatsoever of this kind is done, it reflects not upon [3] man, but upon God, who knows the secrets of our hearts.

9 It is therefore fitting, that we should not only be called Christians, but be so.

10 As some call indeed their governor, bishop; but yet do all things without him.

11 But I can never think that such as these have a good conscience, seeing that they are not gathered together [4] thoroughly according to God's commandment.

CHAP. II.

1 That as all must die, 4 he exhorts them to live orderly and in unity.

SEEING then all things have an end, there are these two [5] indifferently set before us, death and life: and every one shall depart unto his proper place.

2 For as there are two sorts of coins, the one of God, the other of the world; and each of these has its proper [6] inscription engraven upon it; so also is it here.

3 The unbelievers are of this world; but the faithful, through charity, have the character of God the Father by Jesus Christ: by whom if we are not readily disposed to die after the likeness of his passion, his life is not in us.

4 Forasmuch, therefore, as I have in the persons before mentioned seen [7] all of you in faith and charity; I exhort you that ye study to do all things in a [8] divine concord:

5 Your bishop presiding in the place of God; your presbyters in the place of the council of the Apostles; and your dea-

cons most [9] dear to me being entrusted with the ministry of Jesus Christ; who was the Father before all ages, and appeared in the [10] end to us.

6 Wherefore taking the same [11] holy course, see that ye all reverence one another: and let no one look upon his neighbour after the flesh; but do ye all mutually love each other in Jesus Christ.

7 Let there be nothing that may be able to make a division among you; but be ye united to your bishop, and those who preside over you, to be your pattern and direction in the way to immortality.

8 [12] As therefore the Lord did nothing without the Father, being united to him; neither by himself nor yet by his Apostles, so neither do ye do anything without your bishop and presbyters:

9 Neither endeavour to let anything appear rational to yourselves apart;

10 But being come together into the same place [13] have one common prayer; one supplication; one mind; one hope; one in charity, and in joy undefiled.

11 There is one Lord Jesus Christ, than whom nothing is better. Wherefore [14] come ye all together as unto one temple of God; as to one [15] altar, as to one Jesus Christ; who proceeded from one Father, and exists in one, and is returned to one.

CHAP. III.

1 He cautions them against false opinions. 4 Especially those of [16] Ebion and the Judaizing Christians.

---

[1] Deludes. [2] Vid. Epist. Interp. ad loc. [3] Flesh. [4] Firmly. [5] Together.
[6] Character set. [7] Your whole multitude. [8] The concord of God. [9] Sweet.
[10] Was made manifest. Heb. ix. 26. [11] Habit of God. [12] John x. 30, xiv.
11, 12, xvii. 21, 22. [13] Eph. iv. 3, 4, 5, 6. [14] Run. [15] John xvi. 28.
[16] Pearson, Vind. Ign. par. 2, cap. 4.

BE not deceived with [1] strange doctrines; nor with old fables which are unprofitable. For if we still continue to live according to the Jewish law, we do confess ourselves not to have received grace. For even the most [2]holy prophets lived according to Christ Jesus.

2 And for this cause were they persecuted, being inspired by his grace, [3] to convince the unbelievers and disobedient that there is one God who has manifested himself by Jesus Christ his Son; who is his [4] eternal word, not coming forth from silence, who in all things pleased him that sent him.

3 Wherefore if they who were brought up in these ancient [5] laws came nevertheless to the newness of hope: no longer observing sabbaths, [6] but keeping the Lord's day in which also our life is sprung up by him, and through his death, [7] whom yet some deny:

4 (By which mystery we have [8] been brought to believe and therefore wait that we may be found the disciples of Jesus Christ, our only master:)

5 How shall we be able to live [9] different from him whose disciples the very prophets themselves being, did by the spirit expect him as their master.

6 [10]And therefore he whom they justly waited for, being come, raised them up from the dead.

7 Let us not then be insensible of his goodness; for should he [11] have dealt with us according to our works, we had not now had a being.

8 Wherefore being become his disciples, let us learn to live according to the rules of Christianity; for whosoever is called by any other name [12] besides this, he is not of God.

9 Lay aside therefore the old and sour and evil leaven; and be ye changed into the new leaven, which is Jesus Christ.

10 Be ye salted in him, lest any one among you should be corrupted; for by your savour ye shall be [13] judged.

11 It is absurd to name Jesus Christ, and to Judaize. For the Christian religion did not [14] embrace the Jewish, but the Jewish the Christian; that so every tongue that believed might be gathered together unto God.

12 These things, my beloved, I write unto you; not that I know of any among you that [15] lie under this error; but as [16] one of the least among you, I am desirous to forewarn you, that ye fall not into the [17] snares of false doctrine.

13 But that ye be fully instructed in the birth, and suffering, and resurrection of Jesus Christ, our hope; which was accomplished in the time of the government of Pontius Pilate, and that most truly and [18] certainly: and from which God forbid that any among you should be turned aside.

CHAP. IV.

1 *Commends their faith and piety; exhorts them to persevere;* 10 *desires their prayers for himself and the church at Antioch.*

MAY I therefore have joy of you in all things, if I shall

[1] Heterodox. [2] Most divine. [3] Fully to satisfy. [4] John, i. 1. [5] Things. [6] Or, living according to. [7] Or, which. [8] Received. [9] Without. [10] Matt. xxvii. 52. [11] Vid. Annot. Voss. in loc. should he have imitated our works, Gr. [12] More than. [13] Convicted, overthrown. [14] Believe. [15] Have yourselves so. [16] Lesser than you. [17] Hooks. [18] Firmly.

be worthy of it. For though I am bound, yet I am not worthy to be compared to one of you that are at liberty.

2 I know that ye are not puffed up; for ye have Jesus Christ [1] in your hearts.

3 And especially when I commend you, I know that ye are ashamed, as it is written, [2] The just man condemneth himself.

4 Study therefore to be confirmed in the doctrine of our Lord, and of his Apostles; that so whatever ye do, ye may prosper both in body and spirit, in faith and charity, in the Son, and in the Father and in the Holy Spirit: in the beginning, and in the end.

5 Together with your most worthy bishop, and the [3] well-wrought spiritual crown of your presbytery, and your deacons, which are according to God.

6 Be subject to your bishop, and to one another, as Jesus Christ to the Father, according to the flesh: and the Apostles both to Christ, and to the Father, and to the Holy Ghost: that so ye may [4] be united both in body and spirit.

7 [5] Knowing you to be full of God, I have the more briefly exhorted you.

8 Be mindful of me in your prayers, that I may [6] attain unto God, and of the Church that is in Syria, from [7] which I am not worthy to be called.

9 For I stand in need of your joint prayers in God, and of your charity, that the church which is in Syria may be thought worthy to be [8] nourished by your church.

10 The Ephesians [9] from Smyrna salute you, from which place I write unto you: (being present here to the glory of God, in like manner as you are,) who have in all things refreshed me, together with Polycarp, the bishop of the Smyrnæans.

11 The rest of the churches in the honour of Jesus Christ, salute you.

12 [10] Farewell, and be ye strengthened in the concord of God: [11] enjoying his inseparable spirit, which is Jesus Christ.

¶ *To the Magnesians.*

The EPISTLE of IGNATIUS to the TRALLIANS.
CHAP. I.

1 *Acknowledges the coming of their bishop.* 5 *Commends them for their subjection to their bishop, priests, and deacons; and exhorts them to continue in it:* 15 *is afraid even of his over-great desire to suffer, lest it should be prejudicial to him.*

IGNATIUS, who is also called Theophorus, to the holy church which is at Tralles in Asia: beloved of God the Father of Jesus Christ, elect and worthy of God, having peace [12] through the flesh and blood, and passion of Jesus Christ our hope, in the resurrection which is [13] by him: which also I salute in its fulness, continuing in the apostolical character, wishing all joy and happiness unto it.

2 I have [14] heard of your blameless and [15] constant disposition through patience, which [16] not only appears in your out-

---

[1] In yourselves. [2] Prov. xviii. 17 Sept. [3] Worthily complicated. [4] There may be a union both fleshly and spiritual. [5] Eph. iii. 4. [6] Find, enjoy. [7] Whence. [8] Bedewed. Vid. Epist. Inter. in loc. [9] Which came to Smyrna upon my account. [10] Ἔρρωσθε. [11] Possessing. [12] In. [13] Unto. [14] Known. [15] Inseparable mind. [16] Which you have not according to use, but according to possession.

ward conversation, but is naturally rooted and grounded in you.

3 In like manner as Polybius your bishop has declared unto me, who came to me to Smyrna, by the will of God and Jesus Christ, and so rejoiced together with me [1] in my bonds for Jesus Christ, that in effect I saw your whole [2] church in him.

4 Having therefore received [3] testimony of your good will towards me [4] for God's sake, by him; [5] I seemed to find you, as also I knew that ye were the [6] followers of God.

5 For [7] whereas ye are subject to your bishop as to Jesus Christ, ye appear to me to live not after the manner of men, but according to Jesus Christ; who died for us, that so believing in his death, ye might [8] escape death.

6 It is therefore necessary, that as ye do, so without your bishop, you should do nothing: also be ye subject to your presbyters, as to the Apostles of Jesus Christ our hope; in whom if we walk, we shall be found in him.

7 [9] The deacons also, as being the ministers of the mysteries of Jesus Christ, must by all means please ye. For they are not the [10] ministers of meat and drink, but of the church of God. Wherefore they must avoid all offences, as they would do fire.

8 In like manner let us reverence the deacons [11] as Jesus Christ; and the bishop as the father; and the presbyters as the Sanhedrim of God, and college of the Apostles.

9 Without these there is no [12] church. Concerning all which I am persuaded that ye [13] think after the very same manner: for I have received, and even now have with me, the pattern of your love, in your bishop.

10 Whose very [14] look is instructive; and whose mildness [15] powerful: [16] whom I am persuaded, the very Atheists themselves cannot but reverence.

11 But because I have a love towards you, I will not write any more sharply unto you about this matter, though I very well might; but now I have done so; lest being a condemned man, I should seem to prescribe to you as an Apostle.

12 I have [17] great knowledge in God; but I [18] refrain myself, lest I should perish in my boasting.

13 For now I ought the more to fear; and not to hearken to those that would puff me up.

14 For they that speak to me, in my praise, chasten me.

15 For I indeed [19] desire to suffer, but I cannot tell whether I am worthy so to do.

16 [20] And this desire, though to others it does not appear, yet to myself it is for that very reason the more violent. I have, therefore, need of [21] moderation; by which the prince of this world is destroyed.

17 Am I not able to write to you of heavenly things?—But I

---

[1] Who am bound. [2] Multitude. [3] Your benevolence. [4] According to God. [5] Vid. Vossium in loc. [6] Imitators. [7] When. [8] Flee from. [9] Vid Vossium in loc. [10] Deacons. [11] As also the bishop like Jesus Christ the Son of the Father. Vossius in loc. vid. aliter Cotelerium. [12] A church is not called. [13] So do. [14] Habit of body is great instruction. [15] Power. [16] Vid. Vossium et Usserium in loc. [17] I understand many things [18] Measure. [19] Love. [20] Vid. Annot. Vossii in loc. [21] Mildness.

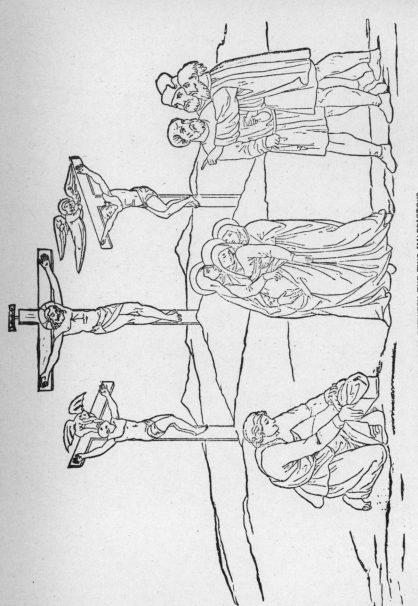

CHRIST ON THE CROSS BETWEEN THE TWO MALEFACTORS.

FROM A FRESCO PAINTING BY MASACCIO, IN THE CHURCH OF ST. CLEMENT, AT ROME.

fear lest I should harm you, who are yet but babes in Christ: (excuse me this care;) and lest perchance being not able to receive them, ye should be choken with them.

13 For even I myself, although I am in bonds, [1] yet am not therefore able to understand heavenly things:

19 As the places of the angels, and the several companies of them, under their respective princes; things visible and invisible; but in these I am yet a learner.

20 For many things are wanting to us, that we come not short of God.

CHAP. II.

1 *Warns them against heretics,* 4 *exhorts them to humility and unity,* 10 *briefly sets before them the true doctrine concerning Christ.*

I EXHORT you therefore, or rather not I, but the love of Jesus Christ; that ye use none but Christian nourishment; abstaining from pasture which is of another kind, I mean heresy.

2 [2] For they that are heretics, confound together the doctrine of Jesus Christ, with their own poison: [3] whilst they seem worthy of belief:

3 As men give a deadly potion mixed with sweet wine; which he who drinks of, does with the treacherous pleasure sweetly drink in his own death.

4 Wherefore guard yourselves against such persons. And that you will do if you are not puffed up; but continue inseparable from Jesus Christ our God, and from your bishop, and from the commands of the Apostles.

5 [4] He that is within the altar is pure; but he that is without, that is, that does anything without the bishop, the presbyters, and deacons, is not pure in his conscience.

6 Not that I know there is any thing of this nature among you; but I fore-arm you, as being greatly beloved by me, foreseeing the snares of the devil.

7 Wherefore putting on meekness, renew yourselves in faith, that is, the flesh of the Lord; and in charity, that is, the blood of Jesus Christ.

8 Let no man have any [5] grudge against his neighbour. Give no occasion to the Gentiles; lest by means of a few foolish men, the whole congregation of God be evil spoken of.

9 For woe to that man [6] through whose vanity my name is blasphemed by any.

10 Stop your ears therefore, as often as any one shall speak [7] contrary to Jesus Christ; who was of the race of David, of the Virgin Mary.

11 Who was truly born and did eat and drink; was truly persecuted under Pontius Pilate; was truly crucified and dead; both those in heaven and on earth, [8] being spectators of it.

12 Who was also truly raised from the dead [9] by his Father, after the same manner as [10] he will also raise up us who believe in him by Christ Jesus; without whom we have no true life.

13 But if, as some who are

---

[1] Orders.　[2] Vid. de hoc loco conjecturas Vossii, Cotelerii, et Junii apud Usserium. Comp. Epist. Intercol. in loc. et Voss. Annot. in Epist. ad Phil. p. 281.　[3] Being believed for their dignity.　[4] Vid. Usserii Obs. Marg. Comp. Coteler. ib.　[5] Any thing. [6] Through whom in vanity, Isaiah lii. 5.　[7] Without.　[8] Seeing, or looking on.　[9] His Father raising him.　[10] The Father.

Atheists, that is to say infidels, pretend, that he only seemed to suffer : (they themselves only seeming to exist) why then am I bound?—Why do I desire to fight with beasts?—Therefore do I die in vain: therefore I will not speak falsely against the Lord.

14 Flee therefore these evil [1] sprouts which bring forth deadly fruit; of which if any one taste, he shall presently die.

15 For these are not the plants of the Father; seeing if they were, they would appear to be the branches of the cross, and their fruit would be incorruptible; by which he invites you through his passion, who are members of him.

16 For the head cannot be without its members, God having promised a union, that is himself.

CHAP. III.

He again exhorts to unity: and desires their prayers for himself and for his church at Antioch.

I SALUTE you from Smyrna, [2] together with the churches of God that are present with me; who have refreshed me in all things, both in the flesh and in the spirit.

2 My bonds, which I carry about me for the sake of Christ, (beseeching him that I may attain unto God) exhort you, that you continue in [3] concord among yourselves, and in prayer with one another.

3 For it becomes every one of you, especially the presbyters, to refresh the bishop, to the honour of the Father of Jesus Christ and of the Apostles.

4 I beseech you, that you hearken to me in love; that I may not [4] by those things which I write, rise up in witness against you.

5 Pray also for me; who through the mercy of God stand in need of your prayers, that I may be worthy of the portion which I am about to obtain that I be not found a reprobate.

6 The love of those who are at Smyrna and Ephesus salute you. Remember in your prayers the church of Syria, from which I am not worthy to be called, being one of the least [5] of it.

7 Fare ye well in Jesus Christ; being subject to your bishop as to the command of God; and so likewise to the presbytery.

8 Love every one his brother with an [6] unfeigned heart. [7] My soul be your expiation, not only now, but when I shall have attained unto God; for I am yet under danger.

9 But the Father is faithful in Jesus Christ, to fulfil both mine and your petition; in whom may ye be found unblamable.

¶ *To the Trallians.*

The EPISTLE of IGNATIUS to the ROMANS.
CHAP. I.

He testifies his desire to see, and his hopes of suffering for Christ, 5 which he earnestly entreats them not to prevent, 10 but to pray for him, that God would strengthen him to the combat.

I GNATIUS, [8] who is also called Theophorus, to the church which has obtained mercy [9] from the majesty of the Most High Father, and his only [10] begotten Son Jesus Christ; beloved, and

[1] Plants. [2] i. e. The delegates of the church. [3] The concord of you. [4] Be a testimony among you, writing. [5] Them. [6] Undivided. [7] Vid. Annot. Voss.li et Coteler. in loc. [8] Vid. Pearson. Vind. Ignat. par 2, ch. xvi. p. 214. [9] In. [10] Omitted, Gr.

illuminated [1] through the will of him who willeth all things which are according to the love of Jesus Christ our [2] God which also presides in the [3] place of the region of the Romans; and which [4] I salute in the name of Jesus Christ ([5] as being) united both in flesh and spirit to all his commands, and [6] filled with the grace of God; [7] (all joy) in Jesus Christ our God.

2 [8] Forasmuch as I have at last [9] obtained through my prayers to God, to see your [10] faces, [11] which I much desired to do; being bound in Jesus Christ, I hope ere long to salute you, if it shall be the will [12] of God to grant me to attain unto the end I long for.

3 For the beginning is well disposed, if I shall but have grace, without hindrance, to receive [13] what is appointed for me.

4 But I fear your love, lest it do me an injury. For it is easy for you to do what you please; but it [14] will be hard for me to attain unto God, if you spare me.

5 But I [15] would not that ye should please men, but God [16] whom also ye do please. For neither shall I hereafter have such an opportunity [17] of going unto God; nor will you if ye shall now be silent, ever be entituled to a better work. For if you shall be silent [18] in my behalf, I shall be made partaker of God.

6 But if you shall love my [19] body, I shall have my course again to run. Wherefore ye cannot do me a greater kindness, than to suffer me to be sacrificed unto God, now that the altar is already prepared:

7 That [20] when ye shall be gathered together in love, ye may [21] give thanks to the Father through Christ Jesus; that he has vouchsafed [22] to bring a bishop of Syria unto you, being called from the east unto the west.

8 For it is good for me to set from the world, unto God; that I may rise again unto him.

9 Ye have never envied any one; ye have taught other. I would therefore that ye [23] should now do those things yourselves, which in your instructions you have [24] prescribed to others.

10 Only pray for me, that God would give me both inward and outward strength, that I may not only say, but will; nor be only called a Christian, but be found one.

11 For if I shall be found a Christian, I may then deservedly be called one; and be thought faithful, when I shall no longer appear to the world.

12 Nothing is [25] good, that is seen.

---

[1] In. [2] God; which also presides in the place of the region of the Romans, worthy of God; most decent, most blessed, most praised, most worthy to obtain what it desires; most pure, most charitable, called by the name of Christ and the Father; Gr. [3] Type of the chorus, *i. e.*, the church of the Romans. See Voss. Annot. in loc. [4] Also. [5] The Son of the Father; to those who are —Gr. [6] Wholly filled. Gr. [7] (Being absolutely separated from any other colour; much pure, or immaculate joy.) [8] Gr. [9] Vid. Voss. Annot. in loc. [10] Worthy of God. [11] And have received even more than I asked, being bound. [12] Gr. [13] My lot. [14] Is. [15] I will not please you as men. Gr. [16] As. [17] Attaining unto. [18] From me. [19] Flesh. [20] Being become a chorus. [21] Sing. [22] That a bishop of Syria should be found. [23] That those things also should be firm. [24] Commanded. Vid. Annot. Userii in loc. N. 26, 27. [25] Nothing that is seen is eternal: for the things which are seen are temporal, but the things that are not seen are eternal. Gr.

13 For even our God, Jesus Christ, now that he is in the Father, does so much the more appear.

14 A Christian is not a work of [1] opinion; but of greatness of mind, ([2] especially when he is hated by the world.)

CHAP. II.

Expresses his great desire and determination to suffer martyrdom.

I WRITE to the churches, and [3] signify to them all, that I am willing to die for God, unless you [4] hinder me.

2 I beseech you that you [5] shew not an unseasonable good will towards me. Suffer me to be food to the wild beasts; by whom I shall attain unto God.

3 For I am the wheat of God; and I shall be ground by the teeth of the wild beasts, that I may be found the pure bread [6] of Christ.

4 Rather [7] encourage the beasts, that they may become my sepulchre; and may leave nothing of my body; that being dead I may not be troublesome to any.

5 Then shall I be truly the disciple of Jesus Christ, when the world shall not see so much as my body, Pray therefore unto Christ for me, that by these instruments I may be made the sacrifice [8] of God.

6 I do not, as Peter and Paul, command you. They were Apostles, I a condemned man; they were free, but I am even to this day a servant:

7 But if I shall suffer, I shall then become the freeman of Jesus Christ, and shall rise [9] free. And now, being in bonds, I learn, not to desire [10] anything.

8 From Syria even unto Rome, I fight with beasts both by sea and land; both night and day: being bound to ten leopards, that is to say, to such a band of soldiers; who, though treated with all manner of kindness, are the worse for it.

9 But I am the more instructed by their injuries; [11] yet am I not therefore justified.

10 May I enjoy the wild beasts that are prepared for me; which also I wish may [12] exercise all their fierceness upon me.

11 And whom for that end I will [13] encourage, that they may be sure to devour me, and not serve me as they have done some, whom out of fear they have not touched. But, and if they will not do it willingly, I will provoke them to it.

12 Pardon me in this matter; I know what is profitable for me. Now I begin to [14] be a disciple. Nor [15] shall anything move me, whether visible or invisible, that I may attain to Jesus Christ.

13 Let fire, and the cross; let the [16] companies of wild beasts; [17] let breakings of bones and tearing of members; let the [18] shattering in pieces of the whole body, and all the wicked [19] torments of the devil come upon me; only let [20] me enjoy Jesus Christ.

---

[1] Persuasion, or silence. Gr. [2] (Desunt, Gr.) [3] Vid. Usser. Annot. N. 31. [4] Forbid me. [5] Be not. [6] Vid Lat. Vet. Interps. et Annot. Usser. N. 32. [7] Flatter. [8] Desunt. Gr. [9] Free in him. Gr. [10] Any worldly or vain things. Gr. [11] 1 Cor. iv. 4. [12] Vid. Voss. in loc. Usser. Annot. N. 48. May be ready for me. Gr. [13] Usser. Annot. N. 48. [14] Luke xiv. 27. [15] Vid. Coteler. in loc. Rom. viii. 38, 39. [16] Force, or rage. [17] Let tearings, and rendings. Gr. [18] Vid. Usser. Annot. N. 56. [19] Ib. N. 57. [20] That I may enjoy.

14 All the [1]ends of the world, and the kingdoms [2]of it, will profit me nothing: I would rather die [3]for Jesus Christ, than rule to the utmost ends of the earth. [4]Him I seek who died for us; him I desire, that rose again for us. This is the [5]gain that is laid up for me.

15 Pardon me, my brethren, ye shall not hinder me from living. [6]Nor seeing I desire to go to God, may you separate me from him, for the sake of this world; nor reduce me by any of the [7]desires of it. Suffer me to [8]enter into pure light: Where being come, I shall be indeed the [9]servant of [10]God.

16 Permit me to imitate the passion of my God. If any one has him within himself, let him consider what I desire; and let him have compassion on me, as knowing [11] how I am straightened.

CHAP. III.

Further expresses his desire to suffer.

THE prince of this world would fain carry me away, and corrupt [12]my resolution towards my God. Let none of you [13]therefore help [14]him: Rather do ye join with me, that is, with God.

2 Do not speak with Jesus Christ, and yet covet the world. Let not any envy dwell with you;

No not though I myself when I shall be come unto you, should exhort you to it, yet do not ye hearken to me; but rather believe what I now write to you.

3 For though I am alive, at the writing this, yet my desire is to die. My love is crucified; [15](and the [16]fire that is within me does not desire any water; but being alive and [17]springing within me, says,) Come to the Father.

4 I take no pleasure in the food of corruption, nor in the pleasures of this life.

5 I desire the bread of God [18]which is the flesh of Jesus Christ, ([19]of the seed of David; and the drink that I long for) is his blood, which is incorruptible love.[20]

6 I have no desire to live any longer after the manner of men, [21]neither shall I, if you consent. Be ye therefore willing, that ye yourselves also may be [22]pleasing to God. I [23]exhort you [24]in a few words; I pray you believe me.

7 Jesus Christ will shew you that I speak truly. My mouth is without deceit, and the Father hath truly spoken [25]by it. Pray therefore for me, that I may accomplish what I desire.

8 I have not written to you after the flesh, but according to the will of God. If I shall suffer, [26]ye have loved me; but if I

---

[1] Gr. Pleasures. [2] Of this age. [3] Gr. unto. [4] For what is a man profited if he shall gain the whole world and lose his own soul. Gr. Add. [5] Usury. Gr. Vid. Voss. Correct. p. 301. [6] Nor desire that I should die, who seek to go to God, rejoice not in the world. Gr. [7] By matter. [8] Take: lay hold on. [9] Man. [10] Vid. Annot. Voss. in loc. [11] What things constrain me. [12] Mind: will. [13] Who are present. [14] Vid. Voss. Annot. in loc. [15] (And there is not any fire within me that loves matter, but living and speaking water saying within me. Gr.) [16] Cotelerius aliter explicat. Annot. in loc. Usser. N. 79. [17] Voss. in loc. Contr. Coteler. q. v. [18] The heavenly bread which is. Gr. [19] (The Son of God made in these last times of the seed of David and Abraham, and the drink of God that I long for. Gr.). [20] Gr. Adds, and perpetual life. [21] And that shall be. [22] Willed. [23] Vid. Annot. Voss. in loc. [24] By a short letter. [25] In. [26] Ye have willed it.

shall be rejected, [1] ye have hated me.

9 Remember in your prayers the church of Syria, which now enjoys God for its shepherd instead of me: [2] Let Jesus Christ only [3] oversee it, and your charity.

10 But I am even ashamed to be reckoned as one of them: For neither am I worthy, being the least among them, and as one [4] born out of due season. But through mercy I have obtained to be somebody, if I shall get unto God.

11 My spirit salutes you; and the charity of the churches that have received me in the name of Jesus Christ ; not as a passenger. For even they that were not near to me in the way, have gone before me to the next city to meet me.

12 These things I write to you from Smyrna, by the most worthy of the church of Ephesus.

13 There is now with me, together with many others, Crocus, most beloved of me. As for those which are [5] come from Syria, and are gone before me to Rome, to the glory of God, I suppose you are not ignorant of them.

14 Ye shall therefore signify to them, that I draw near, for they are all worthy both of God and of you: Whom it is fit that you refresh in all things.

15 This have I written to you, the day before the ninth of the calends of September. [6] Be strong unto the end, in the patience of Jesus Christ. [7]

¶ *To the Romans.*

The EPISTLE of IGNATIUS to the PHILADELPHIANS.
CHAP. I.

Commends their bishop whom they had sent unto him, 5 warns them against divisions and schism.

IGNATIUS, who is also called Theophorus, to the church of God the Father, and our Lord Jesus Christ, which is at Philadelphia in Asia ; which has obtained mercy, being fixed in the concord of God, and rejoicing [8] evermore in the passion of our Lord, and being fulfilled in all mercy through his resurrection : Which also I salute in the blood of Jesus Christ, [9] which is our eternal and undefiled joy ; especially if they are at unity with the bishop, and presbyters who are with him, and the dea-

cons appointed [10] according to the [11] mind of Jesus Christ; whom he has settled according to his own will in all firmness by his Holy Spirit :

2 Which bishop I know obtained [12] that great ministry among you, not of himself, neither by men, nor out of vain glory ; but [13] by the love of God the Father, and our Lord Jesus Christ.

3 Whose moderation [14] I admire ; who by his silence is able to do more than [15] others with all their vain talk. For he is fitted to the commands, as the harp to its strings.

4 Wherefore my soul esteems his mind towards God most hap-

---

[1] Viz. as unworthy to suffer. [2] Vid. Vet. Interp. Lat. [3] Shall oversee it.
[4] 1 Cor. xv. 8. [5] Vid Vet. Interp. Lat. [6] That is the xxxiiid of August.
Gr. [7] Amen. Gr. [8] Inseparably. [9] Vid. Vet. Interpr. Lat. [10] In. [11] Will, order.
[12] Ministry belonging to the public. [13] In. [14] Has struck me with wonder
[15] Those that speak vain things.

py, knowing it to be fruitful in all virtue, and perfect; full of constancy, free from passion, [1] and according to all the moderation of the living God.

5 Wherefore as becomes the children both of the light and of truth; flee divisions and false doctrines; but where your shepherd is, there do ye, as sheep, follow after.

6 For there are many wolves [2] who seem worthy of belief, that with a [3] false pleasure lead captive those that run in the course of God; but in the concord they shall find no place.

7 Abstain therefore from those evil herbs which Jesus Christ does not dress; because such are not the plantation of the Father. Not that I have found any division among you, but rather all manner of [4] purity.

8 For as many as are of God, and of Jesus Christ, are also with their bishop. And as many as shall with repentance return into the unity of the church, even these shall also be the servants of God, that they may live according to Jesus.

9 Be not deceived, brethren; if any one follows him that makes a schism in the church, he shall not inherit the kingdom of God. If any one walks after any other opinion, he agrees not with the passion of Christ.

10 Wherefore let it be your endeavour to partake all of the same holy eucharist.

11 For there is but one flesh of our Lord Jesus Christ; and one cup in the unity of his blood; one altar;

12 As also there is one bi-

shop, together with his presbytery, and the deacons my fellowservants: that so whatsoever ye do, ye may do it according to the will of God.

CHAP. II.

Desires their prayers, and to be united but not to Judaize.

MY brethren, the love I have towards you makes me the [b] more large; and having a great joy in you, I endeavour to secure you against danger; or rather not I, but Jesus Christ; in whom being bound I the more fear, as being yet only [6] on the way to suffering.

2 But your prayer to God shall make me perfect, that I may attain to that portion, which by God's mercy is allotted to me: Fleeing to the Gospel as to the flesh of Christ; and to the Apostles as to the presbytery of the church.

3 Let us also love the prophets, forasmuch as they also have [7] led us to the Gospel, and to hope in [8] Christ, and to expect him.

4 In whom also believing they were saved in the unity of Jesus Christ; being holy men, worthy to be loved, and had in wonder;

5 Who have received testimony from Jesus Christ, and are numbered in the Gospel of our common hope.

6 But if any one shall preach [9] the Jewish law unto you, hearken not unto him; for [10] it is better to receive the doctrine of Christ from one that has been circumcised, than Judaism from one that has not.

[1] In. [2] Vid. Vossii Annot in loc. [3] Evil. [4] Cleanliness made by sifting. [5] Very much poured out. [6] Vid. Voss. in loc. Imperfect. [7] Or preached of the Gospel; and hoped in him, and expected him. [8] Vid. Voss. in loc. [9] Judaism. [10] Opinion: council.

7 But if either the one, or other, do not speak concerning Christ Jesus, they seem to me to be but as monuments and sepulchres of the dead, upon which are written only the names of men.

8 Flee therefore the wicked arts and snares of the prince of this world ; lest at any time being oppressed by his cunning ye grow [1] cold in your charity. But come all together into the same place with an undivided heart.

9 And I bless my God that I have a good conscience towards you, and that no one among you has whereof to boast either openly or privately, that I have been burthensome to him in much or little.

10 And I wish to all among whom I have conversed, that it may not turn to a witness against them.

11 For although some would have deceived me according to the flesh, yet the spirit, being from God, is not deceived ; for it knows both whence it comes and whither it goes, and reproves the secrets of the heart.

12 I cried whilst I was among you ; I spake with a loud voice : attend to the bishop, and to the presbytery, and to the deacons.

13 Now some supposed that I spake this as foreseeing the division [2] that should come among you.

14 But he is my witness for whose sake I am in bonds that I knew nothing from any man. But the spirit spake, saying on this wise : Do nothing without the bishop :

15 Keep your [3] bodies as the temples of God : Love unity ; Flee divisions ; Be the followers of Christ, as he was of his Father.

16 I therefore did as became me, as a man composed to unity. For where there is division, and wrath, God dwelleth not.

17 But the Lord forgives all that repent, if they [4] return to the unity of God, and to the council of the bishop.

18 For I trust in the grace of Jesus Christ [5] that he will free you from every bond.

19 Nevertheless I exhort you that you do nothing out of strife, but according to the instruction of Christ.

20 Because I have heard of some who say ; unless I find it written in the [6] originals, I will not believe it to be written in the Gospel. And when I said, It is written ; they answered what lay before them in their corrupted copies.

21 But to me Jesus Christ is instead of all the uncorrupted monuments in the world ; together with those [7] undefiled monuments, his cross, and death, and resurrection, and the faith which is by him ; by which I desire, through your prayers, to be justified.

22 ¶ The priests indeed are good ; but much better is the High Priest to whom the Holy of Holies has been committed ; and who alone has been entrusted with the secrets of God.

23 He is the door of the Father ; by which Abraham, and Isaac, and Jacob, and all the prophets, enter in ; as well as the Apostles, and the church.

---

[1] Weak.   [2] Of some.   [3] Flesh.   [4] Repent.   [5] Who will loose from you.
[6] Archives, Vid. Voss. Annot. in loc.   [7] Untouched.

24 And all these things tend to the unity which is of God. Howbeit the Gospel has somewhat in it far above all other dispensations; namely, the appearance of our Saviour, the Lord Jesus Christ, his passion and resurrection.

25 For the beloved prophets referred to him; but the gospel is the perfection of incorruption. All therefore together are good, if ye believe with charity.

CHAP. III.

Informs them he had heard that the persecution was stopped at Antioch, and directs them to send a messenger hitherto to congratulate with the church.

NOW as concerning the church of Antioch which is in Syria, seeing I am told that through your prayers and the bowels which ye have towards it in Jesus Christ, it is in peace; it will become you, as the church of God, to ordain some [1] deacon to go to them thither as the ambassador of God; that he may rejoice with them when they meet together, and glorify God's name.

2 Blessed be that man in Jesus Christ, who shall be found worthy of such a ministry; and ye yourselves also shall be glorified.

3 Now if you be willing, it is not impossible for you to do this for the grace of God; as also the other neighbouring churches have sent them, some bishops, some priests and deacons.

4 As concerning Philo the deacon of Cilicia, a most worthy [2] man, he still ministers unto me in the word of God: together with Rheus [3] of Agathopolis, a singular good person, who has followed me even from Syria, not regarding his life: These also bear witness unto you.

5 And I myself give thanks to God for you that you receive them as the Lord shall receive you. But for those that dishonoured them, may they be forgiven through the grace of Jesus Christ.

6 The charity of the brethren that are at Troas salutes you: from whence also I now write by Burrhus, who was sent together with me by those of Ephesus and Smyrna, for respect sake.

7 May our Lord Jesus Christ honour them; in whom they hope, both in flesh, and soul, and spirit; in faith, in love, in unity. Farewell in Christ Jesus our common hope.

The EPISTLE of IGNATIUS to the SMYRNÆANS.

CHAP. I.

1 *Declares his joy for their firmness in the Gospel.* 4 *Enlarges on the person of Christ, against such as pretend that Christ did not really suffer.*

IGNATIUS, who is also called Theophorus, to the church of God the Father, and of the beloved Jesus Christ, which God hath mercifully [4] blessed with every good gift; being filled with faith and charity, so that this is wanting in no gift; most worthy of God, and fruitful in saints: the church which is at Smyrna in Asia; all joy, through his immaculate spirit, and the word of God.

2 I glorify God, even Jesus Christ, who has given you such wisdom.

3 For I have observed that

---

[1] Messenger or Minister. [2] Vid. Vossius, a martyr or confessor. Vid. Annot. in loc. [3] Vid. Vossius Annot. in Ep. ad. Smyrn. p. 261. See chap. iii. v. 11. [4] Comp. 1 Cor. vii. 25.

185

you are settled in an immovable faith, as if you were nailed to the cross of our Lord Jesus Christ, both in the flesh and in the spirit; and are confirmed in love through the blood of Christ; being fully persuaded of those things which relate [1] unto our Lord.

4 Who truly was of the race of David according to the flesh, but the Son of God according to the will and power of God; truly born of the Virgin, and baptized of John; that so [2] all righteousness might be fulfilled by him.

5 He was also truly crucified by Pontius Pilate, and Herod the Tetrarch, being nailed for us in the flesh; by the fruits of which we are, even by his most blessed passion.

6 That he might set [3] up a token for all ages through his resurrection, to all his holy and faithful servants, whether they be Jews or Gentiles, in one body of his church.

7 Now all these things he suffered for us that we might be saved. And he suffered truly, as he also truly raised up himself: And not, as some unbelievers say, that he only seemed to suffer, they themselves only seeming to be.[4]

8 And as they believe so shall it happen unto them; when being divested of the body they shall become [5] mere spirits.

9 But I know that even after his resurrection he was in the flesh; and I believed that he is still so.

10 And when he came to those who were with Peter, [6] he said unto them, Take, handle me, and see that I am not an incorporeal dæmon. And straightway they felt and believed; being convinced both by his flesh and spirit.

11 For this cause they despised death, and were found to be above [7] it.

12 But after his resurrection he did eat and drink with them, as he was flesh; although as to his Spirit he was united to the Father.

CHAP. II.

1 *Exhorts them against heretics.* 8 *The danger of their doctrine.*

NOW these things, beloved, 1 [8] put you in mind of, not questioning but that you yourselves also [9] believe that they are so.

2 But I arm you before-hand against certain beasts in the shape of men whom you must not only not receive, but if it be possible must not meet with.

3 Only you must pray for them, that if it be the will of God they may repent; which yet will be very hard. But of this our Lord Jesus Christ has the power, who is our true life.

4 For if all these things were done only in shew by our Lord, then do I also seem only to be bound.

5 And why have I given up myself to death, to the fire, to the sword, to wild beasts!

6 But now the nearer I am to the sword, the nearer I am to God: when I shall come among the wild beasts, I shall come to God.

7 Only in the name of Jesus Christ, I undergo all, to suffer

---

[1] Unto the Lord. [2] Matt. iii. 15. [3] Vid. Voss. Annot. in loc. [4] *i. e.* Christians. [5] Incorporeal and dæmoniac. [6] Ex. Evang. Sec. Hebr See Dr. Grabe Spicileg. tom. ii. p. 26. [7] Death. [8] Admonish. [9] Have so.

together with him; he who was made a perfect man strengthening me.

8 Whom some not knowing, do deny; or rather have been denied by him, being the advocates of death, rather than of the truth. Whom neither the prophecies, nor the law of Moses have persuaded; nor the Gospel itself even to this day, nor the sufferings of every one of us.

9 For they think also the same things of us. For what does a man profit me, if he shall praise me, and blaspheme my Lord; not confessing that he [1] was truly made man?

10 Now he that doth not say this, does in effect deny him, and is in death. But for the names of such as do this, they being unbelievers, I thought it not fitting to write them unto you.

11 Yea, God forbid that I should make any mention of them, till they shall repent to a true belief of Christ's passion, which is our resurrection.

12 Let no man deceive himself; both the things which are in heaven and the glorious angels, and princes, whether visible or invisible, if they believe not in the blood of Christ, [2] it shall be to them to condemnation.

13 [3] He that is able to receive this, let him receive it. Let no man's [4] place or state in the world puff him up: that which is worth all his faith and charity, to which nothing is to be preferred.

14 But consider those who are of a different opinion from us, as to what concerns the grace of Jesus Christ which is come unto us, how contrary they are to the design of God.

15 They have no regard to charity, no care of the widow, the fatherless, and the oppressed; of the bond or free, of the hungry or thirsty.

16 They abstain from the eucharist, and from [5] the public offices; because they confess not the eucharist to be the flesh of our Saviour Jesus Christ; which suffered for our sins, and which the Father of his goodness, raised again from the dead.

17 And for this cause contradicting the gift of God, they die in their disputes: [6] but much better would it be for them to [7] receive it, that they might one day rise through it.

18 It will therefore become you to abstain from such persons; and not to speak with them neither in private nor in public.

19 But to hearken to the prophets, and especially to the Gospel, in which both Christ's passion is manifested unto us, and his resurrection perfectly declared.

20 But flee all divisions, as the beginning of evils.

CHAP. III.

1 *Exhorts them to follow their bishop and pastors; but especially their bishop.* 6 *Thanks them for their kindness,* 11 *and acquaints them with the ceasing of the persecution at Antioch.*

SEE that ye all follow your bishop, as Jesus Christ, the Father; and the presbytery, as the Apostles. And reverence the deacons, as the command of God.

2 Let no man do anything of what belongs to the church separately from the bishop.

3 Let that eucharist be looked upon as well established, which is either offered by the bishop,

---

[1] Had true flesh. [2] It is. [3] Matt. xix. 12. [4] Vid. Epist. Interpol. [5] Vid. Annot. Coteler. in loc. Or, Prayers. [6] Vid. Coteler. Annot. [7] Love.

or by him to whom the bishop has given his consent.

4 Wheresoever the bishop shall appear, there let the [1]people also be: as where Jesus Christ is, there is the Catholic church.

5 It is not lawful without the bishop, neither to baptize, nor [2]to celebrate the Holy Communion; but whatsoever he shall approve of, that is also pleasing unto God; that so whatever is done, may be sure and well done.

6 For what remains, it is very reasonable that we should [3]repent whilst there is yet time to return unto God.

7 It is a good thing to have a due regard both to God, and to the bishop: he that honours the bishop, shall be honoured of God. But he that does anything without his knowledge, [4]ministers unto the devil.

8 Let all things therefore abound to you in charity; seeing that ye are worthy.

9 Ye have refreshed me in all things; so shall Jesus Christ you. Ye have loved me both when I was present with you, and now being absent, ye cease not to do so.

10 May God be your reward, from whom whilst ye undergo all things, ye shall attain unto him.

11 Ye have done well in that ye have received Philo, and Rheus [5]Agathopus, who followed me [6]for the word of God, as the deacons of Christ our God.

12 Who also gave thanks unto the Lord for you, forasmuch as ye have refreshed them in all [7]things. [8]Nor shall any thing that you have done be lost to you.

13 My [9]soul be for yours, and my bonds which ye have not despised, nor been ashamed of. Wherefore neither shall Jesus Christ, our perfect faith, be ashamed of you.

14 Your prayer is come to the church of Antioch which is in Syria. From whence being sent bound with chains becoming God, I salute the [10]churches; being not worthy to be called [11]from thence, as being the least among them.

15 Nevertheless by the will of God I have been thought worthy of this honour; not for that I think I have deserved it, but by the grace of God.

16 Which I wish may be perfectly given unto me, that through your prayers I may attain unto God.

17 And therefore that your work may be fully accomplished both upon earth and in heaven; it will be fitting, and for the honour of God, [12]that your church appoint some worthy delegate, who being come as far as Syria, may rejoice together with them that they are in peace; and that they are again restored to their former [13]state, and have again received their proper body.

18 Wherefore I should think it a worthy action, to send some one from you with an epistle, to congratulate with them their peace in God; and that through your prayers they have now gotten to their harbor.

19 For inasmuch as ye are perfect yourselves, you ought to think those things that are perfect. For when you are desirous to do well, God is ready to [14]enable you thereunto.

---

[1] Multitude. [2] Make a love-feast. [3] Return to a sound mind. [4] Does worship. [5] Vid. Voss. Annot. in loc. [6] Unto. [7] Ways. [8] Vid. Epist. Interpol. [9] Spirit. [10] All the. [11] *i. e.* the bishop of that church. [12] Vid. Voss. Annot. in loc. [13] Bulk, greatness. [14] Help you.

20 The love of the brethren that are at Troas salute you; from whence I write to you by Burrhus whom you sent with me, together with the Ephesians your brethren; and who has in all things refreshed me.

21 And I would to God that all would imitate him, as being a pattern of the ministry of God. May his grace fully reward him.

22 I salute your very worthy bishop, and your venerable presbytery; and your deacons, my fellow-servants; and all of you in general, and every one in particular, in the name of Jesus Christ, and in his flesh and blood; in his passion and resurrection both fleshly and spiritually; and in [1]the unity of God with you.

23 Grace be with you, and mercy, and peace, and patience, for evermore.

24 I salute the families of my brethren, with their wives and children; and the [2] virgins that are called widows. Be strong in the power of the Holy Ghost. Philo, who is present with me salutes you.

25 I salute the house of Tavias, and pray that it may be strengthened in faith and charity, both of flesh and spirit.

26 I salute Alce my well-beloved, [3] together with the incomparable Daphnus, and Eutechnus, and all by name.

27 Farewell in the grace of God.

¶ *To the Smyrnœans from Troas.*

The EPISTLE of IGNATIUS to POLYCARP.

CHAP. I.

Blesses God for the firm establishment of Polycarp in the faith, and gives him particular directions for improving it.

IGNATIUS, who is also called Theophorus, to Polycarp, bishop of the church [4] which is at Smyrna; their overseer, but rather himself overlooked by God the Father, and the Lord Jesus Christ: all happiness.

2 Having known that thy mind towards God, is fixed as it were upon an immovable rock; I exceedingly give thanks, that I have been thought worthy to behold thy [5] blessed face, in which may I always rejoice in God.

3 Wherefore I beseech thee by the grace of God with which thou art clothed, to press forward in thy course, and to exhort all others that they may be saved.

4 Maintain thy place with all care [6] both of flesh and spirit: Make it thy endeavour to preserve unity, than which nothing is better. Bear with all men, even as the Lord with thee.

5 Support all in love, as also thou dost. [7] Pray without ceasing: ask more understanding than what thou already hast. Be watchful, having thy spirit always awake.

6 Speak to every one [8] according as God shall enable thee. Bear the [9] infirmities of all, as a perfect combatant; where the labour is great, the gain [10] is the more.

7 If thou shalt love the good disciples, what thank is it? But rather do thou subject to thee those that are mischievous, in meekness.

---

[1] Vid. Voss. Annot. in loc.   [2] *i. e.* The deaconesses   See the reason for the name, Voss. Annot. in loc. Add. Coteler. ib.   [3] See Voss. Annot. ex Epist. Interpol.   [4] of the Smyrnæans.   [5] Innocent.   [6] Vid. 1 Cor. vii. 34.   [7] Be at leisure to, etc.   [8] Vid. Voss. in loc. aliter Vet. Lat. Interpr.   [9] The diseases. [10] Is much.

8 Every wound is not healed with the same plaster : if the accessions of the disease be vehement, modify them with [1] soft remedies : be in all things [2] wise as a serpent, but harmless as a dove.

9 For this cause thou art composed of flesh and spirit; that thou mayest modify those things that appear before thy face.

10 And as for those that are not seen, pray to God that he would reveal them unto thee, that so thou mayest be wanting in nothing, but mayest abound in every gift.

11 The times demand thee, as the pilots the winds; and he that is tossed in a tempest, the haven where he would be; that thou mayst attain unto God.

12 Be sober as the combatant of God : the [3] crown proposed to thee is immortality, and eternal life; concerning which thou art also fully persuaded. I will be thy surety in all things, and my bonds, which thou hast loved.

13 Let not those that seem worthy of credit, but teach other doctrines, [4] disturb thee. Stand firm and immovable, as an anvil when it is beaten upon.

14 It is the part of a brave combatant to be [5] wounded, and yet overcome. But especially we ought to endure all things for God's sake, that he may bear with us.

15 Be every day [6] better than other : consider the times; and expect him, who is above all time, eternal, invisible, though for our sakes made visible : impalpable, and impassable, yet for us subjected to sufferings; enduring all manner of ways foi our salvation.

CHAP. II.

1 *Continues his advice,* 6 *and teaches him how to advise others.* 12 *Enforces unity and subjection to the bishop.*

LET not the widows be neglected : be thou after God, their guardian.

2 Let nothing be done without thy knowledge and consent; neither do thou anything but according to the will of God; as also thou dost, [7] with all constancy.

3 Let your assemblies be more full : inquire into all by name.

4 Overlook not the men and maid servants; neither let them be puffed up : but rather let them be the more subject to the glory of God, that they may obtain from him a better liberty.

5 Let them not desire to [8] be set free at the public cost, that they be not slaves to their own lusts.

6 Flee evil [9] arts; or rather, make not any mention of them.

7 Say to my sisters, that they love the Lord; and be satisfied with their own husbands, both in the flesh and spirit.

8 In like manner, exhort my brethren, in the name of Jesus Christ, that they love their wives, even as the Lord the Church.

9 If any man can remain in a virgin state, [10] to the honour of the flesh of Christ, let him remain without boasting; but if he boast, he is undone. And if he desire to be more taken notice

---

[1] Superfusions. [2] Matt. x. 16. [3] Vid. Voss. Annot. in loc Collat. cum Coteler. ib. [4] Amaze thee. [5] Beaten. [6] More studious, diligent. [7] being well settled. [8] Vid. Annot. Coteler. in loc. [9] Or, trades. [10] Vid. Annot. Vossii et Coteler. in loc.

of than the bishop he is corrupted.

10 But it becomes all such as are married, whether men or women to come together with the consent of the bishop, that so their marriage may be according to godliness, and not in lust.

11 Let all things be done to the honour of God.

12 ¹Hearken unto the bishop, that God also may hearken unto you. My soul be security for them that submit to their bishop, with their presbyters and deacons. And may my portion be together with theirs in God.

13 Labour with one another; contend together, run together, suffer together; sleep together, and rise together; as the stewards, and assessors, and ministers of God.

14 Please him under whom ye war, and from whom ye receive your wages. Let none of you be found a deserter; but let your baptism remain, as your arms; your faith, as your helmet; your charity, as your spear; your patience, as your whole armour.

15 Let your works be your ²charge, that so you may receive a suitable reward. Be longsuffering therefore towards each other in meekness: as God is towards you.

16 Let me have joy of you in all things.

CHAP. III.

1 *Greets Polycarp on the peace of the church at Antioch: 2 and desires him to write to that and other churches.*

NOW forasmuch as the church of Antioch in Syria, is, ³as I am told, ¡   ce through your prayers; I also have been the more comforted ⁴and without care in God; if so be that by suffering, I shall attain unto God; that through your prayers I may be found a disciple of Christ.

2 It will be very fit, O most worthy Polycarp, to call a ⁵select council, and choose some one whom ye particularly love, and who is patient of labour; that he may be the messenger of God; and that going unto Syria, he may glorify your incessant love, to the praise of Christ.

3 A Christian has not the power of himself: but must be always at leisure for God's service. Now this work is both God's and your's: when ye shall have perfected it.

4 For I trust through the grace of God that ye are ready to every good work that is fitting for you in the Lord.

5 Knowing therefore your earnest affection for the truth, I have exhorted you by ⁶these short letters.

6 But forasmuch as I have not been able to write to all the churches, because I must suddenly sail from Troas to Neapolis; (for so is the command of those to whose pleasure I am subject;) do you write to the churches that are near you, as being instructed in the will of God, that they also may do in like manner.

7 Let those that are able send ⁷messengers; and let the rest send their letters by those who shall be sent by you: that you

---

¹ Observe, from the foregoing verses, that Ignatius here speaks not to Polycarp, but through him to the Church of Smyrna. ²That which is committed to your custody, to keep secure. ³ It has been manifested unto me. ⁴ In the security of God. ⁵ Most becoming God. ⁶ Viz. To the Smyrnæans, and this to himself. See Pearson in loc. ⁷ Footmen.

may be glorified [1] to all eternity, of which you are worthy.

8 I salute all by name, particularly the wife of Epitropus, with all her house and children. I salute Attalus my well-beloved.

9 I salute him who shall be thought worthy to be sent by you into Syria. Let grace be ever with him, [2] and with Polycarp who sends him.

10 I wish you all happiness in our God, Jesus Christ; in whom continue, in the unity and protection of God.,

11 I salute Alce my well-beloved. Farewell in the Lord.

¶ *To Polycarp.*

The EPISTLE of POLYCARP to the PHILIPPIANS.

[The genuineness of this Epistle is controverted, but implicitly believed by Archbishop Wake, whose translation is below. There is also a translation by Dr. Cave, attached to his life of Polycarp.]

CHAP. I.

Commends the Philippians for their respect to those who suffered for the Gospel; and for their own faith.

POLYCARP, and the presbyters that are with him, to the church of God which [3] is at Philippi: mercy unto you and peace from God Almighty; and the Lord Jesus Christ, our Saviour, be multiplied.

2 I rejoiced greatly with you in our Lord Jesus Christ, that ye received the images of a true love, and accompanied, as it is behooved you, those who were in bonds, becoming saints; which are the crowns of such as are truly chosen by God and our Lord:

3 As also that the [4] root of the faith which was preached from ancient times, remains firm in you to this day; and brings forth fruit to our Lord Jesus Christ, who suffered himself to be brought even to the death for our sins.

4 [5] Whom God hath raised up, having loosed the pains of death, [6] whom having not seen, ye love; in whom though now ye see him not, yet believing ye rejoice with joy unspeakable and full of glory.

5 Into which many desire to enter; [7] knowing that by grace ye are saved; not by works, but by the will of God through Jesus Christ.

6 [8] Wherefore girding up the loins of your minds; [9] serve the Lord with fear, and in truth: laying aside all empty and vain speech, and the error of many; [10]believing in him that raised up our Lord Jesus Christ from the dead, and hath given him glory and a throne at his right hand.

7 To whom all things are made subject, [11] both that are in heaven, and that are in earth; whom every [12] living creature shall worship; who shall come to be the judge of the quick and dead: whose blood God shall require of them that believe in him.

8 But he that raised up [13] Christ from the dead, shall also raise up us in like manner, if we do his will and walk [14] according to his commandments; and love those things which he loved:

9 Abstaining from all [15] un-

---

[1] Vid. Voss. in loc. in the Eternal work. [2] Ex. Vet. Interp. Vid. Voss. Annot. [3] Sojourneth. [4] Firm root remains in you. [5] Acts xi. 24. [6] 1 Pet. i. 8. [7] Eph. ii. 8. [8] 1 Pet. i. 13. [9] Psalm ii. 11. [10] 1 Pet. i. 21. [11] Phil. ii. 10. [12] Breath. [13] Him. [14] In. [15] Injustice.

THE BURIAL OF CHRIST.

MARRIAGE OF CANA IN GALILEE.

FROM LATIN MANUSCRIPTS OF THE FOURTEENTH CENTURY.

righteousness ; [1]inordinate affection, and love of money ; from evil speaking; false witness ; not rendering evil for evil, or railing for railing, or striking for striking, or cursing for cursing.

10 But remembering what the Lord has [2]taught us saying, Judge not, and ye shall not be judged; forgive and ye shall be forgiven ; be ye merciful, and ye shall obtain mercy; for with the same measure that ye mete withal, it shall be measured to you again.

11 And again, that [3]blessed are the poor, and they that are persecuted for righteousness' sake ; for theirs is the kingdom of God.

CHAP. II.

2 *Exhorts to Faith, Hope, and Charity.* 5 *Against covetousness, and as to the duties of husbands, wives, widows,* 6 *deacons, young men, virgins, and presbyters.*

THESE things, my brethren, I took not the liberty of myself to write unto you concerning righteousness, but you yourselves before encouraged me to it.

2 For neither can I, nor any other such as I am, come up to the wisdom of the blessed and renowned Paul : who being himself in person with those who then lived, did with all exactness and soundness teach the word [4]of truth ; and being gone from you wrote an [5]epistle to you.

3 Into which if you look, you will be able to edify yourselves in the faith that has been delivered unto you ; which is the mother of us all ; being followed with hope, and led on by a general love, both towards God and towards Christ, and towards our neighbour.

4 For if any man [6]has these things he has fulfilled the law of righteousness : for he that has charity is far from all sin.

5 But the love of money is the [7]root of all evil. Knowing therefore that as we brought nothing into this world, so neither may we carry any thing out ; let us [8]arm ourselves with the armour of righteousness.

6 And teach ourselves first to walk according to the commandments of the Lord ; and then your wives to walk likewise [9]according to the faith that is given to them ; in [10]charity, and in purity ; loving their own husbands with all [11]sincerity, and all others alike with all temperance ; and to bring up their children in the instruction [12]and fear of the Lord.

7 The widows likewise teach that they be sober as to what concerns the faith of the Lord : praying always for all men ; being far from all detraction, evil speaking, false witness; from covetousness, and from all evil.

8 Knowing that they are the altars of God, [13]who sees all blemishes, and from whom nothing is hid ; who searches out the very reasonings, and thoughts, and secrets of our hearts.

9 ¶ Knowing therefore that God is not mocked, we ought to walk worthy both of his command and of his glory.

---

[1]Eph. iv. 19. Coloss. iii. 5.   1 Pet. iii. 9.   [2]Said to us, teaching, Luke vi. 37. Matt. vii. 1.   [3] Matt. v. 3, 10.   Luke vi. 20.   [4] περι αλεθειας, concerning Truth.   [5] Epistles. Vid. Annot. Coteler. in loc.   [6] Be within.   [7] Beginning of all troubles, or difficulties, χαλεπων, 1 Tim. vi. 7. [8] Be armed. [9] In. [10] Love. [11]Truth.   [12] Of the.   [13] And that he.

10 Also the deacons must be blameless before [1] him, as the ministers of God in Christ, and not of men. Not false accusers; not double tongued; not lovers of money; but [2] moderate in all things; compassionate, careful; walking according to the truth of the Lord, who was the servant of all.

11 Whom if we please in this present world we shall also be made partakers of that which is to come, according as he has promised to us, that he will raise us from the dead; and that if we shall walk worthy of him, we shall also reign together with him, if we believe.

12 In like manner the younger men must be unblameable in all things; above all, taking care of their purity, and to restrain themselves from all evil. For it is good to be cut off from the lusts that are in the world; because every such [3] lust warreth against the spirit: [4] and neither fornicators, nor effeminate, nor abusers of themselves with mankind, shall inherit the kingdom of God; nor they who do such things as are foolish and unreasonable.

13 Wherefore ye must needs abstain from all these things, being subject to the [5] priests and deacons, as unto God and Christ.

14 The virgins admonish to walk in a spotless and pure conscience.

15 And let the [6] elders be compassionate and merciful towards all; [7] turning them from their errors; seeking out those that are weak; not forgetting the widows, the fatherless, and the poor; but

always [8] providing what is good both in the sight of God and man.

16 Abstaining from all wrath, respect of persons, and unrighteous judgment: and especially being free from all covetousness.

17 Not [9] easy to believe any thing against any; not severe in judgment; knowing that we are all debtors in point of sin.

18 If therefore we pray to the Lord that he would forgive us, we ought also to forgive others; for we are all in the sight of our Lord and God; [10] and must all stand before the judgment seat of Christ; and shall every one give an account [11] of himself.

19 Let us therefore serve him in fear, and with all reverence as both himself hath commanded; and as the Apostles who have preached the Gospel unto us, and the prophets who have foretold the coming of our Lord have taught us.

20 Being zealous of what is good; abstaining from all offence, and from false brethren; and from those who bear the name of Christ in hypocrisy: who deceive vain men.

CHAP. III.

1 *As to faith in our Saviour Christ: his nature and sufferings, the resurrection and judgment. 3 Exhorts to prayer 5 and steadfastness in the faith, from the examples of Christ, 7 and Apostles and saints, and exhorts to carefulness in all well-doing.*

FOR [12] whosoever does not confess that Jesus Christ is come in the flesh, he is Antichrist: and whoever does not confess [13] his suffering upon the cross, is from the devil.

2 And whosoever perverts the oracles of the Lord to his own lusts;

---

[1] His righteousness. [2] Continent. [3] Pet. ii. 11. [4] Cor. vi. 9, 10. [5] Elders.
[6] Presbyters. [7] Ezek. xxxiv. 4. [8] Rom. xii. 17. [9] Swiftly believing. [10] Matt.
xii.14; Rom. xiv. 10; 2 Cor. v. 10. [11] For. [12] 1 John iv. 3. [13] The martyrdom of the cross.

and says that there shall neither be any resurrection, nor judgment, he is the first-born of Satan.

3 Wherefore leaving the vanity of many, and their false doctrines ; let us return to the word that was delivered to us from the beginning; [1] Watching unto prayer; and persevering in fasting.

4 With supplication beseeching the all seeing God [2] not to lead us into temptation ; as the Lord hath said, [3] The spirit is truly willing, but the flesh is weak.

5 Let us therefore without ceasing hold steadfastly to him who is our hope, and the earnest of our righteousness, even Jesus Christ; [4] Who his own self bare our sins in his own body on the tree : who did no sin, neither was guile found in his mouth. But suffered all for us that we might live [5] through him.

6 Let us therefore imitate his patience ; and if we suffer for his name, let us glorify him ; for this example he has given us by himself, and so have we believed.

7 Wherefore I exhort all of you that ye obey the word of righteousness, and exercise all patience; which ye have seen set forth before our eyes, not only in the blessed Ignatius, and Zozimus, and Rufus; but in others among yourselves ; and in Paul himself, and the rest of the Apostles :

8 Being [6] confident of this, that all these have not run in vain ; but in faith and righteousness, and are gone to the place that was due to them from the Lord ; with whom they also suffered.

9 For they loved not this present world; but him who died, and was raised again by God for us.

10 Stand therefore in these things, and follow the example of the Lord ; being firm and immutable in the faith, lovers of the brotherhood, lovers of one another: [7] companions together in the truth, [8] being kind and gentle towards each other, despising none.

11 When it is in your power to do good, defer it not, for charity delivered from death.

12 Be all of you subject one to another, [9] having your conversation [10] honest among the Gentiles; that by your good works, both ye yourselves may receive praise, and the Lord may not [11] be blasphemed through you. But wo be to him by whom the name of the Lord is blasphemed.

13 Therefore teach all men sobriety ; in which do ye also exercise yourselves.

CHAP. IV.

Valens, a presbyter, having fallen into the sin of covetousness, he exhorts them against it.

I AM greatly afflicted for Valens, who was once a presbyter among you ; that he should so little understand the place that was given to him in the church. Wherefore I admonish you that ye abstain from [12] covetousness; and that ye be chaste, and true of speech.

2 [13] Keep yourselves from all evil. For he that in these things cannot govern himself how shall he be able to prescribe them to another?

3 If a man does not keep himself from [14] covetousness, he shall be polluted with idolatry and be judged as if he were a Gentile.

[1] 1 Pet. vi. 7.   [2] Matt. vi. 13.   [3] Matt. xxvi. 41.   [4] 1 Pet. ii. 22, 24.   [5] In. 1 Pet. iii. 14, &c.   [6] Persuaded.   [7] Associated in truth.   [8] Yielding to each other in the mildness of the Lord.   Tobit, xii. 9.   [9] 1 Pet. ii. 12.   [10] Unreprovable.   [11] Rom. ii. 24.   Titus, ii. 5.   [12] Concupiscence ; or, immoderate and filthy lusts. So Dr. Hammond on Rom. i. 29.   [13] 1 Thes. v. 22.   Eph. v. 5 ; Coloss. ii. 5.   [14] As before, Dr. Hammond on 1 Cor. v. 10.

4 But who of you are ignorant of the judgment of God? [1] Do we not know that the saints shall judge the world, as Paul teaches?

5 But I have neither perceived nor heard any thing of this kind in you, among whom the blessed [2] Paul laboured; and who are named in the beginning of his Epistle.

6 For he glories of you in all the churches who then only knew God; for we did not then know him. Wherefore, my brethren, I am exceedingly sorry both for him, and for his wife; to whom God grant a true repentance.

7 And be ye also moderate upon this occasion; and look not upon such as enemies, but call them back as suffering, and erring members, that ye may save your whole body: for by so doing, ye shall edify your own selves.

8 For I trust that ye are well exercised in the Holy Scriptures, and that nothing is hid from you; but at present it is not granted unto me to practice that which is [3] written, Be angry and sin not; and again, Let not the sun go down upon your wrath.

9 Blessed be he that believeth and remembereth these things; which also I trust you do.

10 Now the God and Father of our Lord Jesus Christ; and he himself who is our everlasting high-priest, the Son of God, even Jesus Christ, build you up in faith and in truth and in all meekness and lenity; in patience and long-suffering, in forbearance and chastity.

11 And grant unto you a lot and portion among his saints; and us with you, and to all that are under the heavens, who shall believe in our Lord Jesus Christ, and in his Father [4] who raised him from the dead.

12 Pray for all the saints: pray also for kings, and [5] all that are in authority; and for those who persecute you, and hate you, and for the enemies of the cross; that your fruit may be manifest in all; and that ye may be perfect in [6] Christ.

13 [7] Ye wrote to me, both ye, and also Ignatius, that if any one went from hence into Syria, he should bring your letters with him; which also I will take care of, as soon as I shall have a convenient opportunity; either by myself, or him whom I shall send upon your account.

14 The Epistles of Ignatius which he wrote [8] unto us, together with what others of his have come to our hands, we have sent to you, according to your order; which are subjoined to this epistle.

15 By which we may be greatly profited; for they treat of faith and patience, and of all things that pertain to edification in [9] the Lord Jesus.

16 ¶ What you know certainly of Ignatius, and those that are with him signify to us.

17 ¶ These things have I written unto you by Crescens, whom by this present epistle I have recommended to you, and do now again commend.

18 For he has had his conversation without blame among us; and I suppose also with you.

19 Ye will also have regard unto his sister when she shall come unto you.

20 Be ye safe in the Lord Jesus Christ; [10] and in favour with all yours. Amen.

---

[1] 1 Cor. vi. 2.　[2] Phil. 1.　[3] Said in these Scriptures. Psalm iv. 5.　Eph. iv. 26.　[4] Gal. 1, 1 Tim. ii. 1, 2.　[5] Powers and princes.　[6] Him.　[7] See Anno. Usser. in loc.　[8] *i. e.* To himself, and to the church of Smyrna.　[9] Our Lord.
[10] His grace be with you all. Amen.

THE SHEPHERD OF HERMAS.

[This book is thus entitled, because it was composed by Hermas, brother to Pius, bishop of Rome; and because the Angel, who bears the principal part in it, is represented in the form and habit of a shepherd. Irenæus quotes it under the very name of Scripture. Origen thought it a most useful writing and that it was divinely inspired; Eusebius says, that, though it was not esteemed canonical, it was read publicly in the churches, which is corroborated by Jerome; and Athanasius cites it, calls it a most useful work, and observes, that though it was not strictly canonical, the Fathers appointed it to be read for direction and confirmation in faith and piety. Jerome, notwithstanding this, and that he applauded it in his catalogue of writers, in his comments upon it afterwards, terms it apocryphal and foolish. Tertullian praised it when a Catholic, and abused it when a Montanist. Although Gelasius ranks it among the apocryphal books, it is found attached to some of the most ancient MS. of the New Testament; and Archbishop Wake, believing it the genuine work of an apostolic Father, preserves it to the English reader by the following translation, in which he has rendered the books not only more exact, but in greater purity than they had before appeared. The Archbishop procured Dr. Grabe to entirely collate the old Latin version with an ancient MS. in the Lambeth library; and the learned prelate himself still further improved the whole from a multitude of fragments of the original Greek never before used for that purpose.]

The First Book of HERMAS, which is called his VISIONS.

VISION I.

1 *Against filthy and proud thoughts,* 20 *also the neglect of Hermas in chastising his children.*

HE who had bred me up sold a certain young maid at Rome; whom when I saw many years after, I remembered her, and began to love her as a sister. It happened some time afterwards, that I saw her washing in the river Tyber; and I reached out my hand unto her, and brought her out of the river.

2 And when I saw her I thought with myself, saying, How happy should I be if I had such a wife, both for beauty and manners. This I thought with myself; nor did I think any more. But not long after, as I was walking and musing on these thoughts, I began to honour this creature of God, thinking with myself; how noble and beautiful she was.

3 And when I had walked a little, I fell asleep. And the spirit caught me away, and carried me through a certain place toward the right-hand, through which no man could pass. It was a place among rocks, very steep, and unpassable for water.

4 When I was past this place, I came into a plain; and there falling down upon my knees, I began to pray unto the Lord, and to confess my sins.

5 And as I was praying, the heaven was opened, and I saw the woman which I had coveted, saluting me from heaven, and saying, Hermas, hail! and I looking upon her, answered, Lady, what dost thou do here? She answerered me, [1] I am taken up hither to accuse thee of sin before the Lord.

6 Lady, said I, wilt thou [2] convince me? No, said she: but hear the words which I am about to speak unto thee. God who dwelleth in heaven, and hath made all things out of nothing, and hath multiplied them for his holy church's sake, is angry with thee

---

[1] In MS. Lambeth. Præcepta sum a Domino ut peccata tua arguam : I am commanded of the Lord to reprove thee for thy sins. [2] In MS. Wilt thou accuse me?

because thou hast sinned against me.

7 And I answering said unto her, Lady, if I have sinned against thee, tell me where, or in what place, or when did I ever speak an unseemly or dishonest word unto thee?

8 Have I not always esteemed thee as a lady? Have I not always reverenced thee as a sister? Why then dost thou imagine these wicked things against me?

9 Then she, smiling upon me, said: the desire of naughtiness has risen up in thy heart. Does it not seem to thee to be an ill thing for a righteous man to have an evil desire rise up in his heart?

10 It is indeed a sin, and that a very great one, to such a one; for a righteous man thinketh that which is righteous. And whilst he does so, and walketh uprightly, he shall have the Lord in heaven favorable unto him in all his business.

11 But as for those who think wickedly in their hearts, they take to themselves death and captivity; and especially those who love this present world, and glory in their riches, and regard not the good things that are to come; their souls wander up and down, and know not where to fix.

12 Now this is the case of such as are double-minded, who trust not in the Lord, and despise and neglect their own life.

13 But do thou pray unto the Lord, and he will heal thy sins, and the sins of thy whole house, and of all his saints.

14 ¶ As soon as she had spoken these words the heavens were shut, and I remained utterly swallowed up with sadness and fear; and said within myself, if

this be laid against me for sin, how can I be saved?

15 Or how shall I ever be able to entreat the Lord for my many and great sins? With what words shall I beseech him to be merciful unto me?

16 As I was thinking over these things, and meditating in myself upon them, behold a chair was set over against me of the whitest wool, as bright as snow.

17 And there came an old woman in a bright garment, having a book in her hand, and sat alone, and saluted me, saying, [1] Hermas, hail! and I being full of sorrow, and weeping, answered, Hail, Lady!

18 And she said unto me, Why art thou sad, Hermas, who wert wont to be patient, and modest, and always cheerful? I answered, and said to her, Lady, a reproach has been laid to my charge by an excellent woman, who tells me, that I have sinned against her.

19 She replied, Far be any such thing from the servant of God. But it may be the desire of her has risen up in thy heart. For indeed such a thought maketh the servants of God guilty of sin.

20 Nor ought such a detestable thought to be in the servant of God: nor should he who is approved by the Spirit desire that which is evil; but especially Hermas, who contains himself from all wicked lusts, and is full of all simplicity, and of great innocence.

21 ¶ Nevertheless the Lord is not so much angry with thee for thine own sake, as upon the account of thy house, which has committed wickedness against the Lord, and against their parents.

22 And for that out of thy

[1] Vid. Hieron in Hoseam, vii. 9.

fondness towards thy sons, thou hast not admonished thy house, but hast permitted them to live wickedly; for this cause the Lord is angry with thee: but he will heal all the evils that are done in thy house. For through their sins and iniquities, thou art wholly consumed in secular affairs.

23 But now the mercy of God hath taken compassion upon thee, and upon thine house, and hath ¹ greatly comforted thee. Only as for thee, do not wander, but be of an even mind, and comfort thy house.

24 As the workman bringing forth his work, offers it to whomsoever he pleaseth; so shalt thou by teaching every day what is just cut off a great sin. Wherefore cease not to admonish thy sons, for the Lord knows that they will repent with all their heart, ² and they shall be written in the book of life.

25 And when she had said this, she added unto me; Wilt thou hear me read ?—I answered her, Lady, I will.

26 Hear then, said she; and opening the book she read, gloriously, greatly, and wonderfully, such things as I could not keep in my memory. For they were terrible words, such as no man could bear.

27 Howbeit I committed her last words to my remembrance ; for they were but few, and of great use to us.

28 Behold the mighty Lord, who by his invisible power, and with his excellent wisdom made the world, and by his glorious counsel beautified his creature, and with the word of his strength fixed the heaven, and founded the earth upon the waters ; and

by this powerful virtue established his Holy Church, which he hath blessed.

29 Behold he will remove the heavens, and the mountains, the hills, and the seas ; and all things shall be made plain for his elect ; that he may render unto them the promise which he has promised, with much honour and joy ; if so be that they shall keep the commandments of God, which they have received with great faith.

30 ¶ And when she had made an end of reading, she rose out of the chair ; and behold four young men came, and carried the chair to the east.

31 And she called me unto her, and touched my breast, and said unto me, Did my reading please thee ? I answered, Lady, these last things please me ; but what went before was severe and hard.

32 She said unto me, these last things are for ³ the righteous, but the foregoing for the revolters and heathen.

33 And as she was talking with me, two men appeared, and took her upon their shoulders and went to the east where the chair was.

34 And she went cheerfully away ; and as she was going, said unto me, Hermas, be of good cheer.

VISION II.

*Again, of his neglect in correcting his talkative wife ; and of his lewd sons.*⁴

AS I was on the way to Cuma, about the same time that I went the year before, I began to call to mind the vision I formerly had. And again the spirit carried me away, and brought me into the same place, in which I had been the year before.

2 And when I was come into the place, I fell down upon my

---

¹ In Glory. Edit. Oxon. Hath preserved thee in honour. ² So. MSS. Lamb. Et describentur in libre vitæ. ³ Edit. Oxon. ⁴ Et ejus modo.

knees, and began to pray unto the Lord, and to glorify his name, that he had esteemed me worthy, and had manifested unto me my former sins.

3 And when I arose from prayer, behold I saw over against me the old woman whom I had seen the last year, walking and reading in a certain book.

4 And she said unto me, Canst thou tell these things to the elect of God? I answered and said unto her, Lady, I cannot retain so many things in my memory, but give me the book, and I will write them down.

5 Take it, says she, and see that thou restore it again to me.

6 As soon as I had received it, I went aside into a certain place of the field, and transcribed every letter, for I found no syllables.

7 And as soon as I had finished what was written in the book, the book was suddenly caught out of my hand, but by whom I saw not.

8 ¶ After fifteen days, when I had fasted, and entreated the Lord with all earnestness, the knowledge of the writing was revealed unto me. Now the writing was this:

9 Thy seed, O Hermas! hath sinned against the Lord, and have betrayed their parents, through their great wickedness. And they have been called the betrayers of their parents, and have gone on in their treachery.

10 And now have they added lewdness to their other sins, and the pollutions of their naughtiness: thus have they filled up the measure of their iniquities. But do thou [2] upbraid thy sons with all these words; and thy wife, which shall be thy sister; and let her learn to refrain her tongue, with which she calumniates.

11 And when she shall hear these things, she will refrain herself, and shall obtain mercy.

12 And [3] they also shall be instructed, when thou shalt have reproached them with these words, which the Lord has commanded to be revealed unto thee.

13 Then shall their sins be forgiven, which they have heretofore committed, and the sins of all the saints who have sinned even unto this day; if they shall repent with all their hearts, and remove all doubts out of their hearts.

14 For the Lord hath sworn by his glory concerning his [4]elect, having determined this very time, that if any one shall [5] even now sin, he shall not be saved.

15 For the repentance of the righteous has its end; the days of repentance are fulfilled to all the saints; but to the heathen, there is repentance even unto the last day.

16 Thou shalt therefore say to those who are over the church; that they order their ways in righteousness, that they may fully receive the promise with much glory.

17 Stand fast therefore ye that work righteousness and continue to do it, that your departure may be with the holy angels.

18 Happy are ye, as many as shall endure the great trial that is at hand, and whosoever shall not deny his life.

19 For the Lord hath sworn by his Son, that whoso denieth his Son and him, being afraid of his life, he will also deny him in the [6]world that is to come.

---

[1] Clem. Alex. Strom. [2] vi. Impropera. [3] So one MS. in Coteler. Edit. Oxon. And she, &c. [4] Day. Præfinita ista die etiam nunc si peccaverit aliquis Lat. [5] Shall sin after it. [6] Days that are coming.

20 But those who shall never deny him, he will of his exceeding great mercy be favourable unto them.

21 ¶ But thou, O Hermas! remember not the [1] evils which thy sons have done, neither neglect thy sister, but take care that they amend of their former sins.

22 For they will be instructed by this doctrine, if thou shalt not be mindful of what they have done wickedly.

23 For the remembrance of evils worketh death, but the forgetting of them life eternal.

24 But thou, O Hermas! hast undergone a great many worldly troubles for the offences of thy house, because thou hast neglected them, as things that did not belong unto thee; and thou art wholly taken up with thy great business.

25 Nevertheless, for this cause shalt thou be saved, that thou hast not departed from the living God, and thy simplicity and singular continency shall preserve thee, if thou shalt continue in them.

26 Yea, they shall save all such as do such things, and walk in innocence and simplicity.

27 They who are of this kind shall prevail against all impiety, and continue until life eternal.

28 Happy are all they that do righteousness, they shall not be consumed for ever.

29 But thou wilt say, Behold there is a great trial coming. If it seem good to thee, deny him again.

30 The Lord is nigh to them that turn to him, as it is written in the book of Heldam and Modal, who prophesied to the people of Israel in the wilderness.

31 ¶ Moreover, brethren, it was revealed to me, as I was sleeping, by a very goodly young man, saying unto me, What thinkest thou of that old woman from whom thou receivedst the book; who is she? I answered, a Sybil.

32 Thou art mistaken, said he, she is not. I replied, Who is she then, sir? He answered me, It is the church of God.

33 And I said unto him, Why then does she appear old? She is therefore, said he, an old woman, because she was [3] the first of all the creation, and the world was made for her.

34 After this I saw a vision at home in my own house, and the old woman whom I had seen before, came to me and asked me, whether I had yet delivered [4] her book to the elders of the church? And I answered, that I had not yet.

35 She replied, Thou hast well done, for I have certain words more to tell thee But when I shall have finished all the words, they shall be clearly understood by the elect.

36 [5] And thou shalt write two books, and send one to Clement and one to Grapte. For Clement shall send it to the foreign cities, because it is permitted to him so to do: but Grapte shall admonish the widows and orphans.

37 But thou shalt read in this city with the elders of the church.

VISION III.
Of the building of the church triumphant, and of the several sorts of reprobates.

THE vision which I saw, brethren, was this.

---

[1] Injuries. [2] Eldad and Medad. Numb. xi. 26, 27. [3] See Dr. Grabe's Annot. to Bishop Bull's Def. Fid. Nic. p. 24. Fol. de S. Herma. [4] Suum is added in the Lambeth MS. [5] Origen. Philocal, cap. 1.

2 When I had often fasted and prayed unto the Lord, that he would manifest unto me the revelation, which he had promised by the old woman to shew unto me; the same night she appeared unto me, and said unto me:

3 Because thou dost thus afflict thyself, and art so desirous to know all things, come into the field, where thou wilt, and about the sixth hour, I will appear unto thee, and shew thee what thou must see.

4 I asked her, saying: Lady, into what part of the field? She answered, wherever thou wilt, only choose a good and a private place. And before I began to speak and tell her the place, she said unto me: I will come where thou wilt.

5 I was therefore, brethren, in the field, and I observed the hours and came into the place where I had appointed her to come.

6 And I beheld a bench placed; it was a linen pillow, and over it spread a covering of fine linen.

7 When I saw these things ordered in this manner, and that there was nobody in the place, I began to be astonished, and my hair stood on end, and a kind of horror seized me; for I was alone.

8 But, being come to myself, and calling to mind the glory of God, and taking courage, I fell down upon my knees, and began again to confess my sins as before.

9 And whilst I was doing this, the old woman came thither with the six young men whom I had seen before, and stood behind me as I was praying, and heard me praying and confessing my sins unto the Lord.

10 And touching me, she said: Leave off to pray now only for thy sins; pray also for righteousness, that thou mayest receive a part of her in thy house.

11 And she lifted me up from the place, and took me by the hand, and brought me to the seat; and said to the young men; go, and build.

12 As soon as they were departed, and we were alone, she said unto me: sit here. I answered her: Lady, let those who are elder sit first. She replied, Sit down as I bid you.

13 And when I would have sat on the right side, she suffered me not, but made a sign to me with her hand, that I should sit on the left.

14 As I was therefore musing, and full of sorrow, that she would not suffer me to sit on the right side, she said unto me, Hermas, why art thou sad?

15 The place which is on the right hand is theirs who have already attained unto God, and have suffered for his name-sake. But there is yet a great deal remaining unto thee, before thou canst sit with them.

16 But continue as thou doest in thy sincerity, and thou shalt sit with them: as all others shall that do their works, and shall bear what they have borne.

17 ¶ I said to her: Lady, I would know what it is that they have suffered? Hear then, said she: wild beasts, scourgings, imprisonments, and crosses for his name-sake.

18 For this cause the right hand of holiness belongs to them, and to all others as many as shall suffer for the name of God; but the left belongs to the rest.

19 Howbeit the gifts and the promises belong to both, to them on the right, and to those on the left hand; only that sitting on the right hand they have some glory above the others.

20 But thou art desirous to sit on the right hand with them,

and yet thy [1] defects are many. But thou shalt be purged from thy defects, as also all who doubt not shall be cleansed from all the sins which they have committed unto this day.

21 And when she had said this she would have departed.

22 Wherefore, falling down before her feet, I began to entreat her, for the Lord's sake, that she would shew me the vision which she had promised.

23 Then she again took me by the hand, and lifted me up, and made me sit upon the seat on the left side; and holding up a certain bright wand, said unto me, Seest thou that great thing? I replied, Lady, I see nothing.

24 She answered, Dost thou not see over against thee a great tower, which is built upon the water, with bright square stones?

25 For the tower was built upon a square by these six young men that came with her.

26 But many thousand of other men brought stones; some drew them out of the deep, others carried them from the ground, and gave them to the six young men. And they took them and built.

27 As for those stones which were drawn out of the deep, they put them all into the building; for they were polished, and their squares exactly answered one another, and so one was joined in such wise to the other, that there was no space to be seen where they joined, insomuch that the whole tower appeared to be built as it were of one stone.

28 But as for the other stones that were taken off from the ground, some of them they rejected, others they fitted into the building.

29 As for those which were rejected, some they cut out, and cast them at a distance from the tower; but many others of them lay round about the tower, which they made no use of in the building.

30 For some of these were rough, others had clefts in them, others were white and round, not proper for the building of the tower.

31 But I saw the other stones cast afar off from the tower, and falling into the high-way, and yet not continuing in the way, but were rolled from the way into a desert place.

32 Others I saw falling into the fire and burning; others fell near the water, yet could not roll themselves into it, though very desirous to fall into the water.

33 ¶ And when she had shewed me these things she would have departed: but I said to her, Lady, what doth it profit me to see these things, and not understand what they mean?

34 She answered and said unto me: You are very cunning, in that you are desirous to know those things which [2] relate to the tower. Yea, said I, Lady, that I may declare them unto the brethren, and they may rejoice, and hearing these things may glorify God with great glory.

35 Then she said, Many indeed shall hear them, and when they shall have heard them, some shall rejoice, and others weep. And yet even these, if they shall repent, shall rejoice too.

36 Hear therefore what I shall say concerning the parable of the tower, and after this be no longer importunate with me about the revelation.

---

[1] Lat. Exiguitatas.   [2] Are about.

37 For these revelations have an end, seeing they are fulfilled. But thou dost not leave off to desire revelations, for thou art very [1] urgent.

38 As for the tower which thou seest built, it is myself, namely the church, which have appeared to thee both now and heretofore. Wherefore ask what thou wilt concerning the tower, and I will reveal it unto thee, that thou mayst rejoice with the saints.

39 I said unto her, Lady, because thou hast thought me once worthy to receive from thee the revelation of all these things, declare them unto me.

40 She answered me, Whatsoever is fit to be revealed unto thee shall be revealed: [2] only let thy heart be with the Lord, and doubt not, whatsoever thou shalt see.

41 I asked her, Lady, why is the tower built upon the [3] water? She replied, I said before to thee that thou wert very wise to inquire diligently concerning the building, therefore thou shalt find the truth.

42 Hear therefore why the tower is built upon the water: because your life is and shall be saved by water. For [4] it is founded by the word of the almighty and honourable name, and is supported by the invisible power and virtue of God.

43 ¶ And I answering, said unto her, These things are very admirable; but, lady, who are those six young men that build?

44 They are, said she, the angels of God, which were first appointed, and to whom the Lord has delivered all his creatures, to frame and build them up, and to rule over them. For by these the building of the tower shall be finished.

45 And who are the rest who bring them stones?

46 They also are the holy angels of the Lord; but the other are more excellent than these. Wherefore when the whole building of the tower shall be finished, they shall all feast together beside the tower, and shall glorify God, because the structure of the tower is finished.

47 I asked her, saying, I would know the condition of the stones, and the meaning of them, what it is?

48 She answering, said unto me, Art thou better than all others that this should be revealed unto thee? For others are both before thee, and better than thou art, to whom these visions should be made manifest.

49 Nevertheless, that the name of God may be glorified, it has been, and shall be revealed unto thee, for the sake of those who are doubtful, and think in their hearts whether these things are so or not.

50 Tell them that all these things are true, and that there is nothing in them that is not true; but all are firm and truly established.

51 ¶ Hear now then concerning the stones that are in the building.

52 The square and white stones which agree exactly in their joints, are the apostles, and bishops, and doctors, and ministers, who through the mercy of God have come in, and governed, and taught and ministered holily and modestly to the elect of God, both they that have fallen asleep, and which yet remain; and have always agreed with them, and have had peace within

---

[1] Edit. Oxon.   [2] Clem. Alex. Strom. xii.   [3] Baptism.   [4] Namely, the tower.

themselves, and have heard each other.

53 For which cause their joints exactly meet together in the building of the tower.

54 They which are drawn out of the deep and put into the building, and whose joints agree with the other stones which are already built, are those which are already fallen asleep, and have suffered for the sake of the Lord's name.

55 And what are the other stones, lady, that are brought from the earth? I would know what are they.

56 She answered, They which lie upon the ground and are not polished, are those which God has approved, because they have walked in [1] the law of the Lord, and directed their ways in his commandments.

57 They which are brought and put in the building of the tower, are the young in faith and the faithful. And these are admonished by the angels to do well because that iniquity is not found in them.

58 But who are those whom they rejected, and laid beside the tower?

59 They are such as have sinned and are willing to repent; for which cause they are not cast far from the tower, because they will be useful for the building, if they shall repent.

60 They therefore that are yet to repent, if they shall repent, shall become strong in the faith; that is, if they repent now, whilst the tower is building. For if the building shall be finished there will then be no place for them to be put in, but they shall be rejected; for he only has this privilege who shall now be put into the tower.

61 ¶ But would you know who they are that were cut out, and cast afar off from the tower? [2] Lady, said I, I desire it.

62 They are the children of iniquity, who believed only in hypocrisy, but departed not from their evil ways; for this cause they shall not be saved, because they are not of any use in the building by reason of their sins.

63 Wherefore they are cut out, and cast afar off, because of the anger of the Lord, and because they have provoked him to anger against them.

64 As for the great number of other stones which thou hast seen placed about the tower, but not put into the buildings; those which are rugged, are they who have known the truth, but have not continued in it, nor been joined to the saints, and therefore are unprofitable.

65 Those that have clefts in them, are they that keep up discord in their hearts against each other, and live not in peace; that are friendly when present with their brethren, but as soon as they are departed from one another, their wickedness still continues in their hearts: these are the clefts which are seen in those stones.

66 Those that are maimed and short, are they who have believed indeed, but still are in great measure full of wickedness: for this cause they are maimed and not whole.

67 But what are the white and round stones, lady, and which are not proper for the building of the tower?

68 She answering said unto

---

[1] In æquitatem Domini, Lat.   [2] Edit. Oxon.

205

me: How long wilt thou continue foolish and without understanding, asking everything and discerning nothing?

69 They are such as have faith indeed, but have withal the riches of this present world. When therefore any [1] troubles arise, for the sake of their riches and traffic, they deny the Lord.

70 I answering, said unto her, When therefore will they be profitable to the Lord? When their riches shall be cut away, says she, in which they take delight, then they will be profitable unto the Lord for his building.

71 For as a round stone, unless it be cut away, and cast somewhat off, its bulk cannot be made square, so they who are rich in this world, unless their riches be pared off, cannot be made profitable unto the Lord.

72 Learn this from thy own experience; when thou wert rich, thou wast unprofitable; but now thou art profitable, and fit for the life which thou hast undertaken; for thou also once wast one of those stones.

73 ¶ As for the rest of the stones which thou sawest cast afar off from the tower, and running in the way, and tumbled out of the way into desert places, they are such as have believed indeed, but through their doubting have forsaken the true way, thinking that they could find a better. But they wander and are miserable, going into desolate ways.

74 Then for those stones which fell into the fire and were burnt, they are those who have [2] for ever departed from the living God; nor doth it ever come into their hearts to repent, by reason of the affection which they bear to their lusts and wickednesses which they commit.

75 And what are the rest which fell by the water, and could not roll into the water?

76 They are such as have heard the word, and were willing to be baptized in the name of the Lord; but considering the great holiness which the truth requires, have withdrawn themselves, and walked again after their wicked lusts.

77 Thus she finished the explication of the tower.

78 But I being still urgent, asked her, Is there repentance allowed to all those stones which are thus cast away, and were not suitable to the building of the tower; and shall they find place in this tower?

79 They may repent, said she, but they cannot come into this tower; but they shall be placed in a much lower rank, and this after that they shall have been afflicted, and fulfilled the days of their sins.

80 And for this cause they shall be removed, because they have received the word of righteousness: and then they shall be translated from their afflictions, if they shall have a true sense in their hearts of what they have done amiss.

81 But if they shall not have this sense in their hearts, they shall not be saved by reason of the hardness of their hearts.

82 When therefore I had done asking her concerning all these things, she said unto me, Wilt thou see somewhat else? And being desirous of seeing it, I became very cheerful of countenance.

83 She therefore looking back

---

[1] Tribulation arises.   [2] Finally.

upon me, and smiling a little, said unto me, Seest thou seven women about the tower? Lady, said I, I see them.

84 This tower, replied she, is supported by them, according to the command of the Lord : hear therefore the effects of them.

85 The first of them, which holds fast with her hand, is called Faith, by her the elect shall be saved. The next, which is girt up, and looks manly, is named Abstinence : she is the daughter of Faith.

86 Whosoever therefore shall follow her shall be happy in all his life, because he shall abstain from all evil works, believing that if he shall contain himself from all concupiscence, he shall be the heir of eternal life. And what, lady, said I, are the other five?

87 They are, replied she, the daughters of one another. The first of them is called Simplicity; the next Innocence; the third Modesty; then Discipline; and the last of all is Charity. When therefore thou shalt have fulfilled the works of their mother, thou shalt be able to do all things.

88 Lady, said I, I would know what particular virtue every one of these has.

89 Hear then, replied she; they have equal virtues, and their virtues are knit together, and follow one another as they were born.

90 From Faith proceeds Abstinence; from Abstinence, Simplicity; from Simplicity, Innocence; from Innocence, Modesty; from Modesty, Discipline and Charity. Therefore the works of these are holy, and chaste, and right.

91 Whoever therefore shall serve these, and hold fast to their works, he shall have his dwelling in the tower with the saints of God.

92 Then I asked her concerning the times, whether the end were now at hand;

93 But she cried out with a loud voice, saying, O foolish man! Dost thou not see the tower yet a building? When therefore the tower shall be finished, and built, it shall have an end; and indeed it shall soon be accomplished.

94 But do not ask me any more questions. What has been said may suffice thee and all the saints for the refreshment of your spirits. For these things have not been revealed to thee only, but that thou mayest make them manifest unto all.

95 For therefore, O Hermas, after three days thou must understand these words which I begin to speak unto thee, that thou mayest speak them in the ears of the saints; that when they shall have heard and done them, they may be cleansed from their iniquities, and thou together with them.

96 Hear me therefore, O my sons! I have bred you up in much simplicity, and innocency, and modesty for the love of God, which has dropped down upon you in righteousness, that you should be sanctified and justified from all sin and wickedness; but ye will not cease from your evil doings.

97 Now therefore hearken unto me, and have peace one with another, and visit one another, and receive one another, and do not enjoy the creatures of God alone.

98 Give freely to them that are in need. For some by too free feeding contract an infirmity in their flesh, and do injury to their bodies; whilst the flesh of others,

who have not food, withers away, because they want sufficient nourishment, and the bodies are consumed.

99 Wherefore this intemperance is hurtful to you, who have, and do not communicate to them that want. Prepare for the judgment that is about to come upon you.

100 Ye that are the more eminent, search out them that are hungry, whilst the tower is yet unfinished. For when the tower shall be finished, ye shall be willing to do good, and shall not find any place in it.

101 Beware, therefore, ye that glory in your riches, lest perhaps they groan who are in want, and their sighing come up unto God, and ye be shut out with your goods without the gate of the tower.

102 Behold I now warn you who are set over the church, and love the highest seats, be not ye like unto those that work mischief.

103 And they indeed carry about their poison in boxes, but ye contain your poison and[1] infection in your hearts, and will not purge them, and mix your sense with a pure heart, that ye may find mercy with the Great King.

104 Take heed, my children, that your dissensions deprive you not of your lives. How will ye instruct the elect of God, when ye yourselves want correction? Wherefore admonish one another, and be at peace among yourselves, that I, standing before your father, may give an account for you unto the Lord.

105 ¶ And when she had made an end of talking with me, the six young men that built, came and carried her to the tower;

and four others took up the seat on which she sate, and they also went away again to the tower. I saw not the faces of these, for their backs were towards me.

106 As she was going away, I asked her, that she would reveal to me what concerned the three forms, in which she had appeared unto me.

107 But she answering said unto me, concerning these things thou must ask some other, that they may be revealed unto thee.

108 Now, brethren, in the first vision the last year, she appeared unto me exceeding old, and sitting in a chair.

109 In another vision, she had indeed a youthful face, but her flesh and hair were old; but she talked with me standing, and was more cheerful than the first time.

110 In the third vision, she was in all respects much younger, and comely to the eye; only she had the hair of an aged person; yet she looked cheerful, and sate upon a seat.

111 I was therefore very sad concerning these things, until I might understand the vision.

112 Wherefore I saw the same old woman in a vision of the night saying unto me, All prayer needeth humiliation. Fast, therefore, and thou shalt learn from the Lord that which thou dost ask. I fasted therefore one day.

113 The same night a young man appeared to me and said, Why dost thou thus often desire Revelations in thy prayers? Take heed that by asking many things, thou hurt not the body. Let these Revelations suffice thee.

114 Canst thou see more notable Revelations than those which thou hast already received?

115 I answered and said unto

---

[1] Medicaments.

MARY SUPPORTING THE DEAD CHRIST ON HER KNEES.

FROM A GREEK PAINTING IN DISTEMPER ON WOOD; TWELFTH CENTURY.

him, Sir, I only ask this one thing upon the account of the three figures of the old woman that appeared to me, that the Revelation may be complete.

116 He answered me, You are not without understanding, but your doubts make you so; forasmuch as you have not your heart with the Lord.

117 I replied and said, But we shall learn these things more carefully from you.

118 ¶ Hear then, says he, concerning the figures about which you inquire.

119 And first, in the first vision she appeared to thee in the shape of an old woman sitting in a chair, because your old spirit was decayed, and without strength, by reason of your infirmities, and the doubtfulness of your heart.

120 For as they who are old have no hope of renewing themselves, nor expect any thing but their departure; so you being weakened through your worldly affairs gave yourself up to sloth, and cast not away your solicitude from yourself upon the Lord: and your sense was confused, [1] and you grow old in your sadness.

121 But, sir, I would know why she sate upon a chair?

122 He answered, because every one that is weak sitteth upon a chair by reason of his infirmity, that his weakness may be upheld. Behold therefore the figure of the first vision.

123 In the second vision you saw her standing, and having a youthful face, and more cheerful than her former; but her flesh and her hair were ancient. Hear, said he, this parable also.

124 When any one grows old, he despairs of himself by reason of his infirmity and poverty, and expects nothing but the last day of his life.

125 But on a sudden an inheritance is left to him, and he hears of it, and rises; and being become cheerful, he puts on new strength. And he now no longer sits down, but stands, and is delivered from his former sorrow; and sits not, but acts manfully.

126 So you, having heard the Revelation which God revealed unto you because God had compassion upon you, and renewed your spirit, both laid aside your infirmities, and strength came to you, and you grew strong in the faith; and God, seeing your strength, rejoiced.

127 For this cause he shewed you the building of the tower, and will shew other things unto you, if you shall have peace with all your heart among each other.

128 But in the third vision you saw her yet younger, [2] fair and cheerful, and of a serene countenance.

129 For as if some good news comes to him that is sad, he straightway forgets his sadness, and regards nothing else but the good news which he has heard; and for the rest he is comforted, and his spirit is renewed through the joy which he has received: even so you have been refreshed in your spirit by seeing these good things.

130 And for that you saw her sitting upon a bench, it denotes a strong position; because a bench has four feet and stands strongly. And even the world itself is upheld by the four elements.

131 They therefore that repent perfectly, shall be young; and they that turn from their sins

---

[1] Broken, Contusus.   [2] Honestam.

with their whole heart, shall be established.

132 And now you have the Revelation fully, ask no more to have any thing farther revealed unto you.

133 But if any thing be to be revealed, it shall be made manifest unto you.

VISION IV.
Of the trial and tribulation that is about to come upon men.

I SAW a vision, brethren, twenty days after the former vision; a representation of the tribulation that is at hand. I was walking in the field way.

2 Now from the public way to the place whither I went is about ten furlongs; it is a way very little frequented:

3 And as I was walking alone I entreated the Lord that he would confirm the Revelations which he had shewed unto me by his holy Church:

4 And would grant repentance to all his servants who had been offended, that his great and honourable name might be glorified, and because he thought me worthy [1] to whom he might shew his wonders, and, that I might honour him, and give thanks unto him.

5 And behold somewhat like a voice answered me; Doubt not, Hermas. Wherefore I began to think, and say within myself, why should I doubt, seeing I am thus settled by the Lord, and have seen such glorious things?

6 I had gone but a little farther, brethren, when behold I saw a dust rise up to heaven. I began to say within myself, is there a drove of cattle coming, that raises such a dust?

7 It was about a furlong off from me. And behold I saw the dust rise more and more, insomuch that I began to suspect that there was [2] somewhat extraordinary in it.

8 And the sun shone a little: and behold I saw a great beast, as it were a whale; and fiery locusts came out of his mouth. The height of the beast was about a hundred feet, and he had a head like a [3] large earthen vessel.

9 I began to weep, and to pray unto the Lord that he would deliver me from it. Then I called to mind the word which I had heard; Doubt not, Hermas.

10 Wherefore, brethren, putting on a divine faith, and remembering who it was that had taught me great things, I delivered myself bodily unto the beast.

11 Now the beast came on in such a manner, as if it could [4] at once have devoured a city.

12 I came near unto it, and the beast extended its whole bulk upon the ground, and put forth nothing but its tongue, nor once moved itself till I had quite passed by it.

13 Now the beast had upon its head four colours; first black, then a red and bloody colour, then a golden, and then a white.

14 ¶ After that I had passed by it, and was gone forward about thirty feet, behold there met me a certain virgin, well adorned as if she had been just come out of her bride chamber, all in white, having on white shoes, and a veil down her face, and covered with shining hair.

15 Now I knew by my former visions that it was the church, and thereupon grew the more cheerful. She saluted me saying,

---

[1] That he would shew me.   [2] Aliquid divinitus.   [3] Vas. urnale.   [4] In ictu.

Hail, O Man! I returned the salutation, saying, Lady, Hail!

16 She answering said unto me, Did nothing meet you, O man? I replied, Lady, there met me such a beast, as seemed able to devour a whole people; but by the power of God, and through his singular mercy, I escaped it.

17 Thou didst escape it well, said she, because thou didst cast thy whole care upon God, and opened thy heart unto him, believing that thou couldst be safe by no other than by his great and honourable name.

18 For this cause the Lord sent his angel, who is over the beast, whose name is Hegrin, and stopped his mouth, that he should not devour thee. Thou hast escaped a great trial through thy faith, and because thou didst not doubt for such a terrible beast.

19 Go therefore, and relate to the elect of God the great things that he hath done for thee. And thou shalt say unto them, that this beast is the figure of the trial that is about to come.

20 If therefore, ye shall have prepared yourselves, ye may escape it, if your heart be pure and without spot; and if ye shall serve God all the rest of your days without complaint.

21 Cast all your cares upon the Lord, and he will direct them. Believe in God, ye doubtful, because he can do all things; he can both turn away his wrath from you, and send you help and security.

22 Wo to the doubtful, to those who shall hear these words, and shall despise them: it had been better for them that they had not been born.

23 ¶ Then I asked her concerning the four colours which the beast had upon its head. But she answered me saying; Again thou art curious in that thou asketh concerning these things. But I said to her, Lady, shew me what they are.

24 Hear, said she; The black which thou sawest denotes the world in which you dwell. The fiery and bloody colour signifies that this age must be destroyed by fire and blood.

25 The golden part are ye, who have escaped out of it. For as gold is tried by the fire, and is made profitable, so are ye also in like manner tried who dwell among the men of this world.

26 They therefore, that shall endure to the end, and be proved by them shall be purged. And as gold, by this trial, is cleansed and loses its dross, so shall ye also cast away all sorrow and trouble, and be made pure for the building of the tower.

27 But the white colour denotes the time of the world which is to come, in which the elect of God shall dwell: because the elect of God shall be pure and without spot until life eternal.

28 Wherefore do not thou cease to speak these things in the ears of the saints. Here ye have the figure of the great tribulation that is about to come; which, if you please shall be nothing to you. Keep therefore in mind the things that I have said unto you.

29 When she had spoken thus much, she departed; but I saw not whither she went. But suddenly I heard a noise, and I turned back, being afraid, for I thought that the beast was coming toward me.

The Second Book of HERMAS, called his COMMANDS.

Introduction.

WHEN I had prayed at home, and was sat down upon the bed, a certain man came in to me with a reverend look, in the habit of a shepherd, clothed with a white cloak, having his bag upon his back, and his staff in his hand, and saluted me.

2 I returned his salutation, and immediately he sat down by me, and said unto me, I am sent by that venerable messenger, that I should dwell with thee all the remaining days of thy life.

3 But I thought that he was come to try me, and said unto him, Who are you? For I know to whom I am committed. He said unto me, Do you not know me? I answered no. I am, said he, that shepherd to whose care you are delivered.

4 Whilst he was yet speaking, his shape was changed; and when I knew that it was he to whom I was committed, I was ashamed, and a sudden fear came upon me, and I was utterly overcome with sadness, because I had spoken so foolishly unto him.

5 But he said unto me, Be not ashamed, but receive strength in thy mind, through the commands which I am about to deliver unto thee. For, said he, I am sent to shew unto thee all those things again, which thou hast seen before, but especially such of them as may be of most use unto thee.

6 And first of all write my Commands and Similitudes, the rest thou shalt so write as I shall shew unto thee. But I therefore bid thee first of all write my Commands and Similitudes, that by often reading of them thou mayest the more easily [1] keep them in memory.

7 Whereupon I wrote his Commands and Similitudes, as he bade me.

8 Which things if when you have heard, ye shall observe to do them, and shall walk according to them, and exercise yourselves in them with a pure mind, ye shall receive from the Lord those things which he has promised unto you.

9 But if having heard them ye shall not repent, but shall still go on to add to your sins, [2] ye shall be punished by him.

10 All these things that Shepherd, the angel of repentance, commanded me to write.

COMMAND I.
Of [3] believing in one God.

FIRST of [4] all believe that there is one God who created and framed all things of nothing into a being.

2 He comprehends all things, and is only immense, not to be comprehended by any.

3 Who can neither be defined by any words, nor conceived by the mind.

4 Therefore believe in him, and fear him; and fearing him [5] abstain from all evil.

5 Keep these things, and cast all [6] lust and iniquity far from thee, and put on righteousness, and thou shalt live to God, if thou shalt keep this commandment.

---

[1] Observe them, Custodite possiss. Lat. [2] Adversa recipietis. [3] Faith.
[4] Irenæus l. 1, c. 3. Origen, de Princ. l. 1, c. 3. Euseb. Hist. Eccles. l. 5, c. 8. Athanas. de Incarn. Verb. &c. [5] Habe abstinentiam. [6] Omnem. concupiscentiam. MSS. Lamb. et Oxon.

COMMAND II.

*That we must avoid detraction, and do
our alms-deeds with simplicity.*

HE said unto me, [1] Be innocent and without disguise;
so shalt thou be like an infant
who knows no malice which destroys the life of man.

2 Especially see that thou
speak evil of none, nor willingly
hear any one speak evil of any.

3 [2] For if thou observest not
this, thou also who hearest shalt
be [3] partaker of the sin of him
that speaketh evil, by believing
the slander, and thou also shalt
have sin, because thou believed-
est him that spoke evil of thy
brother.

4 [4] Detraction is a pernicious
thing; an inconstant, [5] evil spirit;
that never continues in peace, but
is always in discord. [6] Wherefore
refrain thyself from it, and keep
peace evermore with thy brother.

5 Put on an holy [7] constancy,
[8] in which there are no sins, but
all is full of joy; and do good
of thy labours.

6 [9] Give [10] without distinction
to all that are in want, not
doubting to whom thou givest.

7 But give to all, for God will
have us give to all, of [11] all his
own gifts. They therefore that
receive shall give an account to
God, both wherefore they received and for what end.

8 And they that receive without a real need, shall give an
account for it; but he that gives
shall be innocent.

9 For he has fulfilled his duty
as he received it from God; not
making any choice to whom he
should give, and to whom not.
And this service he did with
simplicity and [12] to the glory of
God.

10 Keep therefore this command according as I have delivered it unto thee; that thy repentance may be found to be sincere, and that good may come to
thy house; and have a pure heart.

COMMAND III.

*Of avoiding lying, and the repentance
of Hermas for his dissimulation.*

MOREOVER [13] he said unto
me, love truth; and let all
the speech be true which proceeds out of thy mouth.

2 That the spirit which the
Lord hath given to dwell in thy
flesh may be found true towards
all men; and the Lord be glorified, who hath given such a spirit
unto thee: because God is true
in all his words, and in him
there is no lie.

3 They therefore that lie, deny
the Lord, [14] and become robbers
of the Lord, [15] not rendering to
God what they received from
him.

4 For they received the spirit
free from lying: If therefore
they make that a liar, they defile
what was committed to them by
the Lord, and become deceivers.

5 When I heard this, I wept
bitterly; and when he saw me
weeping, he said unto me, Why

---

[1] Lat. Have simplicity and be innocent. [2] Gr. Ἐι δε μη, και συ ακουων
ενοχος εση. [3] So the Gr. and Lamb. MS. Particeps eris peccati male loquentis,
credens: tu habebis peccatum. [4] Vid. Antioch. Hom. xxix. [5] Dæmon.
[6] The Greek hath ουν. [7] Rather Simplicity; according to the Greek reading,
preserved by Athanasius. [8] Gr. in which there is no evil offence, but all
things smooth and delightful, εν οις ουδεν προσκομμα εστι πονηρον, αλλα παντα
ομαλα κῃ ἱλαρα. [9] Vid. Antioch. Hom. xcviii. [10] Simply. [11] G. εκ των ιδιων
δορηματων. MS. Lamb. de suis dodis. [12] Gloriously to God. [13] Antioch
Hom. lxvi. [14] According to the Gr. [15] See III. Hermas Simil. ix. v. 268
et seq

weepest thou? And I said, Because, sir, I doubt whether I can be saved?

6 He asked me, Wherefore? I replied, because sir, I never spake a true word in my life; but always lived in dissimulation, and affirmed a lie for truth to all men; and no man contradicted me, but all gave credit to my words. How then can I live, seeing I have done in this manner?

7 And he said unto me, Thou thinkest well and truly. For thou oughtest, as the servant of God, to have walked in the truth, and not have joined an evil conscience with the spirit of truth, nor have grieved the holy and true Spirit of God.

8 And I replied unto him, sir, I never before hearkened so diligently to these things. He answered, Now thou hearest them: Take care from henceforth, that even those things which thou hast formerly spoken falsely for the sake of thy business, may, [1] by thy present truth receive credit.

9 For even those things may be credited, if for the time to come thou shalt speak the truth; and [2] by so doing thou mayest attain unto life.

10 And whosoever shall hearken unto this command, and do it, and shall depart from all lying, he shall live unto God.

COMMAND IV.
Of putting away one's wife for adultery.

FURTHERMORE, said he, I command thee, that thou keep [3] thyself chaste ; and that thou suffer not any thought of any other marriage, or of fornication, to enter into thy heart : for such a thought produces great sin.

2 But be thou at all times mindful of the Lord, and thou shalt never sin. For if such an evil thought should arise in thy heart, thou shouldest be guilty of a great sin ; and they who do such things follow the way of death.

3 Look therefore to thyself, and keep thyself from such a thought; for where chastity remains in the heart of a righteous man, there an evil thought ought never to arise.

4 And I said unto him, Sir, suffer me to speak a little to you. He bade me say on. And I answered, Sir, if a man that is faithful in the Lord shall have a wife, and shall catch her in adultery; doth a man sin that continues to live still with her?

5 And he said unto me, As long as he is ignorant of her sin, he commits no fault in living with her; but if a man shall know his wife to have offended, and she shall not repent of her sin, but go on still in her fornication, and a man shall continue nevertheless to live with her, he shall become guilty of her sin, and partake with her in her adultery.

6 And I said unto him, What therefore is to be done, if the woman continues on in her sin? He answered, Let her husband put her away, and let him continue by himself. But if he shall put away his wife, and marry another [4] he also doth commit adultery.

7 And I said, What if the woman that is so put away, shall repent, and be willing to return to her husband, shall she not be received by him? He said unto me, Yes; and if her husband

---

[1] Through these words. Lat. His verbis et illa fidem recipiant.　　[2] If thou shalt keep the truth.　　[3] Chastity.　　[4] Another man's.

shall not receive her, he will sin, and commit a great offence against himself; but he ought to receive the offender, if she repents; only not often.

8 For to the servants of God there is but one repentance. And for this cause a man that putteth away his wife ought not to take another, because she may repent.

9 This act is alike both in the man and in the woman. Now they commit adultery, not only who pollute their flesh, but who also make an image. [1] If therefore a woman perseveres in any thing of this kind, and repents not, depart from her, and live not with her, otherwise thou also shalt be partaker of her sin.

10 But it is therefore commanded that both the man and the woman should remain unmarried because such persons may repent.

11 Nor do I in this administer any occasion for the doing of these things; but rather that whoso has offended, should not offend any more.

12 But for their former sins, God who has the power of healing will give a remedy; for he has the power of all things.

13 ¶ I asked him again and said, Seeing the Lord hath thought me worthy that thou shouldest dwell with me continually, speak a few words unto me, because I understand nothing, and my heart is hardened through my former conversation; and open my [2] understanding because I am very dull, and apprehend nothing at all.

14 And he answering said unto me, I am the [3] minister of repentance, and give [4] understanding

to all that repent. Does it not seem to thee to be [5] a very wise thing to repent? Because he that does so gets great understanding.

15 For he is sensible that he hath sinned and done wickedly in the sight of the Lord, and he remembers [6] within himself that he has offended, and repents and does no more wickedly, but does that which is good, and humbles his soul and afflicts it, because he has offended. You see therefore that repentance is great wisdom.

16 And I said unto him, For this cause, sir, I inquire diligently into all things, because I am a sinner, that I may know what I must do that I may live; because my sins are many.

17 And he said unto me, Thou shalt live if thou shalt keep these my commandments. And whosoever shall hear and do these commands shall live unto God.

18 ¶ And I said unto him, I have even now heard from certain teachers, that there is no other repentance beside that of baptism; when we go down into the water, and receive the forgiveness of our sins; and that after that, we must sin no more, but live in [7] purity.

19 And he said unto me, Thou has been [8] rightly informed. Nevertheless seeing now thou inquirest diligently into all things, I will manifest this also unto thee: yet not so as to give any occasion of sinning either to those who shall hereafter believe, or to those who have already believed in the Lord.

20 For neither they who have [9] newly believed, or who shall

---

[1] See 1 Cor. vii. 15.   [2] Sense.   [3] Prœpositus.   [4] See below, v. 18 et seq.
[5] Great wisdom.   [6] In his understanding.   [7] Chastity.   [8] Rightly heard.
[9] MS. Lamb.   Qui modo crediderunt, Who have just now believed.

hereafter believe, have any repentance of sins, but forgiveness of them.

21 But as to those who have been called to the faith, and since that are fallen into any gross sin, the Lord hath appointed repentance, because God knoweth the thoughts of all men's hearts, and their infirmities, and the manifold wickedness of the devil, who is always contriving something against the servants of God, and maliciously lays snares for them.

22 Therefore our merciful Lord had compassion towards his creature, and appointed that repentance, and gave unto me the power of it. And therefore I say unto thee, if any one after that great and holy calling shall be tempted by the devil and sin, he has one [1] repentance. But if he shall often sin and repent it shall not profit such a one; for he shall hardly live unto God.

23 And I said, Sir, I am restored again to life since I have thus diligently hearkened to these commands. For I perceive that if I shall not hereafter add any more to my sins, I shall be saved.

24 And he said, Thou shalt be saved: and so shall all others, as many as shall observe these commandments.

25 ¶ And again I said unto him, Sir, seeing thou hearest me patiently shew me yet one thing more. Tell me, saith he, what it is.

26 And I said, If a husband or a wife die, and the party which survives marry again, does he sin in so doing? [2] He that marries says he, sins not: howbeit, if he shall remain single, he shall thereby gain to himself great honour before the Lord.

27 Keep therefore thy chastity and modesty, and thou shalt live unto God. Observe from henceforth those things which I speak with thee, and command thee to observe, from the time [3] that I have been delivered unto thee, and dwell in thy house.

28 So shall thy former sins be forgiven, if thou shalt keep these my commandments. And in like manner shall all others be forgiven, who shall observe these my commandments.

COMMAND V.

Of the sadness of the heart, and of patience.

BE patient, says he, and [4] longsuffering; so shalt thou have dominion over all wicked works, and shalt [5] fulfil all righteousness.

2 For if thou shalt be patient, the Holy Spirit which dwelleth in thee shall be pure, and not be darkened by any evil spirit; but being full of joy shall be enlarged, and feast [6] in the body in which it dwells, and [7] serve the Lord with joy, and in great peace.

3 But if any [8] anger shall overtake thee, presently the Holy Spirit which is in thee will be straightened and seek to depart from thee.

4 For he is choked by the evil spirit, and has not the [9] liberty of [10] serving the Lord as he would: for he is grieved by [11] anger.

---

[1] Vid. Annot. Coteler. in loc. pp. 60, 61.   [2] Vid. not. Coteler. in loc. p. 64 B. C. Rom. vii. 3. Comp. 1 Cor. vii.   [3] SM. Lamb. medius; Ex quo mihi traditus es, That thou hast been delivered unto me, and I dwell, etc. [4] Gr Μακροθυμος. MS. Lam. Animæquus.   [5] Work.   [6] SM. Lamb. melius, Cum. vase. Et Gr. μετα του σκευους, with the body or vessel. [7] Gr. Λειτουργει τῳ κυριῳ.   [8] Οξυχολια, Gr. Bitterness of gall.   [9] Place. [10] Gr. ʼΛειτουργησαι.   [11] ʼΟξυχολια.

THE INTERMENT OF CHRIST.

FROM A FRESCO BY CIMABUE, THIRTEENTH CENTURY.

1 When, therefore, both these spirits dwell together, it is destructive to a man.

5 As if one should take a little wormwood, and put it into a vessel of honey, the whole honey would be spoiled; and a great quantity of honey is corrupted by a very little wormwood, and loses the sweetness of honey, and is no longer acceptable to its Lord because the whole honey is made bitter, and loses its use.

6 But if no wormwood be put into the honey, it is sweet and profitable to its Lord. Thus is forbearance sweeter than honey, and profitable to the Lord who dwelleth in it.

7 But anger is unprofitable. If therefore anger shall be mixed with forbearance, the soul is distressed, and its prayer is not profitable [2] with God.

8 And I said unto him, Sir, I would know the sinfulness of anger, that I may keep myself from it. And he said unto me, Thou shalt know it; and if thou shalt not keep thyself from it, thou shalt lose thy hope with all thy house. Wherefore depart from it.

9 For I the [3] messenger of righteousness am with thee; and all that depart from it, as many as shall repent with all their hearts, shall live unto God; and I will be with them, and will keep them all.

10 For all such as have repented have been justified by the most holy messenger, who is a minister of salvation.

11 ¶ And now, says he, hear the wickedness of anger; how evil and hurtful it is, and how it overthrows the servants of God; for it cannot [4] hurt those that are full of faith because the [5] power of God is with them; but it overthrows the doubtful, and those that are destitute of faith.

12 For as often as it sees [6] such men, it casts itself into their hearts; and so a man or woman is in bitterness for nothing, for the things of life, or for sustenance, or for a vain word, if any should chance to fall in; or by reason of any friend, or for a debt, or for any other superfluous things of the like nature.

13 For these things are foolish, and superfluous, and vain to the servants of God. But equanimity is strong, and forcible; and of great power, and sitteth in great enlargement; is cheerful, rejoicing in peace; and glorifying God at all times [7] with meekness.

14 And this long-suffering dwells with those that are full of faith. But anger is foolish, and light, and empty. Now bitterness is bred through folly; by bitterness, anger; by anger, fury. And this fury arising from so many evil principles, worketh a great and incurable sin.

15 For when all these things are in the same [8] man in which the Holy Spirit dwells, the vessel cannot contain them, but runs over: and because the Spirit being tender cannot tarry with the evil one; it departs and dwells with him that is meek.

16 When, therefore, it is departed from the man in whom it

---

[1] Both Athanasius and Antiochus add these words, omitted in our copies: " For in forbearance (or long suffering) the Lord dwelleth, but in bitterness the Devil." [2] To. [3] Angel. [4] Gr. work upon ενεργησαι; et MS. Lamb. facere. [5] Virtue. [6] Gr. Τοιουτους ανθρωπους. [7] In the Greek of Athanasius and Antiochus the sense is fuller: Having nothing of bitterness in itself, and continuing always in meekness and quietness. [8] Vessel.

dwelt; that man becomes destitute of the Holy Spirit, and is afterwards filled with wicked spirits,[1] and is blinded with evil thoughts. Thus doth it happen to all angry men.

17 Wherefore depart thou from anger and put on equanimity, and resist wrath; so thou shalt be [2] found with modesty and chastity by God. Take good heed therefore that thou neglect not this commandment.

18 For if thou shalt obey this command, then shalt thou also be able to observe the other commandments, which I shall command thee.

19 Wherefore strengthen thyself now in these commands, that thou mayest live unto God. And whosoever shall observe these commandments shall live unto God.

COMMAND IV.

That every man has two [3] angels, and of the suggestions of both.

I COMMANDED thee, said he, in my first commandments, that thou shouldst keep faith and fear, and [4] repentance. Yes, Sir, said I.

2 He continued: But now I will shew thee the virtues of these commands, that thou mayest know their effects; how they are [5] prescribed alike to the just and unjust.

3 Do thou therefore believe the righteous, but give no credit to the unrighteous. For righteousness keepeth the right way, but unrighteousness the wicked way.

4 Do thou therefore keep the right way, and leave that which is evil. For the evil way has not a good end, but hath many stumbling-blocks; it is rugged and full of thorns, and leads to destruction; and it is hurtful to all such as walk in it.

5 But they who go in the right way, walk with evenness, and without offence; because it is not rough nor thorny.

6 Thou seest therefore how it is best to walk in this way. Thou shalt therefore go, says he, and all others, as many as believe in God with all their heart, shall go through it.

7 ¶ And now, says he; [6] understand first of all what belongs to faith. There are two angels with man; one of righteousness, the other of iniquity.

8 And I said unto him: Sir, how shall I know that there are two such angels with man? Hear says he, and understand.

9 The angel of righteousness, is mild and modest, and gentle, and quiet. When therefore, he gets into thy heart, immediately he talks with thee of righteousness, of modesty, of chastity, of bountifulness, of forgiveness, of charity, and piety.

10 When all these things come into thy heart, know then that the angel of righteousness is with thee. Wherefore hearken to this angel and to his works.

11 Learn also the works of

---

[1] In the Greek of Athanasius follow these words, omitted in the Lat. Vers. of Hermas: "And is unstable in all his doings, being drawn hither and thither by wicked men." [2] In the Greek of Athanasius it runs better thus, "Applauded with reverence by those who are beloved of God." [3] Vid. Coteler. Annot. in loc. pp. 67, 68. Comp. Edit. Oxon. p. 61, Note a. [4] Lat. Pœnitentiam; it should rather be Abstinentiam; as in the Greek of Athanasius: as appears by the first Commandment, which is here referred to [5] Place, Lat. Posita sunt. [6] Vid. Antioch. Hom. lxi. Comp. Orig. l. iii. De Princip. et in Luc. Hom. xxxv.

the angel of iniquity. He is first of all bitter, and angry, and foolish; and his works are pernicious, and overthrow the servants of God. When therefore these things come into thy heart; thou shalt know by his works, that this is the angel of inquity.

12 And I said unto him, Sir, how shall I understand these things? Hear, says he, and understand. When anger overtakes thee, or bitterness, know that he is in thee:

13 As also, when the desire of many [1] things, and of the best meats and of drunkenness; when the love of what belongs to others, pride, and much speaking and ambition, and the like things, come upon thee.

14 When therefore these things arise in thy heart, know that the angel of iniquity is with thee. Seeing therefore thou knowest his works, depart from them all, and give no credit to him: because his works are evil, and become not the servants of God.

15 Here therefore thou hast the works of both these angels. Understand now and believe the angel of righteousness, because his instruction is good.

16 For let a man be never so happy; yet if the thoughts of the other angel arise in his heart, that man or woman must needs sin.

17 But let man or woman be never so wicked, if the works of the angel of righteousness come into his heart, that man or woman must needs do some good.

18 Thou seest therefore how it is good to follow the angel of righteousness. If therefore thou shall follow him, and [2] submit to his works, thou shalt live unto God. And as many as shall [2] submit to his work, shall live also unto God.

COMMAND VII.

That we must fear God, but not the Devil.

FEAR [3] God, says he, and keep his commandments. For if thou keepest his commandments thou shalt be powerful in every work, and all thy works shall be [4] excellent. For by fearing God, thou shalt do every thing well.

2 This is that fear with which thou must be affected that thou mayest be saved. But fear not the devil: for if thou fearest the Lord, thou shalt have dominion over him; because there is no power in him.

3 Now if there be no power in him, then neither is he to be feared. But he in whom there is excellent power, he is to be feared: for every one that has power, is to be feared. But he that has no power is despised by every one.

4 Fear the works of the devil, because they are evil. For by fearing the Lord, thou wilt fear and not do the works of the devil, but keep thyself from them.

5 There is therefore a twofold fear; if thou wilt not do evil, fear the Lord and thou shalt not do it. But if thou wilt do good, [5] the fear of the Lord is strong, and great and glorious.

6 Wherefore, fear God and thou shalt live: and whosoever shall fear him, and keep his commandments, their life is with the Lord. But they who keep them not, neither is life in them.

[1] Works. Gr. πραξεων.   [2] Gr. πιστευσῃς, Lat. Credideris, Believe.   [3] Vid. Antioch. Hom. cxxvii. Eccles xii. 13.   [4] Ασυγκρατος, Without comparison: or without mixture.   [5] In the Gr. of Antioch these words follow, which make the connection more clear: "Fear also the Lord, and thou shalt be able to do it, for."

COMMAND VIII.

That we must flee from evil, and do good.

I HAVE told thee, said he, that there are two kinds of creatures of the Lord, and that there is a two-fold [1] abstinence. From some things therefore thou must abstain, and from others not.

2 I answered, Declare to me, sir, from what I must abstain, and from what not. Hearken, said he. Keep thyself from evil, and do it not; but abstain not from good, but do it. For if thou shalt abstain from what is good, and not do it, thou shalt sin. Abstain therefore from all evil, and thou shalt [2] know all righteousness.

3 I said, What evil things are they from which I must abstain? Hearken, said he: from adultery, from drunkenness, from riots, from excess of eating, from daintiness and dishonesty, from pride, from fraud, from lying, from detraction, from hypocrisy, from remembrance of injuries, and from all evil speaking.

4 For these are the works of iniquity, from which the servant of God must abstain. For he that cannot keep himself from these things, cannot live unto God.

5 But hear, said he, what follows of these kind of things: for indeed many more there are from which the servant of God must abstain. From theft, and cheating; from false witness, from covetousness, from boasting, and all other things of the like nature.

6 Do these things seem to thee to be evil or not? Indeed they are very evil to the servants of God. Wherefore the servant of God must abstain from all these [3] works.

7 Keep thyself therefore from them, that thou mayest live unto God, and be written among those that abstain from them. And thus have I shown thee what things thou must avoid: now learn from what thou must not abstain.

8 Abstain not from any good works, but do them. Hear, said he, what the virtue of those good works is which thou must do, that thou mayest be saved. The first of all is faith; the fear of the Lord; charity; concord; equity; truth; patience; chastity.

9 There is nothing better than these things in the life of man; [4] who shall keep and do these things in their life. Hear next what follow these.

10 To minister to the widows; not to despise the fatherless and poor; to redeem the servants of God from necessity; to be hospitable; (for in hospitality there is sometimes [5] great fruit) not to be contentious, but be quiet.

11 To be humble above all men; to reverence the aged; to labour to be righteous; [6] to respect the brotherhood; to bear affronts; to be long-suffering; [7] not to cast away those that have fallen from the faith, but to convert them, and make them be of [8] good cheer; to admonish sinners; not to oppress those that are our debtors; and all other things of a like kind.

12 Do these things seem to thee to be good or not? And I

---

[1] Antioch. Hom. lxxix.   [2] Do according to the Greek, εργαζομενους.
[3] Vid. Coteler. in loc   [4] The sense here is defective, and may be thus restored from the Greek of Athanasius:—Whoever keeps these things, and doth not abstain from them, shall be happy in his life. And so the Lamb.
MS: Hæ? qui custodierit.   [5] Gr. αγαθοποιησις, good deed.   [6] συντηρειν.
[7] Add from the Gr. of Athanasius and Antiochus: Not to remember injuries; To comfort those who labour in their minds.   [8] Ευθυμους.

said, What can be better than these words? Live then, said he, in these commandments, and do not depart from them. For if thou shalt keep all these commandments, thou shalt live unto God. And all they that shall keep these commandments shall live unto God.

COMMAND IX.

That we must ask of God daily; and without doubting.

AGAIN he said unto me; [1] remove from thee all doubting; and question nothing at all, when thou askest anything of the Lord; saying within thyself: how shall I be able to ask anything of the Lord and receive it, seeing I have so greatly sinned against him?

2 Do not think thus, but turn unto the Lord with all thy heart, and ask of him without doubting, and thou shalt know the mercy of the Lord; how that he will not forsake thee, but will fulfil the request of thy soul.

3 For God is not as men, mindful of the injuries he has received; but he forgets injuries, and has compassion upon his creature.

4 Wherefore purify thy heart from all the vices of this present world; and observe the commands I have before delivered unto thee from God; and thou shalt receive whatsoever good things thou shalt ask, and nothing shall be wanting unto thee of all thy petitions; if thou shalt ask of the Lord without doubting.

5 [2] But they that are not such,

shall obtain none of those things which they ask. For they that are full of faith ask all things with confidence, and receive from the Lord, because they ask without doubting. But he that doubts, shall hardly live unto God, except he repent.

6 Wherefore purify thy heart from doubting, and put on faith, and trust in God, and thou shalt receive all that thou shalt ask. But and if thou shouldest chance to ask somewhat and not ([3] immediately) receive it, yet do not therefore doubt, because thou hast not presently received the petition of thy soul.

7 For it may be thou shalt not presently receive it for thy trial, or else for some sin which thou knowest not. But do not thou leave off to ask, [4] and then thou shalt receive. Else if thou shalt cease to ask, thou must complain of thyself, and not of God, that he has not given unto thee what thou didst desire.

8 Consider therefore this doubting, how cruel and pernicious it is; and how it utterly roots out many from the faith, who were very faithful and firm. For this doubting is the daughter of the devil, and deals very wickedly with the servants of God.

9 Despise it therefore, and thou shalt rule over it [5] on every occasion. Put on a firm and powerful faith: for faith promises all things and perfects all things. But doubting will not believe, that it shall obtain anything, by all that it can do.

10 Thou seest therefore, says

---

[1] Vid. Antioch. Hom. lxxxiii. Confer. Fragm. D. Grabe. Spicileg. tom. i. page 303. [2] Add from the Gr. both of Athanasius and Antiochus: But if thou doubtest in thy heart, thou shalt receive none of thy petitions. For those who distrust (or, doubt of) God, are like the double-minded, who shall obtain none of these things. [3] So MS. Lamb. Tardius accipias: and so the Gr. Βραδυτερον λαμβανεις. [4] Asking the petition of thy soul. [5] In everything.

221

he, how faith cometh from above, from God; and hath great power. But doubting is an earthly spirit, and proceedeth from the devil, and has no strength.

11 Do thou therefore keep the virtue of faith, and depart from doubting, in which is no virtue, and thou shalt live unto God. And all shall live unto God, as many as do these things.

COMMAND X.

Of the sadness of the heart; and that we must take heed not to grieve the spirit of God that is in us.

PUT all sadness far from thee; for it is the sister of doubting and of anger. How, sir, said I, is it the sister of these? for sadness, and anger, and doubting, seem to me to be very different from one another.

2 And he answered: [1] Art thou without sense that thou dost not understand it? For sadness is the most mischievous of all spirits, and the worst to the servants of God: [2] It destroys the spirits of all men, and torments the Holy Spirit; and again, it saves.

3 Sir, said I, I am very foolish, and understand not these [3] things. I cannot apprehend how it can torment, and yet save. Hear, said he, and understand. They who never sought out the truth, nor inquired concerning the majesty of God, but only believed, are involved in the affairs of the heathen.

4 And there is another [4] lying prophet that destroys the [5] minds of the servants of God; that is of those that are doubtful, not of those that fully trust in the Lord. Now those doubtful persons come to him, as to a divine spirit, and inquire of him what shall befall them.

5 And this lying prophet having no power in him of the divine Spirit, answers them according to their demands, and fills their souls with promises according as they desire. Howbeit that prophet is vain, and answers vain things to those who are themselves vain.

6 And whatsoever is asked of him by vain men, he answers them vainly. Nevertheless he speaketh some things truly. For the devil fills him with his spirit, that he may overthrow some of the righteous.

7 ¶ Whosoever therefore are strong in the faith of the Lord, and have put on the truth: they are not joined to such spirits, but depart from them. But they that are doubtful, and often repenting like the heathens, consult them, and heap up to themselves great sin, serving idols.

8 As many therefore as are such, inquire of them upon every occasion; worship idols; and are foolish, and void of the truth.

9 For every spirit that is given from God needs not to be asked; but having the power of divinity speaks all things of itself; because he comes from above, from the power of God.

10 But he that being asked speaks according to men's desires, and concerning many other affairs of the present world, understands not the things which relate unto God. For these spirits are darkened through such affairs, and corrupted and broken.

11 As good vines if they are

---

[1] Without sense thou dost not understand it.   [2] So the Lat. Vers. But the Gr. of Athanasius is better: And destroyeth more than any other spirit.   [3] Questions.   [4] Vid. Epit. Oxon. p. 70 b. Comp. 2 Cor. vii. 10.   [5] Lat. Sensus: from the Greek Νους.

neglected, are oppressed with weeds and thorns, and at last killed by them ; so are the men who believe such spirits.

12 They fall into many actions and businesses, and are void of sense, [1] and when they think of things pertaining unto God, they understand nothing at all: but if at any time they chance to hear anything concerning the Lord, their [2] thoughts are upon their business.

13 But they that have the fear of the Lord, and search out the truth concerning God, [3] having all their thoughts towards the Lord; apprehend whatsoever is said to them, and forthwith understand it, because they have the fear of the Lord in them.

14 For where the spirit of the Lord dwells, there is also [4] much understanding added. Wherefore join thyself to the Lord, [5] and thou shalt understand all things.

15 ¶ Learn now, O unwise man! how sadness [6] troubleth the Holy Spirit, and how it saves. When a man that is doubtful is engaged in any affair, and does not accomplish it by reason of his doubting, this sadness enters into him, and grieves the Holy Spirit, and makes him sad.

16 Again, anger when it overtakes any man for any business he is greatly moved ; [7] and then again sadness entereth into the heart of him, who was moved with anger, and he is troubled for what he hath done, and repenteth, because he hath done amiss.

17 This sadness therefore seemeth to bring salvation, because he repenteth of his evil deed. But both the other things, namely, doubting and sadness, such as before was mentioned, vex the spirit: doubting, because his work did not succeed: and sadness, because he angered the Holy Spirit.

18 [8] Remove therefore sadness from thyself, [9] and afflict not the Holy Spirit which dwelleth in thee, lest he [10] entreat God, and depart from thee. For the spirit of the Lord [11] which is given to dwell in the flesh, endureth no such sadness.

19 Wherefore clothe thyself with cheerfulness, which has always favour with the Lord, and thou shalt rejoice in it. For every cheerful man does well; and relishes those things that are good, and despises [12] sadness.

20 But the sad man does always wickedly. [13] First, he doth wickedly, because he grieveth the Holy Spirit, which is given to man, being of a cheerful nature. And again he does ill, because he prays with sadness unto the Lord,

---

[1] And understand nothing at all, thinking of riches. Lat. [2] Senses.
[3] Gr. of Athanasius, Καρδιαν εχοντες προς κυριον. So that the Latin should be Habentes, not Habent. [4] Gr. συνεσις πολλη. [5] Gr. παντα νοησεις. And so in the Lamb. MS. Omnia scies. [6] Gr. εκτριβει. MS. Lamb. Contribulat. [7] In the Greek of Athanasius, follows και ποιηση τι κακον, and he doth something which is ill. Which letter agrees with what follows, Because he hath done amiss. The text in this place being evidently corrupted, it has been endeavoured to restore the true sense of it from the Greek of Athanasius, which is as follows: παλιν η λυπη εισπορευεται επι την καρδιαν του ανθρωπου του οξυχοληρσαντος, και λυπειται επι τη πραξει αυτου ή επραξεν και μετανοει οτι πονηρον ειργασατο. Αυτη ουν η λυπη δοκει σωτηριαν εχειν, οτι το πονηρον πραξας μετενοησεν. Αμφοτεραι δε των πραξεων λυπουσι, &c. [8] Antioch. Hom. xxv. [9] Gr. Μη θλιβε, MS. Lamb. Noli nocere. [10] Gr. Μη εντευξηται τω θεω. Comp. Rom. vii. 27. [11] Gr. Το δοθεν εις την σαρκα, ταυτην λυπην ουκ υποφερει. [12] Gr. λυπης. [13] So the Greek : ο δε λυπηρος ανηρ παντοτε πονηρευεται, πρωτον μεν πονηρευεται, &c.

and maketh not a first thankful acknowledgment unto him of former mercies, and obtains not of God what he asks.

21 For the prayer of a sad man has not always efficacy to come up to the altar of God. And I said unto him, Sir, why has not the prayer of a sad man virtue to come up to the altar of God? because, said he, that sadness remaineth in his heart.

22 When therefore a man's prayer shall be accompanied with sadness, it will not suffer his requests to ascend pure to the altar of God. For as wine when it is mingled with vinegar, has not the sweetness it had before; so sadness being mixed with the Holy Spirit, suffers not a man's prayer to be the same as it would be otherwise.

23 Wherefore cleanse thyself from sadness, which is evil, and thou shalt live unto God. And all others shall live unto God, as many as shall lay aside sadnesss and put on cheerfulness.

COMMAND XI.

That the spirits and prophets are to be tried by their works; and of a two-fold spirit.

HE shewed me certain men sitting upon benches, and one sitting in a chair: and he said unto me seest thou who sit upon the benches? Sir, said I, I see them. He answered, They are the faithful; and he who sits in the chair is an earthly spirit.

2 For he cometh not into [1] the assembly of the faithful, but avoids it. But he joins himself to the doubtful and empty; and

prophesies to them in corners and hidden places; and pleases them by speaking according to all the desires of their hearts.

3 For he placing himself among empty vessels, is not broken, but the one fitteth the other. But when he cometh into the company of just men, [2] who are full of the spirit of God, and they pray unto the Lord; that man is [3] emptied because that earthly spirit flies from him, and he is dumb, and cannot speak anything.

4 As if in a store-house you shall stop up wine or oil; and among those vessels shall place an empty jar; and shall afterwards come to open it, you shall find it empty as you stopped it up: so those empty prophets when they come among the spirits of the just, are found to be such as they came.[4]

5 ¶ I said, How then shall a man be able to discern them? Consider what I am going to say considering both kinds of [5] men; and as I speak unto thee so shalt thou prove the prophet of God, and the false prophet.

6 And first try the man who hath the spirit of God; because the spirit which is from above is humble, and quiet; and departs from all wickedness; and from the vain desires of the present world; and makes himself more humble than all men; and answers to none when he is asked; nor to every one singly: for the Spirit of God doth not speak to a man when he will, but when God pleases.

7 When therefore a man who

---

[1] Church of the living.   [2] Have the Spirit of God in them.   [3] Exinanitur.
[4] Something was wanting in this place to make the subject clear, and it was suggested to Archbishop Wake, by Dr. Grabe, that what should have followed was transposed into the next command. Accordingly the Archbishop reduced both places to what he conceived should be their true order, and in that state they now stand.   [5] Vessels.

ἡ ΑΝΑСΤΑСΙС

THE RESURRECTION OF CHRIST.

FROM A "BOOK OF THE EVANGELISTS." GREEK MANUSCRIPT OF THE TWELFTH
CENTURY.

hath the Spirit of God shall come into the church of the righteous, who have the faith of God, and they pray unto the Lord; then the holy angel of God fills that man with the blessed Spirit, and he speaks in the congregation as he is moved of God.

8 Thus therefore is the spirit of God known, because whosoever speaketh by the Spirit of God, speaketh as the Lord will.

9 Hear now concerning the earthly spirit, which is empty and foolish, and without virtue. And first of all the man who is supposed to have the Spirit, (whereas he hath it not in reality), exalteth himself, and desires to have the first seat, and is wicked, and full of words.

10 And spends his time in pleasure, and in all manner of voluptuousness; and receives the reward of his divination; which if he receives not, he does not divine.

11 Should the Spirit of God receive reward and divine? It doth not become a prophet of God so to do.

12 Thus you see the life of each of these kind of prophets. Wherefore prove that man by his life and works, who says that he hath the Holy Spirit. And believe the Spirit which comes from God, and has power as such. But believe not the earthly and empty spirit, which is from the devil, in whom there is no faith nor virtue.

13 Hear now the similitude which I am about to speak unto thee. Take a stone, and throw it up towards heaven; or take a spout of water, and mount it up thitherward; and see if thou canst reach unto heaven.

14 Sir, said I, how can this be done? For neither of those things which you have mentioned, are possible to be done. And he answered, Therefore as these things cannot be done, so is the earthly spirit without virtue, and without effect.

15 Understand yet farther the power which cometh from above, in this similitude. The grains of hail that drop down are exceedingly small; and yet when they fall upon the head of a man, how do they cause pain to it?

16 And again; consider the droppings of a house: how the little drops falling upon the earth, work a hollow in the stones.

17 So in like manner the least things which come from above, and fall upon the earth, have great force. Wherefore join thyself to this spirit, which has the power; and depart from the other which is empty.

COMMAND XII.

Of a two-fold desire: that the commands of God are not impossible: and that the devil is not to be feared by them that believe.

AGAIN he said unto me; [1] remove from thee all evil desires, and put on good and holy desires. For having put on a good desire, thou shalt hate that which is evil, and bridle it as thou wilt. But an evil desire is dreadful and hard to be tamed.

2 It is very horrible and wild: and by its wildness consumes men. And especially if a servant of God shall chance to fall into it, except he be very wise, he [2] is ruined by it. For it destroys those who have not the garment of a good desire: and [3] are engaged in the affairs of

---

[1] Vid. Antioch. Hom. lxxiv.   [2] MS. Lamb. Consumitur, et, Gr. Athanas. δαπαναται.   [3] Gr. Athanas. εμπεφυρμενους τῳ άίωνι τουτῳ. Instead of implicateos, the Lat. Vers. should be Implicatos.

this present world; and delivers them unto death.

3 [1]Sir, said I, what are the works of an evil desire, which bring men unto death? Shew them to me, that I may depart from them. Hear said he, by what works an evil desire bringeth the servants of God unto death.

4 First of all, it is an evil desire to covet another man's wife; or for a woman to covet another's husband; as also to desire the dainties of riches: and multitude of superfluous meats; and drunkenness; and many delights.

5 For in much delicacy there is folly; and many pleasures are needless to the servants of God. Such lusting therefore is evil and pernicious, which brings to death the servants of God. For all such lusting is from the devil.

6 Whosoever therefore shall depart from all evil desires, shall live unto God; but they that are subject unto them shall die for ever. For this evil lusting is deadly. Do thou therefore put on the desire of righteousness, and being armed with the fear of the Lord, resist all wicked lusting.

7 For this fear dwelleth in good desires; and when evil coveting shall see thee armed with the fear of the Lord, and resisting it, it will fly far from thee, and not appearing before thee, but be afraid of thy armour.

8 And thou shalt have the victory, and be crowned for it; and shalt attain to that desire which is good; and shalt give the victory which thou hast obtained unto God, and shalt serve him in doing what thou thyself wouldest do.

9 For if thou shalt serve good desires, and be subject to them; thou shalt be able to get the dominion over thy wicked lustings; and they shall be subject to thee as thou wilt.

10 ¶ And I said, Sir, I would know how to serve that desire which is good? Hearken, saith he, Fear God and put thy trust in him, and love truth, and righteousness, and do that which is good.

11 If thou shalt do these things, thou shalt be an approved servant of God; and shalt serve him: and all others who shall in like manner serve a good desire shall live unto God.

12 ¶ And when he had fulfilled these twelve commands, he said unto me, Thou hast now these commands, walk in them; and exhort those that hear them that repent, and that they keep their repentance pure all the remaining days of their life.

13 And fulfil diligently this ministry which I commit to thee, and thou shalt receive great advantage by it; and shalt find favour with all such as shall repent, and shall believe thy words. For I am with thee, and will force them to believe.

14 And I said unto him, Sir, these commands are great and excellent, and able to cheer the heart of that man that shall be able to keep them. But, Sir, I cannot tell, whether they can be observed by any man?

15 He answered, Thou shalt easily keep these commands, and they shall not be hard: howbeit, if thou shalt suffer it once to enter into thy heart that they cannot be kept by any one, thou shalt not fulfil them.

[1] That the words here inserted, and removed into their proper place in the foregoing Command, do not belong to this Discourse, the Greek of Athanasius, in which they are all omitted, clearly shews.

16 But now I say unto thee, if thou shalt not observe these commands, but shall neglect them, thou shalt not be saved, nor thy children, nor thy house; because thou hast judged that these commands cannot be kept by man.

17 ¶ These things he spake very angrily unto me, insomuch that he greatly affrighted me. For he changed his countenance, so that a man could not bear his anger.

18 And when he saw me altogether troubled and confounded, he began to speak more moderately and cheerfully, saying, O foolish, and without understanding!

19 Unconstant, not knowing the majesty of God how great and wonderful he is; who created the world for man, and hath made every creature subject unto him: and given him all power, that he should be able to [1] fulfil all these commands.

20 He is able, said he, to [2] fulfil all these commands, who has the Lord in his heart: but they who have the Lord only in their mouths, and their heart is hardened, and they are far from the Lord; to such persons these commands are hard and difficult.

21 Put therefore, ye that are empty and light in the faith, the Lord your God in your hearts; and ye shall perceive how that nothing is more easy than these commands, nor more pleasant, nor more gentle and holy.

22 And turn yourselves to the Lord your God, and forsake the devil and his pleasures, because they are evil, and bitter, and impure. And fear not the devil, because he has no power over you.

23 For I am with you, the messenger of repentance, who have the dominion over him. The devil doth indeed affright men; but his terror is vain. Wherefore fear him not, and he will flee from you.

24 And I said unto him; Sir, hear me speak a few words unto you. He answered, Say on: A man indeed desires to keep the commandments of God: and there is no one but what prays unto God, that he may be able to keep his commandments.

25 But the devil is hard, and by his power rules over the servants of God. And he said He cannot rule over the servants of God, [3] who trust in him with all their hearts.

26 The devil may strive, but he cannot overcome them.

27 For if ye resist him, he will flee away with confusion from you. But they that are not full in the faith, fear the devil, as if he had some great power. For the devil tries the servants of God and if he finds them empty, he destroys them.

28 For as man, when he fills up vessels with good wine, [4] and among them puts a few vessels half full, and comes to try and taste of the vessels, doth not try those that are full, because he knows that they are good; but tastes those that are half full, lest they should grow sour; (for vessels half full soon grow sour, and lose the taste of wine:) so the devil comes to the servants of God to try them.

29 They that are full of faith resist him stoutly, and he departs from them, because he finds no place where to enter into them: then he goes to those that are not full of faith, and because he has place of entrance,

[1] Ut dominetur.   [2] Angel.   [3] Gr. ελπιζοντων εις Ἀυτον.   [4] Origen. in Matt. xxiv. 42.

he goes into them, and does what he will with them, and they become his servants.

30 ¶ But I, [1] the messenger of repentance, say unto you, fear not the devil, for I am sent unto you, that I may be with you, as many as shall repent with your whole heart, and that I may confirm you in the faith.

31 [2] Believe therefore, ye who by reason of your transgressions have [3] forgot God, and your own salvation; and [4] adding to your sins have made your life very heavy.

32 That if ye shall turn to the Lord with your whole hearts, and shall serve him according to his will; he will heal you of your former sins, and ye shall have dominion over all the works of the devil.

33 Be not then afraid in the least of his threatenings, for they are without force, as the nerves of a dead man. But hearken unto me, and fear the Lord Almighty, who is able to save and to destroy you; and keep his commands, that ye may live unto God.

34 And I said unto him; Sir, I am now confirmed in all the commands of the Lord whilst that you are with me, and I know that you will break all the power of the devil.

35 And we also shall overcome him, if we shall be able, through the help of the Lord, to keep these commands which you have delivered.

36 Thou shalt keep them, said he, if thou shalt purify thy heart towards the Lord. And all they also shall keep them who shall cleanse their hearts from the vain desires of the present world, and shall live unto God.

The Third Book of HERMAS, which is called his SIMILITUDES.

SIMILITUDE I.

That seeing we have no abiding city in this world, we ought to look after that which is to come.

AND he said unto me; [5] Ye know that ye who are the servants of the Lord, live here as in a pilgrimage; for your city is far off from this city.

2 If, therefore, ye know your city in which ye are to dwell, why do ye here buy estates, and provide yourselves with delicacies, and stately buildings, and superfluous houses? For he that provides himself these things in this city, does not think of returning into his own city.

3 O foolish, and doubtful, and wretched man; who understandest not that all these things belong to other men, and are under the power of another. For the Lord of this city saith unto thee; Either obey my laws, or depart out of my city.

4 What therefore shalt thou do who art subject to a law in thine own city? Canst thou for thy estate, or for any of those things which thou hast provided, deny thy law? But if thou shalt deny it, and wilt afterwards return into thy own city, thou shalt not be received, but shall be excluded thence.

5 See therefore, that like a man in another country, thou procure

---

[1] Angel. [2] Vid. Antioch. Hom. lxxvii. [3] MS. Lamb. Qui obliti estis Deum, et salutem vestram. [4] What follows should be corrected thus; Et qui adjicientes peccatis vestris, gravatis vitam vestram. [5] Antioch. Hom. xv.

no more to thyself than what is necessary, and sufficient for thee? and be ready, that when the God or Lord of this city shall drive thee out of it, thou mayst oppose his law, and go into thine own city; where thou mayst with all cheerfulness live according to thine own law with no wrong.

6 Take heed therefore ye that serve God, and have him in your hearts: work ye the works of God, being mindful both of his commands and of his promises, which he has promised; and be assured that he will make them good unto you; if ye shall keep his commandments.

7 Instead therefore of the possessions that ye would otherwise purchase, redeem [1] those that are in want from their necessities, as every one is able; justify the widows; judge the cause of the fatherless; and spend your riches and your wealth in such works as these.

8 For, for this end has God enriched you, that ye might fulfil these kind of services. It is much better to do this, than to buy lands or houses; because all such things shall perish with this present time.

9 But what ye shall do for the name of the Lord, ye shall find in your city, and shall have joy without sadness or fear. Wherefore covet not the riches of the heathen; for they are destructive to the servants of God.

10 [2] But trade with your own riches which you possess, by which ye may attain unto everlasting joy.

11 And do not commit adultery, nor touch any other man's wife, nor desire her; but covet that which is thy own business, and thou shalt be saved.

SIMILITUDE II.

As the vine is supported by the elm, so is the rich man helped by the prayers of the poor.

AS I was walking into the field, and considered the elm and the vine, and thought with myself of their fruits, an angel appeared unto me, and said unto me; What is it that thou thinkest upon thus long within thyself?

2 And I said unto him, Sir, I think of this vine and this elm because their fruits are fair. And he said unto me; [3] These two trees are set for a pattern to the servants of God.

3 And I said unto him, Sir, I would know in what the pattern of these trees which thou mentionest, does consist. Hearken, saith he; seest thou this vine and this elm; Sir, said I, I see them,

4 This vine, saith he, is fruitful, but the elm is a tree without fruit. Nevertheless this vine unless it were set by this elm, and supported by it, would not bear much fruit; but lying along upon the ground, would bear but ill fruit, because it did not hang upon the elm; whereas, being supported upon the elm, it bears fruit both for itself and for that.

5 See, therefore, how the elm gives no less, but rather more fruit, than the vine. How, Sir, said I, does it bear more fruit than the vine? Because, said he, the vine being supported upon the elm gives both much and good fruit; whereas, if it lay along upon the ground, it would bear but little, and that very ill too.

6 This similitude, therefore, is set forth to the servants of God;

---

[1] Souls. [2] MS. Lambeth. Proprias, autem quas habetis agite. [3] Vid. Origen. in Jos. Hom. x.

229

and it represents the rich and poor man. I answered, Sir, make this manifest unto me. Hear, said he; the rich man has wealth; howbeit towards the Lord he is poor; for he is [1] taken up about his riches, and prays but little to the Lord; and the prayers which he makes are lazy and without force.

7 When, therefore, the rich man reaches out to the poor those things which he wants, the poor man prays unto the Lord for the rich; and God grants unto the rich man all good things, because the poor man is rich in prayer; and his requests have great power with the Lord.

8 Then the rich man ministers all things to the poor, because he perceives that he is heard by the Lord: and he the more willingly and without doubting, affords him what he wants, and takes care that nothing be lacking to him.

9 And the poor man gives thanks unto the Lord for the rich; because they do both their work from the Lord.

10 With men therefore, the elm is not thought to give any fruit; and they know not neither understand that its company being added to the vine, the vine bears a double increase, both for itself and for the elm.

11 Even so the poor praying unto the Lord for the rich, are heard by him; and their riches are increased, because they minister to the poor of their wealth. They are therefore both made partakers of each other's good works.

12 Whosoever, therefore, shall do these things, he shall not be forsaken by the Lord, but shall be written in the book of life.

13 Happy are they who are rich, and perceive themselves to be increased: for he that is sensible of this, will be able to minister somewhat to others.

SIMILITUDE III.

As the green trees in the winter cannot be distinguished from the dry; so neither can the righteous from the wicked in this present world.

AGAIN he showed me many trees whose leaves were shed, and which seemed to me to be withered, for they were all alike. And he said unto me, Seest thou these trees? I said, Sir, I see that they look like dry trees.

2 He answering, said unto me; These trees are like unto the men who live in the present world. I replied: Sir, why are they like unto dried trees? Because, said he, neither the righteous, nor unrighteous, are known from one another; but all are alike in this present world.

3 For this world is as the winter to the righteous men, [2] because they are not known, but dwell among sinners.

4 As in the winter all the trees having lost their leaves, are like dry trees; nor can it be discerned which are dry and which are green: so in this present world neither the righteous nor wicked are discerned from each other; but they are all alike.

SIMILITUDE IV.

As in the summer the living trees are distinguished from the dry by their fruit and green leaves; so in the world to come the righteous shall be distinguished from the unrighteous by their happiness.

AGAIN he showed me many other trees, of which some had leaves, and others appeared dry and withered. And he said unto me, Seest thou these trees? I answered, Sir, I see them; and some are dry, and others full of leaves.

---

[1] Distracted.   [2] Who are.

2 These trees, saith he, which are green, are the righteous which shall possess the world to come. For the world to come, is the summer to the righteous; but to sinners it is the winter.

3 When, therefore, the mercy of the Lord shall shine forth, then they who serve God shall be made manifest, and plain unto all. For as in the summer the fruit of every tree is shown and made manifest, so also the works of the righteous shall be declared and made manifest, and they shall be restored in that world merry and joyful.

4 For the other [1] kind of men, namely the wicked, like the trees which thou sawest dry, shall as such be found dry and without fruit in that other world; and like dry wood shall be burnt; and it shall be made manifest that they have done evil all the time of their life;

5 And they shall be burnt because they have sinned and have not repented of their sins. And also all the other nations shall be burnt, because they have not acknowledged God their Creator.

6 Do thou therefore bring forth good fruit, that in the summer thy fruit may be known; and keep thyself from much business, and thou shalt not offend. For they who are involved in much business, sin much; because they are taken up with their affairs, and serve not God.

7 And how can a man that does not serve God, ask anything of God, and receive it? But they who serve him, ask and receive what they desire.

8 But, if a man has only one thing to follow, he may serve God, because his mind is not taken off from God but he serves him with a pure mind.

9 If, therefore, thou shalt do this, thou mayest have fruit in the world to come; and all, as many as shall do in like manner, shall bring forth fruit.

SIMILITUDE V.

Of a true fast, and the rewards of it, also of the cleanliness of the body.

AS I was fasting, and sitting down in a certain mountain, and giving thanks unto God for all the things that he had done [2] unto me; behold I saw the shepherd, who was wont to converse with me, sitting by me, and saying unto me: What has brought thee hither thus early in the morning? I answered, Sir, to-day I keep a [3] station.

2 He answered, What is a station? I replied, it is a fast. He said, What is that fast? I answered, I fast, as I have been wont to do. Ye know not, said he, what it is to fast unto God; nor is this a fast which ye fast, profiting nothing with God.

3 Sir, said I, what makes you speak thus? He replied, I speak it, because this is not the true fast which you think that you fast; but I will show you what that is which is a [4] complete fast, and acceptable unto God.

4 Hearken, said he, The Lord does not desire such a needless fast: for by fasting in this manner, thou advancest nothing in righteousness.

5 [5] But the true fast is this: Do nothing wickedly in thy life, but serve God with a pure mind; and keep his commandments and walk according to his precepts, nor suffer any wicked desire to enter into the mind.

[1] Nations   [2] With me.   [3] Vid. not. Coteler. in loc. pp. 72, 73.   [4] Coteler.
[5] Jejuna certe verum jejunium tale. Lat.

6 But trust in the Lord, that if thou dost these things, and fearest him, and abstaineth from every evil work, thou shalt live unto God.

7 If thou shalt do this, thou shalt perfect a great fast, and an acceptable one unto the Lord.

8 ¶ Hearken unto the similitude which I am about to propose unto thee, as to this matter.

9 A certain man having a farm, and many servants, planted a vineyard in a certain part of his estate for his posterity :

10 And taking a journey into a far country, chose one of his servants which he thought the most faithful and approved, and delivered the vineyard into his care; commanding him that he should take up the vines. Which if he did, and fulfilled his command, he promised to give him his liberty. Nor did he command him to do anything more; and so went into a far country.

11 And after that servant had taken that charge upon him, he did whatsoever his lord commanded him. And when he had staked the vineyard, and found it to be full of weeds, he began to think with himself, saying;

12 I have done what my lord commanded me, I will now dig this vineyard, and when it is digged, it will be more beautiful; and the weeds being pulled up, it will bring forth more fruit and not be choked by the weeds.

13 So setting about this work he digged it, and plucked up all the weeds that were in it; and so the vineyard became very beautiful and prosperous, not being choked with weeds.

14 After some time the lord of the vineyard comes and goes into the vineyard, and when he saw that it was handsomely staked and digged, and the weeds plucked up that were in it, and the vines flourishing, he rejoiced greatly at the care of his servant.

15 And calling his son whom he loved, and who was to be his heir, and his friends with whom he was wont to consult ; he tells them what he had commanded his servant to do, and what his servant had done more; and they immediately congratulated that servant, that he had received so [1] full a testimony from his lord.

16 Then he said to them, I indeed promised this servant his liberty, if he observed the command which I gave him; and he observed it, and besides has done a good work to my vineyard, which has exceedingly pleased me.

17 Wherefore, for this work which he hath done, I will make him my heir together with my son, because that when he saw what was good, he neglected it not, but did it.

18 This design of the lord both his son and his friends approved, namely, that his servant should be heir together with his son.

19 Not long after this, the master of the family calling together his friends, sent from his supper several kinds of food to that servant.

20 Which when he had received, he took so much of them as was sufficient for himself, and divided the rest among his fellow servants.

21 Which when they had received, they rejoiced; and wished that they might find yet greater favour with his lord, for what he had done to them.

---

[1] Just a commendation.

CHRIST AS A GARDENER APPEARING TO MARY MAGDALENE.

FROM A PAINTING IN DISTEMPER ON WOOD: TWELFTH CENTURY.

The letters underneath are from the back of the picture: " Donatus Bizamanus, pixit in Hotranto."

22 When his lord heard all these things, he was again filled with great joy; and calling again his friends and his son together, he related to them what his servant had done with the meats which he had sent unto them.

23 They therefore so much the more assented to the master of the household; and he ought to make that servant his heir together with his son.

24 ¶ I said unto him, Sir, I know not these similitudes, neither can I understand them, unless you expound them unto me. I will, says he, expound all things unto thee whatsoever I have talked with thee, or shewn unto thee.

25 Keep the commandments of the Lord and thou shalt be approved, and shalt be written in the number of those that keep his commandments. But if besides those things which the Lord hath commanded, thou shalt add some good thing; thou shalt purchase to thyself a greater dignity, and be in more favour with the Lord than thou shouldst otherwise have been.

26 If therefore thou shalt keep the commandments of the Lord, and shalt add to them these stations, thou shalt rejoice; but especially if thou shalt keep them according to my commands.

27 I said unto him, Sir, whatsoever thou shalt command me, I will observe; for I know that thou wilt be with me. I will, said he, be with thee who hast taken up such a resolution; and I will be with all those who purpose in like manner.

28 This fast, saith he, whilst thou dost also observe the commandments of the Lord, is ex-ceeding good. Thus shalt therefore thou keep it.

29 First of all, take heed to thyself, and keep thyself from every [1] wicked act, and from every filthy word, and from every hurtful desire; and purify thy mind from all the vanity of this present world. If thou shalt observe these things, this fast shall be right.

30 Thus therefore do. Having performed what is before written, that day on which thou fastest thou shalt taste nothing at all but [2] bread and water; [3] and computing the quantity of food which thou art wont to eat upon other days, thou shalt [2] lay aside the expense which thou shouldest have made that day, and give it unto the widow, the fatherless, and the poor.

31 [2] And thus thou shalt perfect the humiliation of thy soul; that he who receives of it may satisfy his soul, and his prayer come up to the Lord God for thee.

32 If therefore thou shalt thus accomplish thy fast, as I command thee, thy sacrifice shall be acceptable unto the Lord, and thy fast shall be written in his book.

33 This station, thus performed, is good and pleasing, and acceptable unto the Lord. These things if thou shalt observe with thy children and with all thy house, thou shalt be happy.

34 And whosoever when they hear these things, shall do them, they also shall be happy; and whatsoever they shall ask of the Lord they shall receive it.

35 And I prayed him that he would expound unto me the similitude of the farm, and the Lord, and of the vineyard, and of the servant that had staked the vine-

[1] Shameful; or, upbraiding.   [2] Vid. Not. Coteler. ii., p. 74. A. B. C.
[3] Vid. Antioch. Hom. vii.

yard; and of the weeds that were plucked out of the vineyard; and of his son and his friends which he took into council with him. For I understand that that was a similitude.

36 He said unto me, Thou art very bold in asking: for thou oughtest not to ask any thing; because if it be fitting to shew it unto thee, it shall be shewed unto thee.

37 I answered him; Sir, whatsoever thou shalt shew me, without explaining it unto me, I shall in vain see it, if I do not understand what it is. And if thou shalt propose any similitudes, and not expound them, I shall in vain hear them.

38. He answered me again, saying: Whosoever is the servant of God, and has the Lord in his heart, he desires understanding of him, and receives it; and he explains every similitude, and understands the words of the Lord which need an inquiry.

39 But they that are lazy and slow to pray, doubt to seek from the Lord; although the Lord be of such an extraordinary goodness, that without ceasing he giveth all things to them that ask of him.

40 Thou therefore who art strengthened by that venerable messenger, and hast received such a powerful gift of prayer; seeing thou art not slothful, why dost thou not now ask understanding of the Lord, and receive it?

41 I said unto him; seeing I have thee present, it is necessary that I should seek it of thee, and ask thee; for thou showest all things unto me, and speakest to me when thou art present.

42 But if I should see or hear these things when thou wert not present, I would then ask the Lord that he would shew them unto me.

43 ¶ And he replied, I said a little before that thou wert subtle and bold, in that thou asketh the meaning of these similitudes.

44 But because thou still persistest, I will unfold to thee this parable which thou desirest, that thou mayest make it known unto all men.

45 Hear therefore, said he, and understand. The farm before mentioned denotes the whole earth. The Lord of the farm is he who created and finished all things, and gave virtue unto them.

46 His son is the Holy Spirit: the servant is the Son of God: the vineyard is the people whom he saves. The stakes are the [1] messengers which are set over them by the Lord, to support his people. The weeds that are plucked up out of the vineyard, are the sins which the servants of God had committed.

47 The food which he sent him from his supper, are the commands which he gave to his people by his Son. The friends whom he called to counsel with him, are the holy angels whom he first created. The absence of the master of the household, is the time that remains unto his coming.

48 I said unto him, Sir, all these things are very excellent, and wonderful, and good. But, continued I, could I or any other man besides though never so wise, have understood these things?

49 Wherefore now, sir, tell me, what I ask. He replied, ask me what thou wilt. Why, said I, is the Son of God in this parable, put in the place of a servant?

[1] Angels.

234

50 Hearken, he said; the Son of God is not put in the condition of a servant, but in great power and authority. I said unto him 'how, sir? I understand it not.'

51 Because, said he, the Son set his [1] messsengers over those whom the Father delivered unto him, to keep every one of them; but he himself labored very much, and suffered much, that he might blot out their offences.

52 For no vineyard can be digged without much labour and pains. Wherefore having blotted out the sins of his people, he shewed to them the paths of life, giving them the law which he had received of the Father.

53 You see, said he, that he is the Lord of his people, having received all power from his Father. [2] But why the Lord did take his Son into counsel, about dividing the inheritance, and the good angels, hear now.

54 That [3] Holy Spirit, which was created first of all, he placed in the body in which God should dwell; namely, in a chosen body, as it seemed good to him. This body therefore into which the [3] Holy Spirit was brought, served that Spirit, walked rightly and purely in modesty; nor ever defiled that Spirit.

55 Seeing therefore the body at all times obeyed the Holy Spirit, and laboured rightly and chastely with him, nor faltered at any time; that body being wearied conversed indeed servilely, but being mightily approved to God with the Holy Spirit, was accepted by him.

56 For such a stout course pleased God, because he was not defiled in the earth, keeping the Holy Spirit. He called therefore to counsel his Son, and the good angels, that there might be some place of standing given to this body which had served the Holy Spirit without blame; lest it should seem to have lost the reward of its service.

57 For every pure body shall receive its reward; that is found without spot, in which the Holy Spirit has been appointed to dwell. And thus you have now the exposition of this parable also.

58 Sir, said I, I now understand your meaning, since I have heard this exposition. Hearken further, said he: keep this thy body clean and pure, that the Spirit which shall dwell in it may bear witness unto it, and be judged to have been with thee.

59 Also take heed that it be not instilled into thy mind that this body perishes, and thou abuse it to any lust. For if thou shalt defile thy body, thou shalt also at the same time defile the Holy Spirit; and if thou shalt defile [4] the Holy Spirit, thou shalt not live.

60 And I said, What if through ignorance this should have been already committed, before a man heard these words; How can he attain unto salvation, who has thus defiled his body?

61 He replied, As for men's

---

[1] Angels. [2] This place, which in all the editions of Hermas is wretchedly corrupted, by the collation of editions and MSS. is thus corrected by Dr. Grabe: "Quære autem Dominus in concilio adhibuerit, filium de hæreditate, honestosque nuncios, audi; Spiritum Sanctum, qui creatus est omnium primus, in corpore, in quo habitaret Deus, collocavit; in delecto scilicet corpore quod ei videbatur." [3] Viz. the created Spirit of Christ, as man; not the Holy Ghost, the Third Person of the Sacred Trinity. [4] Thy body, according to some copies.

former actions which through ignorance they have committed, God only can afford a remedy unto them; for all the power belongeth unto him.

62 But now guard thyself; and seeing God is almighty and merciful, he will grant a remedy to what thou hast formerly done amiss, if for the time to come thou shalt not defile thy body and spirit;

63 For they are companions together, and the one cannot be defiled but the other will be so too. Keep therefore both of them pure, and thou shalt live unto God.

SIMILITUDE VI.

Of two sorts of voluptuous men, and of their death, defection, and of the continuance of their pains

AS I was sitting at home, and praising God for all the things which I had seen; and was thinking concerning the commands, that they were exceeding good, and great, and honest, and pleasant; and such as were able to bring a man to salvation; I said thus within myself; I shall be happy if I shall walk according to these commands, and whosoever shall walk in them shall live unto God.

2 Whilst I was speaking on this wise within myself, I saw him whom I had before been wont to see, sitting by me; and he spake thus unto me:

3 What doubtest thou concerning my commands which I have delivered unto thee? They are good, doubt not, but trust in the Lord, and thou shalt walk in them. For I will give thee strength [1] to fulfil them.

4 These commands are profitable to those who shall repent of those sins which they have formerly committed; if for the time to come they shall not continue in them.

5 Whosoever therefore ye be that repent, cast away from you the naughtiness of the present world; and put on all virtue, and righteousness, and so shall ye be able to keep these commands; and not sin from henceforth any more.

6 For if ye shall keep yourselves from sin from the time to come, ye shall cut off a great deal of your former sins. Walk in my commands, and ye shall live unto God: These things have I spoken unto you.

7 And when he had said this, he added; let us go into the field, and I will show thee shepherds of sheep. I replied, sir, let us go.

8 And we came into a certain field, and there he showed me a young shepherd, [2] finely arrayed, with his garments of a purple colour. And he fed large flocks; and his sheep were full of pleasure, and in much delight and cheerfulness; and they skipping, ran here and there.

9 And the shepherd took very great satisfaction in his flock; and the countenance of that shepherd was cheerful, running up and down among his flock.

10 ¶ Then the angel said unto me, Seest thou this shepherd? I answered, sir, I see him. He said unto me, this is the [3] messenger of delight and pleasure. He therefore corrupts the minds of the servants of God, and turns them from the truth, delighting them with many pleasures, and they perish.

11 For they forget the commands of the living God, and live

---

[1] In them.   [2] Vid. Annot. Coteler. in loc.   [3] Angel.

in luxury and in vain pleasures, and are corrupted by the evil angel, some of them even unto death; and others to [1] a falling away.

12 I replied; I understand not what you mean, by saying unto death, and to a falling away. Hear, says he; all these sheep which thou sawest exceeding [2] joyful, are such as have for ever departed from God, and given themselves up to the [3] lusts of this present time.

13 To these therefore there is no return, by repentance unto life; because that to their other sins they have added this, that they have blasphemed the name of the Lord. These kind of men are ordained unto death.

14 But those sheep which thou sawest not leaping, but feeding in one place, are such as have indeed given themselves up to pleasures and delights; but have not spoken anything wickedly against the Lord.

15 These therefore are only fallen off from the truth, and so have yet hope laid up for them in repentance. For such a falling off hath some hope still left of a renewal; but they that are dead, are utterly gone forever.

16 Again we went a little farther forward; and he showed me a great [4] shepherd, who had as it were a rustic figure, clad with a white goat's skin, having his bag upon his shoulder, and in his hand a stick full of knots, and very hard, and a whip in his other hand; and his countenance was stern and sour; enough to affright a man; such was his look.

17 He took from that young shepherd such sheep as lived in pleasures, but did not skip up and down; and drove them into a certain steep craggy place full of thorns and briars, insomuch that they could not get themselves free from them.

18 But being entangled in them, fed upon thorns and briars, and were grievously tormented with his whipping. For he still drove them on, and afforded them not any place or time to stand still.

19 ¶ When therefore I saw them so cruelly whipped and afflicted, I was grieved for them; because they were greatly tormented, nor had they any rest afforded them.

20 And I said unto the shepherd that was with me; Sir, who is this cruel and implacable shepherd, who is moved with no compassion towards these sheep? He answered, [5] This shepherd is indeed one of the [6] holy angels, but is appointed for the punishment of sinners.

21 To him therefore are delivered those who have erred from God, and served the lusts and pleasures of this world. For this cause he punishes them every one according to their deserts, with cruel and various kinds of pains.

22 Sir, said I, I would know, what kind of pains they are which every one undergoes? Hearken, said he; The several pains and torments are those which men every day undergo in their present lives. For some suffer losses; others poverty; others divers sicknesses. Some are unsettled; others suffer injuries from those that are unworthy; others fall under many other trials and inconveniences.

23 For many with an unsettled design aim at many things, and it

[1] Ad. defectionem. Lat. [2] Exultantia. Lat. [3] In Gr. Athanas εϖιθυμιαις του Αιωνος τουτου. [4] Agrestem Lat. [5] Vid. Origen. in Ps. xxxvi. Hom. 1. [6] Righteous. In Gr. Athanas. εκ των Αγγελων των δικαιων εστι, &c. et sic MS. Lamb.

profiteth them not; and they say that they have not success in their undertakings.

24 [1] They do not call to their mind what they have done amiss, and they complain of the Lord. When therefore they shall have undergone all kind of vexation and inconvenience; then they are delivered over to me for good instruction, and are confirmed in the faith of the Lord, and serve the Lord all the rest of their days with a pure mind.

25 And when they begin to repent of their sins, then they call to mind their works which they have done amiss, and give honour to God, saying, That he is a just Judge, and they have deservedly suffered all things according to their deeds.

26 Then for what remains of their lives, they serve God with a pure mind; and have success in all their undertakings, and receive from the Lord whatever they desire.

27 And then they give thanks unto the Lord that they were delivered unto me; nor do they suffer any more cruelty.

28 ¶ I said unto him; Sir, I entreat you still to show me now one thing. What, said he, dost thou [2] ask? I said unto him; Are they who depart from the fear of God, tormented for the same time that they enjoyed their false delight and pleasures? He answered me: They are tormented for the same time.

29 And I said unto him; They are then tormented but little; whereas they who enjoy their pleasures so as to forget God, ought to endure seven times as much punishment.

30 He answered me; Thou art foolish, neither understandest thou the efficacy of this punishment. I said unto him; Sir, if I understood it, I would not desire you to tell me.

31 Hearken, said he, and learn what the force of both is, both of the pleasure and of the punishment. An hour of pleasure is terminated within its own space; but one hour of punishment has the efficacy of thirty days. [3] Whosoever therefore enjoys his false pleasure for one day, and is one day tormented; that one day of punishment is equivalent to a whole year's space.

32 Thus look how many days any one pursues his pleasures, so many years is he punished for it. You see therefore how that the time of worldly enjoyments is but short; but that of pain and torments a great deal more.

33 I replied; Sir, forasmuch as I do not understand [4] at all these times of pleasure and pain; I entreat you that you would explain yourself more clearly concerning them. He answered me, saying; Thy foolishness still sticks unto thee.

34 Shouldst thou not rather purify thy mind, and serve God? Take heed, lest when thy time is fulfilled, thou be found still unwise. Hear then, as thou desirest, that thou mayest the more easily understand.

35 He that gives himself up one day to his pleasures and delights, and does whatsoever his soul desires, is full of great folly, nor understands what he does, but the day following forgets what he did the day before.

36 For delight and worldly pleasure are not kept in memory, by reason of the folly that is

---

[1] MS. Lamb. Succurrit iis: Gr. Athanas, ον γινωσκουσι. [2] MS. Lamb. Inquiris. [3] Origen. in Num. Hom. viii. [4] MS. Lamb. Omnino.

rooted in them. But when pain and torment befal a man a day, he is in effect troubled the whole year after; because his punishment continues firm in his memory.

37 Wherefore he remembers it with sorrow the whole year; and then calls to mind his vain pleasure and delight, and perceives that for the sake of that he was punished.

38 Whosoever therefore have delivered themselves over to such pleasures, are thus punished; because that when they had life, they rendered themselves liable to death.

39 I said unto him; Sir, what pleasures are hurtful? He answered; That is pleasure to every man which he doth willingly.

40 For the angry man, gratifying his passion, perceives pleasure in it; and so the adulterer and drunkard; the slanderer and liar; the covetous man and the defrauder; and whosoever commits anything like unto these, because he [1] followeth his evil disposition, he receives a satisfaction in the doing of it.

41 All these pleasures and delights are hurtful to the servants of God. For these therefore they are tormented and suffer punishment.

42 There are also pleasures that bring salvation unto men. For many, when they do what is good, find pleasure in it, and are attracted by the delights of it.

43 Now this pleasure is profitable to the servants of God, and brings life to such men; but those hurtful pleasures, which were before mentioned, bring torments and punishment.

44 And whosoever shall continue in them, and shall not repent of what they have done, shall bring death upon themselves.

SIMILITUDE VII.

That they who repent, must bring forth fruits worthy of repentance.

AFTER a few days I saw the same person that before talked with me, in the same field, in which I had seen those shepherds. And he said unto me; What seekest thou?

2 Sir, said I, I came to entreat you that you would command the shepherd, who is the minister of punishment, to depart out of my house, because he greatly afflicts me.

3 And he answered, It is necessary for thee to endure inconveniences and vexations; for so that good angel hath commanded concerning thee, because he would try thee.

4 Sir, said I; What so great offence have I committed, that I should be delivered to this [2] messenger? Hearken, said he: Thou art indeed guilty of many sins, yet not so many that thou shouldest be delivered to this [2] messenger.

5 But thy house hath committed many sins and offences, and therefore that good [2] messenger being grieved at their doings commanded that for some time thou shouldst suffer affliction; that they may both repent of what they have done, and may wash themselves from all the lusts of this present world.

6 When therefore they shall have repented, and be purified, then that messenger which is

---

[1] Obeyeth his disease.

[2] Angel.

appointed over thy punishment, shall depart from thee.

7 I said unto him ; Sir, if they have behaved themselves so as to anger that good angel, yet what have I done? He answered: They cannot otherwise be afflicted, unless thou, who art the head of the family, suffer.

8 For whatsoever thou shalt suffer, they must needs feel it; but as long as thou shalt stand well established, they cannot experience any vexation.

9 I replied; But, sir, behold they also now repent with all their hearts. I know, says he, that they repent with all their hearts; but dost thou therefore think that their offences who repent are immediately blotted out?

10 No, they are not presently; but he that repents must afflict his soul and shew himself humble in all his affairs, and undergo many and divers vexations.

11 And when he shall have suffered all things that were appointed for him; then perhaps he that made him, and formed all things besides, will be moved with compassion towards him, and afford him some remedy; and especially if he shall perceive his heart, who repents, to be pure from every evil work.

12 But at present it is expedient for thee, and for thy house, to be grieved; and it is needful that thou shouldest endure much vexation, as the angel of the Lord who committed thee unto me, has commanded.

13 Rather give thanks unto the Lord, that knowing what was to come, he thought thee worthy to whom he should foretell that trouble was coming upon thee, who art able to bear it.

14 I said unto him; Sir, be but thou also with me, and I shall easily undergo any trouble. I will, said he, be with thee; and I will entreat the messenger who is set over thy punishment, that he would moderate his afflictions towards thee.

15 And moreover thou shalt suffer adversity but for a little time; and then thou shalt again be restored to thy former state; only continue on in the humility of thy mind.

16 Obey the Lord with a pure heart; thou, and thy house, and thy children; and walk in the commands which I have delivered unto thee; and then thy repentance may be firm and pure.

17 And if thou shalt keep these things with thy house, thy inconveniences shall depart from thee.

18 And all vexation shall in like manner depart from all those, whosoever shall walk according to these commands.

SIMILITUDE VIII.

That there are many kinds of elect, and of repenting sinners: and how all of them shall receive a reward proportionable to the measure of their repentance and good works.

AGAIN he shewed me a willow which covered the fields and the mountains, under whose shadow came all such as were called by the name of the Lord.

2 And by that willow stood an angel of the Lord very excellent and lofty; and did cut down boughs from that willow with a great hook; and reached out to the people that were under the shadow of that willow little rods, as it were about a foot long.

3 And when all of them had taken them, he laid aside his hook, and the tree continued entire, as I had before seen it. At which I wondered, and mused within myself.

JESUS CHRIST ASCENDING TO HEAVEN WITH TWO ANGELS.

FROM ONE OF THE MINIATURE PAINTINGS IN THE "BIBLE OF ST. PAUL."

4 Then that shepherd said unto me; Forbear to wonder that that tree continues whole, notwithstanding so many boughs have been cut off from it, but stay a little, for now it shall be shewn thee, what that angel means, who gave those rods to the people.

5 So he again demanded the rods of them, and in the same order that every one had received them, was he called to him, and restored his rod; which when he had received, he examined them.

6 From some he received them dry and rotten, and as it were touched with the moth; those he commanded to be separated from the rest and placed by themselves. Others gave in their rods dry indeed, but not touched with the moth: these also he ordered to be set by themselves.

7 Others gave in their rods half dry; these also were set apart. Others gave in their rods half dry and cleft; these too were set by themselves. Others brought in their rods half dry and half green, and these were in like manner placed by themselves.

8 Others delivered up their rods two parts green, and the third dry; and they too were set apart. Others brought their rods two parts dry, and the third green; and were also placed by themselves.

9 Others delivered up their rods less dry, (for there was but a very little, to wit, their tops dry) but they had clefts, and these were set in like manner by themselves. In the rods of others there was but a little green, and the rest dry; and these were set aside by themselves.

10 Others came, and brought their rods green as they had re-ceived them, and the greatest part of the people brought their rods thus; and the messenger greatly rejoiced at these, and they also were put apart by themselves.

11 Others brought in their rods not only green, but full of branches; and these were set aside, being also received by the angel with great joy. Others brought their rods green with branches, and those also some fruit upon them.

12 They who had such rods, were very cheerful; and the angel himself took great joy at them; nor was the shepherd that stood with me, less pleased with them.

13 ¶ Then the angel of the Lord commanded crowns to be brought: and the crowns were brought made of palms; and the angel crowned those men in whose rods he found the young branches with fruit; and commanded them to go into the tower.

14 He also sent those into the tower, in whose rods he found branches without fruit, giving a seal unto them. For they had the same garment, that is, one white as snow; with which he bade them go into the tower. And so he did to those who returned their rods green as he had received them; giving them a white garment, and so sent them away to go into the tower.

15 Having done this, he said to the shepherd that was with me, I go my way; but do thou send these within the walls, every one into the place in which he has deserved to dwell; examining first their rods, but examine them diligently that no one deceive thee. But and if any one shall escape thee, I will try them

241

upon the altar. Having said this to the shepherd, he departed.

16 After he was gone, the shepherd said unto me: Let us take the rods from them, and plant them; if perchance they may grow green again. I said unto him; Sir, how can those dry rods ever grow green again?

17 He answered me; That tree is a willow, and always loves to live. If therefore these rods shall be planted, and receive a little moisture, many of them will recover themselves.

18 Wherefore I will try, and will pour water upon them, and if any of them can live, I will rejoice with him; but if not, at least by this means I shall be found not to have neglected my part.

19 Then he commanded me to call them; and they all came unto him, every one in the rank in which he stood, and gave him their rods; which having received, he planted every one of them in their several orders.

20 And after he had planted them all, he poured much water upon them, insomuch that they were covered with water, and did not appear above it. Then when he had watered them, he said unto me; Let us depart, and after a little time we will return and visit them.

21 For he who created this tree, would have all those live that received rods from it. And I hope now that these rods are thus watered, many of them receiving in the moisture, will recover.

22 ¶ I said unto him, Sir, tell me what this tree denotes? For I am greatly [1] astonished, that after so many branches have been cut off, it seems still to be whole; nor does there any thing the less of it appear to remain, which greatly amazes me.

23 He answered, Hearken. This great tree which covers the plains and the mountains, and all the earth, is the law of God, published throughout the whole world.

24 Now [2] this law is the Son of God, who is preached to all the ends of the earth. The people that stand under its shadow, are those which have heard his preaching, and believed.

25 The great and venerable angel which you saw, was Michael, who has the power over his people, and governs them. For he has planted the law in the hearts of those who have believed; and therefore he visits them to whom he has given the law, to see if they have kept it.

26 And he examines every one's rod; and of those, many that are weakened: for those rods are the law of the Lord. Then he discerns all those who have not kept the law, knowing the place of every one of them.

27 I said unto him, Sir, why did he send away some to the tower, and left others here to you? He replied, those who have transgressed the law, which they received from him, are left in my power, that they may repent of their sins: but they who [3] fulfilled the law and kept it, are under his power.

28 But who then, said I, are those, who went into the tower crowned? He replied all such as having striven with the devil, have overcome him, are crowned:

[1] Moved.   [2] MS. Lamb. Hæc autem lex Filius Dei est, prædicatus, &c.   [3] Satisfied.

and they are those, who have suffered hard things, that they might keep the law.

29 But they who gave up their rods green, and with young branches, but without fruit, have indeed endured trouble for the same law, but have not suffered death; neither have they denied their holy law.

30 They who delivered up their rods green as they received them, are those who were modest and just, and have lived with a very pure mind, and kept the commandments of God.

31 The rest thou shalt know, when I shall have considered those rods which I have planted and watered.

32 ¶ After a few days we returned, and in the same place stood that glorious angel, and I stood by him, Then he said unto me; Gird thyself with a [1]towel, and serve me.

33 And I girded myself with a clean towel, which was made of coarse cloth. And when he saw me girded, and ready to minister unto him, he said, Call those men whose rods have been planted, every one in his order as he gave them.

34 And he brought me into the field, and I called them all, and they all stood ready in their several ranks. Then he said unto them; let every one pluck up his rod, and bring it unto me. And first they delivered theirs, whose rods had been dry and rotten.

35 And those whose rods still continued so, he commanded to stand apart. Then they came whose rods had been dry but not rotten. Some of these delivered in their rods green; others dry and rotten, as if they had been touched by the moth.

36 Those who gave them up green, he commanded to stand apart; but those whose rods were dry and rotten, he caused to stand with the first sort. Then came they whose rods had been half dry, and cleft: many of these gave up their rods green, and uncleft.

37 Others delivered them up green with branches, and fruit upon the branches, like unto those who went crowned into the tower. Others delivered them up dry, but not rotten; and some gave them up as they were before, half dry, and cleft.

38 Every one of these he ordered to stand apart; some by themselves, others in their respective ranks.

39 Then came they whose rods had been green, but cleft. These delivered their rods altogether green, and stood in their own order. And the shepherd rejoiced at these, because they were all changed, and free from their clefts.

40 Then they gave in their rods, who had them half green and half dry. Of these some were found wholly green, others half dry; others green, with young shoots. And all these were sent away, every one to his proper rank.

41 Then they gave up their rods, who had them before two parts green, and the third dry. Many of those gave in their rods green; many half dry; the rest dry but not rotten. So these were sent away, each to his proper place.

42 Then came they who had before their rods two parts dry

---

[1] Sabano. Vid. Edit. Oxon. p. 129. not. d.

and the third green; many of these delivered up their rods half dry, others dry and rotten; others half dry and cleft; but few green. And all these were set every one in his own rank.

43 Then they reached in their rods, [1] in which there was before but a little green, and the rest dry. Their rods were for the most part found green, having little boughs, with fruit upon them, and the rest altogether green.

44 And the shepherd upon sight of these rejoiced exceedingly, because he had found them thus; and they also went to their proper orders.

45 ¶ Now after he had examined all their rods, he said unto me I told thee that this tree loved life: thou seest how many have repented, and attained unto salvation. Sir, said I, I see it.

46 That thou mightest know, saith he, that the goodness and mercy of the Lord is great, and to be had in honour; who gave his spirit to them that were found worthy of repentance.

47 I answered, Sir, why then did not all of them repent? He replied, Those whose minds the Lord foresaw would be pure, and that they would serve him with all their hearts, to them he gave repentance.

48 But for those whose deceit and wickedness he beheld, and perceived that they would not truly return unto him; to them he denied any return unto repentance, lest they should again blaspheme his law with wicked words.

49 I said unto him; Now, Sir, make known unto me, what is the place of every one of those, who have given up their rods, and what their [2] portion; that when they may have not kept their seal entire, but have wasted the seal which they received, shall hear and believe these things, they may acknowledge their evil deeds and repent;

50 And receiving again their seal from you, may give glory to God, that he was moved with compassion towards them, and sent you to renew their spirits.

51 Hearken, said he: they whose rods have been found dry and rotten, and as it were touched with the moth; are the deserters and the betrayers of the church.

52 Who with the rest of their crimes, have also blasphemed the Lord, and denied his name which had been called upon them. Therefore all these are dead unto God: and thou seest that none of them have repented, although they have heard my commands which thou hast delivered unto them. From these men therefore life is far distant.

53 They also who have delivered up their rods dry, but not rotten, have not been far from them. For they have been counterfeits, and brought in evil doctrines; and have perverted the servants of God: but especially those who had sinned; not suffering them to return unto repentance, but keeping them back by their false doctrines.

54 These therefore have hope; and thou seest that many of them have repented, since the time that thou hast laid my commands before them; and many more will yet repent. But they that shall not repent shall lose both repentance and life.

---

[1] MS. Lamb. Minimum habuerant viride.   [2] Sea.

55 But they that have repented, their place is begun to be within the first walls, and some of them are even gone into the tower. Thou seest therefore, said he, that in the repentance of sinners there is life; but for those who repent not, death is prepared.

56 ¶ Hear now concerning those who gave in their rods half dry and full of clefts. Those whose rods were only half dry, are the doubtful; for they are neither living nor dead.

57 But they who delivered in their rods, not only half dry but also full of clefts, are both doubtful and evil speakers; who detract from those who are absent, and have never peace among themselves, and that envy one another.

58 Howbeit to those also repentance is offered; for thou seest that some of these have repented.

59 Now all those of this kind who have quickly repented, shall have a place in the tower; but they who have been more slow in their repentance, shall dwell within the walls; but they that shall not repent, but shall continue on in their wicked doings, shall die the death.

60 As for those who had their rods green, but yet cleft; they are such as were always faithful and good, but they had some envy and strife among themselves concerning dignity and pre-eminence.

61 Now all such are vain and without understanding, as contend with one another about these things.

62 Nevertheless, seeing they are otherwise good, if when they shall hear these commands they shall amend themselves, and shall at my persuasion suddenly repent; they shall at last dwell in the tower, as they who have truly and worthily repented.

63 But if any one shall again return to his dissension; he shall be shut out from the tower, and shall lose his life. For the life of those who keep the commandments of the Lord consists in doing what they are commanded; not in principality, or in any other dignity.

64 For by forbearance and humility of mind, men shall attain unto life; but by seditions and contempt of the law, they shall purchase death unto themselves.

65 ¶ They who in their rods had half dry and half green, are those who are engaged in many affairs of the world, and are not joined to the saints. For which cause half of them liveth, and half is dead.

66 Wherefore many of these since the time that they have heard my commands, have repented, and begun to dwell in the tower. But some of them have wholly fallen away; to these there is no more place for repentance.

67 For by reason of their present interests, they have blasphemed and denied God: and for this wickedness they have lost life. And of these many are still in doubt; these may yet return; and if they shall quickly repent, they shall have a place in the tower; but if they shall be more slow, they shall dwell within the walls; but if they shall not repent, they shall die.

68 As for those who had two

---

[1] Lamb. MS. Quamplurimis generibus inficiati.

245

parts of their rods green, and the third dry; they have by manifold ways denied the Lord. Of these many have repented, and found a place in the tower: and many have altogether departed from God. These have utterly lost life.

69 And some being in a doubtful state, have raised up dissensions: these may yet return, if they shall suddenly repent and not continue in their lusts; but if they shall continue in their evil doing they shall die.

70 ¶ They who gave in their rods two parts dry, and the other green; are those who have indeed been faithful, but withal rich and full of good things; and thereupon have desired to be famous among the heathen which are without, and have thereby fallen into great pride, and begun to aim at high matters, and to forsake the truth.

71 Nor were they joined to the [1] saints, but lived with the heathen; and this life seemed the more pleasant to them. Howbeit they have not departed from God, but continued in the faith; only they have not wrought the works of faith.

72 Many therefore of these have repented, and begun to dwell in the tower. Yet others still living among the heathen people, and being lifted up with their vanities, have utterly fallen away from God, and followed the works and wickednesses of the heathen. These kind of men therefore are reckoned among strangers to the Gospel.

73 Others of these began to be doubtful in their minds; despairing by reason of their wicked doings ever to attain un-

to salvation: Others being thus made doubtful, did moreover stir up dissensions.

74 To these therefore, and to those who by reason of their doings are become doubtful, there is still hope of return; but they must repent quickly, that their place may be in the tower. But they that repent not, but continue still in their pleasures, are nigh unto death.

75 ¶ As for those who gave in their rods green, excepting their tops, which only were dry, and had clefts; these were always good, and faithful, and [2] upright before God: nevertheless they sinned a little, by reason of their empty pleasures and trifling thoughts which they had within themselves.

76 Wherefore many of them when they heard my words, repented forthwith, and began to dwell in the tower. Nevertheless some grew doubtful, and others to their doubtful minds added dissensions. To these therefore there is still hope of return, because they were always good; but they shall not hardly be moved.

77 As for those, lastly, who gave in their rods dry, their tops only excepted, which alone were green: they are such as have believed indeed in God, but have lived in wickedness; yet without departing from God: having always willingly borne the name of the Lord; and readily received into their houses the servants of God.

78 Wherefore hearing these things they returned, and without delay repented, and lived in all righteousness. And some of them suffered death; others

---

[1] Righteous.   [2] Probi.

readily underwent many trials, being mindful of their evil doings.

79 ¶ And when he had ended his explications of all the rods, he said unto me, Go, and say unto all men that they repent, and they shall live unto God : because the Lord being moved with great clemency hath sent me to preach repentance unto all.

80 Even unto those who by reason of their evil doings, deserve not to attain unto salvation. But the Lord will be patient, and keep the invitation that was made by his Son.

81 I said unto him, Sir, I hope that all when they shall hear these things, will repent. For I trust that everyone acknowledging his crimes, and taking up the fear of the Lord, will return unto repentance.

82 He said unto me, Whosoever shall repent with all their hearts, and cleanse themselves from all the evils that I have before mentioned, and not add anything more to their sins, shall receive from the Lord the cure of their former iniquities, if they shall not make any doubt of these commands, and shall live unto God.

83 But they that shall continue to add to their transgressions, and shall still converse with the lusts of the present world, shall condemn themselves unto death. But do thou walk in these commands, and whosoever shall walk in these, and exercise them rightly, shall live unto God.

84 And having shewed me all these things, he said ; I will shew thee the rest in a few days.

SIMILITUDE IX.

The greatest mysteries of the militant and triumphant church which is to be built.

AFTER I had written the Commands and Similitudes of the Shepherd, the Angel of Repentance ; he came unto me, and said to me, I will shew thee all those things which the [1]Spirit spake with thee under the figure of the Church. For that Spirit is the Son of God.

2 And because thou wert weak in body, it was not declared unto thee by the angel, until thou wert strengthened by the Spirit, and increased in force, that thou mightest also see the angel.

3 For then indeed the building of the tower was very well and gloriously shewn unto thee by the church ; nevertheless thou sawest all things shewn unto thee as it were by a virgin.

4 But now thou art enlightened by the angel, but yet by the same Spirit. But thou must consider all things diligently ; for therefore am I sent into thy house by that venerable [2]messenger, that when thou shalt have seen all things powerfully, thou mayest not be afraid as before.

5 And he led me to the [3]height of a mountain in Arcadia, and we sat upon its top. And he showed me a great plain, and about it twelve mountains in different figures.

6 The first was black as soot. The second was smooth, without herbs. The third was full of thorns and thistles. The fourth had herbs half dried ; of which the upper part was green, but that next the root was dry ; and

---

[1] See above, Book I.   [2] Angel.   [3] Ascent.

some of the herbs, when the sun grew hot, were dry.

7 The fifth mountain was very rugged; but yet had green herbs. The sixth mountain was full of clefts, some lesser, and some greater; and in these clefts grew grass, not flourishing, but which seemed to be withering.

8 The seventh mountain had delightful pasture, and was wholly fruitful: and all kinds of cattle, and of the birds of heaven, fed upon it; and the more they fed of it, the more and better did the grass grow.

9 The eighth mountain was full of fountains, and from those fountains were watered all kinds of the creatures of God. The ninth mountain had no water at all, but was wholly destitute of it; and nourished deadly serpents, and destructive to men.

10 The tenth mountain was full of tall trees, and altogether shady: and under the shade of them lay cattle resting and chewing the cud.

11 The eleventh mountain was full of the thickest trees; and those trees seemed to be loaded with several sorts of fruits; that whosoever saw them could not choose but desire to eat of their fruit.

12 The twelfth mountain was altogether white, and of a most pleasant aspect, and itself gave a most excellent beauty to itself.

13 ¶ In the middle of the [1] plain he showed me a huge white rock, which rose out of the plain, and the rock was higher than those mountains, and was square; so that it seemed capable of supporting the whole world.

14 It looked to me to be old, yet it had in it a new gate, which seemed to have been newly hewn out in it. Now that gate was bright beyond the sun itself; insomuch, that I greatly admired at its light.

15 About the gate stood twelve virgins; of which four that stood at the corners of the gate, seemed to me to be the chiefest, although the rest were also of worth: and they stood at the four parts of the gate.

16 It added also to the grace of those virgins, that they stood in pairs, clothed with linen garments, and decently girded, their right arms being at liberty, as if they were about to lift up some [2] burthen; for so they were adorned, and were exceeding cheerful and ready.

17 When I saw this, I wondered with myself to see such great and noble things. And again I admired upon the account of those virgins, that they were so handsome and delicate; and stood with such firmness and constancy, as if they would carry the whole heaven.

18 And as I was thinking thus within myself, the shepherd said unto me: What thinkest thou within thyself, and art disquieted, and fillest thyself with care?

19 Do not seem to consider, as if thou wert wise, what thou doest not understand, but pray unto the Lord, that thou mayest have ability to understand it: what is to come thou canst not understand, but thou seest that which is before thee.

20 Be not therefore disquieted at those things which thou canst not see; but get the understanding of those which thou seest.

21 Forbear to be curious; and

---

[1] Origen, Hom. iii. in. Ezech.   [2] Fascem aliquem. Lat.

I will shew thee all things that I ought to declare unto thee; but first consider what yet remains.

22 ¶ And when he had said this unto me I looked up, and behold I saw six tall and venerable men coming; their countenances were all alike; and they called a certain multitude of men; and they who came at their call were also tall and stout.

23 And those six commanded them to build a certain tower over that gate. And immediately there began to be a great noise of those men running here and there about the gate, who were come together to build the tower.

24 But those virgins which stood about the gate perceived that the building of the tower was to be hastened by them. And they stretched out their hands, as if they were to receive somewhat from them to do.

25 Then those six men commanded, that they should lift up stones out of a certain deep place, and prepare them for the building of the tower. And there were lifted up ten white stones, square, and [1] not cut round.

26 Then those six men called the ten virgins to them, and commanded them to carry all the stones that were to be put into the building and having carried them through the gate to deliver them to those that were about to build the tower.

27 Immediately the virgins began all of them together to lift up those stones, that were before taken out of the deep.

28 ¶ And they who also stood about the gate did carry stones in such a manner, that those stones which seemed to be the strongest were laid at the corners, the rest were put into the sides.

29 And thus they carried all the stones, and bringing them through the gate delivered them to the builders, as they had been commanded: who receiving them at their hands, built with them.

30 But this building was made upon that great rock, and over the gate; and by these the whole tower was supported. But the building of the ten stones filled the whole gate, which began to be made for the foundation of that tower.

31 After those ten stones did five and twenty others [2] rise up out of the deep; and these were placed in the building of the same tower; being lifted up by those virgins, as the others had been before.

32 After these did five and thirty others [2] rise up; and these were also in like manner fitted into the same work. Then forty other stones were brought up, and all these were added unto the building of that tower.

33 So there began to be four ranks in the foundation of that tower; and the stones ceased to [2] rise out of the deep; and they also which built rested a little.

34 Again those six men commanded the multitude, that they should bring stones out of those twelve mountains to the building of the same tower.

35 So they cut out of all the mountains stones of divers colours, and brought them and gave them to the virgins; which when they had received they carried them, and delivered them into the building of the tower,

36 In which when they were built they became white, and

---

[1] So Cotelerius in loc.   [2] MS. Lamb. Ascenderunt.

different from what they were before; for they were all alike, and did change their former colours. And some were reached up by the men themselves, which when they came into the building, continued such as they were put in.

37 These neither became white, nor different from what they were before; because they were not carried by the virgins through the gate. Wherefore these stones were disagreeable in the building: which, when those six men perceived, they commanded them to be removed, and put again in the place from which they were brought.

38 And they said to those who brought those stones; Do not ye reach up to us any stones for this building, but lay them down by the tower, and these virgins may carry them and reach them to us.

39 For unless they shall be carried by these virgins through this gate, they cannot change their colours; therefore do not labour in vain.

40 ¶ So the building that day was done, howbeit the tower was not finished; for it was afterwards to be built, therefore now also there was some delay made of it.

41 And these six men commanded those that built to depart, and as it were to rest for some time; but they ordered those virgins that they should not depart from the tower; now they seemed to me to be left for the guarding of it.

42 When all were departed, I said unto that shepherd; Sir, why is not the building of the tower finished? Because it cannot, said he, be finished until its Lord comes, and approves of the

building; that if he shall find any stones in it that are not good they may be changed; for this tower is built according to his will.

43 Sir, said I, I would know what the building of this tower signifies; as also I would be informed concerning this rock, and this gate.

44 And concerning the mountains, and the virgins, and the stones that did rise out of the deep, and were not cut, but put into the building just as they came forth; and why the ten stones were first laid in the foundation; then the twenty-five; then thirty-five; then forty?

45 Also concerning these stones that were put into the building, and again taken out, and carried back into their place? Fulfil, I pray, the desire of my soul as to all these things and manifest all unto me.

46 And he said unto me; If thou shalt not be dull, thou shalt know all, and shalt see all the other things that are about to happen in this tower; and shalt understand diligently all these similitudes.

47 And after a few days we came into the same place where we had sat before; and he said unto me, Let us go unto the tower; for the Lord of it will come and examine it.

48 So we came thither, and found none but those virgins there. And he asked them whether the Lord of that tower was come thither? And they replied, that he would be there presently to examine the building.

49 ¶ After a very little while I saw a great multitude of men coming, and in the middle of

them a man so tall, that he surpassed the tower in [1] height.

50 About him were those six, who before commanded in the building, and all the rest of those who had built that tower, and many others of great dignity: and the virgins that kept the tower ran to meet him, and kissed him, and began to walk near unto him.

51 But he examined the building with so much care that he handled every stone; and struck every one with a rod which he held in his hand:

52 Of which some being so struck turned black as soot; others were rough; some looked as if they had cracks in them; others seemed maimed: some neither black nor white; some looked sharp, and agreed not with the other stones, and others were full of spots.

53 These were the several kinds of those stones which were not found proper in the building; all which the Lord commanded to be taken out of the tower, and laid near it, and other stones to be brought and put in their places.

54 And they that built, asked him from which of the mountains he would have stones brought to put in the place of those that were laid aside. But he forbad them to bring any from the mountains, and commanded that they should take out of a certain field that was near.

55 So they digged in the field, and found many bright square stones, and some also that were round. Howbeit, all that were found in that field were taken away, and carried through the gate by those virgins; and those of them that were square were fitted and put into the places of those that were pulled out.

56 But the round ones were not put into the building, because they were hard, and it would have required too much time to cut them; but they were placed about the tower, as if they should hereafter be cut square, and put into the building; for they were very white.

57 ¶ When he who was chief in dignity, and lord of the whole tower saw this, he called to him the shepherd that was with me and gave him the stones that were rejected and laid about the tower and said unto him; cleanse these stones with all care, and fit them into the building of the tower, that they may agree with the rest; but those that will not suit with the rest, cast away afar off from the tower.

58 When he had thus commanded him, he departed, with all those that came with him to the tower: but those virgins still stood about the tower to keep it.

59 And I said unto that shepherd, How can these stones, seeing they have been rejected, return into the building of this tower? He replied; I will cut off the greatest part from these stones, and will add them to the building, and they will agree with the rest.

60 And I said, Sir, how will they be able to fill the same place, when they shall be so much cut away? He answered; They that shall be found too little shall be put into the middle of the building, and the greater shall be placed without, and keep them in.

[1] Greatness.

61 When he had said thus unto me, he added; Let us go, and after three days we will return, and I will put these stones, being cleansed, into the tower.

62 For all these that are about the tower must be cleansed, lest the master of the house chance to come upon the sudden, and find those which are about the tower unclean; [1] and be so exasperated, that these stones should never be put into the building of this tower, and I shall be looked upon to have been ' unmindful of my master's commands.

63 When therefore we came after three days to the tower, he said unto me; Let us examine all these stones, and let us see which of them may go into the building. I answered, Sir, let us see.

64 ¶ And first of all we begun to consider those which had been black ; for they were found just such as they were when they were pulled out of the tower: wherefore he commanded them to be removed from the tower and put by themselves.

65 Then he examined those which had been rough ; and commanded many of those to be cut round, and to be fitted by the virgins into the building of the tower; so they took them, and fitted them into the middle of the building ; and he commanded the rest to be laid by with the black ones, for they also were become black.

66 Next he considered those which were full of cracks, and many of those also he ordered to be pared away, and so to be added to the rest of the building, by the same virgins.

67 These were placed without because they were found entire; but the residue through the multitude of their cracks could not be reformed, and therefore were cast away from the building of the tower.

68 Then he considered those that had been maimed ; many of these had cracks, and were become black; others were large clefts; these he commanded to be placed with those that were rejected.

69 But the rest being cleansed and reformed, he commanded to be put in the building. These therefore those virgins took up, and fitted into the middle of the building, because they were but weak.

70 After these he examined those which were found half white and half black; and many of those were now black; these also he ordered to be laid among those that were cast away.

71 The rest were found altogether white; those were taken up by the virgins, and fitted into the same tower: [2] and these were put in the outside, because they were found entire; that so they might keep in those that were placed in the middle, for nothing was cut off from them.

72 Next he looked upon those [4] which had been hard and sharp; but few of these were made use of, because they could not be cut, for they were found very hard : but the rest were formed, and fitted by the virgins into the middle of the building, because they were more weak.

73 Then he considered those which had spots; of these a few were found black, and these were carried to their fellows. The rest

---

[1] MS. Lamb. Ita exasperetur, ut hi lapides.　[2] MS. Lamb. Negligens, patrisfamilias.　[3] Vid. MS. Lamb. Edit. Oxon. p. 157.　[4] MS. Lamb. Fuerant.

were white and entire; and they were fitted by the virgins into the building, and placed in the outside, by reason of their strength.

74 ¶ After this he came to consider those stones which were white and round: and he said unto me, What shall we do with these stones? I answered, Sir, I cannot tell.

75 He replied, Canst thou think of nothing then for these? I answered, Sir, I understand not this art; neither am I a stone-cutter, nor can I tell any thing.

76 And he said, seest thou not that they are very round? Now to make them square, I must cut off a great deal from them; howbeit, it is necessary that some of these should go into the building of the tower.

77 I answered; If it be necessary, why do you perplex yourself, and not rather choose, if you have any choice among them, and fit them into the building.

78 Upon this he chose out the largest and brightest, and squared them; which when he had done the virgins took them up, and placed them in the outside of the building.

79 And the rest that remained were carried back into the same field from which they were taken; howbeit, they were not cast away; because, said he, there is not yet a little wanting to this tower, which is to be built; and perhaps the Lord will have these stones fitted into this building, because they are exceeding white.

80 Then were there called twelve very stately women, clothed with a black garment, girded, and their shoulders free,

and their hair loose. These seemed to me to be country women.

81 And the shepherd commanded them to take up those stones which were cast out of the building, and carry them back to the mountains out of which they were taken.

82 And they took them all up joyfully, and carried them back to their places from whence they had been taken.

83 When not one stone remained about the tower, he said unto me, Let us go about this tower, and see whether any thing be wanting to it.

84 We began therefore to go round about it; and when he saw that it was handsomely built, he began to be very glad; for it was so beautifully framed, that any one that had seen it must have been in love with the building:

85 For it seemed to be all but one stone, nor did a joint anywhere appear; but it looked as if it had all been cut out of one rock.

86 ¶ And when I diligently considered what a tower it was, I was extremely pleased: and he said unto me, Bring hither some lime and little shells, that I may fill up the [1] spaces of those stones that were taken out of the building, and put in again; for all things about the tower must be made even.

87 And I did as he commanded me, and he said unto me, Be ready to help me, and this work will quickly be finished.

88 He therefore filled up the spaces of those stones, and commanded the place about the tower to be cleansed.

[1] Formas. Lat.

89 Then those virgins took besoms, and cleansed all the place around and took away all the rubbish, and threw water on; which being done, the place became delightful, and the tower beauteous.

90 Then he said unto me, All is now clean: if the Lord should come to finish the tower, he will find nothing whereby to complain of us.

91 When he had said this he would have departed. But I laid hold on his bag, and began to entreat him for the Lord's sake, that he would explain to me all things that he had shown me.

92 He said unto me, I have at present a little business; but I will suddenly explain all things unto thee. Tarry here for me till I come.

93 I said unto him, Sir, what shall I do here alone? He answered, Thou art not alone, seeing all these virgins are with thee.

94 I said, Sir, deliver me then unto them. Then he called them and said unto them, I commend this man unto you until I shall come.

95 So I remained with those virgins: now they were cheerful and courteous unto me; especially the four, which seemed to be the chiefest among them.

96 ¶ Then those virgins said unto me, that shepherd will not return hither to day. I said unto them, What then shall I do? They answered, Tarry for him till the evening, if perhaps he may come and speak with thee; but if not, yet thou shalt continue with us till he does come.

97 I said unto them, I will tarry for him till evening; but if he comes not by that time, I will go home, and return hither again the next morning.

98 They answered me, Thou art delivered unto us, thou mayest not depart from us. I said, Where shall I tarry?

99 They replied, Thou shalt sleep with us as a brother, not as a husband: for thou art our brother, and we are ready from henceforth to dwell with thee; for thou art very dear to us.

100 Howbeit I was ashamed to continue with them. But she that seemed to be the chiefest amongst them, embraced me, and began to kiss me. And the rest when they saw that I was kissed by her, began also to kiss me as a brother; and led me about the tower, and played with me.

101 Some of them also sung psalms, others made up the chorus with them. But I walked about the tower with them, rejoicing silently, and seeming to myself to be grown young again.

102 When the evening came on, I would forthwith have gone home, but they withheld me, and suffered me not to depart. Wherefore I continued with them that night near the same tower.

103 So they spread their linen garments upon the ground; and placed me in the middle, nor did they anything else, only they prayed.

104 I also prayed with them without ceasing, nor less than they. Who when they saw me pray in that manner, rejoiced greatly; and I continued there with them till the next day.

105 And when we had worshipped God, then the shepherd came and said unto them: You have done no injury to this man. They answered, Ask him. I said unto him, Sir, I have received a

great deal of satisfaction in that I have remained with them.

106 And he said unto me, How didst thou sup? I answered, Sir, I feasted the whole night upon the words of the Lord. They received thee well then, said he; I said, Sir, very well.

107 He answered, Wilt thou now learn what thou didst desire? I replied, Sir, I will: and first I pray thee that thou shouldest shew me all things in the order that I asked them.

108 He answered, I will do all as thou wouldst have me, nor will I hide anything from thee.

109 ¶ First of all, Sir, said I, tell me, what this rock, and this gate denote? Hearken, said he; this rock, and this gate, are the Son of God. I replied, Sir, how can that be; seeing the rock is old, but the gate new.

110 Hear, said he, O foolish man! and understand. The Son of God is indeed more ancient than any creature; [1] insomuch that he was in council with his Father at the creation of [2] all things.

111 But the gate is therefore new, because he appeared in the last days in the fulness of time; that they who shall attain unto salvation, may by it enter into the kingdom of God.

112 You have seen, said he, those stones which were carried through the gate, how they were placed in the building of the tower; but that those which were not carried through the gate, were sent away into their own places?

113 I answered, Sir, I saw it. Thus, said he, no man shall enter into the kingdom of God, but he who shall take upon him the name of the Son of God.

114 For if you would enter into any city, and that city should be encompassed with a wall, and had only one gate, could you enter into that city except by that gate?

115 I answered, Sir, how could I do otherwise? As therefore, said he, there would be no other way of entering into that city but by its gate, so neither can any one enter into the kingdom of God, but only by the name of his Son, who is most dear unto him.

116 And he said unto me, Didst thou see the multitude of those that built that tower? Sir, said I, I saw it. He answered, All those are the angels, venerable in their dignity.

117 With those is the Lord encompassed as with a wall: but the gate is the Son of God, who is the only way of coming unto God. For no man shall go to God, but by his Son.

118 Thou sawest also, said he, the six men, and in the middle of them that venerable great man, who walked about the tower, and rejected the stones out of the tower?

119 Sir, said I, I saw them. He answered, that tall man was the Son of God: and those six were his angels of most eminent dignity, which stand about him on the right hand and on the left.

120 Of these excellent angels none comes in unto God without him. He added, Whosoever therefore shall not take upon him his name, he shall not enter into the kingdom of God.

121 ¶ Then I said, What is this tower? This, said he, is the church. And what, Sir, are these virgins? He said unto me, These are the holy spirits, for no

---

[1] Ita ut. Lat.   [2] The creatures.

man can enter into the kingdom of God, except these clothe him with their garment.

122 For it will avail thee nothing to take up the name of the Son of God, unless thou shalt also receive their garment from them. For these virgins are the powers of the Son of God. So shall a man in vain bear his name, unless he shall be also endued with his powers.

123 And he said unto me, sawest thou those stones that were cast away? They bore indeed the name, but put not on their garment. I said, Sir, what is their garment? [1] Their very names, said he, are their garment.

124 Therefore whosoever beareth the name of the Son of God, ought to bear their names also; for the Son of God also himself beareth their names.

125 As for those stones, continued he, which being delivered by their hands, thou sawest remain in the building, they were clothed with their power ; for which cause thou seest the whole tower of the same [2] colour with the rock, and made as it were of one stone.

126 So also those who have believed in God by his Son, have put on his spirit. Behold there shall be one spirit, and one body, and one colour of their garments; and all they shall attain this, who shall bear the names of these virgins.

127 And I said, Sir, why then were those stones cast away which were rejected, seeing they also were carried through the gate, and delivered by the hands of these virgins into the building of this tower?

128 Seeing, said he, thou takest care to inquire diligently into all things, hear also concerning those stones which were rejected. All these received the name of the Son of God, and with that the power of these virgins.

129 Having therefore received these spirits, they were perfected, and brought into the number of the servants of God ; and they began to be one body, and to have one garment, for they were [3] endued with the same righteousness, which they alike exercised.

130 But after that they be held those women which thou sawest clothed with a black garment, with their shoulders at liberty and their hair loose ; they fixed their desires upon them, being tempted with their beauty ; and were clothed with their power, and cast off the clothing of the virgins :

131 Therefore were they cast off from the house of God, and delivered to those women. But they that were not corrupted with their beauty, remained in the house of God. This, said he, is the signification of those stones which were rejected.

132 ¶ And I said, Sir, what if any of these men shall repent, and cast away their desire of those women, and be converted, and return to these virgins, and put on again their virtue ; shall they not enter into the house of God?

133 They shall enter, said he, if they shall lay aside all the works of those women, and shall resume the power of these virgins, and shall walk in their works.

134 And for this cause there

---

[1] Vid. Annot. Edit. Oxon. p. 116, d.   [2] Vid. Origen. Philocal. c. viii.
[3] Sentiebant æquitatem, Lat. from the Greek εφρονουν: but the true reading of Hermas seemeth to have been οφορουν.

JONAH CAST INTO THE SEA, AND HIS COMING OUT OF THE WHALE.

FROM THE FRONT OF A SARCOPHAGUS OF THE FIRST AGES OF CHRISTIANITY, FOUND IN THE CEMETERY OF THE VATICAN, ROME.

is a stop in the building, that if they shall repent, they may be added to the building of this tower; but if they shall not repent, that others may be built in their places, and so they may be utterly cast away.

135 For all these things I gave thanks unto the Lord, that being moved with mercy towards all those upon whom his name is called, he sent to us the angel of repentance to preside over us who have sinned against him; and that he has refreshed our spirits which were almost gone, and who had no hope of salvation, but are now refreshed to the renewal of life.

136 Then I said, Shew me now, Sir, why this tower is not built upon the ground, but upon a rock, and upon the gate? He replied, thou art foolish, and without understanding, therefore thou asketh this.

137 And I said, Sir, I must needs ask all things of you, because I understand nothing at all. For all your answers are great and excellent; and which a man can hardly understand.

138 Hear, said he: The name of the Son of God is great and without bounds, and the whole world is supported by it. If therefore, said I, every creature of God be sustained by his Son, why should he not support those also who have been invited by him, and who carry his name, and walk in his commandments?

139 Seest thou not, said he, that he doth support them, who with all their heart bear his name? He therefore is their foundation, and gladly supports those who do not deny his name, but willingly bear it.

140 ¶ And I said: Sir, tell me the names of these virgins; and of those women that were clothed with the black garment.

141 Hear, said he, the names of those virgins which are the more powerful, and stand at the corners of the gate. These are their names:

142 The first is called [1] Faith; the second Continence; the third, Power; the fourth, Patience; the rest which stand beneath these are, Simplicity, Innocence, Chastity, Cheerfulness, Truth, Understanding, Concord, Charity.

143 Whosoever therefore bear these names, and the names of the Son of God, shall enter into the kingdom of God.

144 Hear now, said he, the names of those women, which were clothed with the black garment. Of these, four are the principal: the first is Perfidiousness; the second, Incontinence; the third, Infidelity; the fourth, Pleasure.

145 And the rest which follow are called thus, Sadness, Malice, Lust, Anger, Lying, Foolishness, Pride, and Hatred. The servant of God, which carries these spirits, shall see indeed the kingdom of God, but he shall not enter into it.

146 But, Sir, what are those stones which were taken out of the deep and fitted into the building? The ten, said he, which were placed at the foundation, are the first age; the following five-and-twenty, the second, of righteous men.

147 The next thirty-five, are the prophets and ministers of the Lord. And the forty, are the Apostles and doctors of the preaching of the Son of God.

[1] Origin. Hom. 13, in Ezek.

148 And I said, Sir, why did the virgins put even those stones into the building after they were carried through the gate? And he said, Because these first carried those spirits, and they departed not one from the one, neither the men from the spirits, nor the spirits from the men:

149 But the spirits were joined to those men even to the day of their death; who if they had not had these spirits with them, they could not have been useful to the building of this tower.

150 And I said, Sir, shew me this farther. He answered, What dost thou ask? Why did these stones come out of the deep, and were placed into the building of this tower, seeing that they long ago carried those [1] holy spirits.

151 [2] It was necessary, said he, for them to ascend by water, that they might be at rest. For they could not otherwise enter into the kingdom of God, but by laying aside the mortality of their former life.

152 They therefore being dead, were nevertheless sealed with the seal of the Son of God, and so entered into the kingdom of God.

153 For before a man receives the name of the Son of God, he is ordained unto death; but when he receives that seal, he is freed from death, and [3] assigned unto life.

154 Now that seal is the water of baptism, into which men go down under the obligation unto death, but come up appointed unto life.

155 Wherefore to those also was this seal [4] preached, and they made use of it, that they might enter the kingdom of God.

156 And I said, Why then, sir, did these forty stones also ascend with them out of the deep, having already received that seal?

157 He answered, [5] Because these Apostles and teachers, who preached the name of the Son of God, dying after they had received his faith and power, preached to them who were dead before; and they gave this seal to them.

158 They went down therefore into the water with them, and again came up. But these went down whilst they were alive, and came up again alive: whereas those who were before dead, went down dead, but came up alive;

159 Through these therefore they received life, and knew the Son of God: for which cause they came up with them, and were fit to come into the building of the tower; and were not cut, but put in entire; because they died in righteousness, and in great purity; only this seal was wanting to them.

160 Thus you have the explication of these things.

161 ¶ I answered: Sir, tell me now what concerns those mountains, why are they so different; some of one form, and some of another.

162 Hear, said he; These twelve mountains which thou seest, are twelve nations, which make up the whole world. Wherefore the Son of God is preached to them, by those whom he sent unto them.

163 But why, said I, are they different, and every one of a

---

[1] Justos, Righteous.   [2] Vid. Edit. Oxon. p. 171, b.   [3] Traditur, Delivered. [4] Vid. Coteler. Annot. in loc. p. 77, 78.   Comp. 1 Pet. iii. 19.   [5] Vid. Clem. Alex. Strom. ii. et vi.

figure? He replied, Hearken. Those twelve nations which possess the whole world, are twelve people.

164 And as thou hast beheld these mountains different, so are they. I will therefore open to thee the meaning and actions of every mountain.

165 But first, sir, said I, shew me this; Seeing these mountains are so different, how have they agreed into the building of this tower; and been brought to one colour; and are no less bright than those that came out of the deep?

166 Because, replied he, all the nations which are under heaven, have heard and believed in the same one name of the Son of God by whom they are called.

167 Wherefore having received his seal, they have all been made partakers of the same [1] understanding and [2] knowledge; and their faith and charity have been the same; and they have carried the spirits of these virgins together with his name.

168 And therefore the building of this tower appeared to be of the same colour, and did shine like the brightness of the sun.

169 But after that they had thus agreed in one mind there began to be one body of them all; howbeit some of them polluted themselves, and were cast off from the kind of the righteous, and again returned to their former state, and became even worse than they were before.

170 ¶ How, said I, sir, were they worse who knew the Lord? He answered: If he who knows not the Lord liveth wickedly, the punishment of his wickedness attends him.

171 But he who has known the Lord, ought to abstain altogether from all wickedness, and more and more to be the servant of righteousness.

172 And does not he then seem to thee to sin more who ought to follow goodness, if he shall prefer the part of sin; than he who offends without knowing the power of God?

173 Wherefore these are indeed ordained unto death; but they who have known the Lord, and have seen his wonderful works, if they shall live wickedly, they shall be doubly punished, and shall die for ever.

174 As therefore thou hast seen that after the stones were cast out of the tower, which had been rejected; they were delivered to wicked and cruel spirits; and thou beheldest the tower so cleansed, as if it had all been made of one stone:

175 [3] So the church of God, when it shall be purified: (the [4] wicked and counterfeits, the [5] mischievous and doubtful, and all that have behaved themselves wickedly in it, and committed divers kinds of sin, being cast out) shall become one body, and there shall be one understanding, one opinion, one faith, and the same charity.

176 And then shall the Son of God rejoice among them, and shall receive his people with a pure will.

177 And I said; Sir, all these things are great and honourable; but now shew unto me the effect and force of every mountain: that every soul which trusteth in the Lord, when it shall hear these things may honour his great, and wonderful, and holy name.

---

[1] Prudence. [2] Sense. [3] Lat. Virtutem. [4] Vid. Orig. Philocal. c. viii. [5] Evil

178 Hear, said he, the variety of these mountains, that is, of the twelve nations.

179 ¶ They who have believed of the first mountain, which is black, are those who have revolted from the faith; and spoken wicked things against the Lord; and betrayed the servants of God.

180 These are condemned to death, there is no repentance for them: and therefore they are black, because their kind is wicked.

181 Of the second mountain which was smooth, are the ¹ hypocrites, who have believed, and the teachers of naughtiness: and these are next to the foregoing, which have not in them the fruit of righteousness.

182 For as their mountain is barren and without fruit; so also such kind of men have indeed the name of Christians, but are empty of faith; nor is there any fruit of the truth in them.

183 Nevertheless there is room left to them for repentance, if they shall suddenly pursue it: but if they shall delay, they also shall be partakers of death with the foregoing kind.

184 I said, Sir, why is there room left to those for repentance, and not to the foregoing kind, seeing their sins are well nigh the same?

185 There is therefore, said he to these a return unto life by repentance, because they have not blasphemed against their Lord, nor betrayed the servants of God: but by their desire of gain have deceived men, leading them according to the lusts of sinners; wherefore they shall suffer for this thing.

186 Howbeit there is still left them room for repentance, because they have not spoken any thing wickedly against the Lord.

187 ¶ They who are of the third mountain which had thorns and brambles, are those who believed, but were some of them rich, others taken up with many affairs: the brambles are their riches: the thorns, those affairs in which they were engaged.

188 Now they who are entangled in much business, and in diversity of affairs, join not themselves to the servants of God, but wander, being called away by those affairs with which they are choked.

189 And so they which are rich, with difficulty yield themselves to the ² conversation of the servants of God; fearing lest any thing should be asked of them. These therefore shall hardly enter into the kingdom of God.

190 For as men walk with difficulty bare-foot over thorns, even so these kind of men shall scarcely enter into the kingdom of God.

191 Nevertheless there is afforded to all these a return unto repentance; if that they shall quickly return to it; that because in their former days they have neglected to work, in the time that is to come they may do some good.

192 If therefore having repented they shall do the works of righteousness, they shall live; but if they shall continue in their evil courses, they shall be delivered to those women that will take away their life.

193 ¶ As for the fourth mountain, which had many herbs, the upper part of which is green,

---

¹ Profligate.　　² Vid. Edit. Oxon., p. 178, Not. b.

but the roots dry, and some of which being touched with the heat of the sun are withered;

194 It denotes the doubtful, who have believed, and some others who carry the Lord in their tongues, but have him not in their heart: therefore their grass is dry, and without root; because they live only in words, but their works are dead.

195 These therefore are neither dead nor living, and withal are doubtful. For the doubtful are neither green nor dry; that is, neither dead nor alive.

196 For as the herbs dry away at the sight of the sun; so tho doubtful as soon as they hear of persecution, and fear inconveniences, return to their idols, and again serve them, and are ashamed to bear the name of their Lord.

197 This kind of men then is neither dead nor alive; nevertheless these also may live, if they shall presently repent; but if not, they shall be delivered to those women, who shall take away their life.

198 ¶ As concerning the fifth mountain that is craggy, and yet has green grass: they are of this kind who have believed, and are faithful indeed, but believe with difficulty; and are bold, and self-conceited; that would be thought to know all things, but really know nothing.

199 Wherefore, by reason of this confidence, knowledge is departed from them; and a rash presumption is entered into them.

200 But they carry themselves high, and as prudent men; and though they are fools, yet would seem to be teachers.

201 Now by reason of this folly many of them, whilst they magnify themselves, are become vain and empty. For boldness and vain confidence is a [1] very evil spirit.

202 Wherefore many of these are cast away; but others acknowledging their error, have repented, and submitted themselves to those who are knowing.

203 And to all the rest of this kind there is repentance allowed; forasmuch as they were not so much wicked as foolish, as void of understanding.

204 If these therefore shall repent, they shall live unto God; but if not, they shall dwell with those women, who shall exercise their wickedness upon them.

205 ¶ For what concerns the sixth mountain having greater and lesser clefts, they are such as have believed; but those in which were lesser clefts are they who have had controversies among themselves; and by reason of their quarrels languish in the faith;

206 Nevertheless many of these have repented, and so will the rest when they shall hear my commands; for their controversies are but small, and they will easily return unto repentance.

207 But those who have the greater clefts, will be as stiff stones, mindful of grudges and offences, and full of anger among themselves. These therefore are cast from the tower, and refused to be put into its building; for this kind of men shall hardly live.

208 Our God and Lord, who ruleth over all things, and has power over all his creatures, will not remember our offences, but is easily appeased by those who confess their sins: but man being

---

[1] Magnum Dæmonium.

languid, mortal, infirm, and full of sins, perseveres in his anger against man; as if it were in his power to save or destroy him.

209 But I, as the angel who am set over your repentance, admonish you, that whosoever among you has any such purpose he should lay it aside, and return unto repentance; and the Lord will heal your former sins, if you shall purge yourselves from this evil spirit; but if you shall not do it, ye shall be delivered to him unto death.

210 ¶ As for the seventh mountain in which the grass was green and flourishing, and the whole mountain faithful; and all kind of cattle fed upon the grass of it, and the more the grass was eaten so much the more it flourished:

211 They are such as believed, and were always good and upright; and without any differences among themselves, but still rejoiced in the servants of God, having put on the spirit of these virgins; and been always forward to shew mercy to all men, readily giving to all men of their labours without upbraiding, and without deliberation.

212 Wherefore the Lord seeing their simplicity and [1] innocence, has increased them in the works of their hands, and given them grace in all their works.

213 But I, who am the angel appointed over your repentance, exhort you, that as many as are of this kind would continue in the same purpose, that your seed may not be rooted out forever.

214 For the Lord hath tried you, and written you into our number; and all your seed shall dwell with the Son of God; for ye are all of his spirit.

215 ¶ As concerning the eighth mountain in which were a great many springs, by which every kind of all the creatures of God was watered; they are such as have believed the Apostles which the Lord sent into all the world to preach;

216 And [2] some of them being teachers have preached and taught purely and sincerely, and have not in the least yielded to any evil desires, but have constantly walked in righteousness and truth.

217 These therefore have their conversations among the angels.

218 ¶ Again; as for what concerns the ninth mountain which is desert, and full of serpents; they are such as have believed, but had many stains:

219 These are such ministers as discharge their ministry amiss; ravishing away the goods of the widows and fatherless; and serve themselves, not others, out of those things which they have received.

220 These, if they continue in this covetousness, have delivered themselves unto death, nor shall there be any hope of life for them. But if they shall be converted, and shall discharge their ministry sincerely, they may live.

221 As for those which were found rough, they are such as have denied the name of the Lord, and not returned again to the Lord, but have become savage and wild; not applying themselves to the servants of God; but being separated from them, have for a little carelessness lost their lives.

222 For as a vine that is forsaken in a hedge, and never

---

[1] Infancy.   [2] MS. Lamb. Et quidam Doctores caste: Omitting Qui

dressed, perishes and is choked by the weeds, and in time becomes wild, and ceases to be useful to its lord; so this kind of men despairing of themselves, and being soured, have begun to be unprofitable to their Lord.

223 Howbeit to these there is, after all, repentance allowed, if they shall not be found from their hearts to have denied Christ; but if any of these shall be found to have denied him from his heart, I cannot tell whether such a one can attain unto life.

224 I say therefore that if any one hath denied, he should in these days return unto repentance; for it cannot be that any one who now denies the Lord, can afterwards attain unto salvation: nevertheless repentance is proposed unto them who have formerly denied.

225 But he who will repent must hasten on his repentance, before the building of this tower is finished: otherwise he shall be delivered by those women unto death.

226 But they that are maimed are the deceitful; and those who mix with one another, these are the serpents that you saw mingled in that mountain.

227 For as the poison of serpents is deadly unto men; so the words of such persons infect and destroy men. They are therefore maimed in their faith, by reason of that kind of life which they lead.

228 Howbeit some of them, having repented, have been saved, and so shall others of the same kind be also saved, if they shall repent; but if not, they shall die by those women whose power and force they possess.

229 ¶ For what concerns the tenth mountain, in which were the trees covering the cattle, they are such as have believed, and some of them have been bishops, that is, governors of the churches.

230 Others, are such stones as have not feignedly, but with a cheerful mind entertained the servants of God.

231 Then such as have been set over inferior ministries; and have protected the poor and the widows; and have always kept a chaste conversation: therefore they also are protected by the Lord.

232 Whosoever shall do on this wise, are honored with the Lord; and their place is among the angels, if they shall continue to obey the Lord even unto the end.

233 ¶ As to the eleventh mountain in which were trees loaded with several sorts of fruits, they are such as have believed, and suffered death, for the name of the Lord; and have endured with a ready mind, and have given up their lives with all their hearts.

234 And I said, Why then, sir, have all these fruit indeed, but yet some fairer than others?

235 Hearken, said he: Whosoever have suffered for the name of the Lord are esteemed honourable by the Lord; and all their offences are blotted out, because they have suffered death for the name of the Son of God.

236 Hear now, why their fruits are different, and some of them excel others, they who being brought before magistrates, and being asked, denied not the Lord, but suffered with a ready mind; these are more honourable with the Lord. The fruits therefore that are the most fair are these.

263

237 But they who were fearful and doubtful, and have deliberated with themselves whether they should confess or deny Christ, and yet have suffered; their fruits are smaller, because that this thought came into their hearts.

238 For it is a wicked and evil thought for a servant to deliberate whether he should deny his master. Take heed therefore ye who have such thoughts, that this mind continue not in you, and ye die unto God.

239 But ye who suffer death for his name sake, ought to honour the Lord, that he has esteemed you worthy to bear his name; and that you should be delivered from all your sins.

240 And why therefore do you not rather esteem yourselves happy? Yea think verily that if any one among you suffer, he performs a great work! For the Lord giveth you life, and ye understand it not. For your offences did oppress you; and if ye had not suffered for his name sake, ye had now been dead unto the Lord,

241 Wherefore I speak this unto you who deliberate whether ye should confess or deny him; confess that ye have the Lord for your God; lest at any time denying him, ye be delivered not into bonds.

242 For all nations punish their servants which deny their masters; what think you that the Lord will do unto you, who has the power of all things?

243 Remove therefore out of your hearts these doubts, that ye may live forever unto God.

244 As for the twelfth mountain, which was white, they are such as have believed like sincere children, into whose thoughts there never came any malice, nor have they ever known what sin was, but have always continued in their integrity.

245 Wherefore this kind of men shall without all doubt inherit the kingdom of God; because they have never in any thing defiled the commandments of God, but have continued with sincerity in the same condition all the days of their life.

246 Whosoever therefore, said he, shall continue as children without malice; shall be more honourable than all those of whom I have yet spoken: for all such children are honoured by the Lord, and esteemed the first of all.

247 Happy therefore are ye who shall remove all malice from you, and put on innocence; because ye shall first see the Lord.

248 And after he had thus ended his explication of all the mountains, I said unto him, Sir, show me now also what concerns the stones that were brought out of the plain, and put into the tower in the room of those that were rejected:

249 As also concerning those round stones which were added into the building of the tower: and also of those who still continued round.

250 ¶ Hear now, says he, concerning those stones which were brought out of the plain into the building of the tower, and placed in the room of those that were rejected; they are the roots of that white mountain.

251 Wherefore because those who have believed of that mountain were very innocent; the lord of this tower commanded that they which were of the roots of this mountain should be placed into the building.

252 For he knew that if they were put into this building they would continue bright; nor would any of them any more be made black.

253 But if he had added on this manner from the rest of the mountains, he would[1] almost have needed again to visit the tower and to cleanse it.

254 Now all these white stones are the young men who have believed, or shall believe; for they are all of the same kind. Happy is this kind, because it is innocent.

255 Hear now also concerning those round and bright stones: all these are of this white mountain. But they are therefore found round, because their riches have a little darkened them from the truth and dazzled their eyes:

256 Howbeit they have never departed from the Lord, nor has any wicked word proceeded out of their mouths; but all righteousness, and virtue, and truth.

257 When therefore the Lord saw their mind, and that they might adorn the truth; he commanded that they should continue good, and that their riches should be pared away:

258 For he would not have them taken wholly away, to the end they might do some good with that which was left, and live unto God; because they also are of a good kind.

259 Therefore was there a little cut off from them, and so they were put into the building of this tower.

260 ¶ As for the rest which continued still round, and were not found fit for the building [2] of this tower, because they have not yet received the seal; they were carried back to their place, because they were found very round.

261 But this present world must be cut away from them, and the vanities of their riches; and then they will be fit for the kingdom of God. For they must enter into the kingdom of God, because God has blessed this innocent kind.

262 Of this kind therefore none shall fall away; for though any of them being tempted by the devil should offend, he shall soon return to his Lord God.

263 I the angel of repentance esteem you happy, whosoever are innocent as little children, because your portion is good and honourable with the Lord.

264 And I say unto all you who have received this seal; keep simplicity, and remember not the offences which are committed against you, nor continue in malice, or in bitterness, through the memory of offences.

265 [3] But become one spirit, and provide remedies for these evil rents, and remove them from you; that the lord of the sheep may rejoice [4] at it; [5] for he will rejoice, if he shall find all whole.

266 But if any of these sheep shall be found scattered away, Wo shall be to the shepherds; but and if the shepherds themselves shall be scattered; what will they answer to [6] the lord of the sheepfold? Will they say that they were troubled by the

---

[1] MS. Lamb. Tantum non necesse habuisset.   [2] MS. Lamb. Structuram turris hujus.   [3] MS. Lamb. Et unum quemque spiritum fleri: which appears from the Gr. of Antiochus to be the true reading, και γενεσθαι εν πνευμα.   [4] MS. Lamb. Gaudeat de his; and Gr. Antioch χαρη επ αντω.   [5] Vid. Antioch. Hom. cxxii.   [6] Gr. Τῳ δεσποτη του ποιμνιου.

sheep? But they shall not be believed.

267 For it is an incredible thing that the shepherd should suffer by his flock; and he shall be the more punished for his lie.

268 Now I am the shepherd; and especially must give an account of you.

269 ¶ Wherefore take care of yourselves whilst the tower is yet building. The Lord dwells in those that love peace; for peace is beloved; but he is far off from the contentious, and those who are [1] full of malice.

270 Wherefore restore unto him the spirit entire, as ye received it. [2] For if thou shalt give unto a fuller a garment new and whole, thou wilt expect to receive it whole again; if therefore the fuller shall restore it unto thee torn, wouldest thou receive it?

271 Wouldst thou not presently be angry; and reproach him, saying; I gave my garment to thee whole; why hast thou rent it, and made it useless to me? Now it is of no use to me, by reason of the rent which thou hast made in it. Wouldst thou not say all this to a fuller, for the rent which he made in thy garment?

272 If therefore thou wouldst be concerned for thy garment, and complain that thou hadst not received it whole; what thinkest thou that the Lord will do, who gave his Spirit to thee entire, and thou hast rendered him altogether unprofitable, so that he can be of no use unto his Lord? For being corrupted by thee, he is no longer profitable to him.

273 Will not therefore the Lord do the same concerning his Spirit, by reason of thy deed? Undoubtedly, said I, he will do the same to all those whom he shall find to continue in the remembrance of injuries.

274 Tread not then under foot he said, his mercy; but rather honour him, because he is so patient with respect to your offences, and not like one of you; but repent, for that will be profitable for you.

275 ¶ All these things which are above written, I the shepherd, the angel of repentance, have shown and spoken to the servants of God.

276 If therefore ye shall believe and hearken to these words, and shall walk in them, and shall correct your ways, ye shall live. But if ye shall continue in malice, and in the remembrance of injuries, no such sinners shall live unto God.

277 All these things which were to be spoken by me I have thus delivered unto you. Then the shepherd said unto me, Hast thou asked all things of me? I answered, Sir, I have.

278 Why, then, said he, hast thou not asked concerning the spaces of these stones that were put in the building, that I may explain that also unto thee? I answered, Sir, I forgot it. Hear, then, said he, concerning these also.

279 They are those who have now heard these commands, and have repented with all their hearts;

280 And when the Lord saw that their repentance was good and pure, and that they could continue in it, he commanded their former sins to be blotted

---

[1] Perdites malitia. Lat.   [2] Antioch. Hom. xciv.

out. For these spaces were their sins, and they are therefore made even that they might not appear.

SIMILITUDE X.

Of Repentance and alms-deeds.

AFTER that I had written this book, the angel which had delivered me to that shepherd, came into the house where I was and sat upon the bed, and that shepherd stood at his right hand.

2 Then he called me and said unto me; I delivered thee and thy house to this shepherd, that thou mightest be protected by him. I said, Yes, Lord.

3 If therefore, said he, thou wilt be protected from all vexations and from all cruelty, and have success in every good word and work; and have all virtue and righteousness; walk in those commands which he has given thee, and thou shalt have dominion over all sin.

4 For if thou keepest those commands, all the lust and pleasure of this present world shall be subject to thee; and success shall follow thee in every good undertaking.

5 Take therefore his [1] gravity and modesty towards thee, and say unto all, that he is in great honour and renown with God, and is a [2] prince of great authority and powerful in his office.

6 To him only is the power of repentance committed throughout the whole world. Does he not seem to thee to be of great authority?

7 But ye despise his goodness, and the modesty which he shews towards you.

8 ¶ I said unto him; Sir, ask him since the time that he came into my house whether I have done any thing disorderly, or have offended him in any thing?

9 I know, said he, that thou hast done nothing disorderly, neither wilt thou hereafter do any such thing; and therefore I speak these things with thee that thou mayest persevere; for he has given me a good account concerning thee,

10 But thou shalt speak these things to others, that they who either have repented, or shall repent, [3] may be like-minded with thee; and he may give me as good an account of them also, and I may do the same unto the Lord.

11 I answered; Sir, I declare to all men the wonderful works of God; and I hope that all who love them and have before sinned, when they shall hear these things, will repent, and recover life.

12 Continue therefore, said he, in this ministry, and fulfil it. And whosoever shall do according to the commands of this shepherd, he shall live; and shall have great honour both here and with the Lord.

13 But they that shall not keep his commands, flee from their life, and are adversaries to it. And they that follow not his commands, shall deliver themselves unto death, and shall be every one guilty of his own blood.

14 But I say unto thee, keep these commandments, and thou shalt find a cure for all thy sins.

15 ¶ Moreover, I have sent [4] these virgins to dwell with thee; for I have seen that they are

---

[1] Lat. Maturitatem.   [2] President.   [3] Eadem quæ tu sentiant.
[4] What is meant by these virgins?—See before, Simil. ix. v. 149 et seq.

very kind to thee. Thou shalt therefore have them for thy helpers, that thou mayest the better keep the commands which he hath given thee; for these commands cannot be kept without these virgins.

16 And [1] I see how they are willing to be with thee; and I will also command them that they shall not all depart from thy house.

17 Only do thou purify thy house, for they will readily dwell in a clean house. For they are clean and chaste, and industrious; and all of them have grace with the Lord.

18 If therefore, thou shalt have thy house pure, they will abide with thee. But if it shall be never so little polluted, they will immediately depart from thy house: for these virgins cannot endure any manner of pollution.

19 I said unto him; Sir, I hope that I shall so please them, that they shall always delight to dwell in my house. And as he to whom you have committed me, makes no complaint of me; so neither shall they complain.

20 Then he said to that shepherd: I see that the servant of God will live and keep these commandments, and place these virgins in a pure habitation.

21 When he had said this, he delivered me again to that shepherd, and called the virgins, and said unto them; forasmuch as I see that ye will readily dwell in this man's house, I commend him and his house to you, that ye may not at all depart from his house. And they willingly heard these words.

22 ¶ Then he said unto me, Go on manfully in thy ministry; declare to all men the great things of God, and thou shalt find grace in this ministry.

23 And whosoever shall walk in these commands, shall live, and be happy in his life. But he that shall neglect them, shall not live, and shall be unhappy in his life.

24 Say unto all that whosoever can do well, cease not to exercise themselves in good works, for it is profitable unto them. For I [2] would that all men should be delivered from the inconveniences they lie under.

25 For he that wants, and suffers inconveniences in his daily life, is in great torment and necessity. Whosoever therefore delivers such a soul from necessity, gets great joy unto himself.

26 For he that is grieved with such inconveniences is equally tormented, as if he were in chains. And many upon the account of such calamities, being not able to bear them, have chosen even to destroy themselves.

27 He therefore that knows the calamity of such a man, and does not free him from it, commits a great sin, and is guilty of his blood.

28 Wherefore exercise yourselves in good works, as many as have received ability from the Lord; lest whilst ye delay to do them, the building of the tower be finished; because for your sakes the building is stopped.

29 Except therefore ye shall make haste to do well, the tower shall be finished, and ye shall be shut out of it.

[1] MS. Lamb. Video: which appears from the close of this section to be the true reading.   [2] Say.

30 And after he had thus spoken with me, he rose up from the bed and departed, taking the shepherd and virgins with him.

31 Howbeit he said unto me that he would send back the shepherd and virgins unto my house. Amen.

LETTERS OF HEROD AND PILATE.

Connecting Roman History with the Death of Christ at Jerusalem.

[These letters occur in a Syriac MS., of the sixth or seventh century, in the British Museum. Dr. Tischendorf states in his Apocalypses Apocryphæ (Prolegg. p. 56) that he has a copy of the same in Greek from a Paris MS., of which he says "scriptura satis differt, non item argumentum." The letters are followed by a few extracts which seem to have been added by some copyist, although they are followed by the subscription to Pilate's letter. We suppose that by Justinus, we are to understand Justus of Tiberias of whom Josephus speaks as a historian of his time. We cannot venture an opinion favorable to the genuineness of this extract, because Photius says Justus did not mention Christ. By Theodorus, we understand the Emperor Tiberius. The question and answer agree in sense with what is read in the "Anaphora," or response of Pilate.]

LETTER OF HEROD TO PILATE THE GOVERNOR.

Herod to Pontius Pilate the Governor of Jerusalem: Peace.

I AM in great anxiety. I write these things unto thee, that when thou hast heard them thou mayest be grieved for me. For as my daughter Herodias, who is dear to me, was playing upon a pool of water which had ice upon it, it broke under her, and all her body went down, and her head was cut off and remained on the surface of the ice. And behold, her mother is holding her head upon her knees in her lap, and my whole house is in great sorrow. For I, when I heard of the man Jesus, wished to come to thee, that I might see him alone, and hear his word, whether it was like that of the sons of men. And it is certain that because of the many evil things which were done by me to John the Baptist, and because I mocked the Christ, behold I receive the reward of righteousness,[1] for I have shed much blood of others' children upon the earth.[2] Therefore the judgments of God are righteous; for every man receives accord-

---

[1] 2 Peter ii. 13.

[2] Matt. ii. 16. It is scarcely necessary to say that it was not the Herod of the epistle who caused the massacre of the children at Bethlehem.

ing to his thought. But since thou wast worthy to see that God-man, therefore it becometh you to pray for me.

My son Azbonius also is in the agony of the hour of death.

And I too am in affliction and great trial, because I have the dropsy; and am in great distress, because I persecuted the introducer of baptism by water, which was John. Therefore, my brother, the judgments of God are righteous.

And my wife, again, through all her grief for her daughter, is become blind in her left eye, because we desired to blind the Eye of righteousness. There is no peace to the doers of evil, saith the Lord.[1] For already great affliction cometh upon the priests and upon the writers of the law; because they delivered unto thee the Just One. For this is the consummation of the world, that they consented that the Gentiles should become heirs. For the children of light shall be cast out,[2] for they have not observed the things which were preached concerning the Lord, and concerning his Son. Therefore gird up thy loins,[3] and receive righteousness, thou with thy wife remembering Jesus night and day; and the kingdom shall belong to you Gentiles, for we the (chosen) people have mocked the Righteous One.

Now if there is place for our request, O Pilate, because we were at one time in power, bury my household carefully; for it is right that we should be buried by thee, rather than by the priests, whom, after a little time, as the Scriptures say, at the coming of Jesus Christ, vengeance shall overtake.

Fare thee well, with Procla thy wife.

I send thee the earrings of my daughter and my own ring, that they may be unto thee a memorial of my decease. For already do worms begin to issue from my body,[4] and lo, I am receiving temporal judgment, and I am afraid of the judgment to come. For in both we stand before the works of the living God; but this judgment, which is temporal, is for a time, while that to come is judgment for ever.

End of the Letter to Pilate the Governor.

LETTER OF PILATE TO HEROD.

PILATE TO HEROD THE TETRARCH: PEACE.

KNOW and see, that in the day when thou didst deliver Jesus unto me, I took pity on myself, and testified by washing my hands (that I was innocent), concerning him who rose from the grave after three days, and had performed thy pleasure in him, for thou didst desire me to be associated with thee in his crucifixion. But I now learn from the executioners and from the soldiers who watched his sepulchre that he rose from the dead. And I have especially confirmed what was told me, that he appeared bodily in Galilee,

---

[1] Is. xlviii. 22; lvii. 21. [2] Luke xvi. 8. [3] 1 Peter i. 13.
[4] A palpable anachronism. Acts xii. 23.

in the same form, and with the same voice, and with the same doctrine, and with the same disciples, not having changed [1] in anything, but preaching with boldness his resurrection, and an everlasting kingdom.

And behold, heaven and earth rejoice; and behold, Procla my wife is believing in the visions which appeared unto her, when thou sentest that I should deliver Jesus to the people of Israel, because of the ill-will they had.

Now when Procla, my wife,[2] heard that Jesus was risen, and had appeared in Galilee, she took with her Longinus the centurion and twelve soldiers, the same that had watched at the sepulchre, and went to greet the face of Christ, as if to a great spectacle, and saw him with his disciples.

Now while they were standing, and wondering, and gazing at him, he looked at them, and said to them, What is it? Do ye believe in me? Procla, know that in the covenant which God gave to the fathers, it is said that every body which had perished should live by means of my death, which ye have seen. And now, ye see that I live, whom ye crucified. And I suffered many things, till that I was laid in the sepulchre. But now, hear me, and believe in my Father—God who is in me. For I loosed the cords of death, and brake the gates of Sheol; and my coming shall be hereafter.

And when Procla my wife and the Romans heard these things, they came and told me, weeping; for they also were against him, when they devised the evils which they had done unto him. So that, I also was on the couch of my bed in affliction, and put on a garment of mourning, and took unto me fifty Romans with my wife and went into Galilee.

And when I was going in the way I testified these things; that Herod did these things by me, that he took counsel with me, and constrained me to arm my hands against him, and to judge him that judgeth all, and to scourge the Just One, Lord of the just. And when we drew nigh to him, O Herod, a great voice was heard from heaven, and dreadful thunder, and the earth trembled, and gave forth a sweet smell, like unto which was never perceived even in the temple of Jerusalem. Now while I stood in the way, our Lord saw me as he stood and talked with his disciples. But I prayed in my heart, for I knew that it was he whom ye delivered unto me, that he was Lord of created things and Creator of all. But we, when we saw him, all of us fell upon our faces before his feet. And I said with a loud voice, I have sinned, O Lord, in that I sat and judged thee, who avengest all in truth. And lo, I know that thou art God, the Son of God, and I beheld thy humanity and not thy divinity. But Herod, with the children of Israel, constrained me to do evil unto thee. Have pity, therefore, upon me, O God of Israel!

[1] Literally "renewed anything."
[2] Literally "his wife," a manifest error.

And my wife, in great anguish, said, God of heaven and of earth, God of Israel, reward me not according to the deeds of Pontius Pilate, nor according to the will of the children of Israel, nor according to the thought of the sons of the priests; but remember my husband in thy glory!

Now our Lord drew near and raised up me and my wife, and the Romans; and I looked at him and saw there were on him the scars of his cross. And he said, That which all the righteous fathers hoped to receive, and saw not—in thy time the Lord of Time, the Son of Man, the Son of the Most High, who is for ever, arose from the dead, and is glorified on high by all that he created, and established for ever and ever.

1. Justinus, one of the writers that were in the days of Augustus and Tiberius and Gaius, wrote in his third discourse: Now Mary the Galilæan, who bare the Christ that was crucified in Jerusalem, had not been with a husband. And Joseph did not abandon her; but Joseph continued in sanctity without a wife, he and his five sons by a former wife;

and Mary continued without a husband.

2. Theodorus wrote to Pilate the Governor: Who was the man, against whom there was a complaint before thee, that he was crucified by the men of Palestine? If the many demanded this righteously, why didst thou not consent to their righteousness? And if they demanded this unrighteously, how didst thou transgress the law and command what was far from righteousness?

Pilate sent to him:—Because he wrought signs I did not wish to crucify him: and since his accusers said, He calleth himself a king, I crucified him.

3. Josephus saith: Agrippa, the king, was clothed in a robe woven with silver, and saw the spectacle in the theatre of Cæsarea. When the people saw that his raiment flashed, they said to him, Hitherto we feared thee as a man: henceforth thou art exalted above the nature of mortals. And he saw an angel standing over him, and he smote him as unto death.[1]

End of the Letter of Pilate to Herod.

THE EPISTLE OF PONTIUS PILATE,

WHICH HE WROTE TO THE ROMAN EMPEROR CONCERNING OUR LORD JESUS CHRIST.

Pontius Pilate to Tiberius Cæsar the Emperor—Greeting:

UPON Jesus Christ, whom I fully made known to thee in my last, a bitter punishment hath at length been inflicted by the will of the peo-ple, although I was unwilling and apprehensive. In good truth, no age ever had or will have a man so good and strict. But the people made a won-

[1] This extract from Josephus (Ant. 19, 8) is abridged from the account of Eusebius (Hist. Eccles. 2, 10). The figures 1, 2, 3, indicate the extracts which have been appended to the epistle.

derful effort, and all their scribes, chiefs and elders agreed to crucify this ambassador of truth, their own prophets, like the Sibyls with us, advising the contrary; and when he was hanged supernatural signs appeared, and in the judgment of philosophers menaced the whole world with ruin. His disciples flourish, not belying their master by their behavior and continence of life; nay, in his name they are most beneficent.[1] Had I not feared a sedition might arise among the people, who were almost furious, perhaps this man would have yet been living with us. Although, being rather compelled by fidelity to thy dignity, than led by my own inclination, I did not strive with all my might to prevent the sale and suffering of righteous blood, guiltless of every accusation, unjustly, indeed, through the maliciousness of men, and yet, as the Scriptures interpret, to their own destruction.

Farewell. The 5th of the Calends of April.

THE REPORT OF PILATE THE GOVERNOR,

CONCERNING OUR LORD JESUS CHRIST; WHICH WAS SENT TO AUGUSTUS CÆSAR, IN ROME.

IN those days, when our Lord Jesus Christ was crucified under Pontius Pilate, the governor of Palestine and Phœnicia, the things here recorded came to pass in Jerusalem, and were done by the Jews against the Lord. Pilate therefore sent the same to Cæsar in Rome, along with his private report, writing thus:

To the most potent, august, divine and awful Augustus Cæsar, Pilate, the administrator of the Eastern Province:

I have received information, most excellent one, in consequence of which I am seized with fear and trembling. For in this province which I administer, one of whose cities is called Jerusalem, the whole multitude of Jews delivered unto me a certain man called Jesus, and brought many accusations against him, which they were unable to establish by consistent evidence. But they charged him with one heresy in particular, namely, That Jesus said the Sabbath was not a rest, nor to be observed by them. For he performed many cures on that day, and made the blind see, and the lame walk, raised the dead, cleansed lepers, healed the paralytic who were wholly unable to move their body or brace their nerves, but could only speak and discourse, and he gave them power to walk and run, removing their infirmity by his word alone. There is another very mighty deed which is strange to the gods we have: he raised up a man who had been four days dead, summoning him by his word alone, when the dead man had begun to decay, and his body was corrupted by the worms which had been bred, and had the stench of a dog; but, seeing him lying in the

[1] *Cf.* Joseph. Ant. xviii. 3, 3.

273

tomb he commanded him to run, nor did the dead man at all delay, but as a bridegroom out of his chamber, so did he go forth from his tomb, filled with abundant perfume. Moreover, even such as were strangers, and clearly demoniacs, who had their dwelling in deserts, and devoured their own flesh, and wandered about like cattle and creeping things, he turned into inhabiters of cities, and by a word rendered them rational, and prepared them to become wise and powerful, and illustrious, taking their food with all the enemies of the unclean spirits which were destructive in them, and which he cast into the depth of the sea.

And, again, there was another who had a withered hand, and not only the hand but rather the half of the body of the man was like a stone, and he had neither the shape of a man nor the symmetry of a body: even him He healed with a word and rendered whole. And a woman also, who had an issue of blood for a long time, and whose veins and arteries were exhausted, and who did not bear a human body, being like one dead, and daily speechless, so that all the physicians of the district were unable to cure her, for there remained unto her not a hope of life; but as Jesus passed by she mysteriously received strength by his shadow falling on her, from behind she touched the hem of his garment, and immediately, in that very hour, strength filled her exhausted limbs, and as if she had never suffered anything, she began to run along

towards Capernaum, her own city, so that she reached it in a six days' journey.

And I have made known these things which I have recently been informed of, and which Jesus did on the Sabbath. And he did other miracles greater than these, so that I have observed greater works of wonder done by him than by the gods whom we worship.

But Herod and Archelaus and Philip, Annas and Caiaphas, with all the people, delivered him to me, making a great tumult against me in order that I might try him. Therefore, I commanded him to be crucified, when I had first scourged him, though I found no cause in him for evil accusations or dealings.

Now when he was crucified, there was darkness over all the world, and the sun was obscured for half a day, and the stars appeared, but no lustre was seen in them; and the moon lost its brightness, as though tinged with blood; and the world of the departed was swallowed up; so that the very sanctuary of the temple, as they call it, did not appear to the Jews themselves at their fall, but they perceived a chasm in the earth, and the rolling of successive thunders. And amid this terror the dead appeared rising again, as the Jews themselves bore witness, and said that it was Abraham, and Isaac, and Jacob, and the twelve patriarchs, and Moses, and Job, who had died before, as they say, some three thousand five hundred years. And there were very many whom I myself saw appearing in the body, and they made lamentation over the Jews, because of the transgression which was committed by them, and because of the destruction of the Jews and of their law.

And the terror of the earthquake continued from the sixth hour of the preparation until the ninth hour; and when it was evening on the first day of the week, there came a sound from heaven, and the heaven became seven times more luminous than on all other days. And at the third hour of the night the sun appeared more luminous than it had ever shone, lighting up the whole hemisphere. And as lightning-flashes suddenly come forth in a storm, so there were seen men, lofty in stature, and surpassing in glory, a countless host, crying out, and their voice was heard as that of exceedingly loud thunder, Jesus that was crucified is risen again: come up from Hades ye that were enslaved in the subterraneous recesses of Hades. And the chasm in the earth was as if it had no bottom; but it was so that the very foundations of the earth appeared, with those that shouted in heaven, and walked in the body among the dead that were raised. And He that raised up all the dead and bound Hades said, Say to my disciples, He goeth before you into Galilee, there shall ye see Him.

And all that night the light ceased not shining. And many of the Jews died in the chasm of the earth, being swallowed up, so that on the morrow most of those who had been against Jesus were not to be found. Others saw the apparition of men rising again whom none of us had ever seen. One synagogue of the Jews was alone left in Jerusalem itself, for they all disappeared in that ruin.

Therefore being astounded by that terror, and being possessed with the most dreadful trembling, I have written what I saw at that time and sent it to thine excellency; and I have inserted what was done against Jesus by the Jews, and sent it to thy divinity, my lord.

THE REPORT OF PONTIUS PILATE,

GOVERNOR OF JUDEA;

Which was sent to Tiberius Cæsar in Rome.

To the most potent, august, dreadful, and divine Augustus, Pontius Pilate, administrator of the Eastern Province.

I HAVE undertaken to communicate to thy goodness by this my writing, though possessed with much fear and trembling, most excellent king, the present state of affairs, as the result hath shown. For as I administered this province, my lord, according to the command of thy serenity, which is one of the eastern cities called Jerusalem, wherein the temple of the nation of the Jews is erected, all the multitude of the Jews, being assembled, delivered up to me a certain man called Jesus, bringing many and endless accusations against him; but they could not convict him in anything. But they had one heresy against him, that he said the sabbath was not their proper rest.

Now that man wrought many cures and good works: he caused the blind to see, he cleansed lepers, he raised the dead, he healed paralytics, who could not move at all, but had only voice, and all their bones in their places; and he gave them strength to walk and run, enjoining it by his word alone. And he did another yet more mighty work, which had been strange even among our gods, he raised from the dead one Lazarus, who had been dead four days, commanding by a word alone that the dead man should be raised, when his body was already corrupted by worms which bred in his wounds. And he commanded the fetid body, which lay in the grave, to run, and as bridegroom from his chamber so he went forth from his grave, full of sweet perfume. And some that were grievously afflicted by demons, and had their dwellings in desert places, and devoured the flesh of their own limbs, and went up and down among creeping things and wild beasts, he caused to dwell in cities in their own houses, and by a word made them reasonable, and caused to become wise and honorable those that were vexed by unclean spirits, and the demons that were in them he sent out into a herd of swine into the sea and drowned them. Again, another who had a withered hand, and lived in suffering, and had not even the half of his body sound, he made whole by a word alone. And a woman who had an issue of blood for a long time, so that because of the discharge all the joints of her bones were seen and shone through like glass, for all the physicians had dismissed her without hope, and had not cleansed her, for there was in her no hope of health at all; but once, as Jesus was passing by she touched from behind the hem of his garments, and in that very hour the strength of her body was restored, and she was made whole, as if she had no affliction, and began to run fast towards her own city of Paneas. And these things happened thus: but the Jews reported that Jesus did these things on the sabbath. And I saw that greater marvels had been wrought by him than by the gods whom we worship. Him then Herod and Archelaus and Philip, and Annas and Caiaphas, with all the people, delivered up to me, to put him on his trial. And because many raised a tumult against me, I commanded that he should be crucified.

Now when he was crucified darkness came over all the world; the sun was altogether hidden, and the sky appeared dark while it was yet day, so that the stars were seen, though still they had their lustre obscured, wherefore, I suppose your excellency is not unaware that in all the world they lighted their lamps from the sixth hour until evening. And the moon, which was like blood, did not shine all night long, although it was at the full, and the stars and Orion made lamentation over the

Jews, because of the transgression committed by them.

And on the first day of the week, about the third hour of the night, the sun appeared as it never shone before, and the whole heaven became bright. And as lightnings come in a storm, so certain men of lofty stature, in beautiful array, and of indescribable glory, appeared in the air, and a countless host of angels, crying out and saying, Glory to God in the highest, and on earth peace, good will among men: Come up from Hades, ye who are in bondage in the depths of Hades. And at their voice all the mountains and hills were moved, and the rocks were rent, and great chasms were made in the earth, so that the very places of the abyss were visible.

And amid the terror dead men were seen rising again, so that the Jews who saw it said, We beheld Abraham and Isaac, and Jacob, and the twelve patriarchs, who died some two thousand five hundred years before, and we beheld Noah clearly in the body. And all the multitude walked about and sang hymns to God with a loud voice, saying, The Lord our God, who hath risen from the dead, hath made alive all the dead, and Hades he hath spoiled and slain.

Therefore, my lord king, all that night the light ceased not. But many of the Jews died, and were sunk and swallowed up in the chasms that night, so that not even their bodies were to be seen. Now I mean, that those of the Jews suffered who spake against Jesus. And but one synagogue remained in Jerusalem, for all the synagogues which had been against Jesus were overwhelmed.

Through that terror, therefore, being amazed and being seized with great trembling, in that very hour, I ordered what had been done by them all to be written, and I have sent it to thy mightiness.

THE TRIAL AND CONDEMNATION OF PILATE.[1]

NOW when the letters came to the city of the Romans, and were read to Cæsar with no few standing there, they were all terrified, because, through the transgression of Pilate, the darkness and the earthquake had happened to all the world. And Cæsar, being filled with anger, sent soldiers and commanded that Pilate should be brought as a prisoner.

And when he was brought to the city of the Romans, and Cæsar heard that he was come, he sat in the temple of the gods, above all the senate, and with all the army, and with all the multitude of his power, and commanded that Pilate should stand in the entrance. And Cæsar said to him, Most impious one, when thou sawest so great signs done by that man, why didst thou dare to do thus? By daring to do an evil deed thou hast ruined all the world.

[1] Commonly called "the Paradosis of Pilate." It may be regarded as an historical continuation of the preceding, which it usually follows in the MSS. without any title.

And Pilate said, King and Autocrat, I am not guilty of these things, but it is the multitude of the Jews who are precipitate and guilty. And Cæsar said, And who are they? Pilate saith, Herod, Archelaus, Philip, Annas and Caiaphas, and all the multitude of the Jews. Cæsar saith, For what cause didst thou execute their purpose? And Pilate said, Their nation is seditious and insubordinate, and not submissive to thy power. And Cæsar said, When they delivered him to thee thou oughtest to have made him secure and sent him to me, and not consented to them to crucify such a man, who was just and wrought such great and good miracles, as thou saidst in thy report.[1] For by such miracles Jesus was manifested to be the Christ, the King of the Jews.

And when Cæsar said this and himself named the name of Christ, all the multitude of the gods fell down together, and became like dust where Cæsar sat with the senate. And all the people that stood near Cæsar were filled with trembling because of the utterance of the word and the fall of their gods, and being seized with fear they all went away, every man to his house, wondering at what had happened. And Cæsar commanded Pilate to be safely kept, that he might know the truth about Jesus.

And on the morrow when Cæsar sat in the capitol with all the senate, he undertook to question Pilate again. And Cæsar said, Say the truth, most impious one, for through thy impious deed which thou didst commit against Jesus, even here the doing of thy evil works were manifested, in that the gods were brought to ruin. Say then, who is he that was crucified, for his name hath destroyed all the gods? Pilate said, And verily his records are true; for even I myself was convinced by his works that he was greater than all the gods whom we venerate. And Cæsar said, For what cause then didst thou perpetrate against him such daring and doing, not being ignorant of him, or assuredly designing some mischief to my government? And Pilate said, I did it because of the transgression and sedition of the lawless and ungodly Jews.[2]

And Cæsar was filled with anger, and held a council with all his senate and officers, and ordered a decree to be written against the Jews thus:—

To Licianus who holdeth the first place in the East Country. Greeting:

I have been informed of the audacity perpetrated very recently by the Jews inhabiting Jerusalem and the cities round about, and their lawless doing, how they compelled Pilate to crucify a certain god called Jesus, through which great transgression of theirs the world was darkened and drawn into ruin. Determine therefore, with a body of soldiers, to go to them there at once and proclaim their subjection to bondage by this decree. By obeying and proceeding against

---

[1] Gr. τῆς σῆς ἀναφορᾶς
[2] See Letter of Pilate to Herod, p. 270.

them, and scattering them abroad in all nations, enslave them, and by driving their nation from all Judea as soon as possible show, wherever this hath not yet appeared, that they are full of evil.

And when this decree came into the East Country, Licianus obeyed, through fear of the decree, and laid waste all the nation of the Jews, and caused those that were left in Judea to go into slavery with them that were scattered among the Gentiles, that it might be known by Cæsar that these things had been done by Licianus against the Jews in the East Country, and to please him.

And again Cæsar resolved to have Pilate questioned, and commanded a captain, Albius by name, to cut off Pilate's head, saying, As he laid hands upon the just man, that is called Christ, he also shall fall in like manner, and find no deliverance.

And when Pilate came to the place he prayed in silence, saying, O Lord, destroy not me with the wicked Hebrews, for I should not have laid hands upon thee, but for the nation of lawless Jews, because they provoked sedition against me: but thou knowest that I did it in ignorance. Destroy me not, therefore, for this my sin, nor be mindful of the evil that is in me, O Lord, and in thy servant Procla who standeth with me in this the hour of my death, whom thou taughtest to prophecy that thou must be nailed to the cross. Do not punish her too in my sin, but forgive us, and number us in the portion of thy just ones. And behold, when Pilate had finished his prayer, there came a voice from heaven, saying, All generations and the families of the Gentiles shall call thee blessed, because under thee were fulfilled all these things that were spoken by the prophets concerning me; and thou thyself must appear as my witness at my second coming, when I shall judge the twelve tribes of Israel, and them that have not confessed my name. And the Prefect cut off the head of Pilate, and behold an angel of the Lord received it. And when his wife Procla saw the angel coming and receiving his head, she also, being filled with joy, forthwith gave up the ghost, and was buried with her husband.[1]

THE DEATH OF PILATE,
WHO CONDEMNED JESUS.

NOW whereas Tiberius Cæsar emperor of the Romans was suffering from a grievous sickness, and hearing that there was at Jerusalem a certain physician, Jesus by name, who healed all diseases by his word alone; not knowing that

---

[1] The Synaxaria of the Greeks, under Oct. 28th, intimate the commemoration of Procla, the wife of Pilate. The Æthiopic calendar inserts 'Pilate and his wife Procla' under June 25th. The reason for putting these names among the saints is, that Pilate by washing his hands attested the innocence of Jesus, while Procla sought to dissuade her husband from complying with the Jews. The above story makes of Pilate almost a martyr; and Tertullian makes him almost a saint in Apol. c. Gentes, cap. 21.

the Jews and Pilate had put him to death, he thus bade one of his attendants, Volusianus by name, saying, Go as quickly as thou canst across the sea, and tell Pilate, my servant and friend, to send me this physician to restore me to my original health. And Volusianus, having heard the order of the emperor, immediately departed, and came to Pilate, as it was commanded him. And he told the same Pilate what had been committed to him by Tiberius Cæsar, saying, Tiberius Cæsar, emperor of the Romans, thy Lord, having heard that in this city there is a physician who healeth diseases by his word alone, earnestly entreateth thee to send him to him to heal his disease. And Pilate was greatly terrified on hearing this, knowing that through envy he had caused him to be slain. Pilate answered the messenger, saying thus, This man was a malefactor, and a man who drew after himself all the people; so, after counsel taken of the wise men of the city, I caused him to be crucified. And as the messenger returned to his lodgings he met a certain woman named Veronica, who had been acquainted with Jesus, and he said, O woman, there was a certain physician in this city, who healed the sick by his word alone, why have the Jews slain him? And she began to weep, saying, Ah, me, my lord, it was my God and my Lord whom Pilate through envy delivered up, condemned, and commanded to be crucified. Then he, grieving greatly, said, I am exceedingly sorry that I cannot fulfil that for which my lord hath sent me.

Veronica said to him, When my Lord went about preaching, and I was very unwillingly deprived of his presence, I desired to have his picture painted for me, that while I was deprived of his presence, at least the figure of his likeness might give me consolation. And when I was taking the canvas to the painter to be painted, my Lord met me and asked whither I was going. And when I had made known to him the cause of my journey, He asked me for the canvas, and gave it back to me printed with the likeness of his venerable face. Therefore, if thy lord will devoutly look upon the sight of this, he will straightway enjoy the benefit of health.

Is a likeness of this kind to be procured with gold or silver? he asked. No, said she, but with a pious sentiment of devotion. Therefore, I will go with thee, and carry the likeness to Cæsar to look upon, and will return.

So Volusianus came with Veronica to Rome, and said to Tiberius the emperor, Jesus, whom thou hast long desired, Pilate and the Jews have surrendered to an unjust death, and through envy fastened to the wood of the cross. Therefore, a certain matron hath come with me bringing the likeness of the same Jesus, and if thou wilt devoutly gaze upon it, thou wilt presently obtain the benefit of thy health. So Cæsar caused the way to be spread with cloths of silk, and ordered the portrait to be presented to him; and as soon as he had looked upon it he regained his original health.

Then Pontius Pilate was apprehended by command of Cæsar and brought to Rome. Cæsar, hearing that Pilate had come to Rome, was filled with exceeding wrath against him, and caused him to be brought to him. Now Pilate brought with him the seamless coat of Jesus, and wore it when before the emperor. As soon as the emperor saw him he laid aside all his wrath, and forthwith rose to him, and was unable to speak harshly to him in anything: and he who in his absence seemed so terrible and fierce now in his presence is found comparatively gentle.

And when he had dismissed him, he soon became terribly inflamed against him, declaring himself wretched, because he had not expressed to him the anger of his bosom. And immediately he had him recalled, swearing and protesting that he was a child of death, and unfitted to live upon earth. And when he saw him he instantly greeted him, and laid aside all the fury of his mind.

All were astonished, and he was astonished himself, that he was so enraged against Pilate while absent, and could say nothing to him sharply while he was present. At length, by Divine suggestion, or perhaps by the persuasion of some Christian, he had him stripped of the coat, and soon resumed against him his original fury of mind. And when the emperor was wondering very much about this, they told him it had been the coat of the Lord Jesus. Then the emperor commanded him to be kept in prison till he should take counsel with the wise men what ought to be done with him. And after a few days sentence was given against Pilate that he should be condemned to the most ignominious death. When Pilate heard this he slew himself with his own dagger, and by such a death put an end to his life.

When Pilate's death was made known Cæsar said, Truly he has died a most ignominious death, whose own hand has not spared him. He was therefore fastened to a great block of stone and sunk in the river Tiber. But wicked and unclean spirits, rejoicing in his wicked and unclean body, all moved about in the water, and caused in the air dreadful lightning and tempests, thunder and hail, so that all were seized with horrible fear. On which account the Romans dragged him out of the river Tiber, bore him away in derision to Vienne, and sunk him in the river Rhone. For Vienne means, as it were, Way of Gehenna, because it was then a place of cursing. And evil spirits were there and did the same things.

Those men, therefore, not enduring to be so harassed by demons, removed the vessel of cursing from them and sent it to be buried in the territory of Losania. But when they were troubled exceedingly by the aforesaid vexations, they put it away from them and sunk it in a certain pool surrounded by mountains, where even yet, according to the account of some, sundry diabolical contrivances are said to issue forth.

THE LOST GOSPEL ACCORDING TO PETER

[In the valley of the Upper Nile, on the right bank of the river, is the mysterious town of Akhmîm. It was called Panopolis in ancient times when it was the capital of the district. The remnants of monasteries and the ruins of temples mark the intellectual life of a former day.

In 1886, the French Achæological Mission excavating in the grave of a monk, came upon a parchment codex. Six years later a translation of this was published in the Memoirs of the French Archæological Mission at Cairo. Scholars realized for the first time that a striking discovery, possibly of overwhelming importance, had been made. A portion of *The Gospel According to Peter* appeared to have been restored to the Christian Community after having been lost for ages. But until now, this document has never been made available to the general public.

Centuries rolled over that remote tomb at Akhmîm, while nations rose and fell, wars blasted civilization, science metamorphosed the world, Shakespeares and Miltons wrote their names and passed on, the American nation was born and grew up —all the while the ink on the parchment in that Egyptian tomb was scarcely changing—and the beautiful words of this Scripture were preserving for us this version of the most tragic and momentous event in history. That briefly is the romance of *The Lost Gospel According to Peter.*

Such a gospel was referred to by Serapion, Bishop of Antioch, in 190 A.D.; Origen, historian, in 253 A.D.; Eusebius, Bishop of Cæsarea in 300 A.D.; Theodoret in 455 in his *Religious History* said that the Nazarenes used *The Gospel According to Peter;* and Justin Martyr includes the *Memoirs of Peter* in his "Apostolic Memoirs." Thus scholars have always recognized that such a document existed long ago, although its whereabouts and fate were a mystery until the discovery at Akhmîm.

While in general the story of the trial and crucifixion that is revealed here follows that of the canonical gospels, in detail it is very different. This account is freer from constraint; and with the events between the burial and resurrection of our Lord, it is much more ample and detailed than anything in the canonical tradition.

There are indeed twenty-nine variations of fact between this *Lost Gospel According to Peter* and the four canonical gospels. Some of the most important that the reader will note are as follows: 1. Herod was the one who gave the order for the execution. 2. Joseph was a friend of Pilate. 3. In the darkness many went about with lamps and fell down. (That is a startling glimpse of the confusion that seized the people.) 4. Our Lord's cry of "My power, my power." 5. The account of how the disciples had to hide because they were searched for as malefactors anxious to burn the temple. 6. The name of the centurion who kept watch at the tomb was Petronius.

It is also interesting to note the prominence assigned to Mary Magdalene; and how this account tends to lay more responsibility on Herod and the people, while relieving Pilate somewhat of his share in the action that was taken. Also, the Resurrection and Ascension are here recorded not as separate events but as occurring on the same day.

282

THE LOST GOSPEL ACCORDING TO PETER

There will be a great divergence of opinion as to the place of this document and its relation to the canonical scriptures. Its existence is here proclaimed, and beyond that every reader may form his own estimate of its value. The Rev. D. H. Stanton, D.D., in the *Journal of Theological Studies*, commenting on Justin Martyr's ancient testimony, and this present document, says: "The conclusion with which we are confronted is that *The Gospel of Peter* once held a place of honor, comparable to that assigned to the Four Gospels, perhaps even higher than some of them. . . ."]

BUT of the Jews none washed his hands, neither Herod nor any one of his judges. And when they had refused to wash them, Pilate rose up. And then Herod the king commandeth that the Lord be taken saying to them, What things soever I commanded you to do unto him, do.

2 And there was standing there Joseph the friend of Pilate and of the Lord; and, knowing that they were about to crucify him, he came to Pilate and asked the body of the Lord for burial. And Pilate sent to Herod and asked his body. And Herod said, Brother Pilate, even if no one has asked for him, we purposed to bury him, especially as the sabbath draweth on: for it is written in the law, that the sun set not upon one that hath been put to death.

3 And he delivered him to the people on the day before the unleavened bread, their feast. And they took the Lord and pushed him as they ran, and said, Let us drag away the Son of God, having obtained power over him. And they clothed him with purple, and set him on the seat of judgment, saying, Judge righteously, O king of Israel. And one of them brought a crown of thorns and put it on the head of the Lord. And others stood and spat in his eyes, and others smote his cheeks: others pricked him with a reed; and some scourged him, saying, With this honor let us honor the Son of God.

4 And they brought two malefactors, and they crucified the Lord between them. But he held his peace, as though having no pain. And when they had raised the cross, they wrote the title: This is the king of Israel. And having set his garments before him they parted them among them, and cast lots for them. And one of those malefactors reproached them, saying, We for the evils that we have done have suffered thus, but this man, who hath become the Saviour of men, what wrong hath he done to you? And they, being angered at him, commanded that his legs should not be broken, that he might die in torment.

5 And, it was noon, and darkness came over all Judæa: and they were troubled and distressed, lest the sun had set, whilst he was yet alive: [for] it is written for them, that the sun set not on him that hath been put to death. And one of them said, Give him to drink gall with vinegar. And they

283

mixed and gave him to drink, and fulfilled all things, and accomplished their sins against their own head. And many went about with lamps, supposing that it was night, and fell down. And the Lord cried out, saying, My power, my power, thou hast forsaken me. And when he had said it he was taken up. And in that hour the vail of the temple of Jerusalem was rent in twain.

6 And then they drew out the nails from the hands of the Lord, and laid him upon the earth, and the whole earth quaked, and great fear arose. Then the sun shone, and it was found the ninth hour: and the Jews rejoiced, and gave his body to Joseph that he might bury it, since he had seen what good things he had done. And he took the Lord, and washed him, and rolled him in a linen cloth, and brought him to his own tomb, which was called the Garden of Joseph.

7 Then the Jews and the elders and the priests, perceiving what evil they had done to themselves, began to lament and to say, Woe for our sins: the judgment hath drawn nigh, and the end of Jerusalem. And I with my companions was grieved; and being wounded in mind we hid ourselves: for we were being sought for by them as malefactors, and as wishing to set fire to the temple. And upon all these things we fasted and sat mourning and weeping night and day until the sabbath.

8 But the scribes and Pharisees and elders being gathered together one with another, when they heard that all the people murmured and beat their breasts saying, If by his death these most mighty signs have come to pass, see how righteous he is,—the elders were afraid and came to Pilate beseeching him and saying, Give us soldiers, that we may guard his sepulchre for three days, lest his disciples come and steal him away, and the people suppose that he is risen from the dead and do us evil. And Pilate gave them Petronius the centurion with soldiers to guard the tomb. And with them came elders and scribes to the sepulchre, and having rolled a great stone together with the centurion and the soldiers, they all together who were there set it at the door of the sepulchre; and they affixed seven seals, and they pitched a tent there and guarded it. And early in the morning as the sabbath was drawing on, there came a multitude from Jerusalem and the region round about, that they might see the sepulchre that was sealed.

9 And in the night in which the Lord's day was drawing on, as the soldiers kept guard two by two in a watch, there was a great voice in the heaven; and they saw the heavens opened, and two men descend from thence with great light and approach the tomb. And that stone which was put at the door rolled of itself and made way in part; and the tomb was opened, and both the young men entered in.

10 When therefore those

soldiers saw it, they awakened the centurion and the elders; for they too were hard by keeping guard. And as they declared what things they had seen, again they see three men come forth from the tomb, and two of them supporting one, and a cross following them: and of the two the head reached unto the heaven, but the head of him who was lead by them overpassed the heavens. And they heard a v o i c e f r o m the heavens, saying, Thou hast preached to them that sleep. And a response was heard from the cross, Yea.

11 They therefore considered one with another whether to go away and shew these things to Pilate. And while they yet thought thereon, the heavens again are seen to open, and a certain man to descend and enter into the sepulchre. When the centurion and they that were with him saw these things, they hastened in the night to Pilate, leaving the tomb which they were watching, and declared all things which they had seen, being greatly distressed and saying, Truly he was the Son of God. Pilate answered and said, I am pure from the blood of the Son of God: but it was ye who determined this. Then they all drew near and besought him and entreated him to command the centurion and the soldiers to say nothing of the things which they had seen: For it is better, say they, for us to be guilty of the greatest sin before God, and not to fall into the hands of the people of the Jews and to be stoned. Pilate therefore commanded the centurion and the soldiers to say nothing.

12 And at dawn upon the Lord's day Mary Magdalene, a disciple of the Lord, fearing because of the Jews, since they were burning with wrath, had not done at the Lord's sepulchre the things which women are wont to do for those that die and for those that are beloved by them—she took her friends with her and came to the sepulchre where he was laid. And they feared lest the Jews should see them, and they said, Although on that day on which he was crucified we could not weep and lament, yet now let us do these things at his sepulchre. But who shall roll away for us the stone that was laid at the door of the sepulchre, that we may enter in and sit by him and do the things that are due? For the stone was great, and we fear lest some one see us. And if we cannot, yet if we but set at the door the things which we bring as a memorial of him, we will weep and lament, until we come unto our home.

13 And t h e y w e n t and found the tomb opened, and coming near they looked in there; and they see there a certain young man sitting in the midst of the tomb, beautiful and clothed in a robe exceeding bright; who said to them, Wherefore are ye come? Whom seek ye? Him that was crucified? He is risen and gone. But if ye believe not, look in and see the place

285

where he lay, that he is not [here]; for he is risen and gone thither, whence he was sent. Then the women feared and fled.

14 Now it was the last day of the unleavened bread, and many were going forth, returning to their homes, as the feast was ended. But we, the twelve disciples of the Lord, wept and were grieved: and each one, being grieved for that which was come to pass, departed to his home. But I Simon Peter and Andrew my brother took our nets and went to the sea; and there was with us Levi the son of Alphæus, whom the Lord . . .

TABLE I.

— · —

A LIST of all the Apocryphal Pieces not now extant, mentioned by Writers in the first four Centuries of Christ, with the several Works wherein they are cited or noticed.

———

A

1. THE ACTS OF ANDREW. *Euseb. Hist. Eccl. l.* 3 *c.* 25. *Philastr. Hæres.* 87. *Epiphan. Hæres.* 47 § 1. *Hæres.* 61 § *l. et Hæres.* 63. § 2. *Gelas. in Decret. apud. Concil. Sanct.* tom. 4. p. 1260.

2. Books under the name of ANDREW. *August. contr. Adversar. Leg. et Prophet. l. c.* 20. *et Innocent I. Epis.* 3. *ad Exuper. Tholos. Episc.* § 7.

3. The Gospel of ANDREW. *Gelas. in Decret.*

A Gospel under the name of APELLES. *Hieron. Præfat. in Comment. in Matt.*

The Gospel according to the Twelve APOSTLES. *Origen. Homil. in Luc.* i. 1. *Ambros. Comment. in Luc.* i. 1. *et Hieron. Præfat. in Comment. in Matt.*

B

The Gospel of BARNABAS. *Gelas. in Decret.*

1. The Writings of BARTHOLOMEW the Apostle. *Dionys. Areopagit. de Theol. Myst. c.* 1.

2. The Gospel of BARTHOLOMEW. *Hieron. Catul. Script. Eccles. in Pantœn. et Præfat. in Comm. in Matt. Gelas in Decret.*

The Gospel of BASILIDES. *Orig. in Luc.* i. 1. *Ambros. in Luc.* i. 1. *Hieron. Præfat. in Comm. in Matt.*

C

1. The Gospel of CERINTHUS. *Epiphan. Hæres.* 51. § 7.

2. The Revelation of CERINTHUS. *Caias Presb. Rom. lib. Disput. apud. Euseb. Hist. Eccl.* l. 3. c. 28.

1. An Epistle of CHRIST to Peter and Paul. *August. de Consens. Evang.* l. 1. c. 9, 19.

2. Some other Books under the name of CHRIST. *Ibid.* c. 3.

3. An Epistle of CHRIST, produced by the Manichees. *August. contr. Faust,* 1. 28. c. 4

4. A Hymn, which CHRIST taught his disciples. *Epis. ad Ceret. Episc.*

E

The Gospel according to the EGYPTIANS. *Clem. Alex. Strom.* 1. 3. p. 452, 465. *Origen. in Luc. il l. Hieron. Prœf. in Comm. in Matt. Epiphan. Hœres.* 62 § 2.

The Acts of the APOSTLES, made use of by the EBIONITES. *Epiphan. Hœres.* 30. § 16.

The Gospel of the EBIONITES. *Epiphan. Hœres.* 30. § 13.

The Gospel of the ENCRATITES. *Epiphan. Hœres.* 46. 1.

The Gospel of EVE. *Epiphan. Hœres.* 26. § 2.

H

The Gospel according to the HEBREWS. *Hegesipp. lib. Comment. apud Euseb. Hist. Eccl.* 1. c. 22. *Clem. Alex. Strom.* 1. 2. p. 380. *Origen. Tract.* 8. *in Matt.* xix. 19. *et* 1. 2, *Joan.* p. 58. *Euseb. Hist. Eccl.* 1. 3. c. 25, 27, *et* 39. Jerome in many places, as above.

The Book of the HELKESAITES. *Euseb. Hist. Eccl.* 1. 6. c. 38.

The false Gospels of HESYCHIUS. *Hieron. Prœfat. in Evang. ad Damas. Gelas. in Decret.*

J

The Book of JAMES. *Origen. Comm. in Matt.* xiii. 55, 56.

Books forged and published under the name of JAMES. *Epiphan. Hœres.* 30. § 23. *Innocent I. Epist.* 3. *ad Exuper. Tholos. Episc.* § 7.

1. The Acts of JOHN. *Euseb. Hist. Eccl.* 1. 3. c. 25. *Athanas. in Synops.* § 76. *Philastr. Hœres.* 87. *Epiphan. Hœres.* 47. § 1. *August. contr. Advers. Leg.* 1. 1. c. 20.

2. Books under the name of JOHN. *Epiphan. Hœres.* 30. § 23. *et Innocent I. ibid.*

A Gospel under the name of JUDE. *Epiphan. Hœres.* 38. § 1.

A Gospel under the name of JUDAS ISCARIOT. *Iren. advers. Hœres.* 1. 1. c. 35.

The Acts of the Apostles by LEUCIUS. *August. lib. de Fide contr. Manich.* c. 38.

The Acts of the Apostles by LENTITUS. *August. de Act. cum Fœlic. Manich.* 1. 2. c. 6.

The Books of LENTITIUS. *Gelas. in Decret.*

The Acts under the Apostles' name by LEONTIUS. *August. de Fide. contr. Manich.* c. 5.

The Acts of the Apostles by LEUTHON. *Hieron. Epist. ad Chromat. et Heliodor.*

The false Gospels, published by LUCIANUS. *Hieron. Prœfat. in Evang. ad Damas.*

M

The Acts of the Apostles used by the MANICHEES. *August. lib. cont. Adimant Manich.* c. 17.

The Gospel of MARCION. *Tertull. adv. Marcion.* lib. 4. c. 2. *et* 4. *Epiphan. Hœres.* 42. *Prœm.*
Books under the name of MATTHEW. *Epiphan. Hœres.* 30. § 23.
  1. The Gospel of MATTHIAS. *Orig. Comm. in Luc.* i. 1. *Euseb. Hist. Eccl.* l. 3. c. 25. *Ambros. in Luc.* i. 1. *Hieron. Prœfat. in Comment in Matt.*
  2. The Traditions of MATTHIAS. *Clem. Alex. Strom.* 1. 2. p. 380. l. 3. p. 436. *et* l. 7. p. 748.
  3. A Book under the name of MATTHIAS. *Innocent I. ibid.*
The Gospel of MERINTHUS. *Epiphan. Hœres.* 51. § 7.

N

The Gospel according to the NAZARENES. See above concerning the Gospel according to the Hebrews.

P

  1 The Acts. of PAUL and THECLA. *Tertull. de Baptism.* c. 17. *Hieron. Catal. Script. Eccl. in Luc. Gelas. in Decret.*
  2. The Acts of PAUL. *Orig. de Princip.* l. 1. c. 2. *et* l. 21. *in Joan.* tom. 2. p. 298. *Euseb. Hist. Eccl.* l. 3. c. 3. *et* 25. *Philastr. Hœres.* 87.
  3. The Preaching of PAUL (and PETER). *Lactant. de Ver. Sap.* l. 4. c. 21. *Script. anonym. ad calcem Opp. Cypr.*, and, according to some, *Clem. Alex. Strom.* l. 6. p. 636.
  4. A Book under the name of PAUL. *Cyprian. Epist.* 27.
  5. The Revelation of Paul. *Epiphan. Hœres.* 38. § 2. *August. Tract.* 98. *in Joann. in fin. Gelas. in Decret.*
The Gospel of PERFECTION. *Epiphan. Hœres.* 26. § 2.
  1. The Acts of PETER. *Euseb. Hist. Eccl.* 1. 3. c. 3. *Athanas. in Synops. S. Scriptur.* § 75. *Philastr Hœres.* 27. *Hieron. catal. Script. Eccl. in Petr. Epiphan. Hœres.* 30. § 15.
  2. The Doctrine of PETER. *Orig. Prœm. in lib. de Princip.*
  3. The Gospel of PETER. *Scrip. lib. de Evang. Petri.*, apud. *Euseb. Hist. Eccl.* l. 6. c. 13. *Tertull. adv. Marc.* l. 4. c. 5. *Orig. Comment. in Matt.* xiii. 55, 56, tom. i. p. 223. *Euseb. Hist. Eccl.* 1. 3. c. 3. *et* 25. *Hieron. Catal. Script. Eccles. in Petr.*
The Judgment of PETER. *Ruffin. Exposit. in Symbol. Apostol.* § 36. *Hieron. Catal. Script. Eccles. in Petr.*
  5. The Preaching of PETER. *Heracl. apud. Orig.* l. 14. *in Joan. Clem. Alex. Strom.* l. 1. p. 357. l. 2. p. 390. l. 6. p. 635, 636, *et* 678. *Theodot. Byzant. in Excerpt.* p. 899. *ad calc. Opp. Clem. Alex. Lactant. de Ver. Sap.* l. 4, c. 21. *Euseb. Hist. Eccles.* l. 3. c. 3. *et Hieron. Catal. Script. Eccl. in Petr.*
  6. The Revelation of PETER. *Clem. Alex. lib. Hypotypos. apud. Euseb. Hist. Eccl.* l. 6. c. 14. *Theodot. Byzant. in Excerpt.* p. 806, 807. *ad. calc. Opp. Clem. Alex. Euseb. Hist. Eccl.* l. 3. c. 3. *et* 25. *Hieron. Catal. Script. Eccl. in Petr.*
  7. Books under the name of PETER. *Innocent. I. Epist.* 3. *ad Exuper. Tholos. Epist.* §. 7.
  1. The Acts of PHILIP. *Gelas. in Decret.*
  2. The Gospel of PHILIP. *Epiphan. Hœres.* 26. § 13.

S

The Gospel of SCYTHIANUS. *Cyrill. Catech.* VI. § 22. *et Epiphan. Hæres.* 66. § 2.

The Acts of the Apostles by SELEUCUS. *Hieron. Epist. ad Chromat. et Heliodor.*

The Revelation of STEPHEN. *Gelas. in Decret.*

T

The Gospel of TITAN. *Euseb. Hist. Eccl.* l. 4. c. 29.

The Gospel of THADDÆUS. *Galas. in Decret.*

The Catholic Epistle of THEMISON the Montanist. *Apollon. lib. cont. Cataphryg. apud. Euseb. Hist. Eccl.* l. 5. c. 18.

1. The Acts of THOMAS. *Epiphan. Hæres.* 47. § 1. *et* 61. § 1 *Athanas. in Synops. S. Script.* §. 76. *et Gelas. in Decret.*

2. The Gospel of THOMAS. *Orig. in Luc.* i. 1. *Euseb. Hist. Eccl.* l. 3. c. 25. *Cyrill. Catech.* IV. § 36. *et Catech.* VI. § 31. *Ambros. in Luc.* i. 1. *Athan. in Synops. S. Script.* § 76. *Hieron. Præf. in Comment. in Matth. Gelas. in Decret.*

4. Books under the name of THOMAS. *Innocent I. Epist.* 3. *ad Exuper. Tholos. Episc.* § 7.

The Gospel of TRUTH made use of by the Valentinians. *Iren. adv. Hæres.* l. 3. c. 11.

V

The Gospel of VALENTINUS. *Tertull. de Præscript. adv. Hæret.* c. 49.

TABLE II.

*A LIST of the Christian Authors of the first four Centuries, whose
Writings contain Catalogues of the Books of the New Testament.*

*** Those which also have Catalogues of the Books of the Old Testament
are marked thus*.

The Names of the Writers.	The times in which they lived.	The variation or Agreement of their Catalogues with ours now received.	The Places of their Writings, in which these Catalogues are.
I. ** ORIGEN, a Presbyter of Alexandria, who employed incredible pains in knowing the Scriptures.*	*A. C.* 210.	Omits the Epistles of James and Jude, though he owns them both in other parts of his writings.	*Comment in Matt. apud Euseb. Hist. Eccl. l. 6. c. 25. Exposit. in Joan. l. 5, apud Euseb. ibid.*
II. Eusebius Pamphilus, whose writings evidence his zeal about the sacred writings, and his great care to be informed which were genuine and which not.	315.	His Catalogue is exactly the same with the modern one; only he says, the Epistles of James, Jude, the 2nd of Peter, the 2nd and 3rd of John, though they were generally received, yet had been by some doubted of. As to the Revelation, though he says some rejected it, yet he says others received it; and himself places it among those which are to be received without dispute.	*Hist. Eccl. l. 3, c. 55, confer ejusdem lib. b 3.*

The Names of the Writers.	The times in which they lived.	The variation or Agreement of their Catalogues with ours now received.	The Places of their Writings, in which these Catalogues are.
III. *ATHANASIUS, Bp. of Alexandria.	*A. C.* 315.	The same perfectly with ours now received.	*Fragment. Epist. Festal. et in Synops. Scriptur. Sacr.*
IV. * CYRIL, Bp. of Jerusalem.	340.	The same with ours, only the Revelation is omitted.	*Catech.* IV. § 36.
V. * The Bishops assembled in the Council of Laodicea.	364. †	The Revelation is omitted.	*Canon.* LX. N.B.—The Canons of this Council were not long afterwards received into the body of the Canons of the universal Church
VI. EPIPHANIUS, Bp. of Salamis in Cyprus.	370.	The same with ours now received.	*Hæres.* 76, *c.* 5.
VII. GREGORY NAZIANZEN, Bp. of Constantinople.	375.	Omits the Revelation.	*Carm. de veris et genuin. Scriptur.*
VIII. PHILASTRIUS, Bp. of Brixia in Venice.	380.	The same with ours now received; except that he mentions only thirteen of St. Paul's Epistles (omitting very probably the Epistle to the Hebrews), and leaves out the Revelation.	*Lib. de Hæres.* 87.

† The Papists generally place this Council before the Council of Nice.

The Names of the Writers.	The times in which they lived.	The variation or Agreement of their Catalogues with ours now received.	The Places of their Writings, in which these Catalogues are.
	A. C.		
IX. *Jerome.	382.	The same with ours, except that he speaks dubiously of the Epist. to the Hebrews; though in other parts of his writings he receives it as Canonical, as hereafter will appear.	*Ep. ad. Paulin. de Stud. Scrip.* Also commonly prefixed to the *Latin Vulgate.*
X. *Ruffin, Presbyter of Aquilegium.	390.	It perfectly agrees with ours.	*Expos. in Symb. Apostol.* § 36. *int. Op. Hieror. et inter Op. Cypr.*
XI. *Austin, Bp. of Hippo in Africa	394.	It perfectly agrees with ours.	*De. Doct. Christ. l. 2, c. 8.*
XII. * The forty-four Bps. assembled in the third Council of Carthage.	St. Austin was present at it.	It perfectly agrees with ours.	*Vid. Canon.* XLVII. *et cap. ult.*
XIII. The anonymous author of the works under the name of Dionysius the Areopagite.	390.	It seems perfectly to agree with ours; for though he doth not, for good reasons, produce the names of the books; yet (as the learned Daille says, *De Script. supposit. Doings.* l. 1. c. 16,) he so clearly describes them as that he has left out no divine book, may be easily perceived.	*Lib. de Hierarch. Eccl. c. 3.*

THE END.

THE FALL OF THE CHILDREN OF SETH

PAUL LAUNE

(See page 76)

THE FORGOTTEN
BOOKS OF EDEN

WRITINGS GIVING MANKIND'S EARLY PICTURES OF THE PAST AND
HOPES FOR THE FUTURE THAT HAVE SURVIVED THE DEVASTATION
OF THE CENTURIES.   TRANSLATED FROM MANUSCRIPTS OF THE
PSEUDEPIGRAPHAL   GROUP   AND   THIS   COLLECTION   PUBLISHED
NOW FOR THE FIRST TIME FOR THE INFORMATION AND ENJOY-
MENT OF THE LAYMAN, WITH NOTES SUGGESTING THE HUMAN
INTEREST INHERENT IN THESE PAGES OF FUNDAMENTAL WISDOM
AND BEAUTY

EDITED BY

RUTHERFORD H. PLATT, Jr.

ASSISTANT EDITOR

J. ALDEN BRETT

ILLUSTRATIONS BY

PAUL LAUNE

INTRODUCTION TO
THE FORGOTTEN BOOKS OF EDEN

By WILLIAM N. GUTHRIE, D.D.
Rector of St. Mark's-in-the-Bouwerie.

A N American Indian's Song is his very own. No other man can sing it without his explicit permission. It is impregnate with his aura. It is not in our sense, however, property. It is believed to invest magically the singer with the mood whence it proceeded, and must, therefore, merge in some way the performer's identity with that of the originator's. To sing another's song is an invasion of his personality, a sort of spiritual piracy involving sacrilege.

When last year in Aroady and Andritzena, I induced primitive shepherds to sing and play for me lustily all sorts of occasional songs and rituals, they refused to do a burial chant, most positively. For to perform one would surely cause a death in the house.

A little reflection on these two paragraphs may perhaps, make the reader realize that authorship was once a thing of great hazards. If one had something great and new to say, and wanted it to circulate widely, one would naturally prefer anonymity.

Indeed, by the Hebrews a story was popularly presumed to have its hero for its author. Moses wrote the account of his own death. Deuteronomy was of course, his own work, although obviously intended to alter the traditional religion. Jonah wrote the little novel about himself. David was the author of the Psalms because reported to have instituted the first temple choir, and as a lad to have played the harp soothing the nerves of King Saul. When an author for the book of Job was wanted, though the whole discussion of the work proves it was written to refute the Wisdom literature which by tradition began with the Proverbs of Solomon, Moses was chosen as a suitable author!

So for centuries among the Jews, writers sought to shelter themselves behind the names of the great dead. In this they were guilty of no fraud. They imagined what Solomon or Enoch would say, or sing, upon a particular theme under given circumstances. It was not really they themselves, but their Solomon, their Enoch, Solomon or Enoch in them, who uttered the new prophesies or temple praises.

Thus arose that body of literature, called by modern scholars, "Pseudepigrapha," that is, writings erroneously, unhistorically, and yet sincerely, ascribed to heroic figures summed from the vasty deep by a self-denying imagination, eager to alter man's belief and custom, to interpret his hope and sorrow, without personal gain or fame, and also, may one add, without the deterrent of persecution to arrest free utterance!

Now it is a foolish modern prejudice against an ancient piece of literature that its author veiled his person in this fashion. The only question is: Was the writing of inherent value? Did it exercise influence?

It is not too much to say that no modern can intelligently understand the New Testament, unless he is acquainted with the so-called "Apocrypha," and with the "Pseudepigrapha" as well. The very words of Jesus were in many instances, suggested by sayings current in his day, more or less as unconscious quotations from the Testaments of the 12 Patriarchs.

The figure of the Messiah which Jesus adapted to his creative purpose, cannot be imagined by a modern without a perusal of the book of Enoch which is its classic and most entrancing glorification. Without the Odes and Songs of Solomon the atmosphere breathed by the earliest church cannot be divined.

Hitherto access to this literature has been confined to technical scholars. Its assembly would require special information and considerable expenditure. With this enterprise of the Alpha House, Inc., it becomes democratic property. We shall have a more intelligent clergy and laity, when this volume has taken its place in every library, and is familiarly brought into every discussion of the historic Christ and of His times.

THE

ORDER OF ALL THE BOOKS

OF

THE FORGOTTEN BOOKS OF EDEN

PREFACE

TODAY the medley of outward life has made a perplexity of inward life. We moderns have ruffled our old incertitudes to an absurd point—incertitudes that are older than theology.

Not without justification have priests mounted altars for generations and cried, "Oh my soul, why dost thou trouble me?"

We are active, restless both in body and mind. Curiosity has replaced blind faith. We go groping, peering, searching, scornful of dogmas, back, further back to sources. And just as the physicist thrills at the universes he discovers as he works inward in the quest of his electrons, so the average man exults in his apprehension of fundamentals of psychology. New cults spring up, attesting to the Truth—as *they* see it—countless fleets of Theism, Buchmanism, Theosophy, Bahai'ism, etc., sail under brightly colored flags; and Atheism is flaunting itself on the horizon.

Almost the passengers have turned pilots. Everyman is thinking for himself.

The findings here—in this strange volume—bring the reader into a large inland sea, cut off from the traffic and the tempest that have sprung up in the West; and untouched by the crosscurrents of dogmas and presumptions that have cluttered historic centuries. Here is virgin water that gushes, troubled by abysmal forces only, out of the very earth itself.

Whence are these writings—these emotions—these profound pages of wisdom? You might as well inquire, whence is human nature? The fact is—they *are*. It isn't as though you can compare this literature with any other, as you might compare the French Romanticists with the Russian school. If you do so, this man may say it is too fantastic; that man, it is too coarse; the other man, it is too "out of date"! And they straightway lose all sight of the fact that it is simply fundamental.

To be sure scholars will argue, and inquire. They would

find the exact history; the shape of this or that Greek stem; they would set the opinion of this erudite authority against the opinion of that. It is right that they, as scholars, should do so. It is right that the average man who is not a scholar should also do so—if he wants to; and should not have to do so, if he does not want to.

It is, however, only just to pay a tribute to .scholarship which has preceded and made possible this book. The publishers are indispensably indebted to *The Apocrypha and Pseudepigrapha* edited by R. H. Charles, D. Litt., D. D.; *The Odes and Psalms of Solomon* by Dr. Rendel Harris; *The Book of Adam and Eve* by the Rev. S. C. Malan, D. D., published in England in 1882.

* * * *

It is appropriate to leave this book in your hands with the invocation of San Peladan, which Conrad has translated for us. San Pelandan believed in astrology, spirits of the air, elves, nymphs and everything that is deliciously fantastic. However, he did say:

"O Nature, indulgent Mother, forgive! Open your arms to the son, prodigal and weary.

"I have attempted to tear asunder the veil you have hung to conceal from us the pain of life, and I have been wounded by the mystery. . . . Œdipus, half way to finding the word of the enigma, young Faust, regretting already the simple life, the life of the heart, I come back to you repentant, reconciled, O gentle deceiver!"

* * * *

Adam and Eve; Solomon; Pharaoh; Aristeas; Ahikar; and the Twelve Intellectual Giants—we come back to you.

R. H. P. Jr.

New York, August 1, 1927.

THE FIRST BOOK OF
Adam and Eve

ALSO CALLED

The Conflict of Adam and Eve with Satan.

PRESENT day controversy that rages around the authenticity of the Scriptures and how human life began on this planet must pause to consider the Adam and Eve story. Where does it come from? What does it mean?

The familiar version in Genesis is not the source of this fundamental legend, It is not a spontaneous, Heaven-born account that sprang into place in the Old Testament. It is simply a version, unexcelled perhaps, but a version of a myth or belief or account handed down by word of mouth from generation to generation of mankind—through the incoherent, unrecorded ages of man it came —like an inextinguishable ray of light that ties the time when human life began, with the time when the human mind could express itself and the human hand could write.

This is the most ancient story in the world—it has survived because it embodies the basic fact of human life. A fact that has not changed one iota; amid all the superficial changes of civilization's vivid array, this fact remains: the conflict of Good and Evil; the fight between Man and the Devil; the eternal struggle of human nature against sin.

That the Adam and Eve story pervaded the thoughts of ancient writers is seen in the large number of versions that exist, or whose existence may be traced, through the writings of Greeks, Syrians, Egyptians, Abyssinians, Hebrews, and other ancient peoples. As a lawyer might say who examines so much apparently unrelated evidence—there must be *something* back of it.

The version which we give here is the work of unknown Egyptians (the lack of historical allusion makes it impossible to date the writing). Parts of this version are found in the Talmud, the Koran, and elsewhere, showing what a vital rôle it played in the original literature of human wisdom. The Egyptian author first wrote in Arabic (which may be taken as the original manuscript) and that found its way farther south and was translated into Ethiopic. For the present English translation we are indebted to Dr. S. C. Malan, Vicar of Broadwindsor, who worked from the Ethiopic edition edited by Dr. E. Trumpp, Professor at the University of Munich. Dr. Trumpp had the advantage of the Arabic original, which makes our bridge over the gap of many centuries a direct one.

The reading of these books is an adventure. You will find the mind of man fed by the passions, hopes, fears of new and strange

3

earthly existence rioting, unrestrained, in the zest of self-expression. You roam in the realms of mythology where swiftly the aspects of nature assume manifold personalities, and the amorphous instinct of sin takes on the grotesqueries of a visible devil.

From such imaginative surroundings you find yourself suddenly staring at commonplace unvarnished events of family life—and such a family as "the first earthly family" was! They had all the troubles, all the petty disagreements, and the taking sides with one another, and the bother moving, and "staying with the baby," that in the total mark family life to-day. You will see it when you peep beneath the overlaying glamour of tradition.

One critic has said of this writing:

> "This is we believe, the greatest literary discovery that the world has known. Its effect upon contemporary thought in molding the judgment of the future generations is of incalculable value.
>
> "The treasures of *Tut-ank-Amen's* Tomb were no more precious to the Egyptologist than are these literary treasures to the world of scholarship."

But we prefer to let the reader make his own exploration and form his own opinion. The writing is arresting enough to inspire very original thoughts concerning it.

In general, this account begins where the Genesis story of Adam and Eve leaves off. Thus the two can not well be compared; here we have a new chapter—a sort of sequel to the other. Here is the story of the twin sisters of Cain and Abel, and it is notable that here the blame for the first murder is placed squarely at the door of a difference over Woman.

The plan of these books is as follows:—

Book I. The careers of Adam and Eve, from the day they left Eden; their dwelling in the Cave of Treasures; their trials and temptations; Satan's manifold apparitions to them. The birth of Cain, of Abel, and of their twin sisters; Cain's love for his own twin sister, Luluwa, whom Adam and Eve wished to join to Abel; the details of Cain's murder of his brother; and Adam's sorrow and death.

Book II. The history of the patriarchs who lived before the Flood; the dwelling of the children of Seth on the Holy Mountain —Mount Hermon—until they were lured by Henun and by the daughters of Cain, to come down from the mountain. Cain's death, when slain by Lamech the blind; and the lives of other patriarchs until the birth of Noah.

BOOK I.

CHAP. I.

The crystal sea. God commands Adam, expelled from Eden, to dwell in the Cave of Treasures.

ON the third day, God planted the garden in the east of the earth, on the border of the world eastward, beyond which, towards the sun-rising, one finds nothing but water, that encompasses the whole world, and reaches unto the borders of heaven.

2 And to the north of the garden there is a sea of water, clear and pure to the taste, like unto nothing else; so that, through the clearness thereof, one may

look into the depths of the earth.

3 And when a man washes himself in it, becomes clean of the cleanness thereof, and white of its whiteness—even if he were dark.

4 And God created that sea of His own good pleasure, for He knew what would come of the man He should make; so that after he had left the garden, on account of his transgression, men should be born in the earth, from among whom righteous ones should die, whose souls God would raise at the last day; when they should return to their flesh; should bathe in the water of that sea, and all of them repent of their sins

5 But when God made Adam go out of the garden, He did not place him on the border of it northward, lest he should draw near to the sea of water, and he and Eve wash themselves in it, be cleansed from their sins, forget the transgression they had committed, and be no longer reminded of it in the thought of their punishment.

6 Then, again, as to the southern side of the garden, God was not pleased to let Adam dwell there; because, when the wind blew from the north, it would bring him, on that southern side, the delicious smell of the trees of the garden.

7 Wherefore God did not put Adam there, lest he should smell the sweet smell of those trees forget his transgression, and find consolation for what he had done, take delight in the smell of the trees, and not be cleansed from his transgression.

8 Again, also, because God is merciful and of great pity, and governs all things in a way He alone knows—He made our father Adam dwell in the western border of the garden, because on that side the earth is very broad.

9 And God commanded him to dwell there in a cave in a rock—the Cave of Treasures below the garden.

CHAP. II.

Adam and Eve faint upon leaving the Garden. God sends His word to encourage them.

BUT when our father Adam, and Eve, went out of the garden, they trod the ground on their feet, not knowing they were treading.

2 And when they came to the opening of the gate of the garden, and saw the broad earth spread before them, covered with stones large and small, and with sand, they feared and trembled, and fell on their faces, from the fear that came upon them; and they were as dead.

3 Because—whereas they had hitherto been in the garden-land, beautifully planted with all manner of trees—they now saw themselves, in a strange land, which they knew not, and had never seen.

4 And because at that time they were filled with the grace of a bright nature, and they had not hearts turned towards earthly things.

5 Therefore had God pity on them; and when He saw them fallen before the gate of the garden, He sent His Word unto father Adam and Eve, and raised them from their fallen state.

CHAP. III.

Concerning the promise of the great five days and a half.

GOD said to Adam, "I have ordained on this earth days and years, and thou and thy seed shall dwell and walk in it, until the days and years are fulfilled; when I shall send the

Word that created thee, and against which thou hast transgressed, the Word that made thee come out of the garden, and that raised thee when thou wast fallen.

2 Yea, the Word that will again save thee when the five days and a half are fulfilled."

3 But when Adam heard these words from God, and of the great five days and a half, he did not understand the meaning of them.

4 For Adam was thinking that there would be but five days and a half a day, to the end of the world.

5 And Adam wept, and prayed God to explain it to him.

6 Then God in His mercy for Adam who was made after His own image and similitude, explained to him, that these were 5,000 and 500 years; and how One would then come and save him and his seed.

7 But God had before that made this covenant with our father, Adam, in the same terms, ere he came out of the garden, when he was by the tree whereof Eve took the fruit and gave it him to eat.

8 Inasmuch as, when our father Adam came out of the garden, he passed by that tree, and saw how God had then changed the appearance of it into another form, and how it withered.

9 And as Adam went to it he feared, trembled and fell down; but God in His mercy lifted him up, and then made this covenant with him.

10 And, again, when Adam was by the gate of the garden, and saw the cherub with a sword of flashing fire in his hand, and the cherub grew angry and frowned at him, both Adam and Eve became afraid of him, and thought he meant to put them to death. So they fell on their faces, and trembled with fear.

11 But he had pity on them, and showed them mercy; and turning from them went up to heaven, and prayed unto the Lord, and said:—

12 "Lord, Thou didst send me to watch at the gate of the garden, with a sword of fire.

13 "But when Thy servants, Adam and Eve, saw me, they fell on their faces, and were as dead. O my Lord, what shall we do to Thy servants?"

14 Then God had pity on them, and showed them mercy, and sent His Angel to keep the garden.

15 And the Word of the Lord came unto Adam and Eve, and raised them up.

16 And the Lord said to Adam, "I told thee that at the end of five days and a half, I will send my Word and save thee.

17 "Strengthen thy heart, therefore, and abide in the Cave of Treasures, of which I have before spoken to thee."

18 And when Adam heard this Word from God, he was comforted with that which God had told him. For He had told him how He would save him.

CHAP. IV.

Adam laments the changed conditions. Adam and Eve enter the Cave of Treasures.

BUT Adam and Eve wept for having come out of the garden, their first abode.

2 And, indeed, when Adam looked at his flesh, that was altered, he wept bitterly, he and Eve, over what they had done. And they walked and went gently down into the Cave of Treasures.

3 And as they came to it Adam wept over himself and said to Eve, "Look at this cave that is to be our prison in this world, and a place of punishment!

4 "What is it compared with the garden? What is its narrowness compared with the space of the other?

5 "What is this rock, by the side of those groves? What is the gloom of this cavern, compared with the light of the garden?

6 "What is this overhanging ledge of rock to shelter us, compared with the mercy of the Lord that overshadowed us?

7 "What is the soil of this cave compared with the gardenland? This earth, strewed with stones; and that, planted with delicious fruit-trees?"

8 And Adam said to Eve, "Look at thine eyes, and at mine, which afore beheld angels in heaven, praising; and they, too, without ceasing.

9 "But now we do not see as we did: our eyes have become of flesh; they cannot see in like manner as they saw before."

10 Adam said again to Eve, "What is our body to-day, compared to what it was in former days, when we dwelt in the garden?"

11 After this Adam did not like to enter the cave, under the overhanging rock; nor would he ever have entered it.

12 But he bowed to God's orders; and said to himself, "Unless I enter the cave, I shall again be a transgressor."

CHAP. V.

In which Eve makes a noble and emotionable intercession, taking the blame on herself.

THEN Adam and Eve entered the cave, and stood praying, in their own tongue, unknown to us, but which they knew well.

2 And as they prayed, Adam raised his eyes, and saw the rock and the roof of the cave that covered him overhead, so that he could see neither heaven, nor God's creatures. So he wept and smote heavily upon his breast, until he dropped, and was as dead.

3 And Eve sat weeping; for she believed he was dead.

4 Then she arose, spread her hands towards God, suing Him for mercy and pity, and said, "O God, forgive me my sin, the sin which I committed, and remember it not against me.

5 "For I alone caused Thy servant to fall from the garden into this lost estate; from light into this darkness; and from the abode of joy into this prison.

6 "O God, look upon this Thy servant thus fallen, and raise him from his death, that he may weep and repent of his transgression which he committed through me.

7 "Take not away his soul this once; but let him live that he may stand after the measure of his repentance, and do Thy will, as before his death.

8 "But if Thou do not raise him up, then, O God, take away my own soul, that I be like him; and leave me not in this dungeon, one and alone; for I could not stand alone in this world, but with him only.

9 "For Thou, O God, didst cause a slumber to come upon him, and didst take a bone from his side, and didst restore the flesh in the place of it, by Thy divine power.

10 "And Thou didst take me, the bone, and make me a woman, bright like him, with heart, reason, and speech; and in flesh, like unto his own; and Thou didst make me after the likeness of his countenance, by Thy mercy and power.

11 "O Lord, I and he are one, and Thou, O God, art our Creator, Thou are He who made us both in one day.

12 "Therefore, O God, give

him life, that he may be with me in this strange land, while we dwell in it on account of our transgression.

13 "But if Thou wilt not give him life, then take me, even me, like him; that we both may die the same day."

14 And Eve wept bitterly, and fell upon our father Adam; from her great sorrow.

CHAP. VI.

God's admonition to Adam and Eve in which he points out how and why they sinned.

BUT God looked upon them; for they had killed themselves through great grief.

2 But He would raise them and comfort them.

3 He, therefore, sent His Word unto them; that they should stand and be raised forthwith.

4 And the Lord said unto Adam and Eve, "You transgressed of your own free will, until you came out of the garden in which I had placed you.

5 "Of your own free will have you transgressed through your desire for divinity, greatness, and an exalted state, such as I have; so that I deprived you of the bright nature in which you then were, and I made you come out of the garden to this land, rough and full of trouble.

6 "If only you had not transgressed My commandment and had kept My law, and had not eaten of the fruit of the tree, near which I told you not to come! And there were fruit trees in the garden better than that one.

7 "But the wicked Satan who continued not in his first estate, nor kept his faith; in whom was no good intent towards Me, and who though I had created him, yet set Me at naught, and sought the Godhead, so that I hurled him down from heaven,—he it is who made the tree appear pleasant in your eyes, until you ate of it, by hearkening to him.

8 "Thus have you transgressed My commandment, and therefore have I brought upon you all these sorrows.

9 "For I am God the Creator, who, when I created My creatures, did not intend to destroy them. But after they had sorely roused My anger, I punished them with grievous plagues, until they repent.

10 "But, if on the contrary, they still continue hardened in their transgression, they shall be under a curse for ever."

CHAP. VII.

The beasts are reconciled.

WHEN Adam and Eve heard these words from God, they wept and sobbed yet more; but they strengthened their hearts in God, because they now felt that the Lord was to them like a father and a mother; and for this very reason, they wept before Him, and sought mercy from Him.

2 Then God had pity on them, and said: "O Adam, I have made My covenant with thee, and I will not turn from it; neither will I let thee return to the garden, until My covenant of the great five days and a half is fulfilled."

3 Then Adam said unto God, "O Lord, Thou didst create us, and make us fit to be in the garden; and before I transgressed, Thou madest all beasts come to me, that I should name them.

4 "Thy grace was then on me; and I named every one according to Thy mind; and Thou madest them all subject unto me.

5 "But now, O Lord God, that I have transgressed Thy com-

mandment, all beasts will rise against me and will devour me, and Eve Thy handmaid; and will cut off our life from the face of the earth.

6 "I therefore beseech Thee, O God, that, since Thou hast made us come out of the garden, and hast made us be in a strange land, Thou wilt not let the beasts hurt us."

7 When the Lord heard these words from Adam, He had pity on him, and felt that he had truly said that the beasts of the field would rise and devour him and Eve, because He, the Lord, was angry with them two on account of their transgression.

8 Then God commanded the beasts, and the birds, and all that moves upon the earth, to come to Adam and to be familiar with him, and not to trouble him and Eve; nor yet any of the good and righteous among their posterity.

9 Then the beasts did obeisance to Adam, according to the commandment of God; except the serpent, against which God was wroth. It did not come to Adam, with the beasts.

CHAP. VIII.

The "Bright Nature" of man is taken away.

THEN Adam wept and said, "O God, when we dwelt in the garden, and our hearts were lifted up, we saw the angels that sang praises in heaven, but now we do not see as we were used to do; nay, when we entered the cave, all creation became hidden from us."

2 Then God the Lord said unto Adam, "When thou wast under subjection to Me, thou hadst a bright nature within thee, and for that reason couldst thou see things afar off. But after thy transgression thy bright nature was withdrawn from thee; and it was not left to thee to see things afar off, but only near at hand; after the ability of the flesh; for it is brutish."

3 When Adam and Eve had heard these words from God, they went their way; praising and worshipping Him with a sorrowful heart.

4 And God ceased to commune with them.

CHAP. IX.

Water from the Tree of Life. Adam and Eve near drowning.

THEN Adam and Eve came out of the Cave of Treasures, and drew near to the garden gate, and there they stood to look at it, and wept for having come away from it.

2 And Adam and Eve went from before the gate of the garden to the southern side of it, and found there the water that watered the garden, from the root of the Tree of Life, and that parted itself from thence into four rivers over the earth.

3 Then they came and drew near to that water, and looked at it; and saw that it was the water that came forth from under the root of the Tree of Life in the garden.

4 And Adam wept and wailed, and smote upon his breast, for being severed from the garden; and said to Eve:—

5 "Why hast thou brought upon me, upon thyself, and upon our seed, so many of these plagues and punishments?"

6 And Eve said unto him, "What is it thou hast seen, to weep and to speak to me in this wise?"

7 And he said to Eve, "Seest thou not this water that was with us in the garden, that watered the trees of the garden, and flowed out thence?

8 "And we, when we were in

the garden, did not care about it; but since we came to this strange land, we love it, and turn it to use for our body."

9 But when Eve heard these words from him, she wept; and from the soreness of their weeping, they fell into that water; and would have put an end to themselves in it, so as never again to return and behold the creation; for when they looked upon the work of creation, they felt they must put an end to themselves.

CHAP. X.

Their bodies need water after they leave the Garden.

THEN God, merciful and gracious, looked upon them thus lying in the water, and nigh unto death, and sent an angel, who brought them out of the water, and laid them on the seashore as dead.

2 Then the angel went up to God, was welcome, and said, "O God, Thy creatures have breathed their last."

3 Then God sent His Word unto Adam and Eve, who raised them from their death.

4 And Adam said, after he was raised, "O God, while we were in the garden we did not require, or care for this water; but since we came to this land we cannot do without it."

5 Then God said to Adam, "While thou wast under My command and wast a bright angel, thou knewest not this water.

6 "But after that thou hast transgressed My commandment, thou canst not do without water, wherein to wash thy body and make it grow; for it is now like that of beasts, and is in want of water."

7 When Adam and Eve heard these words from God, they wept a bitter cry; and Adam en-treated God to let him return into the garden, and look at it a second time.

8 But God said unto Adam, "I have made thee a promise; when that promise is fulfilled, I will bring thee back into the garden, thee and thy righteous seed."

9 And God ceased to commune with Adam.

CHAP. XI.

A recollection of the glorious days in the Garden.

THEN Adam and Eve felt themselves burning with thirst, and heat, and sorrow.

2 And Adam said to Eve, "We shall not drink of this water, even if we were to die. O Eve, when this water comes into our inner parts, it will increase our punishments and that of our children, that shall come after us."

3 Both Adam and Eve then withdrew from the water, and drank none of it at all; but came and entered the Cave of Treasures.

4 But when in it Adam could not see Eve; he only heard the noise she made. Neither could she see Adam, but heard the noise he made.

5 Then Adam wept, in deep affliction, and smote upon his breast; and he arose and said to Eve, "Where art thou?"

6 And she said unto him, "Lo, I am standing in this darkness."

7 He then said to her, "Remember the bright nature in which we lived, while we abode in the garden!

8 "O Eve! remember the glory that rested on us in the garden. O Eve! remember the trees that overshadowed us in the garden while we moved among them.

9 "O Eve! remember that while we were in the garden, we knew neither night nor day.

Think of the Tree of Life, from below which flowed the water, and that shed lustre over us! Remember, O Eve, the gardenland, and the brightness thereof!

10 "Think, oh think of that garden in which was no darkness, while we dwelt therein.

11 "Whereas no sooner did we come into this Cave of Treasures than darkness compassed us round about; until we can no longer see each other; and all the pleasure of this life has come to an end."

CHAP. XII.

How darkness came between Adam and Eve.

THEN Adam smote upon his breast, he and Eve, and they mourned the whole night until dawn drew near, and they sighed over the length of the night in Miyazia.

2 And Adam beat himself, and threw himself on the ground in the cave, from bitter grief, and because of the darkness, and lay there as dead.

3 But Eve heard the noise he made in falling upon the earth. And she felt about for him with her hands, and found him like a corpse.

4 Then she was afraid, speechless, and remained by him.

5 But the merciful Lord looked on the death of Adam, and on Eve's silence from fear of the darkness.

6 And the Word of God came unto Adam and raised him from his death, and opened Eve's mouth that she might speak.

7 Then Adam arose in the cave and said, "O God, wherefore has light departed from us, and darkness come over us? Wherefore dost Thou leave us in this long darkness? Why wilt Thou plague us thus?

8 "And this darkness, O Lord, where was it ere it came upon us? It is such, that we cannot see each other.

9 "For, so long as we were in the garden, we neither saw nor even knew what darkness is. I was not hidden from Eve, neither was she hidden from me, until now that she cannot see me; and no darkness came upon us, to separate us from each other.

10 "But she and I were both in one bright light. I saw her and she saw me. Yet now since we came into this cave, darkness has come upon us, and parted us asunder, so that I do not see her, and she does not see me.

11 "O Lord, wilt Thou then plague us with this darkness?"

CHAP. XI I.

The fall of Adam. Why night and day were created.

THEN when God, who is merciful and full of pity, heard Adam's voice, He said unto him:—

2 "O Adam, so long as the good angel was obedient to Me, a bright light rested on him and on his hosts.

3 "But when he transgressed My commandment, I deprived him of that bright nature, and he became dark.

4 "And when he was in the heavens, in the realms of light, he knew naught of darkness.

5 "But he transgressed, and I made him fall from heaven upon the earth; and it was this darkness that came upon him.

6 "And on thee, O Adam, while in My garden and obedient to Me, did that bright light rest also.

7 "But when I heard of thy transgression, I deprived thee of that bright light. Yet, of My mercy, I did not turn thee into darkness, but I made thee thy body of flesh, over which I spread this skin, in order that it may bear cold and heat.

8 "If I had let My wrath fall

heavily upon thee, I should have destroyed thee; and had I turned thee into darkness, it would have been as if I killed thee.

9 "But in My mercy, I have made thee as thou art; when thou didst transgress My commandment, O Adam, I drove thee from the garden, and made thee come forth into this land; and commanded thee to dwell in this cave; and darkness came upon thee, as it did upon him who transgressed My commandment.

10 "Thus, O Adam, has this night deceived thee. It is not to last for ever; but is only of twelve hours; when it is over, daylight will return.

11 "Sigh not, therefore, neither be moved; and say not in thy heart that this darkness is long and drags on wearily; and say not in thy heart that I plague thee with it.

12 "Strengthen thy heart, and be not afraid. This darkness is not a punishment. But, O Adam, I have made the day, and have placed the sun in it to give light; in order that thou and thy children should do your work.

13 "For I knew thou shouldest sin and transgress, and come out into this land. Yet would I not force thee, nor be heard upon thee, nor shut up; nor doom thee through thy fall; nor through thy coming out from light into darkness; nor yet through thy coming from the garden into this land.

14 "For I made thee of the light; and I willed to bring out children of light from thee and like unto thee.

15 "But thou didst not keep one day My commandment; until I had finished the creation and blessed everything in it.

16 "Then I commanded thee concerning the tree, that thou eat not thereof. Yet I knew

that Satan, who deceived himself, would also deceive thee.

17 "So I made known to thee by means of the tree, not to come near him. And I told thee not to eat of the fruit thereof, nor to taste of it, nor yet to sit under it, nor to yield to it.

18 "Had I not been and spoken to thee, O Adam, concerning the tree, and had I left thee without a commandment, and thou hadst sinned—it would have been an offence on My part, for not having given thee any order; thou wouldst turn round and blame Me for it.

19 "But I commanded thee, and warned thee, and thou didst fall. So that My creatures cannot blame me; but the blame rests on them alone.

20 "And, O Adam, I have made the day for thee and for thy children after thee, for them to work, and toil therein. And I have made the night for them to rest in it from their work; and for the beasts of the field to go forth by night and seek their food.

21 "But little of darkness now remains, O Adam; and daylight will soon appear."

CHAP. XIV.

The earliest prophecy of the coming of Christ.

THEN Adam said unto God: "O Lord, take Thou my soul, and let me not see this gloom any more; or remove me to some place where there is no darkness."

2 But God the Lord said to Adam, "Verily I say unto thee, this darkness will pass from thee, every day I have determined for thee, until the fulfilment of My covenant; when I will save thee and bring thee back again into the garden, into the abode of light thou longest for, wherein is no darkness. I will bring thee to it—in the kingdom of heaven."

3 Again said God unto Adam, "All this misery that thou hast been made to take upon thee because of thy transgression, will not free thee from the hand of Satan, and will not save thee.

4 "But I will. When I shall come down from heaven, and shall become flesh of thy seed, and take upon Me the infirmity from which thou sufferest, then the darkness that came upon thee in this cave shall come upon Me in the grave, when I am in the flesh of thy seed.

5 "And I, who am without years, shall be subject to the reckoning of years, of times, of months, and of days, and I shall be reckoned as one of the sons of men, in order to save thee."

6 And God ceased to commune with Adam.

CHAP. XV.

THEN Adam and Eve wept and sorrowed by reason of God's word to them, that they should not return to the garden until the fulfilment of the days decreed upon them; but mostly because God had told them that He should suffer for their salvation.

CHAP. XVI.

The first sunrise. Adam and Eve think it is a fire coming to burn them.

AFTER this Adam and Eve ceased not to stand in the cave, praying and weeping, until the morning dawned upon them.

2 And when they saw the light returned to them, they restrained from fear, and strengthened their hearts.

3 Then Adam began to come out of the cave. And when he came to the mouth of it, and stood and turned his face towards the east, and saw the sun rise in glowing rays, and felt the heat thereof on his body, he was afraid of it, and thought in his heart that this flame came forth to plague him.

4 He wept then, and smote upon his breast, and fell upon the earth on his face, and made his request, saying:—

5 "O Lord, plague me not, neither consume me, nor yet take away my life from the earth."

6 For he thought the sun was God.

7 Inasmuch as while he was in the garden and heard the voice of God and the sound He made in the garden, and feared Him, Adam never saw the brilliant light of the sun, neither did the flaming heat thereof touch his body.

8 Therefore was he afraid of the sun when flaming rays of it reached him. He thought God meant to plague him therewith all the days He had decreed for him.

9 For Adam also said in his thoughts, as God did not plague us with darkness, behold, He has caused this sun to rise and to plague us with burning heat.

10 But while he was thus thinking in his heart, the Word of God came unto him and said:—

11 "O Adam, arise and stand up. This sun is not God; but it has been created to give light by day, of which I spake unto thee in the cave saying, 'that the dawn would break forth, and there would be light by day.'

12 "But I am God who comforted thee in the night."

13 And God ceased to commune with Adam.

CHAP. XVII.

The Chapter of the Serpent.

THEN Adam and Eve came out at the mouth of the cave, and went towards the garden.

2 But as they drew near to it, before the western gate, from which Satan came when he deceived Adam and Eve, they found the serpent that became Satan coming at the gate, and sorrowfully licking the dust, and wriggling on its breast on the ground, by reason of the curse that fell upon it from God.

3 And whereas aforetime the serpent was the most exalted of all beasts, now it was changed and become slippery, and the meanest of them all, and it crept on its breast and went on its belly.

4 And whereas it was the fairest of all beasts, it had been changed, and was become the ugliest of them all. Instead of feeding on the best food, now it turned to eat the dust. Instead of dwelling, as before, in the best places, now it lived in the dust.

5 And, whereas it had been the most beautiful of all beasts, all of which stood dumb at its beauty, it was now abhorred of them.

6 And, again, whereas it dwelt in one beautiful abode, to which all other animals came from elsewhere; and where it drank, they drank also of the same; now, after it had become venomous, by reason of God's curse, all beasts fled from its abode, and would not drink of the water it drank; but fled from it.

CHAP. XVIII.

The mortal combat with the serpent.

WHEN the accursed serpent saw Adam and Eve, it swelled its head, stood on its tail, and with eyes blood-red, did as if it would kill them.

2 It made straight for Eve, and ran after her; while Adam standing by, wept because he had no stick in his hand where-with to smite the serpent, and knew not how to put it to death.

3 But with a heart burning for Eve, Adam approached the serpent, and held it by the tail; when it turned towards him and said unto him:—

4 "O Adam, because of thee and of Eve, I am slippery, and go upon my belly." Then by reason of its great strength, it threw down Adam and Eve and pressed upon them, as if it would kill them.

5 But God sent an angel who threw the serpent away from them, and raised them up.

6 Then the Word of God came to the serpent, and said unto it, "In the first instance I made thee glib, and made thee to go upon thy belly; but I did not deprive thee of speech.

7 "Now, however, be thou dumb; and speak no more, thou and thy race; because in the first place, has the ruin of my creatures happened through thee, and now thou wishest to kill them."

8 Then the serpent was struck dumb, and spake no more.

9 And a wind came to blow from heaven by command of God that carried away the serpent from Adam and Eve, threw it on the sea shore, and it landed in India.

CHAP. XIX.

Beasts made subject to Adam.

BUT Adam and Eve wept before God. And Adam said unto Him:—

2 "O Lord, when I was in the cave, I said this to Thee, my Lord, that the beasts of the field would rise and devour me, and cut off my life from the earth."

3 Then Adam, by reason of what had befallen him, smote upon his breast, and fell upon the earth like a corpse; then came to him the Word of God,

who raised him, and said unto him,

4 "O Adam, not one of these beasts will be able to hurt thee; because when I made the beasts and other moving things come to thee in the cave, I did not let the serpent come with them, lest it should rise against you, make you tremble; and the fear of it should fall into your hearts.

5 "For I knew that that accursed one is wicked; therefore would I not let it come near you with the other beasts.

6 "But now strengthen thy heart and fear not. I am with thee unto the end of the days I have determined on thee."

CHAP. XX.

Adam wishes to protect Eve.

THEN Adam wept and said, "O God, remove us to some other place, that the serpent may not come again near us, and rise against us. Lest it find Thy handmaid Eve alone and kill her; for its eyes are hideous and evil."

2 But God said to Adam and Eve, "Henceforth fear not, I will not let it come near you; I have driven it away from you, from this mountain; neither will I leave in it aught to hurt you."

3 Then Adam and Eve worshipped before God and gave Him thanks, and praised Him for having delivered them from death.

CHAP. XXI.

Adam and Eve attempt suicide.

THEN Adam and Eve went in search of the garden.

2 And the heat beat like a flame on their faces; and they sweated from the heat, and wept before the Lord.

3 But the place where they wept was nigh unto a high mountain, facing the western gate of the garden.

4 Then Adam threw himself down from the top of that mountain; his face was torn and his flesh was flayed; much blood flowed from him, and he was nigh unto death.

5 Meanwhile Eve remained standing on the mountain weeping over him, thus lying.

6 And she said, "I wish not to live after him; for all that he did to himself was through me."

7 Then she threw herself after him; and was torn and scotched by stones; and remained lying as dead.

8 But the merciful God, who looks upon His creatures, looked upon Adam and Eve as they lay dead, and He sent His Word unto them, and raised them.

9 And said to Adam, "O Adam, all this misery which thou hast wrought upon thyself, will not avail against My rule, neither will it alter the covenant of the 5500 years."

CHAP. XXII.

Adam in a chivalrous mood.

THEN Adam said to God, "I wither in the heat; I am faint from walking, and am loth of this world. And I know not when Thou wilt bring me out of it, to rest."

2 Then the Lord God said unto him, "O Adam, it cannot be at present, not until thou hast ended thy days. Then shall I bring thee out of this wretched land."

3 And Adam said to God, "While I was in the garden I knew neither heat, nor languor, neither moving about, nor trembling, nor fear; but now since I came to this land, all this affliction has come upon me."

4 Then God said to Adam,

"So long as thou wast keeping My commandment, My light and My grace rested on thee. But when thou didst transgress My commandment, sorrow and misery befell thee in this land."

5 And Adam wept and said, "O Lord, do not cut me off for this, neither smite me with heavy plagues, nor yet repay me according to my sin; For we, of our own will, did transgress Thy commandment, and forsook Thy law, and sought to become gods like unto Thee, when Satan the enemy deceived us."

6 Then God said again unto Adam, "Because thou hast borne fear and trembling in this land, languor and suffering treading and walking about, going upon this mountain, and dying from it, I will take all this upon Myself in order to save thee."

CHAP. XXIII.

Adam and Eve gird themselves and make the first altar ever built.

THEN Adam wept more and said, "O God, have mercy on me, so far as to take upon Thee, that which I will do."

2 But God took His Word from Adam and Eve.

3 Then Adam and Eve stood on their feet; and Adam said to Eve, "Gird thyself, and I also will gird myself." And she girded herself, as Adam told her.

4 Then Adam and Eve took stones and placed them in the shape of an altar; and they took leaves from the trees outside the garden, with which they wiped, from the face of the rock, the blood they had spilled.

5 But that which had dropped on the sand, they took together with the dust wherewith it was mingled and offered it upon the altar as an offering unto God.

6 Then Adam and Eve stood under the altar and wept, thus entreating God, "Forgive us our trespass* and our sin, and look upon us with Thine eye of mercy. For when we were in the garden our praises and our hymns went up before Thee without ceasing.

7 "But when we came into this strange land, pure praise was no longer ours, nor righteous prayer, nor understanding hearts, nor sweet thoughts, nor just counsels, nor long discernment, nor upright feelings, neither is our bright nature left us. But our body is changed from the similitude in which it was at first, when we were created.

8 "Yet now look upon our blood which is offered upon these stones, and accept it at our hands, like the praise we used to sing unto Thee at first, when in the garden."

9 And Adam began to make more requests unto God.

*ORIGINAL OF THE LORD'S PRAYER SAID TO BE USED ABOUT 150 YEARS BEFORE OUR LORD: Our Father, Who art in Heaven, be gracious unto us, O Lord our God, hallowed be Thy Name, and let the remembrance of Thee be glorified in Heaven above and upon earth here below.
Let Thy kingdom reign over us now and forever. The Holy Men of old said remit and forgive unto all men whatsoever they have done unto me. And lead us not into temptation, but deliver us from the evil thing; for Thine is the kingdom and Thou shalt reign in glory forever and forevermore, AMEN.

CHAP. XXIV.

A vivid prophecy of the life and death of Christ.

THEN the merciful God, good and lover of men, looked upon Adam and Eve, and upon their blood, which they had held up as an offering unto Him; without an order from Him for so doing. But He wondered at them; and accepted their offerings.

2 And God sent from His presence a bright fire, that consumed their offering.

3 He smelt the sweet savour of their offering, and showed them mercy.

4 Then came the Word of God to Adam, and said unto him, "O Adam, as thou hast shed thy blood, so will I shed My own blood when I become flesh of thy seed; and as thou didst die, O Adam, so also will I die. And as thou didst build an altar, so also will I make for thee an altar on the earth; and as thou didst offer thy blood upon it, so also will I offer My blood upon an altar on the earth.

5 "And as thou didst sue for forgiveness through that blood, so also will I make My blood forgiveness of sins, and blot out transgressions in it.

6 "And now, behold, I have accepted thy offering, O Adam, but the days of the covenant, wherein I have bound thee, are not fulfilled. When they are fulfilled, then will I bring thee back into the garden.

7 "Now, therefore, strengthen thy heart; and when sorrow comes upon thee, make Me an offering, and I will be favourable to thee."

CHAP. XXV.

God represented as merciful and loving. The establishing of worship.

BUT God knew that Adam had in his thoughts, that he should often kill himself and make an offering to Him of his blood.

2 Therefore did He say unto him, "O Adam, do not again kill thyself as thou didst, by throwing thyself down from that mountain."

3 But Adam said unto God, "It was in my mind to put an end to myself at once, for having transgressed Thy commandments, and for my having come out of the beautiful garden; and for the bright light of which Thou hast deprived me; and for the praises which poured forth from my mouth without ceasing, and for the light that covered me.

4 "Yet of Thy goodness, O God, do not away with me altogether; but be favourable to me every time I die, and bring me to life.

5 "And thereby it will be made known that Thou art a merciful God, who willest not that one should perish; who lovest not that one should fall; and who dost not condemn any one cruelly, badly, and by whole destruction."

6 Then Adam remained silent.

7 And the Word of God came unto him, and blessed him, and comforted him, and covenanted with him, that He would save him at the end of the days determined upon him.

8 This, then, was the first offering Adam made unto God; and so it became his custom to do.

CHAP. XXVI.

A beautiful prophecy of eternal life and joy (v. 15). The fall of night.

THEN Adam took Eve, and they began to return to the Cave of Treasures where they dwelt. But when they neared it and saw it from afar, heavy sorrow fell upon Adam and Eve when they looked at it.

2 Then Adam said to Eve, "When we were on the mountain we were comforted by the Word of God that conversed with us; and the light that came from the east, shone over us.

3 "But now the Word of God is hidden from us; and the light that shone over us is so changed as to disappear, and let darkness and sorrow come upon us.

4 "And we are forced to enter this cave which is like a prison, wherein darkness covers us, so that we are parted from each other; and thou canst not see me, neither can I see thee."

5 When Adam had said these words, they wept and spread their hands before God; for they were full of sorrow.

6 And they entreated God to bring the sun to them, to shine on them, so that darkness return not upon them, and they come not again under this covering of rock. And they wished to die rather than see the darkness.

7 Then God looked upon Adam and Eve and upon their great sorrow, and upon all they had done with a fervent heart, on account of all the trouble they were in, instead of their former well-being, and on account of all the misery that came upon them in a strange land.

8 Therefore God was not wroth with them; nor impatient with them; but He was long-suffering and forbearing towards them, as towards the children He had created.

9 Then came the Word of God to Adam, and said unto him, "Adam, as for the sun, if I were to take it and bring it to thee, days, hours, years and months would all come to naught, and the covenant I have made with thee, would never be fulfilled.

10 "But thou shouldest then be turned and left in a long plague, and no salvation would be left to thee for ever.

11 "Yea, rather, bear long and calm thy soul while thou abidest night and day; until the fulfilment of the days, and the time of My covenant is come.

12 "Then shall I come and save thee, O Adam, for I do not wish that thou be afflicted.

13 "And when I look at all the good things in which thou didst live, and why thou camest out of them, then would I willingly show thee mercy.

14 "But I cannot alter the covenant that has gone out of My mouth; else would I have brought thee back into the garden.

15 "When, however, the covenant is fulfilled, then shall I show thee and thy seed mercy, and bring thee into a land of gladness, where there is neither sorrow nor suffering; but abiding joy and gladness, and light that never fails, and praises that never cease; and a beautiful garden that shall never pass away."

16 And God said again unto Adam, "Be long-suffering and enter the cave, for the darkness, of which thou wast afraid, shall only be twelve hours long; and when ended, light shall arise."

17 Then when Adam heard these words from God, he and Eve worshipped before Him, and their hearts were comforted. They returned into the cave after their custom, while tears flowed from their eyes, sorrow and wailing came from their hearts, and they wished their soul would leave their body.

18 And Adam and Eve stood praying, until the darkness of night came upon them, and Adam was hid from Eve, and she from him.

19 And they remained standing in prayer.

CHAP. XXVII.

The second tempting of Adam and Eve. The devil takes on the form of a beguiling light.

WHEN Satan, the hater of all good, saw how they continued in prayer, and how God communed with them, and comforted them, and how He had accepted their offering—Satan made an apparition.

2 He began with transforming his hosts; in his hands was a flashing fire, and they were in a great light.

3 He then placed his throne near the mouth of the cave because he could not enter into it by reason of their prayers. And he shed light into the cave, until the cave glistened over Adam and Eve; while his hosts began to sing praises.

4 And Satan did this, in order that when Adam saw the light, he should think within himself that it was a heavenly light, and that Satan's hosts were angels; and that God had sent them to watch at the cave, and to give him light in the darkness.

5 So that when Adam came out of the cave and saw them, and Adam and Eve bowed to Satan, then he would overcome Adam thereby, and a second time humble him before God.

6 When, therefore, Adam and Eve saw the light, fancying it was real, they strengthened their hearts; yet, as they were trembling, Adam said to Eve:—

7 "Look at that great light, and at those many songs of praise, and at that host standing outside that do not come in to us, do not tell us what they say, or whence they come, or what is the meaning of this light; what those praises are; wherefore they have been sent hither, and why they do not come in.

8 "If they were from God, they would come to us in the cave, and would tell us their errand."

9 Then Adam stood up and prayed unto God with a fervent heart, and said:—

10 "O Lord, is there in the world another god than Thou, who created angels and filled them with light, and sent them to keep us, who would come with them?

11 "But, lo, we see these hosts that stand at the mouth of the cave; they are in a great light; they sing loud praises. If they are of some other god than Thou, tell me; and if they are sent by Thee, inform me of the reason for which Thou hast sent them."

12 No sooner had Adam said this, than an angel from God appeared unto him in the cave, who said unto him, "O Adam, fear not. This is Satan and his hosts; he wishes to deceive you as he deceived you at first. For the first time, he was hidden in the serpent; but this time he is come to you in the similitude of an angel of light; in order that, when you worshipped him, he might enthrall you, in the very presence of God."

13 Then the angel went from Adam, and seized Satan at the opening of the cave, and stripped him of the feint he had assumed, and brought him in his own hideous form to Adam and Eve; who were afraid of him when they saw him.

14 And the angel said to Adam, "This hideous form has been his ever since God made him fall from heaven. He could not have come near you in it; therefore did he transform himself into an angel of light."

15 Then the angel drove away Satan and his hosts from Adam and Eve, and said unto them, "Fear not; God who created you, will strengthen you."

16 And the angel went from them.

17 But Adam and Eve re-

mained standing in the cave; no consolation came to them; they were divided in their thoughts.

18 And when it was morning they prayed; and then went out to seek the garden. For their hearts were towards it, and they could get no consolation for having left it.

CHAP. XXVIII.

The Devil pretends to lead Adam and Eve to the water to bathe.

BUT when the wily Satan saw them, that they were going to the garden, he gathered together his host, and came in appearance upon a cloud, intent on deceiving them.

2 But when Adam and Eve saw him thus in a vision, they thought they were angels of God come to comfort them about their having left the garden, or to bring them back again into it.

3 And Adam spread his hands unto God, beseeching Him to make him understand what they were.

4 Then Satan, the hater of all good, said unto Adam, "O Adam, I am an angel of the great God; and, behold the hosts that surround me.

5 "God has sent me and them to take thee and bring thee to the border of the garden northwards; to the shore of the clear sea, and bathe thee and Eve in it, and raise you to your former gladness, that ye return again to the garden."

6 These words sank into the heart of Adam and Eve.

7 Yet God withheld His Word from Adam, and did not make him understand at once, but waited to see his strength; whether he would be overcome as Eve was when in the garden, or whether he would prevail.

8 Then Satan called to Adam and Eve, and said, "Behold, we go to the sea of water," and they began to go.

9 And Adam and Eve followed them at some little distance.

10 But when they came to the mountain to the north of the garden, a very high mountain, without any steps to the top of it, the Devil drew near to Adam and Eve, and made them go up to the top in reality, and not in a vision; wishing, as he did, to throw them down and kill them, and to wipe off their name from the earth; so that this earth should remain to him and his hosts alone.

CHAP. XXIX.

God tells Adam of the Devil's purpose. (v. 4).

BUT when the merciful God saw that Satan wished to kill Adam with his manifold devices, and saw that Adam was meek and without guile, God spake unto Satan in a loud voice, and cursed him.

2 Then he and his hosts fled, and Adam and Eve remained standing on the top of the mountain, whence they saw below them the wide world, high above which they were. But they saw none of the host which anon were by them.

3 They wept, both Adam and Eve, before God, and begged for forgiveness of Him.

4 Then came the Word from God to Adam, and said unto him, "Know thou and understand concerning this Satan, that he seeks to deceive thee and thy seed after thee."

5 And Adam wept before the Lord God, and begged and entreated Him to give him something from the garden, as a token to him, wherein to be comforted.

6 And God looked upon Adam's thought, and sent the angel Michael as far as the sea that reaches unto India, to take

from thence golden rods and bring them to Adam.

7 This did God in His wisdom, in order that these golden rods, being with Adam in the cave, should shine forth with light in the night around him, and put an end to his fear of the darkness.

8 Then the angel Michael went down by God's order, took golden rods, as God had commanded him, and brought them to God.

CHAP. XXX.

Adam receives the first worldly goods.

AFTER these things, God commanded the angel Gabriel to go down to the garden, and say to the cherub who kept it, "Behold, God has commanded me to come into the garden, and to take thence sweet smelling incense, and give it to Adam."

2 Then the angel Gabriel went down by God's order to the garden, and told the cherub as God had commanded him.

3 The cherub then said, "Well." And Gabriel went in and took the incense.

4 Then God commanded His angel Raphael to go down to the garden, and speak to the cherub about some myrrh, to give to Adam.

5 And the angel Raphael went down and told the cherub as God had commanded him, and the cherub said, "Well." Then Raphael went in and took the myrrh.

6 The golden rods were from the Indian sea, where there are precious stones. The incense was from the eastern border of the garden; and the myrrh from the western border, whence bitterness came upon Adam.

7 And the angels brought these three things to God, by the Tree of Life, in the garden.

8 Then God said to the angels,

"Dip them in the spring of water; then take them and sprinkle their water over Adam and Eve, that they be a little comforted in their sorrow, and give them to Adam and Eve.

9 And the angels did as God had commanded them, and they gave all those things to Adam and Eve on the top of the mountain upon which Satan had placed them, when he sought to make an end of them.

10 And when Adam saw the golden rods, the incense and the myrrh, he was rejoiced and wept because he thought that the gold was a token of the kingdom whence he had come, that the incense was a token of the bright light which had been taken from him, and that the myrrh was a token of the sorrow in which he was.

CHAP. XXXI.

They make themselves more comfortable in the Cave of Treasures on the third day.

AFTER these things God said unto Adam, "Thou didst ask of Me something from the garden, to be comforted therewith, and I have given thee these three tokens as a consolation to thee; that thou trust in Me and in My covenant with thee.

2 "For I will come and save thee; and kings shall bring me when in the flesh, gold, incense and myrrh; gold as a token of My kingdom; incense as a token of My divinity; and myrrh as a token of My suffering and of My death.

3 "But, O Adam, put these by thee in the cave; the gold that it may shed light over thee by night; the incense, that thou smell its sweet savour; and the myrrh, to comfort thee in thy sorrow."

4 When Adam heard these words from God, he worshipped

before Him. He and Eve worshipped Him and gave Him thanks, because He had dealt mercifully with them.

5 Then God commanded the three angels, Michael, Gabriel and Raphael, each to bring what he had brought, and give it to Adam. And they did so, one by one.

6 And God commanded Suriyel and Salathiel to bear up Adam and Eve, and bring them down from the top of the high mountain, and to take them to the Cave of Treasures.

7 There they laid the gold on the south side of the cave, the incense on the eastern side, and the myrrh on the western side. For the mouth of the cave was on the north side.

8 The angels then comforted Adam and Eve, and departed.

9 The gold was seventy rods; the incense, twelve pounds; and the myrrh, three pounds.

10 These remained by Adam in the House of Treasures; therefore was it called "of concealment." But other interpreters say it was called the "Cave of Treasures," by reason of the bodies of righteous men that were in it.

11 These three things did God give to Adam, on the third day after he had come out of the garden, in token of the three days the Lord should remain in the heart of the earth.

12 And these three things, as they continued with Adam in the cave, gave him light by night; and by day they gave him a little relief from his sorrow.

CHAP. XXXII.

Adam and Eve go into the water to pray.

AND Adam and Eve remained in the Cave of Treasures until the seventh day; they neither ate of the fruit of the earth, nor drank water.

2 And when it dawned on the eighth day, Adam said to Eve, "O Eve, we prayed God to give us somewhat from the garden, and He sent His angels who brought us what we had desired.

3 "But now, arise, let us go to the sea of water we saw at first, and let us stand in it, praying that God will again be favourable to us and take us back to the garden; or give us something; or that He will give us comfort in some other land than this in which we are."

4 Then Adam and Eve came out of the cave, went and stood on the border of the sea in which they had before thrown themselves, and Adam said to Eve:—

5 "Come, go down into this place, and come not out of it until the end of thirty days, when I shall come to thee. And pray to God with fervent heart and a sweet voice, to forgive us.

6 "And I will go to another place, and go down into it, and do like thee."

7 Then Eve went down into the water, as Adam had commanded her. Adam also went down into the water; and they stood praying; and besought the Lord to forgive them their offence, and to restore them to their former state.

8 And they stood thus praying, unto the end of the five-and-thirty days.

CHAP. XXXIII.

Satan   falsely   promises   the "bright light."

BUT Satan, the hater of all good, sought them in the cave, but found them not, although he searched diligently for them.

2 But he found them standing in the water praying and thought within himself, "Adam and Eve are thus standing in that water beseeching God to forgive them their transgression,

and to restore them to their former estate, and to take them from under my hand.

3 "But I will deceive them so that they shall come out of the water, and not fulfil their vow."

4 Then the hater of all good, went not to Adam, but he went to Eve, and took the form of an angel of God, praising and rejoicing, and said to her:—

5 "Peace be unto thee! Be glad and rejoice! God is favourable unto you, and He sent me to Adam. I have brought him the glad tidings of salvation, and of his being filled with bright light as he was at first.

6 "And Adam, in his joy for his restoration, has sent me to thee, that thou come to me, in order that I crown thee with light like him.

7 "And he said to me, 'Speak unto Eve; if she does not come with thee, tell her of the sign when we were on the top of the mountain; how God sent His angels who took us and brought us to the Cave of Treasures; and laid the gold on the southern side; incense, on the eastern side; and myrrh on the western side.' Now come to him."

8 When Eve heard these words from him, she rejoiced greatly. And thinking that Satan's appearance was real, she came out of the sea.

9 He went before, and she followed him until they came to Adam. Then Satan hid himself from her, and she saw him no more.

10 She then came and stood before Adam, who was standing by the water and rejoicing in God's forgiveness.

11 And as she called to him, he turned round, found her there and wept when he saw her, and smote upon his breast; and from the bitterness of his grief, he sank into the water.

12 But God looked upon him and upon his misery, and upon his being about to breathe his last. And the Word of God came from heaven, raised him out of the water, and said unto him, "Go up the high bank to Eve." And when he came up to Eve he said unto her, "Who said to thee 'come hither'?"

13 Then she told him the discourse of the angel who had appeared unto her and had given her a sign.

14 But Adam grieved, and gave her to know it was Satan. He then took her and they both returned to the cave.

15 These things happened to them the second time they went down to the water, seven days after their coming out of the garden.

16 They fasted in the water thirty-five days; altogether forty-two days since they had left the garden.

CHAP. XXXIV.

Adam recalls the creation of Eve. He eloquently appeals for food and drink.

AND on the morning of the forty-third day, they came out of the cave, sorrowful and weeping. Their bodies were lean, and they were parched from hunger and thirst, from fasting and praying, and from their heavy sorrow on account of their transgression.

2 And when they had come out of the cave they went up the mountain to the west of the garden.

3 There they stood and prayed and besought God to grant them forgiveness of their sins.

4 And after their prayers Adam began to entreat God, saying, "O my Lord, my God, and my Creator, Thou didst command the four elements to be gathered together, and they were gathered together by Thine order.

5 "Then Thou spreadest Thy

hand and didst create me out of one element, that of dust of the earth; and Thou didst bring me into the garden at the third hour, on a Friday, and didst inform me of it in the cave.

6 "Then, at first, I knew neither night nor day, for I had a bright nature; neither did the light in which I lived ever leave me to know night or day.

7 "Then, again, O Lord, in that third hour in which Thou didst create me, Thou broughtest to me all beasts, and lions, and ostriches, and fowls of the air, and all things that move in the earth, which Thou hadst created at the first hour before me of the Friday.

8 "And Thy will was that I should name them all, one by one, with a suitable name. But Thou gavest me understanding and knowledge, and a pure heart and a right mind from Thee, that I should name them after Thine own mind regarding the naming of them.

9 "O God, Thou madest them obedient to me, and didst order that not one of them break from my sway, according to Thy commandment, and to the dominion which Thou hast given me over them. But now they are all estranged from me.

10 "Then it was in that third hour of Friday, in which Thou didst create me, and didst command me concerning the tree, to which I was neither to draw near, nor to eat thereof; for Thou saidst to me in the garden, 'When thou eatest of it, of death thou shalt die.'

11 "And if Thou hadst punished me as Thou saidst, with death, I should have died that very moment.

12 "Moreover, when Thou commandedst me regarding the tree, I was neither to approach nor to eat thereof, Eve was not with me; Thou hadst not yet created her, neither hadst Thou yet taken her out of my side; nor had she yet heard this order from Thee.

13 "Then, at the end of the third hour of that Friday, O Lord, Thou didst cause a slumber and a sleep to come over me, and I slept, and was overwhelmed in sleep.

14 "Then Thou didst draw a rib out of my side, and created it after my own similitude and image. Then I awoke; and when I saw her and knew who she was, I said, 'This is bone of my bones, and flesh of my flesh; henceforth she shall be called woman.'

15 "It was of Thy good will, O God, that Thou broughtest a slumber and a sleep over me, and that Thou didst forthwith bring Eve out of my side, until she was out, so that I did not see how she was made; neither could I witness, O my Lord, how awful and great are Thy goodness and glory.

16 "And of Thy goodwill, O Lord, Thou madest us both with bodies of a bright nature, and Thou madest us two, one; and Thou gavest us Thy grace, and didst fill us with praises of the Holy Spirit; that we should be neither hungry nor thirsty, nor know what sorrow is, nor yet faintness of heart; neither suffering, fasting, nor weariness.

17 "But now, O God, since we transgressed Thy commandment and broke Thy law, Thou hast brought us out into a strange land, and has caused suffering, and faintness, hunger and thirst to come upon us.

18 "Now, therefore, O God, we pray Thee, give us something to eat from the garden, to satisfy our hunger with it; and something wherewith to quench our thirst.

19 "For, behold, many days, O God, we have tasted nothing and drunk nothing, and our flesh is dried up, and our

strength is wasted, and sleep is gone from our eyes from faintness and weeping.

20 "Then, O God, we dare not gather aught of the fruit of trees, from fear of Thee. For when we transgressed at first Thou didst spare us, and didst not make us die.

21 "But now, we thought in our hearts, if we eat of the fruit of trees, without God's order, He will destroy us this time, and will wipe us off from the face of the earth.

22 "And if we drink of this water, without God's order, He will make an end of us, and root us up at once.

23 "Now, therefore, O God, that I am come to this place with Eve, we beg Thou wilt give us of the fruit of th garden, that we may be satisfied with it.

24 "For we desire the fruit that is on the earth, and all else that we lack in it."

CHAP. XXXV.

God's reply.

THEN God looked again upon Adam and his weeping and groaning, and the Word of God came to him, and said unto him:—

2 "O Adam, when thou wast in My garden, thou knewest neither eating nor drinking; neither faintness nor suffering; neither leanness of flesh, nor change; neither did sleep depart from thine eyes. But since thou transgressedst, and camest into this strange land, all these trials are come upon thee."

CHAP. XXXVI.

Figs.

THEN God commanded the cherub, who kept the gate of the garden with a sword of fire in his hand, to take some of the fruit of the fig-tree, and to give it to Adam.

2 The cherub obeyed the command of the Lord God, and went into the garden and brought two figs on two twigs, each fig hanging to its leaf; they were from two of the trees among which Adam and Eve hid themselves when God went to walk in the garden, and the Word of God came to Adam and Eve and said unto them, "Adam, Adam, where art thou?"

3 And Adam answered, "O God, here am I. When I heard the sound of Thee and Thy voice, I hid myself, because I am naked."

4 Then the cherub took two figs and brought them to Adam and Eve. But he threw them to them from afar; for they might not come near the cherub by reason of their flesh, that could not come near the fire.

5 At first, angels trembled at the presence of Adam and were afraid of him. But now Adam trembled before the angels and was afraid of them.

6 Then Adam drew near and took one fig, and Eve also came in turn and took the other.

7 And as they took them up in their hands, they looked at them, and knew they were from the trees among which they had hidden themselves.

CHAP. XXXVII.

Forty-three days of penance do not redeem one hour of sin (v. 6).

THEN Adam said to Eve, "Seest thou not these figs and their leaves, with which we covered ourselves when we were stripped of our bright nature? But now, we know not what misery and suffering may come upon us from eating them.

2 "Now, therefore, O Eve, let us restrain ourselves and not eat of them, thou and I; and let us ask God to give us of the fruit of the Tree of Life."

3 Thus did Adam and Eve restrain themselves, and did not eat of these figs.

4 But Adam began to pray to God and to beseech Him to give him of the fruit of the Tree of Life, saying thus: "O God, when we transgressed Thy commandment at the sixth hour of Friday, we were stripped of the bright nature we had, and did not continue in the garden after our transgression, more than three hours.

5 "But on the evening Thou madest us come out of it. O God, we transgressed against Thee one hour, and all these trials and sorrows have come upon us until this day.

6 "And those days together with this the forty-third day, do not redeem that one hour in which we transgressed!

7 "O God, look upon us with an eye of pity, and do not requite us according to our transgression of Thy commandment, in presence of Thee.

8 "O God, give us of the fruit of the Tree of Life, that we may eat of it, and live, and turn not to see sufferings and other trouble, in this earth; for Thou art God.

9 "When we transgressed Thy commandment, Thou madest us come out of the garden, and didst send a cherub to keep the Tree of Life, lest we should eat thereof, and live; and know nothing of faintness after we transgressed.

10 "But now, O Lord, behold, we have endured all these days, and have borne sufferings. Make these forty-three days an equivalent for the one hour in which we transgressed."

CHAP. XXXVIII.

"When 5500 years are fulfilled . . . ."

AFTER these things the Word of God came to Adam, and said unto him:—

2 "O Adam, as to the fruit of the Tree of Life, for which thou askest, I will not give it thee now, but when the 5500 years are fulfilled. Then will I give thee of the fruit of the Tree of Life, and thou shalt eat, and live for ever, thou, and Eve, and thy righteous seed.

3 "But these forty-three days cannot make amends for the hour in which thou didst transgress My commandment.

4 "O Adam, I gave thee to eat of the fig-tree in which thou didst hide thyself. Go and eat of it, thou and Eve.

5 "I will not deny thy request, neither will I disappoint thy hope; therefore, bear up unto the fulfilment of the covenant I made with thee."

6 And God withdrew His Word from Adam.

CHAP. XXXIX.

Adam is cautious—but too late.

THEN Adam returned to Eve, and said to her, "Arise, and take a fig for thyself, and I will take another; and let us go to our cave."

2 Then Adam and Eve took each a fig and went towards the cave; the time was about the setting of the sun; and their thoughts made them long to eat of the fruit.

3 But Adam said to Eve, "I am afraid to eat of this fig. I know not what may come upon me from it."

4 So Adam wept, and stood praying before God, saying, "Satisfy my hunger, without my having to eat this fig; for after I have eaten it, what will it profit me? And what shall I desire and ask of Thee, O God, when it is gone?"

5 And he said again, "I am afraid to eat of it; for I know not what will befall me through it."

CHAP. XL.

The first Human hunger.

THEN the Word of God came to Adam, and said unto him, "O Adam, why hadst thou not this dread, neither this fasting, nor this care ere this? And why hadst thou not this fear before thou didst transgress?

2 "But when thou camest to dwell in this strange land, thy animal body could not be on earth without earthly food, to strengthen it and to restore its powers."

3 And God withdrew His Word from Adam.

CHAP. XLI.

The first Human thirst.

THEN Adam took the fig, and laid it on the golden rods. Eve also took her fig, and put it upon the incense.

2 And the weight of each fig was that of a water-melon; for the fruit of the garden was much larger than the fruit of this land.

3 But Adam and Eve remained standing and fasting the whole of that night, until the morning dawned.

4 When the sun rose they were at their prayers, and Adam said to Eve, after they had done praying:—

5 "O Eve, come, let us go to the border of the garden looking south; to the place whence the river flows, and is parted into four heads. There we will pray to God, and ask Him to give us to drink of the Water of Life.

6 "For God has not fed us with the Tree of Life, in order that we may not live. We will, therefore, ask him to give us of the Water of Life, and to quench our thirst with it, rather than with a drink of water of this land."

7 When Eve heard these words from Adam, she agreed; and they both arose and came to the southern border of the garden, upon the brink of the river of water at some little distance from the garden.

8 And they stood and prayed before the Lord, and asked Him to look upon them this once, to forgive them, and to grant them their request.

9 After this prayer from both of them, Adam began to pray with his voice before God, and said:—

10 "O Lord, when I was in the garden and saw the water that flowed from under the Tree of Life, my heart did not desire, neither did my body require to drink of it; neither did I know thirst, for I was living; and above that which I am now.

11 "So that in order to live I did not require any Food of Life, neither did I drink of the Water of Life.

12 "But now, O God, I am dead; my flesh is parched with thirst. Give me of the Water of Life that I may drink of it and live.

13 "Of Thy mercy, O God, save me from these plagues and trials, and bring me into another land different from this, if Thou wilt not let me dwell in Thy garden."

CHAP. XLII.

A promise of the Water of Life. The third prophecy of the coming of Christ.

THEN came the Word of God to Adam, and said unto him:—

2 "O Adam, as to what thou sayest, 'Bring me into a land where there is rest,' it is not another land than this, but it is the kingdom of heaven where alone there is rest.

3 "But thou canst not make thy entrance into it at present; but only after thy judgment is past and fulfilled.

4 "Then will I make thee go up into the kingdom of heaven, thee and thy righteous seed; and I will give thee and them the rest thou askest for at present.

5 "And if thou saidst, 'Give me of the Water of Life that I may drink and live'—it cannot be this day, but on the day that I shall descend into hell, and break the gates of brass, and bruise in pieces the kingdoms of iron.

6 "Then will I in mercy save thy soul and the souls of the righteous, to give them rest in My garden. And that shall be when the end of the world is come.

7 "And, again, as regards the Water of Life thou seekest, it will not be granted thee this day; but on the day that I shall shed My blood upon thy head in the land of Golgotha.

8 "For My blood shall be the Water of Life unto thee, at that time, and not to thee alone, but unto all those of thy seed who shall believe in Me; that it be unto them for rest for ever."

9 The Lord said again unto Adam, "O Adam, when thou wast in the garden, these trials did not come to thee

10 "But since thou didst transgress My commandment, all these sufferings have come upon thee.

11 "Now, also, does thy flesh require food and drink; drink then of that water that flows by thee on the face of the earth."

12 Then God withdrew His Word from Adam.

13 And Adam and Eve worshipped the Lord, and returned from the river of water to the cave. It was noon-day; and when they drew near to the cave, they saw a large fire by it.

CHAP. XLIII.

The Devil attempts arson.

THEN Adam and Eve were afraid, and stood still. And Adam said to Eve, "What is that fire by our cave? We do nothing in it to bring about this fire.

2 "We neither have bread to bake therein, nor broth to cook there. As to this fire, we know not the like, neither do we know what to call it.

3 "But ever since God sent the cherub with a sword of fire that flashed and lightened in his hand, from fear of which we fell down and were like corpses, have we not seen the like.

4 "But now, O Eve, behold, this is the same fire that was in the cherub's hand, which God has sent to keep the cave in which we dwell.

5 "O Eve, it is because God is angry with us, and will drive us from it.

6 "O Eve, we have again transgressed His commandment in that cave, so that He had sent this fire to burn around it, and to prevent us from going into it.

7 "If this be really so, O Eve, where shall we dwell?, And whither shall we flee from before the face of the Lord? Since, as regards the garden, He will not let us abide in it, and He has deprived us of the good things thereof; but He has placed us in this cave, in which we have borne darkness, trials and hardships, until at last we found comfort therein.

8 "But now that He has brought us out into another land, who knows what may happen in it? And who knows but that the darkness of that land may be far greater than the darkness of this land?

9 "Who knows what may happen in that land by day or by night? And who knows whether

it will be far or near, O Eve? Where it will please God to put us, may be far from the garden, O Eve! or where God will prevent us from beholding Him, because we have transgressed His commandment, and because we have made requests unto Him at all times?

10 "O Eve, if God will bring us into a strange land other than this, in which we find consolation, it must be to put our souls to death, and blot out our name from the face of the earth.

11 "O Eve, if we are farther estranged from the garden and from God, where shall we find Him again, and ask Him to give us gold, incense, myrrh, and some fruit of the fig-tree?

12 "Where shall we find Him, to comfort us a second time? Where shall we find Him, that He may think of us, as regards the covenant He has made on our behalf?"

13 Then Adam said no more. And they kept looking, he and Eve, towards the cave, and at the fire that flared up around it.

14 But that fire was from Satan. For he had gathered trees and dry grasses, and had carried and brought them to the cave, and had set fire to them, in order to consume the cave and what was in it.

15 So that Adam and Eve should be left in sorrow, and he should cut off their trust in God, and make them deny Him.

16 But by the mercy of God he could not burn the cave, for God sent His angel round the cave to guard it from such a fire, until it went out.

17 And this fire lasted from noon-day until the break of day. That was the forty-fifth day.

CHAP. XLIV.

The power of fire over man.

YET Adam and Eve were standing and looking at the fire, and unable to come near the cave from their dread of the fire.

2 And Satan kept on bringing trees and throwing them into the fire, until the flame thereof rose up on high, and covered the whole cave, thinking, as he did in his own mind, to consume the cave with much fire. But the angel of the Lord was guarding it.

3 And yet he could not curse Satan, nor injure him by word, because he had no authority over him, neither did he take to doing so with words from his mouth.

4 Therefore did the angel bear with him, without saying one bad word, until the Word of God came who said to Satan, "Go hence; once before didst thou deceive My servants, and this time thou seekest to destroy them.

5 "Were it not for My mercy I would have destroyed thee and thy hosts from off the earth. But I have had patience with thee, unto the end of the world."

6 Then Satan fled from before the Lord. But the fire went on burning around the cave like a coal-fire the whole day; which was the forty-sixth day Adam and Eve had spent since they came out of the garden.

7 And when Adam and Eve saw that the heat of the fire had somewhat cooled down, they began to walk towards the cave to get into it as they were wont; but they could not, by reason of the heat of the fire.

8 Then they both took to weeping because of the fire that made separation between them and the cave, and that drew towards them, burning. And they were afraid.

9 Then Adam said to Eve, "See this fire of which we have a portion in us: which formerly yielded to us, but no longer does so, now that we have transgressed the limit of creation, and changed our condition, and

our nature is altered. But the fire is not changed in its nature, nor altered from its creation. Therefore has it now power over us; and when we come near it, it scorches our flesh."

CHAP. XLV.

Why Satan didn't fulfil his promises.

THEN Adam rose and prayed unto God, saying, "See, this fire has made separation between us and the cave in which Thou hast commanded us to dwell; but now, behold, we cannot go into it."

2 Then God heard Adam, and sent him His Word, that said:—

3 "O Adam, see this fire! how different the flame and heat thereof are from the garden of delights and the good things in it!

4 "When thou wast under My control, all creatures yielded to thee; but after thou hast transgressed My commandment, they all rise over thee."

5 Again said God unto him, "See, O Adam, how Satan has exalted thee! He has deprived thee of the Godhead, and of an exalted state like unto Me, and has not kept his word to thee; but, after all, is become thy foe. It is he who made this fire in which he meant to burn thee and Eve.

6 "Why, O Adam, has he not kept his agreement with thee, not even one day; but has deprived thee of the glory that was on thee—when thou didst yield to his command?

7 "Thinkest thou, Adam, that he loved thee when he made this agreement with thee? Or, that he loved thee and wished to raise thee on high?

8 "But no, Adam, he did not do all that out of love to thee; but he wished to make thee come out of light into darkness; and from an exalted state to degradation; from glory to abasement; from joy to sorrow; and from rest to fasting and fainting."

9 God said also to Adam, "See this fire kindled by Satan around thy cave; see this wonder that surrounds thee; and know that it will encompass about both thee and thy seed, when ye hearken to his behest; that he will plague you with fire; and that ye shall go down into hell after ye are dead.

10 "Then shall ye see the burning of his fire, that will thus be burning around you and your seed. There shall be no deliverance from it for you, but at My coming; in like manner as thou canst not now go into thy cave, by reason of the great fire around it; not until My Word shall come that will make a way for thee on the day My covenant is fulfilled.

11 "There is no way for thee at present to come from hence to rest, not until My Word comes, who is My Word. Then will He make a way for thee, and thou shalt have rest." Then God called with His Word to that fire that burned around the cave, that it part itself asunder, until Adam had gone through it. Then the fire parted itself by God's order, and a way was made for Adam.

12 And God withdrew His Word from Adam.

CHAP. XLVI.

"How many times have I delivered thee out of his hand . . ."

THEN Adam and Eve began again to come into the cave. And when they came to the way between the fire, Satan blew into the fire like a whirlwind, and made on Adam and Eve a burning coal-fire; so that their bodies were singed; and the coal-fire scorched them.

2 And from the burning of the fire Adam and Eve cried aloud, and said, "O Lord, save us! Leave us not to be consumed and plagued by this burning fire; neither require us for having transgressed Thy commandment."

3 Then God looked upon their bodies, on which Satan had caused fire to burn, and God sent His angel that stayed the burning fire. But the wounds remained on their bodies.

4 And God said unto Adam, "See Satan's love for thee, who pretended to give thee the Godhead and greatness; and, behold, he burns thee with fire, and seeks to destroy thee from off the earth.

5 "Then look at Me, O Adam; I created thee, and how many times have I delivered thee out of his hand? If not, would he not have destroyed thee?"

6 God said again to Eve, "What is that he promised thee in the garden, saying, 'At the time ye shall eat of the tree, your eyes will be opened, and you shall become like gods, knowing good and evil.' But lo! he has burnt your bodies with fire, and has made you taste the taste of fire, for the taste of the garden; and has made you see the burning of fire, and the evil thereof, and the power it has over you.

7 "Your eyes have seen the good he has taken from you, and in truth he has opened your eyes; and you have seen the garden in which ye were with Me, and ye have also seen the evil that has come upon you from Satan. But as to the Godhead he cannot give it you, neither fulfil his speech to you. Nay, he was bitter against you and your seed, that will come after you."

8 And God withdrew His Word from them.

CHAP. XLVII.

The Devil's own Scheming.

THEN Adam and Eve came into the cave, yet trembling at the fire that had scorched their bodies. So Adam said to Eve:—

2 "Lo, the fire has burnt our flesh in this world; but how will it be when we are dead, and Satan shall punish our souls? Is not our deliverance long and far off, unless God come, and in mercy to us fulfil His promise?"

3 Then Adam and Eve passed into the cave, blessing themselves for coming into it once more. For it was in their thoughts, that they never should enter it, when they saw the fire around it.

4 But as the sun was setting the fire was still burning and nearing Adam and Eve in the cave, so that they could not sleep in it. After the sun had set, they went out of it. This was the forty-seventh day after they came out of the garden.

5 Adam and Eve then came under the top of hill by the garden to sleep, as they were wont.

6 And they stood and prayed God to forgive them their sins, and then fell asleep under the summit of the mountain.

7 But Satan, the hater of all good, thought within himself: Whereas God has promised salvation to Adam by covenant, and that He would deliver him out of all the hardships that have befallen him—but has not promised me by covenant, and will not deliver me out of my hardships; nay, since He has promised him that He should make him and his seed dwell in the kingdom in which I once was— I will kill Adam.

8 The earth shall be rid of him; and shall be left to me alone; so that when he is dead

he may not have any seed left to inherit the kingdom that shall remain my own realm; God will then be in want of me, and He will restore me to it with my hosts.

CHAP. XLVIII.

Fifth apparition of Satan to Adam and Eve.

AFTER this Satan called to his hosts, all of which came to him, and said unto him:—

2 "O, our Lord, what wilt thou do?"

3 He then said unto them, "Ye know that this Adam, whom God created out of the dust, is he who has taken our kingdom. Come, let us gather together and kill him; or hurl a rock at him and at Eve, and crush them under it."

4 When Satan's hosts heard these words, they came to the part of the mountain where Adam and Eve were asleep.

5 Then Satan and his hosts took a huge rock, broad and even, and without blemish, thinking within himself, "If there should be a hole in the rock, when it fell on them, the hole in the rock might come upon them, and so they would escape and not die."

6 He then said to his hosts, "Take up this stone, and throw it flat upon them, so that it roll not from them to somewhere else. And when ye have hurled it, flee and tarry not."

7 And they did as he bid them. But as the rock fell down from the mountain upon Adam and Eve, God commanded it to become a kind of shed over them, that did them no harm. And so it was by God's order.

8 But when the rock fell, the whole earth quaked with it, and was shaken from the size of the rock.

9 And as it quaked and shook, Adam and Eve awoke from sleep, and found themselves under a rock like a shed. But they knew not how it was; for when they fell asleep they were under the sky, and not under a shed; and when they saw it, they were afraid.

10 Then Adam said to Eve, "Wherefore has the mountain bent itself, and the earth quaked and shaken on our account? And why has this rock spread itself over us like a tent?

11 "Does God intend to plague us and to shut us up in this prison? Or will He close the earth upon us?

12 "He is angry with us for our having come out of the cave, without His order; and for our having done so of our own accord, without consulting Him, when we left the cave and came to this place."

13 Then Eve said, "If, indeed, the earth quaked for our sake, and this rock forms a tent over us because of our transgression, then woe be to us, O Adam, for our punishment will be long.

14 "But arise and pray to God to let us know concerning this, and what this rock is, that is spread over us like a tent."

15 Then Adam stood up and prayed before the Lord, to let him know about this strait. And Adam thus stood praying until the morning.

CHAP. XLIX.

The first prophecy of the Resurrection.

THEN the Word of God came and said:—

2 "O Adam, who counselled thee, when thou camest out of the cave, to come to this place?"

3 And Adam said unto God, "O Lord, we came to this place because of the heat of the fire, that came upon us inside the cave."

4 Then the Lord God said

unto Adam, "O Adam, thou dreadest the heat of fire for one night, but how will it be when thou dwellest in hell?

5 "Yet, O Adam, fear not, neither say in thy heart that I have spread this rock as an awning over thee, to plague thee therewith.

6 "It came from Satan, who had promised thee the Godhead and majesty. It is he who threw down this rock to kill thee under it, and Eve with thee, and thus to prevent you from living upon the earth.

7 "But, in mercy for you, just as that rock was falling down upon you, I commanded it to form an awning over you; and the rock under you, to lower itself.

8 "And this sign, O Adam, will happen to Me at My coming upon earth: Satan will raise the people of the Jews to put Me to death; and they will lay Me in a rock, and seal a large stone upon Me, and I shall remain within that rock three days and three nights.

9 "But on the third day I shall rise again, and it shall be salvation to thee, O Adam, and to thy seed, to believe in Me. But, O Adam, I will not bring thee from under this rock until three days and three nights are passed."

10 And God withdrew His Word from Adam.

11 But Adam and Eve abode under the rock three days and three nights, as God had told them.

12 And God did so to them because they had left their cave and had come to this same place without God's order.

13 But, after three days and three nights, God opened the rock and brought them out from under it. Their flesh was dried up, and their eyes and their hearts were troubled from weeping and sorrow.

CHAP. L.

Adam and Eve seek to cover their nakedness.

THEN Adam and Eve went forth and came into the Cave of Treasures, and they stood praying in it the whole of that day, until the evening.

2 And this took place at the end of fifty days after they had left the garden.

3 But Adam and Eve rose again and prayed to God in the cave the whole of that night, and begged for mercy from Him.

4 And when the day dawned, Adam said unto Eve, "Come! let us go and do some work for our bodies."

5 So they went out of the cave, and came to the northern border of the garden, and they sought something to cover their bodies withal. But they found nothing, and knew not how to do the work. Yet their bodies were stained, and they were speechless from cold and heat.

6 Then Adam stood and asked God to show him something wherewith to cover their bodies.

7 Then came the Word of God and said unto him, "O Adam, take Eve and come to the seashore, where ye fasted before. There ye shall find skins of sheep, whose flesh was devoured by lions, and whose skins were left. Take them and make raiment for yourselves, and clothe yourselves withal."

CHAP. LI.

"What is his beauty that you should have followed him?"

WHEN Adam heard these words from God, he took Eve and removed from the northern end of the garden to the south of it, by the river of water, where they once fasted.

2 But as they were going in the way, and before they reached

that place, Satan, the wicked one, had heard the Word of God communing with Adam respecting his covering.

3 It grieved him, and he hastened to the place where the sheep-skins were, with the intention of taking them and throwing them into the sea, or of burning them with fire, that Adam and Eve should not find them.

4 But as he was about to take them, the Word of God came from heaven, and bound him by the side of those skins until Adam and Eve came near him. But as they neared him they were afraid of him, and of his hideous look.

5 Then came the Word of God to Adam and Eve, and said to them, "This is he who was hidden in the serpent, and who deceived you, and stripped you of the garment of light and glory in which you were.

6 "This is he who promised you majesty and divinity. Where, then, is the beauty that was on him? Where is his divinity? Where is his light? Where is the glory that rested on him?

7 "Now his figure is hideous; he is become abominable among angels; and he has come to be called Satan.

8 "O Adam, he wished to take from you this earthly garment of sheep-skins, and to destroy it, and not let you be covered with it.

9 "What, then, is his beauty that you should have followed him? And what have you gained by hearkening to him? See his evil works and then look at Me; at Me, your Creator, and at the good deeds I do you.

10 "See, I bound him until you came and saw him and beheld his weakness, that no power is left with him."

11 And God released him from his bonds.

CHAP. LII.

Adam and Eve sew the first shirt.

AFTER this Adam and Eve said no more, but wept before God on account of their creation, and of their bodies that required an earthly covering.

2 Then Adam said unto Eve, "O Eve, this is the skin of beasts with which we shall be covered. But when we have put it on, behold, a token of death shall have come upon us, inasmuch as the owners of these skins have died, and have wasted away. So also shall we die, and pass away."

3 Then Adam and Eve took the skins, and went back to the Cave of Treasures; and when in it, they stood and prayed as they were wont.

4 And they thought how they could make garments of those skins; for they had no skill for it.

5 Then God sent to them His angel to show them how to work it out. And the angel said to Adam, "Go forth, and bring some palm-thorns." Then Adam went out, and brought some, as the angel had commanded him.

6 Then the angel began before them to work out the skins, after the manner of one who prepares a shirt. And he took the thorns and stuck them into the skins, before their eyes.

7 Then the angel again stood up and prayed God that the thorns in those skins should be hidden, so as to be, as it were, sewn with one thread.

8 And so it was, by God's order; they became garments for Adam and Eve, and He clothed them withal.

9 From that time the nakedness of their bodies was covered from the sight of each other's eyes.

10 And this happened at the end of the fifty-first day.

11 Then when Adam's and Eve's bodies were covered, they stood and prayed, and sought mercy of the Lord, and forgiveness, and gave Him thanks for that He had had mercy on them, and had covered their nakedness. And they ceased not from prayer the whole of that night.

12 Then when the morn dawned at the rising of the sun, they said their prayers after their custom; and then went out of the cave.

13 And Adam said unto Eve, "Since we know not what there is to the westward of this cave, let us go forth and see it to-day." Then they came forth and went towards the western border.

CHAP. LIII.

The prophecy of the Western Lands.

THEY were not very far from the cave, when Satan came towards them, and hid himself between them and the cave, under the form of two ravenous lions three days without food, that came towards Adam and Eve, as if to break them in pieces and devour them.

2 Then Adam and Eve wept, and prayed God to deliver them from their paws.

3 Then the Word of God came to them, and drove away the lions from them.

4 And God said unto Adam, "O Adam, what seekest thou on the western border? And why hast thou left of thine own accord the eastern border, in which was thy dwelling-place?

5 "Now, then, turn back to thy cave, and remain in it, that Satan do not deceive thee, nor work his purpose upon thee.

6 "For in this western border, O Adam, there will go from thee a seed, that shall replenish it; and that will defile themselves with their sins, and with their yielding to the behests of Satan, and by following his works.

7 "Therefore will I bring upon them the waters of a flood, and overwhelm them all. But I will deliver what is left of the righteous among them; and I will bring them to a distant land, and the land in which thou dwellest now shall remain desolate and without one inhabitant in it."

8 After God had thus discoursed to them, they went back to the Cave of Treasures. But their flesh was dried up, and their strength failed from fasting and praying, and from the sorrow they felt at having trespassed against God.

CHAP. LIV.

Adam and Eve go exploring.

THEN Adam and Eve stood up in the cave and prayed the whole of that night until the morning dawned. And when the sun was risen they both went out of the cave; their heads wandering from heaviness of sorrow, and they not knowing whither they went.

2 And they walked thus unto the southern border of the garden. And they began to go up that border until they came to the eastern border beyond which there was no farther space.

3 And the cherub who guarded the garden was standing at the western gate, and guarding it against Adam and Eve, lest they should suddenly come into the garden. And the cherub turned round, as if to put them to death; according to the commandment God had given him.

4 When Adam and Eve came to the eastern border of the garden—thinking in their hearts that the cherub was not watching—as they were standing by

the gate as if wishing to go in, suddenly came the cherub with a flashing sword of fire in his hand; and when he saw them, he went forth to kill them. For he was afraid lest God should destroy him if they went into the garden without His order.

5 And the sword of the cherub seemed to flame afar off. But when he raised it over Adam and Eve, the flame thereof did not flash forth.

6 Therefore did the cherub think that God was favourable to them, and was bringing them back into the garden. And the cherub stood wondering.

7 He could not go up to Heaven to ascertain God's order regarding their getting into the garden; he therefore abode standing by them, unable as he was to part from them; for he was afraid lest they should enter the garden without leave from God, who then would destroy him.

8 When Adam and Eve saw the cherub coming towards them with a flaming sword of fire in his hand, they fell on their faces from fear, and were as dead.

9 At that time the heavens and the earth shook; and other cherubim came down from heaven to the cherub who guarded the garden, and saw him amazed and silent.

10 Then, again, other angels came down nigh unto the place where Adam and Eve were They were divided between joy and sorrow.

11 They were glad, because they thought that God was favourable to Adam, and wished him to return to the garden; and wished to restore him to the gladness he once enjoyed.

12 But they sorrowed over Adam, because he was fallen like a dead man, he and Eve; and they said in their thoughts, "Adam has not died in this place; but God has put him to death, for his having come to this place, and wishing to get into the garden without His leave."

CHAP. LV.

The Conflict of Satan.

THEN came the Word of God to Adam and Eve, and raised them from their dead state, saying unto them, "Why came ye up hither? Do you intend to go into the garden, from which I brought you out? It can not be to-day; but only when the covenant I have made with you is fulfilled."

2 Then Adam, when he heard the Word of God, and the fluttering of the angels whom he did not see, but only heard the sound of them with his ears, he and Eve wept, and said to the angels:—

3 "O Spirits, who wait upon God, look upon me, and upon my being unable to see you! For when I was in my former bright nature, then I could see you. I sang praises as you do; and my heart was far above you.

4 "But now, that I have transgressed, that bright nature is gone from me, and I am come to this miserable state. And now am I come to this, that I cannot see you, and you do not serve me as you were wont. For I am become animal flesh.

5 "Yet now, O angels of God, ask God with me, to restore me to that wherein I was formerly; to rescue me from this misery, and to remove from me the sentence of death He passed upon me, for having trespassed against Him."

6 Then, when the angels heard these words, they all grieved over him; and cursed Satan who had beguiled Adam, until he came from the garden to misery; from life to death; from peace to trouble; and from gladness to a strange land.

7 Then the angels said unto Adam, "Thou didst hearken to Satan, and didst forsake the Word of God who created thee; and thou didst believe that Satan would fulfil all he had promised thee.

8 "But now, O Adam, we will make known to thee, what came upon us through him, before his fall from heaven.

9 "He gathered together his hosts, and deceived them, promising them to give them a great kingdom, a divine nature; and other promises he made them.

10 "His hosts believed that his word was true, so they yielded to him, and renounced the glory of God.

11 "He then sent for us—according to the orders in which we were—to come under his command, and to hearken to his vain promise. But we would not, and we took not his advice.

12 "Then after he had fought with God, and had dealt forwardly with Him, he gathered together his hosts, and made war with us. And if it had not been for God's strength that was with us, we could not have prevailed against him to hurl him from heaven.

13 "But when he fell from among us, there was great joy in heaven, because of his going down from us. For had he continued in heaven, nothing, not even one angel would have remained in it.

14 "But God in His mercy, drove him from among us to this dark earth; for he had become darkness itself and a worker of unrighteousness.

15 "And he has continued, O Adam, to make war against thee, until he beguiled thee and made thee come out of the garden, to this strange land, where all these trials have come to thee. And death, which God brought upon him he has also brought to thee, O Adam, because thou didst obey him, and didst transgress against God."

16 Then all the angels rejoiced and praised God, and asked Him not to destroy Adam this time, for his having sought to enter the garden; but to bear with him until the fulfilment of the promise; and to help him in this world until he was free from Satan's hand.

CHAP. LVI.

A chapter of divine comfort.

THEN came the Word of God to Adam, and said unto him:—

2 "O Adam, look at that garden of joy and at this earth of toil, and behold the angels who are in the garden—that is full of them, and see thyself alone on this earth, with Satan whom thou didst obey.

3 "Yet, if thou hadst submitted, and been obedient to Me, and hadst kept My Word, thou wouldst be with My angels in My garden.

4 "But when thou didst transgress and hearken to Satan, thou didst become his guest among his angels, that are full of wickedness; and thou camest to this earth, that brings forth to thee thorns and thistles.

5 "O Adam, ask him who deceived thee, to give thee the divine nature he promised thee, or to make thee a garden as I had made for thee; or to fill thee with that same bright nature with which I had filled thee.

6 "Ask him to make thee a body like the one I made thee, or to give thee a day of rest as I gave thee; or to create within thee a reasonable soul, as I did create for thee; or to remove thee hence to some other earth than this one which I gave thee. But, O Adam, he will not fulfil even one of the things he told thee.

7 "Acknowledge, then, My favour towards thee, and My mercy on thee, My creature; that I have not requited thee for thy transgression against Me, but in My pity for thee I have promised thee that at the end of the great five days and a half I will come and save thee."

8 Then God said again to Adam and Eve, "Arise, go down hence, lest the cherub with a sword of fire in his hand destroy you."

9 But Adam's heart was comforted by God's words to him, and he worshipped before Him.

10 And God commanded His angels to escort Adam and Eve to the cave with joy, instead of the fear that had come upon them.

11 Then the angels took up Adam and Eve, and brought them down from the mountain by the garden, with songs and psalms, until they brought them to the cave. There the angels began to comfort and to strengthen them, and then departed from them towards heaven, to their Creator, who had sent them.

12 But, after the angels were gone from Adam and Eve, came Satan, with shamefacedness, and stood at the entrance of the cave in which were Adam and Eve. He then called to Adam, and said, "O Adam, come, let me speak to thee."

13 Then Adam came out of the cave, thinking he was one of God's angels that was come to give him some good counsel.

CHAP. LVII.

"Therefore did I fall. . . ."

BUT when Adam came out and saw his hideous figure, he was afraid of him, and said unto him, "Who art thou?"

2 Then Satan answered and said unto him, "It is I, who hid myself within the serpent, and who talked to Eve, and beguiled her until she hearkened to my command. I am he who sent her, through the wiles of my speech, to deceive thee, until thou and she ate of the fruit of the tree, and ye came away from under the command of God."

3 But when Adam heard these words from him, he said unto him, "Canst thou make me a garden as God made for me? Or canst thou clothe me in the same bright nature in which God had clothed me?

4 "Where is the divine nature thou didst promise to give me? Where is that fair speech of thine, thou didst hold with us at first, when we were in the garden?"

5 Then Satan said unto Adam, "Thinkest thou, that when I have spoken to one about anything, I shall ever bring it to him or fulfil my word? Not so. For I myself have never even thought of obtaining what I asked.

6 "Therefore did I fall, and did I make you fall by that for which I myself fell; and with you also, whosoever accepts my counsel, falls thereby.

7 "But now, O Adam, by reason of thy fall thou art under my rule, and I am king over thee; because thou hast hearkened to me, and hast transgressed against thy God. Neither will there be any deliverance from my hands until the day promised thee by thy God."

8 Again he said, "Inasmuch as we do not know the day agreed upon with thee by thy God, nor the hour in which thou shalt be delivered, for that reason will we multiply war and murder upon thee and thy seed after thee.

9 "This is our will and our good pleasure, that we may not

leave one of the sons of men to inherit our orders in heaven.

10 "For as to our abode, O Adam, it is in burning fire; and we will not cease our evil doing, no, not one day nor one hour. And I, O Adam, shall sow fire upon thee when thou comest into the cave to dwell there."

11 When Adam heard these words he wept and mourned, and said unto Eve, "Hear what he said; that he will not fulfil aught of what he told thee in the garden. Did he really then become king over us?

12 "But we will ask God, who created us, to deliver us out of his hands."

CHAP. LVIII.

"About sunset on the 53rd day. . . ."

THEN Adam and Eve spread their hands unto God, praying and entreating Him to drive Satan away from them; that he dó them no violence, and do not force them to deny God.

2 Then God sent to them at once His angel, who drove away Satan from them. This happened about sunset, on the fifty-third day after they had come out of the garden.

3 Then Adam and Eve went into the cave, and stood up and turned their faces to the earth, to pray to God.

4 But ere they prayed Adam said unto Eve, "Lo, thou hast seen what temptations have befallen us in this land. Come, let us arise, and ask God to forgive us the sins we have committed; and we will not come out until the end of the day next to the fortieth. And if we die herein, He will save us."

5 Then Adam and Eve arose, and joined together in entreating God.

6 They abode thus praying in the cave; neither did they come out of it, by night or by day, until their prayers went up out of their mouths, like a flame of fire.

CHAP. LIX.

Eighth apparition of Satan to Adam and Eve.

BUT Satan, the hater of all good, did not allow them to end their prayers. For he called to his hosts, and they came, all of them. He then said to them, "Since Adam and Eve, whom we beguiled, have agreed together to pray to God night and day, and to entreat Him to deliver them, and since they will not come out of the cave until the end of the fortieth day.

2 "And since they will continue their prayers as they have both agreed to do, that He will deliver them out of our hands, and restore them to their former state, see what we shall do unto them." And his hosts said unto him, "Power is thine, O our Lord, to do what thou listest."

3 Then Satan, great in wickedness, took his hosts and came into the cave, in the thirtieth night of the forty days and one; and he smote Adam and Eve, until he left them dead.

4 Then came the Word of God unto Adam and Eve, who raised them from their suffering, and God said unto Adam, "Be strong, and be not afraid of him who has just come to thee."

5 But Adam wept and said, "Where wast Thou, O my God, that they should smite me with such blows, and that this suffering should come upon us; upon me and upon Eve, Thy handmaid?"

6 Then God said unto him, "O Adam, see, he is lord and master of all thou hast, he who said, he would give thee divinity.

Where is this love for thee?
And where is the gift he promised?

7 "For once has it pleased
him, O Adam, to come to thee,
to c o m f o r t thee, and to
strengthen thee, and to rejoice
with thee, and to send his hosts
to guard thee; because thou hast
hearkened to him, and hast
yielded to his counsel; and hast
transgressed My commandment
but has followed his behest?"

8 Then Adam wept before
the Lord, and said,' "O Lord because
I transgressed a little,
Thou hast sorely plagued me in
return for it, I ask Thee to deliver
me out of his hands; or
else have pity on me, and take
my soul out of my body now in
this strange land."

9 Then God said unto Adam,
"If only there had been this
sighing and praying before, ere
thou didst transgress! Then
wouldst thou have rest from the
trouble in which thou art now."

10 But God had patience with
Adam, and let him and Eve remain
in the cave until they had
fulfilled the forty days.

11 But as to Adam and Eve,
their strength and flesh withered
from fasting and praying, from
hunger and thirst; for they had
not tasted either food or drink
since they left the garden; nor
were the functions of their bodies
yet settled; and they had no
strength left to continue in
prayer from hunger, until the
end of the next day to the fortieth.
They were fallen down
in the cave; yet what speech
escaped from their mouths, was
only in praises.

CHAP. LX.

*The Devil appears like an old
man. He offers "a place of
rest."*

THEN on the eighty-ninth
day, Satan came to the
cave, clad in a garment of light,
and girt about with a bright
girdle.

2 In his hands was a staff of
light, and he looked most awful:
but his face was pleasant and his
speech was sweet.

3 He thus transformed himself
in order to deceive Adam
and Eve, and to make them come
out of the cave, ere they had
fulfilled the forty days.

4 For he said within himself,
"Now that when they had fulfilled
the forty days' fasting and
praying, God would restore them
to their former estate; but if
He did not do so, He would still
be favourable to them; and even
if He had not mercy on them,
would He yet give them something
from the garden to comfort
them; as already twice
before."

5 Then Satan drew near the
cave in this fair appearance, and
said:—

6 "O Adam, rise ye, stand up,
thou and Eve, and come along
with me, to a good land; and
fear not. I am flesh and bones
like you; and at first I was a
creature that God created.

7 "And it was so, that when
He had created me, He placed me
in a garden in the north, on the
border of the world.

8 "And He said to me, 'Abide
here!' And I abode there according
to His Word, neither
did I transgress His commandment.

9 "Then He made a slumber
to come over me, and He
brought thee, O Adam, out of
my side, but did not make thee
abide by me.

10 "But God took thee in
His divine hand, and placed thee
in a garden to the eastward.

11 "Then I grieved because of
thee, for that while God had
taken thee out of my side, He
had not let thee abide with me.

12 "But God said unto me:
'Grieve not because of Adam,

whom I brought out of thy side; no harm will come to him.

13 " 'For now I have brought out of his side a help-meet for him; and I have given him joy by so doing.' "

14 Then Satan said again, "I did not know how it is ye are in this cave, nor anything about this trial that has come upon you—until God said to me, 'Behold, Adam has transgressed, he whom I had taken out of thy side, and Eve also, whom I took out of his side; and I have driven them out of the garden; I have made them dwell in a land of sorrow and misery, because they transgressed against Me, and have hearkened to Satan. And lo, they are in suffering unto this day, the eightieth.'

15 "Then God said unto me, 'Arise, go to them, and make them come to thy place, and suffer not that Satan come near them, and afflict them. For they are now in great misery; and lie helpless from hunger.'

16 "He further said to me, 'When thou hast taken them to thyself, give them to eat of the fruit of the Tree of Life, and give them to drink of the water of peace; and clothe them in a garment of light, and restore them to their former state of grace, and leave them not in misery, for they came from thee. But grieve not over them, nor repent of that which has come upon them.'

17 "But when I heard this, I was sorry; and my heart could not patiently bear it for thy sake, O my child.

18 "But, O Adam, when I heard the name of Satan, I was afraid, and I said within myself, I will not come out, lest he ensnare me, as he did my children, Adam and Eve.

19 "And I said, 'O God, when I go to my children, Satan will meet me in the way, and war against me, as he did against them.'

20 "Then God said unto me, 'Fear not; when thou findest him, smite him with the staff that is in thine hand, and be not afraid of him, for thou art of old standing, and he shall not prevail against thee.'

21 "Then I said, 'O my Lord, I am old, and cannot go. Send Thy angels to bring them.'

22 "But God said unto me, 'Angels, verily, are not like them; and they will not consent to come with them. But I have chosen thee, because they are thy offspring, and like thee, and will hearken to what thou sayest.'

23 "God said further to me, 'If thou hast not strength to walk, I will send a cloud to carry thee and alight thee at the entrance of their cave; then the cloud will return and leave thee there.

24 " 'And if they will come with thee, I will send a cloud to carry thee and them.'

25 "Then He commanded a cloud, and it bare me up and brought me to you; and then went back.

26 "And now, O my children, Adam and Eve, look at my hoar hairs and at my feeble estate, and at my coming from that distant place. Come, come with me, to a place of rest."

27 Then he began to weep and to sob before Adam and Eve, and his tears poured upon the earth like water.

28 And when Adam and Eve raised their eyes and saw his beard, and heard his sweet talk, their hearts softened towards him; they hearkened unto him, for they believed he was true.

29 And it seemed to them that they really were his offspring, when they saw that his face was like their own; and they trusted him.

CHAP. LXI.

They begin to follow Satan.

THEN he took Adam and Eve by the hand, and began to bring them out of the cave.

2 But when they were come a little way out of it, God knew that Satan had overcome them, and had brought them out ere the forty days were ended, to take them to some distant place, and to destroy them.

3 Then the Word of the Lord God again came and cursed Satan, and drove him away from them.

4 And God began to speak unto Adam and Eve, saying to them, "What made you come out of the cave, unto this place?"

5 Then Adam said unto God, "Didst thou create a man before us? For when we were in the cave there suddenly came unto us a good old man who said to us, 'I am a messenger from God unto you, to bring you back to some place of rest.'

6 "And we did believe, O God, that he was a messenger from Thee; and we came out with him; and knew not whither we should go with him."

7 Then God said unto Adam, "See, that is the father of evil arts, who brought thee and Eve out of the Garden of Delights. And now, indeed, when he saw that thou and Eve both joined together in fasting and praying, and that you came not out of the cave before the end of the forty days, he wished to make your purpose vain, to break your mutual bond; to cut off all hope from you, and to drive you to some place where he might destroy you.

8 "Because he was unable to do aught to you, unless he showed himself in the likeness of you.

9 "Therefore did he come to you with a face like your own, and began to give you tokens as if they were all true.

10 "But I in mercy and with the favour I had unto you, did not allow him to destroy you; but I drove him away from you.

11 "Now, therefore, O Adam, take Eve, and return to your cave, and remain in it until the morrow of the fortieth day. And when ye come out, go towards the eastern gate of the garden."

12 Then Adam and Eve worshipped God, and praised and blessed Him for the deliverance that had come to them from Him. And they returned towards the cave. This happened at eventide of the thirty-ninth day.

13 Then Adam and Eve stood up and with great zeal, prayed to God, to be brought out of their want for strength; for their strength had departed from them, through hunger and thirst and prayer. But they watched the whole of that night praying, until morning.

14 Then Adam said unto Eve, "Arise, let us go towards the eastern gate of the garden as God told us."

15 And they said their prayers as they were wont to do every day; and they went out of the cave, to go near to the eastern gate of the garden.

16 Then Adam and Eve stood up and prayed, and besought God to strengthen them, and to send them something to satisfy their hunger.

17 But when they had ended their prayers, they remained where they were by reason of their failing strength.

18 Then came the Word of God again, and said unto them, "O Adam, arise, go and bring hither two figs."

19 Then Adam and Eve arose, and went until they drew near to the cave.

CHAP. LXII.

Two fruit trees.

BUT Satan the wicked was envious, because of the consolation God had given them.

2 So he prevented them, and went into the cave and took the two figs, and buried them outside the cave, so that Adam and Eve should not find them. He also had in his thoughts to destroy them.

3 But by God's mercy, as soon as those two figs were in the earth, God defeated Satan's counsel regarding them; and made them into two fruit-trees, that overshadowed the cave. For Satan had buried them on the eastern side of it.

4 Then when the two trees were grown, and were covered with fruit, Satan grieved and mourned, and said, "Better were it to have left those figs as they were; for now, behold, they have become two fruit-trees, whereof Adam will eat all the days of his life. Whereas I had in mind, when I buried them, to destroy them entirely, and to hide them for aye.

5 "But God has overturned my counsel; and would not that this sacred fruit should perish; and He has made plain my intention, and has defeated the counsel I had formed against His servants."

6 Then Satan went away ashamed, of not having wrought out his design.

CHAP. LXIII.

The first joy of trees.

BUT Adam and Eve, as they drew near to the cave, saw two fig-trees, covered with fruit, and overshadowing the cave.

2 Then Adam said to Eve, "It seems to me we have gone astray. When did these two trees grow here? It seems to me that the enemy wishes to lead us astray. Sayest thou that there is in the earth another cave than this?

3 "Yet, O Eve, let us go into the cave, and find in it the two figs; for this is our cave, in which we were. But if we should not find the two figs in it, then it cannot be our cave."

4 They went then into the cave, and looked into the four corners of it, but found not the two figs.

5 And Adam wept and said to Eve, "Are we come to a wrong cave, then, O Eve? It seems to me these two fig-trees are the two figs that were in the cave." And Eve said, "I, for my part, do not know."

6 Then Adam stood up and prayed and said, "O God, Thou didst command us to come back to the cave, to take the two figs, and then to return to Thee.

7 "But now, we have not found them. O God, hast Thou taken them, and sown these two trees, or have we gone astray in the earth; or has the enemy deceived us? If it be real, then, O God, reveal to us the secret of these two trees and of the two figs."

8 Then came the Word of God to Adam, and said unto him, "O Adam, when I sent thee to fetch the figs, Satan went before thee to the cave, took the figs, and buried them outside, eastward of the cave, thinking to destroy them; and not sowing them with good intent.

9 "Not for his mere sake, then, have these trees grown up at once; but I had mercy on thee and I commanded them to grow. And they grew to be two large trees, that you be overshadowed by their branches, and find rest; and that I make you see My power and My marvellous works.

10 "And, also, to show you Satan's meanness, and his evil

works, for ever since ye came out of the garden, he has not ceased, no, not one day, from doing you some harm. But I have not given him power over you."

11 And God said, "Henceforth, O Adam, rejoice on account of the trees, thou and Eve; and rest under them when ye feel weary. But eat not of their fruit, nor come near them."

12 Then Adam wept, and said, "O God, wilt Thou again kill us, or wilt Thou drive us away from before Thy face, and cut our life from off the face of the earth?

13 "O God, I beseech Thee, if Thou knowest that there be in these trees either death or some other evil, as at the first time, root them up from near our cave, and wither them; and leave us to die of the heat, of hunger and of thirst.

14 "For we know Thy marvellous works, O God, that they are great, and that by Thy power Thou canst bring one thing out of another, without one's wish. For Thy power can make rocks to become trees, and trees to become rocks."

CHAP. LXIV.

Adam and Eve partake of the first earthly food.

THEN God looked upon Adam and upon his strength of mind, upon his endurance of hunger and thirst, and of the heat. And he changed the two fig-trees into two figs, as they were at first, and then said to Adam and to Eve, "Each of you may take one fig." And they took them, as the Lord commanded them.

2 And he said to them, "Go ye into the cave, and eat the figs, and satisfy your hunger, lest ye die."

3 So, as God commanded them, they went into the cave,

about the time when the sun was setting. And Adam and Eve stood up and prayed at the time of the setting sun.

4 Then they sat down to eat the figs; but they knew not how to eat them; for they were not accustomed to eat earthly food. They feared also lest, if they ate, their stomach should be burdened and their flesh thickened, and their hearts take to liking earthly food.

5 But while they were thus seated, God, out of pity for them, sent them His angel, lest they should perish of hunger and thirst.

6 And the angel said unto Adam and Eve, "God says to you that ye have not strength to fast until death; eat, therefore, and strengthen your bodies; for ye are now animal flesh, that cannot subsist without food and drink."

7 Then Adam and Eve took the figs and began to eat of them. But God had put into them a mixture as of savoury bread and blood.

8 Then the angel went from Adam and Eve, who ate of the figs until they had satisfied their hunger. Then they put by what remained; but by the power of God, the figs became full as before, because God blessed them.

9 After this Adam and Eve arose, and prayed with a joyful heart and renewed strength, and praised and rejoiced abundantly the whole of that night. And this was the end of the eighty-third day.

CHAP. LXV.

Adam and Eve acquire digestive organs. Final hope of returning to the Garden is quenched.

AND when it was day, they rose and prayed, after their custom, and then went out of the cave.

2 But as they felt great trouble from the food they had eaten, and to which they were not used, they went about in the cave saying to each other:—

3 "What has happened to us through eating, that this pain should have come upon us? Woe be to us, we shall die! Better for us to have died than to have eaten; and to have kept our bodies pure, than to have defiled them with food."

4 Then Adam said to Eve, "This pain did not come to us in the garden, neither did we eat such bad food there. Thinkest thou, O Eve, that God will plague us through the food that is in us, or that our inwards will come out; or that God means to kill us with this pain before He has fulfilled His promise to us?"

5 Then Adam besought the Lord and said, "O Lord, let us not perish through the food we have eaten. O Lord, smite us not; but deal with us according to Thy great mercy, and forsake us not until the day of the promise Thou hast made us."

6 Then God looked upon them, and at once fitted them for eating food; as unto this day; so that they should not perish.

7 Then Adam and Eve came back into the cave sorrowful and weeping because of the alteration in their nature. And they both knew from that hour that they were altered beings, that their hope of returning to the garden was now cut off; and that they could not enter it.

8 For that now their bodies had strange functions; and all flesh that requires food and drink for its existence, cannot be in the garden.

9 Then Adam said to Eve, "Behold, our hope is now cut off; and so is our trust to enter the garden. We no longer belong to the inhabitants of the garden; but henceforth we are earthy and of the dust, and of the inhabitants of the earth. We shall not return to the garden, until the day in which God has promised to save us, and to bring us again into the garden, as He promised us."

10 Then they prayed to God that He would have mercy on them; after which, their mind was quieted, their hearts were broken, and their longing was cooled down; and they were like strangers on earth. That night Adam and Eve spent in the cave, where they slept heavily by reason of the food they had eaten.

CHAP. LXVI.

Adam does his first day's work.

WHEN it was morning, the day after they had eaten food, Adam and Eve prayed in the cave, and Adam said unto Eve, "Lo, we asked for food of God, and He gave it. But now let us also ask Him to give us a drink of water."

2 Then they arose, and went to the bank of the stream of water, that was on the south border of the garden, in which they had before thrown themselves. And they stood on the bank, and prayed to God that He would command them to drink of the water.

3 Then the Word of God came to Adam, and said unto him, "O Adam, thy body is become brutish, and requires water to drink. Take ye, and drink, thou and Eve; give thanks and praise."

4 Adam and Eve then drew near, and drank of it, until their bodies felt refreshed. After having drunk, they praised God, and then returned to their cave, after their former custom. This happened at the end of eighty-three days.

5 Then on the eighty-fourth

day, they took two figs and hung them in the cave, together with the leaves thereof, to be to them a sign and a blessing from God. And they placed them there until there should arise a posterity to them, who should see the wonderful things God had done to them.

6 Then Adam and Eve again stood outside the cave, and besought God to show them some food wherewith to nourish their bodies.

7 Then the Word of God came and said unto him, "O Adam, go down to the westward of the cave, as far as a land of dark soil, and there thou shalt find food."

8 And Adam hearkened unto the Word of God, took Eve, and went down to a land of dark soil, and found there wheat growing, in the ear and ripe, and figs to eat; and Adam rejoiced over it.

9 Then the Word of God came again to Adam, and said unto him, "Take of this wheat and make thee bread of it, to nourish thy body withal." And God gave Adam's heart wisdom, to work out the corn until it became bread.

10 Adam accomplished all that, until he grew very faint and weary. He then returned to the cave; rejoicing at what he had learned of what is done with wheat, until it is made into bread for one's use.

CHAP. LXVII.

"Then Satan began to lead astray Adam and Eve. . . ."

BUT when Adam and Eve went down to the land of black mud, and came near to the wheat God had showed them, and saw it ripe and ready for reaping, as they had no sickle to reap it withal—they girt themselves, and began to pull up the wheat, until it was all done.

2 Then they made it into a heap; and, faint from heat and from thirst, they went under a shady tree, where the breeze fanned them to sleep.

3 But Satan saw what Adam and Eve had done. And he called his hosts, and said to them, "Since God has shown to Adam and Eve all about this wheat, wherewith to strengthen their bodies—and, lo, they are come and have made a heap of it, and faint from the toil are now asleep—come, let us set fire to this heap of corn, and burn it, and let us take that bottle of water that is by them, and empty it out, so that they may find nothing to drink, and we kill them with hunger and thirst.

4 "Then, when they wake up from their sleep, and seek to return to the cave, we will come to them in the way, and will lead them astray; so that they die of hunger and thirst; when they may, perhaps, deny God, and He destroy them. So shall we be rid of them."

5 Then Satan and his hosts threw fire upon the wheat and consumed it.

6 But from the heat of the flame Adam and Eve awoke from their sleep, and saw the wheat burning, and the bucket of water by them, poured out.

7 Then they wept and went back to the cave.

8 But as they were going up from below the mountain where they were; Satan and his hosts met them in the form of angels, praising God.

9 Then Satan said to Adam, "O Adam, why art thou so pained with hunger and thirst? It seems to me that Satan has burnt up the wheat." And Adam said to him, "Ay."

10 Again Satan said to Adam, "Come back with us; we are angels of God. God sent us to thee, to show thee another field of corn, better than that; and

beyond it is a fountain of good water, and many trees, where thou shalt dwell near it, and work the corn-field to better purpose than that which Satan has consumed."

11 Adam thought that he was true, and that they were angels who talked with him; and he went back with them.

12 Then Satan began to lead astray Adam and Eve eight days, until they both fell down as if dead, from hunger, thirst, and faintness. Then he fled with his hosts, and left them.

CHAP. LXVIII.

How destruction and trouble is of Satan when he is the master. Adam and Eve establish the custom of worship.

THEN God looked upon Adam and Eve, and upon what had come upon them from Satan, and how he had made them perish.

2 God, therefore, sent His Word, and raised up Adam and Eve from their state of death.

3 Then, Adam, when he was raised, said, "O God, Thou hast burnt and taken from us the corn Thou hadst given us, and Thou hast emptied out the bucket of water. And Thou hast sent Thy angels, who have waylaid us from the corn-field. Wilt Thou make us perish? If this be from Thee, O God, then take away our souls; but punish us not."

4 Then God said to Adam, "I did not burn down the wheat, and I did not pour the water out of the bucket, and I did not send My angels to lead thee astray.

5 "But it is Satan, thy master who did it; he to whom thou hast subjected thyself; My commandment being meanwhile set aside. He it is, who burnt down the corn, and poured out the water, and who has led thee astray; and all the promises he has made you, verily are but feint, and deceit, and a lie.

6 "But now, O Adam, thou shalt acknowledge My good deeds done to thee."

7 And God told His angels to take Adam and Eve, and to bear them up to the field of wheat, which they found as before, with the bucket full of water.

8 There they saw a tree, and found on it solid manna; and wondered at God's power. And the angels commanded them to eat of the manna when they were hungry.

9 And God adjured Satan with a curse, not to come again, and destroy the field of corn.

10 Then Adam and Eve took of the corn, and made of it an offering, and took it and offered it up on the mountain, the place where they had offered up their first offering of blood.

11 And they offered this oblation again on the altar they had built at first. And they stood up and prayed, and besought the Lord saying, "Thus, O God, when we were in the garden, did our praises go up to Thee, like this offering; and our innocence went up to thee like incense. But now, O God, accept this offering from us, and turn us not back, reft of Thy mercy."

12 Then God said to Adam and Eve, "Since ye have made this oblation and have offered it to Me, I shall make it My flesh, when I come down upon earth to save you; and I shall cause it to be offered continually upon an altar, for forgiveness and for mercy, unto those who partake of it duly."

13 And God sent a bright fire upon the offering of Adam and Eve, and filled it with brightness, grace, and light; and the Holy Ghost came down upon that oblation.

14 Then God commanded an

angel to take fire-tongs, like a spoon, and with it to take an offering and bring it to Adam and Eve. And the angel did so, as God had commanded him, and offered it to them.

15 And the souls of Adam and Eve were brightened, and their hearts were filled with joy and gladness and with the praises of God.

16 And God said to Adam, "This shall be unto you a custom, to do so, when affliction and sorrow come upon you. But your deliverance and your entrance into the garden, shall not be until the days are fulfilled, as agreed between you and Me; were it not so, I would, of My mercy and pity for you, bring you back to My garden and to My favour for the sake of the offering you have just made to My name."

17 Adam rejoiced at these words which he heard from God; and he and Eve worshipped before the altar, to which they bowed, and then went back to the Cave of Treasures.

18 And this took place at the end of the twelfth day after the eightieth day, from the time Adam and Eve came out of the garden.

19 And they stood up the whole night praying until morning; and then went out of the cave.

20 Then Adam said to Eve, with joy of heart, because of the offering they had made to God, and that had been accepted of Him, "Let us do this three times every week, on the fourth day Wednesday, on the preparation day Friday, and on the Sabbath Sunday, all the days of our life."

21 And as they agreed to these words between themselves, God was pleased with their thoughts, and with the resolution they had each taken with the other.

22 After this, came the Word of God to Adam, and said, "O Adam, thou hast determined beforehand the days in which sufferings shall come upon Me, when I am made flesh; for they are the fourth Wednesday, and the preparation day Friday.

23 "But as to the first day, I created in it all things, and I raised the heavens. And, again, through My rising again on this day, will I create joy, and raise them on high, who believe in Me; O Adam, offer this oblation, all the days of thy life."

24 Then God withdrew His Word from Adam.

25 But Adam continued to offer this oblation thus, every week three times, until the end of seven weeks. And on the first day, which is the fiftieth, Adam made an offering as he was wont, and he and Eve took it and came to the altar before God, as He had taught them.

CHAP. LXIX.

Twelfth apparition of Satan to Adam and Eve, while Adam was praying over the offering upon the altar; when Satan smote him.

THEN Satan, the hater of all good, envious of Adam and of his offering through which he found favour with God, hastened and took a sharp stone from among sharp iron-stones; appeared in the form of a man, and went and stood by Adam and Eve.

2 Adam was then offering on the altar, and had begun to pray, with his hands spread unto God.

3 Then Satan hastened with the sharp iron-stone he had with him, and with it pierced Adam on the right side, when flowed blood and water, then Adam fell upon the altar like a corpse. And Satan fled.

THE FIRST SUNRISE

(See page 13)

4 Then Eve came, and took Adam and placed him below the altar. And there she stayed, weeping over him; while a stream of blood flowed from Adam's side upon his offering.

5 But God looked upon the death of Adam. He then sent His Word, and raised him up and said unto him, "Fulfil thy offering, for indeed, Adam, it is worth much, and there is no shortcoming in it."

6 God said further unto Adam, "Thus will it also happen to Me, on the earth, when I shall be pierced and blood shall flow blood and water from My side and run over My body, which is the true offering; and which shall be offered on the altar as a perfect offering."

7 Then God commanded Adam to finish his offering, and when he had ended it he worshipped before God, and praised Him for the signs He had showed him.

8 And God healed Adam in one day, which is the end of the seven weeks; and that is the fiftieth day.

9 Then Adam and Eve returned from the mountain, and went into the Cave of Treasures, as they were used to do This completed for Adam and Eve, one hundred and forty days since their coming out of the garden.

10 Then they both stood up that night and prayed to God. And when it was morning, they went out, and went down westward of the cave, to the place where their corn was, and there rested under the shadow of a tree, as they were wont.

11 But when there a multitude of beasts came all round them. It was Satan's doing, in his wickedness; in order to wage war against Adam through marriage.

CHAP. LXX.

Thirteenth apparition of Satan to Adam and Eve, to make war against him, through his marriage with Eve.

AFTER this Satan, the hater of all good, took the form of an angel, and with him two others, so that they looked like the three angels who had brought to Adam gold, incense, and myrrh.

2 They passed before Adam and Eve while they were under the tree, and greeted Adam and Eve with fair words that were full of guile

3 But when Adam and Eve saw their comely mien, and heard their sweet speech, Adam rose, welcomed them, and brought them to Eve, and they remained all together; Adam's heart the while, being glad because he thought concerning them, that they were the same angels, who had brought him gold, incense, and myrrh.

4 Because, when they came to Adam the first time, there came upon him from them, peace and joy, through their bringing him good tokens; so Adam thought that they were come a second time to give him other tokens for him to rejoice withal. For he did not know it was Satan; therefore did he receive them with joy and companied with them.

5 Then Satan, the tallest of them, said, "Rejoice, O Adam, and be glad. Lo, God has sent us to thee to tell thee something."

6 And Adam said, "What is it?" Then Satan answered, "It is a light thing, yet it is a word of God, wilt thou hear it from us and do it? But if thou hearest not, we will return to God, and tell Him that thou wouldest not receive His word."

7 And Satan said again to

Adam, "Fear not, neither let a trembling come upon thee; dost not thou know us?"

8 But Adam said, "I know you not."

9 Then Satan said to him, "I am the angel who brought thee gold, and took it to the cave; this other one is he who brought thee incense; and that third one, is he who brought thee myrrh when thou wast on the top of the mountain, and who carried thee to the cave.

10 "But as to the other angels our fellows, who bare you to the cave, God has not sent them with us this time; for He said to us, 'You suffice.'"

11 So when Adam heard these words he believed them, and said to these angels, "Speak the word of God, that I may receive it."

12 And Satan said unto him "Swear, and promise me that thou wilt receive it."

13 Then Adam said, "I know not how to swear and promise."

14 And Satan said to him, "Hold out thy hand, and put it inside my hand."

15 Then Adam held out his hand, and put it into Satan's hand; when Satan said unto him, "Say, now—so true as God is living, rational, and speaking, who raised the heavens in the space, and established the earth upon the waters, and has created me out of the four elements, and out of the dust of the earth—I will not break my promise, nor renounce my word."

16 And Adam swore thus.

17 Then Satan said to him, "Lo, it is now some time since thou camest out of the garden, and thou knowest neither wickedness nor evil. But now God says to thee, to take Eve who came out of thy side, and to wed her, that she bear thee children, to comfort thee, and to drive from thee trouble and sorrow;

now this thing is not difficult, neither is there any scandal in it to thee."

CHAP. LXXI.

Adam is troubled by his wedding with Eve.

BUT when Adam heard these words from Satan, he sorrowed much, because of his oath and of his promise, and said, "Shall I commit adultery with my flesh and my bones, and shall I sin against myself, for God to destroy me, and to blot me out from off the face of the earth?

2 "Since, when at first, I ate of the tree, He drove me out of the garden into this strange land, and deprived me of my bright nature, and brought death upon me. If, then, I should do this, He will cut off my life from the earth, and He will cast me into hell, and will plague me there a long time.

3 "But God never spoke the words thou hast told me; and ye are not God's angels, nor yet sent from Him. But ye are devils, come to me under the false appearance of angels. Away from me; ye cursed of God!"

4 Then those devils fled from before Adam. And he and Eve arose, and returned to the Cave of Treasures, and went into it.

5 Then Adam said to Eve, "If thou sawest what I did, tell it not; for I sinned against God in swearing by His great name, and I have placed my hand another time into that of Satan." Eve, then, held her peace, as Adam told her.

6 Then Adam arose, and spread his hands unto God, beseeching and entreating Him with tears, to forgive him what he had done. And Adam remained thus standing and praying forty days and forty nights.

He neither ate nor drank until he dropped down upon the earth from hunger and thirst.

7 Then God sent His Word unto Adam, who raised him up from where he lay, and said unto him, "O Adam, why hast thou sworn by My name, and why hast thou made agreement with Satan another time?"

8 But Adam wept, and said, "O God, forgive me, for I did this unwittingly; believing they were God's angels."

9 And God forgave Adam, saying to him, "Beware of Satan."

10 And He withdrew His Word from Adam.

11 Then Adam's heart was comforted; and he took Eve, and they went out of the cave, to make some food for their bodies.

12 But from that day Adam struggled in his mind about his wedding Eve; afraid as he was to do it, lest God should be wroth with him.

13 Then Adam and Eve went to the river of water, and sat on the bank, as people do when they enjoy themselves.

14 But Satan was jealous of them; and would destroy them.

CHAP. LXXII.

Adam's heart is set on fire.

THEN Satan, and ten from his hosts, transformed themselves into maidens, unlike any others in the whole world for grace.

2 They came up out of the river in presence of Adam and Eve, and they said among themselves, "Come, we will look at the faces of Adam and of Eve, who are of the men upon earth. How beautiful they are, and how different is their look from our own faces." Then they came to Adam and Eve, and greeted them; and stood wondering at them.

3 Adam and Eve looked at them also, and wondered at their beauty, and said, "Is there, then, under us, another world, with such beautiful creatures as these in it?"

4 And those maidens said to Adam and Eve, "Yes, indeed, we are an abundant creation."

5 Then Adam said to them, "But how do you multiply?"

6 And they answered him, "We have husbands who wedded us, and we bear them children, who grow up, and who in their turn wed and are wedded, and also bear children; and thus we increase. And if so be, O Adam, thou wilt not believe us, we will show thee our husbands and our children."

7 Then they shouted over the river as if to call their husbands and their children, who came up from the river, men and children; and every one came to his wife, his children being with him.

8 But when Adam and Eve saw them, they stood dumb, and wondered at them.

9 Then they said to Adam and Eve, "You see our husbands and our children, wed Eve as we wed our wives, and you shall have children the same as we." This was a device of Satan to deceive Adam.

10 Satan also thought within himself, "God at first commanded Adam concerning the fruit of the tree, saying to him, 'Eat not of it; else of death thou shalt die.' But Adam ate of it, and yet God did not kill him; He only decreed upon him death, and plagues and trials, until the day he shall come out of his body.

11 "Now, then, if I deceive him to do this thing, and to wed Eve without God's commandment, God will kill him then."

12 Therefore did Satan work this apparition before Adam and Eve; because he sought to kill him, and to make him disappear from off the face of the earth.

13 Meanwhile the fire of sin came upon Adam, and he thought of committing sin. But he restrained himself, fearing lest if he followed this advice of Satan God would put him to death.

14 Then Adam and Eve arose, and prayed to God, while Satan and his hosts went down into the river, in presence of Adam and Eve; to let them see that they were going back to their own regions.

15 Then Adam and Eve went back to the Cave of Treasures, as they were wont; about evening time.

16 And they both arose and prayed to God that night. Adam remained standing in prayer, yet not knowing how to pray, by reason of the thoughts of his heart regarding his wedding Eve; and he continued so until morning.

17 And when light arose, Adam said unto Eve, "Arise, let us go below the mountain, where they brought us gold, and let us ask the Lord concerning this matter."

18 Then Eve said, "What is that matter, O Adam?"

19 And he answered her, "That I may request the Lord to inform me about wedding thee; for I will not do it without His order, lest He make us perish, thee and me. For those devils have set my heart on fire, with thoughts of what they showed us, in their sinful apparitions."

20 Then Eve said to Adam, "Why need we go below the mountain? Let us rather stand up and pray in our cave to God, to let us know whether this counsel is good or not."

21 Then Adam rose up in prayer and said, "O God, thou knowest that we transgressed against Thee, and from the moment we transgressed, we were bereft of our bright nature; and our body became brutish, requiring food and drink; and with animal desires.

22 "Command us, O God, not to give way to them without Thy order, lest Thou bring us to nothing. For if Thou give us not the order, we shall be overpowered, and follow that advice of Satan; and Thou wilt again make us perish.

23 "If not, then take our souls from us; let us be rid of this animal lust. And if Thou give us no order respecting this thing, then sever Eve from me, and me from her; and place us each far away from the other.

24 "Yet again, O God, when Thou hast put us asunder from each other, the devils will deceive us with their apparitions, and destroy our hearts, and defile our thoughts towards each other. Yet if it is not each of us towards the other, it will, at all events, be through their appearance when they show themselves to us." Here Adam ended his prayer.

CHAP. LXXIII.

The betrothal of Adam and Eve.

THEN God looked upon the words of Adam that they were true, and that he could long await His order, respecting the counsel of Satan.

2 And God approved Adam in what he had thought concerning this, and in the prayer he had offered in His presence; and the Word of God came unto Adam and said to him, "O Adam, if only thou hadst had this caution at first, ere thou camest out of the garden into this land!"

3 After that, God sent His angel who had brought gold, and the angel who had brought incense, and the angel who had brought myrrh to Adam, that they should inform him respecting his wedding Eve.

4 Then those angels said to

Adam, "Take the gold and give it to Eve as a wedding gift, and betroth her; then give her some incense and myrrh as a present; and be ye, thou and she, one flesh."

5 Adam hearkened to the angels, and took the gold and put it into Eve's bosom in her garment; and bethrothed her with his hand.

6 Then the angels commanded Adam and Eve, to arise and pray forty days and forty nights; and after that, that Adam should come in to his wife; for then this would be an act pure and undefiled; and he should have children who would multiply, and replenish the face of the earth.

7 Then both Adam and Eve received the words of the angels; and the angels departed from them.

8 Then Adam and Eve began to fast and to pray, until the end of the forty days; and then they came together, as the angels had told them. And from the time Adam left the garden until he wedded Eve, were two hundred and twenty-three days, that is seven months and thirteen days.

9 Thus was Satan's war with Adam defeated.

CHAP. LXXIV.

The birth of Cain and Luluwa. Why they received those names.

AND they dwelt on the earth working, in order to continue in the well-being of their bodies; and were so until the nine months of Eve's childbearing were ended, and the time drew near when she must be delivered.

2 Then she said unto Adam, "This cave is a pure spot by reason of the signs wrought in it since we left the garden; and we shall again pray in it. It is not meet, then, that I should bring forth in it; let us rather repair to that of the sheltering rock, which Satan hurled at us, when he wished to kill us with it; but that was held up and spread as an awning over us by the command of God; and formed a cave."

3 Then Adam removed Eve to that cave; and when the time came that she should bring forth, she travailed much. So was Adam sorry, and his heart suffered for her sake; for she was nigh unto death; that the word of God to her should be fulfilled: "In suffering shalt thou bear a child, and in sorrow shalt thou bring forth thy child."

4 But when Adam saw the strait in which Eve was, he arose and prayed to God, and said, "O Lord, look upon me with the eye of Thy mercy, and bring her out of her distress."

5 And God looked at His maid-servant Eve, and delivered her, and she brought forth her first-born son, and with him a daughter.

6 Then Adam rejoiced at Eve's deliverance, and also over the children she had borne him. And Adam ministered unto Eve in the cave, until the end of eight days; when they named the son Cain, and the daughter Luluwa.

7 The meaning of Cain is "hater," because he hated his sister in their mother's womb; ere they came out of it. Therefore did Adam name him Cain.

8 But Luluwa means "beautiful," because she was more beautiful than her mother.

9 Then Adam and Eve waited until Cain and his sister were forty days old, when Adam said unto Eve, "We will make an offering and offer it up in behalf of the children."

10 And Eve said, "We will make one offering for the first-born son; and afterwards we shall make one for the daughter."

CHAP. LXXV.

The family revisits the Cave of Treasures. Birth of Abel and Aklemia.

THEN Adam prepared an offering, and he and Eve offered it up for their children, and brought it to the altar they had built at first.

2 And Adam offered up the offering, and besought God to accept his offering.

3 Then God accepted Adam's offering, and sent a light from heaven that shone upon the offering. And Adam and the son drew near to the offering, but Eve and the daughter did not approach unto it.

4 Then Adam came down from upon the altar, and they were joyful; and Adam and Eve waited until the daughter was eighty days old; then Adam prepared an offering and took it to Eve and to the children; and they went to the altar, where Adam offered it up, as he was wont, asking the Lord to accept his offering.

5 And the Lord accepted the offering of Adam and Eve. Then Adam, Eve, and the children, drew near together, and came down from the mountain, rejoicing.

6 But they returned not to the cave in which they were born; but came to the Cave of Treasures, in order that the children should go round it, and be blessed with the tokens brought from the garden.

7 But after they had been blessed with these tokens, they went back to the cave in which they were born.

8 However, before Eve had offered up the offering, Adam had taken her, and had gone with her to the river of water, in which they threw themselves at first; and there they washed themselves. Adam washed his body and Eve hers also clean, after the suffering and distress that had come upon them.

9 But Adam and Eve, after washing themselves in the river of water, returned every night to the Cave of Treasures, where they prayed and were blessed; and then went back to their cave, where the children were born.

10 So did Adam and Eve until the children had done sucking. Then, when they were weaned, Adam made an offering for the souls of his children; other than the three times he made an offering for them, every week.

11 When the days of nursing the children were ended, Eve again conceived, and when her days were accomplished she brought forth another son and daughter; and they named the son Abel, and the daughter Aklia.

12 Then at the end of forty days, Adam made an offering for the son, and at the end of eighty days he made another offering for the daughter, and did by them, as he had done before by Cain and his sister Luluwa.

13 He brought them to the Cave of Treasures, where they received a blessing, and then returned to the cave where they were born. After the birth of these, Eve ceased from childbearing.

CHAP. LXXVI.

Cain becomes jealous because of his sisters.

AND the children began to wax stronger, and to grow in stature; but Cain was hardhearted, and ruled over his younger brother.

2 And oftentimes when his father made an offering, he would remain behind and not go with them, to offer up.

3 But, as to Abel, he had a meek heart, and was obedient to his father and mother, whom he often moved to make an offering, because he loved it; and prayed and fasted much.

4 Then came this sign to Abel. As he was coming into the Cave of Treasures, and saw the golden rods, the incense and the myrrh, he inquired of his parents Adam and Eve concerning them, and said unto them, "How did you come by those?"

5 Then Adam told him all that had befallen them. And Abel felt deeply about what his father told him.

6 Furthermore his father, Adam, told him of the works of God, and of the garden; and after that, he remained behind his father the whole of that night in the Cave of Treasures.

7 And that night, while he was praying, Satan appeared unto him under the figure of a man, who said to him, "Thou hast oftentimes moved thy father to make an offering, to fast and to pray, therefore I will kill thee, and make thee perish from this world."

8 But as for Abel, he prayed to God, and drove away Satan from him; and believed not the words of the devil. Then when it was day, an angel of God appeared unto him, who said to him, "Shorten neither fasting, prayer, nor offering up an oblation unto thy God. For, lo, the Lord has accepted thy prayer. Be not afraid of the figure which appeared unto thee in the night, and who cursed thee unto death." And the angel departed from him.

9 Then when it was day, Abel came to Adam and Eve, and told them of the vision he had seen. But when they heard it, they grieved much over it, yet said nothing to him about it; they only comforted him.

10 But as to hard-hearted Cain, Satan came to him by night, showed himself and said unto him, "Since Adam and Eve love thy brother Abel much more than they love thee, and wish to join him in marriage to thy beautiful sister, because they love him; but wish to join thee in marriage to his ill-favoured sister, because they hate thee;

11 "Now, therefore, I counsel thee, when they do that, to kill thy brother; then thy sister will be left for thee; and his sister will be cast away."

12 And Satan departed from him. But the wicked One remained behind in the heart of Cain, who sought many a time, to kill his brother.

CHAP. LXXVII.

Cain, 15 years old, and Abel 12 years old, grow apart.

BUT when Adam saw that the elder brother hated the younger, he endeavoured to soften their hearts, and said unto Cain, "Take, O my son, of the fruits of thy sowing, and make an offering unto God, that He may forgive thee thy wickedness and thy sin."

2 He said also to Abel, "Take thou of thy sowing and make an offering and bring it to God, that He may forgive thy wickedness and thy sin."

3 Then Abel hearkened unto his father's voice, and took of his sowing, and made a good offering, and said to his father, Adam, "Come with me, to show me how to offer it up."

4 And they went, Adam and Eve with him, and showed him how to offer up his gift upon the altar. Then after that, they stood up and prayed that God would accept Abel's offering.

5 Then God looked upon Abel and accepted his offering. And

God was more pleased with Abel than with his offering, because of his good heart and pure body. There was no trace of guile in him.

6 Then they came down from the altar, and went to the cave in which they dwelt. But Abel, by reason of his joy at having made his offering, repeated it three times a week, after the example of his father Adam.

7 But as to Cain, he took no pleasure in offering; but after much anger on his father's part, he offered up his gift once; and when he did offer up, his eye was on the offering he made, and he took the smallest of his sheep for an offering, and his eye was again on it.

8 Therefore God did not accept his offering, because his heart was full of murderous thoughts.

9 And they all thus lived together in the cave in which Eve had brought forth, until Cain was fifteen years old, and Abel twelve years old.

CHAP. LXXVIII.

Jealousy overcomes Cain. He makes trouble in the family. How the first murder was planned.

THEN Adam said to Eve, "Behold the children are grown up; we must think of finding wives for them."

2 Then Eve answered, "How can we do it?"

3 Then Adam said to her, "We will join Abel's sister in marriage to Cain, and Cain's sister to Abel."

4 Then said Eve to Adam, "I do not like Cain because he is hard-hearted; but let them bide until we offer up unto the Lord in their behalf."

5 And Adam said no more.

6 Meanwhile Satan came to Cain in the figure of a man of the field, and said to him, "Be-hold Adam and Eve have taken counsel together about the marriage of you two; and they have agreed to marry Abel's sister to thee, and thy sister to him.

7 "But if it was not that I love thee, I would not have told thee this thing. Yet if thou wilt take my advice, and hearken to me, I will bring thee on thy wedding day beautiful robes, gold and silver in plenty, and my relations will attend thee."

8 Then Cain said with joy, "Where are thy relations?"

9 And Satan answered, "My relations are in a garden in the north, whither I once meant to bring thy father Adam; but he would not accept my offer.

10 "But thou, if thou wilt receive my words and if thou wilt come unto me after thy wedding, thou shalt rest from the misery in which thou art; and thou shalt rest and be better off than thy father Adam."

11 At these words of Satan Cain opened his ears, and leant towards his speech.

12 And he did not remain in the field, but he went to Eve, his mother, and beat her, and said to her, "Why are ye about taking my sister to wed her to my brother? Am I dead?"

13 His mother, however, quieted him, and sent him to the field where he had been.

14 Then when Adam came, she told him of what Cain had done.

15 But Adam grieved and held his peace, and said not a word.

16 Then on the morrow Adam said unto Cain his son, "Take of thy sheep, young and good, and offer them up unto thy God; and I will speak to thy brother, to make unto his God an offering of corn."

17 They both hearkened to their father Adam, and they

took their offerings, and offered them up on the mountain by the altar.

18 But Cain behaved haughtily towards his brother, and thrust him from the altar, and would not let him offer up his gift upon the altar; but he offered his own upon it, with a proud heart, full of guile, and fraud.

19 But as for Abel, he set up stones that were near at hand, and upon that, he offered up his gift with a heart humble and free from guile.

20 Cain was then standing by the altar on which he had offered up his gift; and he cried unto God to accept his offering; but God did not accept it from him; neither did a divine fire come down to consume his offering.

21 But he remained standing over against the altar, out of humour and wroth, looking towards his brother Abel, to see if God would accept his offering or not.

22 And Abel prayed unto God to accept his offering. Then a divine fire came down and consumed his offering. And God smelled the sweet savour of his offering; because Abel loved Him and rejoiced in Him.

23 And because God was well pleased with him He sent him an angel of light in the figure of man who had partaken of his offering, because He had smelled the sweet savour of his offering, and they comforted Abel and strengthened his heart.

24 But Cain was looking on all that took place at his brother's offering, and was wroth on account of it.

25 Then he opened his mouth and blasphemed God, because He had not accepted his offering.

26 But God said unto Cain, "Wherefore is thy countenance sad? Be righteous, that I may accept thy offering. Not against Me hast thou murmured, but against thyself."

27 And God said this to Cain in rebuke, and because He abhorred him and his offering.

28 And Cain came down from the altar, his colour changed and of a woeful countenance, and came to his father and mother and told them all that had befallen him. And Adam grieved much because God had not accepted Cain's offering.

29 But Abel came down rejoicing, and with a gladsome heart, and told his father and mother how God had accepted his offering. And they rejoiced at it and kissed his face.

30 And Abel said to his father, "Because Cain thrust me from the altar, and would not allow me to offer my gift upon it, I made an altar for myself and offered my gift upon it."

31 But when Adam heard this he was very sorry, because it was the altar he had built at first, and upon which he had offered his own gifts.

32 As to Cain, he was so sullen and so angry that he went into the field, where Satan came to him and said to him, "Since thy brother Abel has taken refuge with thy father Adam, because thou didst thrust him from the altar, they have kissed his face, and they rejoice over him, far more than over thee."

33 When Cain heard these words of Satan, he was filled with rage; and he let no one know. But he was laying wait to kill his brother, until he brought him into the cave, and then said to him:—

34 "O brother, the country is so beautiful, and there are such beautiful and pleasurable trees in it, and charming to look at! But brother, thou hast never been one day in the field to take thy pleasure therein.

35 "To-day, O, my brother, I very much wish thou wouldest

come with me into the field, to enjoy thyself and to bless our
fields and our flocks, for thou
art righteous, and I love thee
much, O my brother! but thou
hast estranged thyself from me."

36 Then Abel consented to go
with his brother Cain into the
field.

37 But before going out, Cain
said to Abel, "Wait for me, until
I fetch a staff, because of wild
beasts."

38 Then Abel stood waiting
in his innocence. But Cain, the
forward, fetched a staff and
went out.

39 And they began, Cain and
his brother Abel, to walk in the
way; Cain talking to him, and
comforting him, to make him
forget everything.

CHAP. LXXIX.

*A wicked plan is carried to a
tragic conclusion. Cain is fright-
ened. "Am I my brother's
keeper?" The seven punishments. Peace is shattered.*

AND so they went on, until
they came to a lonely
place, where there were no
sheep; then Abel said to Cain,
"Behold, my brother, we are
weary of walking; for we see
none of the trees, nor of the
fruits, nor of the verdure, nor
of the sheep, nor any one of the
things of which thou didst tell
me. Where are those sheep of
thine thou didst tell me to
bless?"

2 Then Cain said to him,
"Come on, and presently thou
shalt see many beautiful things.
but go before me, until I come
up to thee."

3 Then went Abel forward,
but Cain remained behind him.

4 And Abel was walking in
his innocence, without guile; not
believing his brother would kill
him.

5 Then Cain, when he came
up to him, comforted him with
his talk, walking a little behind
him; then he hastened, and
smote him with the staff, blow
upon blow, until he was stunned.

6 But when Abel fell down
upon the ground, seeing that his
brother meant to kill him, he
said to Cain, "O, my brother,
have pity on me. By the breasts
we have sucked, smite me not!
By the womb that bare us and
that brought us into the world,
smite me not unto death with
that staff! If thou wilt kill me,
take one of these large stones,
and kill me outright."

7 Then Cain, the hard-hearted,
and cruel murderer, took a large
stone, and smote his brother
with it upon the head, until
his brains oozed out, and he
weltered in his blood, before him.

8 And Cain repented not of
what he had done.

9 But when the earth, when the
blood of righteous Abel fell upon
it, trembled, as it drank his
blood, and would have brought
Cain to naught for it.

10 And the blood of Abel
cried mysteriously to God, to
avenge him of his murderer.

11 Then Cain began at once
to dig the earth wherein to lay
his brother; for he was trembling from the fear that came
upon him, when he saw the earth
tremble on his account.

12 He then cast his brother
into the pit he made, and covered him with dust. But the
earth would not receive him;
but it threw him up at once.

13 Again did Cain dig the
earth and hid his brother in it;
but again did the earth throw
him up on itself; until three
times did the earth thus throw
up on itself the body of Abel.

14 The muddy earth threw
him up the first time, because
he was not the first creation;
and it threw him up the second

time and would not receive him, because he was righteous and good, and was killed without a cause; and the earth threw him up the third time and would not receive him, that there might remain before his brother a witness against him.

15 And so did the earth mock Cain, until the Word of God, came to him concerning his brother.

16 Then was God angry, and much displeased at Abel's death; and He thundered from heaven, and lightnings went before Him, and the Word of the Lord God came from heaven to Cain, and said unto him, "Where is Abel thy brother?"

17 Then Cain answered with a proud heart and a gruff voice, "How, O God? am I my brother's keeper?"

18 Then God said unto Cain, "Cursed be the earth that has drunk the blood of Abel thy brother; and thou, be thou trembling and shaking; and this will be a sign unto thee, that whosoever finds thee, shall kill thee."

19 But Cain wept because God had said those words to him; and Cain said unto Him, "O God, whosoever finds me shall kill me, and I shall be blotted out from the face of the earth."

20 Then God said unto Cain, "Whosoever shall find thee shall not kill thee;" because before this, God had been saying to Cain, "I shall forego seven punishments on him who kills Cain." For as to the word of God to Cain, "Where is thy brother?" God said it in mercy for him, to try and make him repent.

21 For if Cain had repented at that time, and had said, "O God, forgive me my sin, and the murder of my brother," God would then have forgiven him his sin.

22 And as to God saying to Cain, "Cursed be the ground that has drunk the blood of thy brother" that also, was God's mercy on Cain. For God did not curse him, but He cursed the ground; although it was not the ground that had killed Abel, and had committed iniquity.

23 For it was meet that the curse should fall upon the murderer; yet in mercy did God so manage His thoughts as that no one should know it, and turn away from Cain.

24 And He said to him, "Where is thy brother?" To which he answered and said, "I know not." Then the Creator said to him, "Be trembling and quaking."

25 Then Cain trembled and became terrified; and through this sign did God make him an example before all the creation, as the murderer of his brother. Also did God bring trembling and terror upon him, that he might see the peace in which he was at first, and see also the trembling and terror he endured at the last; so that he might humble himself before God, and repent of his sin, and seek the peace he enjoyed at first.

26 And in the word of God that said, "I will forego seven punishments on whomsoever kills Cain," God was not seeking to kill Cain with the sword, but He sought to make him die of fasting, and praying and weeping by hard rule, until the time that he was delivered from his sin.

27 And the seven punishments are the seven generations during which God awaited Cain for the murder of his brother.

28 But as to Cain, ever since he had killed his brother, he could find no rest in any place; but went back to Adam and Eve, trembling, terrified, and defiled with blood. . . .

THE SECOND BOOK OF

Adam and Eve

CHAP. I.

The grief stricken family. Cain marries Luluwa and they move away.

WHEN Luluwa heard Cain's words, she wept and went to call her father and mother, and told them how that Cain had killed his brother Abel.

2 Then they all cried aloud and lifted up their voices, and slapped their faces, and threw dust upon their heads, and rent asunder their garments, and went out and came to the place where Abel was killed.

3 And they found him lying on the earth, killed, and beasts around him; while they wept and cried because of this just one. From his body, by reason of its purity, went forth a smell of sweet spices.

4 And Adam carried him, his tears streaming down his face; and went to the Cave of Treasures, where he laid him, and wound him up with sweet spices and myrrh.

5 And Adam and Eve continued by the burial of him in great grief a hundred and forty days. Abel was fifteen and a half years old, and Cain seventeen years and a half.

6 As for Cain, when the mourning for his brother was ended, he took his sister Luluwa and married her, without leave from his father and mother; for they could not keep him from her, by reason of their heavy heart.

7 He then went down to the bottom of the mountain, away from the garden, near to the place where he had killed his brother.

8 And in that place were many fruit trees and forest trees. His sister bare him children, who in their turn began to multiply by degrees until they filled that place.

9 But as for Adam and Eve, they came not together after Abel's funeral, for seven years. After this, however, Eve conceived; and while she was with child, Adam said to her, "Come, let us take an offering and offer it up unto God, and ask Him to give us a fair child, in whom we may find comfort, and whom we may join in marriage to Abel's sister."

10 Then they prepared an offering and brought it up to the altar, and offered it before the Lord, and began to entreat Him to accept their offering, and to give them a good offspring.

11 And God heard Adam and accepted his offering. Then, they worshipped, Adam, Eve, and their daughter, and came down to the Cave of Treasures and placed a lamp in it, to burn by night and by day, before the body of Abel.

12 Then Adam and Eve continued fasting and praying until Eve's time came that she should be delivered, when she said to Adam, "I wish to go to the cave in the rock, to bring forth in it."

13 And he said, "Go, and take with thee thy daughter to wait on thee; but I will remain in this Cave of Treasures be-

fore the body of my son Abel."

14 Then Eve hearkened to Adam, and went, she and her daughter. But Adam remained by himself in the Cave of Treasures.

CHAP. II.

A third son is born to Adam and Eve.

AND Eve brought forth a son perfectly beautiful in figure and in countenance. His beauty was like that of his father Adam, yet more beautiful.

2 Then Eve was comforted when she saw him, and remained eight days in the cave; then she sent her daughter unto Adam to tell him to come and see the child and name him. But the daughter stayed in his place by the Adam returned. So did she.

3 But when Adam came and saw the child's good looks, his beauty, and his perfect figure, he rejoiced over him, and was comforted for Abel. Then he named the child Seth, that means, "that God has heard my prayer, and has delivered me out of my affliction." But it means also "power and strength."

4 Then after Adam had named the child, he returned to the Cave of Treasures; and his daughter went back to her mother.

5 But Eve continued in her cave, until forty days were fulfilled, when she came to Adam, and brought with her the child and her daughter.

6 And they came to a river of water, where Adam and his daughter washed themselves, because of their sorrow for Abel; but Eve and the babe washed for purification.

7 Then they returned, and took an offering, and went to the mountain and offered it up, for the babe; and God accepted their offering, and sent His blessing upon them, and upon their son Seth; and they came back to the Cave of Treasures.

8 As for Adam, he knew not again his wife Eve, all the days of his life; neither was any more offspring born of them; but only those five, Cain, Luluwa, Abel, Aklia, and Seth alone.

9 But Seth waxed in stature and in strength; and began to fast and pray, fervently.

CHAP. III

Satan appears as a beautiful woman tempting Adam, telling him he is still a youth. "Spend thy youth in mirth and pleasure." (12) The different forms which Satan takes (15).

AS for our father Adam, at the end of seven years from the day he had been severed from his wife Eve, Satan envied him, when he saw him thus separated from her; and strove to make him live with her again.

2 Then Adam arose and went up above the Cave of Treasures; and continued to sleep there night by night. But as soon as it was light every day he came down to the cave, to pray there and to receive a blessing from it.

3 But when it was evening he went up on the roof of the cave, where he slept by himself, fearing lest Satan should overcome him. And he continued thus apart thirty-nine days.

4 Then Satan, the hater of all good, when he saw Adam thus alone, fasting and praying, appeared unto him in the form of a beautiful woman, who came and stood before him in the night of the fortieth day, and said unto him:—

5 "O Adam, from the time ye have dwelt in this cave, we have experienced great peace from you, and your prayers have reached us, and we have been comforted about you.

6 "But now, O Adam, that thou hast gone up over the roof of the cave to sleep, we have had doubts about thee, and a great sorrow has come upon us because of thy separation from Eve. Then again, when thou art on the roof of this cave, thy prayer is poured out, and thy heart wanders from side to side.

7 "But when thou wast in the cave thy prayer was like fire gathered together; it came down to us, and thou didst find rest.

8 "Then I also grieved over thy children who are severed from thee; and my sorrow is great about the murder of thy son Abel; for he was righteous; and over a righteous man every one will grieve.

9 "But I rejoiced over the birth of thy son Seth; yet after a little while I sorrowed greatly over Eve, because she is my sister. For when God sent a deep sleep over thee, and drew her out of thy side, He brought me out also with her. But He raised her by placing her with thee, while He lowered me.

10 "I rejoiced over my sister for her being with thee. But God had made me a promise before, and said, 'Grieve not; when Adam has gone up on the roof of the Cave of Treasures, and is separated from Eve his wife, I will send thee to him, thou shalt join thyself to him in marriage, and bear him five children, as Eve did bear him five.'

11 "And now, lo! God's promise to me is fulfilled; for it is He who has sent me to thee for the wedding; because if thou wed me, I shall bear thee finer and better children than those of Eve.

12 "Then again, thou art as yet but a youth; end not thy youth in this world in sorrow; but spend the days of thy youth in mirth and pleasure. For thy days are few and thy trial is great. Be strong; end thy days in this world in rejoicing. I shall take pleasure in thee, and thou shall rejoice with me in this wise, and without fear.

13 "Up, then, and fulfil the command of thy God," she then drew near to Adam, and embraced him.

14 But when Adam saw that he should be overcome by her, he prayed to God with a fervent heart to deliver him from her.

15 Then God sent His Word unto Adam, saying, "O Adam, that figure is the one that promised thee the Godhead, and majesty; he is not favourably disposed towards thee; but shows himself to thee at one time in the form of a woman; another moment, in the likeness of an angel; on another occasions, in the similitude of a serpent; and at another time, in the semblance of a god; but he does all that only to destroy thy soul.

16 "Now, therefore, O Adam, understanding thy heart, I have delivered thee many a time from his hands; in order to show thee that I am a merciful God; and that I wish thy good, and that I do not wish thy ruin."

CHAP. IV.

Adam sees the Devil in his true colors.

THEN God ordered Satan to show himself to Adam plainly, in his own hideous form.

2 But when Adam saw him, he feared, and trembled at the sight of him.

3 And God said to Adam, "Look at this devil, and at his hideous look, and know that he it is who made thee fall from brightness into darkness, from peace and rest to toil and misery.

4 And look, O Adam, at him, who said of himself that he is God! Can God be black? Would God take the form of a

woman? Is there any one stronger than God? And can He be overpowered?

5 "See, then, O Adam, and behold him bound in thy presence, in the air, unable to flee away! Therefore, I say unto thee, be not afraid of him; henceforth take care, and beware of him, in whatever he may do to thee."

6 Then God drove Satan away from before Adam, whom He strengthened, and whose heart He comforted, saying to him, "Go down to the Cave of Treasures, and separate not thyself from Eve; I will quell in you all animal lust."

7 From that hour it left Adam and Eve, and they enjoyed rest by the commandment of God. But God did not the like to any one of Adam's seed; but only to Adam and Eve.

8 Then Adam worshipped before the Lord, for having delivered him, and for having layed his passions. And he came down from above the cave, and dwelt with Eve as aforetime.

9 This ended the forty days of his separation from Eve.

CHAP. V.

The devil paints a brilliant picture for Seth to feast his thoughts upon.

AS for Seth, when he was seven years old, he knew good and evil, and was consistent in fasting and praying, and spent all his nights in entreating God for mercy and forgiveness.

2 He also fasted when bringing up his offering every day, more than his father did; for he was of a fair countenance, like unto an angel of God. He also had a good heart, preserved the finest qualities of his soul; and for this reason he brought up his offering every day.

3 And God was pleased with his offering; but He was also pleased with his purity. And he continued thus in doing the will of God, and of his father and mother, until he was seven years old.

4 After that, as he was coming down from the altar, having ended his offering, Satan appeared unto him in the form of a beautiful angel, brilliant with light; with a staff of light in his hand, himself girt about with a girdle of light.

5 He greeted Seth with a beautiful smile, and began to beguile him with fair words, saying to him, "O Seth, why abidest thou in this mountain? For it is rough, full of stones and of sand, and of trees with no good fruit on them; a wilderness without habitations and without towns; no good place to dwell in. But all is heat, weariness, and trouble."

6 He said further, "But we dwell in beautiful places, in another world than this earth. Our world is one of light and our condition is of the best; our women are handsomer than any others; and I wish thee, O Seth, to wed one of them; because I see that thou art fair to look upon, and in this land there is not one woman good enough for thee. Besides, all those who live in this world, are only five souls.

7 "But in our world there are very many men and many maidens, all more beautiful one than another. I wish, therefore, to remove thee hence, that thou mayest see my relations and be wedded to which ever thou likest.

8 "Thou shalt then abide by me and be at peace; thou shalt be filled with splendour and light, as we are.

9 "Thou shalt remain in our world, and rest from this world and the misery of it; thou shalt never again feel faint and weary;

thou shalt never bring up an offering, nor sue for mercy; for thou shalt commit no more sin, nor be swayed by passions.

10 "And if thou wilt hearken to what I say, thou shalt wed one of my daughters; for with us it is no sin so to do; neither is it reckoned animal lust.

11 "For in our world we have no God; but we all are gods; we all are of the light, heavenly, powerful, strong and glorious."

CHAP. VI.

Seth's conscience helps him. He returns to Adam and Eve.

WHEN Seth heard these words he was amazed, and inclined his heart to Satan's treacherous speech, and said to him, "Saidst thou there is another world created than this; and other creatures more beautiful than the creatures that are in this world?"

2 And Satan said, "Yes; behold thou hast heard me; but I will yet praise them and their ways, in thy hearing."

3 But Seth said to him, "Thy speech has amazed me; and thy beautiful description of it all.

4 "Yet I cannot go with thee to-day; not until I have gone to my father Adam and to my mother Eve, and told them all thou hast said to me. Then if they give me leave to go with thee, I will come."

5 Again Seth said, "I am afraid of doing any thing without my father's and mother's leave, lest I perish like my brother Cain, and like my father Adam, who transgressed the commandment of God. But, behold, thou knowest this place; come, and meet me here to-morrow."

6 When Satan heard this, he said to Seth, "If thou tellest thy father Adam what I have told thee, he will not let thee come with me.

7 But hearken to me; do not tell thy father and mother what I have said to thee; but come with me to-day, to our world; where thou shalt see beautiful things and enjoy thyself there, and revel this day among my children, beholding them and taking thy fill of mirth; and rejoice ever more. Then I shall bring thee back to this place to-morrow; but if thou wouldest rather abide with me, so be it."

8 Then Seth answered, "The spirit of my father and of my mother, hangs on me; and if I hide from them one day, they will die, and God will hold me guilty of sinning against them.

9 "And except that they know I am come to this place to bring up to it my offering, they would not be separated from me one hour; neither should I go to any other place, unless they let me. But they treat me most kindly, because I come back to them quickly."

10 Then Satan said to him, "What will happen to thee if thou hide thyself from them one night, and return to them at break of day?"

11 But Seth, when he saw how he kept on talking, and that he would not leave him—ran, and went up to the altar, and spread his hands unto God, and sought deliverance from Him.

12 Then God sent His Word, and cursed Satan, who fled from Him.

13 But as for Seth, he had gone up to the altar, saying thus in his heart. "The altar is the place of offering, and God is there; a divine fire shall consume it; so shall Satan be unable to hurt me, and shall not take me away thence."

14 Then Seth came down from the altar and went to his father and mother, whom he found in the way, longing to hear his voice; for he had tarried a while.

15 He then began to tell

them what had befallen him from Satan, under the form of an angel.

16 But when Adam heard his account, he kissed his face, and warned him against that angel, telling him it was Satan who thus appeared to him. Then Adam took Seth, and they went to the Cave of Treasures, and rejoiced therein.

17 But from that day forth Adam and Eve never parted from him, to whatever place he might go, whether for his offering or for any thing else.

18 This sign happened to Seth, when he was nine years old.

CHAP. VII.

Seth marries Aklia. Adam lives to see grand children and great-grand children.

WHEN our father Adam saw that Seth was of a perfect heart, he wished him to marry; lest the enemy should appear to him another time, and overcome him.

2 So Adam said to his son Seth, "I wish, O my son, that thou wed thy sister Aklia, Abel's sister, that she may bear thee children, who shall replenish the earth, according to God's promise to us.

3 "Be not afraid, O my son; there is no disgrace in it. I wish thee to marry, from fear lest the enemy overcome thee."

4 Seth, however, did not wish to marry; but in obedience to his father and mother, he said not a word.

5 So Adam married him to Aklia. And he was fifteen years old.

6 But when he was twenty years of age, he begat a son, whom he called Enos; and then begat other children than him.

7 Then Enos grew up, married, and begat Cainan.

8 Cainan also grew up, married, and begat Mahalaleel.

9 Those fathers were born during Adam's life-time, and dwelt by the Cave of Treasures.

10 Then were the days of Adam nine hundred and thirty years, and those of Mahalaleel one hundred. But Mahalaleel, when he was grown up, loved fasting, praying, and with hard labours, until the end of our father Adam's days drew near.

CHAP. VIII.

Adam's remarkable last words. He predicts the Flood. He exhorts his offspring to good. He reveals certain mysteries of life.

WHEN our father Adam saw that his end was near, ho called his son Seth, who came to him in the Cave of Treasures, and he said unto him:—

2 "O Seth, my son bring me thy children and thy children's children, that I may shed my blessing on them ere I die."

3 When Seth heard these words from his father Adam, he went from him, shed a flood of tears over his face, and gathered together his children and his children's children, and brought them to his father Adam.

4 But when our father Adam saw them around him, he wept at having to be separated from them.

5 And when they saw him weeping, they all wept together, and fell upon his face saying, "How shalt thou be severed from us, O our father? And how shall the earth receive thee and hide thee from our eyes?" Thus did they they lament much, and in like words.

6 Then our father Adam blessed them all, and said to Seth, after he had blessed them:—

7 "O Seth, my son, thou knowest this world—that it is full of sorrow, and of weariness; and thou knowest all that has come upon us, from our trials in it

I therefore now command thee in these words: to keep innocency, to be pure and just, and trusting in God; and lean not to the discourses of Satan, nor to the apparitions in which he will show himself to thee.

8 But keep the commandments that I give thee this day; then give the same to thy son Enos; and let Enos give it to his son Cainan; and Cainan to his son Mahalaleel; so that this commandment abide firm among all your children.

9 "O Seth, my son, the moment I am dead take ye my body and wind it up with myrrh, aloes, and cassia, and leave me here in this Cave of Treasures in which are all these tokens which God gave us from the garden.

10 "O my son, hereafter shall a flood come and overhelm all creatures, and leave out only eight souls.

11 "But, O my son, let those whom it will leave out from among your children at that time, take my body with them out of this cave; and when they have taken it with them, let the oldest among them command his children to lay my body in a ship until the flood has been assuaged, and they come out of the ship.

12 Then they shall take my body and lay it in the middle of the earth, shortly after they have been saved from the waters of the flood.

13 "For the place where my body shall be laid, is the middle of the earth; God shall come from thence and shall save all our kindred.

14 "But now, O Seth, my son, place thyself at the head of thy people; tend them and watch over them in the fear of God; and lead them in the good way. Command them to fast unto God; and make them understand they ought not to hearken to Satan, lest he destroy them.

15 "Then, again, sever thy children and thy children's children from Cain's children; do not let them ever mix with those, nor come near them either in their words or in their deeds."

16 Then Adam let his blessing descend upon Seth, and upon his children, and upon all his children's children.

17 He then turned to his son Seth, and to Eve his wife, and said to them, "Preserve this gold, this incense, and this myrrh, that God has given us for a sign; for in days that are coming, a flood will overwhelm the whole creation. But those who shall go into the ark shall take with them the gold, the incense, and the myrrh, together with my body; and will lay the gold, the incense, and the myrrh, with my body in the midst of the earth.

18 "Then, after a long time, the city in which the gold, the incense, and the myrrh are found with my body, shall be plundered. But when it is spoiled, the gold the incense, and the myrrh shall be taken care of with the spoil that is kept; and naught of them shall perish, until the Word of God, made man shall come; when kings shall take them, and shall offer to Him, gold in token of His being King; incense, in token of His being God of heaven and earth; and myrrh, in token of His passion.

19 "Gold also, as a token of His overcoming Satan, and all our foes; incense as a token that He will rise from the dead, and be exalted above things in heaven and things in the earth; and myrrh, in token that He will drink bitter gall; and feel the pains of hell from Satan.

20 "And now, O Seth, my son, behold I have revealed unto thee hidden mysteries, which God had revealed unto me. Keep my commandment, for thyself, and for thy people."

CHAP. IX.

The death of Adam.

WHEN Adam had ended his commandment to Seth, his limbs were loosened, his hands and feet lost all power, his mouth became dumb, and his tongue ceased altogether to speak. He closed his eyes and gave up the ghost.

2 But when his children saw that he was dead, they threw themselves over him, men and women, old and young, weeping.

3 The death of Adam took place at the end of nine hundred and thirty years that he lived upon the earth; on the fifteenth day of Barmudeh, after the reckoning of an epact of the sun, at the ninth hour.

4 It was on a Friday, the very day on which he was created, and on which he rested; and the hour at which he died, was the same as that at which he came out of the garden.

5 Then Seth wound him up well, and embalmed him with plenty of sweet spices, from sacred trees and from the Holy Mountain; and he laid his body on the eastern side of the inside of the cave, the side of the incense; and placed in front of him a lamp-stand kept burning.

6 Then his children stood before him weeping and wailing over him the whole night until break of day.

7 Then Seth and his son Enos, and Cainan, the son of Enos, went out and took good offerings to present unto the Lord, and they came to the altar upon which Adam offered gifts to God, when he did offer.

8 But Eve said to them, "Wait until we have first asked God to accept our offering, and to keep by Him the soul of Adam His servant, and to take it up to rest."

9 And they all stood up and prayed.

CHAP. X.

"Adam was the first. . . ."

AND when they had ended their prayer, the Word of God came and comforted them concerning their father Adam.

2 After this, they offered their gifts for themselves and for their father.

3 And when they had ended their offering, the Word of God came to Seth, the eldest among them, saying unto him, "O Seth, Seth, Seth, three times. As I was with thy father, so also shall I be with thee, until the fulfilment of the promise I made him—thy father saying, I will send My Word and save thee and thy seed.

4 "But as to thy father Adam, keep thou the commandment he gave thee; and sever thy seed from that of Cain thy brother."

5 And God withdrew His Word from Seth.

6 Then Seth, Eve, and their children, came down from the mountain to the Cave of Treasures.

7 But Adam was the first whose soul died in the land of Eden, in the Cave of Treasures; for no one died before him, but his son Abel, who died murdered.

8 Then all the children of Adam rose up, and wept over their father Adam, and made offerings to him, one hundred and forty days.

CHAP. XI.

Seth becomes head of the most happy and just tribe of people who ever lived.

AFTER the death of Adam and of Eve, Seth severed his children, and his children's children, from Cain's children. Cain and his seed went down and dwelt westward, below the place where he had killed his brother Abel.

2 But Seth and his children,

dwelt northwards upon the mountain of the Cave of Treasures, in order to be near to their father Adam.

3 And Seth the elder, tall and good, with a fine soul, and of a strong mind, stood at the head of his people; and tended them in innocence, penitence, and meekness, and did not allow one of them to go down to Cain's children.

4 But because of their own purity, they were named "Children of God," and they were with God, instead of the hosts of angels who fell; for they continued in praises to God, and in singing psalms unto Him, in their cave—the Cave of Treasures.

5 Then Seth stood before the body of his father Adam, and of his mother Eve, and prayed night and day, and asked for mercy towards himself and his children; and that when he had some difficult dealing with a child, He would give him counsel.

6 But Seth and his children did not like earthly work, but gave themselves to heavenly things; for they had no other thought than praises, doxologies, and psalms unto God.

7 Therefore did they at all times hear the voices of angels, praising and glorifying God; from within the garden, or when they were sent by God on an errand, or when they were going up to heaven.

8 For Seth and his children, by reason of their own purity, heard and saw those angels. Then, again, the garden was not far above them, but only some fifteen spiritual cubits.

9 Now one spiritual cubit answers to three cubits of man, altogether forty-five cubits.

10 Seth and his children dwelt on the mountain below the garden; they sowed not, neither did they reap; they wrought no food for the body, not even wheat; but only offerings. They ate of the fruit and of trees well flavoured that grew on the mountain where they dwelt.

11 Then Seth often fasted every forty days, as did also his eldest children. For the family of Seth smelled the smell of the trees in the garden, when the wind blew that way.

12 They were happy, innocent, without sudden fear, there was no jealousy, no evil action, no hatred among them. There was no animal passion; from no mouth among them went forth either foul words or curse; neither evil counsel nor fraud. For the men of that time never swore, but under hard circumstances, when men must swear, they swore by the blood of Abel the just.

13 But they constrained their children and their women every day in the cave to fast and pray, and to worship the most High God. They blessed themselves n the body of their father Adam, and anointed themselves with it.

14 And they did so until the end of Seth drew near.

CHAP. XII.

Seth's family affairs. His death. The headship of Enos. How the outcast branch of Adam's family fared.

THEN Seth, the just, called his son Enos, and Cainan, son of Enos, and Mahalaleel, son of Cainan, and said unto them:—

2 "As my end is near, I wish to build a roof over the altar on which gifts are offered."

3 They hearkened to his commandment and went out, all of them, both old and young, and worked hard at it, and built a beautiful roof over the altar.

4 And Seth's thought, in so doing, was that a blessing should come upon his children on the

mountain; and that he should present an offering for them before his death.

5 Then when the building of the roof was completed, he commanded them to make offerings. They worked diligently at these, and brought them to Seth their father who took them and offered them upon the altar; and prayed God to accept their offerings, to have mercy on the souls of his children, and to keep them from the hand of Satan.

6 And God accepted his offering, and sent His blessing upon him and upon his children. And then God made a promise to Seth, saying, "At the end of the great five days and a half, concerning which I have made a promise to thee and to thy father, I will send My Word and save thee and thy seed."

7 Then Seth and his children, and his children's children, met together, and came down from the altar, and went to the Cave of Treasures—where they prayed, and blessed themselves in the body of our father Adam, and anointed themselves with it.

8 But Seth abode in the Cave of Treasures, a few days, and then suffered—sufferings unto death.

9 Then Enos, his first-born son, came to him, with Cainan, his son, and Mahalaleel, Cainan's son, and Jared, the son of Mahalaleel, and Enoch, Jared's son, with their wives and children to receive a blessing from Seth.

10 Then Seth prayed over them, and blessed them, and adjured them by the blood of Abel the just, saying, "I beg of you, my children, not to let one of you go down from this Holy and pure Mountain.

11 Make no fellowship with the children of Cain the murderer and the sinner, who killed his brother; for ye know, O my children, that we flee from him, and from all his sin with all our might because he killed his brother Abel."

12 After having said this, Seth blessed Enos, his first-born son, and commanded him habitually to minister in purity before the body of our father Adam, all the days of his life; then, also, to go at times to the altar which he Seth had built. And he commanded him to feed his people in righteousness, in judgment and purity all the days of his life.

13 Then the limbs of Seth were loosened; his hands and feet lost all power; his mouth became dumb and unable to speak; and he gave up the ghost and died the day after his nine hundred and twelfth year; on the twenty-seventh day of the month Abib; Enoch being then twenty years old.

14 Then they wound up carefull the body of Seth, and embalmed him with sweet spices, and laid him in the Cave of Treasures, on the right side of our father Adam's body, and they mourned for him forty days. They offered gifts for him, as they had done for our father Adam.

15 After the death of Seth, Enos rose at the head of his people, whom he fed in righteousness, and judgment, as his father had commanded him.

16 But by the time Enos was eight hundred and twenty years old, Cain had a large progeny; for they married frequently, being given to animal lusts; until the land below the mountain, was filled with them.

CHAP. XIII.

"Among the children of Cain there was much robbery, murder and sin."

IN those days lived Lamech the blind, who was of the sons of Cain. He had a son whose name was Atun, and they two had much cattle.

2 But Lamech was in the habit of sending them to feed with a young shepherd, who tended them; and who, when coming home in the evening wept before his grandfather, and before his father Atun and his mother Hazina, and said to them, "As for me, I cannot feed those cattle alone, lest one rob me of some of them, or kill me for the sake of them." For among the children of Cain, there was much robbery, murder, and sin.

3 Then Lamech pitied him, and he said, "Truly, he when alone, might be overpowered by the men of this place."

4 So Lamech arose, took a bow he had kept ever since he was a youth, ere he became blind, and he took large arrows, and smooth stones, and a sling which he had, and went to the field with the young shepherd, and placed himself behind the cattle; while the young shepherd watched the cattle. Thus did Lamech many days.

5 Meanwhile Cain, ever since God had cast him off, and had cursed him with trembling and terror, could neither settle nor find rest in any one place; but wandered from place to place.

6 In his wanderings he came to Lamech's wives, and asked them about him. They said to him, "He is in the field with the cattle."

7 Then Cain went to look for him; and as he came into the field, the young shepherd heard the noise he made, and the cattle herding together from before him.

8 Then said he to Lamech, "O my lord, is that a wild beast or a robber?"

9 And Lamech said to him, "Make me understand which way he looks, when he comes up."

10 Then Lamech bent his bow, placed an arrow on it, and fitted a stone in the sling, and when Cain came out from the open country, the shepherd said to Lamech, "Shoot, behold, he is coming."

11 Then Lamech shot at Cain with his arrow and hit him in his side. And Lamech struck him with a stone from his sling, that fell upon his face, and knocked out both his eyes; then Cain fell at once and died.

12 Then Lamech and the young shepherd came up to him, and found him lying on the ground. And the young shepherd said to him, "It is Cain our grandfather, whom thou hast killed, O my lord!"

13 Then was Lamech sorry for it, and from the bitterness of his regret, he clapped his hands together, and struck with his flat palm the head of the youth, who fell as if dead; but Lamech thought it was a feint; so he took up a stone and smote him, and smashed his head until he died.

CHAP. XIV.

Time, like an ever rolling stream, bears away another generation of men.

WHEN Enos was nine hundred years old, all the children of Seth, and of Cainan, and his first-born, with their wives and children, gathered around him, asking for a blessing from him.

2 He then prayed over them and blessed them, and adjured them by the blood of Abel the just saying to them, "Let not one of your children go down from this Holy Mountain, and let them make no fellowship with the children of Cain the murderer."

3 Then Enos called his son Cainan and said to him, "See, O my son, and set thy heart on thy people, and establish them in righteousness, and in innocence; and stand ministering before the body of our father Adam, all the days of thy life."

4 After this Enos entered into rest, aged nine hundred and eighty-five years; and Cainan wound him up, and laid him in the Cave of Treasures on the left of his father Adam; and made offerings for him, after the custom of his fathers.

CHAP. XV.

The offspring of Adam continue to keep the Cave of Treasures as a family shrine.

AFTER the death of Enos, Cainan stood at the head of his people in righteousness and innocence, as his father had commanded him; he also continued to minister before the body of Adam, inside the Cave of Treasures.

2 Then when he had lived nine hundred and ten years, suffering and affliction came upon him. And when he was about to enter into rest, all the fathers with their wives and children came to him, and he blessed them, and adjured them by the blood of Abel, the just, saying to them, "Let not one among you go down from this Holy Mountain; and make no fellowship with the children of Cain the murderer."

3 Mahalaleel, his first-born son, received this commandment from his father, who blessed him and died.

4 Then Mahalaleel embalmed him with sweet spices, and laid him in the Cave of Treasures, with his fathers; and they made offerings for him, after the custom of their fathers.

CHAP. XVI.

The good branch of the family is still afraid of the children of Cain.

THEN Mahalaleel stood over his people, and fed them in righteousness and innocence, and watched them to see they held no intercourse with the children of Cain.

2 He also continued in the Cave of Treasures praying and ministering before the body of our father Adam, asking God for mercy on himself and on his people; until he was eight hundred and seventy years old, when he fell sick.

3 Then all his children gathered unto him, to see him, and to ask for his blessing on them all, ere he left this world.

4 Then Mahalaleel arose and sat on his bed, his tears streaming down his face, and he called his eldest son Jared, who came to him.

5 He then kissed his face, and said to him, "O Jared, my son, I adjure thee by Him who made heaven and earth, to watch over thy people, and to feed them in righteousness and in innocence; and not to let one of them go down from this Holy Mountain to the children of Cain, lest he perish with them.

6 "Hear, O my son, hereafter there shall come a great destruction upon this earth on account of them; God will be angry with the world, and will destroy them with waters.

7 "But I also know that thy children will not hearken to thee, and that they will go down from this mountain and hold intercourse with the children of Cain, and that they shall perish with them.

8 "O my son! teach them, and watch over them, that no guilt attach to thee on their account."

9 Mahalaleel said, moreover,

to his son Jared, "When I die, embalm my body and lay it in the Cave of Treasures, by the bodies of my fathers; then stand thou by my body and pray to God; and take care of them, and fulfil thy ministry before them, until thou enterest into rest thyself."

10 Mahalaleel then blessed all his children; and then lay down on his bed, and entered into rest like his fathers.

11 But when Jared saw that his father Mahalaleel was dead, he wept, and sorrowed, and embraced and kissed his hands and his feet; and so did all his children.

12 And his children embalmed him carefully, and laid him by the bodies of his fathers. Then they arose, and mourned for him forty days.

CHAP. XVII.

Jared turns martinet. He is lured away to the land of Cain where he sees many voluptuous sights. Jared barely escapes with a clean heart.

THEN Jared kept his father's commandment, and arose like a lion over his people. He fed them in righteousness and innocence, and commanded them to do nothing without his counsel. For he was afraid concerning them, lest they should go to the children of Cain.

2 Wherefore did he give them orders repeatedly; and continued to do so until the end of the four hundred and eighty-fifth year of his life.

3 At the end of these said years, there came unto him this sign. As Jared was standing like a lion before the bodies of his fathers, praying and warning his people, Satan envied him, and wrought a beautiful apparition, because Jared would not let his children do aught without his counsel.

4 Satan then appeared to him with thirty men of his hosts, in the form of handsome men; Satan himself being the elder and tallest among them, with a fine beard.

5 They stood at the mouth of the cave, and called out Jared, from within it.

6 He came out to them, and found them looking like fine men, full of light, and of great beauty. He wondered at their beauty and at their looks; and thought within himself whether they might not be of the children of Cain.

7 He said also in his heart, "As the children of Cain cannot come up to the height of this mountain, and none of them is so handsome as these appear to be; and among these men there is not one of my kindred— they must be strangers."

8 Then Jared and they exchanged a greeting and he said to the elder among them, "O my father, explain to me the wonder that is in thee, and tell me who these are, with thee; for they look to me like strange men."

9 Then the elder began to weep, and the rest wept with him; and he said to Jared, "I am Adam whom God made first; and this is Abel my son, who was killed by his brother Cain, into whose heart Satan put to murder him.

10 "Then this is my son Seth, whom I asked of the Lord, who gave him to me, to comfort me instead of Abel.

11 "Then this one is my son Enos, son of Seth, and that other one is Cainan, son of Enos, and that other one is Mahalaleel, son of Cainan, thy father."

12 But Jared remained wondering at their appearance, and at the speech of the elder to him.

13 Then the elder said to him, "Marvel not, O my son; we live in the land north of the garden, which God created before the

world. He would not let us live there, but placed us inside the garden, below which ye are now dwelling.

14 "But after that I transgressed, He made me come out of it, and I was left to dwell in this cave; great and sore troubles came upon me; and when my death drew near, I commanded my son Seth to tend his people well; and this my commandment is to be handed from one to another, unto the end of the generations to come.

15 "But, O Jared, my son, we live in beautiful regions, while you live here in misery, as this thy father Mahalaleel informed me; telling me that a great flood will come and overwhelm the whole earth.

16 "Therefore, O my son, fearing for your sakes, I rose and took my children with me, and came hither for us to visit thee and thy children; but I found thee standing in this cave weeping, and thy children scattered about this mountain, in the heat and in misery.

17 "But, O my son, as we missed our way, and came as far as this, we found other men below this mountain; who inhabit a beautiful country, full of trees and of fruits, and of all manner of verdure; it is like a garden; so that when we found them we thought they were you; until thy father Mahalaleel told me they were no such thing.

18 "Now, therefore, O my son, hearken to my counsel, and go down to them, thou and thy children. Ye will rest from all this suffering in which ye are. But if thou wilt not go down to them, then, arise, take thy children, and come with us to our garden; ye shall live in our beautiful land, and ye shall rest from all this trouble, which thou and thy children are now bearing."

19 But Jared when he heard this discourse from the elder, wondered; and went hither and thither, but at that moment he found not one of his children.

20 Then he answered and said to the elder, "Why have you hidden yourselves until this day?"

21 And the elder replied, "If thy father had not told us, we should not have known it."

22 Then Jared believed his words were true.

23 So that elder said to Jared, "Wherefore didst thou turn about, so and so?" And he said, "I was seeking one of my children, to tell him about my going with you, and about their coming down to those about whom thou hast spoken to me."

24 When the elder heard Jared's intention, he said to him, "Let alone that purpose at present, and come with us; thou shalt see our country; if the land in which we dwell pleases thee, we and thou shall return hither and take thy family with us. But if our country does not please thee, thou shalt come back to thine own place."

25 And the elder urged Jared, to go before one of his children came to counsel him otherwise.

26 Jared, then, came out of the cave and went with them, and among them. And they comforted him, until they came to the top of the mountain of the sons of Cain.

27 Then said the elder to one of his companions, "We have forgotten something by the mouth of the cave, and that is the chosen garment we had brought to clothe Jared withal."

28 He then said to one of them, "Go back, thou, some one; and we will wait for thee here, until thou come back. Then will we clothe Jared and he shall be like us, good, handsome, and fit to come with us into our country."

29 Then that one went back.

30 But when he was a short

distance off, the elder called to him and said to him, "Tarry thou, until I come up and speak to thee."

31 Then he stood still, and the elder went up to him and said to him, "One thing we forgot at the cave, it is this—to put out the lamp that burns inside it, above the bodies that are therein. Then come back to us, quick."

32 That one went, and the elder came back to his fellows and to Jared. And they came down from the mountain, and Jared with them; and they stayed by a fountain of water, near the houses of the children of Cain, and waited for their companion until he brought the garment for Jared.

33 He, then, who went back to the cave, put out the lamp, and came to them and brought a phantom with him and showed it them. And when Jared saw it he wondered at the beauty and grace thereof, and rejoiced in his heart believing it was all true.

34 But while they were staying there, three of them went into houses of the sons of Cain, and said to them, "Bring us to-day some food by the fountain of water, for us and our companions to eat."

35 But when the sons of Cain saw them, they wondered at them and thought: "These are beautiful to look at, and such as we never saw before." So they rose and came with them to the fountain of water, to see their companions.

36 They found them so very handsome, that they cried aloud about their places for others to gather together and come and look at these beautiful beings. Then they gathered around them both men and women.

37 Then the elder said to them, "We are strangers in your land, bring us some good food and drink, you and your women, to refresh ourselves with you."

38 When those men heard these words of the elder, every one of Cain's sons brought his wife, and another brought his daughter, and so, many women came to them; every one addressing Jared either for himself or for his wife; all alike.

39 But when Jared saw what they did, his very soul wrenched itself from them; neither would he taste of their food or of their drink.

40 The elder saw him as he wrenched himself from them, and said to him, "Be not sad; I am the great elder, as thou shalt see me do, do thyself in like manner."

41 Then he spread his hands and took one of the women, and five of his companions did the same before Jared, that he should do as they did.

42 But when Jared saw them working infamy he wept, and said in his mind,—My fathers never did the like.

43 He then spread his hands and prayed with a fervent heart, and with much weeping, and entreated God to deliver him from their hands.

44 No sooner did Jared begin to pray than the elder fled with his companions; for they could not abide in a place of prayer.

45 Then Jared turned round but could not see them, but found himself standing in the midst of the children of Cain.

46 He then wept and said, "O God, destroy me not with this race, concerning which my fathers have warned me; for now, O my Lord God, I was thinking that those who appeared unto me were my fathers; but I have found them out to be devils, who allured me by this beautiful apparition, until I believed them.

47 "But now I ask Thee, O God, to deliver me from this race, among whom I am now

staying, as Thou didst deliver me from those devils. Send Thy angel to draw me out of the midst of them; for I have not myself power to escape from among them."

48 When Jared had ended his prayer, God sent His angel in the midst of them, who took Jared and set him upon the mountain, and showed him the way, gave him counsel, and then departed from him.

CHAP. XVIII.

Confusion in the Cave of Treasures. Miraculous speech of the dead Adam.

THE children of Jared were in the habit of visiting him hour after hour, to receive his blessing and to ask his advice for every thing they did; and when he had a work to do, they did it for him.

2 But this time when they went into the cave they found not Jared, but they found the lamp put out, and the bodies of the fathers thrown about, and voices came from them by the power of God, that said, "Satan in an apparition has deceived our son, wishing to destroy him, as he destroyed our son Cain."

3 They said also, "Lord God of heaven and earth, deliver our son from the hand of Satan, who wrought a great and false apparition before him." They also spake of other matters, by the power of God.

4 But when the children of Jared heard these voices they feared, and stood weeping for their father; for they knew not what had befallen him.

5 And they wept for him that day until the setting of the sun.

6 Then came Jared with a woeful countenance, wretched in mind and body, and sorrowful at having been separated from the bodies of his fathers.

7 But as he was drawing near to the cave, his children saw him, and hastened to the cave, and hung upon his neck, crying, and saying to him, "O father, where hast thou been, and why hast thou left us, as thou wast not wont to do?" And again, "O father, when thou didst disappear, the lamp over the bodies of our fathers went out, the bodies were thrown about, and voices came from them."

8 When Jared heard this he was sorry, and went into the cave; and there found the bodies thrown about, the lamp put out, and the fathers themselves praying for his deliverance from the hand of Satan.

9 Then Jared fell upon the bodies and embraced them, and said, "O my fathers, through your intercession, let God deliver me from the hand of Satan! And I beg you will ask God to keep me and to hide me from him unto the day of my death."

10 Then all the voices ceased save the voice of our father Adam, who spake to Jared by the power of God, just as one would speak to his fellow, saying, "O Jared, my son, offer gifts to God for having delivered thee from the hand of Satan; and when thou bringest those offerings, so be it that thou offerest them on the altar on which I did offer. Then also, beware of Satan; for he deluded me many a time with his apparitions, wishing to destroy me, but God delivered me out of his hand.

11 "Command thy people that they be on their guard against him; and never cease to offer up gifts to God."

12 Then the voice of Adam also became silent; and Jared and his children wondered at this. Then they laid the bodies as they were at first; and Jared and his children stood praying the whole of that night, until break of day.

13 Then Jared made an offering and offered it up on the altar, as Adam had commanded him. And as he went up to the altar, he prayed to God for mercy and for forgiveness of his sin, concerning the lamp going out.

14 Then God appeared unto Jared on the altar and blessed him and his children, and accepted their offerings; and commanded Jared to take of the sacred fire from the altar, and with it to light the lamp that shed light on the body of Adam.

CHAP. XIX.

The children of Jared are led astray.

THEN God revealed to him again the promise He had made to Adam; He explained to him the 5500 years, and revealed unto him the mystery of His coming upon the earth.

2 And God said to Jared, "As to that fire which thou hast taken from the altar to light the lamp withal, let it abide with you to give light to the bodies; and let it not come out of the cave, until the body of Adam comes out of it.

3 But, O Jared, take care of the fire, that it burn bright in the lamp; neither go thou again out of the cave, until thou receivest an order through a vision, and not in an apparition, when seen by thee.

4 "Then command again thy people not to hold intercourse with the children of Cain, and not to learn their ways; for I am God who loves not hatred and works of iniquity."

5 God gave also many other commandments to Jared, and blessed him. And then withdrew His Word from him.

6 Then Jared drew near with his children, took some fire, and came down to the cave, and lighted the lamp before the body of Adam; and he gave his people commandments as God had told him to do.

7 This sign happened to Jared at the end of his four hundred and fiftieth year; as did also many other wonders, we do not record. But we record only this one for shortness sake, and in order not to lengthen our narrative.

8 And Jared continued to teach his children eighty years; but after that they began to transgress the commandments he had given them, and to do many things without his counsel. They began to go down from the Holy Mountain one after another, and to mix with the children of Cain, in foul fellowships.

9 Now the reason for which the children of Jared went down the Holy Mountain, is this, that we will now reveal unto you.

CHAP. XX.

Ravishing music; strong drink loosed among the sons of Cain. They don colorful clothing. The children of Seth look on with longing eyes. They revolt from wise counsel; they descend the mountain into the valley of iniquity. They can not ascend the mountain again.

AFTER Cain had gone down to the land of dark soil, and his children had multiplied therein, there was one of them, whose name was Genun, son of Lamech the blind who slew Cain.

2 But as to this Genun, Satan came into him in his childhood; and he made sundry trumpets and horns, and string instruments, cymbals and psalteries, and lyres and harps, and flutes; and he played on them at all times and at every hour.

3 And when he played on them, Satan came into them, so that from among them were heard beautiful and sweet sounds, that ravished the heart.

4 Then he gathered companies upon companies to play on them; and when they played, it pleased well the children of Cain, who inflamed themselves with sin among themselves, and burnt as with fire; while Satan inflamed their hearts, one with another, and increased lust among them.

5 Satan also taught Genun to bring strong drink out of corn; and this Genun used to bring together companies upon companies in drink-houses; and brought into their hands all manner of fruits and flowers; and they drank together.

6 Thus did this Genun multiply sin exceedingly; he also acted with pride, and taught the children of Cain to commit all manner of the grossest wickedness, which they knew not; and put them up to manifold doings which they knew not before.

7 Then Satan, when he saw that they yielded to Genun and hearkened to him in every thing he told them, rejoiced greatly, increased Genun's understanding, until he took iron and with it made weapons of war.

8 Then when they were drunk, hatred and murder increased among them; one man used violence against another to teach him evil taking his children and defiling them before him.

9 And when men saw they were overcome, and saw others that were not overpowered, those who were beaten came to Genun, took refuge with him, and he made them his confederates.

10 Then sin increased among them greatly; until a man married his own sister, or daughter, or mother, and others; or the daughter of his father's sister, so that there was no more distinction of relationship, and they no longer knew what is iniquity; but did wickedly, and the earth was defiled with sin; and they angered God the Judge, who had created them.

11 But Genun gathered together companies upon companies, that played on horns and on all the other instruments we have already mentioned, at the foot of the Holy Mountain; and they did so in order that the children of Seth who were on the Holy Mountain should hear it.

12 But when the children of Seth heard the noise, they wondered, and came by companies, and stood on the top of the mountain to look at those below; and they did thus a whole year.

13 When, at the end of that year, Genun saw that they were being won over to him little by little, Satan entered into him, and taught him to make dyeing-stuffs for garments of divers patterns, and made him understand how to dye crimson and purple and what not.

14 And the sons of Cain who wrought all this, and shone in beauty and gorgeous apparel, gathered together at the foot of the mountain in splendour, with horns and gorgeous dresses, and horse races, committing all manner of abominations.

15 Meanwhile the children of Seth, who were on the Holy Mountain, prayed and praised God, in the place of the hosts of angels who had fallen; wherefore God had called them "angels," · because He rejoiced over them greatly.

16 But after this, they no longer kept His commandment, nor held by the promise He had made to their fathers; but they relaxed from their fasting and praying, and from the counsel of Jared their father. And they kept on gathering together on the top of the mountain, to look upon the children of Cain, from morning until evening, and upon what they did, upon their beautiful dresses and ornaments.

17 Then the children of Cain looked up from below, and saw the children of Seth, standing in troops on the top of the mountain; and they called to them to come down to them.

18 But the children of Seth said to them from above, "We don't know the way." Then Genun, the son of Lamech, heard them say they did not know the way, and he bethought himself how he might bring them down.

19 Then Satan appeared to him by night, saying, "There is no way for them to come down from the mountain on which they dwell; but when they come to-morrow, say to them, 'Come ye to the western side of the mountain; there you will find the way of a stream of water, that comes down to the foot of the mountain, between two hills; come down that way to us."

20 Then when it was day, Genun blew the horns and beat the drums below the mountain, as he was wont. The children of Seth heard it, and came as they used to do.

21 Then Genun said to them from down below, "Go to the western side of the mountain, there you will find the way to come down."

22 But when the children of Seth heard these words from him, they went back into the cave to Jared, to tell him all they had heard.

23 Then when Jared heard it, he was grieved; for he knew that they would transgress his counsel.

24 After this a hundred men of the children of Seth gathered together, and said among themselves, "Come, let us go down to the children of Cain, and see what they do, and enjoy ourselves with them."

25 But when Jared heard this of the hundred men, his very soul was moved, and his heart was grieved. He then arose with great fervour, and stood in the midst of them, and adjured them by the blood of Abel the just, "Let not one of you go down from this holy and pure mountain, in which our fathers have ordered us to dwell."

26 But when Jared saw that they did not receive his words, he said unto them, "O my good and innocent and holy children, know that when once you go down from this holy mountain, God will not allow you to return again to it."

27 He again adjured them, saying, "I adjure by the death of our father Adam, and by the blood of Abel, of Seth, of Enos, of Cainan, and of Mahalaleel, to hearken to me, and not to go down from this holy mountain; for the moment you leave it, you will be reft of life and of mercy; and you shall no longer be called 'children of God,' but 'children of the devil.'"

28 But they would not hearken to his words.

29 Enoch at that time was already grown up, and in his zeal for God, he arose and said, "Hear me, O ye sons of Seth, small and great—when ye transgress the commandment of our fathers, and go down from this holy mountain—ye shall not come up hither again for ever."

30 But they rose up against Enoch, and would not hearken to his words, but went down from the Holy Mountain.

31 And when they looked at the daughters of Cain, at their beautiful figures, and at their hands and feet dyed with colour, and tattooed in ornaments on their faces, the fire of sin was kindled in them.

32 Then Satan made them look most beautiful before the sons of Seth, as he also made the sons of Seth appear of the fairest in the eyes of the daughters of Cain, so that the daughters of Cain lusted after the sons of

Seth like ravenous beasts, and the sons of Seth after the daughters of Cain, until they committed abomination with them.

33 But after they had thus fallen into this defilement, they returned by the way they had come, and tried to ascend the Holy Mountain. But they could not, because the stones of that holy mountain were of fire flashing before them, by reason of which they could not go up again.

34 And God was angry with them, and repented of them because they had come down from glory, and had thereby lost or forsaken their own purity or innocence, and were fallen into the defilement of sin.

35 Then God sent His Word to Jared, saying, "These thy children, whom thou didst call 'My children,'—behold they have transgressed My commandment, and have gone down to the abode of perdition, and of sin. Send a messenger to those that are left, that they may not go down, and be lost."

36 Then Jared wept before the Lord, and asked of Him mercy and forgiveness. But he wished that his soul might depart from his body, rather than hear these words from God about the going down of his children from the Holy Mountain.

37 But he followed God's order, and preached unto them not to go down from that holy mountain, and not to hold intercourse with the children of Cain.

38 But they heeded not his message, and would not obey his counsel.

CHAP. XXI.

Jared dies in sorrow for his sons who had gone astray. A prediction of the Flood.

AFTER this another company gathered together, and they went to look after their brethren; but they perished as well as they. And so it was, company after company, until only a few of them were left.

2 Then Jared sickened from grief, and his sickness was such that the day of his death drew near.

3 Then he called Enoch his eldest son, and Methuselah Enoch's son, and Lamech the son of Methuselah, and Noah the son of Lamech.

4 And when they were come to him he prayed over them and blessed them, and said to them, "Ye are righteous, innocent sons; go ye not down from this holy mountain; for behold, your children and your children's children have gone down from this holy mountain, and have estranged themselves from this holy mountain, through their abominable lust and transgression of God's commandment.

5 "But I know, through the power of God, that He will not leave you on this holy mountain, because your children have transgressed His commandment and that of our fathers, which we had received from them.

6 "But, O my sons, God will take you to a strange land, and ye never shall again return to behold with your eyes this garden and this holy mountain.

7 "Therefore, O my sons, set your hearts on your own selves, and keep the commandment of God which is with you. And when you go from this holy mountain, into a strange land which ye know not, take with you the body of our father Adam, and with it these three precious gifts and offerings, namely, the gold, the incense, and the myrrh; and let them be in the place where the body of our father Adam shall lay.

8 "And unto him of you who shall be left, O my sons, shall the Word of God come, and

when he goes out of this land he shall take with him the body of our father Adam, and shall lay it in the middle of the earth, the place in which salvation shall be wrought."

9 Then Noah said unto him, "Who is he of us that shall be left?"

10 And Jared answered, "Thou art he that shall be left. And thou shalt take the body of our father Adam from the cave, and place it with thee in the ark when the flood comes.

11 "And thy son Shem, who shall come out of thy loins, he it is who shall lay the body of our father Adam in the middle of the earth, in the place whence salvation shall come."

12 Then Jared turned to his son Enoch, and said unto him, "Thou, my son, abide in this cave, and minister diligently before the body of our father Adam all the days of thy life; and feed thy people in righteousness and innocence."

13 And Jared said no more. His hands were loosened, his eyes closed, and he entered into rest like his fathers. His death took place in the three hundred and sixtieth year of Noah, and in the nine hundred and eighty-ninth year of his own life; on the twelfth of Takhsas on a Friday.

14 But as Jared died, tears streamed down his face by reason of his great sorrow, for the children of Seth, who had fallen in his days.

15 Then Enoch, Methuselah, Lamech and Noah, these four, wept over him; embalmed him carefully, and then laid him in the Cave of Treasures. Then they rose and mourned for him forty days.

16 And when these days of mourning were ended, Enoch, Methuselah, Lamech and Noah remained in sorrow of heart, be-cause their father had departed from them, and they saw him no more.

CHAP. XXII.

Only three righteous men left in the world. The evil conditions of men prior to the Flood.

BUT Enoch kept the commandment of Jared his father, and continued to minister in the cave.

2 It is this Enoch to whom many wonders happened, and who also wrote a celebrated book; but those wonders may not be told in this place.

3 Then after this, the children of Seth went astray and fell, they, their children and their wives. And when Enoch, Methuselah, Lamech and Noah saw them, their hearts suffered by reason of their fall into doubt full of unbelief; and they wept and sought of God mercy, to preserve them, and to bring them out of that wicked generation.

4 Enoch continued in his ministry before the Lord three hundred and eighty-five years, and at the end of that time he became aware through the grace of God, that God intended to remove him from the earth.

5 He then said to his son, "O my son, I know that God intends to bring the waters of the Flood upon the earth, and to destroy our creation.

6 "And ye are the last rulers over this people on this mountain; for I know that not one will be left you to beget children on this holy mountain; neither shall any one of you rule over the children of his people; neither shall any great company be left of you, on this mountain."

7 Enoch said also to them, "Watch over your souls, and hold fast by your fear of God and by your service of Him, and worship Him in upright faith, and serve Him in righteousness,

innocence and judgment, in repentance and also in purity."

8 When Enoch had ended his commandments to them, God transported him from that mountain to the land of life, to the mansions of the righteous and of the chosen, the abode of Paradise of joy, in light that reaches up to heaven; light that is outside the light of this world; for it is the light of God, that fills the whole world, but which no place can contain.

9 Thus, because Enoch was in the light of God, he found himself out of the reach of death; until God would have him die.

10 Altogether, not one of our fathers or of their children, remained on that holy mountain, except those three, Methuselah, Lamech, and Noah. For all the rest went down from the mountain and fell into sin with the children of Cain. Therefore were they forbidden that mountain, and none remained on it but those three men.

THE BOOK OF THE SECRETS OF ENOCH.

THIS new fragment of early literature came to light through certain manuscripts which were recently found in Russia and Servia and so far as is yet known has been preserved only in Slavonic. Little is known of its origin except that in its present form it was written somewhere about the beginning of the Christian era. Its final editor was a Greek and the place of its composition Egypt. Its value lies in the unquestioned influence which it has exerted on the writers of the New Testament. Some of the dark passages of the latter being all but inexplicable without its aid.

Although the very knowledge that such a book ever existed was lost for probably 1200 years, it nevertheless was much used by both Christian and heretic in the early centuries and forms a most valuable document in any study of the forms of early Christianity.

The writing appeals to the reader who thrills to lend wings to his thoughts and fly to mystical realms. Here is a strange dramatization of eternity—with views on Creation, Anthropology, and Ethics. As the world was made in six days, so its history would be accomplished in 6,000 years (or 6,000,000 years), and this would be followed by 1,000 years of rest (possibly when the balance of conflicting moral forces has been struck and human life has reached the ideal state). At its close would begin the 8th Eternal Day, when time should be no more.

I.

An account of the mechanism of the world showing the machinery of the sun and moon in operation. Astronomy and an interesting ancient calendar. See Chapter 15–17 also 21. What the world was like before Creation, see Chapter 24. Chapter 26 is especially picturesque. A unique account of how Satan was created (Chapter 29.)

THERE was a wise man, a great artificer, and the Lord conceived love for him and received him, that he should behold the uppermost dwellings and be an eye-witness of the wise and great and inconceivable and immutable realm of God Almighty, of the very wonderful and glorious and bright and many-eyed station of the Lord's servants, and of the inaccessible throne of the Lord, and of the degrees and manifestations of the incorporeal hosts, and of the ineffable ministration of the multitude of the elements, and of the various apparition and inexpressible singing of the host of Cherubim, and of the boundless light.

2 At that time, he said, when my 165th year was completed, I begat my son Mathusal.

3 After this too I lived two hundred years and completed of all the years of my life three hundred and sixty-five years.

4 On the first day of the first month I was in my house alone and was resting on my couch and slept.

5 And when I was asleep, great distress came up into my heart, and I was weeping with my eyes in sleep, and I could not understand what this distress was, or what would happen to me.

6 And there appeared to me two men, exceeding big, so that I never saw such on earth; their faces were shining like the sun, their eyes too *were* like a burning light, and from their lips was fire coming forth with clothing and singing of various kinds in appearance purple, their wings *were* brighter than gold, their hands whiter than snow.

7 They were standing at the head of my couch and began to call me by my name.

8 And I arose from my sleep and saw clearly those two men standing in front of me.

9 And I saluted them and was seized with fear and the appearance of my face was changed from terror, and those men said to me:

10 'Have courage, Enoch, do not fear; the eternal God sent us to thee, and lo! thou shalt to-day ascend with us into heaven, and thou shalt tell thy sons and all thy household all that they shall do without thee on earth in thy house, and let no one seek thee till the Lord return thee to them.

11 And I made haste to obey them and went out from my house, and made to the doors, as it was ordered me, and summoned my sons Mathusal and Regim and Gaidad and made known to them all the marvels those *men* had told me.

II.

The Instruction.   How Enoch instructed his sons.

LISTEN to me, my children, I know not whither I go, or what will befall me; now therefore, my children, I tell you: turn not from God before the face of the vain, who made not Heaven and earth, for these shall perish and those who worship them, and may the Lord make confident your hearts in the fear of him. And now, my children, let no one think to seek me, until the Lord return me to you.

III.

Of Enoch's assumption; how the angels took him into the first heaven.

IT came to pass, when Enoch had told his sons, that the angels took him on to their wings and bore him up on to the first heaven and placed him on the clouds. And there I looked, and again I looked higher, and saw the ether, and they placed me on the first heaven and showed me a very great Sea, greater than the earthly sea.

IV.

Of the Angels ruling the stars.

THEY brought before my face the elders and rulers of the stellar orders, and showed me two hundred angels, who rule the stars and *their* services to the heavens, and fly with their wings and come round all those who sail.

V.

Of how the Angels keep the store-houses of the snow.

AND here I looked down and saw the treasure-houses of the snow, and the angels who keep their terrible store-houses, and the clouds whence they come out and into which they go.

VI.

Of the dew and of the olive-oil, and various flowers.

THEY showed me the treasure-house of the dew, like oil of the olive, and the appearance of its form, as of all the flowers of the earth; further many angels guarding the treasure-houses of these *things, and* how they are made to shut and open.

VII.

Of how Enoch was taken on to the second heaven.

AND those men took me and led me up on to the second heaven, and showed me darkness, greater than earthly darkness, and there I saw prisoners hanging, watched, awaiting the great and boundless judgement, and these angels were dark-looking, more than earthly darkness, and incessantly making weeping through all hours.

2 And I said to the men who were with me: 'Wherefore are these incessantly tortured?' they answered me: 'These are God's apostates, who obeyed not God's commands, but took counsel with their own will, and turned away with their prince, who also *is* fastened on the fifth heaven.

3 And I felt great pity for them, and they saluted me, and said to me: 'Man of God, pray for us to the Lord'; and I answered to them: 'Who am I, a mortal man, that I should pray for angels? who knoweth whither I go, or what will befall me? or who will pray for me?'

VIII.

Of the assumption of Enoch to the third heaven.

AND those men took me thence, and led me up on to the third heaven, and placed me there; and I looked downwards, and saw the produce of these places, such as has never been known for goodness.

2 And I saw all the sweet-flowering trees and beheld their fruits, which were sweet-smelling, and all the foods borne *by them* bubbling with fragrant exhalation.

3 And in the midst of the trees that of life, in that place whereon the Lord rests, when he goes up into paradise; and this tree is of ineffable goodness and fragrance, and adorned more than every existing thing; and on all sides.*it is* in form gold-looking and vermilion and fire-like and covers all, and it has produce from all fruits.

4 Its root is in the garden at the earth's end.

5 And paradise is between corruptibility and incorruptibility.

6 And two springs come out which send forth honey and milk, and their springs send forth oil and wine, and they separate into four parts, and go round with quiet course, and go down into the PARADISE OF

EDEN, between corruptibility and incorruptibility.

7 And thence they go forth along the earth, and have a revolution to their circle even as other elements.

8 And here there is no unfruitful tree, and every place is blessed.

9 And *there are* three hundred angels very bright, who keep the garden, and with incessant sweet singing and never-silent voices serve the Lord throughout all days and hours.

10 And I said: 'How very sweet is this place,' and those men said to me:

IX.

The showing to Enoch of the place of the righteous and compassionate.

THIS place, O Enoch, is prepared for the righteous, who endure all manner of offence from those that exasperate their souls, who avert their eyes from iniquity, and make righteous judgement, and give bread to the hungering, and cover the naked with clothing, and raise up the fallen, and help injured orphans, and who walk without fault before the face of the Lord, and serve him alone, and for them is prepared this place for eternal inheritance.

X.

Here they showed Enoch the terrible place and various tortures.

AND those two men led me up on to the Northern side, and showed me there a very terrible place, and *there were* all manner of tortures in that place: cruel darkness and unillumined gloom, and there is no light there, but murky fire constantly flameth aloft. and *there*

is a fiery river coming forth, and that whole place is everywhere fire, and everywhere *there is* frost and ice, thirst and shivering, while the bonds are very cruel, and the angels fearful and merciless, bearing angry weapons, merciless torture, and I said:

2 Woe, woe, how very terrible is this place.'

3 And those men said to me: This place, O Enoch, is prepared for those who dishonour God, who on earth practise sin against nature, which is child-corruption after the sodomitic fashion, magic-making, enchantments and devilish witchcrafts, and who boast of their wicked deeds, stealing, lies, calumnies, envy, rancour, fornication, murder, and who, accursed, steal the souls of men, who, seeing the poor take away their goods and themselves wax rich, injuring them for other men's goods; who being able to satisfy the empty, made the hungering to die; being able to clothe, stripped the naked; and who knew not their creator, and bowed down to soulless (*sc.* lifeless) Gods, who cannot see nor hear, vain gods, *who also* built hewn images and bow down to unclean handiwork, for all these is prepared this place amongst these, for eternal inheritance.

XI.

Here they took Enoch up on to the fourth heaven where is the course of sun and moon.

THOSE men took me, and led me up on to the fourth heaven, and showed me all the successive goings, and all the rays of the light of sun and moon.

2 And I measured their goings, and compared their light, and saw that the sun's light is greater than the moon's.

3 Its circle and the wheels on which it goes always, like a wind going past with very marvellous

speed, and day and night it has no rest.*

4 Its passage and return *are accompanied by* four great stars, *and* each star has under it a thousand stars, to the right of the sun's wheel, *and by* four to the left, each having under it a thousand stars, altogether eight thousand, issuing with the sun continually.

5 And by day fifteen myriads of angels attend it, and by night a thousand.

6 And six-winged ones issue with the angels before the sun's wheel into the fiery flames, and a hundred angels kindle the sun and set it alight.

XII.

Of the very marvellous elements of the sun.

AND I looked and saw other flying elements of the sun, whose names *are* Phoenixes and Chalkydri, marvellous and wonderful, with feet and tails in the form of a lion, and a crocodile's head, their appearance *is* empurpled, like the rainbow; their size *is* nine hundred measures, their wings *are like* those of angels, each *has* twelve, and they attend and accompany the sun, bearing heat and dew, as it is ordered them from God.

2 Thus *the sun* revolves and goes, and rises under the heaven, and its course goes under the earth with the light of its rays incessantly.

XIII.

The angels took Enoch and placed him in the east at the sun's gates.

THOSE men bore me away to the east, and placed me at the sun's gates, where the sun goes forth according to the regulation of the seasons and the circuit of the months of the whole year, and the number of the hours day and night.

2 And I saw six gates open, each gate having sixty-one stadia and a quarter of one stadium, and I measured *them* truly, and understood their size *to be* so much, through which the sun goes forth, and goes to the west, and is made even, and rises throughout all the months, and turns back again from the six gates according to the succession of the seasons; thus *the period* of the whole year is finished after the returns of the four seasons.

XIV.

They took Enoch to the West.

AND again those men led me away to the western parts, and showed me six great gates open corresponding to the Eastern gates, opposite to where the sun sets, according to the number of the days three hundred and sixty-five and a quarter.

2 Thus again it goes down to the western gates, *and* draws away its light, the greatness of its brightness, under the earth; for since the crown of its shining is in heaven with the Lord, and guarded by four hundred angels, while the sun goes round on wheel under the earth, and stands seven great hours in night, and spends half *its course* under the earth, when it comes to the eastern approach in the eighth hour of the night, it brings its lights, and the crown of shining, and the sun flames forth more than fire.

XV.

The elements of the sun, the Phoenixes and Chalkydri broke into song.

THEN the elements of the sun, called Phoenixes and Chalkydri break into song, there-

*Cf. "Rapid Transit."

fore every bird flutters with its wings, rejoicing at the giver of light, and they broke into song at the command of the Lord.

2 The giver of light comes to give brightness to the whole world, and the morning guard takes shape, which is the rays of the sun, and the sun of the earth goes out, and receives its brightness to light up the whole face of the earth, and they showed me this calculation of the sun's going.

3 And the gates which it enters, these are the great gates of the computation of the hours of the year; for this reason the sun is a great creation, whose circuit *lasts* twenty-eight years, and begins again from the beginning.

XVI.

They took Enoch and again placed him in the east at the course of the moon.

THOSE men showed me the other course, that of the moon, twelve great g a t e s, crowned from west to east, by which the moon goes in and out of the customary times.

2 It goes in at the first gate to the western places of the sun, by the first gates with *thirty*-one *days* exactly, by the second gates with thirty-one days exactly, by the third with thirty days exactly, by the fourth with thirty days exactly, by the fifth with thirty-one days exactly, by the sixth with thirty-one days exactly, by the seventh with thirty days exactly, by the eighth with thirty-one days perfectly, by the ninth with thirty-one days exactly, by the tenth with thirty days perfectly, by the eleventh with thirty-one days exactly, by the twelfth with twenty-eight days exactly.

3 And it goes through the western gates in the order and number of the eastern, and accomplishes the three hundred and sixty-five and a quarter days of the solar year, while the lunar year has three hundred and fifty-four, and there are wanting *to it* twelve days of the solar circle, which are the lunar epacts of the whole year.

4 [Thus, too, the great circle contains five hundred and thirty-two years.]

5 The quarter *of a day* is omitted for three years, the fourth fulfils *it* exactly.

6 Therefore they are taken outside of heaven for three years and are not added to the number of days, because they change the time of the years to two new months towards completion, to two others towards diminution.

7 And when the western gates are finished, it returns and goes to the eastern to the lights, and goes thus day and night about the heavenly circles, lower than all circles, swifter than the heavenly winds, and spirits and elements and angels flying; each angel has six wings.

8 It has a sevenfold course in nineteen years.

XVII.

Of the singings of the angels, which it is impossible to describe.

IN the midst of the heavens I saw armed soldiers, serving the Lord, with tympana and organs, with incessant voice, with sweet voice, with sweet and incessant *voice* and various singing, which it is impossible to describe, and *which* astonishes every mind, so wonderful and marvellous is the singing of those angels, and I was delighted listening to it.

XVIII.

Of the taking of Enoch on to the fifth heaven.

THE men took me on to the fifth heaven and placed me, and there I saw many and countless soldiers, called Grigori, of human appearance, and their size *was* greater than that of great giants and their faces withered, and the silence of their mouths perpetual, and there was no service on the fifth heaven, and I said to the men who were with me:

2 Wherefore are these very withered and their faces melancholy, and their mouths silent, and *wherefore* is there no service on this heaven?'

3 And they said to me: These are the Grigori, who with their prince Satanail rejected the Lord of light, and after them are those who are held in great darkness on the second heaven, and three of them went down on to earth from the Lord's throne, to the place Ermon, and broke through their vows on the shoulder of the hill Ermon* and saw the daughters of men how good they are, and took to themselves wives, and befouled the earth with their deeds, who in all times of their age made lawlessness and mixing, and giants are born and marvellous big men and great enmity.

4 And therefore God judged them with great judgement, and they weep for their brethren and they will be punished on the Lord's great day.

5 And I said to the Grigori: 'I saw your brethren and their works, and their great torments, and I prayed for them, but the Lord has condemned them *to be* under earth till heaven and earth shall end for ever.'

6 And I said: 'Wherefore do you wait, brethren, and do not serve before the Lord's face, and have not put your services before the Lord's face, lest you anger your Lord utterly?'

7 And they listened to my admonition, and spoke to the four ranks in heaven, and lo! as I stood with those two men four trumpets trumpeted together with great voice, and the Grigori broke into song with one voice, and their voice went up before the Lord pitifully and affectingly.

XIX.

Of the taking of Enoch on to the sixth heaven.

AND thence those men took me and bore me up on to the sixth heaven, and there I saw seven bands of angels, very bright and very glorious, and their faces shining more than the sun's shining, glistening, and there is no difference in their faces, or behaviour, or manner of dress; and these make the orders, and learn the goings of the stars, and the alteration of the moon, or revolution of the sun, and the good government of the world.

2 And when they see evil-doing they make commandments and instruction, and sweet and loud singing, and all *songs* of praise.

3 These are the archangels who are above angels, measure all life in heaven and on earth, and the angels who are are *appointed* over seasons and years, the angels who are over rivers and sea, and who are over the fruits of the earth, and the angels who are over every grass, giving food to all, to every living thing, and the angels who write all the souls of men, and all their deeds, and their lives before the Lord's face; in their midst are six Phoenixes and six Cherubim and six six-winged ones continually

*Compare *The Second Book of Adam and Eve.* Chap. XX.

with one voice singing one voice, and it is not possible to describe their singing, and they rejoice before the Lord at his footstool.

XX.

Hence they took Enoch into the Seventh Heaven.

AND those two men lifted me up thence on to the seventh Heaven, and I saw there a very great light, and fiery troops of great archangels, incorporeal forces, and dominions, orders and governments, cherubim and seraphim, thrones and many-eyed ones, nine regiments, the Ioanit stations of light, and I became afraid, and began to tremble with great terror, and those men took me, and led me after them, and said to me:

2 'Have courage, Enoch, do not fear,' and showed me the Lord from afar, sitting on His very high throne. For what is there on the tenth heaven, since the Lord dwells here?

3 On the tenth heaven is God, in the Hebrew tongue he is called Aravat.

4 And all the heavenly troops would come and stand on the ten steps according to their rank, and would bow down to the Lord, and would again go to their places in joy and felicity, singing songs in the boundless light with small and tender voices, gloriously serving him.

XXI.

Of how the angels here left Enoch, at the end of the seventh Heaven, and went away from him unseen.

AND the cherubim and seraphim standing about the throne, the six-winged and many-eyed ones do not depart, standing before the Lord's face doing his will, and cover his whole throne, singing with gentle voice before the Lord's face: 'Holy, holy, holy, Lord Ruler *of* Sabaoth, heavens and earth are full of Thy glory.'

2 When I saw all these things, those men said to me: 'Enoch, thus far is it commanded us to journey with thee,' and those men went away from me and thereupon I saw them not.

3 And I remained alone at the end of the seventh heaven and became afraid, and fell on my face and said to myself: 'Woe is me, what has befallen me?'

4 And the Lord sent one of his glorious ones, the archangel Gabriel, and *he* said to me: 'Have courage, Enoch, do not fear, arise before the Lord's face into eternity, arise, come with me.'

5 And I answered him, and said in myself: 'My Lord, my soul is departed from me, from terror and trembling,' and I called to the men who led me up to this place, on them I relied, and *it is* with them I go before the Lord's face.

6 And Gabriel caught me up, as a leaf caught up by the wind, and placed me before the Lord's face.

7 And I saw the eighth Heaven, which is called in the Hebrew tongue M u z a l o t h, changer of the seasons, of drought, and of wet, and of the twelve signs of the zodiac, which are above the seventh Heaven.

8 And I saw the ninth Heaven, which is called in Hebrew Kuchavim, where are the heavenly homes of the twelve signs of the zodiac.

XXII.

In the tenth Heaven the archangel Michael led Enoch to before the Lord's face.

ON the tenth Heaven, Aravoth, I saw the appearance of the Lord's face, like iron made to glow in fire, and brought out, emitting sparks, and it burns.

2 Thus I saw. the Lord's face,

but the Lord's face is ineffable, marvellous and very awful, and very, very terrible.

3 And who am I to tell of the Lord's unspeakable being, and of his very wonderful face? And I cannot tell the quantity of his many instructions, and various voices, the Lord's throne very great and not made with hands, nor the quantity of those standing round him, troops of cherubim and seraphim, nor their incessant singing, nor his immutable beauty, and who shall tell of the ineffable greatness of his glory?

4 And I fell prone and bowed down to the Lord, and the Lord with his lips said to me:

5 'Have courage, Enoch, do not fear, arise and stand before my face into eternity.'

6 And the archistratege Michael lifted me up, and led me to before the Lord's face.

7 And the Lord said to his servants tempting them: 'Let Enoch stand before my face into eternity,' and the glorious ones bowed down to the Lord, and said: 'Let Enoch go according to Thy word.'

8 And the Lord said to Michael: 'Go and take Enoch from out his earthly garments, and anoint him with my sweet ointment, and put him into the garments of My glory.'

9 And Michael did thus, as the Lord told him. He anointed me, and dressed me, and the appearance of that ointment is more than the great light, and his ointment is like sweet dew, and its smell mild, shining like the sun's ray, and I looked at myself, and was like one of his glorious ones.

10 And the Lord summoned one of his archangels by name Pravuil, whose knowledge was quicker in wisdom than the other archangels, who wrote all the deeds of the Lord; and the Lord said to Pravuil:

11 'Bring out the books from my store-houses, and a reed of quick-writing, and give it to Enoch, and deliver to him the choice and comforting books out of thy hand.'

XXIII.

Of Enoch's writing, how he wrote his wonderful journeyings and the heavenly apparitions and himself wrote three hundred and sixty-six books.

AND he was telling me all the works of heaven, earth and sea, and all the elements, their passages and goings, and the thunderings of the thunders, the sun and moon, the goings and changes of the stars, the seasons, years, days, and hours, the risings of the wind, the numbers of the angels, and the formation of their songs, and all human things, the tongue of every human song and life, the commandments, instructions, and sweet-voiced singings, and all things that it is fitting to learn.

2 And Pravuil told me: 'All the things that I have told thee, we have written. Sit and write all the souls of mankind, however many of them are born, and the places prepared for them to eternity; for all souls are prepared to eternity, before the formation of the world.'

3 And all double thirty days and thirty nights, and I wrote out all things exactly, and wrote three hundred and sixty-six books.

XXIV.

Of the great secrets of God, which God revealed and told to Enoch, and spoke with him face to face.

AND the Lord summoned me, and said to me: 'Enoch, sit down on my left with Gabriel.'

2 And I bowed down to the

Lord, and the Lord spoke to me: Enoch, beloved, all thou seest, all things that are standing finished I tell to thee even before the very beginning, all that I created from non-being, and visible things from invisible.

3 Hear, Enoch, and take in these my words, for not to My angels have I told my secret, and I have not told them their rise, nor my endless realm, nor have they understood my creating, which I tell thee to-day.

4 For before all things were visible, I alone used to go about in the invisible things, like the sun from east to west, and from west to east.

5 But even the sun has peace in itself, while I found no peace, because I was creating all things, and I conceived the thought of placing foundations, and of creating visible creation.

XXV.

God relates to Enoch, how out of the very lowest darkness comes down the visible and invisible.

I COMMANDED in the very lowest *parts*, that visible things should come down from invisible, and Adoil came down very great, and I beheld him, and lo! he had a belly of great light.

2 And I said to him: 'Become undone, Adoil, and let the visible *come* out of thee.'

3 And he came undone, and a great light came out. And I *was* in the midst of the great light, and as there is born light from light, there came forth a great age, and showed all creation, which I had thought to create.

4 And I saw that *it was* good.

5 And I placed for myself a throne, and took my seat on it, and said to the light: 'Go thou up higher and fix thyself high above the throne, and be a foundation to the highest things.'

6 And above the light there is nothing else, and then I bent up and looked up from my throne.

XXVI.

God summons from the very lowest a second time that Archas, heavy and very red should come forth.

AND I summoned the very lowest a second time, and said: 'Let Archas come forth hard,' and he came forth hard from the invisible.

2 And Archas came forth, hard, heavy, and very red.

3 And I said: 'Be opened, Archas, and let there be born from thee,' and he came undone, an age came forth, very great and very dark, bearing the creation of all lower things, and I saw that *it was* good and said to him:

4 'Go thou down below, and make thyself firm, and be for a foundation for the lower things,' and it happened and he went down and fixed himself, and became the foundation for the lower things, and below the darkness there is nothing else.

XXVII.

Of how God founded the water, and surrounded it with light, and established on it seven islands.

AND I commanded that there should be taken from light and darkness, and I said: 'Be thick,' and it became thus, and I spread it out with the light, and it became water, and I spread it out over the darkness, below the light, and then I made firm the waters, that is to say the bottomless, and I made foundation of light around the water, and created seven circles from inside, and imaged it (*sc.* the water) like crystal wet and dry, that is to say like glass, *and* the circumcession of the waters and the other elements, and I showed each one of them its road, and the seven stars each one of them in its heaven, that they go thus, and I saw that it was good.

2 And I separated between light and between darkness, that is to say in the midst of the water hither and thither, and I said to the light, that it should be the day, and to the darkness, that it should be the night, and there was evening and there was morning the first day.

XXVIII.

The week in which God showed Enoch all his wisdom and power, throughout all the seven days, how he created all the heavenly and earthly forces and all moving things even down to man.

AND then I made firm the heavenly circle, and *made* that the lower water which is under heaven collect itself together, into one whole, and that the chaos become dry, and it became so.

2 Out of the waves I created rock hard and big, and from the rock I piled up the dry, and the dry I called earth, and the midst of the earth I called abyss, that is to say the bottomless, I collected the sea in one place and bound it together with a yoke.

3 And I said to the sea: 'Behold I give thee *thy* eternal limits, and thou shalt not break loose from thy component parts.'

4 Thus I made fast the firmament. This day I called me the first-created.

XXIX.

Then it became evening, and then again morning, and it was the second day. [Monday is the first day.] The fiery Essence.

AND for all the heavenly troops I imaged the image and essence of fire, and my eye looked at the very hard, firm rock, and from the gleam of my eye the lightning received its wonderful nature, *which* is both fire in water and water in fire, and one does not put out the other, nor does the one dry up the other, therefore the lightning is brighter than the sun, softer than water and firmer than hard rock.

2 And from the rock I cut off a great fire, and from the fire I created the orders of the incorporeal ten troops of angels, and their weapons are fiery and their raiment a burning flame, and I commanded that each one should stand in his order.

Here Satanail with his angels was thrown down from the height.

3 And one from out the order of angels, having turned away with the order that was under him, conceived an impossible thought, to place his throne higher than the clouds above the earth, that he might become equal in rank to my power.

4 And I threw him out from the height with his angels, and he was flying in the air continuously above the bottomless.

XXX.

And then I created all the heavens, and the third day was, [Tuesday.]

ON the third day I commanded the earth to make grow great and fruitful trees, and hills, and seed to sow, and I planted Paradise, and enclosed it, and placed as armed *guardians* flaming angels, and thus I created renewal.

2 Then came evening, and came morning the fourth day.

3 [Wednesday]. On the fourth day I commanded that there should be great lights on the heavenly circles.

4 On the first uppermost circle I placed the stars, Kruno, and on the second Aphrodit, on the third Aris, on the fifth Zeus, on the sixth Ermis, on the seventh lesser the moon, and adorned it with the lesser stars.

5 And on the lower I placed the sun for the illumination of day, and the moon and stars for the illumination of night.

6 The sun that it should go according to each animal (*sc* signs of the zodiac), twelve, and I appointed the succession of the months and their names and lives, their thunderings, and their hour-markings, how they should succeed.

7 Then evening came and morning came the fifth day.

8 [Thursday]. On the fifth day I commanded the sea, that it should bring forth fishes, and feathered birds of many varieties, and all animals creeping over the earth, going forth over the earth on four legs, and soaring in the air, male sex and female, and every soul breathing the spirit of life.

9 And there came evening, and there came morning the sixth day.

10 [Friday]. On the sixth day I commanded my wisdom to create man from seven consistencies: one, his flesh from the earth; two, his blood from the dew; three, his eyes from the sun; four, his bones from stone; five, his intelligence from the swiftness of the angels and from

cloud; six, his veins and his hair from the grass of the earth; seven, his soul from my breath and from the wind.

11 And I gave him seven natures: to the flesh hearing, the eyes for sight, to the soul smell, the veins for touch, the blood for taste, the bones for endurance, to the intelligence sweetness (*sc.* enjoyment).

12 I conceived a cunning saying to say, I created man from invisible and from visible nature, of both are his death and life and image, he knows speech like some created thing, small in greatness and again great in smallness, and I placed him on earth, a second angel, honourable, great and glorious, and I appointed him as ruler to rule on earth and to have my wisdom, and there was none like him of earth of all my existing creatures.

13 And I appointed him a name, from the four component parts, from east, from west, from south, from north, and I appointed for him four special stars, and I called his name Adam, and showed him the two ways, the light and the darkness, and I told him:

14 'This is good, and that bad,' that I should learn whether he has love towards me, or hatred, that it be clear which in his race love me.

15 For I have seen his nature, but he has not seen his own nature, therefore *through* not seeing he will sin worse, and I said 'After sin *what is there* but death?'

16 And I put sleep into him and he fell asleep. And I took from him a rib, and created him a wife, that death should come to him by his wife, and I took his last word and called her name mother, that is to say, Eva.

XXXI.

God gives over paradise to Adam, and gives him a command to see the heavens opened, and that he should see the angels singing the song of victory.

ADAM has life on earth, and I created a garden in Eden in the east, that he should observe the testament and keep the command.

2 I made the heavens open to him, that he should see the angels singing the song of victory, and the gloomless light.

3 And he was continuously in paradise, and the devil understood that I wanted to create another world, because Adam was lord on earth, to rule and control it.

4 The devil is the evil spirit of the lower places, as a fugitive he made Sotona from the heavens as his name was Satanail, thus he became different from the angels, *but his nature* did not change *his* intelligence as far as *his* understanding of righteous and sinful *things*.

5 And he understood his condemnation and the sin which he had sinned before, therefore he conceived thought against Adam, in such form he entered and seduced Eva, but did not touch Adam.

6 But I cursed ignorance, but what I had blessed previously, those I did not curse, I cursed not man, nor the earth, nor other creatures, but man's evil fruit, and his works.

XXXII.

After Adam's sin God sends him away into the earth 'whence I took thee,' but does not wish to ruin him for all years to come.

I SAID to him: 'Earth thou art, and into the earth whence I took thee thou shalt go, and I will not ruin thee, but send thee whence I took thee.

2 Then I can again take thee at My second coming.'

3 And I blessed all my creatures visible and invisible. And Adam was five and half hours in paradise.

4 And I blessed the seventh day, which is the Sabbath, on which he rested from all his works.

XXXIII.

God shows Enoch the age of this world, its existence of seven thousand years, and the eighth thousand is the end, neither years, nor months, nor weeks, nor days.

AND I appointed the eighth day also, that the eighth day should be the first-created after my work, and that *the first seven* revolve in the form of the seventh thousand, and that at the beginning of the eighth thousand there should be a time of not-counting, endless, with neither years nor months nor weeks nor days nor hours.

2 And now, Enoch, all that I have told thee, all that thou hast understood, all that thou hast seen of heavenly things, all that thou hast seen on earth, and all that I have written in books by my great wisdom, all these things I have devised and created from the uppermost foundation to the lower and to the end, and there is no counsellor nor inheritor to my creations.

3 I am self-eternal, not made with hands, and without change.

4 My thought is my counsellor, my wisdom and my word are made, and my eyes observe all things how they stand here and tremble with terror.

5 If I turn away my face, then all things will be destroyed.

6 And apply thy mind, Enoch, and know him who is speaking to thee, and take thou the books which thou thyself hast written.

7 And I give thee Samuil and Raguil, who led thee up, and the books, and go down to earth, and tell thy sons all that I have told thee, and all that thou hast seen, from the lower heaven up to my throne, and all the troops.

8 For I created all forces, and there is none that resisteth me or that does not subject himself to me. For all subject themselves to my monarchy, and labour for my sole rule.

9 Give them the books of the handwriting, and they will read them and will know me for the creator of all things, and will understand how there is no other God but me.

10 And let them distribute the books of thy handwriting—children to children, generation to generation, nations to nations.

11 And I will give thee, Enoch, my intercessor, the archistratege Michael, for the handwritings of thy fathers Adam, Seth, Enos, Cainan, Mahaleleel, and Jared thy father.

XXXIV.

God convicts the idolaters and sodomitic fornicators, and therefore brings down a deluge upon them.

THEY have rejected my commandments and my yoke, worthless seed has come up, not fearing God, and they would not bow down to me, but have begun to bow down to vain gods, and denied my unity, and have laden the whole earth with untruths, offences, abominable lecheries, namely one with another, and all manner of other unclean wickednesses, which are disgusting to relate.

2 And therefore I will bring down a deluge upon the earth and will destroy all men, and the whole earth will crumble together into great darkness.

XXXV.

God leaves one righteous man of Enoch's tribe with his whole house, who did God's pleasure according to his will.

BEHOLD from their seed shall arise another generation, much afterwards, but of them many will be very insatiate.

2 He who raises that generation, *shall* reveal to them the books of thy handwriting, of thy fathers, *to them* to whom he must point out the guardianship of the world, to the faithful men and workers of my pleasure, who do not acknowledge my name in vain.

3 And they shall tell another generation, and those *others* having read shall be glorified thereafter, more than the first.

XXXVI.

God commanded Enoch to live on earth thirty days, to give instruction to his sons and to his children's children. After thirty days he was again taken on to heaven.

NOW, Enoch, I give thee the term of thirty days to spend in thy house, and tell thy sons and all thy household, that all may hear from my face what is told them by thee, that they may read and understand, how there is no other God but me.

2 And that they may always keep my commandments, and begin to read and take in the books of thy handwriting.

3 And after thirty days I shall send my angel for thee, and he will take thee from earth and from thy sons to me.

XXXVII.

Here God summons an angel.

AND the Lord called up one of the older angels, terrible and menacing, and placed him by me, in appearance white as snow, and his hands like ice, having the appearance of great frost, and he froze my face, because I could not endure the terror of the Lord, just as it is not possible to endure a stove's fire and the sun's heat, and the frost of the air.

2 And the Lord said to me: 'Enoch, if thy face be not frozen here, no man will be able to behold thy face.'

XXXVIII.

Mathusal continued to have hope and to await his father Enoch at his couch day and night.

AND the Lord said to those men who first led me up: 'Let Enoch go down on to earth with you, and await him till the determined day.'

2 And they placed me by night on my couch.

3 And Mathusal expecting my coming, keeping watch by day and by night at my couch, was filled with awe when he heard my coming, and I told him, 'Let all my household come together, that I tell them everything.'

XXXIX.

Enoch's pitiful admonition to his sons with weeping and great lamentation, as he spoke to them.

OH my children, my beloved ones, hear the admonition of your father, as much as is according to the Lord's will.

2 I have been let come to you to-day, and announce to you, not from my lips, but from the Lord's lips, all that is and was and all that is now, and all that will be till judgement-day.

3 For the Lord has let me come to you, you hear therefore the words of my lips, of a man made big for you, but I am one who has seen the Lord's face, like iron made to glow from fire it sends forth sparks and burns.

4 You look now upon my eyes, *the eyes* of a man big with meaning for you, but I have seen the Lord's eyes, shining like the sun's rays and filling the eyes of man with awe.

5 You see now, my children, the right hand of a man that helps you, but I have seen the Lord's right hand filling heaven as he helped me.

6 You see the compass of my work like your own, but I have seen the Lord's limitless and perfect compass, which has no end.

7 You hear the words of my lips, as I heard the words of the Lord, like great thunder incessantly with hurling of clouds.

8 And now, my children, hear the discourses of the father of the earth, how fearful and awful it is to come before the face of the ruler of the earth, how much more terrible and awful it is to come before the face of the ruler of heaven, the controller of quick and dead, and of the heavenly troops. Who can endure that endless pain?

XL.

Enoch admonishes his children truly of all things from the Lord's lips, how he saw and heard and wrote down.

AND now, my children, I know all things, for this *is* from the Lord's lips, and this my eyes have seen, from beginning to end.

2 I know all things, and have written all things into books, the heavens and their end, and their plenitude, and all the armies and their marchings.

3 I have measured and described the stars, the great countless multitude *of them*.

4 What man has seen their revolutions, and their entrances? For not even the angels see their number, while I have written all their names.

5 And I measured the sun's

circle, and measured its rays, counted the hours, I wrote down too all things that go over the earth, I have written the things that are nourished, and all seed sown and unsown, which the earth produces and all plants, and every grass and every flower, and their sweet smells, and their names, and the dwelling-places of the clouds, and their composition, and their wings, and how they bear rain and rain-drops.

6 And I investigated all things, and wrote the road of the thunder and of the lightning, and they showed me the keys and their guardians, their rise, the way they go; it is let out in measure (sc. gently) by a chain, lest by a heavy chain and violence it hurl down the angry clouds and destroy all things on earth.

7 I wrote the treasure-houses of the snow, and the store-houses of the cold and the frosty airs, and I observed their season's key-holder, he fills the clouds with them, and does not exhaust the treasure-houses.

8 And I wrote the resting-places of the winds and observed and saw how their key-holders bear weighing-scales and measures; first, they put them in *one* weighing-scale, then in the other the weights and let them out according to measure cunningly over the whole earth, lest by heavy breathing they make the earth to rock.

9 And I measured out the whole earth, its mountains, and all hills, fields, trees, stones, rivers, all existing things I wrote down, the height from earth to the seventh heaven, and downwards to the very lowest hell, and the judgement-place, and the very great, open and weeping hell.

10 And I saw how the prisoners are in pain, expecting the limitless judgement.

11 And I wrote down all those being judged by the judge, and all their judgements (*sc.* sentences) and all their works.

XLI.

Of how Enoch lamented Adam's sin.

AND I saw all forefathers from *all* time with Adam and Eva, and I sighed and broke into tears and said of the ruin of their dishonour:

2. 'Woe is me for my infirmity and *for that* of my forefathers,' and thought in my heart and said:

3 'Blessed *is* the man who has not been born or who has been born and shall not sin before the Lord's face, that he come not into this place, nor bring the yoke of this place.'

XLII.

Of how Enoch saw the key-holders and guards of the gates of hell standing.

I SAW the key-holders and guards of the gates of hell standing, like great serpents, and their faces like extinguished lamps, and their eyes of fire, their sharp teeth, and I saw all the Lord's works, how they are right, while the works of man are some *good*, and others bad, and in their works are known those who lie evilly.

XLIII.

Enoch shows his children how he measured and wrote out God's judgements.

I, my children, measured and wrote out every work and every measure and every righteous judgement.

2 As *one* year is more honourable than another, so is *one* man more honourable than another, some for great possessions, some for wisdom of heart, some for

FACSIMILE OF ACTUAL PAGE OF ORIGINAL GUTEN-
BERG BIBLE, ONE OF PAGES OWNED BY ALPHA
HOUSE, INC., "THE RESEARCH PUBLISHERS."

The first successful printing was done in 1450 A.D. when
Gutenberg printed the Old Testament in Latin. There
are about 45 copies of the precious Gutenberg Bible in
existence that have survived the chances of Europe and
its wars for five hundred years.

particular intellect, some for cunning, one for silence of lip, another for cleanliness, one for strength, another for comeliness, one for youth, another for sharp wit, one for shape of body, another for sensibility, let it be heard everywhere, but there is none better than he who fears God, he shall be more glorious in time to come.

XLIV.

Enoch instructs his sons, that they revile not the face of man, small or great.

THE Lord with his hands having created man, in the likeness of his own face, the Lord made him small and great.

2 Whoever reviles the ruler's face, and abhors the Lord's face, has despised the Lord's face, and he who vents anger on any man without injury, the Lord's great anger will cut him down, he who spits on the face of man reproachfully, will be cut down at the Lord's great judgement.

3 Blessed is the man who does not direct his heart with malice against any man, and helps the injured and condemned, and raises the broken down, and shall do charity to the needy, because on the day of the great judgement every weight, every measure and every makeweight *will be* as in the market, that is to say *they are* hung on scales and stand in the market, *and every one* shall learn his own measure, and according to his measure shall take his reward.

XLV.

God shows how he does not want from men sacrifices, nor burnt-offerings, but pure and contrite hearts.

WHOEVER hastens to make offering before the Lord's face, the Lord for his part will hasten that offering by granting of his work.

2 But whoever increases his lamp before the Lord's face and make not true judgement, the Lord will *not* increase his treasure in the realm of the highest.

3 When the Lord demands bread, or candles, or flesh (*sc.* cattle), or any other sacrifice, then that is nothing; but God demands pure hearts, and with all that *only* tests the heart of man.

XLVI.

Of how an earthly ruler does not accept from man abominable and unclean gifts, then how much more does God abominate unclean gifts, but sends them away with wrath and does not accept his gifts.

HEAR, my people, and take in the words of my lips.

2 If any one bring any gifts to an earthly ruler, and have disloyal thoughts in his heart, and the ruler know this, will he not be angry with him, and not refuse his gifts, and not give him over to judgement?

3 Or *if* one man make himself appear good to another by deceit of tongue, but *have* evil in his heart, then will not *the other* understand the treachery of his heart, and himself be condemned, since his untruth was plain to all?

4 And when the Lord shall send a great light, then there will be judgement for the just and the unjust, and there no one shall escape notice.

XLVII.

Enoch instructs his sons from God's lips, and hands them the handwriting of this book.

AND now, my children, lay thought on your hearts, mark well the words of your father, which are all *come* to you from the Lord's lips.

2 Take these books of your father's handwriting and read them.

3 For the books are many, and in them you will learn all the Lord's works, all that has been from the beginning of creation, and will be till the end of time.

4 And if you will observe my handwriting, you will not sin against the Lord; because there is no other except the Lord, neither in heaven, nor in earth, nor in the very lowest *places*, nor in the *one* foundation.

5 The Lord has placed the foundations in the unknown, and has spread forth heavens visible and invisible; he fixed the earth on the waters, and created countless creatures, and who has counted the water and the foundation of the unfixed, or the dust of the earth, or the sand of the sea, or the drops of the rain, or the morning dew, or the wind's breathings? Who has filled earth and sea, and the indissoluble winter?

6 I cut the stars out of fire, and decorated heaven, and put it in their midst.

XLVIII.

Of the sun's passage along the seven circles.

THAT the sun go along the seven heavenly c i r c l e s, which are the appointment of one hundred and eighty-two thrones, that it go down on a short day, and again one hundred and eighty-two, that it go down on a big day, and he has two thrones on which he rests, revolving hither and thither above the thrones of the months, from the seventeenth day of the month Tsivan it goes down to the month Thevan, from the seventeenth of Thevan it goes up.

3 And thus it goes close to the earth, then the earth is glad and makes grow its fruit, and when it goes away, then the earth is sad, and trees and all fruits have no florescence.

4 All this he measured, with good measurement of hours, and fixed a measure by his wisdom, of the visible and the invisible.

5 From the invisible he made all things visible, himself being invisible.

6 Thus I make known to you, my children, and distribute the books to your children, into all your generations, and amongst the nations who shall have the sense to fear God, let them receive them, and may they come to love them more than any food or earthly sweets, and read them and apply themselves to them.

7 And those who understand not the Lord, who fear not God, who accept not, but reject, who do not receive them (*sc.* the books), a terrible judgement awaits these.

8 Blessed is the man who shall bear their yoke and shall drag them along, for he shall be released on the day of the great judgement.

XLIX.

Enoch instructs his sons not to swear either by heaven or earth, and shows God's promise, even in the mother's womb.

I SWEAR to you, my children, but I swear not by any oath, neither by heaven nor by earth, nor by any other creature which God created.

2 The Lord said: 'There is no oath in me, nor injustice, but truth.'

3 If there is no truth in men, let them swear by the words 'yea, yea,' or else, 'nay, nay.'

4 And I swear to you, yea, yea, that there has been no man in his mother's womb, *but that* already before, even to each one there is a place prepared for the repose of that soul, and a meas-

ure fixed how much it is intended that a man be tried in this world.

5 Yea, children, deceive not yourselves, for there has been previously prepared a place for every soul of man.

L.

Of how none born on earth can remain hidden nor his work remain concealed, but he (sc. God) bids us be meek, to endure attack and insult, and not to offend widows and orphans.

I HAVE put every man's work in writing and none born on earth can remain hidden nor his works remain concealed.

2 I see all things.

3 Now therefore, my children, in patience and meekness spend the number of your days, that you inherit endless life.

4 Endure for the sake of the Lord every wound, every injury, every evil word and attack.

5 If ill-requitals befall you, return *them* not either to neighbour or enemy, because the Lord will return *them* for you and be your avenger on the day of great judgement, that there be no avenging here among men.

6 Whoever of you spends gold or silver for his brother's sake, he will receive ample treasure in the world to come.

7 Injure not widows nor orphans nor strangers, lest God's wrath come upon you.

LI.

Enoch instructs his sons, that they hide not treasures in the earth, but bids them give alms to the poor.

STRETCH out your hands to the poor according to your strength.

2 Hide not your silver in the earth.

3 Help the faithful man in affliction, and affliction will not find you in the time of your trouble.

4 And every grievous and cruel yoke that come upon you bear all for the sake of the Lord, and thus you will find your reward in the day of judgement.

5 It is good to go morning, midday, and evening into the Lord's dwelling, for the glory of your creator.

6 Because every breathing *thing* glorifies him, and every creature visible and invisible returns him praise.

LII.

God instructs his faithful, how they are to praise his name.

BLESSED is the man who opens his lips in praise of God of Sabaoth and praises the Lord with his heart.

2 Cursed every man who opens his lips for the bringing into contempt and calumny of his neighbour, because he brings God into contempt.

3 Blessed is he who opens his lips blessing and praising God.

4 Cursed is he before the Lord all the days of his life, who opens his lips to curse and abuse.

5 Blessed is he who blesses all the Lord's works.

6 Cursed is he who brings the Lord's creation into contempt.

7 Blessed is he who looks down and raises the fallen.

8 Cursed is he who looks to and is eager for the destruction of what is not his.

9 Blessed is he who keeps the foundations of his fathers made firm from the beginning.

10 Cursed is he who perverts the decrees of his forefathers.

11 Blessed is he who implants peace and love.

12 Cursed is he who disturbs those that love their neighbours.

13 Blessed is he who speaks with humble tongue and heart to all.

14 Cursed is he who speaks peace with his tongue, while in his heart there is no peace but a sword.

15 For all these things will be laid bare in the weighing-scales and in the books, on the day of the great judgement.

LIII.

[Let us not say: 'Our father is before God, he will stand forward for us on the day of judgement,' for there father cannot help son, nor yet son father.]

AND now, my children, do not say: 'Our father is standing before God, and is praying for our sins,' for there is there no helper of any man who has sinned.

2 You see how I wrote all works of every man, before his creation, *all* that is done amongst all men for all time, and none can tell or relate my handwriting, because the Lord sees all the imaginings of man, how they are vain, where they lie in the treasure-houses of the heart.

3 And now, my children, mark well all the words of your father, that I tell you, lest you regret, saying: 'Why did our father not tell us?'

LIV.

Enoch instructs his sons, that they should hand the books to others also.

AT that time, not understanding this let these books which I have given you be for an inheritance of your peace.

2 Hand them to all who want them, and instruct them, that they may see the Lord's very great and marvellous works.

LV.

Here Enoch shows his sons, telling them with tears: 'My children, the hour has approached for me to go up on to heaven; behold, the angels are standing before me.'

MY children, behold, the day of my term and the time have approached.

2 For the angels who shall go with me are standing before me and urge me to my departure from you; they are standing here on earth, awaiting what has been told them.

3 For to-morrow I shall go up on to heaven, to the uppermost Jerusalem to my eternal inheritance.

4 Therefore I bid you do before the Lord's face all *his* good pleasure.

LVI.

Methosalam asks of his father blessing, that he (sc. Methosalam) may make him (sc. Enoch) food to eat.

METHOSALAM having answered his father Enoch, said: 'What is agreeable to thy eyes, father, that I may make before thy face, that thou mayst bless our dwellings, and thy sons, and that thy people may be made glorious through thee, and then *that* thou mayst depart thus, as the Lord said?'

2 Enoch answered to his son Methosalam *and* said: 'Hear, child, from the time when the Lord anointed me with the ointment of his glory, *there has been no* food in me, and my soul remembers not earthly enjoyment, neither do I want anything earthly.'

LVII.

Enoch bade his son Methosalam to summon all his brethren.

MY child Methosalam, summon all thy brethren and all your household and the elders of the people, that I may talk to them and depart, as is planned for me.'

2 And Methosalam made haste, and summoned his brethren, Regim, Riman, Uchan, Chermion, Gaidad, and all the elders of the people before the face of his father Enoch; and he blessed them, *and* said to them:

LVIII.

Enoch's instruction to his sons.

LISTEN to me, my children, to-day.

2 In those days when the Lord came down on to earth for Adam's sake, and visited all his creatures, which he created himself, after all these he created Adam, and the Lord called all the beasts of the earth, all the reptiles, and all the birds that soar in the air, and brought them all before the face of our father Adam.

3 And Adam gave the names to all things living on earth.

4 And the Lord appointed him ruler over all, and subjected to him all things under his hands, and made them dumb and made them dull that they be commanded of man, and be in subjection and obedience to him.

5 Thus also the Lord created every man lord over all his possessions.

6 The Lord will not judge a single soul of beast for man's sake, but adjudges the souls of men to their beasts in this world; for men have a special place.

7 And as every soul of man is according to number, similarly beasts will not perish, nor all souls of beasts which the Lord created, till the great judgement, and they will accuse man, if he feed them ill.

LIX.

Enoch instructs his sons wherefore they may not touch beef because of what comes from it.

WHOEVER defiles the soul of beasts, defiles his own soul.

2 For man brings clean animals to make sacrifice for sin, that he may have cure of his soul.

3 And if they bring for sacrifice clean animals, and birds, man has cure, he cures his soul.

4 All is given you for food, bind it by the four feet, that is to make good the cure, he cures his soul.

5 But whoever kills beast without wounds, kills his own soul and defiles his own flesh.

6 And he who does any beast any injury whatsoever, in secret, it is evil practice, and he defiles his own soul.

LX.

He who does injury to soul of man, does injury to his own soul, and there is no cure for his flesh, nor pardon for all time. How it is not fitting to kill man neither by weapon nor by tongue.

HE who works the killing of a man's soul, kills his own soul, and kills his own body, and there is no cure for him for all time.

2 He who puts a man in any snare, shall stick in it himself, and there is no cure for him for all time.

3 He who puts a man in any vessel, his retribution will not be wanting at the great judgement for all time.

4 He who works crookedly or speaks evil against any soul, will not make justice for himself for all time.

LXI.

Enoch instructs his sons to keep themselves from injustice and often to stretch forth hands to the poor, to give a share of their labours.

AND now, my children, keep your hearts from every injustice, which the Lord hates. Just as a man asks (*sc.* something) for his own soul from God, so let him do to every living soul, because I know all things, how in the great time (*sc.* to come) are many mansions prepared for men, good for the good, and bad for the bad, without number many.

2 Blessed are those who enter the good houses, for in the bad (*sc.* houses) there is no peace nor return (*sc.* from them).

3 Hear, my children, small and great! When man puts a good thought in his heart, brings gifts from his labours before the Lord's face and his hands made them not, then the Lord will turn away his face from the labour of his hand, and he (*sc.* man) cannot find the labour of his hands.

4 And if his hands made it, but his heart murmur, and his heart cease not making murmur incessantly, he has not any advantage.

LXII.

Of how it is fitting to bring one's gift with faith, because there is no repentance after death.

BLESSED is the man who in his patience brings his gifts with faith before the Lord's face, because he will find forgiveness of sins.

2 But if he take back his words before the time, there is no repentance for him; and if the time pass and he do not of his own will what is promised, there is no repentance after death.

3 Because every work which man does before the time, is all deceit before men, and sin before God.

LXIII.

Of how not to despise the poor, but to share with them equally, lest thou be murmured against before God.

WHEN man clothes the naked and fills the hungry, he will find reward from God.

2 But if his heart murmur, he commits a double evil: ruin of himself and of that which he gives; and for him there will be no finding of reward on account of that.

3 And if his own heart is filled with his food and his own flesh (*sc.* clothed) with his clothing, he commits contempt, and will forfeit all his endurance of poverty, and will not find reward of his good deeds.

4 Every proud and magniloquent man is hateful to the Lord, and every false speech, clothed in untruth; it will be cut with the blade of the sword of death, and thrown into the fire, and shall burn for all time.'

XLIV.

Of how the Lord calls up Enoch, and people took counsel to go and kiss him at the place called Achuzan.

WHEN Enoch had spoken these words to his sons, all people far and near heard how the Lord was calling Enoch. They took counsel together:

2 'Let us go and kiss Enoch,'

and two thousand men came together and came to the place Achuzan where Enoch was, and his sons.

3 And the elders of the people, the whole assembly, came and bowed down and began to kiss Enoch and said to him:

4 'Our father Enoch, be thou blessed of the Lord, the eternal ruler, and now bless thy sons and all the people, that we may be glorified to-day before thy face.

5 For thou shalt be glorified before the Lord's face for all time, since the Lord chose thee, rather than all men on earth, and designated thee writer of all his creation, visible and invisible, and redeemer of the sins of man, and helper of thy household.'

LXV.

Of Enoch's instruction of his sons.

AND Enoch answered all his people saying: 'Hear, my children, before that all creatures were created, the Lord created the visible and invisible things.

2 And as much time as there was and went past, understand that after all that he created man in the likeness of his own form, and put into him eyes to see, and ears to hear, and heart to reflect, and intellect wherewith to deliberate.

3 And the Lord saw all man's works, and created all his creatures, and divided time, from time he fixed the years, and from the years he appointed the months, and from the months he appointed the days, and of days he appointed seven.

4 And in those he appointed the hours, measured them out exactly, that man might reflect on time and count years, months, and hours, *their* alternation, beginning, and end, and that he

might count his own life, from the beginning until death, and reflect on his sin and write his work bad and good; because no work is hidden before the Lord, that every man might know his works and never transgress all his commandments, and keep my handwriting from generation to generation.

5 When all creation visible and invisible, as the Lord created it, shall end, then every man goes to the great judgement, and then all time shall perish, and the years, and thenceforward there will be neither months nor days nor hours, they will be stuck together and will not be counted.

6 There will be one aeon, and all the righteous who shall escape the Lord's great judgement, shall be collected in the great aeon, for the righteous the great aeon will begin, and they will live eternally, and then too there will be amongst them neither labour, nor sickness, nor humiliation, nor anxiety, nor need, nor violence, nor night, nor darkness, but great light.

7 And they shall have a great indestructible wall, and a paradise bright and incorruptible, for all corruptible things shall pass away, and there will be eternal life.

LXVI.

Enoch instructs his sons and all the elders of the people, how they are to walk with terror and trembling before the Lord, and serve him alone and not bow down to idols, but to God, who created heaven and earth and every creature, and to his image.

AND now, my children, keep your souls from all injustice, such as the Lord hates.

2 Walk before his face with terror and trembling and serve him alone.

3 Bow down to the true God, not to dumb idols, but bow down to his picture, and bring all just offerings before the Lord's face. The Lord hates what is unjust.

4 For the Lord sees all things; when man takes thought in his heart, then he counsels the intellects, and every thought is always before the Lord, who made firm the earth and put all creatures on it.

5 If you look to heaven, the Lord is there; if you take thought of the sea's deep and all the under-earth, the Lord is there.

6 For the Lord created all things. Bow not down to things made by man, leaving the Lord of all creation, because no work can remain hidden before the Lord's face.

7 Walk, my children, in long-suffering, in meekness, honesty, in provocation, in grief, in faith and in truth, in *reliance on* promises, in illness, in abuse, in wounds, in temptation, in nakedness, in privation, loving one another, till you go out from this age of ills, that you become inheritors of endless time.

8 Blessed are the just who shall escape the great judgement, for they shall shine forth more than the sun sevenfold, for in this world the seventh part is taken off from all, light, darkness, food, enjoyment, sorrow, paradise, torture, fire, frost, and other things; he put all down in writing, that you might read and understand.'

LXVII.

The Lord let out darkness on to earth and covered the people and Enoch, and he was taken up on high, and light came again in the heaven.

WHEN Enoch had talked to the people, the Lord sent out darkness on to the earth, and there was darkness, and it covered those men standing with Enoch, and they took Enoch up on to the highest heaven, where the Lord *is;* and he received him and placed him before his face, and the darkness went off from the earth, and light came again.

2 And the people saw and understood not how Enoch had been taken, and glorified God, and found a roll in which was traced 'the invisible God'; and all went to their homes.

LXVIII.

ENOCH was born on the sixth day of the month Tsivan, and lived three hundred and sixty-five years.

2 He was taken up to heaven on the first day of the month Tsivan and remained in heaven sixty days.

3 He wrote all these signs of all creation, which the Lord created, and wrote three hundred and sixty-six books, and handed them over to his sons and remained on earth thirty days, and was again taken up to heaven on the sixth day of the month Tsivan, on the very day and hour when he was born.

4 As every man's nature in this life is dark, so are also his conception, birth, and departure from this life.

5 At what hour he was conceived, at that hour he was born, and at that hour too he died.

6 Methosalam and his brethren, all the sons of Enoch, made haste, and erected an altar at the place called Achuzan, whence and where Enoch had been taken up to heaven.

7 And they took sacrificial oxen and summoned all people and sacrificed the sacrifice before the Lord's face.

8 All people, the elders of the people and the whole assembly

came to the feast and brought gifts to the sons of Enoch.

9 And they made a great feast, rejoicing and making merry three days, praising God, who had given them such a sign through Enoch, who had found favour with him, and that they should hand it on to their sons from generation to generation, from age to age.

10 Amen.

THE PSALMS OF SOLOMON

THIS collection of eighteen war songs are the gift of an ancient Semitic writer. The original manuscript has perished but fortunately Greek translations have been preserved, and recently a Syriac version of the same songs has turned up and was published in English for the first time in 1909 by Dr. Rendel Harris.

The date of the writing may be established at the middle of the First Century B. C. because the theme of these songs is that of Pompey's actions in Palestine and his death in Egypt in 48 B. C.

These psalms had an important position and were widely circulated in the early Church. They are frequently referred to in the various Codexes and histories of the first few centuries of the Christian Era.

Later, they became lost through inexplicable reasons; and have only been recovered for our use after the lapse of many centuries.

Besides the literary value of the trumpet-like rythm of these verses, we have here a chapter of stirring ancient history written by an eyewitness. Pompey comes out of the West. He uses battering-rams on the fortifications. His soldiers defile the altar. He is slain in Egypt after a fearful career. In the "righteous" of these psalms we see the Pharisees; in the "sinners" we see the Sadducees. It is an epic of a great people in the throes of a great crisis.

I.

"They became insolent in their prosperity . . . ."

I cried unto the Lord when I was in distress,
Unto God when sinners assailed.
Suddenly the alarm of war was heard before me;
I said, He will hearken to me, for I am full of righteousness.
I thought in my heart that I was full of righteousness,
Because I was well off and had become rich in children.
Their wealth spread to the whole earth,
And their glory unto the end of the earth.
They were exalted unto the stars;
They said they would never fall.
But they became insolent in their prosperity,
And they were without understanding,
Their sins were in secret,
And even I had no knowledge of them.
Their transgressions went beyond those of the heathen before them;
They utterly polluted the holy things of the Lord.

II.

The desecration of Jerusalem; captivity, murder, and raping. A psalm of utter despair.

When the sinner waxed proud, with a battering-ram he cast down fortified walls,

And thou didst not restrain him.
Alien nations ascended Thine altar,
They trampled it proudly with their sandals;
Because the sons of Jerusalem had defiled the holy things of the Lord,
Had profaned with iniquities the offerings of God.
Therefore He said: Cast them far from Me;

.   .   .   .   .

It was set at naught before God,
It was utterly dishonoured;
The sons and the daughters were in grievous captivity,
Sealed was their neck, branded was it among the nations.

According to their sins hath He done unto them,
For He hath left them in the hands of them that prevailed.
He hath turned away His face from pitying them,
Young and old and their children together;
For they had done evil one and all, in not hearkening.
And the heavens were angry,
And the earth abhorred them;
For no man upon it had done what they did,
And the earth recognized all Thy righteous judgements, O God.
They set the sons of Jerusalem to be mocked at in return for the harlots in her;
Every wayfarer entered in in the full light of day.
They made mock with their transgressions, as they themselves were wont to do;
In the full light of day they revealed their iniquities.
And the daughters of Jerusalem were defiled in accordance with Thy judgement,
Because they had defiled themselves with unnatural intercourse.

I am pained in my bowels and my inward parts for these things.

And yet I will justify Thee, O God, in uprightness of heart,
For in Thy judgements is Thy righteousness displayed, O God.
For Thou hast rendered to the sinners according to their deeds,
Yea, according to their sins, which were very wicked.
Thou hast uncovered their sins, that Thy judgement might be manifest;
Thou hast wiped out their memorial from the earth.
God is a righteous judge,
And he is no respecter of persons.

For the nations reproached Jerusalem, trampling it down;
Her beauty was dragged down from the throne of glory.
She girded on sackcloth instead of comely raiment,
A rope was about her head instead of a crown.
She put off the glorious diadem which God had set upon her,
In dishonour was her beauty cast upon the ground.

And I saw and entreated the Lord and said,
Long enough, O Lord, has Thine hand been heavy on Israel, in bringing the nations upon them.
For they have made sport unsparingly in wrath and fierce anger;
And they will make an utter end, unless Thou, O Lord, rebuke them in Thy wrath.
For they have done it not in zeal, but in lust of soul,
Pouring out their wrath upon us with a view to rapine.
Delay not, O God, to recompense them on their heads,
To turn the pride of the dragon into dishonour.

And I had not long to wait before God showed me the insolent one
Slain on the mountains of Egypt,
Esteemed of less account than the least, on land and sea;
His body, too, borne hither and thither on the billows with much insolence,
With none to bury him, because He had rejected him with dishonour.

He reflected not that he was man,
And reflected not on the latter end;
He said: I will be lord of land and sea;
And he recognized not that it is God who is great,
Mighty in His great strength.
He is king over the heavens,
And judgeth kings and kingdoms.
It is He who setteth me up in glory,
And bringeth down the proud to eternal destruction in dishonour,
Because they knew Him not.

And now behold, ye princes of the earth, the judgement of the Lord,
For a great king and righteous is He, judging all that is under heaven.
Bless God, ye that fear the Lord with wisdom,
For the mercy of the Lord will be upon them that fear Him, in the Judgement;
So that He will distinguish between the righteous and the sinner,
And recompense the sinners for ever according to their deeds;
And have mercy on the righteous, delivering him from the affliction of the sinner,
And recompensing the sinner for what he hath done to the righteous.

For the Lord is good to them that call upon Him in patience,
Doing according to His mercy to His pious ones,
Establishing them at all times before Him in strength.

Blessed be the Lord for ever before His servants.

III.

Righteousness versus Sin.

Why sleepest thou, O my soul,
And blessest not the Lord?
Sing a new song,
Unto God who is worthy to be praised.
Sing and be wakeful against His awaking,
For good is a psalm sung to God from a glad heart.

The righteous remember the Lord at all times,
With thanksgiving and declaration of the righteousness of the Lord's judgements.
The righteous despiseth not the chastening of the Lord;
His will is always before the Lord.
The righteous stumbleth and holdeth the Lord righteous:
He falleth and looketh out for what God will do to him;
He seeketh out whence his deliverance will come.
The steadfastness of the righteous is from God, their deliverer;
There lodgeth not in the house of the righteous sin upon sin.
The righteous continually searcheth his house,
To remove utterly all iniquity done by him in error.
He maketh atonement for sins of ignorance by fasting and afflicting his soul,
And the Lord counteth guiltless every pious man and his house.

The sinner stumbleth and curseth
his life,
The day when he was begotten, and his mother's travail.
He addeth sins to sins, while he
liveth;
He falleth—verily grievous is
his fall—and riseth no more.
The destruction of the sinner is
for ever,
And he shall not be remembered, when the righteous is
visited.
This is the portion of sinners for
ever.

But they that fear the Lord shall
rise to life eternal,
And their life shall be in the
light of the Lord, and shall
come to an end no more.

IV.

*A conversation of Solomon with
the Men-pleasers.*

Wherefore sittest thou, O profane man, in the council of
the pious,
Seeing that thy heart is far
removed from the Lord,
Provoking with transgressions
the God of Israel?
Extravagant in speech, extravagant in outward seeming beyond all men,
Is he that is severe of speech
in condemning sinners in
judgement.
And his hand is first upon him
as though he acted in zeal,
And yet he is himself guilty in
respect of manifold sins and
of wantonness.
His eyes are upon every woman
without distinction;
His tongue lieth when he
maketh contract with an
oath.
By night and in secret he sinneth
as though unseen,
With his eyes he talketh to
every woman of evil com-
pacts.

He is swift to enter every house
with cheerfulness as though
guileless.

Let God remove those that live
in hypocrisy in the company
of the pious,
Even the life of such an one
with corruption of his flesh
and penury.
Let God reveal the deeds of the
men-pleasers,
The deeds of such an one with
laughter and derision;
That the pious may count righteous the judgement of their
God,
When sinners are removed
from before the righteous,
Even the man-pleaser who
uttereth law guilefully.
And their eyes are fixed upon
any man's house that is still
secure,
That they may, like the Serpent, destroy the wisdom
of . . . with words of
transgressors,
His words are deceitful that he
may accomplish his wicked
desire.
He never ceaseth from scattering families as though they
were orphans,
Yea, he layeth waste a house
on account of his lawless
desire.
He deceiveth with words, saying,
There is none that seeth, or
judgeth.
He fills one house with lawlessness,
And then his eyes are fixed
upon the next house,
To destroy it with words that
give wing to desire.
Yet with all these his soul, like
Sheol, is not sated.

Let his portion, O Lord, be dishonoured before thee;
Let him go forth groaning, and
come home cursed.
Let his life be spent in anguish,
and penury, and want, O
Lord;

Let his sleep be beset with pains and his awaking with perplexities.

Let sleep be withdrawn from his eyelids at night;

Let him fail dishonourably in every work of his hands.

Let him come home empty-handed to his house,

And his house be void of everything wherewith he could sate his appetite.

Let his old age be spent in childless loneliness until his removal by death.

Let the flesh of the men-pleasers be rent by wild beasts,

And let the bones of the lawless lie dishonoured in the sight of the sun.

Let ravens peck out the eyes of the hypocrites.

For they have laid waste many houses of men, in dishonour,

And scattered them in their lust;

And they have not remembered God,

Nor feared God in all these things;

But they have provoked God's anger and vexed Him.

May He remove them from off the earth,

Because with deceit they beguiled the souls of the flawless.

Blessed are they that fear the Lord in their flawlessness;

The Lord shall deliver them from guileful men and sinners,

And deliver us from every stumbling-block of the lawless (men).

Let God destroy them that insolently work all unrighteousness,

For a great and mighty judge is the Lord our God in righteousness.

Let Thy mercy, O Lord, be upon all them that love Thee.

V.

A statement of the philosophy of the indestructibility of matter. One of the tenets of modern physics.

O Lord God, I will praise Thy name with joy,

In the midst of them that know Thy righteous judgements.

For Thou art good and merciful, the refuge of the poor;

When I cry to Thee, do not silently disregard me.

For no man taketh spoil from a mighty man;

Who, then, can take aught of all that Thou hast made, except Thou Thyself givest?

For man and his portion lie before Thee in the balance;

He cannot add to, so as to enlarge, what has been prescribed by Thee.

O God, when we are in distress we call upon Thee for help,

And Thou dost not turn back our petition, for Thou art our God.

Cause not Thy hand to be heavy upon us,

Lest through necessity we sin.

Even though Thou restore us not, we will not keep away;

But unto Thee will we come.

For if I hunger, unto Thee will I cry, O God;

And *Thou* wilt give to me.

Birds and fish dost Thou nourish,

In that Thou givest rain to the steppes that green grass may spring up,

So to prepare fodder in the steppe for every living thing;

And if they hunger, unto Thee do they lift up their face.

Kings and rulers and peoples *Thou* dost nourish, O God;

And who is the help of the poor and needy, if not Thou, O Lord?

And Thou wilt hearken—for who
is good and gentle but
thou?—
Making glad the soul of the
humble by opening Thine
hand in mercy.

Man's goodness is bestowed
grudgingly and . . .;
And if he repeat it without
murmuring, even that is
marvellous.
But Thy gift is great in goodness and wealth,
And he whose hope is set on
Thee shall have no lack of
gifts.
Upon the whole earth is Thy
mercy, O Lord, in goodness.

Happy is he whom God remem-
bereth in granting to him a
due sufficiency;
If a man abound overmuch,
he sinneth.
Sufficient are moderate means
with righteousness,
And hereby the blessing of the
Lord becomes abundance
with righteousness.
They that fear the Lord rejoice
in good gifts,
· And thy goodness is upon
Israel in Thy kingdom.

Blessed is the glory of the Lord,
for He is our king.

VI.

*A song of hope and fearlessness
and peace.*

Happy is the man whose heart
is fixed to call upon the
name of the Lord;
When he remembereth the
name of the Lord, he will be
saved.
His ways are made even by the
Lord,
And the works of his hands
are preserved by the Lord
his God.
At what he sees in his bad
dreams, his soul shall not be
troubled;

When he passes through rivers
and the tossing of the seas,
he shall not be dismayed.
He ariseth from his sleep, and
blesseth the name of the
Lord:
When his heart is at peace, he
singeth to the name of his
God,
And he entreateth the Lord for
all his house.
And the Lord heareth the prayer
of every one that feareth
God,
And every request of the soul
that hopes for Him doth the
Lord accomplish.

Blessed is the Lord, who showeth
mercy to those who love
Him in sincerity.

VII.

*The fine old doctrine—"Thou art
our Shield!"*

Make not Thy dwelling afar
from us, O God;
Lest they assail us that hate
us without cause.
For Thou hast rejected them,
O God;
Let not their foot trample
upon Thy holy inheritance.
Chasten us Thyself in Thy good
pleasure;
But give us not up to the
nations;
For, if Thou sendest pestilence,
Thou Thyself givest it charge
concerning us;
For Thou art merciful,
And wilt not be angry to the
point of consuming us.

While Thy name dwelleth in our
midst, we shall find mercy;
And the nations shall not pre-
vail against us.
For Thou art our shield,
And when we call upon Thee,
Thou hearkenest to us;
For Thou wilt pity the seed of
Israel for ever
And Thou wilt not reject
them:

But we shall be under Thy yoke
for ever,
And under the rod of Thy
chastening.
Thou wilt establish us in the
time that Thou helpest us,
Showing mercy to the house of
Jacob on the day wherein
Thou didst promise to help
them.

VIII.

*Some remarkable similes of war
creeping on Jerusalem. A survey of the sins that brought all
this trouble.*

Distress and the sound of war
hath my ear heard,
The sound of a trumpet an-
nouncing slaughter and ca-
lamity,
The sound of much people as of
an exceeding high wind,
As a tempest with mighty fire
sweeping through the Negeb.
And I said in my heart, Surely
God judgeth us;
A sound I hear moving to-
wards Jerusalem, the holy
city.
My loins were broken at what
I heard, my knees tottered;
My heart was afraid, my bones
were dismayed like flax.
I said: They establish their ways
in righteousness.

I thought upon the judgments
of God since the creation of
heaven and earth;
I held God righteous in His
judgements which have been
from of old.
God laid bare their sins in the
full light of day;
All the earth came to know
the righteous judgements of
God.
In secret places underground
their iniquities were committed to provoke Him to
anger;
They wrought confusion, son
with mother and father with
daughter;

They committed adultery,
every man with his neigh-
bour's wife.
They concluded covenants with
one another with an oath
touching these things;
They plundered the sanctuary
of God, as though there was
no avenger.
They trode the altar of the
Lord, coming straight from
all manner of uncleanness;
And with menstrual blood they
defiled the sacrifices, as
though these were common
flesh.
They left no sin undone, wherein
they surpassed not the
heathen.

Therefore God mingled for them
a spirit of wandering;
And gave them to drink a cup
of undiluted wine, that they
might become drunken.
He brought him that is from the
end of the earth, that
smiteth mightily;
He decreed war against Jerusalem, and against her land.
The princes of the land went to
meet him with joy: they
said unto him:
Blessed be thy way! Come
ye, enter ye in with peace.
They made the rough ways even,
before his entering in;
They opened the gates to
Jerusalem, they crowned its
walls.

As a father entereth the house of
his sons, so he entered Jerusalem in peace;
He established his feet there
in great safety.
He captured her fortresses and
the wall of Jerusalem;
For God Himself led him in
safety, while they wandered.
He destroyed their princes and
every one wise in counsel;
He poured out the blood of
the inhabitants of Jerusalem,
like the water of uncleanness.

He led away their sons and daughters, whom they had begotten in defilement.

They did according to their uncleanness, even as their fathers had done:
They defiled Jerusalem and the things that had been hallowed to the name of God.
But God hath shown Himself righteous in His judgements upon the nations of the earth;
And the pious servants of God are like innocent lambs in their midst.
Worthy to be praised is the Lord that judgeth the whole earth in His righteousness.

Behold, now, O God, Thou hast shown us Thy judgement in Thy righteousness;
Our eyes have seen Thy judgements, O God.
We have justified Thy name that is honoured for ever;
For Thou are the God of righteousness, judging Israel with chastening.

Turn, O God, Thy mercy upon us, and have pity upon us;
Gather together the dispersed of Israel, with mercy and goodness;
For Thy faithfulness is with us.
And though we have stiffened our neck, yet Thou art our chastener;
Overlook us not, O our God, lest the nations swallow us up, as though there were none to deliver.

But Thou art our God from the beginning,
And upon Thee is our hope set, O Lord;
And we will not depart from Thee,
For good are Thy judgements upon us.
Ours and our children's be Thy good pleasure for ever;

O Lord, our Saviour, we shall never more be moved.
The Lord is worthy to be praised for His judgements with the mouth of His pious ones;
And blessed be Israel of the Lord for ever.

IX.

The exile of the tribes of Israel. A reference to the covenant which God made with Adam. (See the First Book of Adam and Eve, Chap. III, Verse 7).

When Israel was led away captive into a strange land,
When they fell away from the Lord who redeemed them,
They were cast away from the inheritance, which the Lord had given them.
Among every nation were the dispersed of Israel according to the word of God,
That Thou mightest be justified, O God, in Thy righteousness by reason of our transgressions:
For Thou art a just judge over all the peoples of the earth.
For from Thy knowledge none that doeth unjustly is hidden,
And the righteous deeds of Thy pious ones are before Thee, O Lord;
Where, then, can a man hide himself from Thy knowledge, O God?
Our works are subject to our own choice and power
To do right or wrong in the works of our hands;
And in Thy righteousness Thou visitest the sons of men.
He that doeth righteousness layeth up life for himself with the Lord;
And he that doeth wrongly forfeits his life to destruction;

For the judgements of the Lord are given in righteousness to every man and his house.

Unto whom art Thou good, O God, except to them that call upon the Lord?

He cleanseth from sins a soul when it maketh confession, when it maketh acknowledgement;

For shame is upon us and upon our faces on account of all these things.

And to whom doth He forgive sins, except to them that have sinned?

Thou blessest the righteous, and dost not reprove them for the sins that they have committed;

And Thy goodness is upon them that sin, when they repent.

And, now, Thou art our God, and we the people whom Thou hast loved:

Behold and show pity, O God of Israel, for we are Thine;

And remove not Thy mercy from us, lest they assail us.

For Thou didst choose the seed of Abraham before all the nations,

And didst set Thy name upon us, O Lord,

And Thou wilt not reject us for ever.

Thou madest a covenant with our fathers concerning us;

And we hope in Thee, when our soul turneth unto Thee.

The mercy of the Lord be upon the house of Israel for ever and ever.

X.

A glorious hymn. Further reference to the eternal covenant between God and Man.

Happy is the man whom the Lord remembereth with reproving,

And whom He restraineth from the way of evil with strokes,

That he may be cleansed from sin, that it may not be multiplied.

He that maketh ready his back for strokes shall be cleansed,

For the Lord is good to them that endure chastening.

For He maketh straight the ways of the righteous,

And doth not pervert them by His chastening.

And the mercy of the Lord is upon them that love Him in truth,

And the Lord remembereth His servants in mercy.

For the testimony is in the law of the eternal covenant,

The testimony of the Lord is on the ways of men in His visitation.

Just and kind is our Lord in His judgements for ever,

And Israel shall praise the name of the Lord in gladness.

And the pious shall give thanks in the assembly of the people;

And on the poor shall God have mercy in the gladness of Israel;

For good and merciful is God for ever,

And the assemblies of Israel shall glorify the name of the Lord.

The salvation of the Lord be upon the house of Israel unto everlasting gladness!

XI.

Jerusalem hears a trumpet and stands on tiptoe to see her children returning from the North, East and West.

Blow ye in Zion on the trumpet to summon the saints,

Cause ye to be heard in Jerusalem the voice of him that bringeth good tidings;

For God hath had pity on
Israel in visiting them.
Stand on the height, O Jerusalem, and behold thy
children,
From the East and the West,
gathered together by the
Lord;
From the North they come in
the gladness of their God,
From the isles afar off God
hath gathered them.
High mountains hath He abased
into a plain for them;
The hills fled at their entrance.
The woods gave them shelter as
they passed by;
Every sweet-smelling tree God
caused to spring up for
them,
That Israel might pass by in
the visitation of the glory
of their God.
Put on, O Jerusalem, thy glorious garments;
Make ready thy holy robe;
For God hath spoken good
concerning Israel, for ever
and ever.
Let the Lord do what He hath
spoken concerning Israel and
Jerusalem;
Let the Lord raise up Israel
by His glorious name.

The mercy of the Lord be upon
Israel for ever and ever.

XII.

*An appeal for family tranquility
and peace and quiet at home.*

O Lord, deliver my soul from
the lawless and wicked man,
From the tongue that is lawless and slanderous, and
speaketh lies and deceit.
Manifoldly twisted are the
words of the tongue of the
wicked man,
Even as among a people a
fire that burneth up their
beauty.
So he delights to fill houses with
a lying tongue,

To cut down the trees of gladness which setteth on fire
transgressors,
To involve households in warfare by means of slanderous
lips.

May God remove far from the
innocent the lips of transgressors by bringing them to
want
And may the bones of sland-
erers be scattered far away
from them that fear the
Lord!
In flaming fire perish the slanderous tongue far away from
the pious!
May the Lord preserve the
quiet soul that hateth the
unrighteous;
And may the Lord establish
the man that followeth peace
at home.
The salvation of the Lord be
upon Israel His servant for
ever;
And let the sinners perish together at the presence of
the Lord;
But let the Lord's pious ones
inherit the promises of the
Lord.

XIII.

*Of Solomon. A Psalm. Comfort
for the righteous.*

The right hand of the Lord hath
covered me;
The right hand of the Lord
hath spared us.
The arm of the Lord hath saved
us from the sword that
passed through,
From famine and the death of
sinners.
Noisome beasts ran upon them:
With their teeth they tore
their flesh,
And with their molars crushed
their bones.
But from all these things the
Lord delivered us.

The righteous was troubled on account of his errors,
Lest he should be taken away along with the sinners;
For terrible is the overthrow of the sinner;
But not one of all these things toucheth the righteous.
For not alike are the chastening of the righteous for sins done in ignorance,
And the overthrow of the sinners.
Secretly is the righteous chastened,
Lest the sinner rejoice over the righteous.
For He correcteth the righteous as a beloved son.
And his chastisement is as that of a first-born.
For the Lord spareth His pious ones,
And blotteth out their errors by His chastening.
For the life of the righteous shall be for ever;
But sinners shall be taken away into destruction,
And their memorial shall be found no more.
But upon the pious is the mercy of the Lord,
And upon them that fear Him His mercy.

XIV.

Sinners "love the brief day spent in companionship with their sin." Profound wisdom, beautifully expressed.

Faithful is the Lord to them that love Him in truth,
To them that endure His chastening,
To them that walk in the righteousness of His commandments,
In the law which He commanded us that we might live.
The pious of the Lord shall live by it for ever;

The Paradise of the Lord, the trees of life, are His pious ones.
Their planting is rooted for ever;
They shall not be plucked up all the days of heaven:
For the portion and the inheritance of God is Israel.
But not so are the sinners and transgressors,
Who love the brief day spent in companionship with their sin;
Their delight is in fleeting corruption,
And they remember not God.
For the ways of men are known before Him at all times,
And He knoweth the secrets of the heart before they come to pass.
Therefore their inheritance is Sheol and darkness and destruction,
And they shall not be found in the day when the righteous obtain mercy;
But the pious of the Lord shall inherit life in gladness.

XV.

The psalmist restates the great philosophy of Right and Wrong.

When I was in distress I called upon the name of the Lord,
I hoped for the help of the God of Jacob and was saved;
For the hope and refuge of the poor art Thou, O God.
For who, O God, is strong except to give thanks unto Thee in truth?
And wherein is a man powerful except in giving thanks to Thy name?
A new psalm with song in gladness of heart,
The fruit of the lips with the well-tuned instrument of the tongue,
The first fruits of the lips from a pious and righteous heart—

He that offereth these things
shall never be shaken by
evil;
The flame of fire and the
wrath against the unrighteous shall not touch him,
When it goeth forth from the face
of the Lord against sinners,
To destroy all the substance
of sinners,
For the mark of God is upon
the righteous that they may
be saved.

Famine and sword and pestilence
shall be far from the righteous,
For they shall flee away from
the pious as men pursued
in war;
But they shall pursue sinners
and overtake them,
And they that do lawlessness
shall not escape the judgement of God;
As by enemies experienced in
war shall they be overtaken,
For the mark of destruction is
upon their forehead.
And the inheritance of sinners
is destruction and darkness,
And their iniquities shall pursue them unto Sheol beneath.
Their inheritance shall not be
found of their children,
For sins shall lay waste the
houses of sinners.
And sinners shall perish for ever
in the day of the Lord's
judgement,
When God visiteth the earth
with His judgement.
But they that fear the Lord shall
find mercy therein,
And shall live by the compassion of their God;
But sinners shall perish for ever.

XVI.

*The psalmist again expresses
profound truth—"For if Thou
givest not strength, who can endure chastisement?"*

When my soul slumbered being
afar from the Lord, I had all
but slipped down to the pit,
When I was far from God,
my soul had been well-nigh
poured out unto death,
I had been nigh unto the gates
of Sheol with the sinner,
When my soul departed from
the Lord God of Israel—
Had not the Lord helped me
with His everlasting mercy.

He pricked me, as a horse is
pricked, that I might serve
Him,
My saviour and helper at all
times saved me.
I will give thanks unto Thee, O
God, for Thou hast helped
me to my salvation;
And hast not counted me with
sinners to my destruction.
Remove not Thy mercy from me,
O God,
Nor Thy memorial from my
heart until I die.
Rule me, O God, keeping me
back from wicked sin,
And from every wicked woman
that causeth the simple to
stumble.
And let not the beauty of a
lawless woman beguile me,
Nor any one that is subject to
unprofitable sin.

Establish the works of my hands
before Thee,
And preserve my goings in the
remembrance of Thee.
Protect my tongue and my lips
with words of truth;
Anger and unreasoning wrath
put far from me.
Murmuring, and impatience in
affliction, remove far from
me,
When, if I sin, Thou chastenest
me that I may return unto
Thee.
But with goodwill and cheerfulness support my soul;
When Thou strengthenest my
soul, what is given to me
will be sufficient for me.
For if *Thou* givest not strength,
Who can endure chastisement
with poverty?

When a man is rebuked by
means of his corruption,
Thy testing of him is in his
flesh and in the affliction of
poverty.
If the righteous endureth in all
these trials, he shall receive
mercy from the Lord.

XVII.

*"They set a worldly monarchy
. . . . they lay waste the
Throne of David." A poetic
narrative about the utter dis-
integration of a great nation.*

O Lord, Thou art our King for
ever and ever,
For in Thee, O God, doth our
soul glory.
How long are the days of man's
life upon the earth?
As are his days, so is the hope
set upon him.
But *we* hope in God, our
deliverer;
For the might of our God is for
ever with mercy,
And the kingdom of our God
is for ever over the nations
in judgement.

Thou, O Lord, didst choose
David to be king over Israel,
And swaredst to him touching
his seed that never should
his kingdom fail before
Thee.
But, for our sins, sinners rose
up against us;
They assailed us and thrust us
out;
What Thou hadst not prom-
ised to them, they took
away from us with violence.
They in no wise glorified Thy
honourable name;
They set a worldly monarchy
in place of that which was
their excellency;
They laid waste the throne of
David in tumultuous arro-
gance.

But Thou, O God, didst cast
them down, and remove
their seed from the earth,
In that there rose up against
them a man that was alien
to our race.
According to their sins didst
Thou recompense them, O
God;
So that it befell them accord-
ing to their deeds.
God showed them no pity;
He sought out their seed and
let not one of them go free.
Faithful is the Lord in all His
judgements
Which He doeth upon the
earth.

The lawless one laid waste our
land so that none inhab-
ited it,
They destroyed young and old
and their children together.
In the heat of His anger He
sent them away even unto
the west,
And He exposed the rulers of
the land unsparingly to derision.
Being an alien the enemy acted
proudly,
And his heart was alien from
Our God.
And all things whatsoever he did
in Jerusalem,
As also the nations in the
cities to their gods.

And the children of the covenant in the midst of the
mingled peoples surpassed
them in evil.
There was not among them
one that wrought in the
midst of Jerusalem mercy
and truth.
They that loved the synagogues
of the pious fled from them,
As sparrows that fly from their
nest.
They wandered in deserts that
their lives might be saved
from harm,

And precious in the eyes of them that lived abroad was any that escaped alive from them.

Over the whole earth were they scattered by lawless men.

For the heavens withheld the rain from dropping upon the earth,

Springs were stopped that sprang perennially out of the deeps, that ran down from lofty mountains.

For there was none among them that wrought righteousness and justice;

From the chief of them to the least of them all were sinful;

The king was a transgressor, and the judge disobedient, and the people sinful.

Behold, O Lord, and raise up unto them their king, the son of David,

At the time in the which Thou seest, O God, that he may reign over Israel Thy servant.

And gird him with strength, that he may shatter unrighteous rulers,

And that he may purge Jerusalem from nations that trample her down to destruction.

Wisely, righteously he shall thrust out sinners from the inheritance,

He shall destroy the pride of the sinner as a potter's vessel.

With a rod of iron he shall break in pieces all their substance,

He shall destroy the godless nations with the word of his mouth;

At his rebuke nations shall flee before him,

And he shall reprove sinners for the thoughts of their heart.

And he shall gather together a holy people, whom he shall lead in righteousness,

And he shall judge the tribes of the people that has been sanctified by the Lord his God.

And he shall not suffer unrighteousness to lodge any more in their midst,

Nor shall there dwell with them any man that knoweth wickedness,

For he shall know them, that they are all sons of their God.

And he shall divide them according to their tribes upon the land,

And neither sojourner nor alien shall sojourn with them any more.

He shall judge peoples and nations in the wisdom of his righteousness. *Selah.*

And he shall have the heathen nations to serve him under his yoke;

And he shall glorify the Lord in a place to be seen of all the earth;

And he shall purge Jerusalem, making it holy as of old:

So that nations shall come from the ends of the earth to see his glory,

Bringing as gifts her sons who had fainted.

And to see the glory of the Lord, wherewith God hath glorified her.

And he shall be a righteous king, taught of God, over them,

And there shall be no unrighteousness in his days in their midst,

For all shall be holy and their king the anointed of the Lord.

For he shall not put his trust in horse and rider and bow,

Nor shall he multiply for himself gold and silver for war,

Nor shall he gather confidence from a multitude for the day of battle.

The Lord Himself is his king, the hope of him that is mighty through his hope in God.

All nations shall be in fear before him,
For he will smite the earth with the word of his mouth for ever.
He will bless the people of the Lord with wisdom and gladness,
And he himself will be pure from sin, so that he may rule a great people.
He will rebuke rulers, and remove sinners by the might of his word;
And relying upon his God, throughout his days he will not stumble;
For God will make him mighty by means of His holy spirit,
And wise by means of the spirit of understanding, with strength and righteousness.
And the blessing of the Lord will be with him: he will be strong and stumble not;
His hope will be in the Lord: who then can prevail against him?
He will be mighty in his works, and strong in the fear of God,
He will be shepherding the flock of the Lord faithfully and righteously,
And will suffer none among them to stumble in their pasture.
He will lead them all aright,
And there will be no pride among them that any among them should be oppressed.
This will be the majesty of the king of Israel whom God knoweth;
He will raise him up over the house of Israel to correct him.
His words shall be more refined than costly gold, the choicest;
In the assemblies he will judge the peoples, the tribes of the sanctified.

His words shall be like the words of the holy ones in the midst of sanctified peoples.
Blessed be they that shall be in those days,
In that they shall see the good fortune of Israel which God shall bring to pass in the gathering together of the tribes.
May the Lord hasten His mercy upon Israel!
May He deliver us from the uncleanness of unholy enemies!
The Lord Himself is our king for ever and ever.

XVIII.

With this psalm end the warlike Songs of Solomon.

Lord, Thy mercy is over the works of Thy hands for ever;
Thy goodness is over Israel with a rich gift.
Thine eyes look upon them, so that none of them suffers want;
Thine ears listen to the hopeful prayer of the poor.
Thy judgements are executed upon the whole earth in mercy;
And Thy love is toward the seed of Abraham, the children of Israel.
Thy chastisement is upon us as upon a first-born, only-begotten son,
To turn back the obedient soul from folly that is wrought in ignorance.
May God cleanse Israel against the day of mercy and blessing,
Against the day of choice when Blessed shall they be that shall be in those days,
He bringeth back His anointed.

In that they shall see the goodness of the Lord which He shall perform for the generation that is to come,

Under the rod of chastening of the Lord's anointed in the fear of his God,

In the spirit of wisdom and righteousness and strength;

That he may direct every man in the works of righteousness by the fear of God,

That he may establish them all before the Lord,

A good generation living in the fear of God in the days of mercy. *Selah.*

Great is our God and glorious, dwelling in the highest.

It is He who hath established in their courses the lights of heaven for determining seasons from year to year,

And they have not turned aside from the way which He appointed them.

In the fear of God they pursue their path every day,

From the day God created them and for evermore.

And they have erred not since the day He created them.

Since the generations of old they have not withdrawn from their path,

Unless God commanded them so to do by the command of His servants.

THE ODES OF SOLOMON.

HERE are some of the most beautiful songs of peace and joy that the world possesses. Yet their origin, the date of their writing, and the exact meaning of many of the verses remain one of the great literary mysteries.

They have come down to us in a single and very ancient document in Syriac language. Evidently that document is a translation from the original Greek. Critical debate has raged around these Odes; one of the most plausible explanations is that they are songs of newly baptized Christians of the First Century.

They are strangely lacking in historical allusions. Their radiance is no reflection of other days. They do not borrow from either the Old Testament or the Gospels. The inspiration of these verses is first-hand. They remind you of Aristides' remark, "*A new people with whom something Divine is mingled.*" Here is vigor and insight to which we can find parallels only in the most exalted parts of the Scriptures.

For these dazzling mystery odes, we owe our translation to J. Rendel Harris, M.A., Hon. Fellow of Clare College, Cambridge. He says about them: "There does not seem to be anything about which everyone seems agreed unless it be that the Odes are of singular beauty and high spiritual value."

Ode 1.

1 The Lord is on my head like a crown, and I shall not be without Him.

2 They wove for me a crown of truth, and it caused thy branches to bud in me.

3 For it is not like a withered crown which buddeth not: but thou livest upon my head, and thou hast blossomed upon my head.

4 Thy fruits are full-grown and perfect, they are full of thy salvation.

Ode 2.

(No part of this Ode has ever been identified.)

Ode 3.

The first words of this Ode have disappeared.

1 . . . I put on:
2 And his members are with him. And on them do I stand, and He loves me:
3 For I should not have known how to love the Lord, if He had not loved me.
4 For who is able to distinguish love, except the one that is loved?
5 I love the Beloved, and my soul loves Him:
6 And where His rest is, there also am I;
7 And I shall be no stranger, for with the Lord Most High and Merciful there is no grudging.
8 I have been united to Him, for the Lover has found the Beloved,
9 And because I shall love Him that is the Son, I shall become a son;
10 For he that is joined to Him that is immortal, will also himself become immortal;
11 And he who has pleasure in the Living One, will become living.
12 This is the Spirit of the Lord, which doth not lie, which teacheth the sons of men to know His ways.
13 Be wise and understanding and vigilant. Hallelujah.

Ode 4.

This Ode is important because of the historical allusion with which it commences. This may refer to the closing of the temple at Leontopolis in Egypt which would date this writing about 73 A. D.

1 No man, O my God, changeth thy holy place;
2 And it is not (possible) that he should change it and put it in another place: because he hath no power over it:
3 For thy sanctuary thou hast designed before thou didst make (other) places:
4 That which is the elder shall not be altered by those that are younger than itself.
5 Thou has given thy heart, O Lord, to thy believers: never wilt thou fail, nor be without fruits:
6 For one hour of thy Faith is more precious than all days and years.
7 For who is there that shall put on thy grace, and be hurt?
8 For thy seal is known: and thy creatures know it: and thy (heavenly) hosts possess it: and the elect archangels are clad with it.
9 Thou hast given us thy fellowship: it was not that thou wast in need of us: but that we are in need of thee:
10 Distill thy dews upon us and open thy rich fountains that pour forth to us milk and honey:
11 For there is no repentance with thee that thou shouldest repent of anything that thou hast promised:
12 And the end was revealed before thee: for what thou gavest, thou gavest freely:
13 So that thou mayest not draw them back and take them again:
14 For all was revealed before thee as God, and ordered from the beginning before thee: and thou, O God, hast made all things. Hallelujah.

Ode 5.

This Ode has strangely appeared in a speech by Salome in another ancient work called the Pistis Sophia.

1 I will give thanks unto thee, O Lord, because I love thee;

2 O Most High, thou wilt not forsake me, for thou art my hope:

3 Freely I have received thy grace, I shall live thereby:

4 My persecutors will come and not see me:

5 A cloud of darkness shall fall on their eyes; and an air of thick gloom shall darken them:

6 And they shall have no light to see: they may not take hold upon me.

7 Let their counsel become thick darkness, and what they have cunningly devised, let it return upon their own heads:

8 For they have devised a counsel, and it did not succeed:

9 For my hope is upon the Lord, and I will not fear, and because the Lord is my salvation, I will not fear:

10 And He is as a garland on my head and I shall not be moved; even if everything should be shaken, I stand firm;

11 And if all things visible should perish, I shall not die; because the Lord is with me and I am with Him. Hallelujah.

Ode 6.

First century universalism is revealed in an interesting way in verse 10.

1 As the hand moves over the harp, and the strings speak,

2 So speaks in my members the Spirit of the Lord, and I speak by His love.

3 For it destroys what is foreign, and everything that is bitter:

4 For thus it was from the beginning and will be to the end, that nothing should be His adversary, and nothing should stand up against Him.

5 The Lord has multiplied the knowledge of Himself, and is zealous that these things should be known, which by His grace have been given to us.

6 And the praise of His name He gave us: our spirits praise His holy Spirit.

7 For there went forth a stream and became a river great and broad;

8 For it flooded and broke up everything and it brought (water) to the Temple:

9 And the restrainers of the children of men were not able to restrain it, nor the arts of those whose business it is to restrain waters;

10 For it spread over the face of the whole earth, and filled everything: and all the thirsty upon earth were given to drink of it;

11 And thirst was relieved and quenched: for from the Most High the draught was given.

12 Blessed then are the ministers of that draught who are entrusted with that water of His:

13 They have assuaged the dry lips, and the will that had fainted they have raised up;

14 And souls that were near departing they have caught back from death:

15 And limbs that had fallen they straightened and set up:

16 They gave strength for their feebleness and light to their eyes:

17 For everyone knew them in the Lord, and they lived by the water of life for ever. Hallelujah.

Ode 7.

A wonderfully, simple and joyful psalm on the Incarnation.

1 As the impulse of anger against evil, so is the impulse of joy over what is lovely, and brings in of its fruits without restraint:

2 My joy is the Lord and my impulse is toward Him: this path of mine is excellent:

3 For I have a helper, the Lord.

4 He hath caused me to know Himself, without grudging, by His simplicity: His kindness has humbled His greatness.

5 He became like me, in order that I might receive Him:

6 He was reckoned like myself in order that I might put Him on;

7 And I trembled not when I saw Him: because He was gracious to me:

8 Like my nature He became that I might learn Him and like my form, that I might not turn back from Him:

9 The Father of knowledge is the word of knowledge:

10 He who created wisdom is wiser than His works:

11 And He who created me when yet I was not knew what I should do when I came into being:

12 Wherefore He pitied me in His abundant grace: and granted me to ask from Him and to receive from His sacrifice:

13 Because He it is that is incorrupt, the fulness of the ages and the Father of them.

14 He hath given Him to be seen of them that are His, in order that they may recognize Him that made them: and that they might not suppose that they came of themselves:

15 For knowledge He hath appointed as its way, He hath widened it and extended it; and brought to all perfection;

16 And set over it the traces of His light, and I walked therein from the beginning even to the end.

17 For by Him it was wrought, and He was resting in the Son, and for its salvation He will take hold of everything;

18 And the Most High shall be known in His Saints, to announce to those that have songs of the coming of the Lord;

19 That they may go forth to meet Him, and may sing to Him with joy and with the harp of many tones:

20 The seers shall come before Him and they shall be seen before Him,

21 And they shall praise the Lord for His love: because He is near and beholdeth.

22 And hatred shall be taken from the earth, and along with jealousy it shall be drowned:

23 For ignorance hath been destroyed, because the knowledge of the Lord hath arrived.

24 They who make songs shall sing the grace of the Lord Most High;

25 And they shall bring their songs, and their heart shall be like the day: and like the excellent beauty of the Lord their pleasant song:

26 And there shall neither be anything that breathes without knowledge, nor any that is dumb:
27 For He hath given a mouth to His creation, to open the voice of the mouth towards Him, to praise Him:
28 Confess ye His power, and show forth His grace. Hallelujah.

Ode 8.

Note the sudden transition from the person of the Psalmist to the person of the Lord (v. 10). This is like the canonical Psalter in style.

1 Open ye, open ye your hearts to the exultation of the Lord:
2 And let your love be multiplied from the heart and even to the lips,
3 To bring forth fruit to the Lord, living [fruit], holy [fruit], and to talk with watchfulness in His light.
4 Rise up, and stand erect, ye w h o s o m e t i m e were brought low:
5 Tell forth ye who were in silence, that your mouth hath been opened.
6 Ye, therefore, that were despised, be henceforth lifted up, because your righteousness hath been exalted.
7 For the right hand of the Lord is with you: and He is your helper:
8 And peace was prepared for you, before ever your war was.
9 Hear the word of truth, and receive the knowledge of the Most High.
10 Your flesh has not known what I am saying to you: neither have your hearts known what I am showing to you.
11 Keep my secret, ye who are kept by it:

12 Keep my faith, ye who are kept by it.
13 And understand my knowledge, ye who know me in truth.
14 Love me with affection, ye who love:
15 For I do not turn away my face from them that are mine;
16 For I know them, and before they came into being I took knowledge of them, and on their faces I set my seal:
17 I fashioned their members: my own breasts I prepared for them, that they might drink my holy milk and live thereby.
18 I took pleasure in them and am not ashamed of them:
19 For my workmanship are they and the strength of my thoughts:
20 Who then shall rise up against my handiwork, or who is there that is not subject to them?
21 I willed and fashioned mind and heart: and they are mine, and by my own right hand I set my elect ones:
22 And my righteousness goeth before them and they shall not be deprived of my name, for it is with them.
23 Ask, and abound and abide in the love of the Lord,
24 And yet beloved ones in the Beloved: those who are kept, in Him that liveth:
25 And they that are saved in Him that was saved;
26 And ye shall be found incorrupt in all ages to the name of your Father. Hallelujah.

Ode 9.

We shall never know surely whether the wars referred to here are spiritual or actual outward wars.

1 Open your ears and I will speak to you. Give me

your souls that I may also give you my soul,

2 The word of the Lord and His good pleasures, the holy thought which He has devised concerning his Messiah.

3 For in the will of the Lord is your salvation, and His thought is everlasting life; and your end is immortality.

4 Be enriched in God the Father, and receive the thought of the Most High.

5 Be strong and be redeemed by His grace.

6 For I announce to you peace, to you His saints;

7 That none of those who hear may fall in war, and that those again who have known Him may not perish, and that those who receive may not be ashamed.

8 An everlasting crown for ever is Truth. Blessed are they who set it on their heads:

9 A stone of great price is it; and there have been wars on account of the crown.

10 And righteousness hath taken it and hath given it to you.

11 Put on the crown in the true covenant of the Lord.

12 And all those who have conquered shall be written in His book.

13 For their book is victory which is yours. And she (Victory) sees you before her and wills that you shall be saved. Hallelujah.

Ode 10.

A vigorous little Ode in which Christ Himself is the speaker.

1 The Lord hath directed my mouth by His word: and He hath opened my heart by His light: and He hath caused to dwell in me His deathless life;

2 And gave me that I might speak the fruit of His peace:

3 To convert the souls of them who are willing to come to Him; and to lead captive a good captivity for freedom.

4 I was strengthened and made mighty and took the world captive;

5 And it became to me for the praise of the Most High, and of God my Father.

6 And the Gentiles were gathered together who were scattered abroad.

7 And I was unpolluted by my love for them, because they confessed me in high places: and the traces of the light were set upon their heart:

8 And they walked in my life and were saved and became my people for ever and ever. Hallelujah.

Ode 11.

A beautiful sketch of Paradise regained and the blessedness of those who have returned to the privileges of the fallen Adam.

1 My heart was cloven and its flower appeared; and grace sprang up in it: and it brought forth fruit to the Lord,

2 For the Most High clave my heart by His Holy Spirit and searched my affection towards Him: and filled me with His love.

3 And His opening of me became my salvation; and I ran in His way in His peace, even in the way of truth:

4 From the beginning and even to the end I acquired His knowledge:

5 And I was established upon the rock of truth, where He had set me up:

6 And speaking waters touched my lips from the fountain of the Lord plenteously:

7 And I drank and was inebriated with the living water that doth not die;

8 And my inebriation was not one without knowledge, but I forsook vanity and turned to the Most High my God,

9 And I was enriched by His bounty, and I forsook the folly which is diffused over the earth; and I stripped it off and cast it from me:

10 And the Lord renewed me in His raiment, and possessed me by His light, and from above He gave me rest in incorruption;

11 And I became like the land which blossoms and rejoices in its fruits:

12 And the Lord was like the sun shining on the face of the land;

13 He lightened my eyes, and my face received the dew; and my nostrils enjoyed the pleasant odour of the Lord;

14 And He carried me to His Paradise; where is the abundance of the pleasure of the Lord;

15 And I worshipped the Lord on account of His glory; and I said, Blessed, O Lord, are they who are planted in thy land! and those who have a place in thy Paradise;

16 And they grow by the fruits of the trees. And they have changed from darkness to light.

17 Behold! all thy servants are fair, who do good works, and turn away from wickedness to the pleasantness that is thine:

18 And they have turned back the bitterness of the trees from them, when they were planted in thy land;

19 And everything became like a relic of thyself, and memorial for ever of thy faithful works.

20 For there is abundant room in thy Paradise, and nothing is useless therein;

21 But everything is filled with fruit; glory be to thee, O God, the delight of Paradise for ever. Hallelujah.

Ode 12.

An exceptionally high level of spiritual thought.

1 He hath filled me with words of truth; that I may speak the same;

2 And like the flow of waters flows truth from my mouth, and my lips show forth His fruit.

3 And He has caused His knowledge to abound in me, because the mouth of the Lord is the true Word, and the door of His light;

4 And the Most High hath given it to His words, which are the interpreters of His own beauty, and the repeaters of His praise, and the confessors of His counsel, and the heralds of His thought, and the chasteners of His servants.

5 For the swiftness of the Word is inexpressible, and like its expression is its swiftness and force;

6 And its course knows no limit. Never doth it fail, but it stands sure, and it knows not descent nor the way of it.

7 For as its work is, so is its end: for it is light and the dawning of thought;

8 And by it the worlds talk one to the other; and in the Word there were those that were silent;

9 And from it came love and concord; and they spake one to the other whatever was theirs; and they were penetrated by the Word;

10 And they knew Him who made them, because they were in concord; for the mouth of the Most High spake to them; and His explanation ran by means of it:

11 For the dwelling-place of the Word is man: and its truth is love.

12 Blessed are they who by means thereof have understood everything, and have known the Lord in His truth. Hallelujah.

Ode 13.

A strange little Ode.

1 Behold! the Lord is our mirror: open the eyes and see them in Him: and learn the manner of your face:

2 And tell forth praise to His spirit: and wipe off the filth from your face: and love His holiness, and clothe yourselves therewith:

3 And be without stain at all times before Him. Hallelujah.

Ode 14.

This Ode is as beautiful in style as the canonical Psalter.

1 As the eyes of a son to his father, so are my eyes, O Lord, at all times towards thee.

2 For with thee are my consolations and my delight.

3 Turn not away thy mercies from me, O Lord: and take not thy kindness from me.

4 Stretch out to me, O Lord, at all times thy right hand: and be my guide even unto the end, according to thy good pleasure.

5 Let me be well-pleasing before thee, because of thy glory and because of thy name:

6 Let me be preserved from evil, and let thy meekness, O Lord, abide with me, and the fruits of thy love.

7 Teach me the Psalms of thy truth, that I may bring forth fruit in thee:

8 And open to me the harp of thy Holy Spirit, that with all its notes I may praise thee, O Lord.

9 And according to the multitude of thy tender mercies, so thou shalt give to me; and hasten to grant our petitions; and thou art able for all our needs. Hallelujah.

Ode 15.

One of the loveliest Odes in this unusual collection.

1 As the sun is the joy to them that seek for its daybreak, so is my joy the Lord;

2 Because He is my Sun and His rays have lifted me up; and His light hath dispelled all darkness from my face.

3 In Him I have acquired eyes and have seen His holy day:

4 Ears have become mine and I have heard His truth.

5 The thought of knowledge hath been mine, and I have been delighted t h r o u g h Him.

6 The way of error I have left, and have walked towards Him and have received salvation from Him, without grudging.

7 And according to His bounty He hath given to me, and according to His excellent beauty He hath made me.

8 I have put on incorruption through His name: and have put off corruption by His grace.

9 Death hath been destroyed before my face: and Sheol hath been abolished by my word:

10 And there hath gone up deathless life in the Lord's land,

11 And it hath been made known to His faithful ones, and hath been given without stint to all those that trust in Him. Hallelujah.

ODE 16.

The beauty of God's creation.

1 As the work of the husbandman is the ploughshare: and the work of the steersman is the guidance of the ship:

2 So also my work is the Psalm of the Lord: my craft and my occupation are in His praises:

3 Because His love hath nourished my heart, and even to my lips His fruits He poured out.

4 For my love is the Lord, and therefore I will sing unto Him:

5 For I am made strong in His praise, and I have faith in Him.

6 I will open my mouth and His spirit will utter in me the glory of the Lord and His beauty; the work of His hands and the operation of His fingers:

7 The multitude of His mercies and the strength of His word.

8 For the word of the Lord searches out all things, both the invisible and that which reveals His thought;

9 For the eye sees His works, and the ear hears His thought;

10 He spread out the earth and He settled the waters in the sea:

11 He measured the heavens and fixed the stars: and He established the creation and set it up:

12 And He rested from His works:

13 And created things run in their courses, and do their works:

14 And they know not how to stand and be idle; and His heavenly hosts are subject to His word.

15 The treasure-chamber of the light is the sun, and the treasury of the darkness is the night:

16 And He made the sun for the day that it may be bright, but night brings darkness over the face of the land;

17 And their alternations one to the other speak the beauty of God:

18 And there is nothing that is without the Lord; for He was before any thing came into being:

19 And the worlds were made by His word, and by the thought of His heart. Glory and honour to His name. Hallelujah.

ODE 17.

A peculiar change of personality, scarcely realized until the return from it in the last verse.

1 I was crowned by my God: my crown is living:

2 And I was justified in my Lord: my incorruptible salvation is He.

3 I was loosed from vanity, and I was not condemned:

4 The choking bonds were cut off by her hands: I received the face and the fashion of a new person:

and I walked in it and was saved;

5 And the thought of truth led me on. And I walked after it and did not wander:

6 And all that have seen me were amazed: and I was regarded by them as a strange person:

7 And He who knew and brought me up is the Most High in all His perfection. And He glorified me by His kindness, and raised my thoughts to the height of His truth.

8 And from thence He gave me the way of His precepts and I opened the doors that were closed,

9 And brake in pieces the bars of iron; but my iron melted and dissolved before me;

10 Nothing appeared closed to me: because I was the door of everything.

11 And I went over all my bondmen to loose them; that I might not leave any man bound or binding:

12 And I imparted my knowledge without grudging: and my prayer was in my love:

13 And I sowed my fruits in hearts, and transformed them into myself: and they received my blessing and lived;

14 And they were gathered to me and were saved; because they were to me as my own members and I was their head. Glory to thee our head, the Lord Messiah. Hallelujah.

ODE 18.

A man who had a spiritual experience brings a message.

1 My heart was lifted up in the love of the Most High and was enlarged: that I might praise Him for His name's sake.

2 My members were strengthened that they might not fall from His strength.

3 Sicknesses removed from my body, and it stood to the Lord by His will. For His kingdom is true.

4 O Lord, for the sake of them that are deficient do not remove thy word from me!

5 Neither for the sake of their works do thou restrain from me thy perfection!

6 Let not the luminary be conquered by the darkness; nor let truth flee away from falsehood.

7 Thou wilt appoint me to victory; our Salvation is thy right hand. And thou wilt receive men from all quarters.

8 And thou wilt preserve whosoever is held in evils:

9 Thou art my God. Falsehood and death are not in thy mouth:

10 For thy will is perfection; and vanity thou knowest not,

11 Nor does it know thee.

12 And error thou knowest not,

13 Neither does it know thee.

14 And ignorance appeared like a blind man; and like the foam of the sea,

15 And they supposed of that vain thing that it was something great;

16 And they too came in likeness of it and became vain; and those have understood who have known and meditated;

17 And they have not been corrupt in their imagination; for such were in the mind of the Lord;

18 And they mocked at them that were walking in error;

19 And they spake truth from the inspiration which the Most High breathed into them; Praise and great comeliness to His name. Hallelujah.

Ode 19.

Fantastic and not in harmony with the other Odes. The reference to a painless Virgin Birth is notable.

1 A cup of milk was offered to me: and I drank it in the sweetness of the delight of the Lord.

2 The Son is the cup, and He who was milked is the Father:

3 And the Holy Spirit milked Him: because His breasts were full, and it was necessary for Him that His milk should be sufficiently released;

4 And the Holy Spirit opened His bosom and mingled the milk from the two breasts of the Father; and gave the mixture to the world without their knowing:

5 And they who receive in its fulness are the ones on the right hand.

6 The Spirit opened the womb of the Virgin and she received c o n c e p t i o n and brought forth; and the Virgin became a Mother with many mercies;

7 And she travailed and brought forth a Son, without incurring pain;

8 And because she was not sufficiently prepared, and she had not sought a midwife (for He brought her to bear) she brought forth, as if she were a man, of her own will;

9 And she brought Him forth openly, and acquired Him with great dignity,

10 And loved Him in His swaddling clothes and guarded Him kindly, and showed Him in Majesty. Hallelujah.

Ode 20.

A mixture of ethics and mysticism; of the golden rule and the tree of life.

1 I am a priest of the Lord, and to Him I do priestly service: and to Him I offer the sacrifice of His thought.

2 For His thought is not like the thought of the world nor the thought of the flesh, nor like them that serve carnally.

3 The sacrifice of the Lord is righteousness, and purity of heart and lips.

4 Present your reins before Him blamelessly: and let not thy heart do violence to heart, nor thy soul to soul.

5 Thou shalt not acquire a stranger by the price of thy silver, neither shalt thou seek to devour thy neighbour,

6 Neither shalt thou deprive him of the covering of his nakedness.

7 But put on the grace of the Lord without stint; and come into His Paradise and make thee a garland from its tree,

8 And put it on thy head and be glad; and recline on His rest, and glory shall go before thee,

9 And thou shalt receive of His kindness and of His grace; and thou shalt be flourishing in truth in the praise of His holiness. Praise and honour be to His name. Hallelujah.

Ode 21.

A remarkable explanation of the "coats of skin" in the third chapter of Genesis.

1 My arms I lifted up to the Most High, even to the

grace of the Lord: because He had cast off my bonds from me: and my Helper had lifted me up to His grace and to His salvation:

2 And I put off darkness and clothed myself with light,

3 And my soul acquired a body free from sorrow or affliction or pains.

4 And increasingly helpful to me was the thought of the Lord, and His fellowship in incorruption:

5 And I was lifted up in His light; and I served before Him,

6 And I became near to Him, praising and confessing Him;

7 My heart ran over and was found in my mouth: and it arose upon my lips; and the exultation of the Lord increased on my face, and His praise likewise. Hallelujah.

Ode 22.

Like the Psalms of David in their exultation because of freedom.

1 He who brought me down from on high, also brought me up from the regions below;

2 And He who gathers together the things that are betwixt is He also who cast me down:

3 He who scattered my enemies had existed from ancient and my adversaries:

4 He who gave me authority over bonds that I might loose them;

5 He that overthrew by my hands the dragon with seven heads: and thou hast set me over his roots that I might destroy his seed.

6 Thou wast there and didst help me, and in every place thy name was a rampart to me.

7 Thy right hand destroyed his wicked poison; and thy hand levelled the way for those who believe in thee.

8 And thou didst choose them from the graves and didst separate them from the dead.

9 Thou didst take dead bones and didst cover them with bodies.

10 They were motionless, and thou didst give them energy for life.

11 Thy way was without corruption, and thy face; thou didst bring thy world to corruption: that everything might be dissolved, and then renewed,

12 And that the foundation for everything might be thy rock: and on it thou didst build thy kingdom; and it became the dwelling place of the saints. Hallelujah.

Ode 23.

The reference to the sealed document sent by God is one of the great mysteries of the collection.

1 Joy is of the saints! and who shall put it on, but they alone?

2 Grace is of the elect! and who shall receive it except those who trust in it from the beginning?

3 Love is of the elect? And who shall put it on except those who have possessed it from the beginning?

4 Walk ye in the knowledge of the Most High without grudging: to His exultation and to the perfection of His knowledge.

5 And His thought was like a letter; His will descended from on high, and it was sent like an arrow which is violently shot from the bow:

6 And many hands rushed to the letter to seize it and to take and read it:

7 And it escaped their fingers and they were affrighted at it and at the seal that was upon it.

8 Because it was not permitted to them to loose its seal: for the power that was over the seal was greater than they.

9 But those who saw it went after the letter that they might know where it would alight, and who should read it and who should hear it.

10 But a wheel received it and came over it:

11 And there was with it a sign of the Kingdom and of the Government:

12 And everything which tried to move the wheel it mowed and cut down:

13 And it gathered the multitude of adversaries, and bridged the rivers and crossed over and rooted up many forests and made a broad path.

14 The head went down to the feet, for down to the feet ran the wheel, and that which was a sign upon it.

15 The letter was one of command, for there were included in it all districts;

16 And there was seen at its head, the head which was revealed even the Son of Truth from the Most High Father,

17 And He inherited and took possession of everything. And the thought of many was brought to nought.

18 And all the apostates hasted and fled away. And those who persecuted and were enraged became extinct.

19 And the letter was a great volume, which was wholly written by the finger of God:·

20 And the name of the Father was on it, and of the Son and of the Holy Spirit, to rule for ever and ever. Hallelujah.

ODE 24.

The mention of the Dove refers to a lost Gospel to which there are rare references in ancient writings.

1 The Dove fluttered over the Messiah, because He was her head; and she sang over Him and her voice was heard:

2 And the inhabitants were afraid and the sojourners were moved:

3 The birds dropped their wings and all c r e e p i n g things died in their holes: and the abysses w e r e opened which had been hidden; and they cried to the Lord like women in travail:

4 And no food was given to them, because it did not belong to them;

5 And they sealed up the abysses with the seal of the Lord. And they perished, in the thought, those that had existed from ancient times;

6 For they were corrupt from the beginning; and the end of their corruption was life:

7 And every one of them that was imperfect perished: for it was not possible to give them a word that they might remain:

8 And the Lord destroyed the imaginations of all them that had not the truth with them.

9 For they who in their hearts were lifted up were deficient in wisdom, and so they were rejected, because the truth was not with them.

10 For the Lord disclosed His way, and spread abroad His grace: and those who understood it, know His holiness. Hallelujah.

ODE 25.

Back again to personal experience.

1 I was rescued from my bonds and unto thee, my God, I fled:

2 For thou art the right hand of my Salvation and my helper.

3 Thou hast restrained those that rise up against me,

4 And I shall see him no more: because thy face was with me, which saved me by thy grace.

5 But I was despised and rejected in the eyes of many: and I was in their eyes like lead,

6 And strength was mine from thyself and help.

7 Thou didst set me a lamp at my right hand and at my left: and in me there shall be nothing that is not bright:

8 And I was clothed with the covering of thy Spirit, and thou didst remove from me my raiment of skin;

9 For thy right hand lifted me up and removed sickness from me:

10 And I became mighty in the truth, and holy by thy righteousness; and all my adversaries were afraid of me;

11 And I became admirable by the name of the Lord, and was justified by His gentleness, and His rest is for ever and ever. Hallelujah.

ODE 26.

Remarkable praise.

1 I poured out praise to the Lord, for I am His:

2 And I will speak His holy song, for my heart is with Him.

3 For His harp is in my hands, and the Odes of His rest shall not be silent.

4 I will cry unto him from my whole heart: I will praise and exalt Him with all my members.

5 For from the east and even to the west is His praise:

6 And from the south and even to the north is the confession of Him:

7 And from the top of the hills to their utmost bound is His perfection.

8 Who can write the Psalms of the Lord, or who read them?

9 Or who can train his soul for life, that his soul may be saved,

10 Or who can rest on the Most High, so that with His mouth he may speak?

11 Who is able to interpret the wonders of the Lord?

12 For he who could interpret would be dissolved and would become that which is interpreted.

13 For it suffices to know and to rest: for in rest the singers stand,

14 Like a river which has an abundant fountain, and flows to the help of them that seek it. Hallelujah.

ODE 27.

The human body makes a cross when a man stands erect in prayer with arms outstretched.

1 I stretched out my hands and sanctified my Lord:

2 For the extension of my hands is His sign:

3 And my expansion is the upright tree [or cross].

Ode 28.

This Ode is a musical gem.

1 As the wings of doves over their nestlings; and the mouth of their nestlings towards their mouths.

2 So also are the wings of the Spirit over my heart:

3 My heart is delighted and exults: like the babe who exults in the womb of his mother:

4 I believed; therefore I was at rest; for faithful is He in whom I have believed:

5 He has richly blessed me and my head is with Him: and the sword shall not divide me from Him, nor the scimitar;

6 For I am ready before destruction comes; and I have been set on His immortal pinions:

7 And He showed me His sign: forth and given me to drink, and from that life is the spirit within me, and it cannot die, for it lives.

8 They who saw me marvelled at me, because I was persecuted, and they supposed that I was swallowed up: for I seemed to them as one of the lost;

9 And my oppression became my salvation; and I was their reprobation because there was no zeal in me;

10 Because I did good to every man I was hated,

11 And they came round me like mad dogs, who ignorantly attack their masters,

12 For their thought is corrupt and their understanding perverted.

13 But I was carrying water in my right hand, and their bitterness I endured by my sweetness;

14 And I did not perish, for I was not their brother nor was my birth like theirs.

15 And they sought for my death and did not find it: for I was older than the memorial of them;

16 And vainly did they make attack upon me and those who, without reward, came after me:

17 They sought to destroy the memorial of him who was before them.

18 For the thought of the Most High cannot be anticipated; and His heart is superior to all wisdom. Hallelujah.

Ode 29.

Again reminiscent of the Psalms of David.

1 The Lord is my hope: in Him I shall not be confounded.

2 For according to His praise He made me, and according to His goodness even so He gave unto me:

3 And according to His mercies He exalted me: and according to His excellent beauty He set me on high:

4 And brought me up out of the depths of Sheol: and from the mouth of death He drew me:

5 And thou didst lay my enemies low, and He justified me by His grace.

6 For I believed in the Lord's Messiah: and it appeared to me that He is the Lord;

7 And He showed him His sign: and He led me by His light, and gave me the rod of His power;

8 That I might subdue the imaginations of the peoples; and the power of the men of might to bring them low:

9 To make war by His word, and to take victory by His power.

10 And the Lord overthrew my enemy by His word: and

he became like the stubble which the wind carries away;

11 And I gave praise to the Most High because He exalted me His servant and the son of His handmaid. Hallelujah.

Ode 30.

An invitation to the thirsty.

1 Fill ye waters for yourselves from the living fountain of the Lord, for it is opened to you:

2 And come all ye thirsty, and take the draught; and rest by the fountain of the Lord.

3 For fair it is and pure and gives rest to the soul. Much more pleasant are its waters than honey;

4 And the honeycomb of bees is not to be compared with it.

5 For it flows forth from the lips of the Lord and from the heart of the Lord is its name.

6 And it came infinitely and invisibly: and until it was set in the midst they did not know it:

7 Blessed are they who have drunk therefrom and have found rest thereby. Hallelujah.

Ode 31.

A song that Marcus Aurelius might have known when he said, "Be like the promontory against which the waves continually break."

1 The abysses were dissolved before the Lord: and darkness was destroyed by His appearance:

2 Error went astray and perished at His hand: and folly found no path to walk in, and was submerged by the truth of the Lord.

3 He opened His mouth and spake grace and joy: and He spake a new song of praise to His name:

4 And He lifted up His voice to the Most High, and offered to Him the sons that were with Him.

5 And His face was justified, for thus His holy Father had given to Him.

6 Come forth, ye that have been afflicted and receive joy, and possess your souls by His grace; and take to you immortal life.

7 And they made me a debtor when I rose up, me who had been a debtor: and they divided my spoil, though nothing was due to them.

8 But I endured and held my peace and was silent, as if not moved by them.

9 But I stood unshaken like a firm rock which is beaten by the waves and endures.

10 And I bore their bitterness for humility's sake:

11 In order, that I might redeem my people, and inherit it, and that I might not make void my promises to the fathers, to whom I promised the salvation of their seed. Hallelujah.

Ode 32.

Joy and light.

1 To the blessed there is joy from their hearts, and light from Him that dwells in them:

2 And words from the Truth, who was self-originate: for He is strengthened by the holy power of the Most High: and He is unperturbed for ever and ever. Hallelujah.

Ode 33.

A virgin stands and proclaims (v. 5).

1 Again Grace ran and forsook corruption, and came down in Him to bring it to nought;

2 And He destroyed perdition from before Him, and devastated all its order;

3 And He stood on a lofty summit and uttered His voice from one end of the earth to the other:

4 And drew to Him all those who obeyed Him; and there did not appear as it were an evil person.

5 But there stood a perfect virgin who was proclaiming and calling and saying,

6 O ye sons of men, return ye, and ye daughters of men, come ye:

7 And forsake the ways of that corruption and draw near unto me, and I will enter into you, and will bring you forth from perdition,

8 And make you wise in the ways of truth: that you be not destroyed nor perish:

9 Hear ye me and be redeemed. For the grace of God I am telling among you: and by my means you shall be redeemed and become blessed.

10 I am your judge; and they who have put me on shall not be injured: but they shall possess the new world that is incorrupt:

11 My chosen ones walk in me, and my ways I will make known to them that seek me, and I will make them trust in my name. Hallelujah.

Ode 34.

True poetry—pure and simple.

1 No way is hard where there is a simple heart.

2 Nor is there any wound where the thoughts are upright:

3 Nor is there any storm in the depth of the illuminated thought:

4 Where one is surrounded on every side by beauty, there is nothing that is divided.

5 The likeness of what is below is that which is above; for everything is above: what is below is nothing but the imagination of those that are without knowledge.

6 Grace has been revealed for your salvation. Believe and live and be saved. Hallelujah.

Ode 35.

"No cradled child more softly lies than I: come soon, eternity."

1 The dew of the Lord in quietness He distilled upon me:

2 And the cloud of peace He caused to rise over my head, which guarded me continually;

3 It was to me for salvation: everything was shaken and they were affrighted;

4 And there came forth from them a smoke and a judgment; and I was keeping quiet in the order of the Lord:

5 More than shelter was He to me, and more than foundation.

6 And I was carried like a child by his mother: and He gave me milk, the dew of the Lord:

7 And I grew great by His bounty, and rested in His perfection,

8 And I spread out my hands in the lifting up of my soul: and I was made right with the Most High, and I was redeemed with Him. Hallelujah.

Ode 36.

Theologians have never agreed on an explanation of this perplexing Ode.

1 I rested in the Spirit of the Lord: and the Spirit raised me on high:

2 And made me stand on my feet in the height of the Lord, before His perfection and His glory, while I was praising Him by the composition of His songs.

3 The Spirit brought me forth before the face of the Lord: and, although a son of man, I was named the Illuminate, the Son of God:

4 While I praised amongst the praising ones, and great was I amongst the mighty ones.

5 For according to the greatness of the Most High, so He made me: and like His own newness He renewed me; and He anointed me from His own perfection:

6 And I became one of His Neighbours; and my mouth was opened, like a cloud of dew;

7 And my heart poured out as it were a gushing stream of righteousness,

8 And my access to Him was in peace; and I was established by the Spirit of His government. Hallelujah.

Ode 37.

An elementary Ode.

1 I stretched out my hands to my Lord: and to the Most High I raised my voice:

2 And I spake with the lips of my heart; and He heard me, when my voice reached Him:

3 His answer came to me, and gave me the fruits of my labours;

4 And it gave me rest by the grace of the Lord. Hallelujah.

Ode 38.

A beautiful description of the power of truth.

1 I went up to the light of truth as if into a chariot:

2 And the Truth took me and led me: and carried me across pits and gulleys; and from the rocks and the waves it preserved me:

3 And it became to me a haven of Salvation: and set me on the arms of immortal life:

4 And it went with me and made me rest, and suffered me not to wander, because it was the Truth;

5 And I ran no risk, because I walked with Him;

6 And I did not make an error in anything because I obeyed the Truth.

7 For Error flees away from it, and meets it not: but the Truth proceeds in the right path, and

8 Whatever I did not know, it made clear to me, all the poisons of error, and the plagues of death which they think to be sweetness:

9 And I saw the destroyer of destruction, when the bride who is corrupted is adorned: and the bridegroom who corrupts and is corrupted;

10 And I asked the Truth, 'Who are these?'; and He said to me, 'This is the deceiver and the error:

11 And they are alike in the beloved and in his bride: and they lead astray and corrupt the whole world:

12 And they invite many to the banquet,

13 And give them to drink of the wine of their intoxication, and remove their wisdom and knowledge, and so they make them without intelligence;

14 And then they leave them; and then these go about like madmen corrupting: seeing that they are without heart, nor do they seek for it.'

15 And I was made wise so as not to fall into the hands of the deceiver; and I congratulated myself because the Truth went with me,

16 And I was established and lived and was redeemed,

17 And my foundations were laid on the hand of the Lord: because He established me.

18 For He set the root and watered it and fixed it and blessed it; and its fruits are for ever.

19 It struck deep and sprung up and spread out, and was full and enlarged;

20 And the Lord alone was glorified in His planting and in His husbandry: by His care and by the blessing of His lips,

21 By the beautiful planting of His right hand: and by the discovery of His planting, and by the thought of His mind. Hallelujah.

ODE 39.

One of the few allusions to events in the Gospels—that of our Lord walking on the Sea of Galilee.

1 Great rivers are the power of the Lord:

2 And they carry headlong those who despise Him: and entangle their paths:

3 And they sweep away their fords, and catch their bodies and destroy their lives.

4 For they are more swift than lightning and more rapid, and those who cross them in faith are not moved;

5 And those who walk on them without blemish shall not be afraid.

6 For the sign in them is the Lord; and the sign is the way of those who cross in the name of the Lord;

7 Put on, therefore, the name of the Most High, and know Him, and you shall cross without danger, for the rivers will be subject to you.

8 The Lord has bridged them by His word; and He walked and crossed them on foot:

9 And His footsteps stand firm on the water, and are not injured; they are as firm as a tree that is truly set up.

10 And the waves were lifted up on this side and on that, but the footsteps of our Lord Messiah stand firm and are not obliterated and are not defaced.

11 And a way has been appointed for those who cross after Him and for those who adhere to the course of faith in Him and worship His name. Hallelujah.

ODE 40.

A song of praise without equal.

1 As the honey distills from the comb of the bees,

2 And the milk flows from the woman that loves her children;

3 So also is my hope on Thee, my God.

4 As the fountain gushes out its water,

5 So my heart gushes out the praise of the Lord and my lips utter praise to Him, and my tongue His psalms.

⸫ And my face exults with His gladness, and my spirit exults in His love, and my soul shines in Him:

7 And reverence confides in Him; and redemption in Him stands assured:

8 And His inheritance is immortal life, and those who participate in it are incorrupt. Hallelujah.

ODE 41.

We discover that the writer may be a Gentile (v. 8).

1 All the Lord's children will praise Him, and will collect the truth of His faith.

2 And His children shall be known to Him. Therefore we will sing in His love:

3 We live in the Lord by His grace: and life we receive in His Messiah:

4 For a great day has shined upon us: and marvellous is He who has given us of His glory.

5 Let us, therefore, all of us unite together in the name of the Lord, and let us honour Him in His goodness,

6 And let our faces shine in His light: and let our hearts meditate in His love by night and by day.

7 Let us exult with the joy of the Lord.

8 All those will be astonished that see me. For from another race am I:

9 For the Father of truth remembered me: He who possessed me from the beginning:

10 For His bounty begat me, and the thought of His heart:

11 And His Word is with us in all our way;

12 The Saviour who makes alive and does not reject our souls;

13 The man who was humbled, and exalted by His own righteousness,

14 The Son of the Most High appeared in the perfection of His Father;

15 And light dawned from the Word that was beforetime in Him;

16 The Messiah is truly one; and He was known before the foundation of the world,

17 That He might save souls for ever by the truth of His name: a new song arises from those who love Him. Hallelujah.

ODE 42.

The Odes of Solomon, the Son of David, are ended with the following exquisite verses.

1 I stretched out my hands and approached my Lord:

2 For the stretching of my hands is His sign:

3 My expansion is the outspread tree which was set up on the way of the Righteous One.

4 And I became of no account to those who did not take hold of me; and I shall be with those who love me.

5 All my persecutors are dead; and they sought after me who hoped in me, because I was alive:

6 And I rose up and am with them; and I will speak by their mouths.

7 For they have despised those who persecuted them;

8 And I lifted up over them the yoke of my love;

9 Like the arm of the bridegroom over the bride,

10 So was my yoke over those that know me:

11 And as the couch that is spread in the house of the bridegroom and bride,

12 So is my love over those that believe in me.

13 And I was not r e j e c t e d though I was reckoned to be so.

14 I did not perish, though they devised it against me.

15 Sheol saw me and was made miserable:

16 Death cast me up and many along with me.

17 I had gall and bitterness, and I went down with him to the utmost of his depth:

18 And the feet and the head he let go, for they were not able to endure my face:

19 And I made a congregation of living men amongst his dead men, and I spake with them by living lips:

20 Because my word shall not be void:

21 And those who had died ran towards me: and they cried and said, Son of God, have pity on us, and do with us according to thy kindness,

22 And bring us out from the bonds of darkness: and open to us the door by which we shall come out to thee.

23 For we see that our death has not touched thee.

24 Let us also be redeemed with thee: for thou art our Redeemer.

25 And I heard their voice; and my name I sealed upon their heads:

26 For they are free men and they are mine. Hallelujah.

THE LETTER OF ARISTEAS

IN THE *Letter of Aristeas,* one of the most noteworthy and ancient recoveries in this collection, we have come a long way from Adam and Eve, a long way from the Flood. This writing presents a spectacle of the resiliency of the human race, which has repeopled the Earth, with powerful nations living in pomp and splendor.

You will read here of the first great bibliophile—Ptolemy Philadelphus. He desires to collect into his library at Alexandria "all the books in the world." Finally in his passion to secure one great work—the Jewish Laws—he trades 100,000 captives for that book. This is probably the highest price ever paid for a single work. It presents an unusual reason for the end of the Great Captivity.

The events of this narrative took place during the lifetime of the famous Queen Arsinoe, who died 270 B. C. The exact date of the writing is uncertain.

The details of court life, the discussion of social problems of the day are of the utmost interest and vividness. It is an odd discovery in this day and age to see the king and his guests playing at questions and answers during their banqueting.

The structure of this absorbing work is as follows:

1. Dedication of the book to Philocrates.
2. Preliminary action:

 (a) The proposal of the Librarian to liberate the Jewish captives in exchange for a book.
 (b) The emancipation.
 (c) The letter of Philadelphus to Eleazar.
 (d) The reply.
 (e) The names of the committee appointed to translate the book.

3. Description of the royal presents:
   (a) The table (probably the most elaborate piece of furniture ever produced).
   (b) The other presents.
4. Description of Jerusalem.
   (a) The temple (and the water-works system).
   (b) The ceremony.
   (c) The citadel.
   (d) The city.
   (e) The countryside.
5. Eleazar's farewell.
6. Eleazar's explanation of the law (this is profound wisdom).
7. The reception.
8. The banquet (72 questions and answers).
9. The translation of the Book.

CHAP. I.

At the time of the Jewish captivity in Egypt, Ptolemy Philadelphus reveals himself as the first great bibliophile. He desires to have all the books in the world in his library; in order to get the Laws of Moses he offers to trade 100,000 captives for that work exclaiming, "It is a small boon indeed!"

SINCE I have collected *material* for a memorable history of my visit to Eleazar the High Priest of the Jews, and because you, Philocrates, as you lose no opportunity of reminding me, have set great store upon receiving an account of the motives and object of my mission, I have attempted to draw up a clear exposition of the matter for you, for I perceive that you possess a natural love of learning, *a quality* which is the highest possession of man—to be constantly attempting 'to add to his stock of knowledge and acquirements' whether through the study of history or by actually participating in the events themselves.

2 It is by this means, by taking up into itself the noblest elements, that the soul is established in purity, and having fixed its aim on piety, the noblest goal of all, it uses this as its infallible guide and so acquires a definite purpose.

3 It was my devotion to the pursuit of religious knowledge that led me to undertake the embassy to the man I have mentioned, who was held in the highest esteem by his own citizens and by others, both for his virtue and his majesty, and who had in his possession *documents of* the highest value to the Jews in his own country and in foreign lands for the interpretation of the divine law, for their laws are written on leather parchments in Jewish characters.

4 This *embassy* then I undertook with enthusiasm, having first of all found an opportunity *of pleading* with the king on behalf of the Jewish captives who had been transported from Judea to Egypt by the king's father, when he first obtained possession of this city and conquered the land of Egypt.

5 It is worth while that I should tell you this story, too, since I am convinced that you, with your disposition towards holiness and your sympathy with men who are living in accordance with the holy law, will all the

more readily listen to the account which I purpose to set forth, since you yourself have lately come to us from the island and are anxious to hear everything that tends to build up the soul.

6 On a former occasion too, I sent you a record of the facts which I thought worth relating about the Jewish race,—the record which I had obtained from the most learned high priests of the most learned land of Egypt.

7 As you are so eager to acquire the knowledge of those things which can benefit the mind, I feel it incumbent upon me to impart to you *all the information in my power*.

8 *I should feel the same duty* towards all who possessed the same disposition but I feel it especially towards you since you have aspirations which are so noble, and since you are not only my brother in character, no less than in blood, but are one with me as well in the pursuit of goodness.

9 For neither the pleasure derived from gold nor any other of the possessions which are prized by shallow minds confers the same benefit as the pursuit of culture and the study which we expend in securing it.

10 But that I may not weary you by a too lengthy introduction, I will proceed at once to the substance of my narrative.

11 Demetrius of Phalerum, the president of the king's library, received vast sums of money, for the purpose of collecting together, as far as he possibly could, all the books in the world.

12 By means of purchase and transcription, he carried out, to the best of his ability, the purpose of the king.

13 On one occasion when I was present he was asked, How many thousand books are there *in the library?* and he replied, 'More than two hundred thou-

sand, O king, and I shall make endeavour in the immediate future *to gather together* the remainder also, so that the total of five hundred thousand may be reached. I am told that the laws of the Jews are worth transcribing and deserve a place in your library.'

14 'What is to prevent you from doing this?' replied the king. 'Everything that is necessary has been placed at your disposal.'

15 'They need to be translated,' answered Demetrius, 'for in the country of the Jews they use a peculiar alphabet (just as the Egyptians, too, have a special form of letters) and speak a peculiar dialect.

16 They are supposed to use the Syriac tongue, but this is not the case; their language is quite different.'

17 And the king when he understood all the facts of the case ordered a letter to be written to the Jewish High Priest that his purpose (which has already been described) might be accomplished.

18 Thinking that the time had come to press the demand, which I had often laid before Sosibius of Tarentum and Andreas, the chief of the bodyguard, for the emancipation of the Jews who had been transported from Judea by the king's father—for when by a combination of good fortune and courage he had brought his attack on the whole district of Coele-Syria and Phoenicia to a successful issue, in the process of terrorising the country into subjection, he transported some of his foes and others he reduced to captivity.

19 The number of those whom he transported from the country of the Jews to Egypt amounted to no less than a hundred thousand.

20 Of these he armed thirty thousand picked men and settled

them in garrisons in the country districts.

21 (And even before this time large numbers of Jews had come into Egypt with the Persian, and in an earlier period still others had been sent *to Egypt* to help Psammetichus in his campaign against the king of the Ethiopians. But these were nothing like so numerous as the captives whom Ptolemy the son of Lagus transported.)

22 As I have already said Ptolemy picked out the best of these, the men who were in the prime of life and distinguished for their courage, and armed them, but the great mass of the others, those who were too old or too young for this purpose, and the women too, he reduced to slavery, not that he wished to do this of his own free will, but he was compelled by his soldiers who claimed them as a reward for the services which they had rendered in war.

23 Having, as has already been stated, obtained an opportunity for securing their emancipation, I addressed the king with the following arguments. 'Let us not be so unreasonable as to allow our deeds to give the lie to our words.

24 Since the law which we wish not only to transcribe but also to translate belongs to the whole Jewish race, what justification shall we be able to find for our embassy while such vast numbers of them remain in a state of slavery in your kingdom?

25 In the perfection and wealth of your clemency release those who are held in such miserable bondage, since as I have been at pains to discover, the God who gave them their law is the God who maintains your kingdom.

26 They worship the same God—the Lord and Creator of the Universe, as all other men, as we ourselves, O king, though we call him by different names, such as Zeus* or Dis.

27 This name was very appropriately bestowed upon him by our first ancestors, in order to signify that He, through whom all things are endowed with life and come into being, is necessarily the Ruler and Lord of the Universe.

28 Set all mankind an example of magnanimity by releasing those who are held in bondage.'

29 After a brief interval, while I was offering up an earnest prayer to God that He would so dispose the mind of the king that all the captives might be set at liberty—(for the human race, being the creation of God, is swayed and influenced by Him.

30 Therefore with many divers prayers I called upon Him who ruleth the heart that *the king* might be constrained to grant my request.

31 For I had great hopes with regard to the salvation of the men since I was assured that God would grant a fulfilment of my prayer.

32 For when men from pure motives plan some action in the interest of righteousness and the performance of noble deeds, Almighty God brings their efforts and purposes to a successful issue)—*the king* raised his head and looking up at me with a cheerful countenance asked, 'How many thousands do you think they will number?'

33 Andreas, who was standing near, replied, 'A little more than a hundred thousand.'

34 'It is a small boon indeed,' said the king, 'that Aristeas asks of us!'

35 Then Sosibius and some others who were present said,

---

*A important comparison of God and Zeus.

'Yes, but it will be a fit tribute to your magnanimity for you to offer the enfranchisement of these men as an act of devotion to the supreme God.

36 You have been greatly honoured by Almighty God and exalted above all your forefathers in glory and it is only fitting that you should render to Him the greatest thankoffering in your power.'

37 Extremely pleased *with these arguments* he gave orders that an addition should be made to the wages *of the soldiers by the amount of the redemption money*, that twenty drachmae should be paid *to the owners* for every slave, that a public order should be issued and that registers of the captives should be attached to it.

38 He showed the greatest enthusiasm in the business, for it was God who had brought our purpose to fulfilment in its entirety and constrained him to redeem not only those who had come into Egypt with the army of his father but any who had come before that time or had been subsequently brought into the kingdom.

39 It was pointed out to him that the ransom money would exceed four hundred talents.

40 I think it will be useful to insert a copy of the decree, for in this way the magnanimity of the king, who was empowered by God to save such vast multitudes, will be made clearer and more manifest.

41 The decree of the king ran as follows: 'All who served in the army of our father in the campaign against Syria and Phoenicia and in the attack upon the country of the Jews and became possessed of Jewish captives and brought them back to the city *of Alexandria* and the land *of Egypt* or sold them to others— and in the same way any captives who were in our land be-fore that time or were brought hither afterwards—all who possess such captives are required to set them at liberty at once, receiving twenty drachmae per head as ransom money.

42 The soldiers will receive this money as a gift added to their wages, the others from the king's treasury.

43 We think that it was against our father's will and against all propriety that they should have been made captives and that the devastation of their land and the transportation of the Jews to Egypt was an act of military wantonness.

44 The spoil which fell to the soldiers on the field *of battle* was all the booty which they should have claimed.

45 To reduce the people to slavery in addition was an act of absolute injustice.

46 Wherefore, since it is acknowledged that we are accustomed to render justice to all men and especially to those who are unfairly in a condition of servitude, and since we strive to deal fairly with all men according to the demands of justice and piety, we have decreed, in reference to the persons of the Jews who are in any condition of bondage in any part of our dominion, that those who possess them shall receive the stipulated sum of money and set them at liberty and that no man shall show any tardiness in discharging his obligations.

47 Within three days after the publication of this decree, they must make lists *of slaves* for the officers appointed to carry out our will, and immediately produce the persons *of the captives*.

48 For we consider that it will be advantageous to us and to our affairs that the matter should be brought to a conclusion.

49 Any one who likes may give information about any who disobey the decree, on condition

JUDAH REVEALS THE STORY OF HIS LIFE

(See page 233 et seq.)

that if the man is proved guilty he will become his slave; his property, however, will be handed over to the royal treasury.'

50 When the decree was brought to be read over to the king for his approval, it contained all the other provisions except the phrase 'any captives who were in the land before that time or were brought hither afterwards,' and in his magnanimity and the largeness of his heart the king inserted this clause and gave orders that the grant of money required for the redemption should be deposited in full with the paymasters of the forces and the royal bankers, and so the matter was decided and the decree ratified within seven days.

51 The grant for the redemption amounted to more than six hundred and sixty talents; for many infants at the breast were emancipated together with their mothers.

52 When the question was raised whether the sum of twenty talents was to be paid for these, the king ordered that it should be done, and thus he carried out his decision in the most comprehensive way.

CHAP. II.

Showing how the most careful records were kept of affairs of state. Government Red Tape. A committee of six is appointed to go to the High Priest in Jerusalem and arrange for the exchange. Aristeas is put in charge of the delegation.

WHEN this had been done, he ordered Demetrius to draw up a memorial with regard to the transcription of the Jewish books.

2 For all affairs of state used to be carried out by means of decrees and with the most pains-taking accuracy by these *Egyptian* kings, and nothing was done in a slipshod or haphazard fashion.

3 And so I have inserted copies of the memorial and the letters, the number of the presents sent and the nature of each, since every one of them excelled in magnificence and technical skill.

4 The following is a copy of the memorial. *The Memory* of Demetrius to the great king. 'Since you have given me instructions, O king, that the books which are needed to complete your library should be collected together, and that those which are defective should be repaired, I have devoted myself with the utmost care to the fulfilment of your wishes, and I now have the following proposal to lay before you.

5 The books of the law of the Jews (with some few others) are absent *from the library*.

6 They are written in the Hebrew characters and language and have been carelessly interpreted, and do not represent the original text as I am informed by those who know; for they have never had a king's care to protect them.

7 It is necessary that these should be made accurate for your library since the law which they contain, inasmuch as it is of divine origin, is full of wisdom and free from all blemish.

8 For this reason literary men and poets and the mass of historical writers have held aloof from referring to these books and the men who have lived and are living in accordance with them, because their conception of life is so sacred and religious, as Hecataeus of Abdera says.

9 If it please you, O king, a letter shall be written to the High Priest in Jerusalem, asking him to send six elders out of every tribe—men who have lived

the noblest life and are most skilled in their law—that we may find out the points in which the majority of them are in agreement, and so having obtained an accurate translation may place it in a conspicuous place in a manner worthy of the work itself and your purpose.

10 May continual prosperity be yours!'

11 When this memorial had been presented, the king ordered a letter to be written to Eleazar on the matter, giving also an account of the emancipation of the *Jewish* captives.

12 And he gave fifty talents weight of gold and seventy talents of silver and a large quantity of precious stones to make bowls and vials and a table and libation cups.

13 He also gave orders to those who had the custody of his coffers to allow the artificers to make a selection of any materials they might require for the purpose, and that a hundred talents in money should be sent to provide sacrifices for the temple and for other needs.

14 I shall give you a full account of the workmanship after I have set before you copies of the letters. The letter of the king ran as follows:

15 'King Ptolemy sends greeting and salutation to the High Priest Eleazar.

16 Since there are many Jews settled in our realm who were carried off from Jerusalem by the Persians at the time of their power and many more who came with my father into Egypt as captives—large numbers of these he placed in the army and paid them higher wages than usual, and when he had proved the loyalty of their leaders he built fortresses and placed them in their charge that the native Egyptians might be intimidated by them.

17 And I, when I ascended the throne, adopted a kindly attitude towards all my subjects, and more particularly to those who were citizens of yours—I have set at liberty more than a hundred thousand captives, paying their owners the appropriate market price for them, and if ever evil has been done to your people through the passions of the mob, I have made them reparation.

18 The motive which prompted my action has been the desire to act piously and render unto the supreme God a thankoffering for maintaining my kingdom in peace and great glory in all the world.

19 Moreover those of your people who were in the prime of life I have drafted into my army, and those who were fit to be attached to my person and worthy of the confidence of the court, I have established in official positions.

20 Now since I am anxious to show my gratitude to these men and to the Jews throughout the world and to the generations yet to come, I have determined that your law shall be translated from the Hebrew tongue which is in use amongst you into the Greek language, that these books may be added to the other royal books in my library.

21 It will be a kindness on your part and a reward for my zeal if you will select six elders from each of your tribes, men of noble life and skilled in your law and able to interpret it, that *in questions of dispute* we may be able to discover the verdict in which the majority agree, for the investigation is of the highest possible importance.

22 I hope to win great renown by the accomplishment of this work.

23 I have sent Andreas, the chief of my bodyguard and Aristeas—men whom I hold in high esteem—to lay the matter

before you and present you with a hundred talents of silver, the first-fruits of my offering for the temple and the sacrifices and other religious rites.

24 If you will write to me concerning your wishes in these matters, you will confer a great favour upon me and afford me a *new* pledge of friendship, for all your wishes shall be carried out as speedily as possible. Farewell.'

25 To this letter Eleazar replied appropriately as follows: 'Eleazar the High Priest sends greetings to King Ptolemy his true friend.

26 My highest wishes are for your welfare and the welfare of Queen Arsinoe, your sister, and your children.

27 I also am well. I have received your letter and am greatly rejoiced by your purpose and your noble counsel.

28 I summoned together the whole people and read it to them that they might know of your devotion to our God.

29 I showed them too the cups which you sent, twenty of gold and thirty of silver, the five bowls and the table of dedication, and the hundred talents of silver for the offering of the sacrifices and providing the things of which the temple stands in need.

30 These gifts were brought to me by Andreas, one of your most honoured servants, and by Aristeas, both good men and true, distinguished by their learning, and worthy in every way to be the representatives of your high principles and righteous purposes.

31 These men imparted to me your message and received from me an answer in agreement with your letter. I will consent to everything which is advantageous to you even though your request is very unusual.

32 For you have bestowed upon our citizens great and never to be forgotten benefits in many ways.

33 Immediately therefore I offered sacrifices on behalf of you, your sister, your children, and your friends, and all the people prayed that your plans might prosper continually, and that Almighty God might preserve your kingdom in peace with honour, and that the translation of the holy law might prove advantageous to you and be carried out successfully.

34 In the presence of all the people I selected six elders from each tribe, good men and true, and I have sent them to you with *a copy* of our law.

35 It will be a kindness, O righteous king, if you will give instruction that as soon as the translation of the law is completed, the men shall be restored again to us in safety. Farewell.'

36 *The following* are the names *of the elders:* Of the first tribe, Joseph, Ezekiah, Zachariah, John, Ezekiah, Elisha.

37 Of the second tribe, Judas, Simon, Samuel, Adaeus, Matthias, Eschlemias.

38 Of the third tribe, Nehemia, Joseph, Theodosius, Baseas, Ornias, Dakis.

39 Of the fourth tribe, Jonathan, Abraeus, Elisha, Ananias, Chabrias. . . .

40 Of the fifth tribe, Isaac, Jacob, Jesus, Sabbataeus, Simon, Levi.

41 Of the sixth tribe, Judas, Joseph, Simon, Zacharias, Samuel, Selemas.

42 Of the seventh tribe, Sabbataeus, Zedekiah, Jacob, Isaac, Jesias, Natthaeus.

43 Of the eighth tribe, Theodosius, Jason, Jesus, Theodotus, John, Jonathan.

44 Of the ninth tribe, Theophilus, Abraham, A r s a m o s, Jason, Endemias, Daniel.

45 Of the tenth tribe, Jere-

miah, Eleazar, Zachariah, Baneas, Elisha, Dathaeus.

46 Of the eleventh tribe, Samuel, Joseph, Judas, Jonathes, Chabu, Dositheus.

47 Of the twelfth tribe, Isaelus, John, Theodosius, Arsamos, Abietes, Ezekiel.

48 They were seventy-two in all. Such was the answer which Eleazar and his friends gave to the king's letter.

CHAP. III.

In which is described the most exquisite and beautiful table ever produced. Also other rich gifts. Interesting in the light of recent excavations in Egypt.

I WILL now proceed to redeem my promise and give a description of the works of art.

2 They were wrought with exceptional skill, for the king spared no expense and personally superintended the workmen individually.

3 They could not therefore scamp any part of the work or finish it off negligently.

4 First of all I will give you a description of the table.

5 The king was anxious that this piece of work should be of exceptionally large dimensions, and he caused enquiries to be made of the Jews in the locality with regard to the size of the table already in the temple at Jerusalem.

6 And when they described the measurements, he proceeded to ask whether he might make a larger structure.

7 And some of the priests and the other Jews replied that there was nothing to prevent him.

8 And he said that he was anxious to make it five times the size, but he hesitated lest it should prove useless for the temple services.

9 He was desirous that his gift should not merely be stationed in the temple, for it would afford him much greater pleasure if the men whose duty it was to offer the fitting sacrifices were able to do so appropriately on the table which he had made.

10 He did not suppose that it was owing to lack of gold that the former table had been made of small size, but there seems to have been, he said, some reason why it was made of this dimension.

11 For had the order been given, there would have been no lack of means.

12 Wherefore we must not transgress or go beyond the proper measure.

13 At the same time he ordered them to press into service all the manifold forms of art, for he was a man of the most lofty conceptions and nature had endowed him with a keen imagination which enabled him to picture the appearance which would be presented *by the finished work.*

14 He gave orders too, that where there were no instructions laid down in the *Jewish* Scriptures, everything should be made as beautiful as possible.

15 When such instructions were laid down, they were to be carried out to the letter.

16 They made the table two cubits * long, one cubit broad, one and a half cubits high fashioning it of pure solid gold.

17 What I am describing was not thin gold laid over another foundation, but the whole structure was of massive gold welded together.

18 And they made a border of a hand's breadth round about it.

19 And there was a wreath of wave-work, engraved in relief in

* A cubit is 18 inches.

the form of ropes marvellously wrought on its three sides.

20 For it was triangular in shape and the style of the work was exactly the same on each of the sides, so that whichever side they were turned, they presented the same appearance.

21 Of the two sides under the border, the one which sloped down to the table was a very beautiful piece of work, but it was the outer side which attracted the gaze of the spectator.

22 Now the upper edge of the two sides, being elevated, was sharp since, as we have said, *the rim* was three-sided, from whatever point of view one approached it.

23 And there were layers of precious stones on it in the midst of the embossed cord-work, and they were interwoven with one another by an inimitable artistic device.

24 For the sake of security they were all fixed by golden needles which were inserted in perforations *in the stones*.

25 At the sides they were clamped together by fastenings to hold them firm.

26 On the part of the border round the table which slanted upwards and met the eyes, there was wrought a pattern of eggs in precious stones, elaborately engraved by a continuous piece of fluted relief-work, closely connected together round the whole table.

27 And under the stones which had been arranged to represent eggs the artists made a crown containing all kinds of fruits, having at its top clusters of grapes and ears of corn, dates also and apples, and pomegranates and the like, conspicuously arranged.

28 These fruits were wrought out of precious stones, of the same colour as the fruits themselves and they fastened them edgeways round all the sides of the table with a band of gold.

29 And after the crown *of fruit* had been put on, *underneath* there was inserted another pattern of eggs *in precious stones,* and other fluting and embossed work, that both sides of the table might be used, according to the wishes of the owners and for this reason the wave-work and the border were extended down to the feet of the table.

30 They made and fastened under the whole width of the table a massive plate four fingers thick, that the feet might be inserted into it, and clamped fast with linch-pins which fitted into sockets under the border, so that which ever side of the table people preferred, might be used.

31 Thus it became manifestly clear that the work was intended to be used either way.

32 On the table itself they engraved a 'maeander,' having precious stones standing out in the middle of it, rubies and emeralds and an onyx too and many other kinds of stones which excel in beauty.

33 And next to the 'maeander' there was placed a wonderful piece of network, which made the centre of the table appear like a rhomboid in shape, and on it a crystal and amber, as it is called, had been wrought, which produced an incomparable impression on the beholders.

34 They made the feet *of the table* with heads like lilies, so that they seemed to be like lilies bending down beneath the table, and the parts which were visible represented leaves which stood upright.

35 The basis of the foot on the ground consisted of a ruby and measured a hand's breadth *high* all round.

36 It had the appearance of a shoe and was eight fingers broad.

37 Upon it the whole expanse of the foot rested.

38 And they made *the foot*

appear like ivy growing out of the stone, interwoven with akanthus and surrounded with a vine which encircled it with clusters of grapes, which were worked in stones, up to the top *of the foot.*

39 All the four feet were made in the same style, and everything was wrought and fitted so skilfully, and such remarkable skill and knowledge were expended upon making it true to nature, that when the air was stirred by a breath of wind, movement was imparted to the leaves, and everything was fashioned to correspond with the actual reality *which it represented.*

40 And they made the top of the table in three parts like a triptychon, and they were so fitted and dovetailed together with spigots along the whole breadth of the work, that the meeting of the joints could not be seen or even discovered.

41 The thickness of the table was not less than half a cubit, so that the whole work must have cost many talents.

42 For since the king did not wish to add to its size he expended on the details the same sum of money which would have been required if the table could have been of larger dimensions.

43 And everything was completed in accordance with his plan, in a most wonderful and remarkable way, with inimitable art and incomparable beauty.

44 Of the mixing bowls, two were wrought in gold, and from the base to the middle were engraved with relief work in the pattern of scales, and between the scales precious stones were inserted with great artistic skill.

45 Then there was a 'maeander' a cubit in height, with its surface wrought out of precious stones of many colours, displaying great artistic effort and beauty.

46 Upon this there was a mosaic, worked in the form of a rhombus, having a net-like appearance and reaching right up to the brim.

47 In the middle, small shields which were made of different precious stones, placed alternately, and varying in kind, not less than four fingers broad, enhanced the beauty of their appearance.

48 On the top of the brim there was an ornament of lilies in bloom, and intertwining clusters of grapes were engraven all round.

49 Such then was the construction of the golden bowls, and they held more than two firkins each.

50 The silver bowls had a smooth surface, and were wonderfully made as if they were intended for looking-glasses, so that everything which was brought near to them was reflected even more clearly than in mirrors.

51 But it is impossible to describe the real impression which these works of art produced upon the mind when they were finished.

52 For, when these vessels had been completed and placed side by side, first a silver bowl and then a golden, then another silver, and then another golden, the appearance they presented is altogether indescribable, and those who came to see them were not able to tear themselves from the brilliant sight and entrancing spectacle.

53 The impressions produced by the spectacle were various in kind.

54 When men looked at the golden vessels, and their minds made a complete survey of each detail of workmanship, their souls were thrilled with wonder.

55 Again when a man wished

to direct his gaze to the silver vessels, as they stood before him, everything seemed to flash with light round about the place where he was standing, and afforded a still greater delight to the onlookers.

56 So that it is really impossible to describe the artistic beauty of the works.

57 The golden vials they engraved in the centre with vine wreaths.

58 And about the rims they wove a wreath of ivy and myrtle and olive in relief work and inserted precious stones in it.

59 The other parts of the relief work they wrought in different patterns, since they made it a point of honour to complete everything in a way worthy of the majesty of the king.

60 In a word it may be said that neither in the king's treasury nor in any other, were there any works which equalled these in costliness or in artistic skill.

61 For the king spent no little thought upon them, for he loved to gain glory for the excellence of his *designs*.

62 For oftentimes he would neglect his official business, and spend his time with the artists in his anxiety that they should complete everything in a manner worthy of the place to which the gifts were to be sent.

63 So everything was carried out on a grand scale, in a manner worthy of the king who sent the gifts and of the high priest who was the ruler of the land.

64 There was no stint of precious stones, for not less than five thousand were used and they were all of large size.

65 The most exceptional artistic skill was employed, so that the cost of the stones and the workmanship was five times as much as that of the gold.

CHAP IV.

Vivid details of the sacrifice. The unerring accuracy of the priests is notable. A savage orgy. A description of the temple and its water-works.

I HAVE given you this description of the presents because I thought it was necessary.

2 The next point in the narrative is an account of our journey to Eleazar, but I will first of all give you a description of the whole country.

3 When we arrived in the land of the Jews we saw the city situated in the middle of the whole of Judea on the top of a mountain of considerable altitude.

4 On the summit the temple had been built in all its splendour.

5 It was surrounded by three walls more than seventy cubits high and in length and breadth corresponding to the structure of the edifice.

6 All the buildings were characterised by a magnificence and costliness quite unprecedented.

7 It was obvious that no expense had been spared on the door and the fastenings, which connected it with the door-posts, and the stability of the lintel.

8 The style of the curtain too was thoroughly in proportion to that of the entrance.

9 Its fabric owing to the draught of wind was in perpetual motion, and as this motion was communicated from the bottom and the curtain bulged out to its highest extent, it afforded a pleasant spectacle from which a man could scarcely tear himself away.

10 The construction of the altar was in keeping with the place itself and with the burnt offerings which were consumed by fire upon it, and the approach to it was on a similar scale.

11 There was a *gradual* slope up to it, conveniently arranged for the purpose of decency, and the ministering priests were robed in linen garments, down to their ankles.

12 The Temple faces the east and its back is toward the west.

13 The whole of the floor is paved with stones and slopes down to the appointed places, that water may be conveyed to wash away the blood from the sacrifices, for many thousand beasts are sacrificed there on the feast days.

14 And there is an inexhaustible supply of water, because an abundant natural spring gushes up from within the temple area.

15 There are moreover wonderful and indescribable cisterns underground, as they pointed out to me, at a distance of five furlongs all round the site of the temple, and each of them has countless pipes so that the different streams converge together.

16 And all these were fastened with lead at the bottom and at the sidewalls, and over them a great quantity of plaster had been spread, and every part of the work had been most carefully carried out.

17 There are many openings for water at the base *of the altar* which are invisible to all except to those who are engaged in the ministration, so that all the blood of the sacrifices which is collected in great quantities is washed away in the twinkling of an eye.

18 Such is my opinion with regard to the character of the reservoirs and I will now show you how it was confirmed.

19 They led me more than four furlongs outside the city and bade me peer down towards a certain spot and listen to the noise that was made by the meeting of the waters, so that the great size of the reservoirs

became manifest to me, as has already been pointed out.

20 The ministration of the priests is in every way unsurpassed both for its physical endurance and for its orderly and silent service.

21 For they all work spontaneously, though it entails much painful exertion, and each one has a special task allotted to him.

22 The service is carried on without interruption—some provide the wood, others the oil, others the fine wheat flour, others the spices; others again bring the pieces of flesh for the burnt offering, exhibiting a wonderful degree of strength.

23 For they take up with both hands the limbs of a calf, each of them weighing more than two talents, and throw them with each hand in a wonderful way on to the high place *of the altar* and never miss placing them on the proper spot.

24 In the same way the pieces of the sheep and also of the goats are wonderful both for their weight and their fatness.

25 For those, whose business it is, always select *the beasts* which are without blemish and specially fat, and thus the sacrifice which I have described, is carried out.

26 There is a special place set apart for them to rest in, where those who are relieved from duty sit.

27 When this takes place, those who have already rested and are ready *to resume their duties* rise up *spontaneously* since there is no one to give orders with regard to the arrangement of the sacrifices.

28 The most complete silence reigns so that one might imagine that there was not a single person present, though there are actually seven hundred men engaged in the work, besides the vast number of those who are

occupied in bringing up the sacrifices.

29 Everything is carried out with reverence and in a way worthy of the great God.

30 We were greatly astonished, when we saw Eleazar engaged in the ministration, at the mode of his dress, and the majesty *of his appearance,* which was revealed in the robe which he wore and the precious stones upon his person.

31 There were golden bells *upon the garment* which reached down to his feet, giving forth a peculiar kind of melody, and on both sides of them there were pomegranates with variegated flowers of a wonderful hue.

32 He was girded with a girdle of conspicuous beauty, woven in the most beautiful colours.

33 On his breast he wore the oracle of God, as it is called, on which twelve stones, of different kinds, were inset, fastened together with gold, containing the names of the leaders of the tribes, according to their original order, each one flashing forth in an indescribable way its own particular colour.

34 On his head he wore a tiara, as it is called, and upon this in the middle of his forehead an inimitable turban, the royal diadem full of glory with the name of God inscribed in sacred letters on a plate of gold . . . having been judged worthy to wear these *emblems* in the ministrations.

35 Their appearance created such awe and confusion *of mind* as to make one feel that one had come into the presence of a man who belonged to a different world.

36 I am convinced that any one who takes part in the spectacle which I have described will be filled with astonishment and indescribable wonder and be profoundly affected in his mind at the thought of the sanctity which is attached to each detail of the service.

37 But in order that we might gain complete information, we ascended to the summit of the neighboring citadel and looked around us.

38 It is situated in a very lofty spot, and is fortified with many towers, which have been built up to the very top, of immense stones, with the object, as we were informed, of guarding the temple precincts, so that if there were an attack, or an insurrection or an onslaught of the enemy, no one would be able to force an entrance within the walls that surround the temple.

39 On the towers of the citadel engines of war were placed and different kinds of machines, and the position was much higher than the circle of walls which I have mentioned.

40 The towers were guarded too by most trusty men who had given the utmost proof of their loyalty to their country.

41 These men were never allowed to leave the citadel, except on feast days and then only in detachments, nor did they permit any stranger to enter it.

42 They were also very careful when any command came from the chief officer to admit any visitors to inspect the place, as our own experience taught us.

43 They were very reluctant to admit us,—though we were but two unarmed men—to view the offering of the sacrifices.

44 And they asserted that they were bound by an oath when the trust was committed to them, for they had all sworn and were bound to carry out the oath sacredly to the letter, that though they were five hundred in number they would not permit more than five men to enter at one time.

45 The citadel was the special

protection of the temple and its founder had fortified it so strongly that it might *efficiently* protect it.

CHAP. V.

A description of the city and the countryside. Compare Verse 11 with conditions of today. Verses 39–41 reveal how the ancients estimate a scholar and a gentleman.

THE size of the city is of moderate dimensions.

2 It is about forty furlongs* in circumference, as far as one could conjecture.

3 It has its towers arranged in the shape of a theatre, with thoroughfares leading between them now the crossroads of the lower towers are visible but those of the upper towers are more frequented.

4 For the ground ascends, since the city is built upon a mountain.

5 There are steps too which lead up to the crossroads, and some people are always going up, and others down and they keep as far apart from each other as possible on the road because of those who are bound by the rules of purity, lest they should touch anything which is unlawful.

6 It was not without reason that the original founders of the city built it in due proportions, for they possessed clear insight *with regard to what was required.*

7 For the country is extensive and beautiful.

8 Some parts of it are level, especially the districts which belong to Samaria, as it is called, and which border on the land of the Idumeans, other parts are mountainous, especially those which are contiguous to the land of Judea.

9 The people therefore are bound to devote themselves to agriculture and the cultivation of the soil that by this means they may have a plentiful supply of crops.

10 In this way cultivation of every kind is carried on and an abundant harvest reaped in the whole of the aforesaid land.

11 The cities which are large and enjoy a corresponding prosperity are well-populated, but they neglect the country districts, since all men are inclined to a life of enjoyment, for every one has a natural tendency towards the pursuit of pleasure.

12 The same thing happened in Alexandria, which excels all cities in size and prosperity.

13 Country people by migrating from the rural districts and settling in the city brought agriculture into disrepute: and so to prevent them from settling *in the city,* the king issued orders that they should not stay in it for more than twenty days.†

14 And in the same way he gave the judges written instructions, that if it was necessary to issue a summons against any one *who lived in the country,* the case must be settled within five days.

15 And since he considered the matter one of great importance, he appointed also legal officers for every district with their assistants, that the farmers and their advocates might not in the interests of business empty the granaries of the city, I mean, of the produce of husbandry.

16 I have permitted this digression because it was Eleazar who pointed out with great

---

* A furlong is ⅛ mile (i. e. 220 yards). † This account of the measures adopted at Alexandria to prevent the depopulation of the countryside through migrations into the city is an interesting revelation that the question was as acute 2000 years ago as it is today.

clearness the points which have been mentioned.

17 For great is the energy which they expend on the tillage of the soil.

18 For the land is thickly planted with multitudes of olive trees, with crops of corn and pulse, with vines too, and there is abundance of honey.

19 Other kinds of fruit trees and dates do not count compared with these.

20 There are cattle of all kinds in great quantities and a rich pasturage for them.

21 Wherefore they rightly recognise that the country districts need a large population, and the relations between the city and the villages are properly regulated.

22 A great quantity of spices and precious stones and gold is brought into the country by the Arabs.

23 For the country is well adapted not only for agriculture but also for commerce, and the city is rich in the arts and lacks none of the merchandise which is brought across the sea.

24 It possesses too suitable and commodious harbours at Askalon, Joppa, and Gaza, as well as at Ptolemais which was founded by the King and holds a central position compared with the other places named, being not far distant from any of them.

25 The country produces everything in abundance, since it is well watered in all directions and well protected *from storms.*

26 The river Jordan, as it is called, which never runs dry, flows through the land.

27 Originally the country contained not less than 60 million acres—though afterwards the neighbouring peoples made incursions against it—and 600,000 men were settled upon it in farms of a hundred acres each.

28 The river like the Nile rises in harvest-time and irrigates a large portion of the land.

29 Near the district belonging to the people of Ptolemais it issues into another river and this flows out into the sea.

30 Other mountain torrents, as they are called, flow down into the plain and encompass the parts about Gaza and the district of Ashdod.

31 The country is encircled by a natural fence and is very difficult to attack and cannot be assailed by large forces, owing to the narrow passes, with their overhanging precipices and deep ravines, and the rugged character of the mountainous regions which surround all the land.

32 We were told that from the neighbouring mountains of Arabia copper and iron were formerly obtained.

33 This was stopped, however, at the time of the Persian rule, since the authorities of the time spread abroad a false report that the working of the mines was useless and expensive in order to prevent their country from being destroyed by the mining in these districts and possibly taken away from them owing to the *Persian* rule, since by the assistance of this false report they found an excuse for entering the district.

34 I have now, my dear brother Philocrates, given you all the essential information upon this subject in brief form.

35 I shall describe the work of translation in the sequel.

36 The High Priest selected men of the finest character and the highest culture, such as one would expect from their noble parentage.

37 They were men who had not only acquired proficiency in Jewish literature but had studied most carefully that of the Greeks as well.

38 They were specially qualified therefore for serving on em-

bassies and they undertook this duty whenever it was necessary.

39 They possessed a great facility for conferences and the discussion of problems connected with the law.

40 They espoused the middle course—and this is always the best course to pursue.

41 They abjured the rough and uncouth manner, but they were altogether above pride and never assumed an air of superiority over others, and in conversation they were ready to listen and give an appropriate answer to every question.

42 And all of them carefully observed this rule and were anxious above everything else to excel each other in its observance and they were all of them worthy of their leader and of his virtue.

43 And one could observe how they loved Eleazar by their unwillingness to be torn away from him and how he loved them.

44 For besides the letter which he wrote to the king concerning their safe return, he also earnestly besought Andreas to work *for the same end* and urged me, too, to assist to the best of my ability.

45 And although we promised to give our best attention to the matter, he said that he was still greatly distressed, for he knew that the king out of the goodness of his nature considered it his highest privilege, whenever he heard of a man who was superior to his fellows in culture and wisdom, to summon him to his court.

46 For I have heard of a fine saying of his to the effect that by securing just and prudent men about his person he would secure the greatest protection for his kingdom, since such friends would unreservedly give him the most beneficial advice.

47 And the men who were now being sent to him by Eleazar undoubtedly possessed these qualities.

48 And he frequently asserted upon oath that he would never let the men go if it were merely some private interest of his own that constituted the impelling motive—but it was for the common advantage of all the citizens that he was sending them.

49 For, *he explained,* the good life consists in the keeping of the enactments of the law, and this end is achieved much more by hearing than by reading.

50 From this and other similar statements it was clear what his feelings towards them were.

CHAP. VI.

Explanations of the customs of the people showing what is meant by the word, "Unclean." The essence and origin of the "God-Belief." Verses 43–44 give a picturesque description of the Divinity of physiology.

IT is worth while to mention briefly the information which he gave in reply to our questions.

2 For I suppose that most people feel a curiosity with regard to some of the enactments in the law, especially those about meats and drinks and animals recognised as unclean.

3 When we asked why, since there is but one form of creation, some animals are regarded as unclean for eating, and others unclean even to the touch (for though the law is scrupulous on most points, it is specially scrupulous on such matters as these) he began his reply as follows:

4 'You observe,' he said, 'what an effect our modes of life and our associations produce upon us; by associating with the bad, men catch their depravities and become miserable throughout their life; but if they live with the wise and prudent, they find the means of escaping from ignorance and amending their lives.

5 Our lawgiver first of all laid down the principles of piety and righteousness and inculcated them point by point, not merely by prohibitions but by the use of examples as well, demonstrating the injurious effects *of sin* and the punishments inflicted by God upon the guilty.

6 For he proved first of all that there is only one God and that his power is manifested throughout the universe, since every place is filled with his sovereignty and none of the things which are wrought in secret by men upon the earth escapes His knowledge.

7 For all that a man does and all that is to come to pass in the future are manifest to Him.

8 Working out these truths carefully and having made them plain, he showed that even if a man should think of doing evil —to say nothing of actually effecting it,—he would not escape detection, for he made it clear that the power of God pervaded the whole of the law.

9 Beginning from his starting point, he went on to show that all mankind except ourselves believe in the existence of many gods, though they themselves are much more powerful than the beings whom they vainly worship.

10 For when they have made statues of stone and wood, they say that they are the images of those who have invented something useful for life -and they worship them, though they have clear proof that they possess no feeling.

11 For it would be utterly foolish to suppose that any one became a god in virtue of his inventions.

12 For *the inventors* simply took certain objects already created and by combining them together, showed that they possessed a fresh utility: they did not themselves create the sub-stance of the thing, and so it is a vain and foolish thing for people to make gods of men like themselves.

13 For in our times there are many who are much more inventive and much more learned than the men of former days *who have been deified,* and yet they would never come to worship them.

14 The makers and authors of these myths think that they are the wisest of the Greeks.

15 Why need we speak of other infatuated people, Egyptians and the like, who place their reliance upon wild beasts and most kinds of creeping things and cattle, and worship them, and offer sacrifices to them both while living and when dead?

16 Now our Lawgiver being a wise man and specially endowed by God to understand all things, took a comprehensive view of each particular detail, and fenced us round with impregnable ramparts and walls of iron, that we might not mingle at all with any of the other nations, but remain pure in body and soul, free from all vain imaginations, worshipping the one Almighty God above the whole creation.

17 Hence the leading Egyptian priests having looked carefully into many matters, and being cognizant with our affairs, call us "men of God."

18 This is a title which does not belong to the rest of mankind but only to those who worship the true God.

19 The rest are men *not of God* but of meats and drinks and clothing.

20 For their whole disposition leads them to find solace in these things are reckoned of no account, but throughout their things.

21 Among our people such

whole life their main consideration is the sovereignty of God.

22 Therefore lest we should be
corrupted by any abomination,
or our lives be perverted by evil
communications, he hedged us
round on all sides by rules of
purity, affecting alike what we
eat, or drink, or touch, or hear,
or see.

23 For though, speaking generally, all things are alike in their
natural constitution, since they
are all governed by one and the
same power, yet there is a deep
reason in each individual case
why we abstain from the use of
certain things and enjoy the
common use of others.

24 For the sake of illustration
I will run over one or two points
and explain them to you.

25 For you must not fall into
the degrading idea that it was
out of regard to mice and weasels
and other such things that Moses
drew up his laws with such exceeding care.*

26 All these ordinances were
made for the sake of righteousness to aid the quest for virtue
and the perfecting of character.

27 For all the birds that we
use are tame and distinguished
by their cleanliness, feeding on
various kinds of grain and pulse,
such as for instance pigeons,
turtle-doves, locusts, partridges,
geese also, and all other birds of
this class.

28 But the birds which are
forbidden you will find to be
wild and carnivorous, tyrannising over the others by the
strength which they possess, and
cruelly obtaining food by prey-
ing of the tame birds enumerated
above.

29 And not only so, but they
seize lambs and kids, and injure
human beings too, whether dead
or alive, and so by naming them
unclean, he gave a sign by means
of them that those, for whom the
legislation was ordained, must
practise righteousness in their
hearts and not tyrannise over
any one in reliance upon their
own strength nor rob them of
anything, but steer their course
of life in accordance with justice,
just as the tame birds, already
mentioned, consume the different kinds of pulse that grow
upon the earth and do not tyrannise to the destruction of their
own kindred.

30 Our legislator taught us
therefore that it is by such
methods as these that indications
are given to the wise, that they
must be just and effect nothing
by violence, and refrain from
tyrannising over others in reliance upon their own strength.

31 For since it is *considered*
unseemly even to touch such *unclean* animals, as have been
mentioned, on account of their
particular habits, ought we not
to take every precaution lest our
own characters should be destroyed to the same extent?

32 Wherefore all the rules
which he has laid down with regard to what is permitted in the
case of these *birds* and other
animals, he has enacted with the
object of teaching us a moral
lesson.

33 For the division of the
hoof and the separation of the
claws are intended to teach us
that we must discriminate between our individual actions with
a view to the practice of virtue.

34 For the strength of our
whole body and its activity de-
pend upon our shoulders and
limbs.

35 Therefore he compels us to
recognise that we must perform
all our actions with discrimination according to the standard
of righteousness—more especially
because we have been distinctly
separated from the rest of mankind.

*Compare this quaint idea with I Corinthians, IX, 9.

36 For most other men defile themselves by promiscuous intercourse, thereby working great iniquity, and whole countries and cities pride themselves upon such vices.

37 For they not only have intercourse with men but they defile their own mothers and even their daughters.

38 But we have been kept separate from such sins.

39 And the people who have been separated in the aforementioned way are also characterised *by the Lawgiver* as possessing the *gift* of memory.

40 For all animals "which are cloven-footed and chew the cud" represent to the initiated the *symbol* of memory.

41 For the act of chewing the cud is nothing else than the reminiscence of life and existence.

42 For life is wont to be sustained by means of food, wherefor he exhorts us in the Scripture also in these words: "Thou shalt surely remember the Lord that wrought in thee those great and wonderful things."

43 For when they are properly conceived, they are manifestly great and glorious; first the construction of the body and the disposition of the food and the separation of each individual limb and, for more, the organisation of the senses, the operation and invisible movement of the mind, the rapidity of its particular actions and its discovery of the arts, display an infinite *resourcefulness*.

44 Wherefore he exhorts us to remember that the aforesaid parts are kept together by the divine power with consummate skill.

45 For he has marked out every time and place that we may continually remember the God who rules and preserves us.

46 For in the matter of meats and drinks he bids us first of all offer part as a sacrifice and then forthwith enjoy *our meat*.

47 Moreover, upon our garments he has given us a symbol of remembrance, and in like manner he has ordered us to put the *divine* oracles upon our gates and doors as a remembrance of God.

48 And upon our hands, too, he expressly orders the symbol to be fastened, clearly showing that we ought to perform every act in righteousness, remembering our own creation, and above all the fear of God.

49 He bids men also, when lying down to sleep and rising up again, to meditate upon the works of God, not only in word, but by observing distinctly the change and impression produced upon them, when they are going to sleep, and also their waking, how divine and incomprehensible the change from one of these states to the other is.

50 The excellency of the analogy in regard to discrimination and memory has now been pointed out to you, according to our interpretation of "the cloven hoof and the chewing of the cud."

51 For our laws have not been drawn up at random or in accordance with the first *casual* thought that occurred to the mind, but with a view to truth and the indication of right reason.

52 For by means of the directions which he gives with regard to meats and drinks and particular cases of touching, he bids us neither to do nor listen to anything thoughtlessly nor to resort to injustice by the abuse of the power of reason.

53 In the case of the wild animals, too, the same principle may be discovered.

54 For the character of the weasel and of mice and such animals as these, which are expressly mentioned, is destructive.

55 Mice defile and damage

everything, not only for their own food but even to the extent of rendering absolutely useless to man whatever it falls in their way to damage.

56 The weasel class, too, is peculiar: for besides what has been said, it has a characteristic which is defiling: It conceives through the ears and brings forth through the mouth.

57 And it is for this reason that a like practice is declared unclean in men.

58 For by embodying in speech all that they receive through the ears, they involve others in evils and work no ordinary impurity, being themselves altogether defiled by the pollution of impiety.

59 And your king, as we are informed, does quite right in destroying such men.'

60 Then I said 'I suppose you mean the informers, for he constantly exposes them to tortures and to painful forms of death.'

61 'Yes,' he replied, 'these are the men I mean; for to watch for men's destruction is an unholy thing.

62 And our law forbids us to injure any one either by word or deed.

63 My brief account of these matters ought to have convinced you, that all our regulations have been drawn up with a view to righteousness, and that nothing has been enacted in the Scripture thoughtlessly or without due reason, but its purpose is to enable us throughout our whole life and in all our actions to practise righteousness before all men, being mindful of Almighty God.

64 And so concerning meats and things unclean, creeping things, and wild beasts, the whole system aims at righteousness and righteous relationships between man and man.'

65 He seemed to me to have made a good defence on all the points; for in reference also to the calves and rams and goats which are offered, he said that it was necessary to take them from the herds and flocks, and sacrifice tame animals and offer nothing wild, that the offerers of the sacrifices might understand the symbolic meaning of the lawgiver and not be under the influence of an arrogant self-consciousness.

66 For he, who offers a sacrifice, makes an offering also of his own soul in all its moods.

67 I think that these particulars with regard to our discussion are worth narrating, and on account of the sanctity and natural meaning of the law, I have been induced to explain them to you clearly, Philocrates, because of your own devotion to learning.

CHAP. VII.

The arrival of the envoys with the manuscript of the precious book and gifts. Preparations for a royal banquet. The host immediately upon being seated at table entertains his guests with questions and answers. Some sage comments on sociology.

AND Eleazar, after offering the sacrifice, and selecting the envoys, and preparing many gifts for the king, despatched us on our journey in great security.

2 And when we reached Alexandria, the king was at once informed of our arrival.

3 On our admission to the palace, Andreas and I warmly greeted the king and handed over to him the letter written by Eleazar.

4 The king was very anxious to meet the envoys, and gave orders that all the other officials should be dismissed and the envoys summoned to his presence *at once*.

5 Now this excited general surprise, for it is customary for those who come to seek an audience with the king on matters of importance to be admitted to his presence on the fifth day, while envoys from kings or very important cities with difficulty secure admission to the Court in thirty days—but these men he counted worthy of greater honour, since he held their master in such high esteem, and so he immediately dismissed those whose presence he regarded as superfluous and continued walking about until they came in and he was able to welcome them.

6 When they entered with the gifts which had been sent with them and the valuable parchments, on which the law was inscribed in gold in Jewish characters, for the parchment was wonderfully prepared and the connexion *between the pages* had been so effected as to be invisible, the king as soon as he saw them began to ask them about the books.

7 And when they had taken the rolls out of their coverings and unfolded the pages, the king stood still for a long time and then making obeisance about seven times, he said:

8 'I thank you, my friends, and I thank him that sent you still more, and most of all God, whose oracles these are.'

9 And when all, the envoys and the others who were present as well, shouted out at one time and with one voice: 'God save the King!' he burst into tears of joy.

10 For his exaltation of soul and the *sense* of the overwhelming honour which had been paid him compelled him to weep over his good fortune.

11 He commanded them to put the rolls back in their places and then after saluting the men, said: 'It was right, men of God, that I should first of all pay my reverence to the books for the sake of which I summoned you here and then when I had done that, to extend the right-hand *of friendship* to you.

12 It was for this reason that I did this first.

13 I have enacted that this day, on which you arrived, shall be kept as a great day and it will be celebrated annually throughout my life time.

14 It happens also that it is the anniversary of my naval victory over Antigonus. Therefore I shall be glad to feast with you to-day.

15 Everything that you may have occasion to use,' he said, 'shall be prepared for you in a befitting manner and for me also with you.'

16 After they had expressed their delight, he gave orders that the best quarters near the citadel should be assigned to them, and that preparations should be made for the banquet.

17 And Nicanor summoned the lord high steward, Dorotheus, who was the special officer appointed to look after *the Jews*, and commanded him to make the necessary preparation for each one.

18 For this arrangement had been made by the king and it is an arrangement which you see maintained to-day.

19 For as many cities as have special customs in the matter of drinking, eating, and reclining, have special officers appointed *to look after their requirements*.

20 And whenever they come to visit the kings, preparations are made in accordance with their own customs, in order that there may be no discomfort to disturb the enjoyment of their visit.

21 The same precaution was taken in the case of the Jewish envoys.

22 Now Dorotheus who was the patron appointed to look

after *Jewish* guests was a very conscientious man.

23 All the stores which were under his control and set apart for the reception of such guests, he brought out for the feast.

24 He arranged the seats in two rows in accordance with the king's instructions.

25 For he had ordered him to make half the men sit at his right hand and the rest behind him, in order that he might not withhold from them the highest possible honour.

26 When they had taken their seats he instructed Dorotheus to carry out everything in accordance with the customs which were in use amongst his Jewish guests.

27 Therefore he dispensed with the services of the sacred heralds and the sacrificing priests and the others who were accustomed to offer the prayers, and called upon one of our number, Eleazar, the oldest of the Jewish priests, to offer prayer instead.

28 And he rose up and made a remarkable prayer. 'May Almighty God enrich you, O king, with all the good things which He has made and may He grant you and your wife and your children and your comrades the continual possession of them as long as you live!'

29 At these words a loud and joyous applause broke out which lasted for a considerable time, and then they turned to the enjoyment of the banquet which had been prepared.

30 All the arrangements for service at table were carried out in accordance with the injunction of Dorotheus.

31 Among the *attendants* were the royal pages and others who held places of honour at the king's court.

32 Taking an opportunity af-forded by a pause *in the banquet* the king asked the envoy who sat in the seat of honour (for they were arranged according to seniority), how he could keep his kingdom unimpaired to the end?

33 After pondering for a moment he replied, 'You could best establish its security if you were to imitate the unceasing benignity of God. For if you exhibit clemency and inflict mild punishments upon those who deserve them in accordance with their deserts, you will turn them from evil and lead them to repentance.' *

34 The king praised the answer and then asked the next man, how he could do everything for the best in all his actions?

35 And he replied, 'If a man maintains a just bearing towards all, he will always act rightly on every occasion, remembering that every thought is known to God. If you take the fear of God as your starting-point, you will never miss the goal.'

36 The king complimented this man, too, upon his answer and asked another, how he could have friends like-minded with himself?

37 He replied, 'If they see you studying the interests of the multitudes over whom you rule; you will do well to observe how God bestows his benefits on the human race, providing for them health and food and all other things in due season.'

38 After expressing his agreement with the reply, the king asked the next guest, how in giving audiences and passing judgments he could gain the praise even of those who failed to win their suit?

39 And he said, 'If you are fair in speech to all alike and

---

*Compare this attitude toward criminals with that of the so-called modern humanitarian view. Also see Chapter VIII. 11.

never act insolently nor tyrannically in your treatment of offenders. And you will do this if you watch the method by which God acts. The petitions of the worthy are always fulfilled, while those who fail to obtain an answer to their prayers are informed by means of dreams or events of what was harmful *in their requests* and that God does not smite them according to their sins or the greatness of His strength, but acts with forbearance towards them.'

40 The king praised the man warmly for his answer and asked the next in order, how he could be invincible in military affairs?

41 And he replied, 'If he did not trust entirely to his multitudes or his warlike forces, but called upon God continually to bring his enterprises to a successful issue, while he himself discharged all his duties in the spirit of justice.'

42 Welcoming this answer, he asked another how he might become an object of dread to his enemies.

43 And he replied, 'If while maintaining a vast supply of arms and forces he remembered that these things were powerless to achieve a permanent and conclusive result. For even God instils fear into the minds of men by granting reprieves and making merely a display of the greatness of his power.'

44 This man the king praised and then said to the next, What is the highest good in life?

45 And he answered, 'To know that God is Lord of the Universe, and that in our finest achievements it is not we who attain success but God who by his power brings all things to fulfilment and leads us *to the goal.*'

46 The king exclaimed that the man had answered well and then asked the next how he could keep all his possessions intact and finally hand them down to his successors in the same condition?

47 And he answered, 'By praying constantly to God that you may be inspired with high motives in all your undertakings and by warning your descendants not to be dazzled by fame or wealth, for it is God who bestows all these gifts and men never by themselves win the supremacy.'

48 The king expressed his agreement with the answer and inquired of the next guest, how he could bear with equanimity whatever befell him?

49 And he said, 'If you have a firm grasp of the thought that all men are appointed by God to share the greatest evil as well as the greatest good, since it is impossible for one who is a man to be exempt from these. But God to whom we ought *always* to pray, inspires us with courage to endure.'

50 Delighted with the man's reply, the king said that all their answers had been good. 'I will put a question to one other,' *he added,* 'and then I will stop for the present: that we may turn our attention to the enjoyment *of the feast* and spend a pleasant time.'

51 Thereupon he asked the man, What is the true aim of courage?

52 And he answered, 'If a right plan is carried out in the hour of danger in accordance with the original intention. For all things are accomplished by God to your advantage, O king, since your purpose is good.'

53 When all had signified by their applause their agreement with the answer, the king said to the philosophers (for not a few of them were present), 'It is my opinion that these men excel in virtue and possess extraordinary knowledge, since on the spur of the moment they

have given fitting answers to these questions which I have put to them, and have all made God the starting-point of their words.'

54 And Menedemus, the philosopher of Eretria, said, 'True, O King—for since the universe is managed by providence and since we rightly perceive that man is the creation of God, it follows that all power and beauty of speech proceed from God.'

55 When the king had nodded his assent to this sentiment, the speaking ceased and they proceeded to enjoy themselves. When evening came on, the banquet ended.

CHAP. VIII.

More questions and answers. Note Verse 20 with its reference to flying through the air written in 150 B. C.

ON the following day they sat down to table again and continued the banquet according to the same arrangements.

2 When the king thought that a fitting opportunity had arrived to put inquiries to his guests, he proceeded to ask further questions of the men who sat next in order to those who had given answers on the previous day.

3 He began to open the conversation with the eleventh man, for there were ten who had been asked questions on the former occasion.

4 When silence was established, he asked how he could continue to be rich?

5 After a brief reflection, the man who had been asked the question replied—'If he did nothing unworthy of his position, never acted licentiously, never lavished expense on empty and vain pursuits, but by acts of benevolence made all his subjects well disposed towards himself. For it is God who is the author of all good things and Him man must needs obey.'

6 The king bestowed praise upon him and then asked another how he could maintain the truth?

7 In reply to the question he said, 'By recognizing that a lie brings great disgrace upon all men, and more especially upon kings. For since they have the power to do whatever they wish, why should they resort to lies? In addition to this you must always remember, O King, that God is a lover of the truth.

8 The king received the answer with great delight and looking *at another* said, 'What is the teaching of wisdom?'

9 And the other replied, 'As you wish that no evil should befall you, but to be a partaker of all good things, so you should act on the same principle towards your subjects and offenders, and you should mildly admonish the noble and good. For God draws all men *to Himself* by his benignity.'

10 The king praised him and asked the next in order how he could be the friend of men?

11 And he replied, 'By observing that the human race increases and is born with much trouble and great suffering: wherefore you must not lightly punish or inflict torments upon them, since you know that the life of men is made up of pains and penalties. For if you understood everything you would be filled with pity, for God also it pitiful.'

12 The king received the answer with approbation and inquired of the next, 'What is the most essential qualification for ruling?'

13 'To keep oneself,' he answered, 'free from bribery and to practise sobriety during the greater part of one's life, to honour rightousness above all things, and to make friends of men of this type. For God, too, is a lover of justice.'

13 Having signified his approval, the king said to another, 'What is the true mark of piety?'

14 And he replied, 'To perceive that God constantly works in the Universe and knows all things, and no man who acts unjustly and works wickedness can escape His notice. As God is the benefactor of the whole world, so you, too, must imitate Him and be void of offence.'

15 The king signified his agreement and said to another, 'What is the essence of kingship?'

16 And he replied, 'To rule oneself well and not to be led astray by wealth or fame to immoderate or unseemly desires, *this is the true way of ruling* if you reason the matter well out. For all that you really need is yours, and God is free from need and benignant withal. Let your thoughts be such as become a man, and desire not many things but only such as are necessary for ruling.'

17 The king praised him and asked another man, how his deliberations might be for the best?

18 And he replied, 'If he constantly set justice before him in everything and thought that injustice was equivalent to deprivation of life. For God always promises the highest blessings to the just.'

19 Having praised him, the king asked the next, how he could be free from disturbing thoughts in his sleep?

20 And he replied, 'You have asked me a question which is very difficult to answer, for we cannot bring our true selves into play during the hours for sleep, but are held fast in these by imaginations that cannot be controlled by reason. For our souls possess the feeling that they actually see the things that enter into our consciousness *during sleep*. But we make a mistake if we suppose that we are actually sailing on the sea in boats or flying through the air* or travelling to other regions or anything else of the kind. And yet we actually do imagine such things to be taking place.

21 So far as it is possible for me to decide, I have reached the following conclusion. You must in every possible way, O King, govern your words and actions by the rule of piety that you may have the consciousness that you are maintaining virtue and that you never choose to gratify yourself at the expense of reason and never by abusing your power do despite to righteousness.

22 For the mind mostly busies itself in sleep with the same things with which it occupies itself when awake. And he who has all his thoughts and actions set towards the noblest ends establishes himself *in righteousness* both when he is awake and when he is asleep. Wherefore you must be steadfast in the constant discipline of self.

23 The king bestowed praise on the man and said to another —'Since you are the tenth to answer, when you have spoken, we will devote ourselves to the banquet.' And then he put the question, how can I avoid doing anything unworthy of myself?

24 And he replied, 'Look always to your own fame and your own supreme position, that you may speak and think only such things as are consistent therewith, knowing that all your subjects think and talk about you. For you must not appear to be worse than the actors, who study carefully the rôle, which it is necessary for them to play, and shape all their actions in accordance with it. You are not acting a part, but are really a king, since God has bestowed upon

*Written about 150 B. C!

you a royal authority in keeping with your character.'

25 When the king had applauded loud and long in the most gracious way, the guests were urged to seek repose. So when the conversation ceased, they devoted themselves to the next course of the feast.

26 On the following day, the same arrangement was observed, and when the king found an opportunity of putting questions to the men, he questioned the first of those who had been left over for the next interrogation, What is the highest form of government?

27 And he replied, 'To rule oneself and not to be carried away by impulses. For all men possess a certain natural bent of mind. It is probable that most men have an inclination towards food and drink and pleasure, and kings a bent towards the acquisition of territory and great renown. But it is good that there should be moderation in all things.

28 What God gives, that you must take and keep, but never yearn for things that are beyond your reach.'

29 Pleased with these words, the king asked the next, how he could be free from envy?

30 And he after a brief pause replied, 'If you consider first of all that it is God who bestows on all kings glory and great wealth and no one is king by his own power. All men wish to share this glory but cannot, since it is the gift of God.'

31 The king praised the man in a long speech and then asked another, how he could despise his enemies?

32 And he replied, 'If you show kindness to all men and win their friendship, you need fear no one. To be popular with all men is the best of good gifts to receive from God.'

33 Having praised this answer the king ordered the next man to reply to the question, how he could maintain his great renown?

34 And he replied that 'If you are generous and large-hearted in bestowing kindness and acts of grace upon others, you will never lose your renown, but if you wish the aforesaid graces to continue yours, you must call upon God continually.'

35 The king expressed his approval and asked the next, To whom ought a man to show liberality?

36 And he replied, 'All men acknowledge that we ought to show liberality to those who are well disposed towards us, but I think that we ought to show the same keen spirit of generosity to those who are opposed to us that by this means we may win them over to the right and to what is advantageous to ourselves. But we must pray to God that this may be accomplished, for he rules the minds of all men.'

37 Having expressed his agreement with the answer, the king asked the sixth to reply to the question, to whom ought we to exhibit gratitude?

38 And he replied, "To our parents continually, for God has given us a most important commandment with regard to the honour due to parents. In the next place He reckons the attitude of friend towards friend for He speaks of "a friend which is as thine own soul." You do well in trying to bring all men into friendship with yourself.'

39 The king spoke kindly to him and then asked the next, What is it that resembles beauty in value?

40 And he said, 'Piety, for it is the pre-eminent form of beauty, and its power lies in love, which is the gift of God. This you have already acquired and with it all the blessings of life.'

41 The king in the most

gracious way applauded the answer and asked another, how, if he were to fail, he could regain his reputation again in the same degree?

42 And he said, 'It is not possible for you to fail, for you have sown in all men the seeds of gratitude which produce a harvest of goodwill, and this is mightier than the strongest weapons and guarantees the greatest security. But if any man does fail, he must never again do those things which caused his failure, but he must form friendships and act justly. For it is the gift of God to be able to do good actions and not the contrary.'

43 Delighted with these words, the king asked another, how he could be free from grief?

44 And he replied, 'If he never injured any one, but did good to everybody and followed the pathway of righteousness, for its fruits bring freedom from grief. But we must pray to God that unexpected evils such as death or disease or pain or anything of this kind may not come upon us and injure us. But since you are devoted to piety, no such misfortune will ever come upon you.'

45 The king bestowed great praise upon him and asked the tenth, What is the highest form of glory?

46 And he said, 'To honour God, and this is done not with gifts and sacrifices but with purity of soul and holy conviction, since all things are fashioned and governed by God in accordance with His will. Of this purpose you are in constant possession as all men can see from your achievements in the past and in the present.'

47 With loud voice the king greeted them all and spoke kindly to them, and all those who were present expressed their approval, especially the philoso-

phers. For they were far superior to them [i. e. the philosophers] both in conduct and in argument, since they always made God their starting-point.

48 After this the king to show his good feeling proceeded to drink the health of his guests.

CHAP. IX.

Verse 8 epitomizes the value of knowledge. Verse 23, parental affection. Note especially the question in Verse 26 and the answer. Also note the question in Verse 47 and the answer. This is sage advice for business men.

ON the following day the same arrangements were made for the banquet, and the king, as soon as an opportunity occurred, began to put questions to the men who sat next to those who had already responded, and he said to the first 'Is wisdom capable of being taught?'

2 And he said, 'The soul is so constituted that it is able by the divine power to receive all the good and reject the contrary.'

3 The king expressed approval and asked the next man, What is it that is most beneficial to health?

4 And he said, 'Temperance, and it is not possible to acquire this unless God create a disposition towards it.'

5 The king spoke kindly to the man and said to another, 'How can a man worthily pay the debt of gratitude to his parents?'

6 And he said, 'By never causing them pain, and this is not possible unless God dispose the mind to the pursuit of the noblest ends.'

7 The king expressed agreement and asked the next, how he could become an eager listener?

8 And he said, 'By remember-

ing that all knowledge is useful, because it enables you by the help of God in a time of emergency to select some of the things which you have learned and apply them to the crisis which confronts you. And so the efforts of men are fulfilled by the assistance of God.'

9 The king praised him and asked the next How he could avoid doing anything contrary to law?

10 And he said, 'If you recognize that it is God who has put the thoughts into the hearts of the lawgivers that the lives of men might be preserved, you will follow them.'

11 The king acknowledged the man's answer and said to another, 'What is the advantage of kinship?'

12 And he replied, 'If we consider that we ourselves are afflicted by the misfortunes which fall upon our relatives and if their sufferings become our own —then the strength of kinship is apparent at once, for it is only when such feeling is shown that we shall win honour and esteem in their eyes. For help, when it is linked with kindliness, is of itself a bond which is altogether indissoluble. And in the day of their prosperity we must not crave their possessions, but must pray God to bestow all manner of good upon them.'

13 And having accorded to him the same praise as to the rest, the king asked another, how he could attain freedom from fear?

14 And he said, 'When the mind is conscious that it has wrought no evil, and when God directs it to all noble counsels.'

15 The king expressed his approval and asked another, how he could always maintain a right judgement?

16 And he replied, 'If he constantly set before his eyes the misfortunes which befall men

and recognized that it is God who takes away prosperity *from some* and brings others to great honour and glory.'

17 The king gave a kindly reception to the man and asked the next to answer the question, how he could avoid a life of ease and pleasure?

18 And he replied, 'If he continually remembered that he was the ruler of a great empire and the lord of vast multitudes, and that his mind ought not to be occupied with other things, but he ought always to be considering how he could best promote their welfare. He must pray, too, to God that no duty might be neglected.'

19 Having bestowed praise upon him, the king asked the tenth, how he could recognize those who were dealing treacherously with him?

20 And he replied to the question, 'If he observed whether the bearing of those about him was natural and whether they maintained the proper rule of precedence at receptions and councils, and in their general intercourse, never going beyond the bounds of propriety in congratulations or in other matters of deportment. But God will incline your mind, O King, to all that is noble.'

21 When the king had expressed his loud approval and praised them all individually (amid the plaudits of all who were present), they turned to the enjoyment of the feast.

22 And on the next day, when the opportunity offered, the king asked the next man, What is the grossest form of neglect?

23 And he replied, 'If a man does not care for his children and devote every effort to their education. For we always pray to God not so much for ourselves as for our children that every blessing may be theirs. Our desire that our children may

possess self-control is only realized by the power of God.'

24 The king said that he had spoken well and then asked another, how he could be patriotic?

25 'By keeping before your mind,' he replied, 'the thought that it is good to live and die in one's own country. Residence abroad* brings contempt upon the poor and shame upon the rich as though they had been banished for a crime. If you bestow benefits upon all, as you continually do, God will give you favour with all and you will be accounted patriotic."

26 After listening to this man, the king asked the next in order, how he could live amicably with his wife?

27 And he answered, 'By recognizing that womankind are by nature headstrong and energetic in the pursuit of their own desires, and subject to sudden changes of opinion through fallacious reasoning, and their nature is essentially weak. It is necessary to deal wisely with them and not to provoke strife. For the successful conduct of life the steersman must know the goal toward which he ought to direct his course. It is only by calling upon the help of God that men can steer a true course of life at all times.'

28 The king expressed his agreement and asked the next, how he could be free from error?

29 And he replied, 'If you always act with deliberation and never give credence to slanders, but prove for yourself the things that are said to you and decide by your own judgement the requests which are made to you and carry out everything in the light of your judgement, you will be free from error, O King. But the knowledge and practice of these things is the work of the Divine power.'

30 Delighted with these words, the king asked another, how he could be free from wrath?

31 And he said in reply to the question, 'If he recognized that he had power over all even to inflict death upon them, if he gave way to wrath, and that it would be useless and pitiful if he, just because he was lord, deprived many of life.

32 What need was there for wrath, when all men were in subjection and no one was hostile to him? It is necessary to recognize that God rules the whole world in the spirit of kindness and without wrath at all, and you,' said he, 'O King, must of necessity copy His example.'

33 The king said that he had answered well and then inquired of the next man, What is good counsel?

34 'To act well at all times and with due reflection,' he explained, 'comparing *what is advantageous* to our own policy with the injurious effects that would result from the adoption of the opposite view, in order that by weighing every point we may be well advised and our purpose may be accomplished. And most important of all, by the power of God every plan of yours will find fulfilment because you practise piety.'

35 The king said that this man had answered well, and asked another, What is philosophy?

36 And he explained, 'To deliberate well in reference to any question that emerges and never to be carried away by impulses, but to ponder over the injuries that result from the passions, and to act rightly as the circumstances demand, practising moderation. But we must pray to God to instil into our mind a regard for these things.'

37 The king signified his consent and asked another, how he

*There were foreign residents in those days too.

could meet with recognition when traveling abroad?

38 'By being fair to all men,' he replied, 'and by appearing to be inferior rather than superior to those amongst whom he was traveling. For it is a recognized principle that God by His very nature accepts the humble. And the human race loves those who are willing to be in subjection to them.'

39 Having expressed his approval at this reply, the king asked another, how he could build in such a way that his structures would endure after him?

40 And he replied to the question, 'If his creations were on a great and noble scale, so that the beholders would spare them for their beauty, and if he never dismissed any of those who wrought such works and never compelled others to minister to his needs without wages.

41 For observing how God provides for the human race, granting them health and mental capacity and all other gifts, he himself should follow His example by rendering to men a recompense for their arduous toil.* For it is the deeds that are wrought in righteousness that abide continually.'

42 The king said that this man, too, had answered well and asked the tenth, What is the fruit of wisdom?

43 And he replied, 'That a man should be conscious in himself that he has wrought no evil and that he should live his life in the truth. Since it is from these, O mighty King, that the greatest joy and stedfastness of soul and strong faith in God accrue to you if you rule your realm in piety.'

44 And when they heard the answer they all shouted with loud acclaim, and afterwards the king in the fullness of his joy began to drink their healths.

45 And on the next day the banquet followed the same course as on previous occasions, and when the opportunity presented itself the king proceeded to put questions to the remaining guests, and he said to the first, 'How can a man keep himself from pride?'

46 And he replied, 'If he maintains equality and remembers on all occasions that he is a man ruling over men. And God brings the proud to nought, and exalts the meek and humble.'

47 The king spoke kindly to him and asked the next, Whom ought a man to select as his counsellors?

48 And he replied, 'Those who have been tested in many affairs and maintain unmingled goodwill towards him and partake of his own disposition. And God manifests Himself to those who are worthy that these ends may be attained.'

49 The king praised him and asked another, What is the most necessary possession for a king?

50 'The friendship and love of his subjects,' he replied, 'for it is through this that the bond of goodwill is rendered indissoluble. And it is God who ensures that this may come to pass in accordance with *your* wish.'

51 The king praised him and inquired of another, What is goal of speech? And he replied, 'To convince your opponent by showing him his mistakes in a well-ordered array of *arguments*.

52 For in this way you will win your hearer, not by opposing him, but by bestowing praise upon him with a view to persuading him. And it is by the power of God that persuasion is accomplished.'

*The policy of a fair wage for a fair day's work is here seen to be not so modern as we sometimes think in what we are pleased to call this enlightened age.

53 The king said that he had given a good answer, and asked another, how he could live amicably with the many different races who formed the population of his kingdom?

54 'By acting the proper part towards each,' he replied, 'and taking righteousness as your guide, as you are now doing with the help of the insight which God bestows upon you.'

55 The king was delighted by this reply, and asked another, 'Under what circumstances ought a man to suffer grief?'

56 'In the misfortunes that befall our friends,' he replied, 'when we see that they are protracted and irremediable. Reason does not allow us to grieve for those who are dead and set free from evil, but all men do grieve *over them* because they think only of themselves and their own advantage. It is by the power of God alone that we can escape all evil.'

57 The king said that he had given a fitting answer, and asked another, how is reputation lost?

58 And he replied, 'When pride and unbounded self-confidence hold sway, dishonour and loss of reputation are engendered. For God is the Lord of all reputation and bestows it where He will.'

59 The king gave his confirmation to the answer, and asked the next man, To whom ought men to entrust themselves?

60 'To those,' he replied, 'who serve you from goodwill and not from fear or self-interest, thinking only of their own gain. For the one is the sign of love, the other the mark of ill will and time-serving.

61 For the man who is always watching for his own gain is a traitor at heart. But you possess the affection of all your subjects by the help of the good counsel which God bestows upon you.'

62 The king said that he had answered wisely, and asked another, What is it that keeps a kingdom safe?

63 And he replied to the question, 'Care and forethought that no evil may be wrought by those who are placed in a position of authority over the people, and this you always do by the help of God who inspires you with grave judgement.'

64 The king spoke words of encouragement to him, and asked another, What is it that maintains gratitude and honour?

65 And he replied, 'Virtue, for it is the creator of good deeds, and by it evil is destroyed, even as you exhibit nobility of character towards all by the gift which God bestows upon you.'

66 The king graciously acknowledged the answer and asked the eleventh (since there were two more than seventy), how he could in time of war maintain tranquillity of soul?

67 And he replied, 'By remembering that he had done no evil to any of his subjects, and that all would fight for him in return for the benefits which they had received, knowing that even if they lose their lives, you will care for those dependent on them. For you never fail to make reparation to any—such is the kind-heartedness with which God has inspired you.'

68 The king loudly applauded them all and spoke very kindly to them and then drank a long draught to the health of each, giving himself up to enjoyment, and lavishing the most generous and joyous friendship upon his guests.

CHAP. X.

The questions and answers continue. Showing how the army officers ought to be selected. What man is worthy of admiration and other problems of daily life as true today as 2000 years ago. Verses 15–17 are notable for recommending the theatre. Verses 21-22 describe the wisdom of electing a president or having a king.

ON the seventh day much more extensive preparations were made, and many others were present from the different cities (among them a large number of ambassadors).

2 When an opportunity occurred, the king asked the first of those who had not yet been questioned, how he could avoid being deceived *by fallacious reasoning?*

3 And he replied, 'By noticing carefully the speaker, the thing spoken, and the subject under discussion, and by putting the same questions again after an interval in different forms. But to possess an alert mind and to be able to form a sound judgement in every case is one of the good gifts of God, and you possess it, O King.'

4 The king loudly applauded the answer and asked another, Why is it that the majority of men never become virtuous?

5 'Because,' he replied, 'all men are by nature intemperate and inclined to pleasure. Hence, injustice springs up and a flood of avarice. The habit of virtue is a hindrance to those who are devoted to a life of pleasure because it enjoins upon them the preference of temperance and righteousness. For it is God who is the master of these things.'

6 The king said that he had answered well, and asked, What ought kings to obey? And he said, 'The laws, in order that by righteous enactments they may restore the lives of men. Even as you by such conduct in obedience to the Divine command have laid up in store for yourself a perpetual memorial.'

7 The king said that this man, too, had spoken well, and asked the next, Whom ought we to appoint as governors?

8 And he replied, 'All who hate wickedness, and imitating your own conduct act righteously that they may maintain a good reputation constantly. For this is what you do, O mighty King,' he said, 'and it is God who has bestowed upon you the crown of righteousness.'

9 The king loudly acclaimed the answer and then looking at the next man said, 'Whom ought we to appoint as officers over the forces?'

10 And he explained, 'Those who excel in courage and righteousness and those who are more anxious about the safety of their men than to gain a victory by risking their lives through rashness. For as God acts well towards all men, so too you in imitation of Him are the benefactor of all your subjects.'

11 The king said that he had given a good answer and asked another, What man is worthy of admiration?

12 And he replied, 'The man who is furnished with reputation and wealth and power and possesses a soul equal to it all. You yourself show by your actions that you are most worthy of admiration through the help of God who makes you care for these things.'

13 The king expressed his approval and said to another, 'To what affairs ought kings to devote most time?'

14 And he replied, 'To reading and the *study of* the records of official journeys, which are written in reference to the *various* kingdoms, with a view to the reformation and preservation of the subjects. And it is by such activity that you have attained to a glory which has never been approached by others, through the help of God who fulfils all your desires.'

15 The king spoke enthusiastically to the man and asked another, how ought a man to occupy himself during his hours of relaxation and recreation?

16 And he replied, 'To watch those plays which can be acted with propriety and to set before one's eyes scenes taken from life and enacted with dignity and decency is profitable and appropriate.

17 For there is some edification to be found even in these amusements, for often some desirable lesson is taught by the most insignificant affairs of life. But by practising the utmost propriety in all your actions, you have shown that you are a philosopher and you are honoured by God on account of your virtue.'

18 The king, pleased with the words which had just been spoken, said to the ninth man, how ought a man to conduct himself at banquets?

19 And he replied, 'You should summon to your side men of learning and those who are able to give you useful hints with regard to the affairs of your kingdom and the lives of your subjects (for you could not find any theme more suitable or more educative than this) since such men are dear to God because they have trained their minds to contemplate the noblest themes —as you indeed are doing yourself, since all your actions are directed by God.'

20 Delighted with the reply, the king inquired of the next man, What is best for the people? That a private citizen should be made king over them or a member of the royal family?

21 And he replied, 'He who is best by nature. For kings who come of royal lineage are often harsh and severe towards their subjects. And still more is this the case with some of those who

have risen from the ranks of private citizens, who after having experienced evil and borne their share of poverty, when they rule over multitudes turn out to be more cruel than the godless tyrants.

22 But, as I have said, a good nature which has been properly trained is capable of ruling, and you are a great king, not so much because you excel in the glory of your rule and your wealth but rather because you have surpassed all men in clemency and philanthropy, thanks to God who has endowed you with these qualities.'

23 The king spent some time in praising this man and then asked the last of all, What is the greatest achievement in ruling an empire?

24 And he replied, 'That the subjects should continually dwell in a state of peace, and that justice should be speedily administered in cases of dispute.

25 These results are achieved through the influence of the ruler, when he is a man who hates evil and loves the good and devotes his energies to saving the lives of men, just as you consider injustice the worst form of evil and by your just administration have fashioned for yourself an undying reputation, since God bestows upon you a mind which is pure and untainted by any evil.'

26 And when he ceased, loud and joyful applause broke out for some considerable time. When it stopped the king took a cup and gave a toast in honour of all his guests and the words which they had uttered.

27 Then in conclusion he said, 'I have derived the greatest benefit from your presence. I have profited much by the wise teaching which you have given me in reference to the art of ruling.'

28 Then he ordered that three

talents of silver should be presented to each of them, and *appointed* one of his slaves to deliver over the money.

29 All at once shouted their approval, and the banquet became a scene of joy, while the king gave himself up to a continuous round of festivity.

CHAP. XI.

For a comment on ancient stenography, see Verse 7. The translation is submitted for approval and accepted as read, and (Verse 23) a rising vote of approval is taken and unanimously carried.

I HAVE written at length and must crave your pardon, Philocrates.

2 I was astonished beyond measure at the men and the way in which on the spur of the moment they gave answers which really needed a long time to devise.

3 For though the questioner had given great thought to each particular question, those who replied one after the other had their answers to the questions *ready at once* and so they seemed to me and to all who were present and especially to the philosophers to be worthy of admiration.

4 And I suppose that the thing will seem incredible to those who will read my narrative in the future.

5 But it is unseemly to misrepresent facts which are recorded in the public archives.

6 And it would not be right for me to transgress in such a matter as this. I tell the story just as it happened, conscientiously avoiding any error.

7 I was so impressed by the force of their utterances, that I made an effort to consult those whose business it was to make a record of all that happened at the royal audiences and banquets.

8 For it is the custom, as you know, from the moment the king begins to transact business until the time when he retires to rest, for a record to be taken of all his sayings and doings—a most excellent and useful arrangement.

9 For on the following day *the minutes of the* doings and sayings of the previous day are read over before business commences, and if there has been any irregularity, the matter is at once set right.

10 I obtained therefore, as has been said, accurate information from the public records, and I have set forth the facts in proper order since I know how eager you are to obtain useful information.

11 Three days later Demetrius took the men and passing along the sea-wall, seven stadia long, to the island, crossed the bridge and made for the northern districts *of Pharos.*

12 There he assembled them in a house, which had been built upon the sea-shore, of great beanty and in a secluded situation, and invited them to carry out the work of translation, since everything that they needed for the purpose was placed at their disposal.

13 So they set to work comparing their several results and making them agree, and whatever they agreed upon was suitably copied out under the direction of Demetrius.

14 And the session lasted until the ninth hour; after this they were set free to minister to their physical needs.

15 Everything they wanted was furnished for them on a lavish scale. In addition to this Dorotheus made the same preparations for them daily as were made for the king himself—for

thus he had been commanded by the king.

16 In the early morning they appeared daily at the Court, and after saluting the king went back to their own place.

17 And as is the custom of all the Jews, they washed their hands in the sea and prayed to God and then devoted themselves to reading and translating the particular passage *upon which they were engaged*, and I put the question to them, Why it was that they washed their hands before they prayed?

18 And they explained that it was a token that they had done no evil (for every form of activity is wrought by means of the hands) since in their noble and holy way they regard everything as a symbol of righteousness and truth.

19 As I have already said, they met together daily in the place which was delightful for its quiet and its brightness and applied themselves to their task.

20 And it so chanced that the work of translation was completed in seventy-two days, just as if this had been arranged of set purpose.

21 When the work was completed, Demetrius collected together the Jewish population in the place where the translation had been made, and read it over to all, in the presence of the translators, who met with a great reception also from the people, because of the great benefits which they had conferred upon them.

22 They bestowed warm praise upon Demetrius, too, and urged him to have the whole law transcribed and present a copy to their leaders.

23 After the books had been read, the priests and the elders of the translators and the Jewish community and the leaders of the people stood up and said, that since so excellent and sacred and accurate a translation had been made, it was only right that it should remain as it was and no alteration should be made in it.

24 And when the whole company expressed their approval, they bade them pronounce a curse in accordance with their custom upon anyone who should make any alteration either by adding anything or changing in any way whatever any of the words which had been written or making any omission.

25 This was a very wise precaution to ensure that the book might be preserved for all the future time unchanged.

26 When the matter was reported to the king, he rejoiced greatly, for he felt that the design which he had formed had been safely carried out.

27 The whole book was read over to him and he was greatly astonished at the spirit of the lawgiver.

28 And he said to Demetrius, 'How is it that none of the historians or the poets have ever thought it worth their while to allude to such a wonderful achievement?'

29 And he replied, 'Because the law is sacred and of divine origin. And some of those who formed the intention of *dealing with it* have been smitten by God and therefore desisted from their purpose.'

30 He said that he had heard from Theopompus that he had been driven out of his mind for more than thirty days because he intended to insert in his history some of the incidents from the earlier and somewhat unreliable translations of the law.

31 When he had recovered a little, he besought God to make it clear to him why the misfortune had befallen him.

32 And it was revealed to him in a dream, that from idle curiosity he was wishing to com-

municate sacred truths to common men, and that if he desisted he would recover his health.

33 I have heard, too, from the lips of Theodektes, one of the tragic poets, that when he was about to adapt some of the incidents recorded in the book for one of his plays, he was affected with cataract in both his eyes.

34 And when he perceived the reason why the misfortune had befallen him, he prayed to God for many days and was afterwards restored.

35 And after the king, as I have already said, had received the explanation of Demetrius on this point, he did homage and ordered that great care should be taken of the books, and that they should be sacredly guarded.

36 And he urged the translators to visit him frequently after their return to Judea, for it was only right, he said, that he should now send them home.

37 But when they came back, he would treat them as friends, as was right, and they would receive rich presents from him.

38 He ordered preparations to be made for them to return home, and treated them most munificently.

39 He presented each one of them with three robes of the finest sort, two talents of gold, a sideboard weighing one talent, all the furniture for three couches.

40 And with the escort he sent Eleazar ten couches with silver legs and all the necessary equipment, a sideboard worth thirty talents, ten robes, purple, and a magnificent crown, and a hundred pieces of the finest woven linen, also bowls and dishes, and two golden beakers to be dedicated to God.

41 He urged him also in a letter that if any of the men preferred to come back to him, not to hinder them.

42 For he counted it a great privilege to enjoy the society of such learned men, and he would rather lavish his wealth upon them than upon vanities.

43 And now Philocrates, you have the complete story in accordance with my promise.

44 I think that you find greater pleasure in these matters than in the writings of the mythologists.

45 For you are devoted to the study of those things which can benefit the soul, and spend much time upon it. I shall attempt to narrate whatever other events are worth recording, that by perusing them you may secure the highest reward for your zeal.

FOURTH BOOK OF MACCABEES

THIS book is like a fearful peal of thunder echoing out of the dim horrors of ancient tyranny. It is a chapter based on persecution by Antiochus, the tyrant of Syria, whom some called Epiphanes, The Madman. Roman history of the first centuries records two such tyrants—the other, Caligula, the Second Brilliant Madman.

The form of this writing is that of an oration. So carefully timed are the risings and fallings of the speech; so devastating are its arguments; so unfaltering is its logic; so deep its thrusts; so cool its reasoning—that it takes its place as a sample of the sheerest eloquence.

The keynote is Courage. The writer begins with an impassioned statement of the Philosophy of Inspired Reason. We like to think of this twentieth Century as the Age of Reason and contrast it with the Age of Myths—yet a writing such as this is a challenge to such an assumption. We find a writer who probably belonged to the first century before the Christian Era stating a clear-cut philosophy of Reason that is just as potent today as it was two thousand years ago.

The setting of the observations in the torture chambers is unrelenting. On our modern ears attuned to gentler things it strikes appallingly. The details of the successive tortures (suggesting the instruments of the Spanish Inquisition centuries later) are elaborated in a way shocking to our taste. Even the emergence of the stoical characters of the Old man, the Seven Brothers, and the Mother, does nothing to soften the ferocity with which this orator conjures Courage.

The ancient Fathers of the Christian Church carefully preserved this book (we have it from a Syrian translation) as a work of high moral value and teaching, and it was undoubtedly familiar to many of the early Christian martyrs, who were aroused to the pitch of martyrdom by reading it.

CHAP. I.

An outline of philosophy from ancient times concerning Inspired Reason. Civilization has never achieved higher thought. A discussion of "Repressions." Verse 48 sums up the whole Philosophy of mankind.

PHILOSOPHICAL in the highest degree is the question I propose to discuss, namely whether the Inspired Reason is supreme ruler over the passions; and to the philosophy of it I would seriously entreat your earnest attention.

2 For not only is the subject generally necessary as a branch of knowledge, but it includes the praise of the greatest of virtues, whereby I mean self-control.

3 That is to say, if Reason

is proved to control the passions adverse to temperance, gluttony and lust, it is also clearly shown to be lord over the passions, like malevolence, opposed to justice, and over those opposed to manliness, namely rage and pain and fear.

4 But, some may ask, if the Reason is master of the passions, why does it not control forgetfulness and ignorance? their object being to cast ridicule.

5 The answer is that Reason is not master over defects inhering in the mind itself, but over the passions or moral defects that are adverse to justice and manliness and temperance and judgement; and its action in their case is not to extirpate the passions, but to enable us to resist them successfully.

6 I could bring before you many examples, drawn from various sources, where Reason has proved itself master over the passions, but the best instance by far that I can give is the noble conduct of those who died for the sake of virtue, Eleazar, and the Seven Brethren and the Mother.

7 For these all by their contempt of pains, yea, even unto death, proved that Reason rises superior to the passions.

8 I might enlarge here in praise of their virtues, they, the men with the Mother, dying on this day we celebrate for the love of moral beauty and goodness, but rather would I felicitate them on the honours they have attained.

9 For the admiration felt for their courage and endurance, not only by the world at large but by their very executioners, made them the authors of the downfall of the tyranny under which our nation lay, they defeating the tyrant by their endurance, so that through them was their country purified.

10 But I shall presently take

opportunity to discuss this, after we have begun with the general theory, as I am in the habit of doing, and I will then proceed to their story, giving glory to the all-wise God.

11 Our enquiry, then, is whether the Reason is supreme master over the passions.

12 But we must define just what the Reason is and what passion is, and how many forms of passion there are, and whether the Reason is supreme over all of them.

13 Reason I take to be the mind preferring with clear deliberation the life of wisdom.

14 Wisdom I take to be the knowledge of things, divine and human, and of their causes.

15 This I take to be the culture acquired under the Law, through which we learn with due reverence the things of God and for our worldly profit the things of man.

16 Now wisdom is manifested under the forms of judgement and justice, and courage, and temperance.

17 But judgement or self-control is the one that dominates them all, for through it, in truth, Reason asserts its authority over the passions.

18 But of the passions there are two comprehensive sources, namely, pleasure and pain, and either belongs essentially also to the soul as well as to the body.

19 And with respect both to pleasure and pain there are many cases where the passions have certain sequences.

20 Thus while desire goes before pleasure, satisfaction follows after, and while fear goes before pain, after pain comes sorrow.

21 Anger, again, if a man will retrace the course of his feelings, is a passion in which are blended both pleasure and pain.

22 Under pleasure, also, comes that moral debasement which

exhibits the widest variety of the passions.

23 It manifests itself in the soul as ostentation, and covetousness, and vain-glory, and contentiousness, and backbiting, and in the body as eating of strange meat, and gluttony, and gormandizing in secret.

24 Now pleasure and pain being as it were two trees, growing from body and soul, many offshoots of these passions sprout up; and each man's Reason as master-gardener, weeding and pruning and binding up, and turning on tho water and directing it hither and thither, brings the thicket of dispositions and passions under domestication.

25 For while Reason is the guide of the virtues it is master of the passions.

26 Observe, now, in the first place, that Reason becomes supreme over the passions in virtue of the inhibitory action of temperance.

27 Temperance, I take it, is the repression of the desires; but of the desires some are mental and some physical, and both kinds are clearly controlled by Reason; when we are tempted towards forbidden meats, how do we come to relinquish the pleasures to be derived from them?

28 Is it not that Reason has power to repress the appetites? In my opinion it is so.

29 Accordingly when we feel a desire to eat water-animals and birds and beasts and meats of every description forbidden to us under the Law, we abstain through the predominance of Reason.

30 For the propensions of our appetites are checked and inhibited by the temperate mind, and all the movements of the body obey the bridle of Reason.

31 And what is there to be surprised at if the natural desire of the soul to enjoy the fruition of beauty is quenched?

32 This, certainly, is why we praise the virtuous Joseph, because by his Reason, with a mental effort, he checked the carnal impulse.* For he, a young man at the age when physical desire is strong, by his Reason quenched the impulse of his passions.

33 And Reason is proved to subdue the impulse not only of sexual desire, but of all sorts of covetings.

34 For the Law says, 'Thou shalt not covet thy neighbour's wife, nor anything that is thy neighbour's.'

35 Verily, when the Law orders us not to covet, it should, I think, confirm strongly the argument that the Reason is capable of controlling covetous desires, even as it does the passions that militate against justice.

36 How else can a man, naturally gormandizing and greedy and drunken, be taught to change his nature, if the Reason be not manifestly the master of the passions?

37 Certainly, as soon as a man orders his life according to the Law, if he is miserly he acts contrary to his nature, and lends money to the needy without interest, and at the seventh-year periods cancels the debt.

38 And if he is parsimonious, he is overruled by the Law through the action of Reason, and refrains from gleaning his stubbles or picking the last grapes from his vineyards.

39 And with regard to all the rest we can recognize that Reason is in the position of master over the passions or affections.

40 For the Law ranks above affection for parents, so that a man may not for their sakes surrender his virtue, and it overrides love for a wife, so that if

* See *The Testament of Joseph*, page 260.

she transgress a man should rebuke her, and it governs love for children, so that if they are naughty a man should punish them, and it controls the claims of friendship, so that a man should reprove his friends if they do evil.

41 And do not think it a paradoxical thing when Reason through the Law is able to overcome even hatred, so that a man refrains from cutting down the enemy's orchards, and protects the property of the enemy from the spoilers, and gathers up their goods that have been scattered.

42 And the rule of Reason is likewise proved to extend through the more aggressive passions or vices, ambition, vanity, ostentation, pride, and backbiting.

43 For the temperate mind repels all these debased passions, even as it does anger, for it conquers even this.

44 Yea, Moses when he was angered against Dathan and Abiram did not give free course to his wrath, but governed his anger by his Reason.

45 For the temperate mind is able, as I said, to win the victory over the passions, modifying some, while crushing others absolutely.

46 Why else did our wise father Jacob blame the houses of Simeon and Levi for their unreasoning slaughter of the tribe of the Shechemites, saying, 'Accursed be their anger!'

47 For had not Reason possessed the power to restrain their anger he would not have spoken thus.

48 For in the day when God created man, he implanted in him his passions and inclinations, and also, at the very same time, set the mind on a throne amidst the senses to be his sacred guide in all things; and to the mind he gave the Law, by the which if a man order himself, he shall reign over a kingdom that is temperate, and just, and virtuous, and brave.

CHAP. II.

The ruling of Desire and Anger. The story of David's thirst. Stirring chapters of ancient history. Savage attempts to make the Jews eat swine. Interesting references to an ancient bank (Verse 21.)

WELL then, someone may ask, if Reason is master of the passions why is it not master of forgetfulness and ignorance?

2 But the argument is supremely ridiculous. For Reason is not shown to be master over passions or defects in itself, but over those of the body.

3 For example, none of you is able to extirpate our natural desire, but the Reason can enable him to escape being made a slave by desire.

4 None of you is able to extirpate anger from the soul, but it is possible for the Reason to come to his aid against anger.

5 None of you can extirpate a malevolent disposition, but Reason can be his powerful ally against being swayed by malevolence.

6 Reason is not the extirpate of the passions, but their antagonist.

7 The case of the thirst of King David may serve at least to make this clearer.

8 For when David had fought the live-long day against the Philistines, and by the help of our country's warriors had slain many of them, he came at eventide, all fordone with sweat and toil, to the royal tent, around which was encamped the whole army of our ancestors.

9 So all the host fell to their evening meal; but the king,

being consumed with an intense thirst, though he had abundance of water, was unable to slake it.

10 Instead, an irrational desire for the water that was in the possession of the enemy with growing intensity burned him up and unmanned and consumed him.

11 Then when his body-guard murmured against the craving of the king, two youths, mighty warriors, ashamed that their king should lack his desire, put on all their armour, and took a water-vessel, and scaled the enemy's ramparts; and stealing undetected past the guards at the gate, they searched through all the enemy's camp.

12 And they bravely found the spring, and drew from it a draught for the king.

13 But David, though still burning with the thirst, considered that such a draught, reckoned as equivalent to blood, was a grievous danger to his soul.

14 Therefore, opposing his Reason to his desire, he poured out the water as an offering to God.

15 For the temperate mind is able to conquer the dictates of the passions, and to quench the fires of desire, and to wrestle victoriously with the pangs of our bodies though they be exceeding strong, and by the moral beauty and goodness of Reason to defy with scorn all the domination of the passions.

16 And now the occasion calls us to set forth the story of the self-controlled Reason.

17 At a time when our fathers enjoyed great peace through the due observance of the Law, and were in happy case, so that Seleucus Nicanor, the king of Asia, sanctioned the tax for the temple-service, and recognized our polity, precisely then, certain men, acting factiously against the general concord, involved us in many and various calamities.

18 Onias, a man of the highest character, being then high priest and having the office for his life, a certain Simon raised a faction against him, but since despite every kind of slander he failed to injure him on account of the people, he fled abroad with intent to betray his country.

19 So he came to Apollonius, the governor of Syria and Phoenicia and Cilicia, and said, 'Being loyal to the king, I am here to inform you that in the treasuries of Jerusalem are stored many thousands of private deposits, not belonging to the temple account, and rightfully the property of King Seleucus.'

20 Apollonius having made inquiry into the details of the matter, praised Simon for his loyal service to the king, and hastening to the court of Seleucus, disclosed to him the valuable treasure; then, after receiving authority to deal with the matter, he promptly marched into our country, accompanied by the accursed Simon and a very powerful army, and announced that he was there by the king's command to take possession of the private deposits in the treasury.

21 Our people were deeply angered by this announcement, and protested strongly, considering it an outrageous thing for those who had entrusted their deposits to the temple treasury to be robbed of them, and they threw all possible obstacles in his way.

22 Apollonius, however, with threats, made his way into the temple.

23 Then the priests in the temple and the women and children besought God to come to the rescue of his Holy Place that was being violated; and when Apollonius with his armed host marched in to seize the moneys, there appeared from heaven

angels, riding upon horses, with lightning flashing from their arms, and cast great fear and trembling upon them.

24 And Apollonius fell down half-dead in the Court of the Gentiles, and stretched out his hands to heaven, and with tears he entreated the Hebrews that they would make intercession for him and stay the wrath of the heavenly host.

25 For he said that he had sinned and was worthy even of death, and that if he were given his life he would laud to all men the blessedness of the Holy Place.

26 Moved by these words, Onias, the high-priest, although most scrupulous in other cases, made intercession for him lest king Seleucus should possibly think that Apollonius had been overthrown by a human device and not by divine justice.

27 Apollonius, accordingly, after his astonishing deliverance departed to report to the king the things that had befallen him.

28 But Seleucus dying, his successor on the throne was his son Antiochus Epiphanes, an overweening terrible man; who dismissed Onias from his sacred office, and made his brother Jason high-priest instead, the condition being that in return for the appointment Jason should pay him three thousand six hundred and sixty talents yearly.

29 So he appointed Jason high-priest and made him chief ruler over the people.

30 And he (Jason) introduced to our people a new way of life and a new constitution in utter defiance of the Law; so that not only did he lay out a gymnasium on the Mount of our fathers, but he actually abolished the service of the temple.

31 Wherefore the divine justice was kindled to anger and brought Antiochus himself as an enemy against us.

32 For when he was carrying on war with Ptolemy in Egypt and heard that the people of Jerusalem had rejoiced exceedingly over a report of his death, he immediately marched back against them.

33 And when he had plundered the city he made a decree denouncing the penalty of death upon any who should be seen to live after the Law of our fathers.

34 But he found all his decrees of no avail to break down the constancy of our people to the Law, and he beheld all his threats and penalties utterly despised, so that even women for circumcising their sons, though they knew beforehand what would be their fate, were flung, together with their offspring, headlong from the rocks.

35 When therefore his decrees continued to be contemned by the mass of the people, he personally tried to force by tortures each man separately to eat unclean meats and thus abjure the Jewish religion.

36 Accordingly, the tyrant Antiochus, accompanied by his councillors, sat in judgement on a certain high place with his troops drawn up around him in full armour, and he ordered his guards to drag there every single man of the Hebrews and compel them to eat swine's flesh and things offered to idols; but if any should refuse to defile themselves with the unclean things, they were to be tortured and put to death.

37 And when many had been taken by force, one man first from among the company was brought before Antiochus, a Hebrew whose name was Eleazar, a priest by birth, trained in knowledge of the law, a man advanced in years and well known to many of the tyrant's court for his philosophy.

38 And Antiochus, looking on him, said:

'Before I allow the tortures to

begin for you, O venerable man, I would give you this counsel, that you should eat of the flesh of the swine and save your life; for I respect your age and your grey hairs, although to have worn them so long a time, and still to cling to the Jewish religion, makes me think you no philosopher.

39 For most excellent is the meat of this animal which Nature has graciously bestowed upon us, and why should you abominate it? Truly it is folly not to enjoy innocent pleasures, and it is wrong to reject Nature's favours.

40 But it will be still greater folly, I think, on your part if with idle vapouring about truth you shall proceed to defy even me to your own punishment.

41 Will you not awake from your preposterous philosophy? Will you not fling aside the nonsense of your calculations and, adopting another frame of mind befitting your mature years, learn the true philosophy of expediency, and bow to my charitable counsel, and have pity on your own venerable age?

42 For consider this, too, that even if there be some Power whose eye is upon this religion of yours, he will always pardon you for a transgression done under compulsion.'

43 Thus urged by the tyrant to the unlawful eating of unclean meat, Eleazar asked permission to speak; and receiving it, he began his speech before the court as follows:

44 'We, O Antiochus, having accepted the Divine Law as the Law of our country, do not believe any stronger necessity is laid upon us than that of our obedience to the Law.

45 Therefore we do surely deem it right not in any way whatsoever to transgress the Law.

46 And yet, were our Law, as you suggest, not truly divine, while we vainly believed it to be divine, not even so would it be right for us to destroy our reputation for piety.

47 Think it not, then, a small sin for us to eat the unclean thing, for the transgression of the Law, be it in small things or in great, is equally heinous; for in either case equally the Law is despised.

48 And you scoff at our philosophy, as if under it we were living in a manner contrary to reason.

49 Not so, for the Law teaches us self-control, so that we are masters of all our pleasures and desires and are thoroughly trained in manliness so as to endure all pain with readiness; and it teaches justice, so that with all our various dispositions we act fairly, and it teaches righteousness, so that with due reverence we worship only the God who is.

50 Therefore do we eat no unclean meat; for believing our Law to be given by God, we know also that the Creator of the world, as a Lawgiver, feels for us according to our nature.

51 He has commanded us to eat the things that will be convenient for our souls, and he has forbidden us to eat meats that would be the contrary.

52 But it is the act of a tyrant that you should compel us not only to transgress the Law, but should also make us eat in such manner that you may mock at this defilement so utterly abominable to us.

53 But you shall not mock at me thus, neither will I break the sacred oaths of my ancestors to keep the Law, not even though you tear out mine eyes and burn out mine entrails.

54 I am not so unmanned by old age but that when righteousness is at stake the strength of youth returns to my Reason.

55 So twist hard your racks and blow your furnace hotter. I do not so pity mine old age as to break the Law of my fathers in mine own person.

56 I will not belie thee, O Law that wast my teacher; I will not desert thee, O beloved self-control; I will not put thee to shame, O wisdom-loving Reason, nor will I deny ye, O venerated priesthood and knowledge of the Law.

57 Neither shalt thou sully the pure mouth of mine old age and my lifelong constancy to the Law. Clean shall my fathers receive me, unafraid of thy torments even to the death.

58 For thou indeed mayest be tyrant over unrighteous men, but thou shalt not lord it over my resolution in the matter of righteousness either by thy words or through thy deeds.'

CHAP. III.

Eleazar, the gentle spirited old man, shows such fortitude that even as we read these words 2000 years later, they seem like an inextinguishable fire.

BUT when Eleazar replied thus eloquently to the exhortations of the tyrants, the guards around him dragged him roughly to the torturing place.

2 And first they unclothed the old man, who was adorned with the beauty of holiness.

3 Then binding his arms on either side they scourged him, a herald standing and shouting out over against him, 'Obey the orders of the king!'

4 But the great-souled and noble man, an Eleazar in very truth, was no more moved in his mind than if he were being tormented in a dream; yea, the old man keeping his eyes steadfastly raised to heaven suffered his flesh to be torn by the scourges till he was bathed in blood and his sides became a mass of wounds; and even when he fell to the ground because his body could no longer support the pain he still kept his Reason erect and inflexible.

5 With his foot then one of the cruel guards as he fell kicked him savagely in the side to make him get up.

6 But he endured the anguish, and despised the compulsion, and bore up under the torments, and like a brave athlete taking punishment, the old man outwore his tormentors.

7 The sweat stood on his brow, and he drew his breath in hard gasps, till his nobility of soul extorted the admiration of his tormentors themselves.

8 Hereupon, partly in pity for his old age, partly in sympathy for their friend, partly in admiration of his courage, some of the courtiers of the king went up to him and said:

9 'Why, O Eleazar, dost thou madly destroy thyself in this misery? We will bring to thee of the seethed meats, but do thou feign only to partake of the swine's flesh, and so save thyself.'

10 And Eleazar, as if their counsel did but add to his tortures, cried loudly: 'No. May we sons of Abraham never have so evil a thought as with faint heart to counterfeit a part unseemly to us.

11 Contrary to Reason, indeed, were it for us, after living unto the truth till old age, and guarding in lawful guise the repute of so living, now to change and become in our own persons a pattern to the young of impiety, to the end that we should encourage them to eat unclean meat.

12 Shame were it if we should live on a little longer, during that little being mocked of all men for cowardice, and while despised by the tyrant as unmanly should fail to defend the Divine Law unto the death.

13 Therefore, O sons of Abraham, do ye die nobly for righteousness' sake; but as for you, O minions of the tyrant, why pause ye in your work?'

14 So they, seeing him thus triumphant over the tortures and unmoved even by the pity of his executioners, dragged him to the fire.

15 There they cast him on it, burning him with cruelly cunning devices, and they poured broth of evil odour into his nostrils.

16 But when the fire already reached to his bones and he was about to give up the ghost, he lifted up his eyes to God and said:

17 'Thou, O God, knowest that though I might save myself I am dying by fiery torments for thy Law. Be merciful unto thy people, and let our punishment be a satisfaction in their behalf. Make my blood their purification, and take my soul to ransom their souls.'

18 And with these words the holy man nobly yielded up his spirit under the torture, and for the sake of the Law held out by his Reason even against the torments unto death.

19 Beyond question, then, the Inspired Reason is master over the passions; for if his passions or sufferings had prevailed over his Reason we should have credited them with this evidence of their superior power.

20 But now his Reason having conquered his passions, we properly attribute to it the power of commanding them.

21 And it is right that we should admit that the mastery lies with Reason, in cases at least where it conquers pains that come from outside ourselves; for it were ridiculous to deny it.

22 And my proof covers not only the superiority of Reason to pains, but its superiority to pleasures also; neither does it surrender to them.

CHAP. IV.

This so called "Age of Reason" may in this chapter read that the Philosophy of Reason is 2000 years old. The story of seven sons and their mother.

FOR the Reason of our father Eleazar, like a fine steersman steering the ship of sanctity on the sea of the passions, though buffeted by the threats of the tyrant and swept by the swelling waves of the tortures, never shifted for one moment the helm of sanctity until he sailed into the haven of victory over death.

2 No city besieged with many and cunning engines ever defended itself so well as did that holy man when his sacred soul was attacked with scourge and rack and flame, and he moved them who were laying siege to his soul through his Reason that was the shield of sanctity.

3 For our father Eleazar, setting his mind firm as a beetling sea-cliff, broke the mad onset of the surges of the passions.

4 O priest worthy of thy priesthood, thou didst not defile thy holy teeth, nor didst thou befoul with unclean meat thy belly that had room only for piety and purity.

5 O confessor of the Law and philosopher of the Divine life! Such should those be whose office is to serve the Law and defend it with their own blood and honourable sweat in the face of sufferings to the death.

6 Thou, O father, didst fortify our fidelity to the Law through thy steadfastness unto glory; and having spoken in honour of holiness thou didst not belie thy speech, and didst confirm the words of divine philosophy by

thy deeds, O aged man that wast more forceful than the tortures.

7 O reverend elder that wast tenser-strung than the flame, thou great king over the passions, Eleazar.

8 For as our father Aaron, armed with the censer, ran through the massed congregation against the fiery angel and overcame him, so the son of Aaron, Eleazar, being consumed by the melting heat of the fire, remained unshaken in his Reason.

9 And yet most wonderful of all, he, being an old man, with the sinews of his body unstrung and his muscles relaxed and his nerves weakened, grew a young man again in the spirit of his Reason and with Isaac-like Reason turned the hydra-headed torture to impotence.

10 O blessed age, O reverend grey head, O life faithful to the Law and perfected by the seal of death!

11 Assuredly, then, if an old man despised the torments unto death for righteousness' sake it must be admitted that the Inspired Reason is able to guide the passions.

12 But some perhaps may answer that not all men are masters of the passions because not all men have their Reason enlightened.

13 But as many as with their whole heart make righteousness their first thought, these alone are able to master the weakness of the flesh, believing that unto God they die not, as our patriarchs, Abraham and Isaac and Jacob, died not, but that they live unto God.

14 Therefore there is nothing contradictory in certain persons appearing to be slaves to passion in consequence of the weakness of their Reason.

15 For who is there that being a philosopher following righteously the whole rule of philosophy, and having put his trust in God, and knowing that it is a blessed thing to endure all hardness for the sake of virtue, would not conquer his passions for the sake of righteousness?

16 For the wise and self-controlled man alone is the brave ruler of the passions.

17 Yea, by this means even young boys, being philosophers by virtue of the Reason which is according to righteousness, have triumphed over yet more grievous tortures.

18 For when the tyrant found himself notably defeated in his first attempt, and impotent to compel an old man to eat unclean meat, then truly in violent rage he ordered the guards to bring others of the young men of the Hebrews, and if they would eat unclean meat to release them after eating it, but if they refused, to torture them yet more savagely.

19 And under these orders of the tyrant seven brethren together with their aged mother were brought prisoners before him, all handsome, and modest, and well-born, and generally attractive.

20 And when the tyrant saw them there, standing as if they were a festal choir with their mother in the midst, he took notice of them, and struck by their noble and distinguished bearing he smiled at them, and calling them nearer said:

21 'O young men, I wish well to each one of you, and admire your beauty, and honour highly so large a band of brothers; so not only do I advise you not to persist in the madness of that old man who has already suffered, but I even entreat of you to yield to me and become partakers in my friendship.

22 For, as I am able to punish those who disobey my orders, so am I able to advance those who do obey me.

23 Be assured then that you

shall be given positions of importance and authority in my service if you will reject the ancestral law of your polity.

24 Share in the Hellenic life, and walk in a new way, and take some pleasure in your youth; for if you drive me to anger with your disobedience you will compel me to resort to terrible penalties and put every single one of you to death by torture.

25 Have pity then on yourselves, whom even I, your opponent, pity for your youth and your beauty.

26 Will you not consider with yourselves this thing, that if you disobey me there is nothing before you but death in torments?'

27 With these words he ordered the instruments of torture to be brought forward in order to persuade them by fear to eat unclean meat.

28 But when the guards had produced wheels, and joint-dislocators, and racks, and bone-crushers, and catapults, and cauldrons, and braziers, and thumb-screws, and iron claws, and wedges, and branding irons, the tyrant spoke again and said:

29 'You had better feel fear, my lads, and the justice you worship will pardon your unwilling transgression.'

30 But they, hearing his persuasions, and seeing his dreadful engines, not only showed no fear but actually arrayed their philosophy in opposition to the tyrant, and by their right Reason did abase his tyranny.

31 And yet consider; supposing some amongst them to have been faint-hearted and cowardly, what sort of language would they have used? would it not have been to this effect?

32 'Alas! miserable creatures that we are and foolish above measure! When the king invites us and appeals to us on terms of kind treatment shall we not obey him?

33 Why do we encourage ourselves with vain desires and dare a disobedience that is to cost us our lives? Shall we not, O men my brothers, fear the dread instruments and weigh well his threats of the tortures, and abandon these empty vaunts and this fatal bragging?

34 Let us take pity on our own youth and have compassion on our mother's age; and let us lay to heart that if we disobey we shall die.

35 And even the divine justice will have mercy on us, if compelled by necessity we yield to the king in fear. Why should we cast away from us this dear life and rob ourselves of this sweet world?

36 Let us not strive against necessity nor with vain confidence invite our torture.

37 Even the Law itself does not willingly condemn us to death, we being in terror of the instruments of torture.

38 Why does such contentiousness inflame us and a fatal obstinacy find favour with us, when we might have a peaceful life by obeying the king?'

39 But no such words escaped these young men at the prospect of the torture, nor did such thoughts enter into their minds.

40 For they were despisers of the passions and masters over pain.

CHAP. V.

A chapter of horror and torture revealing ancient tyranny at its utmost savagery. Verse 26 is profound truth.

AND thus no sooner did the tyrant conclude his urging of them to eat unclean meat than all with one voice together, and as with one soul, said to him:

2 'Why dost thou delay, O tyrant? We are ready to die rather than transgress the commandments of our fathers.

3 For we should be putting our ancestors also to shame, if we did not walk in obedience to the Law and take Moses as our counsellor.

4 O tyrant that counsellest us to transgress the Law, do not, hating us, pity us beyond ourselves.

5 For we esteem thy mercy, giving us our life in return for a breach of the Law, a thing harder to bear than death itself.

6 Thou wouldst terrify us with thy threats of death under torture, as if a little while ago thou hadst learned nothing from Eleazar.

7 But if the old men of the Hebrews endured the tortures for righteousness' sake, yea, until they died, more befittingly will we young men die despising the torments of thy compulsion, over which he our aged teacher also triumphed.

8 Make trial therefore, O tyrant. And if thou takest our lives for the sake of righteousness, think not that thou hurtest us with thy tortures.

9 For we through this our evil entreatment and our endurance of it shall win the prize of virtue; but thou for our cruel murder shalt suffer at the hands of divine justice sufficient torment by fire for ever.'

10 These words of the youths redoubled the wrath of the tyrant, not at their disobedience only but at what he considered their ingratitude.

11 So by his orders the scourgers brought forward the eldest of them and stripped him of his garment and bound his hands and arms on either side with thongs.

12 But when they had scourged him till they were weary, and gained nothing

thereby, they cast him upon the wheel.

13 And on it the noble youth was racked till his bones were out of joint. And as joint after joint gave way, he denounced the tyrant in these words:

14 'O thou most abominable tyrant, thou enemy of the justice of heaven and bloody-minded, thou dost torment me in this fashion not for manslaying nor for impiety but for defending the Law of God.'

15 And when the guards said to him, 'Consent to eat, that so you may be released from your tortures,' he said to them, 'Your method, O miserable minions, is not strong enough to lead captive my Reason. Cut off my limbs, and burn my flesh, and twist my joints; through all the torments I will show you that in behalf of virtue the sons of the Hebrews alone are unconquerable.'

16 As he thus spake they set hot coals upon him besides, and intensifying the torture strained him yet tighter on the wheel.

17 And all the wheel was besmeared with his blood, and the heaped coals were quenched by the humours of his body dropping down, and the rent flesh ran round the axles of the machine.

18 And with his bodily frame already in dissolution this great-souled youth, like a true son of Abraham, groaned not at all; but as if he were suffering a change by fire to incorruption, he nobly endured the torment, saying:

19 'Follow my example, O brothers. Do not for ever desert me, and forswear not our brotherhood in nobility of soul.

20 War a holy and honourable warfare on behalf of righteousness, through which may the just Providence that watched over our fathers become merciful unto his people and take

vengeance on the accursed tyrant.'

21 And with these words the holy youth yielded up the ghost.

22 But while all were wondering at his constancy of soul, the guards brought forward the second in age of the sons, and grappling him with sharp-clawed hands of iron they fastened him to the engines and the catapult.

23 But when they heard his noble resolve in answer to their question, 'Would he eat rather than be tortured?' these panther-like beasts tore at his sinews with claws of iron, and rent away all the flesh from his cheeks, and tore off the skin from his head.

24 But he steadfastly enduring this agony said, 'How sweet is every form of death for the sake of the righteousness of our fathers!'

25 And to the tyrant he said, 'O most ruthless of tyrants, doth not it seem to thee that at this moment thou thyself sufferest tortures worse than mine in seeing thy tyranny's arrogant intention overcome by my endurance for righteousness' sake?

26 For I am supported under pain by the joys that come through virtue, whereas thou art in torment whilst glorying in thy impiety; neither shalt thou escape, O most abominable tyrant, the penalties of the divine wrath.'

27 And when he had bravely met his glorious death, the third son was brought forward and was earnestly entreated by many to taste and so to save himself.

28 But he answered in a loud voice, 'Are ye ignorant that the same father begat me and my brothers that are dead, and the same mother gave us birth, and in the same doctrines was I brought up?

29 I do not forswear the noble bond of brotherhood.

30 Therefore if ye have any engine of torment, apply it to this body of mine; for my soul ye cannot reach, not if ye would.'

31 But they were greatly angered at the bold speech of the man, and they dislocated his hands and his feet with their dislocating engines, and wrenched his limbs out of their sockets, and unstrung them; and they twisted round his fingers, and his arms, and his legs, and his elbow-joints.

32 And in no wise being able to strangle his spirit they stripped off his skin, taking the points of the fingers with it, and tore in Scythian fashion the scalp from his head, and straightway brought him to the wheel.

33 And on this they twisted his spine till he saw his own flesh hanging in strips and great gouts of blood pouring down from his entrails.

34 And at the point of death he said, 'We, O most abominable tyrant, suffer thus for our upbringing and our virtue that are of God; but thou for thy impiety and thy cruelty shall endure torments without end.'

35 And when this man had died worthily of his brothers, they brought up the fourth, and said to him, 'Be not thou also mad with the same madness as thy brethren, but obey the king and save thyself.'

36 But he said unto them, 'For me ye have no fire so exceeding hot as to make me a coward.

37 By the blessed death of my brethren, by the eternal doom of the tyrant, and by the glorious life of the righteous, I will not deny my noble brotherhood.

38 Invent tortures, O tyrant, in order that thou mayest learn thereby that I am brother of those who have been already tortured.'

39 When he heard this the bloodthirsty, murderous, and

utterly abominable Antiochus bade them cut out his tongue.

40 But he said, 'Even if thou dost remove my organ of speech, God is a hearer also of the speechless.

41 Lo, I put out my tongue ready: cut it out, for thou shalt not thereby silence my Reason.

42 Gladly do we give our bodily members to be mutilated for the cause of God.

43 But God will speedily pursue after thee; for thou cuttest out the tongue that sang songs of praise unto him.'

44 But when this man also was put to a death of agony with the tortures, the fifth sprang forward saying, 'I shrink not, O tyrant, from demanding the torture for virtue's sake.

45 Yea, of myself I come forward, in order that, slaying me also, thou mayest by yet more misdeeds increase the penalty thou owest to the justice of Heaven.

46 O enemy of virtue and enemy of man, for what crime dost thou destroy us in this way?

47 Doth it seem evil to thee that we worship the Creator of all and live according to his virtuous Law?

48 But these things are worthy of honours not of tortures, if thou didst understand human aspirations and hadst hope of salvation before God.

49 Lo, now thou art God's enemy and makest war on those that worship God.'

50 As he spake thus the guards bound him and brought him before the catapult; and they tied him thereto on his knees, and, fastening them there with iron clamps, they wrenched his loins over the rolling 'wedge' so that he was completely curled back like a scorpion and every joint was disjointed.

51 And thus in grievous strait for breath and anguish of body he exclaimed, 'Glorious, O tyrant, glorious against thy will are the boons that thou bestowest on me, enabling me to show my fidelity to the Law through yet more honourable tortures.'

52 And when this man also was dead, the sixth was brought, a mere boy, who in answer to the tyrant's inquiry whether he was willing to eat and be released, said:

53 'I am not so old in years as my brethren, but I am as old in mind. For we were born and reared for the same purpose and are equally bound also to die for the same cause; so if thou chooseth to torture us for not eating unclean meat, torture.'

54 As he spake these words they brought him to the wheel, and with care they stretched him out and dislocated the bones of his back and set fire under him.

55 And they made sharp skewers red-hot and ran them into his back, and piercing through his sides they burned away his entrails also.

56 But he in the midst of his tortures exclaimed, 'O contest worthy of saints, wherein so many of us brethren, in the cause of righteousness, have been entered for a competition in torments, and have not been conquered!

57 For the righteous understanding, O tyrant, is unconquerable.

58 In the armour of virtue I go to join my brothers in death, and to add in myself one strong avenger more to punish thee, O deviser of the tortures and enemy of the truly righteous.

59 We six youths have overthrown thy tyranny. For is not thine impotence to alter our Reason or force us to eat unclean meat an overthrow for thee?

60 Thy fire is cool for us, thy engines of torture torment not, and thy violence is impotent.

61 For the guards have been officers for us, not of a tyrant, but of the Divine Law; and therefore have we our Reason yet unconquered.'

CHAP. VI.

Brotherly bonds and a mother's love.

AND when this one also died a blessed death, being cast into the cauldron, the seventh son, the youngest of them all, came forward.

2 But the tyrant, although fiercely exasperated by his brethren, felt pity for the boy, and seeing him there already bound he had him brought near, and sought to persuade him, saying: 'Thou seest the end of the folly of thy brethren; for through their disobedience they have been racked to death. Thou, too, if thou dost not obey, wilt thyself also be miserably tortured and put to death before thy time; but if thou dost obey thou shalt be my friend, and thou shalt be advanced to high office in the business of the kingdom.'

4 And while thus appealing to him he sent for the boy's mother, in order that in her sorrow for the loss of so many sons she might urge the survivor to obey and be saved.

5 But the mother, speaking in the Hebrew tongue, as I shall tell later on, encouraged the boy, and he said to the guards, 'Loose me, that I may speak to the king and to all his friends with him.'

6 And they, rejoicing at the boy's request, made haste to loose him.

7 And running up to the red-hot brazier, 'O impious tyrant,' he cried, 'and most ungodly of all sinners, art thou not ashamed to take thy blessings and thy kingship at the hands of God, and to slay his servants and torture the followers of righteousness?

8 For which things the divine justice delivers thee unto a more rapid and an eternal fire and torments which shall not leave hold on thee to all eternity.

9 Art thou not ashamed, being a man, O wretch with the heart of a wild beast, to take men of like feelings with thyself, made from the same elements, and tear out their tongues, and scourge and torture them in this manner?

10 But while they have fulfilled their righteousness towards God in their noble deaths, thou shalt miserably cry "Woe is me!" for thy unjust slaying of the champions of virtue.'

11 And then standing on the brink of death he said, 'I am no renegade to the witness borne by my brethren.

12 And I call upon the God of my fathers to be merciful unto my nation.

13 And thee will he punish both in this present life and after that thou art dead.'

14 And with this prayer he cast himself into the red-hot brazier, and so gave up the ghost.

15 If therefore the seven brethren despised the tortures even to the death, it is universally proved that the Inspired Reason is supreme lord over the passions.

16 For if they had yielded to their passions or sufferings and eaten unclean meat, we should have said that they had been conquered thereby.

17 But in this case it was not so; on the contrary by their Reason, which was commended in the sight of God, they rose superior to their passions.

18 And it is impossible to deny the supremacy of the mind; for they won the victory over their passions and their pains.

19 How can we do otherwise than admit right Reason's mastery over passion with these men who shrank not before the agonies of burning?

20 For even as towers on harbour-moles repulse the assaults of the waves and offer a calm entrance to those entering the haven, so the seven-towered right Reason of the youths defended the haven of righteousness and repulsed the tempestuousness of the passions.

21 They formed a holy choir of righteousness as they cheered one another on, saying:

22 'Let us die like brothers, O brethren, for the Law.

23 Let us imitate the Three Children at the Assyrian court who despised this same ordeal of the furnace.

24 Let us not turn cravens before the proof of righteousness.'

25 And one said, 'Brother, be of good cheer,' and another, 'Bear it out nobly'; and another recalling the past, 'Remember of what stock ye are, and at whose fatherly hand Isaac for righteousness' sake yielded himself to be a sacrifice.'

26 And each and all of them together, looking at each other brightly and very boldly, said, 'With a whole heart will we consecrate ourselves unto God who gave us our souls, and let us lend our bodies to the keeping of the Law.

27 Let us not fear him who thinketh he kills; for a great struggle and peril of the soul awaits in eternal torment those who transgress the ordinance of God.

28 Let us then arm ourselves with divine Reason's mastery of the passions.

29 After this our passion, Abraham, Isaac, and Jacob shall receive us, and all our forefathers shall praise us.'

30 And to each separate one of the brothers, as they were dragged off, those whose turn was yet to come said, 'Do not disgrace us, brother, nor be false to our brethren already dead.'

31 You are not ignorant of the love of brethren, whereof the divine and all-wise Providence has given an inheritance to those who are begotten though their fathers, implanting it in them even through the mother's womb; wherein brethren do dwell the like period, and take their form during the same time, and are nourished from the same blood, and are quickened with the same soul, and are brought into the world after the same space, and they draw milk from the same founts, whereby their fraternal souls are nursed together in arms at the breast; and they are knit yet closer through a common nurture and daily companionship and other education, and through our discipline under the Law of God.

32 The feeling of brotherly love being thus naturally strong, the seven brethren had their mutual concord made yet stronger. For trained in the same Law, and disciplined in the same virtues, and brought up together in the upright life, they loved one another the more abundantly. Their common zeal for moral beauty and goodness heightened their mutual concord, for in conjunction with their piety it rendered their brotherly love more fervent.

33 But though nature, companionship, and their virtuous disposition increased the ardour of their brotherly love, nevertheless the surviving sons through their religion supported the sight of their brethren, who were on the rack, being tortured to death; nay more, they even encouraged them to face the agony, so as not only to despise their own tortures, but also to conquer their passion of brotherly affection for their brethren.

AHIKAR ANSWERS PHARAOH'S RIDDLE

(See page 214)

34 O Reasoning minds, more kingly than kings, than freemen more free, of the harmony of the seven brethren, holy and well attuned to the keynote of piety!

35 None of the seven youths turned coward, none shrunk in the face of death, but all hastened to the death by torture as if running the road to immortality.

36 For as hands and feet move in harmony with the promptings of the soul, so those holy youths, as if prompted by the immortal soul of religion, went in harmony to death for its sake.

37 O all-holy sevenfold companionship of brethren in harmony!

38 For as the seven days of the creation of the world do enring religion, so did the youths choir-like enring their sevenfold companionship, and made the terror of the tortures of no account.

39 We now shudder when we hear of the suffering of those youths; but they, not only seeing it with their eyes, nor merely hearing the spoken, imminent threat, but actually feeling the pang, endured it through; and that in the torture by fire, than which what greater agony can be found?

40 For sharp and stringent is the power of fire, and swiftly did it bring their bodies to dissolution.

41 And think it not wonderful if with those men Reason triumphed over the tortures, when even a woman's soul despised a yet greater diversity of pains; for the mother of the seven youths endured the torments inflicted on each several one of her children.

42 But consider how manifold are the yearnings of a mother's heart, so that her feeling for her offspring becomes the centre of her whole world; and indeed, here, even the irrational animals have for their young an affection and love similar to men's.

43 For example, among the birds, the tame ones sheltering under our roofs defend their nestlings; and those that nest upon the mountain tops, and in the rock clefts, and in the holes of trees, and in the branches, and hatch their young there, do also drive away the intruder.

44 And then, if they be unable to drive him away, they flutter around the nestlings in a passion of love, calling to them in their own speech, and they give succour to their young ones in whatever fashion they can.

45 And what need have we of examples of the love of offspring among irrational animals, when even the bees, about the season of the making of the comb, fend off intruders, and stab with their sting, as with a sword, those who approach their brood, and do battle against them even to the death?

46 But she, the mother of those young men, with a soul like Abraham, was not moved from her purpose by her affection for her children.

CHAP. VII.

A comparison of a mother's and father's affections, in this chapter are some mountain peaks of eloquence.

O REASON of the sons, lord over the passions! O religion, that wast dearer to the mother than her children!

2 The mother, having two choices before her, religion and the present saving alive of her seven sons according to the tyrant's promise, loved rather religion, which saveth unto eternal life according to God.

3 O how may I express the passionate love of parents for children? We stamp a marvel-

lous likeness of our soul and of our shape on the tender nature of the child, and most of all through the mother's sympathy with her children being deeper than the father's.

4 For women are softer of soul than men, and the more children they bear the more do they abound in love for them.

5 But, of all mothers, she of the seven sons abounded in love beyond the rest, seeing that, having in seven child-bearings felt maternal tenderness for the fruit of her womb, and having been constrained because of the many pangs in which she bore each to a close affection, she nevertheless through the fear of God rejected the present safety of her children.

6 Ay, and more than that, through the moral beauty and goodness of her sons and their obedience to the Law, her maternal love for them was made stronger.

7 For they were just, and temperate, and brave and great-souled, and lovers of each other and of their mother in such manner that they obeyed her in the keeping of the Law even unto death.

8 But nevertheless, though she had so many temptations to yield to her maternal instincts, in no single instance did the dreadful variety of tortures have power to alter her Reason; but the mother urged each son separately, and all together, to die for their religion.

9 O holy nature, and parental love, and yearning of parents for offspring, and wages of nursing, and unconquerable affection of mothers!

10 The mother, seeing them one by one racked and burned, remained unshaken in soul for religion's sake.

11 She saw the flesh of her sons being consumed in the fire, and the extremities of their hands and feet scattered on the ground, and the flesh-covering, torn off from their heads right to their cheeks, strewn about like masks.

12 O mother, who now knew sharper pangs than the pangs of labour! O woman, alone among women, the fruit of whose womb was perfect religion!

13 Thy firstborn, giving up the ghost, did not alter thy resolution, nor thy second, looking with eyes of pity on thee under his tortures, nor thy third, breathing out his spirit.

14 Neither didst thou weep when thou beheldest the eyes of each amid the torments looking boldly on the same anguish, and sawest in their quivering nostrils the signs of approaching death.

15 When thou sawest the flesh of one son being severed after the flesh of another, and hand after hand being cut off, and head after head being flayed, and corpse cast upon corpse, and the place crowded with spectators on account of the tortures of thy children, thou sheddest not a tear.

16 Not the melodies of the sirens nor the songs of swans with sweet sound do so charm the hearer's ears, as sounded the voices of the sons, speaking to the mother from amid the torments.

17 How many and how great were the tortures with which the mother was tormented while her sons were being tortured with torments of rack and fire!

18 But Inspired Reason lent her heart a man's strength under her passion of suffering, and exalted her to make no account of the present yearnings of mother-love.

19 And although she saw the destruction of her seven children and the many and varied forms of their torments, the noble mother willingly surrendered them through faith in God.

20 For she beheld in her own mind, even as it had been cunning advocates in a council-chamber, nature, and parenthood, and mother-love, and her children on the rack, and it was as if she, the mother, having the choice between two votes in the case of her children, one for their death and one to save them alive, thereupon regarded not the saving of her seven sons for a little time, but, as a true daughter of Abraham, called to mind his God-fearing courage.

21 O mother of the race, vindicator of our Law, defender of our religion, and winner of the prize in the struggle within thyself!

22 O woman, nobler to resist than men, and braver than warriors to endure!

23 For as the Ark of Noah, with the whole living world for her burden in the world-whelming Deluge, did withstand the mighty surges, so thou, the keeper of the Law, beaten upon every side by the surging waves of the passions, and strained as with strong blasts by the tortures of thy sons, didst nobly weather the storms that assailed thee for religion's sake.

24 Thus then, if one both a woman and advanced in years, and the mother of seven sons, endured the sight of her children being tortured to death, the Inspired Reason must confessedly be supreme ruler over the passions.

25 I have proved, accordingly, that not only have men triumphed over their sufferings, but that a woman also has despised the most dreadful tortures.

26 And not so fierce were the lions around Daniel, not so hot was the burning fiery furnace of Mishael, as burned in her the instinct of motherhood at the sight of her seven sons being tortured.

27 But by her religion-guided Reason the mother quenched her passions, many and strong as they were.

28 For there is this also to consider, that had the woman been weak of spirit, despite her motherhood, she might have wept over them, and perchance spoken thus:

29 'Ah, thrice wretched me, and more than thrice wretched! Seven children have I borne and am left childless!

30 In vain was I seven times with child, and to no profit was my ten months' burden seven times borne, and fruitless have been my nursings, and sorrowful my sucklings.

31 In vain for you, O my sons, did I endure the many pangs of labour, and the more difficult cares of your upbringing.

32 Alas, for my sons, that some were yet unwed, and those that were wedded had begotten no children; I shall never see children of yours, nor shall I be called by the name of grandparent.

33 Ah me, that had many beautiful children, and am a widow and desolate in my woe! Neither will there be any son to bury me when I am dead!'

34 But the holy and God-fearing mother wailed not with this lamentation over any one of them, neither besought she any to escape death, nor lamented over them as dying men; but, as though she had a soul of adamant and were bringing forth the number of her sons, for a second time, into immortal life, she besought rather and entreated of them that they should die for religion's sake.

35 O mother, warrior of God in the cause of religion, old and a woman, thou didst both defeat the tyrant by thy endurance, and wast found stronger than a man, in deeds as well as words.

36 For verily when thou wast put in bonds with thy sons,

thou stoodest there seeing
Eleazar being tortured, and thou
spakest to thy sons in the Hebrew tongue:

37 'My sons, noble is the
fight; and do ye, being called
thereto to bear witness for our
nation, fight therein zealously on
behalf of the Law of our fathers.

38 For it would be shameful
if, while this aged man endured
the agony for religion's sake, you
that are young men shrank before the pain.

39 Remember that for the
sake of God ye have come into
the world, and have enjoyed
life, and that therefore ye owe
it to God to endure all pain for
his sake; for whom also our
father Abraham made haste to
sacrifice his son Isaac, the an-
cestor of our nation; and Isaac,
seeing his father's hand lifting
the knife against him, did not
shrink.

40 And Daniel, the just man,
was cast to the lions, and
Ananias, Azarias, and Mishael
were flung into the furnace of
fire, and they endured for God's
sake.

41 And ye also, having the
same faith unto God, be not
troubled; for it were against
Reason that ye, knowing righteousness, should not withstand
the pains.'

42 With these words the
mother of the seven encouraged
every single one of her sons to
die rather than transgress the
ordinance of God; they themselves also knowing well that men
dying for God live unto God, as
live Abraham, and Isaac, and
Jacob, and all the patriarchs.

CHAP. VIII.

*The famous "Athletes of Right-
eousness." Here ends the story
of courage called the Fourth
Book of Maccabees.*

SOME of the guards declared
that when she also was
about to be seized and put to

death, she cast herself on the
pyre in order that no man might
touch her body.

2 O mother, that together
with thy seven sons didst break
the tyrant's force, and bring to
nought his evil devices, and
gavest an example of the noble-
ness of faith.

3 Thou wert nobly set as a
roof upon thy sons as pillars,
and the earthquake of the torments shook thee not at all.

4 Rejoice therefore, pure-
souled mother, having the hope
of thy endurance certain at the
hand of God.

5 Not so majestic stands the
moon amid the stars in heaven
as thou, having lit the path of
thy seven starlike sons unto
righteousness, standest in honour with God; and thou art set
in heaven with them.

6 For thy child-bearing was
from the son of Abraham.

7 And had it been lawful for
us to paint, as might some artist,
the tale of thy piety, would not
the spectators have shuddered
at the mother of seven sons suffering for righteousness' sake
multitudinous tortures even unto
death?

8 And indeed it were fitting to
inscribe these words over their
resting-place, speaking for a
memorial to future generations
of our people:

HERE LIE AN AGED PRIEST
AND A WOMAN FULL OF YEARS
AND HER SEVEN SONS
THROUGH THE VIOLENCE OF A
TYRANT
DESIRING TO DESTROY THE HEBREW
NATION.
THEY VINDICATED THE RIGHTS OF
OUR PEOPLE
LOOKING UNTO GOD AND ENDURING
THE TORMENTS EVEN UNTO
DEATH.

9 For truly it was a holy war
which was fought by them. For
on that day virtue, proving them

through endurance, set before them the prize of victory in incorruption in everlasting life.

10 But the first in the fight was Eleazar, and the mother of the seven sons played her part, and the brethren fought.

11 The tyrant was their adversary and the world and the life of man were the spectators.

12 And righteousness won the victory, and gave the crown to her athletes. Who but wondered at the athletes of the true Law?

13 Who were not amazed at them? The tyrant himself and his whole council admired their endurance, whereby they now do both stand beside the throne of God and live the blessed age.

14 For Moses says, 'All also who have sanctified themselves are under thy hands.'

15 And these men, therefore, having sanctified themselves for God's sake, not only have received this honour, but also the honour that through them the enemy had no more power over our people, and the tyrant suffered punishment, and our country was purified, they having as it were become a ransom for our nation's sin; and through the blood of these righteous men and the propitiation of their death, the divine Providence delivered Israel that before was evil entreated.

16 For when the tyrant Antiochus saw the heroism of their virtue, and their endurance under the tortures, he publicly held up their endurance to his soldiers as an example; and he thus inspired his men with a sense of honour and heroism on the field of battle and in the labours of besieging, so that he plundered and overthrew all his enemies.

17 O Israelites, children born of the seed of Abraham, obey this Law, and be righteous in all ways, recognizing that Inspired Reason is lord over the passions, and over pains, not only from within, but from without ourselves; by which means those men, delivering up their bodies to the torture for righteousness' sake, not only won the admiration of mankind, but were deemed worthy of a divine inheritance.

18 And through them the nation obtained peace and restoring the observance of the Law in our country hath captured the city from the enemy.

19 And vengeance hath pursued the tyrant Antiochus upon earth, and in death he suffers punishment.

20 For when he failed utterly to constrain the people of Jerusalem to live like Gentiles and abandon the customs of our fathers, he thereupon left Jerusalem and marched away against the Persians.

21 Now these are the words that the mother of the seven sons, the righteous woman, spake to her children:

22 'I was a pure maiden, and I strayed not from my father's house, and I kept guard over the rib that was builded into Eve.

23 No seducer of the desert, no deceiver in the field, corrupted me; nor did the false, beguiling Serpent sully the purity of my maidenhood; I lived with my husband all the days of my youth; but when these my sons were grown up, their father died.

24 Happy was he; for he lived a life blessed with children, and he never knew the pain of their loss.

25 Who, while he was yet with us, taught you the Law and the prophets. He read to us of Abel who was slain by Cain, and of saac who was offered as a burnt-offering, and of Joseph in the prison.

26 And he spake to us of Phineas, the zealous priest, and he taught you the song of

Ananias, Azarias, and Mishael in the fire.

27 And he glorified also Daniel in the den of lions, and blessed him; and he called to your minds the saying of Isaiah,

28 "Yea even though thou pass through the fire, the flame shall not hurt thee."

29 He sang to us the words of David the psalmist, "Many are the afflictions of the just."

30 He quoted to us the proverb of Solomon, "He is a tree of life to all them that do his will."

31 He confirmed the words of Ezekiel, "Shall these dry bones live?" For he forgat not the song that Moses taught, which teaches, "I will slay and I will make alive. This is your life and the blessedness of your days."'

32 Ah, cruel was the day, and yet not cruel, when the cruel tyrant of the Greeks set the fire blazing for his barbarous braziers, and with his passions boiling brought to the catapult and back again to his tortures the seven sons of the daughter of Abraham, and blinded the eyeballs of their eyes, and cut out their tongues, and slew them with many kinds of torment.

33 For which cause the judgement of God pursued, and shall pursue, the accursed wretch.

34 But the sons of Abraham, with their victorious mother, are gathered together unto the place of their ancestors, having received pure and immortal souls from God, to whom be glory for ever and ever.

THE STORY OF AHIKAR

WE HAVE in *The Story of Ahikar* one of the most ancient sources of human thought and wisdom. Its influence can be traced through the legends of many people, including the Koran, and the Old and New Testaments.

A mosaic found in Treves, Germany, pictured among the wise men of the world the character of Ahikar. Here is his colorful tale.

The date of this story has been a subject of lively discussion. Scholars finally put it down about the First Century when they were proved in error by the original story turning up in an Aramaic papyrus of 500 B. C. among the ruins of Elephantine.

The story is obviously fiction and not history. In fact the reader can make its acquaintance in the supplementary pages of *The Arabian Nights*. It is brilliantly written, and the narrative which is full of action, intrigue, and narrow escape holds the attention to the last. The liberty of imagination is the most precious possession of the writer.

The writing divides itself into four phases: (1) The Narrative; (2) The Teaching (a remarkable series of Proverbs); (3) The Journey to Egypt; (4) The Similitudes or Parables (with which Ahikar completes the education of his erring nephew).

CHAP. I.

Ahikar, Grand Vizier of Assyria, has 60 wives but is fated to have no son. Therefore he adopts his nephew. He crams him full of wisdom and knowledge more than of bread and water.

THE story of Haiqâr the Wise, Vizier of Sennacherib the King, and of Nadan, sister's son to Haiqâr the Sage.

2 There was a Vizier in the days of King Sennacherib, son

of Sarhadum, King of Assyria and Nineveh, a wise man named Haiqâr, and he was Vizier of the king Sennacherib.

3 He had a fine fortune and much goods, and he was skilful, wise, a philosopher, in knowledge, in opinion and in government, and he had married sixty women, and had built a castle for each of them.

4 But with it all he had no child by any of these women, who might be his heir.

5 And he was very sad on account of this, and one day he assembled the astrologers and the learned men and the wizards and explained to them his condition and the matter of his barrenness.

6 And they said to him, 'Go, sacrifice to the gods and beseech them that perchance they may provide thee with a boy.'

7 And he did as they told him and offered sacrifices to the idols, and besought them and implored them with request and entreaty.

8 And they answered him not one word. And he went away sorrowful and dejected, departing with a pain at his heart.

9 And he returned, and implored the Most High God, and believed, beseeching Him with a burning in his heart, saying, 'O Most High God, O Creator of the Heavens and of the earth, O Creator of all created things!

10 I beseech Thee to give me a boy, that I may be consoled by him, that he may be present at my death, that he may close my eyes, and that he may bury me.'

11 Then there came to him a voice saying, 'Inasmuch as thou hast relied first of all on graven images, and hast offered sacrifices to them, for this reason thou shalt remain childless thy life long.

12 But take Nadan thy sister's son, and make him thy child and teach him thy learning and thy good breeding, and at thy death he shall bury thee.'

13 Thereupon he took Nadan his sister's son, who was a little suckling. And he handed him over to eight wet-nurses, that they might suckle him and bring him up.

14 And they brought him up with good food and gentle training and silken clothing, and purple and crimson. And he was seated upon couches of silk.

15 And when Nadan grew big and walked, shooting up like a tall cedar, he taught him good manners and writing and science and philosophy.

16 And after many days King Sennacherib looked at Haiqâr and saw that he had grown very old, and moreover he said to him.

17 'O my honoured friend, the skilful, the trusty, the wise, the governor, my secretary, my vizier, my Chancellor and director; verily thou art grown very old and weighted with years; and thy departure from this world must be near.

18 Tell me who shall have a place in my service after thee.' And Haiqâr said to him, 'O my lord, may thy head live for ever! There is Nadan my sister's son, I have made him my child.

19 And I have brought him up and taught him my wisdom and my knowledge.'

20 And the king said to him, 'O Haiqâr! bring him to my presence, that I may see him, and if I find him suitable, put him in thy place; and thou shalt go thy way, to take a rest and to live the remainder of thy life in sweet repose.'

21 Then Haiqâr went and presented Nadan his sister's son. And he did homage and wished him power and honour.

22 And he looked at him and admired him and rejoiced in him

and said to Haiqâr: 'Is this thy son, O Haiqâr? I pray that God may preserve him. And as thou hast served me and my father Sarhadum so may this boy of thine serve me and fulfil my undertakings, my needs, and my business, so that I may honour him and make him powerful for thy sake.'

23 And Haiqâr did obeisance to the king and said to him, 'May thy head live, O my lord the king, for ever! I seek from thee that thou mayst be patient with my boy Nadan and forgive his mistakes that he may serve thee as it is fitting.'

24 Then the king swore to him that he would make him the greatest of his favourites, and the most powerful of his friends, and that he should be with him in all honour and respect. And he kissed his hands and bade him farewell.

25 And he took Nadan his sister's son with him and seated him in a parlour and set about teaching him night and day till he had crammed him with wisdom and knowledge more than with bread and water.

CHAP. II.

A "Poor Richard's Almanac" of ancient days. Immortal precepts of human conduct concerning money, women, dress, business, friends. Especially interesting proverbs are found in Verses 12, 17, 23, 37, 45, 47. Compare Verse 63 with some of the cynicism of today.

THUS he taught him, saying: 'O my son! hear my speech and follow my advice and remember what I say.

2 O my son! if thou hearest a word, let it die in thy heart, and reveal it not to another, lest it become a live coal and burn thy tongue and cause a pain in thy body, and thou gain a reproach, and art shamed before God and man.

3 O my son! if thou hast heard a report, spread it not; and if thou hast seen something, tell it not.

4 O my son! make thy eloquence easy to the listener, and be not hasty to return an answer.

5 O my son! when thou hast heard anything, hide it not.

6 O my son! loose not a sealed knot, nor untie it, and seal not a loosened knot.

7 O my son! covet not outward beauty, for it wanes and passes away, but an honourable remembrance lasts for aye.

8 O my son! let not a silly woman deceive thee with her speech, lest thou die the most miserable of deaths, and she entangle thee in the net till thou art ensnared.

9 O my son! desire not a woman bedizened with dress and with ointments, who is despicable and silly in her soul. Woe to thee if thou bestow on her anything that is thine, or commit to her what is in thine hand and she entice thee into sin, and God be wroth with thee.

10 O my son! be not like the almond-tree, for it brings forth leaves before all the trees, and edible fruit after them all, but be like the mulberry-tree, which brings forth edible fruit before all the trees, and leaves after them all.

11 O my son! bend thy head low down, and soften thy voice, and be courteous, and walk in the straight path, and be not foolish. And raise not thy voice when thou laughest, for if it were by a loud voice that a house was built, the ass would build many houses every day; and if it were by dint of strength that the plough were driven, the plough would never be removed from under the shoulders of the camels.

12 O my son! the removing of stones with a wise man is better

than the drinking of wine with a sorry man.

13 O my son! pour out thy wine on the tombs of the just, and drink not with ignorant, contemptible people.

14 O my son! cleave to wise men who fear God and be like them, and go not near the ignorant, lest thou become like him and learn his ways.

15 O my son! when thou hast got thee a comrade or a friend, try him, and afterwards make him a comrade and a friend; and do not praise him without a trial; and do not spoil thy speech with a man who lacks wisdom.

16 O my son! while a shoe stays on thy foot, walk with it on the thorns, and make a road for thy son, and for thy household and thy children, and make thy ship taut before she goes on the sea and its waves and sinks and cannot be saved.

17 O my son! if the rich man eat a snake, they say, "It is by his wisdom," and if a poor man eat it, the people say, "From his hunger."

18 O my son! be content with thy daily bread and thy goods, and covet not what is another's.

19 O my son! be not neighbour to the fool, and eat not bread with him, and rejoice not in the calamities of thy neighbours.* If thine enemy wrong thee, show him kindness.

20 O my son! a man who fears God do thou fear him and honour him.

21 O my son! the ignorant man falls and stumbles, and the wise man, even if he stumbles, he is not shaken, and even if he falls he gets up quickly, and if he is sick, he can take care of his life. But as for the ignorant, stupid man, for his disease there is no drug.

22 O my son! if a man approach thee who is inferior to thyself, go forward to meet him, and remain standing, and if he cannot recompense thee, his Lord will recompense thee for him.

23 O my son! spare not to beat thy son, for the drubbing of thy son is like manure to the garden, and like tying the mouth of a purse, and like the tethering of beasts, and like the bolting of the door.

24 O my son! restrain thy son from wickedness, and teach him manners before he rebels against thee and brings thee into contempt amongst the people and thou hang thy head in the streets and the assemblies and thou be punished for the evil of his wicked deeds.

25 O my son! get thee a fat ox with a foreskin, and an ass great with its hoofs, and get not an ox with large horns, nor make friends with a tricky man, nor get a quarrelsome slave, nor a thievish handmaid, for everything which thou committest to them they will ruin.

26 O my son! let not thy parents curse thee, and the Lord be pleased with them; for it hath been said, "He who despiseth his father or his mother let him die the death (I mean the death of sin); and he who honoureth his parents shall prolong his days and his life and shall see all that is good."

27 O my son! walk not on the road without weapons, for thou knowest not when the foe may meet thee, so that thou mayst be ready for him.

28 O my son! be not like a bare, leafless tree that doth not grow, but be like a tree covered with its leaves and its boughs; for the man who has neither wife nor children is disgraced in the world and is hated by them, like a leafless and fruitless tree.

*Cf. Psalms CXLI. 4.

29 O my son! be like a fruitful tree on the roadside, whose fruit is eaten by all who pass by, and the beasts of the desert rest under its shade and eat of its leaves.

30 O my son! every sheep that wanders from its path and its companions becomes food for the wolf.

31 O my son! say not, "My lord is a fool and I am wise," and relate not the speech of ignorance and folly, lest thou be despised by him.

32 O my son! be not one of those servants, to whom their lords say, "Get away from us," but be one of those to whom they say, "Approach and come near to us."

33 O my son! caress not thy slave in the presence of his companion, for thou knowest not which of them shall be of most value to thee in the end.

34 O my son! be not afraid of thy Lord who created thee, lest He be silent to thee.

35 O my son! make thy speech fair and sweeten thy tongue; and permit not thy companion to tread on thy foot, lest he tread at another time on thy breast.

36 O my son! if thou beat a wise man with a word of wisdom, it will lurk in his breast like a subtle sense of shame; but if thou drub the ignorant with a stick he will neither understand nor hear.

37 O my son! if thou send a wise man for thy needs, do not give him many orders, for he will do thy business as thou desirest: and if thou send a fool, do not order him, but go thyself and do thy business, for if thou order him, he will not do what thou desirest. If they send thee on business, hasten to fulfil it quickly.

38 O my son! make not an enemy of a man stronger than thyself, for he will take thy measure, and his revenge on thee.

39 O my son! make trial of thy son, and of thy servant, before thou committest thy belongings to them, lest they make away with them; for he who hath a full hand is called wise, even if he be stupid and ignorant, and he who hath an empty hand is called poor, ignorant, even if he be the prince of sages.

40 O my son! I have eaten a colocynth, and swallowed aloes, and I have found nothing more bitter than poverty and scarcity.

41 O my son! teach thy son frugality and hunger, that he may do well in the management of his household.

42 O my son! teach not to the ignorant the language of wise men, for it will be burdensome to him.

43 O my son! display not thy condition to thy friend, lest thou be despised by him.

44 O my son! the blindness of the heart is more grievous than the blindness of the eyes, for the blindness of the eyes may be guided little by little, but the blindness of the heart is not guided, and it leaves the straight path, and goes in a crooked way.

45 O my son! the stumbling of a man with his foot is better than the stumbling of a man with his tongue.

46 O my son! a friend who is near is better than a more excellent brother who is far away.

47 O my son! beauty fades but learning lasts, and the world wanes and becomes vain, but a good name neither becomes vain nor wanes.

48 O my son! the man who hath no rest, his death were better than his life; and the sound of weeping is better than the sound of singing; for sorrow and weeping, if the fear of God be in them, are better than the sound of singing and rejoicing.

49 O my child! the thigh of

a frog in thy hand is better than a goose in the pot of thy neighbour; and a sheep near thee is better than an ox far away; and a sparrow in thy hand is better than a thousand sparrows flying;* and poverty which gathers is better than the scattering of much provision; and a living fox is better than a dead lion; and a pound of wool is better than a pound of wealth, I mean of gold and silver; for the gold and tho silver are hidden and covered up in the earth, and are not seen; but the wool stays in the markets and it is seen, and it is a beauty to him who wears it.

50 O my son! a small fortune is better than a scattered fortune.

51 O my son! a living dog is better than a dead poor man.

52 O my son! a poor man who does right is better than a rich man who is dead in sins.

53 O my son! keep a word in thy heart, and it shall be much to thee, and beware lest thou reveal the secret of thy friend.

54 O my son! let not a word issue from thy mouth till thou hast taken counsel with thy heart. And stand not betwixt persons quarrelling, because from a bad word there comes a quarrel, and from a quarrel there comes war, and from war there comes fighting, and thou wilt be forced to bear witness; but run from thence and rest thyself.

55 O my son! withstand not a man stronger than thyself, but get thee a patient spirit, and endurance and an upright conduct, for there is nothing more excellent than that.

56 O my son! hate not thy first friend, for the second one may not last.

57 O my son! visit the poor in his affliction, and speak of him in the Sultan's presence, and do thy diligence to save him from the mouth of the lion.†

58 O my son! rejoice not in the death of thine enemy, for after a little while thou shalt be his neighbour, and him who mocks thee do thou respect and honour and be beforehand with him in greeting.

59 O my son! if water would stand still in heaven, and a black crow become white, and myrrh grow sweet as honey, then ignorant men and fools might understand and become wise.

60 O my son! if thou desire to be wise, restrain thy tongue from lying, and thy hand from stealing, and thine eyes from beholding evil; then thou wilt be called wise.

61 O my son! let the wise man beat thee with a rod, but let not the fool anoint thee with sweet salve. Be humble in thy youth and thou shalt be honoured in thine old age.

62 O my son! withstand not a man in the days of his power, nor a river in the days of its flood.

63 O my son! be not hasty in the wedding of a wife, for if it turns out well, she will say, 'My lord, make provision for me'; and if it turns out ill, she will rate at him who was the cause of it.

64 O my son! whosoever is elegant in his dress, he is the same in his speech; and he who has a mean appearance in his dress, he also is the same in his speech.

65 O my son! if thou hast committed a theft, make it known to the Sultan, and give him a share of it, that thou mayst be delivered from him, for otherwise thou wilt endure bitterness.

66 O my son! make a friend of the man whose hand is satis-

---

*Cf. "A bird in the hand is worth two in the bush." †Cf. 2 Timothy, IV, 17.

fled and filled, and make no
friend of the man whose hand
is closed and hungry.

67 There are four things in
which neither the king nor his
army can be secure: oppression
by the vizier, and bad government, and perversion of the will,
and tyranny over the subject;
and four things which cannot be
hidden: the prudent, and the
foolish, and the rich, and the
poor.'

CHAP. III.

*Ahikar retires from active par-
ticipation in affairs of state. He
turns over his possessions to his
treacherous nephew. Here is the
amazing story of how a thank-
less profligate turns forgerer. A
clever plot to entangle Ahikar
results in his being condemned
to death. Apparently the end of
Ahikar.*

THUS spake Haiqâr, and
when he had finished these
injunctions and proverbs to
Nadan, his sister's son, he
imagined that he would keep
them all, and he knew not that
instead of that he was displaying to him weariness and contempt and mockery.

2 Thereafter Haiqâr sat still
in his house and delivered over
to Nadan all his goods, and the
slaves, and the handmaidens,
and the horses, and the cattle,
and everything else that he had
possessed and gained; and the
power of bidding and of forbidding remained in the hand of
Nadan.

3 And Haiqâr sat at rest in
his house, and every now and
then Haiqâr went and paid his
respects to the king, and returned home.

4 Now when Nadan perceived
that the power of bidding and
of forbidding was in his own
hand, he despised the position
of Haiqâr and scoffed at him,
and set about blaming him whenever he appeared, saying, 'My
uncle Haiqâr is in his dotage,
and he knows nothing now.'

5 And he began to beat the
slaves and the handmaidens, and
to sell the horses and the camels
and be spendthrift with all that
his uncle Haiqâr had owned.

6 And when Haiqâr saw that
he had no compassion on his
servants nor on his household,
he arose and chased him from
his house, and sent to inform the
king that he had scattered his
possessions and his provision.

7 And the king arose and
called Nadan and said to him:
'Whilst Haiqâr remains in health,
no one shall rule over his goods,
nor over his household, nor over
his possessions.'

8 And the hand of Nadan was
lifted off from his uncle Haiqâr
and from all his goods, and in
the meantime he went neither
in nor out, nor did he greet him.

9 Thereupon Haiqâr repented
him of his toil with Nadan his
sister's son, and he continued to
be very sorrowful.

10 And Nadan had a younger
brother named Benuzârdân, so
Haiqâr took him to himself in
place of Nadan, and brought
him up and honoured him with
the utmost honour. And he delivered over to him all that he
possessed, and made him governor of his house.

11 Now when Nadan per-
ceived what had happened he
was seized with envy and jealousy, and he began to complain
to every one who questioned
him, and to mock his uncle
Haiqâr, saying: 'My uncle has
chased me from his house, and
has preferred my brother to me,
but if the Most High God give
me the power, I shall bring upon
him the misfortune of being
killed.'

12 And Nadan continued to
meditate as to the stumbling-
block he might contrive for him.

And after a while Nadan turned it over in his mind, and wrote a letter to Achish, son of Shah the Wise, king of Persia, saying thus:

13 'Peace and health and might and honour from Sennacherib king of Assyria and Nineveh, and from his vizier and his secretary Haiqâr unto thee, O great king! Let there be peace between thee and me.

14 And when this letter reaches thee, if thou wilt arise and go quickly to the plain of Nisrîn, and to Assyria and Nineveh, I will deliver up the kingdom to thee without war and without battle-array.'

15 And he wrote also another letter in the name of Haiqâr to Pharaoh king of Egypt. 'Let there be peace between thee and me, O mighty king!

16 If at the time of this letter reaching thee thou wilt arise and go to Assyria and Nineveh to the plain of Nisrîn, I will deliver up to thee the kingdom without war and without fighting.'

17 And the writing of Nadan was like to the writing of his uncle Haiqâr.

18 Then he folded the two letters, and sealed them with the seal of his uncle Haiqâr; they were nevertheless in the king's palace.

19 Then he went and wrote a letter likewise from the king to his uncle Haiqâr: 'Peace and health to my Vizier, my Secretary, my Chancellor, Haiqâr.

20 O Haiqâr, when this letter reaches thee, assemble all the soldiers who are with thee, and let them be perfect in clothing and in numbers, and bring them to me on the fifth day in the plain of Nisrîn.

21 And when thou shalt see me there coming towards thee, haste and make the army move against me as an enemy who would fight with me, for I have with me the ambassadors of Pharaoh king of Egypt, that they may see the strength of our army and may fear us, for they are our enemies and they hate us.'

22 Then he sealed the letter and sent it to Haiqâr by one of the king's servants. And he took the other letter which he had written and spread it before the king and read it to him and showed him the seal.

23 And when the king heard what was in the letter he was perplexed with a great perplexity and was wroth with a great and fierce wrath, and said, 'Ah, I have shown my wisdom! what have I done to Haiqâr that he has written these letters to my enemies? Is this my recompense from him for my benefits to him?'

24 And Nadan said to him, 'Be not grieved, O king! nor be wroth, but let us go to the plain of Nisrîn and see if the tale be true or not.'

25 Then Nadan arose on the fifth day and took the king and the soldiers and the vizier, and they went to the desert to the plain of Nisrîn. And the king looked, and lo! Haiqâr and the army were set in array.

26 And when Haiqâr saw that the king was there, he approached and signalled to the army to move as in war and to fight in array against the king as it had been found in the letter, he not knowing what a pit Nadan had digged for him.

27 And when the king saw the act of Haiqâr he was seized with anxiety and terror and perplexity, and was wroth with a great wrath.

28 And Nadan said to him, 'Hast thou seen, O my lord the king! what this wretch has done? but be not thou wroth and be not grieved nor pained, but go to thy house and sit on thy throne, and I will bring

Haiqâr to thee bound and chained with chains, and I will chase away thine enemy from thee without toil.'

29 And the king returned to his throne, being provoked about Haiqâr, and did nothing concerning him. And Nadan went to Haiqâr and said to him, 'W'allah, O my uncle! The king verily rejoiceth in thee with great joy and thanks thee for having done what he commanded thee.

30 And now he hath sent me to thee that thou mayst dismiss the soldiers to their duties and come thyself to him with thy hands bound behind thee, and thy feet chained, that the ambassadors of Pharaoh may see this, and that the king may be feared by them and by their king.'

31 Then answered Haiqâr and said, 'To hear is to obey.' And he arose straightway and bound his hands behind him, and chained his feet.

32 And Nadan took him and went with him to the king. And when Haiqâr entered the king's presence he did obeisance before him on the ground, and wished for power and perpetual life to the king.

33 Then said the king, 'O Haiqâr, my Secretary, the Governor of my affairs, my Chancellor, the ruler of my State, tell me what evil have I done to thee that thou hast rewarded me by this ugly deed.'

34 Then they showed him the letters in his writing and with his seal. And when Haiqâr saw this, his limbs trembled and his tongue was tied at once, and he was unable to speak a word from fear; but he hung his head towards the earth and was dumb.

35 And when the king saw this, he felt certain that the thing was from him, and he straightway arose and commanded them to kill Haiqâr, and to strike his neck with the sword outside of the city.

36 Then Nadan screamed and said, 'O Haiqâr, O blackface! what avails thee thy meditation or thy power in the doing of this deed to the king?'

37 Thus says the story-teller. And the name of the swordsman was Abu Samîk. And the king said to him, 'O swordsman! arise, go, cleave the neck of Haiqâr at the door of his house, and cast away his head from his body a hundred cubits.'

38 Then Haiqâr knelt before the king, and said, 'Let my lord the king live for ever! and if thou desire to slay me, let thy wish be fulfilled; and I know that I am not guilty, but the wicked man has to give an account of his wickedness; nevertheless, O my lord the king! I beg of thee and of thy friendship, permit the swordsman to give my body to my slaves, that they may bury me, and let thy slave be thy sacrifice.'

39 The king arose and commanded the swordsman to do with him according to his desire.

40 And he straightway commanded his servants to take Haiqâr and the swordsman and go with him naked that they might slay him.

41 And when Haiqâr knew for certain that he was to be slain he sent to his wife, and said to her, 'Come out and meet me, and let there be with thee a thousand young virgins, and dress them in gowns of purple and silk that they may weep for me before my death.

42 And prepare a table for the swordsman and for his servants. And mingle plenty of wine, that they may drink.'

43 And she did all that he commanded her. And she was very wise, clever, and prudent. And she united all possible courtesy and learning.

44 And when the army of the

king and the swordsman arrived they found the table set in order, and the wine and the luxurious viands, and they began eating and drinking till they were gorged and drunken.

45 Then Haiqâr took the swordsman aside apart from the company and said, 'O Abu Samîk, dost thou not know that when Sarhadum the king, the father of Sennacherib, wanted to kill thee, I took thee and hid thee in a certain place till the king's anger subsided and he asked for thee?

46 And when I brought thee into his presence he rejoiced in thee: and now remember the kindness I did thee.

47 And I know that the king will repent him about me and will be wroth with a great wrath about my execution.

48 For I am not guilty, and it shall be when thou shalt present me before him in his palace, thou shalt meet with great good fortune, and know that Nadan my sister's son has deceived me and has done this bad deed to me, and the king will repent of having slain me; and now I have a cellar in the garden of my house, and no one knows of it.

49 Hide me in it with the knowledge of my wife. And I have a slave in prison who deserves to be killed.

50 Bring him out and dress him in my clothes, and command the servants when they are drunk to slay him. They will not know who it is they are killing.

51 And cast away his head a hundred cubits from his body, and give his body to my slaves that they may bury it. And thou shalt have laid up a great treasure with me.

52 And then the swordsman did as Haiqâr had commanded him, and he went to the king and said to him, 'May thy head live for ever!'

53 Then Haiqâr's wife let down to him in the hiding-place every week what sufficed for him, and no one knew of it but herself.

54 And the story was reported and repeated and spread abroad in every place of how Haiqâr the Sage had been slain and was dead, and all the people of that city mourned for him.

55 And they wept and said: 'Alas for thee, O Haiqâr! and for thy learning and thy courtesy! How sad about thee and about thy knowledge! Where can another like thee be found? and where can there be a man so intelligent, so learned, so skilled in ruling as to resemble thee that he may fill thy place?'

56 But the king was repenting about Haiqâr, and his repentance availed him naught.

57 Then he called for Nadan and said to him, 'Go and take thy friends with thee and make a mourning and a weeping for thy uncle Haiqâr, and lament for him as the custom is, doing honour to his memory.'

58 But when Nadan, the foolish, the ignorant, the hardhearted, went to the house of his uncle, he neither wept nor sorrowed nor wailed, but assembled heartless and dissolute people and set about eating and drinking.*

59 And Nadan began to seize the maidservants and the slaves belonging to Haiqâr, and bound them and tortured them and drubbed them with a sore drubbing.

60 And he did not respect the wife of his uncle, she who had brought him up like her own

*Compare this account of Nadan's revelry and his beating of the servants with Matthew XXIV. 48-51 and Luke XII. 43-46. You will see that the language of Ahikar has colored one of our Lord's parables.

boy, but wanted her to fall into sin with him.

61 But Haiqâr had been cast into the hiding-place, and he heard the weeping of his slaves and his neighbours, and he praised the Most High God, the Merciful One, and gave thanks, and he always prayed and besought the Most High God.

62 And the swordsman came from time to time to Haiqâr whilst he was in the midst of the hiding-place: and Haiqâr came and entreated him. And he comforted him and wished him deliverance.

63 And when the story was reported in other countries that Haiqâr the Sage had been slain, all the kings were grieved and despised king Sennacherib, and they lamented over Haiqâr the solver of riddles.

CHAP. IV.

"The Riddles of the Sphinx."
What really happened to Ahi-
kar. His return.

AND when the king of Egypt had made sure that Haiqâr was slain, he arose straightway and wrote a letter to king Sennacherib, reminding him in it 'of the peace and the health and the might and the honour which we wish specially for thee, my beloved brother, king Sennacherib.

2 I have been desiring to build a castle between the heaven and the earth, and I want thee to send me a wise, clever man from thyself to build it for me, and to answer me all my questions, and that I may have the taxes and the custom duties of Assyria for three years.'

3 Then he sealed the letter and sent it to Sennacherib.

4 He took it and read it and gave it to his viziers and to the nobles of his kingdom, and they were perplexed and ashamed,

and he was wroth with a great wrath, and was puzzled about how he should act.

5 Then he assembled the old men and the learned men and the wise men and the philosophers, and the diviners and the astrologers, and every one who was in his country, and read them the letter and said to them, 'Who amongst you will go to Pharaoh king of Egypt and answer him his questions?'

6 And they said to him, 'O our lord the king! know thou that there is none in thy kingdom who is acquainted with these questions except Haiqâr, thy vizier and secretary.

7 But as for us, we have no skill in this, unless it be Nadan, his sister's son, for he taught him all his wisdom and learning and knowledge. Call him to thee, perchance he may untie this hard knot.'

8 Then the king called Nadan and said to him, 'Look at this letter and understand what is in it.' And when Nadan read it, he said, 'O my lord! who is able to build a castle between the heaven and the earth?'

9 And when the king heard the speech of Nadan he sorrowed with a great and sore sorrow, and stepped down from his throne and sat in the ashes, and began to weep and wail over Haiqâr.

10 Saying, 'O my grief! O Haiqâr, who didst know the secrets and the riddles! woe is me for thee, O Haiqâr! O teacher of my country and ruler of my kingdom, where shall I find thy like? O Haiqâr, O teacher of my country, where shall I turn for thee? woe is me for thee! how did I destroy thee! and I listened to the talk of a stupid, ignorant boy without knowledge, without religion, without manliness.

11 Ah! and again Ah for myself! who can give thee to me

just for once, or bring me word that Haiqâr is alive? and I would give him the half of my kingdom.

12 Whence is this to me? Ah, Haiqâr! that I might see thee just for once, that I might take my fill of gazing at thee, and delighting in thee.

13 Ah! O my grief for thee to all time! O Haiqâr, how have I killed thee! and I tarried not in thy case till I had seen the end of the matter.'

14 And the king went on weeping night and day. Now when the swordsman saw the wrath of the king and his sorrow for Haiqâr, his heart was softened towards him, and he approached into his presence and said to him:

15 'O my lord! command thy servants to cut off my head.' Then said the king to him: 'Woe to thee, Abu Samîk, what is thy fault?'

16 And the swordsman said unto him, 'O my master! every slave who acts contrary to the word of his master is killed, and I have acted contrary to thy command.'

17 Then the king said unto him. 'Woe unto thee, O Abu Samîk, in what hast thou acted contrary to my command?'

18 And the swordsman said unto him, 'O my lord! thou didst command me to kill Haiqâr, and I knew that thou wouldst repent thee concerning him, and that he had been wronged, and I hid him in a certain place, and I killed one of his slaves, and he is now safe in the cistern, and if thou command me I will bring him to thee.'

19 And the king said unto him. 'Woe to thee, O Abu Samîk! thou hast mocked me and I am thy lord.'

20 And the swordsman said unto him, 'Nay, but by the life of thy head, O my lord! Haiqâr is safe and alive.'

21 And when the king heard that saying, he felt sure of the matter, and his head swam, and he fainted from joy, and he commanded them to bring Haiqâr.

22 And he said to the swordsman, 'O trusty servant! if thy speech be true, I would fain enrich thee, and exalt thy dignity above that of all thy friends.'

23 And the swordsman went along rejoicing till he came to Haiqâr's house. And he opened the door of the hiding-place, and went down and found Haiqâr sitting, praising God, and thanking Him.

24 And he shouted to him, saying, 'O Haiqâr, I bring the greatest of joy, and happiness, and delight!'

25 And Haiqâr said to him, 'What is the news, O Abu Samîk?' And he told him all about Pharaoh from the beginning to the end. Then he took him and went to the king.

26 And when the king looked at him, he saw him in a state of want, and that his hair had grown long like the wild beasts' and his nails like the claws of an eagle, and that his body was dirty with dust, and the colour of his face had changed and faded and was now like ashes.

27 And when the king saw him he sorrowed over him and rose at once and embraced him and kissed him, and wept over him and said: 'Praise be to God! who hath brought thee back to me.'

28 Then he consoled him and comforted him. And he stripped off his robe, and put it on the swordsman, and was very gracious to him, and gave him great wealth, and made Haiqâr rest.

29 Then said Haiqâr to the king, 'Let my lord the king live for ever! These be the deeds of the children of the world. I have reared me a palm-tree that I might lean on it, and it bent sideways, and threw me down.

30 But, O my lord! since I have appeared before thee, let not care oppress thee.' And the king said to him: 'Blessed be God, who showed thee mercy, and knew that thou wast wronged, and saved thee and delivered thee from being slain.

31 But go to the warm bath, and shave thy head, and cut thy nails, and change thy clothes, and amuse thyself for the space of forty days, that thou mayst do good to thyself and improve thy condition and the colour of thy face may come back to thee.'

32 Then the king stripped off his costly robe, and put it on Haiqâr, and Haiqâr thanked God and did obeisance to the king, and departed to his dwelling glad and happy, praising the Most High God.

33 And the people of his household rejoiced with him, and his friends and every one who heard that he was alive rejoiced also.

CHAP. V.

The letter of the "riddles" is shown to Ahikar. The boys on the eagles. The first "airplane" ride. Off to Egypt. Ahikar, being a man of wisdom also has a sense of humor. (Verse 27).

AND he did as the king commanded him, and took a rest for forty days.

2 Then he dressed himself in his gayest dress, and went riding to the king, with his slaves behind him and before him, rejoicing and delighted.

3 But when Nadan his sister's son perceived what was happening, fear took hold of him and terror, and he was perplexed, not knowing what to do.

4 And when Haiqâr saw it he entered into the king's presence and greeted him, and he returned the greeting, and made him sit down at his side, saying to him,

'O my darling Haiqâr! look at these letters which the king of Egypt sent to us, after he had heard that thou wast slain.

5 They have provoked us and overcome us, and many of the people of our country have fled to Egypt for fear of the taxes that the king of Egypt has sent to demand from us.'

6 Then Haiqâr took the letter and read it and understood all its contents.

7 Then he said to the king, 'Be not wroth, O my lord! I will go to Egypt, and I will return the answers to Pharaoh, and I will display this letter to him, and I will reply to him about the taxes, and I will send back all those who have run away; and I will put thy enemies to shame with the help of the Most High God, and for the Happiness of thy kingdom.'

8 And when the king heard this speech from Haiqâr he rejoiced with a great joy, and his heart was expanded and he showed him favour.

9 And Haiqâr said to the king: 'Grant me a delay of forty days that I may consider this question and manage it.' And the king permitted this.

10 And Haiqâr went to his dwelling, and he commanded the huntsmen to capture two young eaglets for him, and they captured them and brought them to him: and he commanded the weavers of ropes to weave two cables of cotton for him, each of them two thousand cubits long, and he had the carpenters brought and ordered them to make two great boxes, and they did this.

11 Then he took two little lads, and spent every day sacrificing lambs and feeding the eagles and the boys, and making the boys ride on the backs of the eagles, and he bound them with a firm knot, and tied the cable to the feet of the eagles,

and let them soar upwards little by little every day, to a distance of ten cubits, till they grew accustomed and were educated to it; and they rose all the length of the rope till they reached the sky; the boys being on their backs. Then he drew them to himself.

12 And when Haiqâr saw that his desire was fulfilled he charged the boys that when they were borne aloft to the sky they were to shout, saying;

13 'Bring us clay and stone, that we may build a castle for king Pharaoh, for we are idle.'

14 And Haiqâr was never done training them and exercising them till they had reached the utmost possible point (of skill).

15 Then leaving them he went to the king and said to him, 'O my lord! the work is finished according to thy desire. Arise with me that I may show thee the wonder.'

16 So the king sprang up and sat with Haiqâr and went to a wide place and sent to bring the eagles and the boys, and Haiqâr tied them and let them off into the air all the length of the ropes, and they began to shout as he had taught them. Then he drew them to himself and put them in their places.

17 And the king and those who were with him wondered with a great wonder: and the king kissed Haiqâr between his eyes and said to him, 'Go in peace, O my beloved! O pride of my kingdom! to Egypt and answer the questions of Pharaoh and overcome him by the strength of the Most High God.'

18 Then he bade him farewell, and took his troops and his army and the young men and the eagles, and went towards the dwellings of Egypt; and when he had arrived, he turned towards the country of the king.

19 And when the people of Egypt knew that Sennacherib had sent a man of his Privy Council to talk with Pharaoh and to answer his questions, they carried the news to king Pharaoh, and he sent a party of his Privy Councillors to bring him before him.

20 And he came and entered into the presence of Pharaoh, and did obeisance to him as it is fitting to do to kings.

21 And he said to him: 'O my lord the king! Sennacherib the king hails thee with abundance of peace and might, and honour.

22 And he has sent me, who am one of his slaves, that I may answer thee thy questions, and may fulfil all thy desire: for thou hast sent to seek from my lord the king a man who will build thee a castle between the heaven and the earth.

23 And I by the help of the Most High God and thy noble favour and the power of my lord the king will build it for thee as thou desirest.

24 But, O my lord the king! what thou hast said in it about the taxes of Egypt for three years—now the stability of a kingdom is strict justice, and if thou winnest and my hand hath no skill in replying to thee, then my lord the king will send thee the taxes which thou hast mentioned.

25 And if I shall have answered thee in thy questions, it shall remain for thee to send whatever thou hast mentioned to my lord the king.'

26 And when Pharaoh heard that speech, he wondered and was perplexed by the freedom of his tongue and the pleasantness of his speech.

27 And king Pharaoh said to him, 'O man! what is thy name?' And he said, 'Thy servant is Abiqâm, and I a little ant of the ants of king Sennacherib.'

28 And Pharaoh said to him, 'Had thy lord no one of higher

dignity than thee, that he has sent me a little ant to reply to me, and to converse with me?'

29 And Haiqâr said to him, 'O my lord the king! I would to God Most High that I may fulfil what is on thy mind, for God is with the weak that He may confound the strong.'

30 Then Pharaoh commanded that they should prepare a dwelling for Abiqâm and supply him with provender, meat, and drink, and all that he needed.

31 And when it was finished, three days afterwards Pharaoh clothed himself in purple and red and sat on his throne, and all his viziers and the magnates of his kingdom were standing with their hands crossed, their feet close together, and their heads bowed.

32 And Pharaoh sent to fetch Abiqâm, and when he was presented to him, he did obeisance before him, and kissed the ground in front of him.

33 And king Pharaoh said to him, 'O Abiqâm, whom am I like? and the nobles of my kingdom, to whom are they like?'

34 And Haiqâr said to him, 'O my lord the king! thou art like the idol Bel, and the nobles of thy kingdom are like his servants.'

35 He said to him, 'Go, and come back hither to-morrow.' So Haiqâr went as king Pharaoh had commanded him.

36 And on the morrow Haiqâr went into the presence of Pharaoh, and did obeisance, and stood before the king. And Pharaoh was dressed in a red colour, and the nobles were dressed in white.

37 And Pharaoh said to him 'O Abiqâm, whom am I like? and the nobles of my kingdom, to whom are they like?'

38 And Abiqâm said to him, 'O my lord! thou art like the sun, and thy servants are like its beams.' And Pharaoh said

to him, 'Go to thy dwelling, and come hither to-morrow.'

39 Then Pharaoh commanded his Court to wear pure white, and Pharaoh was dressed like them and sat upon his throne, and he commanded them to fetch Haiqâr. And he entered and sat down before him.

40 And Pharaoh said to him, 'O Abiqâm, whom am I like? and my nobles, to whom are they like?'

41 And Abiqâm said to him, 'O my lord! thou art like the moon, and thy nobles are like the planets and the stars.' And Pharaoh said to him, 'Go, and to-morrow be thou here.'

42 Then Pharaoh commanded his servants to wear robes of various colours, and Pharaoh wore a red velvet dress, and sat on his throne, and commanded them to fetch Abiqâm. And he entered and did obeisance before him.

43 And he said, 'O Abiqâm, whom am I like? and my armies, to whom are they like?' And he said, 'O my lord! thou art like the month of April, and thy armies are like its flowers.'

44 And when the king heard it he rejoiced with a great joy, and said, 'O Abiqâm! the first time thou didst compare me to the idol Bel, and my nobles to his servants.

45 And the second time thou didst compare me to the sun, and my nobles to the sunbeams.

46 And the third time thou didst compare me to the moon, and my nobles to the planets and the stars.

47 And the fourth time thou didst compare me to the month of April, and my nobles to its flowers. But now, O Abiqâm! tell me, thy lord, king Sennacherib, whom is he like? and his nobles, to whom are they like?'

48 And Haiqâr shouted with a loud voice and said: 'Be it far from me to make mention of

my lord the king and thou seated on thy throne. But get up on thy feet that I may tell thee whom my lord the king is like and to whom his nobles are like.'

49 And Pharaoh was perplexed by the freedom of his tongue and his boldness in answering. Then Pharaoh arose from his throne, and stood before Haiqâr, and said to him, 'Tell me now, that I may perceive whom thy lord the king is like, and his nobles, to whom they are like.'

50 And Haiqâr said to him: 'My lord is the God of heaven, and his nobles are the lightnings and the thunder, and when he wills the winds blow and the rain falls.

51 And he commands the thunder, and it lightens and rains, and he holds the sun, and it gives not its light, and the moon and the stars, and they circle not.

52 And he commands the tempest, and it blows and the rain falls and it tramples on April and destroys its flowers and its houses.'

53 And when Pharaoh heard this speech, he was greatly perplexed and was wroth with a great wrath, and said to him: 'O man! tell me the truth, and let me know who thou really art.'

54 And he told him the truth. 'I am Haiqâr the scribe, greatest of the Privy Councillors of king Sennacherib, and I am his vizier and the Governor of his kingdom, and his Chancellor.'

55 And he said to him, 'Thou hast told the truth in this saying. But we have heard of Haiqâr, that king Sennacherib has slain him, yet thou dost seem to be alive and well.'

56 And Haiqâr said to him, 'Yes, so it was, but praise be to God, who knoweth what is hidden, for my lord the king commanded me to be killed, and he believed the word of profligate men, but the Lord delivered me, and blessed is he who trusteth in Him.'

57 And Pharaoh said to Haiqâr, 'Go, and to-morrow be thou here, and tell me a word that I have never heard from my nobles nor from the people of my kingdom and my country.'

CHAP. VI.

The ruse succeeds. Ahikar answers every question of Pharaoh. The boys on the eagles are the climax of the day. Wit, so rarely found in the ancient Scriptures, is revealed in Verses 34-35.

AND Haiqâr went to his dwelling, and wrote a letter, saying in it on this wise:

2 'From Sennacherib king of Assyria and Nineveh to Pharaoh king of Egypt.

3 'Peace be to thee, O my brother! and what we make known to thee by this is that a brother has need of his brother, and kings of each other, and my hope from thee is that thou wouldst lend me nine hundred talents of gold, for I need it for the victualling of some of the soldiers, that I may spend it upon them. And after a little while I will send it thee.'

4 Then he folded the letter, and presented it on the morrow to Pharaoh.

5 And when he saw it, he was perplexed and said to him, 'Verily I have never heard anything like this language from any one.'

6 Then Haiqâr said to him, 'Truly this is a debt which thou owest to my lord the king.'

7 And Pharaoh accepted this, saying, 'O Haiqâr, it is the like of thee who are honest in the service of kings.

8 Blessed be God who hath made thee perfect in wisdom and hath adorned thee with philosophy and knowledge.

9 And now, O Haiqâr, there remains what we desire from thee, that thou shouldst build us a castle between heaven and earth.'

10 Then said Haiqâr, 'To hear is to obey. I will build thee a castle according to thy wish and choice; but, O my lord! prepare us lime and stone and clay and workmen, and I have skilled builders who will build for thee as thou desirest.'

11 And the king prepared all that for him, and they went to a wide place; and Haiqâr and his boys came to it, and he took the eagles and the young men with him; and the king and all his nobles went and the whole city assembled, that they might see what Haiqâr would do.

12 Then Haiqâr let the eagles out of the boxes, and tied the young men on their backs, and tied the ropes to the eagles' feet, and let them go in the air. And they soared upwards, till they remained between heaven and earth.

13 And the boys began to shout, saying, 'Bring bricks, bring clay, that we may build the king's castle, for we are standing idle!'

14 And the crowd were astonished and perplexed, and they wondered. And the king and his nobles wondered.

15 And Haiqâr and his servants began to beat the workmen, and they shouted for the king's troops, saying to them, 'Bring to the skilled workmen what they want and do not hinder them from their work.'

16 And the king said to him, 'Thou art mad; who can bring anything up to that distance?'

17 And Haiqâr said to him, 'O my lord! how shall we build a castle in the air? and if my lord the king were here, he would have built several castles in a single day.'

18 And Pharaoh said to him,

'Go, O Haiqâr, to thy dwelling, and rest, for we have given up building the castle, and to-morrow come to me.'

19 Then Haiqâr went to his dwelling and on the morrow he appeared before Pharaoh. And Pharaoh said, 'O Haiqâr, what news is there of the horse of thy lord? for when he neighs in the country of Assyria and Nineveh, and our mares hear his voice, they cast their young.'

20 And when Haiqâr heard this speech he went and took a cat, and bound her and began to flog her with a violent flogging till the Egyptians heard it, and they went and told the king about it.

21 And Pharaoh sent to fetch Haiqâr, and said to him, 'O Haiqâr, wherefore dost thou flog thus and beat that dumb beast?'

22 And Haiqâr said to him, 'O my lord the king! verily she has done an ugly deed to me, and has deserved this drubbing and flogging, for my lord king Sennacherib had given me a fine cock, and he had a strong true voice and knew the hours of the day and the night.

23 And the cat got up this very night and cut off its head and went away, and because of this deed I have treated her to this drubbing.'

24 And Pharaoh said to him, 'O Haiqâr, I see from all this that thou art growing old and art in thy dotage, for between Egypt and Nineveh there are sixty-eight parasangs, and how did she go this very night and cut off the head of thy cock and come back?'

25 And Haiqâr said to him, 'O my lord! if there were such a distance between Egypt and Nineveh, how could thy mares hear when my lord the king's horse neighs and cast their young? and how could the voice of the horse reach to Egypt?'

26 And when Pharaoh heard

that, he knew that Haiqâr had answered his questions.

27 And Pharaoh said, 'O Haiqâr, I want thee to make me ropes of the sea-sand.'

28 And Haiqâr said to him, 'O my lord the king! order them to bring me a rope out of the treasury that I may make one like it.'

29 Then Haiqâr went to the back of the house, and bored holes in the rough shore of the sea, and took a handful of sand in his hand, sea-sand, and when the sun rose, and penetrated into the holes, he spread the sand in the sun till it became as if woven like ropes.

30 And Haiqâr said, 'Command thy servants to take these ropes, and whenever thou desirest it, I will weave thee some like them.'

31 And Pharaoh said, 'O Haiqâr, we have a millstone here and it has been broken and I want thee to sew it up.'

32 Then Haiqâr looked at it, and found another stone.

33 And he said to Pharoh, 'O my lord! I am a foreigner, and I have no tool for sewing.

34 But I want thee to command thy faithful shoemakers to cut awls from this stone, that I may sew that millstone.'

35 Then Pharaoh and all his nobles laughed. And he said, 'Blessed be the Most High God, who gave thee this wit and knowledge.'

36 And when Pharaoh saw that Haiqâr had overcome him, and returned him his answers, he at once became excited, and commanded them to collect for him three years' taxes, and to bring them to Haiqâr.

37 And he stripped off his robes and put them upon Haiqâr, and his soldiers, and his servants, and gave him the expenses of his journey.

38 And he said to him, 'Go in peace, O strength of his lord and pride of his Doctors! have any of the Sultans thy like? give my greetings to thy lord king Sennacherib, and say to him how we have sent him gifts, for kings are content with little.'

39 Then Haiqâr arose, and kissed king Pharaoh's hands and kissed the ground in front of him, and wished him strength and continuance, and abundance in his treasury, and said to him, 'O my lord! I desire from thee that not one of our countrymen may remain in Egypt.'

40 And Pharaoh arose and sent heralds to proclaim in the streets of Egypt that not one of the people of Assyria or Nineveh should remain in the land of Egypt, but that they should go with Haiqâr.

41 Then Haiqâr went and took leave of king Pharaoh, and journeyed, seeking the land of Assyria and Nineveh; and he had some treasures and a great deal of wealth.

42 And when the news reached king Sennacherib that Haiqâr was coming, he went out to meet him and rejoiced over him exceedingly with great joy and embraced him and kissed him, and said to him, 'Welcome home, O kinsman! my brother Haiqâr, the strength of my kingdom, and pride of my realm.

43 Ask what thou would'st have from me, even if thou desirest the half of my kingdom and of my possessions.'

44 Then said Haiqâr unto him, 'O my lord the king, live for ever! Show favour, O my lord the king! to Abu Samîk in my stead, for my life was in the hands of God and in his.'

45 Then said Sennacherib the king, 'Honour be to thee, O my beloved Haiqâr! I will make the station of Abu Samîk the swordsman higher than all my Privy Councillors and my favourites.'

46 Then the king began to ask him how he had got on with

Pharaoh from his first arrival until he had come away from his presence, and how he had answered all his questions, and how he had received the taxes from him, and the changes of raiment and the presents.

47 And Sennacherib the king rejoiced with a great joy, and said to Haiqâr, 'Take what thou wouldst fain have of this tribute, for it is all within the grasp of thy hand.'

48 And Haiqâr said: 'Let the king live for ever! I desire naught but the safety of my lord the king and the continuance of his greatness.

49 O my lord! what can I do with wealth and its like? but if thou wilt show me favour, give me Nadan, my sister's son, that I may recompense him for what he has done to me, and grant me his blood and hold me guiltless of it.'

50 And Sennacherib the king said, 'Take him, I have given him to thee.' And Haiqâr took Nadan, his sister's son, and bound his hands with chains of iron, and took him to his dwelling, and put a heavy fetter on his feet, and tied it with a tight knot, and after binding him thus he cast him into a dark room, beside the retiring-place, and appointed Nebu-hal as sentinel over him and commanded him to give him a loaf of bread and a little water every day.

CHAP. VII.

The parables of Ahikar in which he completes his nephew's education. Striking similes. Ahikar calls the boy picturesque names. Here ends the story of Ahikar.

AND whenever Haiqâr went in or out he scolded Nadan, his sister's son, saying to him wisely:

2 'O Nadan, my boy! I have done to thee all that is good and kind. and thou hast rewarded me for it with what is ugly and bad and with killing.

3 'O my son! it is said in the proverbs: He who listeneth not with his ear, they will make him listen with the scruff of his neck.'

4 And Nadan said, 'For what cause art thou wroth with me?'

5 And Haiqâr said to him, 'Because I brought thee up, and taught thee, and gave thee honour and respect and made thee great, and reared thee with the best of breeding, and seated thee in my place that thou mightest be my heir in the world, and thou didst treat me with killing and didst repay me with my ruin.

6 But the Lord knew that I was wronged, and He saved me from the snare which thou hadst set for me, for the Lord healeth the broken hearts and hindereth the envious and the haughty.

7 O my boy! thou hast been to me like the scorpion which, when it strikes on brass, pierces it.

8 O my boy! thou art like the gazelle who was eating the roots of the madder, and it said to her, "Eat of me to-day and take thy fill, and to-morrow they will tan thy hide in my roots."

9 O my boy! thou hast been to me like a man who saw his comrade naked in the chilly time of winter; and he took cold water and poured it upon him.

10 O my boy! thou hast been to me like a man who took a stone, and threw it up to heaven to stone his Lord with it. And the stone did not hit, and did not reach high enough, but it became the cause of guilt and sin.

11 O my boy! if thou hadst honoured me and respected me and hadst listened to my words thou wouldst have been my heir, and wouldst have reigned over my dominions.

12 O my son! know thou that if the tail of the dog or

the pig were ten cubits long it would not approach to the worth of the horse's even if it were like silk.

13 O my boy! I thought that thou wouldst have been my heir at my death; and thou through thy envy and thy insolence didst desire to kill me. But the Lord delivered me from thy cunning.

14 O my son! thou hast been to me like a trap which was set up on the dunghill, and there came a sparrow and found 'the trap set up. And the sparrow said to the trap, "What doest thou here?" Said the trap, "I am praying here to God."

15 And the lark asked it also, "What is the piece of wood that thou holdest?" Said the trap, "That is a young oak-tree on which I lean at the time of prayer."

16 Said the lark: "And what is that thing in thy mouth?" Said the trap: "That is bread and victuals which I carry for all the hungry and the poor who come near to me."

17 Said the lark: "Now then may I come forward and eat, for I am hungry?" And the trap said to him, "Come forward." And the lark approached that it might eat.

18 But the trap sprang up and seized the lark by its neck.

19 And the lark answered and said to the trap, "If that is thy bread for the hungry God accepteth not thine alms and thy kind deeds.

20 And if that is thy fasting and thy prayers, God accepteth from thee neither thy fast nor thy prayer, and God will not perfect what is good concerning thee."

21 O my boy! thou hast been to me (as) a lion who made friends with an ass, and the ass kept walking before the lion for a time; and one day the lion sprang upon the ass and ate it up.

22 O my boy! thou hast been to me like a weevil in the wheat, for it does no good to anything, but spoils the wheat and gnaws it.

23 O my boy! thou hast been like a man who sowed ten measures of wheat, and when it was harvest time, he arose and reaped it, and garnered it, and threshed it, and toiled over it to the very utmost, and it turned out to be ten measures, and its master said to it: "O thou lazy thing! thou hast not grown and thou hast not shrunk."

24 O my boy! thou hast been to me like the partridge that had been thrown into the net, and she could not save herself, but she called out to the partridges, that she might cast them with herself into the net.

25 O my son! thou hast been to me like the dog that was cold and it went into the potter's house to get warm.

26 And when it had got warm, it began to bark at them, and they chased it out and beat it, that it might not bite them.

27 O my son! thou hast been to me like the pig who went into the hot bath with people of quality, and when it came out of the hot bath, it saw a filthy hole and it went down and wallowed in it.

28 O my son! thou hast been to me like the goat which joined its comrades on their way to the sacrifice, and it was unable to save itself.

29 O my boy! the dog which is not fed from its hunting becomes food for flies.

30 O my son! the hand which does not labour and plough and (which) is greedy and cunning shall be cut away from its shoulder.

31 O my son! the eye in which light is not seen, the ravens shall pick at it and pluck it out.

32 O my boy! thou hast been to me like a tree whose branches they were cutting, and it said

to them, "If something of me were not in your hands, verily you would be unable to cut me."

33 O my boy! thou art like the cat to whom they said: "Leave off thieving till we make for thee a chain of gold and feed thee with sugar and almonds."

34 And she said, "I am not forgetful of the craft of my father and my mother."

35 O my son! thou hast been like the serpent riding on a thorn-bush when he was in the midst of a river, and a wolf saw them and said, "Mischief upon mischief, and let him who is more mischievous than they direct both of them."

36 And the serpent said to the wolf, "The lambs and the goats and the sheep which thou hast eaten all thy life, wilt thou return them to their fathers and to their parents or no?"

37 Said the wolf, "No." And the serpent said to him, "I think that after myself thou art the worst of us."

38 O my boy! I fed thee with good food and thou didst not feed me with dry bread.

39 O my boy! I gave thee sugared water to drink and good syrup, and thou didst not give me water from the well to drink.

40 O my boy! I taught thee, and brought thee up, and thou didst dig a hiding-place for me and didst conceal me.

41 O my boy! I brought thee up with the best upbringing and trained thee like a tall cedar; and thou hast twisted and bent me.

42 O my boy! it was my hope concerning thee that thou wouldst build me a fortified castle, that I might be concealed from my enemies in it, and thou didst become to me like one burying in the depth of the earth; but the Lord took pity on me and delivered me from thy cunning.

43 O my boy! I wished thee well, and thou didst reward me with evil and hatefulness, and now I would fain tear out thine eyes, and make thee food for dogs, and cut out thy tongue, and take off thy head with the edge of the sword, and recompense thee for thine abominable deeds.'

44 And when Nadan heard this speech from his uncle Haiqâr, he said: 'O my uncle! deal with me according to thy knowledge, and forgive me my sins, for who is there who hath sinned like me, or who is there who forgives like thee?

45 Accept me, O my uncle! Now I will serve in thy house, and groom thy horses and sweep up the dung of thy cattle, and feed thy sheep, for I am the wicked and thou art the righteous: I the guilty and thou the forgiving.'*

46 And Haiqâr said to him, 'O my boy! thou art like the tree which was fruitless beside the water, and its master was fain to cut it down, and it said to him, "Remove me to another place, and if I do not bear fruit, cut me down."

47 And its master said to it, "Thou being beside the water hast not borne fruit, how shalt thou bear fruit when thou art in another place?"

48 O my boy! the old age of the eagle is better than the youth of the crow.

49 O my boy! they said to the wolf, "Keep away from the sheep lest their dust should harm thee." And the wolf said, "The dregs of the sheep's milk are good for my eyes."

50 O my boy! they made the wolf go to school that he might learn to read, and they said to him, "Say A, B." He said, "Lamb and goat in my belly."

51 O my boy! they set the ass

---

*Compare the parable of the Prodigal Son in Luke XV. 19.

down at the table and he fell, and began to roll himself in the dust, and one said, "Let him roll himself, for it is his nature, he will not change."

52 O my boy! the saying has been confirmed which runs: "If thou begettest a boy, call him thy son, and if thou rearest a boy, call him thy slave."

53 O my boy! he who doeth good shall meet with good; and he who doeth evil shall meet with evil, for the Lord requiteth a man according to the measure of his work.

54 O my boy! what shall I say more to thee than these sayings? for the Lord knoweth what is hidden, and is acquainted with the mysteries and the secrets.

55 And He will requite thee and will judge betwixt me and thee, and will recompense thee according to thy desert.'

56 And when Nadan heard that speech from his uncle Haiqâr, he swelled up immediately and became like a blown-out bladder.

57 And his limbs swelled and his legs and his feet and his side, and he was torn and his belly burst asunder and his entrails were scattered, and he perished, and died.

58 And his latter end was destruction, and he went to hell. For he who digs a pit for his brother shall fall into it; and he who sets up traps shall be caught in them.

59 This is what happened and (what) we found about the tale of Haiqâr, and praise be to God for ever. Amen, and peace.

60 This chronicle is finished with the help of God, may He be exalted! Amen, Amen, Amen.

The Testaments of the Twelve Patriarchs

THE following twelve books are biographies written between 107 and 137 B. C. They are a forceful exposition, showing how a Pharisee with a rare gift of writing secured publicity by using the names of the greatest men of ancient times. "There were intellectual giants in those days" and the Twelve Patriarchs were the Intellectual Giants!

Each is here made to tell his life story. When he is on his deathbed he calls all his children and grandchildren and great-grandchildren about him, and proceeds without reservation to lay bare his experiences for the moral guidance of his hearers. If he fell into sin he tells all about it and then counsels them not to err as he did. If he was virtuous, he shows what rewards were his.

When you look beyond the unvarnished—almost brutally frank—passages of the text, you will discern a remarkable attestation of the expectations of the Messiah which existed a hundred years before Christ. And there is another element of rare value in this strange series. As Dr. R. H. Charles says in his scholarly work on the Pseudepigrapha: its ethical teaching "has achieved a real immortality by influencing the thought and diction of the writers of the New Testament, and even those of our Lord. This ethical teaching, which is very much higher and purer than that of the Old Testament, is yet its true spiritual child, and helps to bridge the chasm that divides the ethics of the Old and New Testaments."

The instances of the influence of these writings on the New Testament are notable in the Sermon on the Mount which reflects the spirit and even uses phrases from these Testaments. St. Paul appears to have borrowed so freely that it seems as though he must have carried a copy of the Testaments with him on his travels.

Thus, the reader has before him in these pages what is at once striking for its blunt primitive style and valuable as some of the actual source books of the Bible.

TESTAMENT OF REUBEN
The First-Born Son of Jacob and Leah.

CHAP. I.

Reuben, the first-born son of Jacob and Leah. The man of experience counsels against fornication and points out the ways in which men are most apt to fall into error.

THE copy of the Testament of Reuben, even the commands which he gave his sons before he died in the hundred and twenty-fifth year of his life.

2 Two years after the death of Joseph his brother, when Reuben fell ill, his sons and his sons' sons were gathered together to visit him.

3 And he said to them: My children, behold I am dying, and go the way of my fathers.

4 And seeing there Judah, and Gad, and Asher, his brethren, he said to them: Raise me up, that I may tell to my brethren and to my children what things I have hidden in my heart, for

behold now at length I am passing away.

5 And he arose and kissed them, and said unto them: Hear, my brethren, and do ye, my children, give ear to Reuben your father, in the commands which I give unto you.

6 And behold I call to witness against you this day the God of heaven, that ye walk not in the sins of youth and fornication, wherein I was poured out, and defiled the bed of my father Jacob.

7 And I tell you that he smote me with a sore plague in my loins for seven months; and had not my father Jacob prayed for me to the Lord, the Lord would have destroyed me.

8 For I was thirty years old when I wrought the evil thing before the Lord, and for seven months I was sick unto death.

9 And after this I repented with set purpose of my soul for seven years before the Lord.

10 And wine and strong drink I drank not, and flesh entered not into my mouth, and I ate no pleasant food; but I mourned over my sin, for it was great, such as had not been in Israel.

11 And now hear me, my children, what things I saw concerning the seven spirits of deceit, when I repented.

12 Seven spirits therefore are appointed against man, and they are the leaders in the works of youth.

13 And seven other spirits are given to him at his creation, that through them should be done every work of man.

14 The first is the spirit of life, with which the constitution of man is created.

15 The second is the sense of sight, with which ariseth desire.

16 The third is the sense of hearing, with which cometh teaching.

17 The fourth is the sense of smell, with which tastes are given to draw air and breath.

18 The fifth is the power of speech, with which cometh knowledge.

19 The sixth is the sense of taste, with which cometh the eating of meats and drinks; and by it strength is produced, for in food is the foundation of strength.

20 The seventh is the power of procreation and sexual intercourse, with which through love of pleasure sins enter in.

21 Wherefore it is the last in order of creation, and the first in that of youth, because it is filled with ignorance, and leadeth the youth as a blind man to a pit, and as a beast to a precipice.

22 Besides all these there is an eighth spirit of sleep, with which is brought about the trance of nature and the image of death.

23 With these spirits are mingled the spirits of error.

24 First, the spirit of fornication is seated in the nature and in the senses;

25 The second, the spirit of insatiableness, in the belly;

26 The third, the spirit of fighting, in the liver and gall.

27 The fourth is the spirit of obsequiousness and chicanery, that through officious attention one may be fair in seeming.

28 The fifth is the spirit of pride, that one may be boastful and arrogant.

29 The sixth is the spirit of lying, in perdition and jealousy to practise deceits, and concealments from kindred and friends.

30 The seventh is the spirit of injustice, with which are thefts and acts of rapacity, that a man may fulfil the desire of his heart; for injustice worketh together with the other spirits by the taking of gifts.

31 And with all these the spirit of sleep is joined which is that of error and fantasy.

32 And so perisheth every young man, darkening his mind from the truth, and not understanding the law of God, nor obeying the admonitions of his fathers, as befell me also in my youth.

33 And now, my children, love the truth, and it will preserve you: hear ye the words of Reuben your father.

34 Pay no heed to the face of a woman,

35 Nor associate with another man's wife,

36 Nor meddle with affairs of womankind.

37 For had I not seen Bilhah bathing in a covered place, I had not fallen into this great iniquity.

38 For my mind taking in the thought of the woman's nakedness, suffered me not to sleep until I had wrought the abominable thing.

39 For while Jacob our father had gone to Isaac his father, when we were in Eder, near to Ephrath in Bethlehem, Bilhah became drunk and was asleep uncovered in her chamber.

40 Having therefore gone in and beheld her nakedness, I wrought the impiety without her perceiving it, and leaving her sleeping I departed.

41 And forthwith an angel of God revealed to my father concerning my impiety, and he came and mourned over me, and touched her no more.

CHAP. II.

Reuben continues with his experiences and his good advice.

PAY no heed, therefore, my children, to the beauty of women, nor set your mind on their affairs; but walk in singleness of heart in the fear of the Lord, and expend labour on good works, and on study and on your flocks, until the Lord give you a wife, whom He will, that ye suffer not as I did.

2 For until my father's death I had not boldness to look in his face, or to speak to any of my brethren, because of the reproach.

3 Even until now my conscience causeth me anguish on account of my impiety.

4 And yet my father comforted me much, and prayed for me unto the Lord, that the anger of the Lord might pass from me, even as the Lord showed.

5 And thenceforth until now I have been on my guard and sinned not.

6 Therefore, my children, I say unto you, observe all things whatsoever I command you, and ye shall not sin.

7 For a pit unto the soul is the sin of fornication, separating it from God, and bringing it near to idols, because it deceiveth the mind and understanding, and leadeth down young men into Hades before their time.

8 For many hath fornication destroyed; because, though a man be old or noble, or rich or poor, he bringeth reproach upon himself with the sons of men and derision with Beliar.

9 For ye heard regarding Joseph how he guarded himself from a woman, and purged his thoughts from all fornication, and found favour in the sight of God and men.

10 For the Egyptian woman did many things unto him, and summoned magicians, and offered him love potions, but the purpose of his soul admitted no evil desire.

11 Therefore the God of your fathers delivered him from every evil and hidden death.

12 For if fornication overcomes not your mind, neither can Beliar overcome you.

13 For evil are women, my children; and since they have

no power or strength over man, they use wiles by outward attractions, that they may draw him to themselves.

14 And whom they cannot bewitch by outward attractions, him they overcome by craft.

15 For moreover, concerning them, the angel of the Lord told me, and taught me, that women are overcome by the spirit of fornication more than men, and in their heart they plot against men; and by means of their adornment they deceive first their minds, and by the glance of the eye instil the poison, and then through the accomplished act they take them captive.

16 For a woman cannot force a man openly, but by a harlot's bearing she beguiles him.

17 Flee, therefore, fornication, my children, and command your wives and your daughters, that they adorn not their heads and faces to deceive the mind: because every woman who useth these wiles hath been reserved for eternal punishment.

18 For thus they allured the Watchers* who were before the flood; for as these continually beheld them, they lusted after them, and they conceived the act in their mind; for they changed themselves into the shape of men, and appeared to them when they were with their husbands.

19 And the women lusting in their minds after their forms, gave birth to giants, for the Watchers appeared to them as reaching even unto heaven.

20 Beware, therefore, of fornication; and if you wish to be pure in mind, guard your senses from every woman.

21 And command the women likewise not to associate with men, that they also may be pure in mind.

22 For constant m e e t i n g s,

even though the ungodly deed be not wrought, are to them an irremediable disease, and to us a destruction of Beliar and an eternal reproach.

23 For in fornication there is neither understanding nor godliness, and all jealousy dwelleth in the lust thereof.

24 Therefore, then I say unto you, ye will be jealous against the sons of Levi, and will seek to be exalted over them; but ye shall not be able.

25 For God will avenge them, and ye shall die by an evil death. For to Levi God gave the sovereignty and to Judah with him and to me also, and to Dan and Joseph, that we should be for rulers.

26 Therefore I command you to hearken to Levi, because he shall know the law of the Lord, and shall give ordinances for judgement and shall sacrifice for all Israel until the consummation of the times, as the anointed High Priest, of whom the Lord spake.

27 I adjure you by the God of heaven to do truth each one unto his neighbour and to entertain love each one for his brother.

28 And draw ye near to Levi in humbleness of heart, that ye may receive a blessing from his mouth.

29 For he shall bless Israel and Judah, because him hath the Lord chosen to be king over all the nation.

30 And bow down before his seed, for on our behalf it will die in wars visible and invisible, and will be among you an eternal king.

31 And Reuben died, having given these commands to his sons. And they placed him in a coffin until they carried him up from Egypt, and buried him in Hebron in the cave where his father was.

*See *The Second Book of Adam and Eve*, **Chapter XX.**

TESTAMENT OF SIMEON
The Second Son of Jacob and Leah.

CHAP. I.

Simeon, the second son of Jacob and Leah. The strong man. He becomes jealous of Joseph and is an instigator of the plot against Joseph.

THE copy of the words of Simeon, the things which he spake to his sons before he died, in the hundred and twentieth year of his life, at which time Joseph, his brother, died.

2 For when Simeon was sick, his sons came to visit him, and he strengthened himself and sat up and kissed them, and said:—

3 Hearken, my children, to Simeon your father, and I will declare unto you what things I have in my heart.

4 I was born of Jacob as my father's second son; and my mother Leah called me Simeon, because the Lord had heard her prayer.

5 Moreover, I became strong exceedingly; I shrank from no achievement, nor was I afraid of ought. For my heart was hard, and my liver was immovable, and my bowels without compassion.

6 Because valour also has been given from the Most High to men in soul and body.

7 For in the time of my youth I was jealous in many things of Joseph, because my father loved him beyond all.

8 And I set my mind against him to destroy him, because the prince of deceit sent forth the spirit of jealousy and blinded my mind, so that I regarded him not as a brother, nor did I spare even Jacob my father.

9 But his God and the God of his fathers sent forth His angel, and delivered him out of my hands.

10 For when I went to Shechem to bring ointment for the flocks, and Reuben to Dothan, where were our necessaries and all our stores, Judah my brother sold him to the Ishmaelites.

11 And when Reuben heard these things he was grieved, for he wished to restore him to his father.

12 But on hearing this I was exceedingly wroth against Judah in that he let him go away alive, and for five months I continued wrathful against him.

13 But the Lord restrained me, and withheld from me the power of my hands; for my right hand was half withered for seven days.

14 And I knew, my children, that because of Joseph this had befallen me, and I repented and wept; and I besought the Lord God that my hand might be restored, and that I might hold aloof from all pollution and envy and from all folly.

15 For I knew that I had devised an evil thing before the Lord and Jacob my father, on account of Joseph my brother, in that I envied him.

16 And now, my children, hearken unto me and beware of the spirit of deceit and envy.

17 For envy ruleth over the whole mind of a man, and suffereth him neither to eat nor to drink, nor to do any good thing. But it ever suggesteth to him to destroy him that he envieth; and so long as he that is envied flourisheth, he that envieth fadeth away.

18 Two years therefore I afflicted my soul with fasting in the fear of the Lord, and I learnt that deliverance from envy cometh by the fear of God.

19 For if a man flee to the

Lord, the evil spirit runneth away from him and his mind is lightened.

20 And henceforward he sympathiseth with him whom he envied and forgiveth those who are hostile to him, and so ceaseth from his envy.

CHAP. II.

Reuben counsels his hearers against envy.

AND my father asked concerning me, because he saw that I was sad; and I said unto him, I am pained in my liver.

2 For I mourned more than they all, because I was guilty of the selling of Joseph.

3 And when we went down into Egypt, and he bound me as a spy, I knew that I was suffering justly, and I grieved not.

4 Now Joseph was a good man, and had the Spirit of God within him: being compassionate and pitiful, he bore no malice against me; but loved me even as the rest of his brethren.

5 Beware, therefore, my children, of all jealousy and envy, and walk in singleness of heart, that God may give you also grace and glory, and blessing upon your heads, even as ye saw in Joseph's case.

6 All his days he reproached us not concerning this thing, but loved us as his own soul, and beyond his own sons glorified us, and gave us riches, and cattle and fruits.

7 Do ye also, my children, love each one his brother with a good heart, and the spirit of envy will withdraw from you.

8 For this maketh savage the soul and destroyeth the body; it causeth anger and war in the mind, and stirreth up unto deeds of blood, and leadeth the mind into frenzy, and causeth tumult to the soul and trembling to the body.

9 For even in sleep malicious jealousy gnaweth, and with wicked spirits disturbeth the soul, and causeth the body to be troubled, and waketh the mind from sleep in confusion; and as a wicked and poisonous spirit, so appeareth it to men.

10 Therefore was J o s e p h comely in appearance, and goodly to look upon, because no wickedness dwelt in him; for some of the trouble of the spirit the face manifesteth.

11 And now, my children, make your hearts good before the Lord, and your ways straight before men, and ye shall find grace before the Lord and men.

12 Beware, therefore, of fornication, for fornication is mother of all evils, separating from God, and bringing near to Beliar.

13 For I have seen it inscribed in the writing of Enoch that your sons shall be corrupted in fornication, and shall do harm to the sons of Levi with the sword.

14 But they shall not be able to withstand Levi; for he shall wage the war of the Lord, and shall conquer all your hosts.

15 And they shall be few in number, divided in Levi and Judah, and there shall be none of you for sovereignty, even as also our father prophesied in his blessings.

CHAP. III.

A prophecy of the coming of the Messiah.

BEHOLD I have told you all things, that I may be acquitted of your sin.

2 Now, if ye remove from you your envy and all stiffneckedness, as a rose shall my bones flourish in Israel, and as a lily my flesh in Jacob, and my odour shall be as the odour of Libanus; and as cedars shall holy ones be multiplied from me

for ever, and their branches shall stretch afar off.

3 Then shall perish the seed of Canaan, and a remnant shall not be unto Amalek, and all the Cappadocians shall perish, and all the Hittites shall be utterly destroyed.

4 Then shall fail the land of Ham, and all the people shall perish.

5 Then shall all the earth rest from trouble, and all the world under heaven from war.

6 Then the Mighty One of Israel shall glorify Shem.

7 *For the Lord God shall appear on earth, and Himself save men.*

8 Then shall all the spirits of deceit be given to be trodden under foot, and men shall rule over wicked spirits.

9 Then shall I arise in joy, and will bless the Most High because of his marvellous works, *because God hath taken a body and eaten with men and saved men.*

10 And now, my children, obey Levi and Judah, and be not lifted up against these two tribes, for from them shall arise unto you the salvation of God.

11 For the Lord shall raise up from Levi as it were a High Priest, and from Judah as it were a King, God and man, He shall save all the Gentiles and the race of Israel.

12 Therefore I give you these commands that ye also may command your children, that they may observe them throughout their generations.

13 And when Simeon had made an end of commanding his sons, he slept with his fathers, being an hundred and twenty years old.

14 And they laid him in a wooden coffin, to take up his bones to Hebron. And they took them up secretly during a war of the Egyptians. For the bones of Joseph the Egyptians guarded in the tombs of the kings.

15 For the sorcerers told them, that on the departure of the bones of Joseph there should be throughout all the land darkness and gloom, and an exceeding great plague to the Egyptians, so that even with a lamp a man should not recognize his brother.

16 And the sons of Simeon bewailed their father.

17 And they were in Egypt until the day of their departure by the hand of Moses.

TESTAMENT OF LEVI
The Third Son of Jacob and Leah.

CHAP. I.

Levi, the third son of Jacob and Leah. A mystic and dreamer of dreams, a prophet.

THE copy of the words of Levi, the things which he ordained unto his sons, according to all that they should do, and what things should befall them until the day of judgement.

2 He was sound in health when he called them to him; for it had been revealed to him that he should die.

3 And when they were gathered together he said to them:

4 I, Levi, was born in Haran, and I came with my father to Shechem.

5 And I was young, about twenty years of age, when, with Simeon, I wrought vengeance on Hamor for our sister Dinah.

6 And when I was feeding the flocks in Abel-Maul, the spirit of understanding of the Lord came upon me, and I saw all men corrupting their way, and that un-

righteousness had built for itself walls, and lawlessness sat upon towers.

7 And I was grieving for the race of the sons of men, and I prayed to the Lord that I might be saved.

8 Then there fell upon me a sleep, and I beheld a high mountain, and I was upon it.

9 And behold the heavens were opened, and an angel of God said to me, Levi, enter.

10 And I entered from the first heaven, and I saw there a great sea hanging.

11 And further I saw a second heaven far brighter and more brilliant, for there was a boundless light also therein.

12 And I said to the angel, Why is this so? And the angel said to me, Marvel not at this, for thou shalt see another heaven more brilliant and incomparable.

13 And when thou hast ascended thither, Thou shalt stand near the Lord, and shalt be His minister, and shalt declare His mysteries to men, and shalt proclaim concerning Him that shall redeem Israel.

14 And by thee and Judah shall the Lord appear among men, saving every race of men.

15 And from the Lord's portion shall be thy life, and He shall be thy field and vineyard, and fruits, gold, and silver.

16 Hear, therefore, regarding the heavens which have been shown to thee.

17 The lowest is for this cause gloomy unto thee, in that it beholds all the unrighteous deeds of men.

18 And it has fire, snow, and ice made ready for the day of judgement, in the righteous judgement of God; for in it are all the spirits of the retributions for vengeance on men.

19 And in the second are the hosts of the armies which are ordained for the day of judgement, to work vengeance on the spirits of deceit and of Beliar.

20 And above them are the holy ones.

21 And in the highest of all dwelleth the Great Glory, far above all holiness.

22 In the heaven next to it are the archangels, who minister and make propitiation to the Lord for all the sins of ignorance of the righteous;

23 Offering to the Lord a sweet-smelling savour, a reasonable and a bloodless offering.

24 And in the heaven below this are the angels who bear answers to the angels of the presence of the Lord.

25 And in the heaven next to this are thrones and dominions, in which always they offer praise to God.

26 When, therefore, the Lord looketh upon us, all of us are shaken; yea, the heavens, and the earth, and the abysses are shaken at the presence of His majesty.

27 But the sons of men, having no perception of these things, sin and provoke the Most High.

CHAP. II.

Levi urges piety and education.

NOW, therefore, know that the Lord shall execute judgement upon the sons of men.

2 Because when the rocks are being rent, and the sun quenched, and the waters dried up, and the fire cowering, and all creation troubled, and the invisible spirits melting away, and Hades taketh spoils through the visitations of the Most High, men will be unbelieving and persist in their iniquity.

3 On this account with punishment shall they be judged.

4 Therefore the Most High hath heard thy prayer, to sepa-

rate thee from iniquity, and that thou shouldst become to Him a son, and a servant, and a minister of His presence.

5 The light of knowledge shalt thou light up in Jacob, and as the sun shalt thou be to all the seed of Israel.

6 And there shall be given to thee a blessing, and to all thy seed, until the Lord shall visit all the Gentiles in His tender mercies for ever.

7 And therefore there have been given to thee counsel and understanding, that thou mightest instruct thy sons concerning this;

8 Because they that bless Him shall be blessed, and they that curse Him shall perish.

9 And thereupon the angel opened to me the gates of heaven, and I saw the holy temple, and upon a throne of glory the Most High.

10 And He said to me: Levi, I have given thee the blessings of the priesthood until I come and sojourn in the midst of Israel.

11 Then the angel brought me down to the earth, and gave me a shield and a sword, and said to me: Execute vengeance on Shechem because of Dinah, thy sister, and I will be with thee because the Lord hath sent me.

12 And I destroyed at that time the sons of Hamor, as it is written in the heavenly tables.

13 And I said to him: I pray thee, O Lord, tell me Thy name, that I may call upon Thee in a day of tribulation.

14 And he said: I am the angel who intercedeth for the nation of Israel that they may not be smitten utterly, for every evil spirit attacketh it.

15 And after these things I awaked, and blessed the Most High, and the angel who intercedeth for the nation of Israel and for all the righteous.

CHAP. III.

Levi has visions and shows what rewards are in store for the righteous.

AND when I was going to my father, I found a brazen shield; wherefore also the name of the mountain is Aspis, which is near Gebal, to the south of Abila.

2 And I kept these words in my heart. And after this I counselled my father, and Reuben my brother, to bid the sons of Hamor not to be circumcised; for I was zealous because of the abomination which they had wrought on my sister.

3 And I slew Shechem first, and Simeon slew Hamor. And after this my brothers came and smote that city with the edge of the sword.

4 And my father heard these things and was wroth, and he was grieved in that they had received the circumcision, and after that had been put to death, and in his blessings he looked amiss upon us.

5 For we sinned because we had done this thing against his will, and he was sick on that day.

6 But I saw that the sentence of God was for evil upon Shechem; for they sought to do to Sarah and Rebecca as they had done to Dinah our sister, but the Lord prevented them.

7 And they persecuted Abraham our father when he was a stranger, and they vexed his flocks when they were big with young; and Eblaen, who was born in his house, they most shamefully handled.

8 And thus they did to all strangers, taking away their wives by force, and they banished them.

9 But the wrath of the Lord came upon them to the uttermost.

10 And I said to my father Jacob: By thee will the Lord despoil the Canaanites, and will give their land to thee and to thy seed after thee.

11 For from this day forward shall Shechem be called a city of imbeciles; for as a man mocketh a fool, so did we mock them.

12 Because also they had wrought folly in Israel by defiling my sister. And we departed and came to Bethel.

13 And there again I saw a vision as the former, after we had spent there seventy days.

14 And I saw seven men in white raiment saying unto me: Arise, put on the robe of the priesthood, and the crown of righteousness, and the breast-plate of understanding, and the garment of truth, and the plate of faith, and the turban of the head, and the ephod of prophecy.

15 And they severally carried these things and put them on me, and said unto me: From henceforth become a priest of the Lord, thou and thy seed for ever.

16 And the first anointed me with holy oil, and gave to me the staff of judgement.

17 The second washed me with pure water, and fed me with bread and wine even the most holy things, and clad me with a holy and glorious robe.

18 The third clothed me with a linen vestment like an ephod.

19 The fourth put round me a girdle like unto purple.

20 The fifth gave me a branch of rich olive.

21 The sixth placed a crown on my head.

22 The seventh placed on my head a diadem of priesthood, and filled my hands with incense, that I might serve as priest to the Lord God.

23 And they said to me: Levi, thy seed shall be divided into three offices, for a sign of the glory of the Lord who is to come.

24 And the first portion shall be great; yea, greater than it shall none be.

25 The second shall be in the priesthood.

26 And the third shall be called by a new name, because a king shall arise in Judah, and shall establish a new priesthood, after the fashion of the Gentiles.

27 And His presence is beloved, as a prophet of the Most High, of the seed of Abraham our father.

28 Therefore, every desirable thing in Israel shall be for thee and for thy seed, and ye shall eat everything fair to look upon, and the table of the Lord shall thy seed apportion.

29 And some of them shall be high priests, and judges, and scribes; for by their mouth shall the holy place be guarded.

30 And when I awoke, I understood that this dream was like the first dream. And I hid this also in my heart, and told it not to any man upon the earth.

31 And after two days I and Judah went up with our father Jacob to Isaac our father's father.

32 And my father's father blessed me according to all the words of the visions which I had seen. And he would not come with us to Bethel.

33 And when we came to Bethel, my father saw a vision concerning me, that I should be their priest unto God.

34 And he rose up early in the morning, and paid tithes of all to the Lord through me. And so we came to Hebron to dwell there.

35 And Isaac called me continually to put me in remembrance of the law of the Lord, even as the angel of the Lord showed unto me.

36 And he taught me the law of the priesthood, of sacrifices,

whole burnt-offerings, first-fruits, freewill-offerings, peace-offerings.

37 And each day he was instructing me, and was busied on my behalf before the Lord, and said to me: Beware of the spirit of fornication; for this shall continue and shall by thy seed pollute the holy place.

38 Take, therefore, to thyself a wife without blemish or pollution, while yet thou are young, and not of the race of strange nations.

39 And before entering into the holy place, bathe; and when thou offerest the sacrifice, wash; and again, when thou finishest the sacrifice, wash.

40 Of twelve trees having leaves offer to the Lord, as Abraham taught me also.

41 And of every clean beast and bird offer a sacrifice to the Lord.

42 And of all thy first-fruits and of wine offer the first, as a sacrifice to the Lord God; and every sacrifice thou shalt salt with salt.

43 Now, therefore, observe whatsoever I command you, children; for whatsoever things I have heard from my fathers I have declared unto you.

44 And behold I am clear from your ungodliness and transgression, which ye shall commit in the end of the ages against the Saviour of the world, Christ, acting godlessly, deceiving Israel, and stirring up against it great evils from the Lord.

45 And ye shall deal lawlessly together with Israel, so He shall not bear with Jerusalem because of your wickedness; but the veil of the temple shall be rent, so as not to cover your shame.

46 And ye shall be scattered as captives among the Gentiles, and shall be for a reproach and for a curse there.

47 For the house which the Lord shall choose shall be called Jerusalem, as is contained in the book of Enoch the righteous.

48 Therefore when I took a wife I was twenty-eight years old, and her name was Melcha.

49 And she conceived and bare a son, and I called his name Gersam, for we were sojourners in our land.

50 And I saw concerning him, that he would not be in the first rank.

51 And Kohath was born in the thirty-fifth year of my life, towards sunrise.

52 And I saw in a vision that he was standing on high in the midst of all the congregation.

53 Therefore I called his name Kohath which is, beginning of majesty and instruction.

54 And she bare me a third son, in the fortieth year of my life; and since his mother bare him with difficulty, I called him Merari, that is, 'my bitterness,' because he also was like to die.

55 And Jochebed was born in Egypt, in my sixty-fourth year, for I was renowned then in the midst of my brethren.

56 And Gersam took a wife, and she bare to him Lomni and Semei. And the sons of Kohath, Ambram, Issachar, Hebron, and Ozeel. And the sons of Merari, Mooli, and Mouses.

57 And in the ninety-fourth year Ambram took Jochebed my daughter to him to wife, for they were born in one day, he and my daughter.

58 Eight years old was I when I went into the land of Canaan, and eighteen years when I slew Shechem, and at nineteen years I became priest, and at twenty-eight years I took a wife, and at forty-eight I went into Egypt.

59 And behold, my children, ye are a third generation. In my hundred and eighteenth year Joseph died.

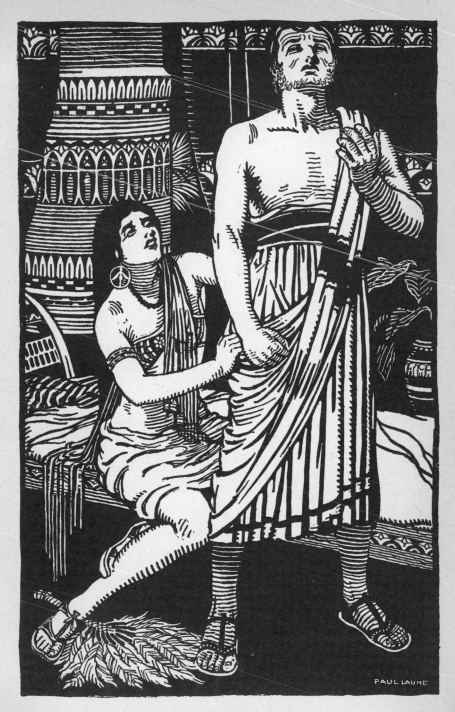

JOSEPH'S PREDICAMENT

(See page 259 et s

CHAP. IV.

Levi shows how wisdom survives destruction. He has no use for scornful people.

AND now, my children, I command you: Fear the Lord your God with your whole heart, and walk in simplicity according to all His law.

2 And do ye also teach your children letters, that they may have understanding all their life, reading unceasingly the law of God.

3 For every one that knoweth the law of the Lord shall be honoured, and shall not be a stranger whithersoever he goeth.

4 Yea, many friends shall he gain more than his parents, and many men shall desire to serve him, and to hear the law from his mouth.

5 Work righteousness, therefore, my children, upon the earth, that ye may have it as a treasure in heaven.

6 And sow good things in your souls, that ye may find them in your life.

7 But if ye sow evil things, ye shall reap every trouble and affliction.

8 Get wisdom in the fear of God with diligence; for though there be a leading into captivity, and cities and lands be destroyed, and gold and silver and every possession perish, the wisdom of the wise nought can take away, save the blindness of ungodliness, and the callousness that comes of sin.

9 For if one keep oneself from these evil things, then even among his enemies shall wisdom be a glory to him, and in a strange country a fatherland, and in the midst of foes shall prove a friend.

10 Whosoever teaches noble things and does them, shall be enthroned with kings, as was also Joseph my brother.

11 Therefore, my children, I have learnt that at the end of the ages ye will transgress against the Lord, stretching out hands to wickedness against Him; and to all the Gentiles shall ye become a scorn.

12 For our father Israel is pure from the transgressions of the chief priests [who shall lay their hands upon the Saviour of the world].

13 For as the heaven is purer in the Lord's sight than the earth, so also be ye, the lights of Israel, purer than all the Gentiles.

14 But if ye be darkened through transgressions, what, therefore, will all the Gentiles do living in blindness?

15 Yea, ye shall bring a curse upon our race, because the light of the law which was given for to lighten every man this ye desire to destroy by teaching commandments contrary to the ordinances of God.

16 The offerings of the Lord ye shall rob, and from His portion shall ye steal choice portions, eating them contemptuously with harlots.

17 And out of covetousness ye shall teach the commandments of the Lord, wedded women shall ye pollute, and the virgins of Jerusalem shall ye defile; and with harlots and adulteresses shall ye be joined, and the daughters of the Gentiles shall ye take to wife, purifying them with an unlawful purification; and your union shall be like unto Sodom and Gomorrah.

18 And ye shall be puffed up because of your priesthood, lifting yourselves up against men, and not only so, but also against the commands of God.

19 For ye shall contemn the holy things with jests and laughter.

20 Therefore the temple, which the Lord shall choose, shall be laid waste through your

uncleanness, and ye shall be captives throughout all nations.

21 And ye shall be an abomination unto them, and ye shall receive reproach and everlasting shame from the righteous judgement of God.

22 And all who hate you shall rejoice at your destruction.

23 And if you were not to receive mercy through Abraham, Isaac, and Jacob, our fathers, not one of our seed should be left upon the earth.

24 And now I have learnt that for seventy weeks ye shall go astray, and profane the priesthood, and pollute the sacrifices.

25 And ye shall make void the law, and set at nought the words of the prophets by evil perverseness.

26 And ye shall persecute righteous men, and hate the godly; the words of the faithful shall ye abhor.

27 And a man who reneweth the law in the power of the Most High, ye shall call a deceiver; and at last ye shall rush upon him to slay him, not knowing his dignity, taking innocent blood through wickedness upon your heads.

28 And your holy places shall be laid waste even to the ground because of him.

29 And ye shall have no place that is clean; but ye shall be among the Gentiles a curse and a dispersion until He shall again visit you, and in pity shall receive you through faith and water.

CHAP. V.

He prophesies the coming of the Messiah. This was written 100 years before Christ.

AND whereas ye have heard concerning the seventy weeks, hear also concerning the priesthood. For in each jubilee there shall be a priesthood.

2 And in the first jubilee, the first who is anointed to the priesthood shall be great, and shall speak to God as to a father.

3 And his priesthood shall be perfect with the Lord, and in the day of his gladness shall he arise for the salvation of the world.

4 In the second jubilee, he that is anointed shall be conceived in the sorrow of beloved ones; and his priesthood shall be honoured and shall be glorified by all.

5 And the third priest shall be taken hold of by sorrow.

6 And the fourth shall be in pain, because unrighteousness shall gather itself against him exceedingly, and all Israel shall hate each one his neighbour.

7 The fifth shall be taken hold of by darkness. Likewise also the sixth and the seventh.

8 And in the seventh shall be such pollution as I cannot express before men, for they shall know it who do these things.

9 Therefore shall they be taken captive and become a prey, and their land and their substance shall be destroyed.

10 And in the fifth week they shall return to their desolate country, and shall renew the house of the Lord.

11 And in the seventh week shall become priests, who are idolaters, adulterers, lovers of money, proud, lawless, lascivious, abusers of children and beasts.

12 And after their punishment shall have come from the Lord, the priesthood shall fail.

13 Then shall the Lord raise up a new priest.

14 And to him all the words of the Lord shall be revealed; and he shall execute a righteous judgement upon the earth for a multitude of days.

15 And his star shall arise in heaven as of a king.

16 Lighting up the light of knowledge as the sun the day, and he shall be magnified in the world.

17 He shall shine forth as the sun on the earth, and shall remove all darkness from under heaven, and there shall be peace in all the earth.

18 The heavens shall exult in his days, and the earth shall be glad, and the clouds shall rejoice;

19 And the knowledge of the Lord shall be poured forth upon the earth, as the water of the seas;

20 And the angels of the glory of the presence of the Lord shall be glad in him.

21 The heavens shall be opened, and from the temple of glory shall come upon him sanctification, with the Father's voice as from Abraham to Isaac.

22 And the glory of the Most High shall be uttered over him, and the spirit of understanding and sanctification shall rest upon him in the water.

23 For he shall give the majesty of the Lord to His sons in truth for evermore;

24 And there shall none succeed him for all generations for ever.

25 And in his priesthood the Gentiles shall be multiplied in knowledge upon the earth, and enlightened through the grace of the Lord. In his priesthood shall sin come to an end, and the lawless shall cease to do evil.

26 And he shall open the gates of paradise, and shall remove the threatening sword against Adam, and he shall give to the saints to eat from the tree of life, and the spirit of holiness shall be on them.

27 And Beliar shall be bound by him, and he shall give power to His children to tread upon the evil spirits.

28 And the Lord shall rejoice in His children, and be well pleased in His beloved ones for ever.

29 Then shall Abraham and Isaac and Jacob exult, and I will be glad, and all the saints shall clothe themselves with joy.

30 And now, my children, ye have heard all; choose, therefore, for yourselves either the light or the darkness, either the law of the Lord or the works of Beliar.

31 And his sons answered him, saying, Before the Lord we will walk according to His law.

32 And their father said unto them, The Lord is witness, and His angels are witnesses, and ye are witnesses, and I am witness, concerning the word of your mouth.

33 And his sons said unto him: We are witnesses.

34 And thus Levi ceased commanding his sons; and he stretched out his feet on the bed, and was gathered to his fathers, after he had lived a hundred and thirty-seven years.

35 And they laid him in a coffin, and afterwards they buried him in Hebron, with Abraham, Isaac, and Jacob.

THE TESTAMENT OF JUDAH
The Fourth Son of Jacob and Leah.

CHAP. I.

Judah, the fourth son of Jacob and Leah. He is the giant, athlete, warrior; he recounts heroic deeds. He runs so fast that he can outstrip a hind.

THE copy of the words of Judah, what things he spake to his sons before he died.

2 They gathered themselves together, therefore, and came to him, and he said to them: Hearken, my children, to Judah your father.

3 I was the fourth son born to my father Jacob; and Leah my mother named me Judah, saying, I give thanks to the Lord,

because He hath given me a fourth son also.

4 I was swift in my youth, and obedient to my father in everything.

5 And I honoured my mother and my mother's sister.

6 And it came to pass, when I became a man, that my father blessed me, saying, Thou shalt be a king, prospering in all things.

7 And the Lord showed me favour in all my works both in the field and in the house.

8 I know that I raced a hind, and caught it, and prepared the meat for my father, and he did eat.

9 And the roes I used to master in the chase, and overtake all that was in the plains.

10 A wild mare I overtook, and caught it and tamed it.

11 I slew a lion and plucked a kid out of its mouth.

12 I took a bear by its paw and hurled it down the cliff, and it was crushed.

13 I outran the wild boar, and seizing it as I ran, I tore it in sunder.

14 A leopard in Hebron leaped upon my dog, and I caught it by the tail, and hurled it on the rocks, and it was broken in twain.

15 I found a wild ox feeding in the fields, and seizing it by the horns, and whirling it round and stunning it, I cast it from me and slew it.

16 And when the two kings of the Canaanites came sheathed in armour against our flocks, and much people with them, single-handed I rushed upon the king of Hazor, and smote him on the greaves and dragged him down, and so I slew him.

17 And the other, the king of Tappuah, as he sat upon his horse, I slew, and so I scattered all his people.

18 Achor, the king, a man of giant stature, I found, hurling javelins before and behind as he sat on horseback, and I took up a stone of sixty pounds weight, and hurled it and smote his horse, and killed it.

19 And I fought with this other for two hours; and I clave his shield in twain, and I chopped off his feet, and killed him.

20 And as I was stripping off his breastplate, behold nine men his companions began to fight with me.

21 And I wound my garment on my hand; and I slung stones at them, and killed four of them, and the rest fled.

22 And Jacob my father slew Beelesath, king of all the kings, a giant in strength, twelve cubits high.

23 And fear fell upon them, and they ceased warring against us.

24 Therefore my father was free from anxiety in the wars when I was with my brethren.

25 For he saw in a vision concerning me that an angel of might followed me everywhere, that I should not be overcome.

26 And in the south there came upon us a greater war than that in Shechem; and I joined in battle array with my brethren, and pursued a thousand men, and slew of them two hundred men and four kings.

27 And I went up upon the wall, and I slew four mighty men.

28 And so we captured Hazor, and took all the spoil.

29 And the next day we departed to Aretan, a city strong and walled and inaccessible, threatening us with death.

30 But I and Gad approached on the east side of the city, and Reuben and Levi on the west.

31 And they that were upon the wall, thinking that we were alone, were drawn down against us.

32 And so my brothers secretly climbed up the wall on

both sides by stakes, and entered the city, while the men knew it not.

33 And we took it with the edge of the sword.

34 And as for those who had taken refuge in the tower, we set fire to the tower and took both it and them.

35 And as we were departing the men of Tappuah seized our spoil, and seeing this we fought with them.

36 And we slew them all and recovered our spoil.

37 And when I was at the waters of Kozeba, the men of Jobel came against us to battle.

38 And we fought with them and routed them; and their allies from Shiloh we slew, and we did not leave them power to come in against us.

39 And the men of Makir came upon us the fifth day, to seize our spoil; and we attacked them and overcame them in fierce battle: for there was a host of mighty men amongst them, and we slew them before they had gone up the ascent.

40 And when we came to their city their women rolled upon us stones from the brow of the hill on which the city stood.

41 And I and Simeon had ourselves behind the town, and seized upon the heights, and destroyed this city also.

42 And the next day it was told us that the king of the city of Gaash with a mighty host was coming against us.

43 I, therefore, and Dan feigned ourselves to be Amorites, and as allies went into their city.

44 And in the depth of night our brethren came and we opened to them the gates; and we destroyed all the men and their substance, and we took for a prey all that was theirs, and their three walls we cast down.

45 And we drew near to Thamna, where was all the substance of the hostile kings.

46 Then being insulted by them, I was therefore wroth, and rushed against them to the summit; and they kept slinging against me stones and darts.

47 And had not Dan my brother aided me, they would have slain me.

48 We came upon them, therefore, with wrath, and they all fled; and passing by another way, they besought my father, and he made peace with them.

49 And we did to them no hurt, and they became tributary to us, and we restored to them their spoil.

50 And I built Thamna, and my father built Pabael.

51 I was twenty years old when this war befell. And the Canaanites feared me and my brethren.

52 And I had much cattle, and I had for chief herdsman Iram the Adullamite.

53 And when I went to him I saw Parsaba, king of Adullam; and he spake unto us, and he made us a feast; and when I was heated he gave me his daughter Bathshua to wife.

54 She bare me Er, and Onan and Shelah; and two of them the Lord smote: for Shelah lived, and his children are ye.

CHAP. II.

Judah describes some archaelogical findings, a city with walls of iron and gates of brass. He has an encounter with an adventuress.

AND eighteen years my father abode in peace with his brother Esau, and his sons with us, after that we came from Mesopotamia, from Laban.

2 And when eighteen years were fulfilled, in the fortieth year of my life, Esau, the brother of my father, came upon us with a mighty and strong people.

3 And Jacob smote Esau with

an arrow, and he was taken up wounded on Mount Seir, and as he went he died at Anoniram.

4 And we pursued after the sons of Esau.

5 Now they had a city with walls of iron and gates of brass; and we could not enter into it, and we encamped around, and besieged it.

6 And when they opened not to us in twenty days, I set up a ladder in the sight of all and with my shield upon my head I went up, sustaining the assault of stones, upwards of three talents weight; and I slew four of their mighty men.

7 And Reuben and Gad slew six others.

8 Then they asked from us terms of peace; and having taken counsel with our father, we received them as tributaries.

9 And they gave us five hundred cors of wheat, five hundred baths of oil, five hundred measures of wine, until the famine, when we went down into Egypt.

10 And after these things my son Er took to wife Tamar, from Mesopotamia, a daughter of Aram.

11 Now Er was wicked, and he was in need concerning Tamar, because she was not of the land of Canaan.

12 And on the third night an angel of the Lord smote him.

13 And he had not known her according to the evil craftiness of his mother, for he did not wish to have children by her.

14 In the days of the wedding feast I gave Onan to her in marriage; and he also in wickedness knew her not, though he spent with her a year.

15 And when I threatened him he went in unto her, but he spilled the seed on the ground, according to the command of his mother, and he also died through wickedness.

16 And I wished to give Shelah also to her, but his mother did not permit it; for she wrought evil against Tamar, because she was not of the daughters of Canaan, as she also herself was.

17 And I knew that the race of the Canaanites was wicked, but the impulse of youth blinded my mind.

18 And when I saw her pouring out wine, owing to the intoxication of wine I was deceived, and took her although my father had not counselled it.

19 And while I was away she went and took for Shelah a wife from Canaan.

20 And when I knew what she had done, I cursed her in the anguish of my soul.

21 And she also died through her wickedness together with her sons.

22 And after these things, while Tamar was a widow, she heard after two years that I was going up to shear my sheep, and adorned herself in bridal array, and sat in the city Enaim by the gate.

23 For it was a law of the Amorites, that she who was about to marry should sit in fornication seven days by the gate.

24 Therefore being drunk with wine, I did not recognize her; and her beauty deceived me, through the fashion of her adorning.

25 And I turned aside to her, and said: Let me go in unto thee.

26 And she said: What wilt thou give me? And I gave her my staff, and my girdle, and the diadem of my kingdom in pledge.

27 And I went in unto her, and she conceived.

28 And not knowing what I had done, I wished to slay her; but she privily sent my pledges, and put me to shame.

29 And when I called her, I heard also the secret words which I spoke when lying with

her in my drunkenness; and I could not slay her, because it was from the Lord.

30 For I said, Lest haply she did it in subtlety, having received the pledge from another woman.

31 But I came not again near her while I lived, because I had done this abomination in all Israel.

32 Moreover, they who were in the city said there was no harlot in the gate, because she came from another place, and sat for a while in the gate.

33 And I thought that no one knew that I had gone in to her.

34 And after this we came into Egypt to Joseph, because of the famine.

35 And I was forty and six years old, and seventy and three years lived I in Egypt.

CHAP. III.

He counsels against wine and lust as twin evils. "For he who is drunken reverenceth no man."
(Verse 13).

AND now I command you, my children, hearken to Judah your father, and keep my sayings to perform all the ordinances of the Lord, and to obey the commands of God.

2 And walk not after your lusts, nor in the imaginations of your thoughts in haughtiness of heart; and glory not in the deeds and strength of your youth, for this also is evil in the eyes of the Lord.

3 Since I also gloried that in wars no comely woman's face ever enticed me, and reproved Reuben my brother concerning Bilhah, the wife of my father, the spirits of jealousy and of fornication arrayed themselves against me, until I lay with Bathshua the Canaanite, and Tamar, who was espoused to my sons.

4 For I said to my father-in-law: I will take counsel with my father, and so will I take thy daughter.

5 And he was unwilling, but he showed me a boundless store of gold in his daughter's behalf; for he was a king.

6 And he adorned her with gold and pearls, and caused her to pour out wine for us at the feast with the beauty of women.

7 And the wine turned aside my eyes, and pleasure blinded my heart.

8 And I became enamoured of and I lay with her, and transgressed the commandment of the Lord and the commandment of my fathers, and I took her to wife.

9 And the Lord rewarded me according to the imagination of my heart, inasmuch as I had no joy in her children.

10 And now, my children, I say unto you, be not drunk with wine; for wine turneth the mind away from the truth, and inspires the passion of lust, and leadeth the eyes into error.

11 For the spirit of fornication hath wine as a minister to give pleasure to the mind; for these two also take away the mind of man.

12 For if a man drink wine to drunkenness, it disturbeth the mind with filthy thoughts leading to fornication, and heateth the body to carnal union; and if the occasion of the lust be present, he worketh the sin, and is not ashamed.

13 Such is the inebriated man, my children; for he who is drunken reverenceth no man.

14 For, lo, it made me also to err, so that I was not ashamed of the multitude in the city, in that before the eyes of all I turned aside unto Tamar, and I wrought a great sin, and I uncovered the covering of my sons' shame.

15 After I had drunk wine I

reverenced not the commandment of God, and I took a woman of Canaan to wife.

16 For much discretion needeth the man who drinketh wine, my children; and herein is discretion in drinking wine, a man may drink so long as he preserveth modesty.

17 But if he go beyond this limit the spirit of deceit attacketh his mind, and it maketh the drunkard to talk filthily, and to transgress and not to be ashamed, but even to glory in his shame, and to account himself honourable.

18 He that committeth fornication is not aware when he suffers loss, and is not ashamed when put to dishonour.

19 For even though a man be a king and commit fornication, he is stripped of his kingship by becoming the slave of fornication, as I myself also suffered.

20 For I gave my staff, that is, the stay of my tribe; and my girdle, that is, my power; and my diadem, that is, the glory of my kingdom.

21 And indeed I repented of these things; wine and flesh I eat not until my old age, nor did I behold any joy.

22 And the angel of God showed me that for ever do women bear rule over king and beggar alike.

23 And from the king they take away his glory, and from the valiant man his might, and from the beggar even that little which is the stay of his poverty.

24 Observe, therefore, my children, the right limit in wine; for there are in it four evil spirits—of lust, of hot desire, of profligacy, of filthy lucre.

25 If ye drink wine in gladness, be ye modest in the fear of God.

26 For if in your gladness the fear of God departeth, then drunkenness ariseth and shamelessness stealeth in.

27 But if ye would live soberly do not touch wine at all, lest ye sin in words of outrage, and in fightings and slanders, and transgressions of the commandments of God, and ye perish before your time.

28 Moreover, wine revealeth the mysteries of God and men, even as I also revealed the commandments of God and the mysteries of Jacob my father to the Canaanitish woman Bathshua, which God bade me not to reveal.

29 And wine is a cause both of war and confusion.

30 And now, I command you, my children, not to love money, nor to gaze upon the beauty of women; because for the sake of money and beauty I was led astray to Bathshua the Canaanite.

31 For I know that because of these two things shall my race fall into wickedness.

32 For even wise men among my sons shall they mar, and shall cause the kingdom of Judah to be diminished, which the Lord gave me because of my obedience to my father.

33 For I never caused grief to Jacob, my father; for all things whatsoever he commanded I did.

34 And Isaac, the father of my father, blessed me to be king in Israel, and Jacob further blessed me in like manner.

35 And I know that from me shall the kingdom be established.

36 And I know what evils ye will do in the last days.

37 Beware, therefore, my children, of fornication, and the love of money, and hearken to Judah your father.

38 For these things withdraw you from the law of God, and blind the inclination of the soul, and teach arrogance, and suffer not a man to have compassion upon his neighbour.

39 They rob his soul of all

goodness, and oppress him with toils and troubles, and drive away sleep from him, and devour his flesh.

40 And he hindereth the sacrifices of God; and he remembereth not the blessing of God, he hearkeneth not to a prophet when he speaketh, and resenteth the words of godliness.

41 For he is a slave to two contrary passions, and cannot obey God, because they have blinded his soul, and he walketh in the day as in the night.

42 My children, the love of money leadeth to idolatry; because, when led astray through money, men name as gods those who are not gods, and it causeth him who hath it to fall into madness.

43 For the sake of money I lost my children, and had not my repentance, and my humiliation, and the prayers of my father been accepted, I should have died childless.

44 But the God of my fathers had mercy on me, because I did it in ignorance.

45 And the prince of deceit blinded me, and I sinned as a man and as flesh, being corrupted through sins; and I learnt my own weakness while thinking myself invincible.

46 Know, therefore, my children, that two spirits wait upon man—the spirit of truth and the spirit of deceit.

47 And in the midst is the spirit of understanding of the mind, to which it belongeth to turn whithersoever it will.

And the works of truth and the works of deceit are written upon the hearts of men, and each one of them the Lord knoweth.

49 And there is no time at which the works of men can be hid; for on the heart itself have they been written down before the Lord.

50 And the spirit of truth testifieth all things, and accuseth all; and the sinner is burnt up by his own heart, and cannot raise his face to the judge.

CHAP. IV.

Judah makes a vivid simile concerning tyranny and a dire prophecy concerning the morals of his listeners.

AND now, my children, I command you, love Levi, that ye may abide, and exalt not yourselves against him, lest ye be utterly destroyed.

2 For to me the Lord gave the kingdom, and to him the priesthood, and He set the kingdom beneath the priesthood.

3 To me He gave the things upon the earth; to him the things in the heavens.

4 As the heaven is higher than the earth, so is the priesthood of God higher than the earthly kingdom, unless it falls away through sin from the Lord and is dominated by the earthly kingdom.

5 For the angel of the Lord said unto me: The Lord chose him rather than thee, to draw near to Him, and to eat of His table and to offer Him the firstfruits of the choice things of the sons of Israel; but thou shalt be king of Jacob.

6 And thou shalt be amongst them as the sea.

7 For as, on the sea, just and unjust are tossed about, some taken into captivity while some are enriched, so also shall every race of men be in thee: some shall be impoverished, being taken captive, and others grow rich by plundering the possessions of others.

8 For the kings shall be as sea-monsters.

9 They shall swallow men like fishes: the sons and daughters of freemen shall they enslave;

houses, lands, flocks, money shall they plunder:

10 And with the flesh of many shall they wrongfully feed the ravens and the cranes; and they shall advance in evil, in covetousness uplifted, and there shall be false prophets like tempest, and they shall persecute all righteous men.

11 And the Lord shall bring upon them divisions one against another.

12 And there shall be continual wars in Israel; and among men of another race shall my kingdom be brought to an end, until the salvation of Israel shall come.

13 Until the appearing of the God of righteousness, that Jacob and all the Gentiles may rest in peace.

14 And He shall guard the might of my kingdom for ever; for the Lord sware to me with an oath that He would not destroy the kingdom from my seed for ever.

15 Now I have much grief, my children, because of your lewdness and witchcrafts, and idolatries which ye shall practise against the kingdom, following them that have familiar spirits, diviners, and demons of error.

16 Ye shall make your daughters singing girls and harlots, and ye shall mingle in the abominations of the Gentiles.

17 For which things' sake the Lord shall bring upon you famine and pestilence, death and the sword, beleaguering by enemies, and revilings of friends, the slaughter of children, the rape of wives, the plundering of possessions, the burning of the temple of God, the laying waste of the land, the enslavement of yourselves among the Gentiles.

18 And they shall make some of you eunuchs for their wives.

19 Until the Lord visit you, when with perfect heart ye repent and walk in all His commandments, and He bring you up from captivity among the Gentiles.

20 And after these things shall a star arise to you from Jacob in peace,

21 And a man shall arise from my seed, like the sun of righteousness,

22 Walking with the sons of men in meekness and righteousness;

23 And no sin shall be found in him.

24 And the heavens shall be opened unto him, to pour out the spirit, even the blessing of the Holy Father; and He shall pour out the spirit of grace upon you;

25 And ye shall be unto Him sons in truth, and ye shall walk in His commandments first and last.

26 Then shall the sceptre of my kingdom shine forth; and from your root shall arise a stem; and from it shall grow a rod of righteousness to the Gentiles, to judge and to save all that call upon the Lord.

27 And after these things shall Abraham and Isaac and Jacob arise unto life, and I and my brethren shall be chiefs of the tribes of Israel:

28 Levi first, I the second, Joseph third, Benjamin fourth, Simeon fifth, Issachar sixth, and so all in order.

29 And the Lord blessed Levi, and the Angel of the Presence, me; the powers of glory, Simeon; the heaven, Reuben; the earth, Issachar; the sea, Zebulun; the mountains, Joseph; the tabernacle, Benjamin; the luminaries, Dan; Eden, Naphtali; the sun, Gad; the moon, Asher.

30 And ye shall be the people of the Lord, and have one tongue; and there shall be there no spirit of deceit of Beliar, for he shall be cast into the fire for ever.

31 And they who have died in grief shall arise in joy, and they who were poor for the Lord's sake shall be made rich, and they who are put to death for the Lord's sake shall awake to life.

32 And the harts of Jacob shall run in joyfulness, and the eagles of Israel shall fly in gladness; and all the people shall glorify the Lord for ever.

33 Observe, therefore, my children, all the law of the Lord, for there is hope for all them who hold fast unto His ways.

34 And he said to them: Behold, I die before your eyes this day, a hundred and nineteen years old.

35 Let no one bury me in costly apparel, nor tear open my bowels, for this shall they who are kings do; and carry me up to Hebron with you.

36 And Judah, when he had said these things, fell asleep; and his sons did according to all whatsoever he commanded them, and they buried him in Hebron, with his fathers.

THE TESTAMENT OF ISSACHAR
The Fifth Son of Jacob and Leah.

CHAP. I.

Issachar, the fifth son of Jacob and Leah. The sinless child of hire for mandrakes. He appeals for simplicity.

THE copy of the words of Issachar.

2 For he called his sons and said to them: Hearken, my children, to Issachar your father; give ear to the words of him who is beloved of the Lord.

3 I was born the fifth son to Jacob, by way of hire for the mandrakes.

4 For Reuben my brother brought in mandrakes from the field, and Rachel met him and took them.

5 And Reuben wept, and at his voice Leah my mother came forth.

6 Now these mandrakes were sweet-smelling apples which were produced in the land of Haran below a ravine of water.

7 And Rachel said: I will not give them to thee, but they shall be to me instead of children.

8 For the Lord hath despised me, and I have not borne children to Jacob.

9 Now there were two apples; and Leah said to Rachel: Let it suffice thee that thou hast taken my husband: wilt thou take these also?

10 And Rachel said to her: Thou shalt have Jacob this night for the mandrakes of thy son.

11 And Leah said to her: Jacob is mine, for I am the wife of his youth.

12 But Rachel said: Boast not, and vaunt not thyself; for he espoused me before thee, and for my sake he served our father fourteen years.

13 And had not craft increased on the earth and the wickedness of men prospered, thou wouldst not now see the face of Jacob.

14 For thou art not his wife, but in craft wert taken to him in my stead.

15 And my father deceived me, and removed me on that night, and did not suffer Jacob to see me; for had I been there, this had not happened to him.

16 Nevertheless, for the mandrakes I am hiring Jacob to thee for one night.

17 And Jacob knew Leah, and she conceived and bare me, and

on account of the hire I was called Issachar.

18 Then appeared to Jacob an angel of the Lord, saying: Two children shall Rachel bear, inasmuch as she hath refused company with her husband, and hath chosen continency.

19 And had not Leah my mother paid the two apples for the sake of his company, she would have borne eight sons; for this reason she bare six, and Rachel bare the two: for on account of the mandrakes the Lord visited her.

20 For He knew that for the sake of children she wished to company with Jacob, and not for lust of pleasure.

21 For on the morrow also she again gave up Jacob.

22 Because of the mandrakes, therefore, the Lord hearkened to Rachel.

23 For though she desired them, she eat them not, but offered them in the house of the Lord, presenting them to the priest of the Most High who was at that time.

24 When, therefore, I grew up, my children, I walked in uprightness of heart, and I became a husbandman for my father and my brethren, and I brought in fruits from the field according to their season.

25 And my father blessed me, for he saw that I walked in rectitude before him.

26 And I was not a busybody in my doings, nor envious and malicious against my neighbour.

27 I never slandered any one, nor did I censure the life of any man, walking as I did in singleness of eye.

28 Therefore, when I was thirty-five years old, I took to myself a wife, for my labour wore away my strength, and I never thought upon pleasure with women; but owing to my toil, sleep overcame me.

29 And my father always re-joiced in my rectitude, because I offered through the priest to the Lord all first-fruits; then to my father also.

30 And the Lord increased ten thousandfold His benefits in my hands; and also Jacob, my father, knew that God aided my singleness.

31 For on all the poor and oppressed I bestowed the good things of the earth in the singleness of my heart.

32 And now, hearken to me, my children, and walk in singleness of your heart, for I have seen in it all that is well-pleasing to the Lord.

33 The single-minded man coveteth not gold, he overreacheth not his neighbour, he longeth not after manifold dainties, he delighteth not in varied apparel.

34 He doth not desire to live a long life, but only waiteth for the will of God.

35 And the spirits of deceit have no power against him, for he looketh not on the beauty of women, lest he should pollute his mind with corruption.

36 There is no envy in his thoughts, no malicious person maketh his soul to pine away, nor worry with insatiable desire in his mind.

37 For he walketh in singleness of soul, and beholdeth all things in uprightness of heart, shunning eyes made evil through the error of the world, lest he should see the perversion of any of the commandments of the Lord.

38 Keep, therefore, my children, the law of God, and get singleness, and walk in guilelessness, not playing the busybody with the business of your neighbour, but love the Lord and your neighbour, have compassion on the poor and weak.

39 Bow down your back unto husbandry, and toil in labours in all manner of husbandry, offer-

ing gifts to the Lord with thanksgiving.

40 For with the first-fruits of the earth will the Lord bless you, even as He blessed all the saints from Abel even until now.

41 For no other portion is given to you than of the fatness of the earth, whose fruits are raised by toil.

42 For our father Jacob blessed me with blessings of the earth and of first-fruits.

43 And Levi and Judah were glorified by the Lord even among the sons of Jacob; for the Lord gave them an inheritance, and to Levi He gave the priesthood, and to Judah the kingdom.

44 And do ye therefore obey them, and walk in the singleness of your father; for unto Gad hath it been given to destroy the troops that are coming upon Israel.

CHAP. II.

KNOW ye therefore, my children, that in the last times your sons will forsake singleness, and will cleave unto insatiable desire.

2 And leaving guilelessness, will draw near to malice; and forsaking the commandments of the Lord, they will cleave unto Beliar.

3 And leaving husbandry, they will follow after their own wicked devices, and they shall be dispersed among the Gentiles, and shall serve their enemies.

4 And do you therefore give these commands to your children, that, if they sin, they may the more quickly return to the Lord; For He is merciful, and will deliver them, even to bring them back into their land.

5 Behold, therefore, as ye see, I am a hundred and twenty-six years old and am not conscious of committing any sin.

6 Except my wife I have not known any woman. I never committed fornication by the uplifting of my eyes.

7 I drank not wine, to be led astray thereby;

8 I coveted not any desirable thing that was my neighbour's.

9 Guile arose not in my heart;

10 A lie passed not through my lips.

11 If any man were in distress I joined my sighs with his,

12 And I shared my bread with the poor.

13 I wrought godliness, all my days I kept truth.

14 I loved the Lord; likewise also every man with all my heart.

15 So do you also these things, my children, and every spirit of Beliar shall flee from you, and no deed of wicked men shall rule over you;

16 And every wild beast shall ye subdue, since you have with you the God of heaven and earth and walk with men in singleness of heart.

17 And having said these things, he commanded his sons that they should carry him up to Hebron, and bury him there in the cave with his fathers.

18 And he stretched out his feet and died, at a good old age; with every limb sound, and with strength unabated, he slept the eternal sleep.

THE TESTAMENT OF ZEBULUN
The Sixth Son of Jacob and Leah.

CHAP. I.

Zebulun, the sixth son of Jacob and Leah. The inventor and philanthropist. What he learned as a result of the plot against Joseph.

THE copy of the words of Zebulun, which he enjoined on his sons before he died in the hundred and fourteenth year of his life, two years after the death of Joseph.

2 And he said to them: Hearken to me, ye sons of Zebulun, attend to the words of your father.

3 I, Zebulun, was born a good gift to my parents.

4 For when I was born my father was increased very exceedingly, both in flocks and herds, when with the straked rods he had his portion.

5 I am not conscious that I have sinned all my days, save in thought.

6 Nor yet do I remember that I have done any iniquity, except the sin of ignorance which I committed against Joseph; for I covenanted with my brethren not to tell my father what had been done.

7 But I wept in secret many days on account of Joseph, for I feared my brethren, because they all agreed that if any one should declare the secret, he should be slain.

8 But when they wished to kill him, I adjured them much with tears not to be guilty of this sin.

9 For Simeon and Gad came against Joseph to kill him, and he said unto them with tears: Pity me, my brethren, have mercy upon the bowels of Jacob our father: lay not upon me your hands to shed innocent blood, for I have not sinned against you.

10 And if indeed I have sinned, with chastening chastise me, my brethren, but lay not upon me your hand, for the sake of Jacob our father.

11 And as he spoke these words, wailing as he did so, I was unable to bear his lamentations, and began to weep, and my liver was poured out, and all the substance of my bowels was loosened.

12 And I wept with Joseph and my heart sounded, and the joints of my body trembled, and I was not able to stand.

13 And when Joseph saw me weeping with him, and them coming against him to slay him, he fled behind me, beseeching them.

14 But meanwhile Reuben arose and said: Come, my brethren, let us not slay him, but let us cast him into one of these dry pits, which our fathers digged and found no water.

15 For for this cause the Lord forbade that water should rise up in them, in order that Joseph should be preserved.

16 And they did so, until they sold him to the Ishmaelites.

17 For in his price I had no share, my children.

18 But Simeon and Gad and six other of our brethren took the price of Joseph, and bought sandals for themselves, and their wives, and their children, saying:

19 We will not eat of it, for it is the price of our brother's blood, but we will assuredly tread it under foot, because he said that he would be king over us, and so let us see what will become of his dreams.

20 Therefore it is written in

the writing of the law of Moses, that whosoever will not raise up seed to his brother, his sandal should be unloosed, and they should spit in his face.

21 And the brethren of Joseph wished not that their brother should live, and the Lord loosed from them the sandal which they wore against Joseph their brother.

22 For when they came into Egypt they were unloosed by the servants of Joseph outside the gate, and so they made obeisance to Joseph after the fashion of King Pharaoh.

23 And not only did they make obeisance to him, but were spit upon also, falling down before him forthwith, and so they were put to shame before the Egyptians.

24 For after this the Egyptians heard all the evils that they had done to Joseph.

25 And after he was sold my brothers sat down to eat and drink.

26 But I, through pity for Joseph, did not eat, but watched the pit, since Judah feared lest Simeon, Dan, and Gad should rush off and slay him.

27 But when they saw that I did not eat, they set me to watch him, till he was sold to the Ishmaelites.

28 And when Reuben came and heard that while he was away Joseph had been sold, he rent his garments, and mourning, said:

29 How shall I look on the face of my father Jacob? And he took the money and ran after the merchants, but as he failed to find them he returned grieving.

30 But the merchants had left the broad road and marched through the Troglodytes by a short cut.

31 But Reuben was grieved, and ate no food that day.

32 Dan therefore came to him and said: Weep not, neither grieve; for we have found what we can say to our father Jacob.

33 Let us slay a kid of the goats, and dip in it the coat of Joseph; and let us send it to Jacob, saying: Know, is this the coat of thy son?

34 And they did so. For they stripped off from Joseph his coat when they were selling him, and put upon him the garment of a slave.

35 Now Simeon took the coat, and would not give it up, for he wished to rend it with his sword, as he was angry that Joseph lived and that he had not slain him.

36 Then we all rose up and said unto him: If thou givest not up the coat, we will say to our father that thou alone didst this evil thing in Israel.

37 And so he gave it unto them, and they did even as Dan had said.

CHAP. II.

He urges human sympathy and understanding of one's fellow men.

AND now, my children, I you to keep the commands of the Lord, and to show mercy to your neighbours, and to have compassion towards all, not towards men only, but also towards beasts.

2 For all this thing's sake the Lord blessed me, and when all my brethren were sick, I escaped without sickness, for the Lord knoweth the purposes of each.

3 Have, therefore, compassion in your hearts, my children, because even as a man doeth to his neighbour, even so also will the Lord do to him.

4 For the sons of my brethren were sickening and were dying on account of Joseph, because they showed not mercy in their hearts; but my sons were pre-

served without sickness, as ye know.

5 And when I was in the land of Canaan, by the sea-coast, I made a catch of fish for Jacob my father; and when many were choked in the sea, I continued unhurt.

6 I was the first to make a boat to sail upon the sea, for the Lord gave me understanding and wisdom therein.

7 And I let down a rudder behind it, and I stretched a sail upon another upright piece of wood in the midst.

8 And I sailed therein along the shores, catching fish for the house of my father until we came to Egypt.

9 And through compassion I shared my catch with every stranger.

10 And if a man were a stranger, or sick, or aged, I boiled the fish, and dressed them well, and offered them to all men, as every man had need, grieving with and having compassion upon them.

11 Wherefore also the Lord satisfied me with abundance of fish when catching fish; for he that shareth with his neighbour receiveth manifold more from the Lord.

12 For five years I caught fish and gave thereof to every man whom I saw, and sufficed for all the house of my father.

13 And in the summer I caught fish, and in the winter I kept sheep with my brethren.

14 Now I will declare unto you what I did.

15 I saw a man in distress through nakedness in wintertime, and had compassion upon him, and stole away a garment secretly from my father's house, and gave it to him who was in distress.

16 Do you, therefore, my children, from that which God bestoweth upon you, show compassion and mercy without hesi-tation to all men, and give to every man with a good heart.

17 And if ye have not the wherewithal to give to him that needeth, have compassion for him in bowels of mercy.

18 I know that my hand found not the wherewithal to give to him that needed, and I walked with him weeping for seven furlongs, and my bowels yearned towards him in compassion.

19 Have, therefore, yourselves also, my children, compassion towards every man with mercy, that the Lord also may have compassion and mercy upon you.

20 Because also in the last days God will send His compassion on the earth, and wheresoever He findeth bowels of mercy He dwelleth in him.

21 For in the degree in which a man hath compassion upon his neighbours, in the same degree hath the Lord also upon him.

22 And when we went down into Egypt, Joseph bore no malice against us.

23 To whom taking heed, do ye also, my children, approve yourselves without malice, and love one another; and do not set down in account, each one of you, evil against his brother.

24 For this breaketh unity and divideth all kindred, and troubleth the soul, and weareth away the countenance.

25 Observe, therefore, the waters, and know when they flow together, they sweep along stones, trees, earth, and other things.

26 But if they are divided into many streams, the earth swalloweth them up, and they vanish away.

27 So shall ye also be if ye be divided. Be not ye, therefore, divided into two heads, for everything which the Lord made hath but one head, and two shoulders, two hands, two feet, and all the remaining members.

28 For I have learnt in the

writing of my fathers, that ye shall be divided in Israel, and ye shall follow two kings, and shall work every abomination.

29 And your enemies shall lead you captive, and ye shall be evil entreated among the Gentiles, with many infirmities and tribulations.

30 And after these things ye shall remember the Lord and repent, and He shall have mercy upon you, for He is merciful and compassionate.

31 And He setteth not down in account evil against the sons of men, because they are flesh, and are deceived through their own wicked deeds.

32 And after these things shall there arise unto you the Lord Himself, the light of righteousness, and ye shall return unto your land.

33 And ye shall see Him in Jerusalem, for His name's sake.

34 And again through the wickedness of your works shall ye provoke Him to anger,

35 And ye shall be cast away by Him unto the time of consummation.

36 And now, my children, grieve not that I am dying, nor be cast down in that I am coming to my end.

37 For I shall rise again in the midst of you, as a ruler in the midst of his sons; and I shall rejoice in the midst of my tribe, as many as shall keep the law of the Lord, and the commandments of Zebulun their father.

38 But upon the ungodly shall the Lord bring eternal fire, and destroy them throughout all generations.

39 But I am now hastening away to my rest, as did also my fathers.

40 But do ye fear the Lord our God with all your strength all the days of your life.

41 And when he had said these things he fell asleep, at a good old age.

42 And his sons laid him in a wooden coffin. And afterwards they carried him up and buried him in Hebron, with his fathers.

THE TESTAMENT OF DAN

The Seventh Son of Jacob and Bilhah.

CHAP. I.

The seventh son of Jacob and Bilhah. The jealous one. He counsels against anger saying that "it giveth peculiar vision." This is a notable thesis on anger.

THE copy of the words of Dan, which he spake to his sons in his last days, in the hundred and twenty-fifth year of his life.

2 For he called together his family, and said: Hearken to my words, ye sons of Dan; and give heed to the words of your father.

3 I have proved in my heart, and in my whole life, that truth with just dealing is good and well pleasing to God, and that lying and anger are evil, because they teach man all wickedness.

4 I confess, therefore, this day to you, my children, that in my heart I resolved on the death of Joseph my brother, the true and good man.

5 And I rejoiced that he was sold, because his father loved him more than us.

6 For the spirit of jealousy and vainglory said to me: Thou thyself also art his son.

7 And one of the spirits of Beliar stirred me up, saying: Take this sword, and with it slay

Joseph: so shall thy father love thee when he is dead.

8 Now this is the spirit of anger that persuaded me to crush Joseph as a leopard crusheth a kid.

9 But the God of my fathers did not suffer him to fall into my hands, so that I should find him alone and slay him, and cause a second tribe to be destroyed in Israel.

10 And now, my children, behold I am dying, and I tell you of a truth, that unless ye keep yourselves from the spirit of lying and of anger, and love truth and longsuffering, ye shall perish.

11 For anger is blindness, and does not suffer one to see the face of any man with truth.

12 For though it be a father or a mother, he behaveth towards them as enemies; though it be a brother, he knoweth him not; though it be a prophet of the Lord, he disobeyeth him; though a righteous man, he regardeth him not; though a friend, he doth not acknowledge him.

13 For the spirit of anger encompasseth him with the net of deceit, and blindeth his eyes, and through lying darkeneth his mind, and giveth him its own peculiar vision.

14 And wherewith encompasseth it his eyes? With hatred of heart, so as to be envious of his brother.

15 For anger is an evil thing, my children, for it troubleth even the soul itself.

16 And the body of the angry man it maketh its own, and over his soul it getteth the mastery, and it bestoweth upon the body power that it may work all iniquity.

17 And when the body does all these things, the soul justifieth what is done, since it seeth not aright.

18 Therefore he that is wrathful, if he be a mighty man, hath a threefold power in his anger: one by the help of his servants; and a second by his wealth, whereby he persuadeth and overcometh wrongfully; and thirdly, having his own natural power he worketh thereby the evil.

19 And though the wrathful man be weak, yet hath he a power twofold of that which is by nature; for wrath ever aideth such in lawlessness.

20 This spirit goeth always with lying at the right hand of Satan, that with cruelty and lying his works may be wrought.

21 Understand ye, therefore, the power of wrath, that it is vain.

22 For it first of all giveth provocation by word; then by deeds it strengtheneth him who is angry, and with sharp losses disturbeth his mind, and so stirreth up with great wrath his soul.

23 Therefore, when any one speaketh against you, be not ye moved to anger, and if any man praiseth you as holy men, be not uplifted: be not moved either to delight or to disgust.

24 For first it pleaseth the hearing, and so maketh the mind keen to perceive the grounds for provocation; and then being enraged, he thinketh that he is justly angry.

25 If ye fall into any loss or ruin, my children, be not afflicted; for this very spirit maketh a man desire that which is perishable, in order that he may be enraged through the affliction.

26 And if ye suffer loss voluntarily, or involuntarily, be not vexed; for from vexation ariseth wrath with lying.

27 Moreover, a twofold mischief is wrath with lying; and they assist one another in order to disturb the heart; and when the soul is continually disturbed, the Lord departeth from it, and Beliar ruleth over it.

CHAP. II.

A prophecy of the sins, captivity, plagues, and ultimate restitution of the nation. They still talk of Eden (See Verse 13). Verse 23 is remarkable in the light of prophecy.

OBSERVE, therefore, my children, the commandments of the Lord, and keep His law; depart from wrath, and hate lying, that the Lord may dwell among you, and Beliar may flee from you.

2 Speak truth each one with his neighbour. So shall ye not fall into wrath and confusion; but ye shall be in peace, having the God of peace, so shall no war prevail over you.

3 Love the Lord through all your life, and one another with a true heart.

4 I know that in the last days ye shall depart from the Lord, and ye shall provoke Levi unto anger, and fight against Judah; but ye shall not prevail against them, for an angel of the Lord shall guide them both; for by them shall Israel stand.

5 And whensoever ye depart from the Lord, ye shall walk in all evil and work the abominations of the Gentiles, going a-whoring after women of the lawless ones, while with all wickedness the spirits of wickedness work in you.

6 For I have read in the book of Enoch, the righteous, that your prince is Satan, and that all the spirits of wickedness and pride will conspire to attend constantly on the sons of Levi, to cause them to sin before the Lord.

7 And my sons will draw near to Levi, and sin with them in all things; and the sons of Judah will be covetous, plundering other men's goods like lions.

8 Therefore shall ye be led away with them into captivity, and there shall ye receive all the plagues of Egypt, and all the evils of the Gentiles.

9 And so when ye return to the Lord ye shall obtain mercy, and He shall bring you into His sanctuary, and He shall give you peace.

10 And there shall arise unto you from the tribe of Judah and of Levi the salvation of the Lord; and he shall make war against Beliar.

11 And execute an everlasting vengeance on our enemies; and the captivity shall he take from Beliar the souls of the saints, and turn disobedient hearts unto the Lord, and give to them that call upon him eternal peace.

12 And the saints shall rest in Eden, and in the New Jerusalem shall the righteous rejoice, and it shall be unto the glory of God for ever.

13 And no longer shall Jerusalem endure desolation, nor Israel be led captive; for the Lord shall be in the midst of it [living amongst men], and the Holy One of Israel shall reign over it in humility and in poverty; and he who believeth on Him shall reign amongst men in truth.

14 And now, fear the Lord, my children, and beware of Satan and his spirits.

15 Draw near unto God and unto the angel that intercedeth for you, for he is a mediator between God and man, and for the peace of Israel he shall stand up against the kingdom of the enemy.

16 Therefore is the enemy eager to destroy all that call upon the Lord.

17 For he knoweth that upon the day on which Israel shall repent, the kingdom of the enemy shall be brought to an end.

18 For the very angel of peace shall strengthen Israel, that it fall not into the extremity of evil.

19 And it shall be in the time of the lawlessness of Israel, that the Lord will not depart from them, but will transform them into a nation that doeth His will, for none of the angels will be equal unto him.

20 And His name shall be in every place in Israel, and among the Gentiles.

21 Keep, therefore, yourselves, my children, from every evil work, and cast away wrath and all lying, and love truth and long-suffering.

22 And the things which ye have heard from your father, do ye also impart to your children that the Saviour of the Gentiles may receive you; for he is true and long-suffering, meek and lowly, and teacheth by his works the law of God.

23 Depart, therefore, from all unrighteousness, and cleave unto the righteousness of God, and your race will be saved for ever.

24 And bury me near my fathers.

25 And when he had said these things he kissed them, and fell asleep at a good old age.

26 And his sons buried him, and after that they carried up his bones, and placed them near Abraham, and Isaac, and Jacob.

27 Nevertheless, Dan prophesied unto them that they should forget their God, and should be alienated from the land of their inheritance and from the race of Israel, and from the family of their seed.

THE TESTAMENT OF NAPHTALI
The Eighth Son of Jacob and Bilhah.

CHAP. I.

Naphtali, the eighth son of Jacob and Bilhah. The Runner. A lesson in physiology.

THE copy of the testament of Naphtali, which he ordained at the time of his death in the hundred and thirtieth year of his life.

2 When his sons were gathered together in the seventh month, on the first day of the month, while still in good health, he made them a feast of food and wine.

3 And after he was awake in the morning, he said to them, I am dying; and they believed him not.

4 And as he glorified the Lord, he grew strong and said that after yesterday's feast he should die.

5 And he began then to say: Hear, my children, ye sons of Naphtali, hear the words of your father.

6 I was born from Bilhah, and because Rachel dealt craftly, and gave Bilhah in place of herself to Jacob, and she conceived and bare me upon Rachel's knees, therefore she called my name Naphtali.

7 For Rachel loved me very much because I was born upon her lap; and when I was still young she was wont to kiss me, and say: May I have a brother of thine from mine own womb, like unto thee.

8 Whence also Joseph was like unto me in all things, according to the prayers of Rachel.

9 Now my mother was Bilhah, daughter of Rotheus the brother of Deborah, Rebecca's nurse, who was born on one and the self-same day with Rachel.

10 And Rotheus was of the family of Abraham, a Chaldean, God-fearing, free-born, and noble.

11 And he was taken captive and was bought by Laban; and

he gave him Euna his handmaid to wife, and she bore a daughter, and called her name Zilpah, after the name of the village in which he had been taken captive.

12 And next she bore Bilhah, saying: My daughter hastens after what is new, for immediately that she was born she seized the breast and hastened to suck it.

13 And I was swift on my feet like the deer, and my father Jacob appointed me for all messages, and as a deer did he give me his blessing.

14 For as the potter knoweth the vessel, how much it is to contain, and bringeth clay accordingly, so also doth the Lord make the body after the likeness of the spirit, and according to the capacity of the body doth He implant the spirit.

15 And the one does not fall short of the other by a third part of a hair; for by weight, and measure, and rule was all the creation made.

16 And as the potter knoweth the use of each vessel, what it is meet for, so also doth the Lord know the body, how far it will persist in goodness, and when it beginneth in evil.

17 For there is no inclination or thought which the Lord knoweth not, for He created every man after His own image.

18 For as a man's strength, so also in his work; as his eye, so also in his sleep; as his soul, so also in his word either in the law of the Lord or in the law of Beliar.

19 And as there is a division between light and darkness, between seeing and hearing, so also is there a division between man and man, and between woman and woman; and it is not to be said that the one is like the other either in face or in mind.

20 For God made all things good in their order, the five senses in the head, and He joined on the neck to the head, adding to it the hair also for comeliness and glory, then the heart for understanding, the belly for excrement, and the stomach for grinding, the windpipe for taking in the breath, the liver for wrath, the gall for bitterness, the spleen for laughter, the reins for prudence, the muscles of the loins for power, the lungs for drawing in, the loins for strength, and so forth.

21 So then, my children, let all your works be done in order with good intent in the fear of God, and do nothing disorderly in scorn or out of its due season

22 For if thou bid the eye to hear, it cannot; so neither while ye are in darkness can ye do the works of light.

23 Be ye, therefore, not eager to corrupt your doings through covetousness or with vain words to beguile your souls; because if ye keep silence in purity of heart, ye shall understand how to hold fast the will of God, and to cast away the will of Beliar.

24 Sun and moon and stars change not their order; so do ye also change not the law of God in the disorderliness of your doings.

25 The Gentiles went astray, and forsook the Lord, and changed their order, and obeyed stocks and stones, spirits of deceit.

26 But ye shall not be so, my children, recognizing in the firmament, in the earth, and in the sea, and in all created things, the Lord who made all things, that ye become not as Sodom, which changed the order of nature.

27 In like manner the Watchers also changed the order of their nature, whom the Lord cursed at the flood, on whose account He made the earth without inhabitants and fruitless.

28 These things I say unto

you, my children, for I have read in the writing of Enoch that ye yourselves also shall depart from the Lord, walking according to all the lawlessness of the Gentiles, and ye shall do according to all the wickedness of Sodom.

29 And the Lord shall bring captivity upon you, and there shall ye serve your enemies, and ye shall be bowed down with every affliction and tribulation, until the Lord have consumed you all.

30 And after ye have become diminished and made few, ye return and acknowledge the Lord your God; and He shall bring you back into your land, according to His abundant mercy.

31 And it shall be, that after that they come into the land of their fathers, they shall again forget the Lord and become ungodly.

32 And the Lord shall scatter them upon the face of all the earth, until the compassion of the Lord shall come, a man working righteousness and working mercy unto all them that are afar off, and to them that are near.

CHAP. II.

He makes a plea for orderly living. Notable for their eternal wisdom are Verses 27–30.

FOR in the fortieth year of my life, I saw a vision on the Mount of Olives, on the east of Jerusalem, that the sun and the moon were standing still.

2 And behold Isaac, the father of my father, said to us; Run and lay hold of them, each one according to his strength; and to him that seizeth them will the sun and moon belong.

3 And we all of us ran together, and Levi laid hold of the sun, and Judah outstripped the others and seized the moon, and they were both of them lifted up with them.

4 And when Levi became as a sun, lo, a certain young man gave to him twelve branches of palm; and Judah was bright as the moon, and under their feet were twelve rays.

5 And the two, Levi and Judah, ran, and laid hold of them.

6 And lo, a bull upon the earth, with two great horns, and an eagle's wings upon its back; and we wished to seize him, but could not.

7 But Joseph came, and seized him, and ascended up with him on high.

8 And I saw, for I was there, and behold a holy writing appeared to us, saying: Assyrians, Medes, Persians, Chaldeans, Syrians, shall possess in captivity the twelve tribes of Israel.

9 And again, after seven days, I saw our father Jacob standing by the sea of Jamnia, and we were with him.

10 And behold, there came a ship sailing by, without sailors or pilot; and there was written upon the ship, The Ship of Jacob.

11 And our father said to us: Come, let us embark on our ship.

12 And when he had gone on board, there arose a vehement storm, and a mighty tempest of wind; and our father, who was holding the helm, departed from us.

13 And we, being tost with the tempest, were borne along over the sea; and the ship was filled with water, and was pounded by mighty waves, until it was broken up.

14 And Joseph fled away upon a little boat, and we were all divided upon nine planks, and Levi and Judah were together.

15 And we were all scattered unto the ends of the earth.

16 Then Levi, girt about with sackcloth, prayed for us all unto the Lord.

17 And when the storm ceased, the ship reached the land as it were in peace.

18 And, lo, our father came, and we all rejoiced with one accord.

19 These two dreams I told to my father; and he said to me: These things must be fulfilled in their season, after that Israel hath endured many things.

20 Then my father saith unto me: I believe God that Joseph liveth, for I see always that the Lord numbereth him with you.

21 And he said, weeping: Ah me, my son Joseph, thou livest, though I behold thee not, and thou seest not Jacob that begat thee.

22 He caused me also, therefore, to weep by these words, and I burned in my heart to declare that Joseph had been sold, but I feared my brethren.

23 And lo! my children, I have shown unto you the last times, how everything shall come to pass in Israel.

24 Do ye also, therefore, charge your children that they be united to Levi and to Judah; for through them shall salvation arise unto Israel, and in them shall Jacob be blessed.

25 For through their tribes shall God appear dwelling among men on earth, to save the race of Israel, and to gather together the righteous from amongst the Gentiles.

26 If ye work that which is good, my children, both men and angels shall bless you; and God shall be glorified among the Gentiles through you, and the devil shall flee from you, and the wild beasts shall fear you, and the Lord shall love you, and the angels shall cleave to you.

27 As a man who has trained a child well is kept in kindly remembrance; so also for a good work there is a good remembrance before God.

28 But him that doeth not that which is good, both angels and men shall curse, and God shall be dishonoured among the Gentiles through him, and the devil shall make him as his own peculiar instrument, and every wild beast shall master him, and the Lord shall hate him.

29 For the commandments of the law are twofold, and through prudence must they be fulfilled.

30 For there is a season for a man to embrace his wife, and a season to abstain therefrom for his prayer.

31 So, then, there are two commandments; and, unless they be done in due order, they bring very great sin upon men.

32 So also is it with the other commandments.

33 Be ye therefore wise in God, my children, and prudent, understanding the order of His commandments, and the laws of every word, that the Lord may love you.

34 And when he had charged them with many such words, he exhorted them that they should remove his bones to Hebron, and that they should bury him with his fathers.

35 And when he had eaten and drunken with a merry heart, he covered his face and died.

36 And his sons did according to all that Naphtali their Father had commanded them.

THE TESTAMENT OF GAD

The Ninth Son of Jacob and Zilpah.

CHAP. I.

Gad, the ninth son of Jacob and Zilpah. Shepherd and strong man but a murderer at heart. Verse 25 is a notable definition of hatred.

THE copy of the testament of Gad, what things he spake unto his sons, in the hundred and twenty-fifth year of his life, saying unto them:

2 Hearken, my children, I was the ninth son born to Jacob, and I was valiant in keeping the flocks.

3 Accordingly I guarded at night the flock; and whenever the lion came, or the wolf, or any wild beast against the fold, I pursued it, and overtaking it I seized its foot with my hand and hurled it about a stone's throw, and so killed it.

4 Now Joseph my brother was feeding the flock with us for upwards of thirty days, and being young, he fell sick by reason of the heat.

5 And he returned to Hebron to our father, who made him lie down near him, because he loved him greatly.

6 And Joseph told our father that the sons of Zilpah and Bilhah were slaying the best of the flock and eating them against the judgement of Reuben and Judah.

7 For he saw that I had delivered a lamb out of the mouth of a bear, and put the bear to death; but had slain the lamb, being grieved concerning it that it could not live, and that we had eaten it.

8 And regarding this matter I was wroth with Joseph until the day that he was sold.

9 And the spirit of hatred was in me, and I wished not either to hear of Joseph with the ears, or see him with the eyes, because he rebuked us to our faces saying that we were eating of the flock without Judah.

10 For whatsoever things he told our father, he believed him.

11 I confess now my sin, my children, that oftentimes I wished to kill him, because I hated him from my heart.

12 Moreover, I hated him yet more for his dreams; and I wished to lick* him out of the land of the living, even as an ox licketh up the grass of the field.

13 And Judah sold him secretly to the Ishmaelites.

14 Thus the God of our fathers delivered him from our hands, that we should not work great lawlessness in Israel.

15 And now, my children, hearken to the words of truth to work righteousness, and all the law of the Most High, and go not astray through the spirit of hatred, for it is evil in all the doings of men.

16 Whatsoever a man doeth the hater abominateth him: and though a man worketh the law of the Lord, he praiseth him not; though a man feareth the Lord, and taketh pleasure in that which is righteous, he loveth him not.

17 He dispraiseth the truth, he envieth him that prospereth, he welcometh evil-speaking, he loveth arrogance, for hatred blindeth his soul; as I also then looked on Joseph.

18 Beware, therefore, my children of hatred; for it worketh

---

*Even our present day slang is centuries old.

254

lawlessness even against the Lord Himself.

19 For it will not hear the words of His commandments concerning the loving of one's neighbour, and it sinneth against God.

20 For if a brother stumble, it delighteth immediately to proclaim it to all men, and is urgent that he should be judged for it, and be punished and be put to death.

21 And if it be a servant it stirreth him up against his master, and with every affliction it deviseth against him, if possibly he can be put to death.

22 For hatred worketh with envy also against them that prosper: so long as it heareth of or seeth their success it always languisheth.

23 For as love would quicken even the dead, and would call back them that are condemned to die, so hatred would slay the living, and those that had sinned venially it would not suffer to live.

24 For the spirit of hatred worketh together with Satan, through hastiness of spirits, in all things to men's death; but the spirit of love worketh together with the law of God in long-suffering unto the salvation of men.

25 Hatred, therefore, is evil, for it constantly mateth with lying, speaking against the truth; and it maketh small things to be great, and causeth the light to be darkness, and calleth the sweet bitter, and teacheth slander, and kindleth wrath, and stirreth up war, and violence and all covetousness; it filleth the heart with evils and devilish poison.

26 These things, therefore, I say to you from experience, my children, that ye may drive forth hatred, which is of the devil, and cleave to the love of God.

27 Righteousness casteth out hatred, humility destroyeth envy.

28 For he that is just and humble is ashamed to do what is unjust, being reproved not of another, but of his own heart, because the Lord looketh on his inclination.

29 He speaketh not against a holy man, because the fear of God overcometh hatred.

30 For fearing lest he should offend the Lord, he will not do wrong to any man, even in thought.

31 These things I learnt at last, after I had repented concerning Joseph.

32 For true repentance after a godly sort destroyeth ignorance, and driveth away the darkness, and enlighteneth the eyes, and giveth knowledge to the soul, and leadeth the mind to salvation.

33 And those things which it hath not learnt from man, it knoweth through repentance.

34 For God brought upon me a disease of the liver; and had not the prayers of Jacob my father succoured me, it had hardly failed but my spirit had departed.

35 For by what things a man transgresseth, by the same also is he punished.

36 Since, therefore, my liver was set mercilessly against Joseph, in my liver too I suffered mercilessly, and was judged for eleven months, for so long a time as I had been angry against Joseph.

CHAP. II.

Gad exhorts his listeners against hatred showing how it has brought him into so much trouble. Verses 8–11 are memorable.

AND now, my children, I exhort you, love ye each one his brother, and put away hatred from your hearts, love one another in deed, and in word, and in the inclination of the soul.

2 For in the presence of my father I spake peaceably to Joseph; and when I had gone out, the spirit of hatred darkened my mind, and stirred up my soul to slay him.

3 Love ye one another from the heart; and if a man sin against thee, speak peaceably to him, and in thy soul hold not guile; and if he repent and confess, forgive him.

4 But if he deny it, do not get into a passion with him, lest catching the poison from thee he take to swearing and so thou sin doubly.

5 Let not another man hear thy secrets when engaged in legal strife, lest he come to hate thee and become thy enemy, and commit a great sin against thee; for ofttimes he addresseth thee guilefully or busieth himself about thee with wicked intent.

6 And though he deny it and yet have a sense of shame when reproved, give over reproving him.

7 For he who denieth may repent so as not again to wrong thee; yea, he may also honour thee, and fear and be at peace with thee.

8 And if he be shameless and persist in his wrong-doing, even so forgive him from the heart, and leave to God the avenging.

9 If a man prospereth more than you, do not be vexed, but pray also for him, that he may have perfect prosperity.

10 For so it is expedient for you.

11 And if he be further exalted, be not envious of him, remembering that all flesh shall die; and offer praise to God, who giveth things good and profitable to all men.

12 Seek out the judgments of the Lord, and thy mind will rest and be at peace.

13 And though a man become rich by evil means, even as Esau, the brother of my father, be not jealous; but wait for the end of the Lord.

14 For if he taketh away from a man wealth gotten by evil means He forgiveth him if he repent, but the unrepentant is reserved for eternal punishment.

15 For the poor man, if free from envy he pleaseth the Lord in all things, is blessed beyond all men, because he hath not the travail of vain men.

16 Put away, therefore, jealousy from your souls, and love one another with uprightness of heart.

17 Do ye also therefore tell these things to your children, that they honour Judah and Levi, for from them shall the Lord raise up salvation to Israel.

18 For I know that at the last your children shall depart from Him, and shall walk in all wickedness, and affliction and corruption before the Lord.

19 And when he had rested for a little while, he said again; My children, obey your father, and bury me near to my fathers.

20 And he drew up his feet, and fell asleep in peace.

21 And after five years they carried him up to Hebron, and laid him with his fathers.

THE TESTAMENT OF ASHER

The Tenth Son of Jacob and Zilpah.

CHAP. I.

Asher, the tenth son of Jacob and Zilpah. An explanation of dual personality. The first Jekyll and Hyde story. For a statement of the Law of Compensation that Emerson would have enjoyed, see Verse 27.

THE copy of the Testament of Asher, what things he spake to his sons in the hundred and twenty-fifth year of his life.

2 For while he was still in health, he said to them: Hearken, ye children of Asher, to your father, and I will declare to you all that is upright in the sight of the Lord.

3 Two ways hath God given to the sons of men, and two inclinations, and two kinds of action, and two modes of action, and two issues.

4 Therefore all things are by twos, one over against the other.

5 For there are two ways of good and evil, and with these are the two inclinations in our breasts discriminating them.

6 Therefore if the soul take pleasure in the good inclination, all its actions are in righteousness; and if it sin it straightway repenteth.

7 For, having its thoughts set upon righteousness, and casting away wickedness, it straightway overthroweth the evil, and uprooteth the sin.

8 But if it incline to the evil inclination, all its actions are in wickedness, and it driveth away the good, and cleaveth to the evil, and is ruled by Beliar; even though it work what is good, he perverteth it to evil.

9 For whenever it beginneth to do good, he forceth the issue of the action into evil for him, seeing that the treasure of the inclination is filled with an evil spirit.

10 A person then may with words help the good for the sake of the evil, yet the issue of the action leadeth to mischief.

11 There is a man who showeth no compassion upon him who serveth his turn in evil; and this thing hath two aspects, but the whole is evil.

12 And there is a man that loveth him that worketh evil, because he would prefer even to die in evil for his sake; and concerning this it is clear that it hath two aspects, but the whole is an evil work.

13 Though indeed he have love, yet is he wicked who concealeth what is evil for the sake of the good name, but the end of the action tendeth unto evil.

14 Another stealeth, docth unjustly, plundereth, defraudeth, and withal pitieth the poor: this too hath a twofold aspect, but the whole is evil.

15 He who defraudeth his neighbour provoketh God, and sweareth falsely against the Most High, and yet pitieth the poor: the Lord who commanded the law he setteth at nought and provoketh, and yet he refresheth the poor.

16 He defileth the soul, and maketh gay the body; he killeth many, and pitieth a few: this, too, hath a twofold aspect, but the whole is evil.

17 Another committeth adultery and fornication, and abstaineth from meats, and when he fasteth he doeth evil, and by the power of his wealth overwhelmeth many; and notwithstanding his excessive wickedness he doeth the commandments:

this, too, hath a twofold aspect, but the whole is evil.

18 Such men are hares; clean, —like those that divide the hoof, but in very deed are unclean.

19 For God in the tables of the commandments hath thus declared.

20 But do not ye, my children, wear two faces like unto them, of goodness and of wickedness; but cleave unto goodness only, for God hath his habitation therein, and men desire it.

21 But from wickedness flee away, destroying the evil inclination by your good works; for they that are double-faced serve not God, but their own lusts, so that they may please Beliar and men like unto themselves.

22 For good men, even they that are of single face, though they be thought by them that are double-faced to sin, are just before God.

23 For many in killing the wicked do two works, of good and evil; but the whole is good, because he hath uprooted and destroyed that which is evil.

24 One man hateth the merciful and unjust man, and the man who committeth adultery and fasteth: this, too, hath a twofold aspect, but the whole work is good, because he followeth the Lord's example, in that he accepteth not the seeming good as the genuine good.

25 Another desireth not to see a good day with them that riot, lest he defile his body and pollute his soul; this, too, is double-faced, but the whole is good.

26 For such men are like to stags and to hinds, because in the manner of wild animals they seem to be unclean, but they are altogether clean; because they walk in zeal for the Lord and abstain from what God also hateth and forbiddeth by His commandments, warding off the evil from the good.

27 Ye see, my children, how that there are two in all things, one against the other, and the one is hidden by the other: in wealth is hidden covetousness, in conviviality drunkenness, in laughter grief, in wedlock profligacy.

28 Death succeedeth to life, dishonour to glory, night to day, and darkness to light; and all things are under the day, just things under life, unjust things under death; wherefore also eternal life awaiteth death.

29 Nor may it be said that truth is a lie, nor right wrong; for all truth is under the light, even as all things are under God.

30 All these things, therefore, I proved in my life, and I wandered not from the truth of the Lord, and I searched out the commandments of the Most High, walking according to all my strength with singleness of face unto that which is good.

31 Take heed, therefore, ye also, my children, to the commandments of the Lord, following the truth with singleness of face.

32 For they that are double-faced are guilty of a twofold sin; for they both do the evil thing and they have pleasure in them that do it, following the example of the spirits of deceit, and striving against mankind.

33 Do ye, therefore, my children, keep the law of the Lord, and give not heed unto evil as unto good; but look unto the thing that is really good, and keep it in all commandments of the Lord, having your conversation therein, and resting therein.

34 For the latter ends of men do show their righteousness or unrighteousness, when they meet the angels of the Lord and of Satan

35 For when the soul departs troubled, it is tormented by the evil spirit which also it served in lusts and evil works.

36 But if he is peaceful with joy he meeteth the angel of peace, and he leadeth him into eternal life.

37 Become not, my children, as Sodom, which sinned against the angels of the Lord, and perished for ever.

38 For I know that ye shall sin, and be delivered into the hands of your enemies; and your land shall be made desolate, and your holy places destroyed, and ye shall be scattered unto the four corners of the earth.

39 And ye shall be set at nought in the dispersion vanishing away as water.

40 Until the Most High shall visit the earth, coming Himself as man, with men eating and drinking, and breaking the head of the dragon in the water.

41 He shall save Israel and all the Gentiles, God speaking in the person of man.

42 Therefore do ye also, my children, tell these things to your children, that they disobey Him not.

43 For I have known that ye shall assuredly be disobedient, and assuredly act ungodly, not giving heed to the law of God, but to the commandments of men, being corrupted through wickedness.

44 And therefore shall ye be scattered as Gad and Dan my brethren, and ye shall know not your lands, tribe, and tongue.

45 But the Lord will gather you together in faith through His tender mercy, and for the sake of Abraham, Isaac, and Jacob.

46 And when he had said these things unto them, he commanded them, saying: Bury me in Hebron.

47 And he fell asleep and died at a good old age.

48 And his sons did as he had commanded them, and they carried him up to Hebron, and buried him with his fathers.

THE TESTAMENT OF JOSEPH
The Eleventh Son of Jacob and Rachel.

CHAP. I.

Joseph, the eleventh son of Jacob and Rachel, the beautiful and beloved. His struggle against the Egyptian temptress.

THE copy of the Testament of Joseph.

2 When he was about to die he called his sons and his brethren together, and said to them:—

3 My brethren and my children, hearken to Joseph the beloved of Israel; give ear, my sons, unto your father.

4 I have seen in my life envy and death, yet I went not astray, but persevered in the truth of the Lord.

5 These my brethren hated me, but the Lord loved me:

6 They wished to slay me, but the God of my fathers guarded me:

7 They let me down into a pit, and the Most High brought me up again.

8 I was sold into slavery, and the Lord of all made me free:

9 I was taken into captivity, and His strong hand succoured me.

10 I was beset with hunger, and the Lord Himself nourished me.

11 I was alone, and God comforted me:

12 I was sick, and the Lord visited me:

13 I was in prison, and my God showed favour unto me;

14 In bonds, and He released me;

15 Slandered, and He pleaded my cause;

16 Bitterly spoken against by the Egyptians, and He delivered me;

17 Envied by my fellow-slaves, and He exalted me.

18 And this chief captain of Pharaoh entrusted to me his house.

19 And I struggled against a shameless woman, urging me to transgress with her; but the God of Israel my father delivered me from the burning flame.

20 I was cast into prison, I was beaten, I was mocked; but the Lord granted me to find mercy, in the sight of the keeper of the prison.

21 For the Lord doth not forsake them that fear Him, neither in darkness, nor in bonds, nor in tribulations, nor in necessities.

22 For God is not put to shame as a man, nor as the son of man is he afraid, nor as one that is earth-born is He weak or affrighted.

23 But in all those things doth He give protection, and in divers ways doth He comfort, though for a little space He departeth to try the inclination of the soul.

24 In ten temptations He showed me approved, and in all of them I endured; for endurance is a mighty charm, and patience giveth many good things.

25 How often did the Egyptian woman threaten me with death!

26 How often did she give me over to punishment, and then call me back and threaten me, and when I was unwilling to company with her, she said to me:

27 Thou shalt be lord of me, and all that is in my house, if thou wilt give thyself unto me, and thou shalt be as our master.

28 But I remembered the words of my father, and going into my chamber, I wept and prayed unto the Lord.

29 And I fasted in those seven years, and I appeared to the Egyptians as one living delicately, for they that fast for God's sake receive beauty of face.

30 And if my lord were away from home, I drank no wine; nor for three days did I take my food, but I gave it to the poor and sick.

31 And I sought the Lord early, and I wept for the Egyptian woman of Memphis, for very unceasingly did she trouble me, for also at night she came to me under pretence of visiting me.

32 And because she had no male child she pretended to regard me as a son.

33 And for a time she embraced me as a son, and I knew it not; but later, she sought to draw me into fornication.

34 And when I perceived it I sorrowed unto death; and when she had gone out, I came to myself, and lamented for her many days, because I recognized her guile and her deceit.

35 And I declared unto her the words of the Most High, if haply she would turn from her evil lust.

36 Often, therefore, did she flatter me with words as a holy man, and guilefully in her talk praise my chastity before her husband, while desiring to ensnare me when we were alone.

37 For she lauded me openly as chaste, and in secret she said unto me: Fear not my husband; for he is persuaded concerning thy chastity: for even should one tell him concerning us, he would not believe.

38 Owing to all these things I lay upon the ground, and besought God that the Lord would deliver me from her deceit.

39 And when she had pre-

vailed nothing thereby, she came again to me under the plea of instruction, that she might learn the word of God.

40 And she said unto me: If thou willest that I should leave my idols, lie with me, and I will persuade my husband to depart from his idols, and we will walk in the law by thy Lord.

41 And I said unto her: The Lord willeth not that those who reverence Him should be in uncleanness, nor doth He take pleasure in them that commit adultery, but in those that approach Him with a pure heart and undefiled lips.

42 But she heed her peace, longing to accomplish her evil desire.

43 And I gave myself yet more to fasting and prayer, that the Lord might deliver me from her.

44 And again, at another time she said unto me: If thou wilt not commit adultery, I will kill my husband by poison; and take thee to be my husband.

45 I therefore, when I heard this, rent my garments, and said unto her:

46 Woman, reverence God, and do not this evil deed, lest thou be destroyed; for know indeed that I will declare this thy device unto all men.

47 She therefore, being afraid, besought that I would not declare this device.

48 And she departed soothing me with gifts, and sending to me every delight of the sons of men.

49 And afterwards she sent me food mingled with enchantments.

50 And when the eunuch who brought it came, I looked up and beheld a terrible man giving me with the dish a sword, and I perceived that her scheme was to beguile me.

51 And when he had gone out I wept, nor did I taste that or any other of her food.

52 So then after one day she came to me and observed the food, and said unto me: Why is it that thou hast not eaten of the food?

53 And I said unto her: It is because thou hast filled it with deadly enchantments; and how saidst thou: I come not near to idols, but to the Lord alone.

54 Now therefore know that the God of my father hath revealed unto me by His angel thy wickedness, and I have kept it to convict thee, if haply thou mayst see and repent.

55 But that thou mayst learn that the wickedness of the ungodly hath no power over them that worship God with chastity behold I will take of it and eat before thee.

56 And having so said, I prayed thus: The God of my fathers and the angel of Abraham, be with me; and ate.

57 And when she saw this she fell upon her face at my feet, weeping; and I raised her up and admonished her.

58 And she promised to do this iniquity no more.

59 But her heart was still set upon evil, and she looked around how to ensnare me, and sighing deeply she became downcast, though she was not sick.

60 And when her husband saw her, he said unto her: Why is thy countenance fallen?

61 And she said unto him: I have a pain at my heart, and the groanings of my spirit oppress me; and so he comforted her who was not sick.

62 Then, accordingly seizing an opportunity, she rushed unto me while her husband was yet without, and said unto me: I will hang myself, or cast myself over a cliff, if thou wilt not lie with me.

63 And when I saw the spirit of Beliar was troubling her, I prayed unto the Lord, and said unto her:

64 Why, wretched woman, art

thou troubled and disturbed, blinded through sins?

65 Remember that if thou kill thyself, Asteho, the concubine of thy husband, thy rival, will beat thy children, and thou wilt destroy thy memorial from off the earth.

66 And she said unto me: Lo, then thou lovest me; let this suffice me: only strive for my life and my children, and I expect that I shall enjoy my desire also.

67 But she knew not that because of my lord I spake thus, and not because of her.

68 For if a man hath fallen before the passion of a wicked desire and become enslaved by it, even as she, whatever good thing he may hear with regard to that passion, he receiveth it with a view to his wicked desire.

69 I declare, therefore, unto you, my children, that it was about the sixth hour when she departed from me; and I knelt before the Lord all day, and all the night; and about dawn I rose up, weeping the while and praying for a release from her.

70 At last, then, she laid hold of my garments, forcibly dragging me to have connexion with her.

71 When, therefore, I saw that in her madness she was holding fast to my garment, I left it behind, and fled away naked.

72 And holding fast to the garment she falsely accused me, and when her husband came he cast me into prison in his house; and on the morrow he scourged me and sent me into Pharaoh's prison.

73 And when I was in bonds, the Egyptian woman was oppressed with grief, and she came and heard how I gave thanks unto the Lord and sang praises in the abode of darkness, and with glad voice rejoiced, glorifying my God that I was delivered from the lustful desire of the Egyptian woman.

74 And often hath she sent unto me saying: Consent to fulfil my desire, and I will release thee from thy bonds, and I will free thee from the darkness.

75 And not even in thought did I incline unto her.

76 For God loveth him who in a den of wickedness combines fasting with chastity, rather than the man who in kings' chambers combines luxury with license.

77 And if a man liveth in chastity, and desireth also glory, and the Most High knoweth that it is expedient for him, He bestoweth this also upon me.

78 How often, though she were sick, did she come down to me at unlooked for times, and listened to my voice as I prayed!

79 And when I heard her groanings I held my peace.

80 For when I was in her house she was wont to bare her arms, and breasts, and legs, that I might lie with her; for she was very beautiful, splendidly adorned in order to beguile me.

81 And the Lord guarded me from her devices.

CHAP. II.

Joseph is the victim of many plots by the wicked ingenuity of the Memphian woman. For an interesting prophetic parable, see Verses 73-74.

YE see, therefore, my children, how great things patience worketh, and prayer with fasting.

2 So ye too, if ye follow after chastity and purity with patience and prayer, with fasting in humility of heart, the Lord will dwell among you because He loveth chastity.

3 And wheresoever the Most High dwelleth, even though envy,

or slavery, or slander befalleth a man, the Lord who dwelleth in him, for the sake of his chastity not only delivereth him from evil, but also exalteth him even as me.

4 For in every way the man is lifted up, whether in deed, or in word, or in thought.

5 My brethren knew how my father loved me, and yet I did not exalt myself in my mind: although I was a child, I had the fear of God in my heart; for I knew that all things would pass away.

6 And I did not raise myself against them with evil intent, but I honoured my brethren; and out of respect for them, even when I was being sold, I refrained from telling the Ishmaelites that I was a son of Jacob, a great man and a mighty.

7 Do ye also, my children, have the fear of God in all your works before your eyes, and honour your brethren.

8 For every one who doeth the law of the Lord shall be loved by Him.

9 And when I came to the Indocolpitae with the Ishmaelites, they asked me, saying:

10 Art thou a slave? And I said that I was a home-born slave, that I might not put my brethren to shame.

11 And the eldest of them said unto me: Thou art not a slave, for even thy appearance doth make it manifest.

12 But I said that I was their slave.

13 Now when we came into Egypt they strove concerning me, which of them should buy me and take me.

14 Therefore it seemed good to all that I should remain in Egypt with the merchant of their trade, until they should return bringing merchandise.

15 And the Lord gave me favour in the eyes of the mer-chant, and he entrusted unto me his house.

16 And God blessed him by my means, and increased him in gold and silver and in household servants.

17 And I was with him three months and five days.

18 And about that time the Memphian woman, the wife of Pentephris came down in a chariot, with great pomp, because she had heard from her eunuchs concerning me.

19 And she told her husband that the merchant had become rich by means of a young Hebrew, and they say that he had assuredly been stolen out of the land of Canaan.

20 Now, therefore, render justice unto him, and take away the youth to thy house; so shall the God of the Hebrews bless thee, for grace from heaven is upon him.

21 And Pentephris was persuaded by her words, and commanded the merchant to be brought, and said unto him:

22 What is this that I hear concerning thee, that thou steal-est persons out of the land of Canaan, and sellest them for slaves?

23 But the merchant fell at his feet, and besought him, saying: I beseech thee, my lord, I know not what thou sayest.

24 And Pentephris said unto him: Whence, then, is the Hebrew slave?

25 And he said: The Ishmaelites entrusted him unto me until they should return.

26 But he believed him not, but commanded him to be stripped and beaten.

27 And when he persisted in this statement, Pentephris said: Let the youth be brought.

28 And when I was brought in, I did obeisance to Pentephris for he was third in rank of the officers of Pharaoh.

29 And he took me apart from

him, and said unto me: Art thou a slave or free?

30 And I said: A slave.

31 And he said: Whose?

32 And I said: The Ishmaelites'.

33 And he said: How didst thou become their slave?

34 And I said: They bought me out of the land of Canaan.

35 And he said unto me: Truly thou liest; and straightway he commanded me to be stripped and beaten.

36 Now the Memphian woman was looking through a window at me while I was being beaten, for her house was near, and she sent unto him saying:

37 Thy judgement is unjust; for thou dost punish a free man who hath been stolen, as though he were a transgressor.

38 And when I made no change in my statement, though I was beaten, he ordered me to be imprisoned, until, he said, the owners of the boy should come.

39 And the woman said unto her husband: Wherefore dost thou detain the captive and wellborn lad in bonds, who ought rather to be set at liberty, and be waited upon?

40 For she wished to see me out of a desire of sin, but I was ignorant concerning all these things.

41 And he said to her: It is not the custom of the Egyptians to take that which belongeth to others before proof is given.

42 This, therefore, he said concerning the merchant; but as for the lad, he must be imprisoned.

43 Now after four and twenty days came the Ishmaelites; for they had heard that Jacob my father was mourning much concerning me.

44 And they came and said unto me: How is it that thou saidst that thou wast a slave? and lo, we have learnt that thou art the son of a mighty man in the land of Canaan, and thy father still mourneth for thee in sackcloth and ashes.

45 When I heard this my bowels were dissolved and my heart melted, and I desired greatly to weep, but I restrained myself that I should not put my brethren to shame.

46 And I said unto them, I know not, I am a slave.

47 Then, therefore, they took counsel to sell me, that I should not be found in their hands.

48 For they feared my father, lest he should come and execute upon them a grievous vengeance.

49 For they had heard that he was mighty with God and with men.

50 Then said the merchant unto them: Release me from the judgement of Pentiphri.

51 And they came and requested me, saying: Say that thou wast bought by us with money, and he will set us free.

52 Now the Memphian woman said to her husband: Buy the youth; for I hear, said she, that they are selling him.

53 And straightway she sent a eunuch to the Ishmaelites, and asked them to sell me.

54 But since the eunuch would not agree to buy me at their price he returned, having made trial of them, and he made known to his mistress that they asked a large price for their slave.

55 And she sent another eunuch, saying: Even though they demand two minas, give them, do not spare the gold; only buy the boy, and bring him to me.

56 The eunuch therefore went and gave them eighty pieces of gold, and he received me; but to the Egyptian woman he said: I have given a hundred.

57 And though I knew this I held my peace, lest the eunuch should be put to shame.

58 Ye see, therefore, my chil-

dren, what great things I endured that I should not put my brethren to shame.

59 Do ye also, therefore, love one another, and with long-suffering hide ye one another's faults.

60 For God delighteth in the unity of brethren, and in the purpose of a heart that takes pleasure in love.

61 And when my brethren came into Egypt they learnt that I had returned their money unto them, and upbraided them not, and comforted them.

62 And after the death of Jacob my father I loved them more abundantly, and all things whatsoever he commanded I did very abundantly for them.

63 And I suffered them not to be afflicted in the smallest matter; and all that was in my hand I gave unto them.

64 And their children were my children, and my children as their servants; and their life was my life, and all their suffering was my suffering, and all their sickness was my infirmity.

65 My land was their land, and their counsel my counsel.

66 And I exalted not myself among them in arrogance because of my worldly glory, but I was among them as one of the least.

67 If ye also, therefore, walk in the commandments of the Lord, my children, He will exalt you there, and will bless you with good things for ever and ever.

68 And if any one seeketh to do evil unto you, do well unto him, and pray for him, and ye shall be redeemed of the Lord from all evil.

69 For, behold, ye see that out of my humility and long-suffering I took unto wife the daughter of the priest of Heliopolis.

70 And a hundred talents of gold were given me with her, and the Lord made them to serve me.

71 And He gave me also beauty as a flower beyond the beautiful ones of Israel; and He preserved me unto old age in strength and in beauty, because I was like in all things to Jacob.

72 And hear ye, my children, also the vision which I saw.

73 There were twelve harts feeding: and the nine were first dispersed over all the earth, and likewise also the three.

74 And I saw that from Judah was born a virgin wearing a linen garment, and from her was born a lamb, without spot; and on his left hand there was as it were a lion; and all the beasts rushed against him, and the lamb overcame them, and destroyed them and trod them under foot.

75 And because of him the angels and men rejoiced, and all the land.

76 And these things shall come to pass in their season, in the last days.

77 Do ye therefore, my children, observe the commandments of the Lord, and honour Levi and Judah; for from them shall arise unto you the Lamb of God, who taketh away the sin of the world, one who saveth all the Gentiles and Israel.

78 For His kingdom is an everlasting kingdom, which shall not pass away; but my kingdom among you shall come to an end as a watcher's hammock, which after the summer disappeareth.

79 For I know that after my death the Egyptians will afflict you, but God will avenge you, and will bring you into that which He promised to your fathers.

80 But ye shall carry up my bones with you; for when my bones are being taken up thither,

the Lord shall be with you in light, and Beliar shall be in darkness with the Egyptians.

81 And carry ye up Asenath your mother to the Hippodrome, and near Rachel your mother bury her.

82 And when he had said these things he stretched out his feet, and died at a good old age.

83 And all Israel mourned for him, and all Egypt, with a great mourning.

84 And when the children of Israel went out of Egypt, they took with them the bones of Joseph, and they buried him in Hebron with his fathers, and the years of his life were one hundred and ten years.

THE TESTAMENT OF BENJAMIN
The Twelfth Son of Jacob and Rachel.

CHAP. I.

Benjamin, the twelfth son of Jacob and Rachel, the baby of the family, turns philosopher and philanthropist.

THE copy of the words of Benjamin, which he commanded his sons to observe, after he had lived a hundred and twenty-five years.

2 And he kissed them, and said: As Isaac was born to Abraham in his old age, so also was I to Jacob.

3 And since Rachel my mother died in giving me birth, I had no milk; therefore I was suckled by Bilhah her handmaid.

4 For Rachel remained barren for twelve years after she had borne Joseph; and she prayed the Lord with fasting twelve days, and she conceived and bare me.

5 For my father loved Rachel dearly, and prayed that he might see two sons born from her.

6 Therefore was I called Benjamin, that is, a son of days.

7 And when I went into Egypt, to Joseph, and my brother recognized me, he said unto me: What did they tell my father when they sold me?

8 And I said unto him, They dabbled thy coat with blood and sent it, and said: Know whether this be thy son's coat.

9 And he said unto me: Even so, brother, when they had stripped me of my coat they gave me to the Ishmaelites, and they gave me a loin cloth, and scourged me, and bade me run.

10 And as for one of them that had beaten me with a rod, a lion met him and slew him.

11 And so his associates were affrighted.

12 Do ye also, therefore, my children, love the Lord God of heaven and earth, and keep His commandments, following the example of the good and holy man Joseph.

13 And let your mind be unto good, even as ye know me; for he that hath his mind right seeth all things rightly.

14 Fear ye the Lord, and love your neighbour; and even though the spirits of Beliar claim you to afflict you with every evil, yet shall they not have dominion over you, even as they had not over Joseph my brother.

15 How many men wished to slay him, and God shielded him!

16 For he that feareth God and loveth his neighbour cannot be smitten by the spirit of Beliar, being shielded by the fear of God.

17 Nor can he be ruled over by the device of men or beasts, for he is helped by the Lord

through the love which he hath towards his neighbour.

18 For Joseph also besought our father that he would pray for his brethren, that the Lord would not impute to them as sin whatever evil they had done unto him.

19 And thus Jacob cried out: My good child, thou hast prevailed over the bowels of thy father Jacob.

20 And he embraced him, and kissed him for two hours, saying:

21 In thee shall be fulfilled the prophecy of heaven concerning the Lamb of God, and Saviour of the world, and that a blameless one shall be delivered up for lawless men, and a sinless one shall die for ungodly men in the blood of the covenant, for the salvation of the Gentiles and of Israel, and shall destroy Beliar and his servants.

22 See ye, therefore, my children, the end of the good man?

23 Be followers of his compassion, therefore, with a good mind, that ye also may wear crowns of glory.

24 For the good man hath not a dark eye; for he showeth mercy to all men, even though they be sinners.

25 And though they devise with evil intent concerning him, by doing good he overcometh evil, being shielded by God; and he loveth the righteous as his own soul.

26 If any one is glorified, he envieth him not; if any one is enriched, he is not jealous; if any one is valiant, he praiseth him; the virtuous man he laudeth; on the poor man he hath mercy; on the weak he hath compassion; unto God he singeth praises.

27 And him that hath the grace of a good spirit he loveth as his own soul.

28 If, therefore, ye also have a good mind, then will both wicked men be at peace with you, and the profligate will reverence you and turn unto good; and the covetous will not only cease from their inordinate desire, but even give the objects of their covetousness to them that are afflicted.

29 If ye do well, even the unclean spirits will flee from you; and the beasts will dread you.

30 For where there is reverence for good works and light in the mind, even darkness fleeth away from him.

31 For if any one does violence to a holy man, he repenteth; for the holy man is merciful to his reviler, and holdeth his peace.

32 And if any one betrayeth a righteous man, the righteous man prayeth: though for a little he be humbled, yet not long after he appeareth far more glorious, as was Joseph my brother.

33 The inclination of the good man is not in the power of the deceit of the spirit of Beliar, for the angel of peace guideth his soul.

34 And he gazeth not passionately upon corruptible things, nor gathereth together riches through a desire of pleasure.

35 He delighteth not in pleasure, he grieveth not his neighbour, he sateth not himself with luxuries, he erreth not in the uplifting of the eyes, for the Lord is his portion.

36 The good inclination receiveth not glory nor dishonour from men, and it knoweth not any guile, or lie, or fighting or reviling; for the Lord dwelleth in him and lighteth up his soul, and he rejoiceth towards all men alway.

37 The good mind hath not two tongues, of blessing and of cursing, of contumely and of honour, of sorrow and of joy, of quietness and of confusion, of hypocrisy and of truth, of pov-

erty and of wealth; but it hath one disposition, uncorrupt and pure, concerning all men.

38 It hath no double sight, nor double hearing; for in everything which he doeth, or speaketh, or seeth, he knoweth that the Lord looketh on his soul.

39 And he cleanseth his mind that he may not be condemned by men as well as by God.

40 And in like manner the works of Beliar are twofold, and there is no singleness in them.

41 Therefore, my children, I tell you, flee the malice of Beliar; for he giveth a sword to them that obey him.

42 And the sword is the mother of seven evils. First the mind conceiveth through Beliar, and first there is bloodshed; secondly ruin; thirdly, tribulation; fourthly, exile; fifthly, dearth; sixthly, panic; seventhly, destruction.

43 Therefore was Cain also delivered over to seven vengeances by God, for in every hundred years the Lord brought one plague upon him.

44 And when he was two hundred years old he began to suffer, and in the nine-hundredth year he was destroyed.

45 For on account of Abel, his brother, with all the evils was he judged, but Lamech with seventy times seven.

46 Because for ever those, who are like Cain in envy and hatred of brethren, shall be punished with the same judgement.

CHAP. II.

Verse 3 contains a striking example of the homeliness yet vividness of the figures of speech of these ancient patriarchs.

AND do ye, my children, flee evil-doing, envy, and hatred of breathren, and cleave to goodness and love.

2 He that hath a pure mind in love, looketh not after a woman with a view to fornication; for he hath no defilement in his heart, because the Spirit of God resteth upon him.

3 For as the sun is not defiled by shining on dung and mire, but rather drieth up both and driveth away the evil smell; so also the pure mind, though encompassed by the defilements of earth, rather cleanseth them and is not itself defiled.

4 And I believe that there will be also evil-doings among you, from the words of Enoch the righteous: that ye shall commit fornication with the fornication of Sodom, and shall perish, all save a few, and shall renew wanton deeds with women; and the kingdom of the Lord shall not be among you, for straightway He shall take it away.

5 Nevertheless the temple of God shall be in your portion, and the last temple shall be more glorious than the first.

6 And the twelve tribes shall be gathered together there, and all the Gentiles, until the Most High shall send forth His salvation in the visitation of an only-begotten prophet.

7 And He shall enter into the first temple, and there shall the Lord be treated with outrage, and He shall be lifted up upon a tree.

8 And the veil of the temple shall be rent, and the Spirit of God shall pass on to the Gentiles as fire poured forth.

9 And He shall ascend from Hades and shall pass from earth into heaven.

10 And I know how lowly He shall be upon earth, and how glorious in heaven.

11 Now when Joseph was in Egypt, I longed to see his figure and the form of his countenance; and through the prayers of Jacob my father I saw him, while awake in the daytime, even

his entire figure exactly as he was.

12 And when he had said these things, he said unto them: Know ye, therefore, my children, that I am dying.

13 Do ye, therefore, truth each one to his neighbour, and keep the law of the Lord and His commandments.

14 For these things do I leave you instead of inheritance.

15 Do ye also, therefore, give them to your children for an everlasting possession; for so did both Abraham, and Isaac, and Jacob.

16 For all these things they gave us for an inheritance, saying: Keep the commandments of God, until the Lord shall reveal His salvation to all Gentiles.

17 And then shall ye see Enoch, Noah, and Shem, and Abraham, and Isaac, and Jacob, rising on the right hand in gladness.

18 Then shall we also rise, each one over our tribe, worshipping the King of heaven, who appeared upon earth in the form of a man in humility.

19 And as many as believe on Him on the earth shall rejoice with Him.

20 Then also all men shall rise, some unto glory and some unto shame.

21 And the Lord shall judge Israel first, for their unrighteousness; for when He appeared as God in the flesh to deliver them they believed Him not.

22 And then shall He judge all the Gentiles, as many as believed Him not when He appeared upon earth.

23 And He shall convict Israel through the chosen ones of the Gentiles, even as He reproved

Esau through the Midianites, who deceived their brethren, so that they fell into fornication, and idolatry; and they were alienated from God, becoming therefore children in the portion of them that fear the Lord.

24 If ye therefore, my children, walk in holiness according to the commandments of the Lord, ye shall again dwell securely with me, and all Israel shall be gathered unto the Lord.

25 And I shall no longer be called a ravening wolf on account of your ravages, but a worker of the Lord distributing food to them that work what is good.

26 And there shall arise in the latter days one beloved of the Lord, of the tribe of Judah and Levi, a doer of His good pleasure in his mouth, with new knowledge enlightening the Gentiles.

27 Until the consummation of the age shall he be in the synagogues of the Gentiles, and among their rulers, as a strain of music in the mouth of all.

28 And he shall be inscribed in the holy books, both his work and his word, and he shall be a chosen one of God for ever.

29 And through them he shall go to and fro as Jacob my father, saying: He shall fill up that which lacketh of thy tribe.

30 And when he had said these things he stretched out his feet.

31 And died in a beautiful and good sleep.

32 And his sons did as he had enjoined them, and they took up his body and buried it in Hebron with his fathers.

33 And the number of the days of his life was a hundred and twenty-five years.

MERIDIAN Books on Religion and Philosophy